Evidence-Based Practices for Supporting Individuals with Autism Spectrum Disorder

■ ■ ■

SPECIAL EDUCATION LAW, POLICY, AND PRACTICE
Series Editors
Mitchell L. Yell, PhD, University of South Carolina
David F. Bateman, PhD, Shippensburg University of Pennsylvania

The Special Education Law, Policy, and Practice series highlights current trends and legal issues in the education of students with disabilities. The books in this series link legal requirements with evidence-based instruction and highlight practical applications for working with students with disabilities. The titles in the Special Education Law, Policy, and Practices series are designed not only to be required textbooks for general education and special education preservice teacher education programs but are also designed for practicing teachers, education administrators, principals, school counselors, school psychologists, parents, and others interested in improving the lives of students with disabilities. The Special Education Law, Policy, and Practice series is committed to research-based practices working to provide appropriate and meaningful educational programming for students with disabilities and their families.

Titles in Series:
The Essentials of Special Education Law by Andrew M. Markelz and David F. Bateman

Special Education Law Annual Review 2020 by David F. Bateman, Mitchell L. Yell, and Kevin P. Brady

Developing Educationally Meaningful and Legally Sound IEPs by Mitchell L. Yell, David F. Bateman, and James G. Shriner

Sexuality Education for Students with Disabilities edited by Thomas C. Gibbon, Elizabeth A. Harkins Monaco, and David F. Bateman

Creating Positive Elementary Classrooms: Preventing Behavior Challenges to Promote Learning by Stephen W. Smith and Mitchell L. Yell

Service Animals in Schools: A Comprehensive Guide for Administrators, Teachers, Parents, and Students by Anne O. Papalia, Kathy B. Ewoldt, and David F. Bateman

Evidence-Based Practices for Supporting Individuals with Autism Spectrum Disorder by Laura C. Chezan, Katie Wolfe, and Erik Drasgow

Evidence-Based Practices for Supporting Individuals with Autism Spectrum Disorder

■ ■ ■

Edited by

Laura C. Chezan
Old Dominion University

Katie Wolfe
University of South Carolina

Erik Drasgow
University of South Carolina

ROWMAN & LITTLEFIELD
Lanham • Boulder • New York • London

Acquisitions Editor: Courtney Packard
Acquisitions Assistant: Ivy Roberts
Sales and Marketing Inquiries: textbooks@rowman.com

Credits and acknowledgments for material borrowed from other sources, and reproduced with permission, appear on the appropriate pages within the text.

Published by Rowman & Littlefield
An imprint of The Rowman & Littlefield Publishing Group, Inc.
4501 Forbes Boulevard, Suite 200, Lanham, Maryland 20706
www.rowman.com

86-90 Paul Street, London EC2A 4NE

British Library Cataloguing in Publication Information Available

Library of Congress Cataloging-in-Publication Data
Names: Chezan, Laura Claudia, editor.
Title: Evidence-Based Practices for Supporting Individuals with Autism Spectrum Disorder / edited by Laura C. Chezan, Old Dominion University, Katie Wolfe, University of South Carolina, Erik Drasgow, University of South Carolina.
Description: Lanham : Rowman & Littlefield, [2023] | Series: Special education law, policy, and practice | Includes bibliographical references and index.
Identifiers: LCCN 2022016754 (print) | LCCN 2022016755 (ebook) | ISBN 9781538149256 (cloth) | ISBN 9781538149263 (paperback) | ISBN 9781538149270 (epub)
Subjects: LCSH: Autism spectrum disorders—Treatment. | Evidence-based psychiatry.
Classification: LCC RC553.A88 G85 2023 (print) | LCC RC553.A88 (ebook) | DDC 616.85/882—dc23/eng/20220713
LC record available at https://lccn.loc.gov/2022016754
LC ebook record available at https://lccn.loc.gov/2022016755

♾️™ The paper used in this publication meets the minimum requirements of American National Standard for Information Sciences—Permanence of Paper for Printed Library Materials, ANSI/NISO Z39.48-1992.

Brief Contents

■ ■ ■

Contents

■ ■ ■

Preface

■ ■ ■

One of the critical aspects of education and service delivery for learners with autism spectrum disorder (ASD) is designing and implementing meaningful educational programs that are likely to promote independence, community participation, valued group membership, and life satisfaction. Designing and implementing meaningful, high-quality, and effective educational programs encompasses myriad factors including the identification of socially valid, functional, and chronologically age-appropriate behaviors; the adoption and use of evidence-based practices; the understanding of contextual variables and their influence on program implementation; the consideration of preferences, values, and cultural norms of linguistically and ethnically diverse learners; and collaboration with families and practitioners from other disciplines within the context of ethical and professional relationships. Despite the critical importance of designing educational programs that equip learners with ASD with the behaviors needed to become self-sufficient and productive members of their communities, many educational programs focus exclusively on academic outcomes without consideration of behaviors required to successful functioning across quality-of-life domains, such as interpersonal relationships, self-advocacy, self-determination, personal development, and participation in inclusive environments.

Evidence-Based Practices for Supporting Individuals with Autism Spectrum Disorder is a resource to assist practitioners in identifying, selecting, implementing, and evaluating evidence-based practices to promote successful functioning of learners with ASD in current and future environments and enhance their quality of life. Throughout the book, we highlight the importance of using evidence-based practices to facilitate the acquisition, generalization, and maintenance of socially valid, functional, and chronologically age-appropriate behaviors required for learners with ASD to be active and valued members in inclusive environments. We are hopeful that this book will convey to our audience not only the importance of using scientifically supported interventions to teach socially significant behaviors, but it also will provide a framework to inform the selection, use, and evaluation of such interventions to better meet the individualized needs of this population of learners in the context of ethical, professional, and collaborative partnerships with families and practitioners from different disciplines.

The primary audience for *Evidence-Based Practices for Supporting Individuals with Autism Spectrum Disorder* consists of undergraduate and graduate students in education preparation programs. Although students within regular and special education preparation programs are the intended audience of this book, practitioners and other professionals from related fields such as psychology, behavior analysis, counseling, or speech and language pathology may find its content relevant and informative.

Chapters in this book were authored by national and international scholars with extensive experience and research expertise in special education, behavior analysis, speech-language pathology, and educational psychology. Each chapter included in this book provides practitioner-friendly but scientifically supported information to describe a framework of conducting assessments, selecting and using evidence-based practices with fidelity, adhering to ethical and professional standards, and collaborating with families and practitioners from different disciplines to design and implement meaningful educational programs leading to independence and enhanced quality of life in learners with ASD.

Chapter 1 discusses the concept of quality of life and the principles of normalization and social-role valorization in relation to assessment and program development to promote active and valued membership, self-determination, and quality of life in learners with ASD. Chapter 2 overviews characteristics of learners with ASD, including diagnostic characteristics and co-occurring medical conditions and diagnoses. Chapter 3 provides an overview of the assessment process to inform instructional planning, including characteristics of meaningful assessment and methods to identify socially valid, functional, and chronologically age-appropriate behaviors. Chapter 4 defines and describes evidence-based practices for learners with ASD, including core elements, individual and group applications, and an evidence-based intervention selection model encompassing professional judgment, research evidence, and individual and contextual variables. Chapter 5 highlights the importance of effective training and discusses empirically supported training strategies, including technology-delivered training, to facilitate the implementation with fidelity and sustained use of evidence-based practices for learners with ASD. Chapter 6 focuses on progress monitoring and evaluation, with emphasis on describing practitioner-friendly methods for data collection, display, analysis, and interpretation to inform instructional decisions.

Chapter 7 presents ethical aspects related to the selection and implementation of evidence-based practices within the context of a model for problem solving and decision making when confronted with ethical dilemmas. Chapter 8 offers a comprehensive discussion of evidence-based practices to enhance social competence in learners with ASD, with an emphasis on requesting and rejecting, gaining attention, greeting behavior, conversation, joint attention, and peer-interaction skills. Chapter 9 examines evidence-based practices to facilitate the acquisition, generalization, and maintenance of academic outcomes related to reading and mathematics for learners with ASD. Chapter 10 concentrates on the relationship between communication and problem behavior with an emphasis on functional behavioral assessment and function-based interventions to promote socially appropriate behavior in learners with ASD. Chapter 11 is devoted to evidence-based practices for transition planning with an emphasis on secondary transition frameworks and practices. Chapter 12 highlights the importance of family involvement and engagement in successful implementation of evidence-based practices while presenting effective strategies to develop collaborative partnerships with families of learners with ASD. Chapter 13 emphasizes the importance of interprofessional collaboration while discussing the problem-solving framework as an effective approach to promoting collaborations among practitioners. Chapter 14 overviews the most important aspects discussed throughout the book to assist practitioners with the development and implementation of meaningful and high-quality educational programs to promote independence and improve the quality of life of learners with ASD.

1

Quality of Life

Laura C. Chezan and Erik Drasgow

■ ■ ■

INTRODUCTION AND OVERVIEW

Accessing meaningful education, developing friendships and romantic relationships, engaging in leisure and recreational activities, living independently, or obtaining and maintaining employment are several aspects that influence one's quality of life. Quality of life refers to one's satisfaction with life or well-being (Schalock et al., 2011). Researchers have demonstrated that learners with disabilities who make choices, access inclusive educational environments, engage in positive relationships, make friends, obtain a job, and participate in community activities have an enhanced quality of life (Baker & Palmer, 2006; Kober & Eggleton, 2005; Lachapelle et al., 2005; Tobin et al., 2014).

Historically, learners with autism spectrum disorder (ASD) have demonstrated lower levels of quality of life compared to learners without disabilities because of their unique social communication and behavioral characteristics (Ayres et al., 2018; van Heijst & Geurts, 2015). According to the *Diagnostic and Statistical Manual of Mental Disorders* (5th ed.; DSM-5; American Psychiatric Association, 2013), learners with ASD are characterized by deficits in social communication and social interaction and by restricted and repetitive patterns of behavior, interests, and activities. Deficits in social communication and social interaction have been correlated with limited friendships and social isolation (Bauminger & Schulman, 2003; Kuhlthau et al., 2010; Laugeson & Ellingsen, 2014; Locke et al., 2010) and with difficulties in obtaining and maintaining employment (Baldwin et al., 2014; Chiang et al., 2013; Walsh et al., 2017). Moreover, restricted and repetitive patterns of behavior, interests, and activities pose challenges to social inclusion and interpersonal relationships and, consequently, result in low levels of quality of life in learners with ASD (de Vries & Geurts, 2015; Rodriguez & Thompson, 2015; Wolfe et al., 2019).

Several factors including challenges posed by the social communication and behavioral patterns characteristic to learners with ASD, the increased prevalence of ASD (i.e., 1 in 54 children is diagnosed with ASD; Centers for Disease Control and Prevention, 2020), the emphasis on evidence-based practices, and the increase in accountability have emphasized the critical importance of quality of life as a component of educational planning. Specifically, experts and researchers have advocated for the development and implementation of educational programs that target goals related to quality of life and for the inclusion of quality of life as an outcome to evaluate the effectiveness of interventions and services received by learners with ASD in the fields of education, health care, and social services (Burgess & Gutstein, 2007; Cholewicki et al., 2019; Downs et al., 2019; Schalock & Verdugo, 2013).

In other words, practitioners are urged to design educational programs that promote the acquisition, generalization, and maintenance of behaviors that lead to successful outcomes across quality-of-life domains, such as interpersonal relations, self-advocacy and self-determination, personal development, school and community inclusion, and active participation in current and future environments. When learners with ASD acquire the behaviors needed to function successfully in the natural environment, they are more likely to be valued members in their community and, consequently, experience a better quality of life and a sense of belonging.

Developing meaningful educational programs that focus not only on academic achievement but are also likely to promote community participation, valued group membership, social interactions, independence, and life satisfaction is a critical aspect of education and service delivery for learners with ASD. Our purpose in this chapter is to provide an overview of the concept of quality of life and discuss its importance to educational planning and service delivery for learners with ASD. First, we will define the quality-of-life concept. Second, we will provide a historical overview of the factors that have contributed to its development and application to learners with disabilities. Third, we will present some considerations for promoting quality of life in learners with ASD by discussing quality-of-life domains and outcomes and by highlighting best practices for incorporating quality of life in educational planning and assessment. Finally, we will end by discussing quality of life at the organizational and system level.

DEFINING QUALITY OF LIFE

Numerous definitions of quality of life have been proposed in the literature over the past several decades. For example, the World Health Organization (WHO) defines *quality of life* as "an individual's perception of their position in life in the context of the culture and value systems in which they live and in relation to their goals, expectations, standards, and concerns" (World Health Organization and Division of Mental Health and Prevention of Substance Abuse, 1997, p. 1). Quality of life has also been referred to as one's satisfaction with his or her well-being across multiple life domains, including physical and emotional health, interpersonal relationships, social inclusion, self-esteem, and self-determination (Cummings, 1997; Schalock et al., 2011; Tavernor et al., 2013). Furthermore, one's ability to function successfully and live happily within his or her environment have also been emphasized as significant factors comprising the concept of quality of life (Brown & Brown, 2005).

Although no universally accepted definition of quality of life exists, there is growing consensus that four common principles guide the conceptualization of quality of life across disciplines and populations. The first conceptualization principle refers to quality of life as a *multidimensional construct* consisting of domains and indicators that represent the factors related to one's well-

Table 1.1. The Quality-of-Life Conceptual Model Proposed by Schalock and Alonso (2002)

Domain	Indicator
Material well-being	• Financial resources • Material possessions (e.g., residence, car) • Employment status (paid/unpaid job, unemployed) • Benefits and health insurance
Physical well-being	• Health status and co-occurring medical conditions • Activities of daily living (mobility, feeding, toileting)
Emotional well-being	• Satisfaction, happiness, and enjoyment • Self-esteem and identity • Lack of stress
Rights	• Dignity, equality, freedom • Access to education, opportunities, and due process
Social inclusion	• Participation in community activities and events • Valued roles and membership in groups and community
Interpersonal relations	• Interactions with social partners in the natural environment • Relationships with family, friends, and peers
Self-determination	• Choices • Autonomy and decision making • Goals based on interests, preferences, and values
Personal development	• Education and competence • Personal accomplishments and achievements

Source: Adapted from Schalock, R. L., & Alonso, M. A. V. (2002). *Handbook on quality of life for human service practitioners.* American Association on Mental Retardation.

being (Claes et al., 2010; Dardas & Ahmad, 2014; White-Koning et al., 2008). For example, the conceptualization of quality of life in the field of intellectual and other developmental disabilities consists of eight core domains: emotional well-being, personal development, interpersonal relations, social inclusion, physical well-being, self-determination, material well-being, and rights (Schalock & Alonso, 2002). Furthermore, each domain consists of specific indicators that allow the evaluation of one's quality of life within the context of his or her personal life experiences and circumstances (Cholewicki et al., 2019; Claes et al., 2010). For example, indicators of the interpersonal relations domain include social interactions and relationships, whereas indicators of the self-determination domain include autonomy, goals, and choices. Table 1.1 provides an overview of the quality-of-life domains and indicators based on the conceptual model proposed by Schalock and Alonso (2002).

The second conceptualization principle emphasizes the idea that quality of life is a *universal construct* consisting of the same components for all individuals regardless of their race or ethnicity, culture, socioeconomic status, or the presence or absence of a disability (Schalock & Keith, 2016). Specifically, researchers have demonstrated that domains, such as interpersonal relationships, social inclusion, health, rights, or personal development are considered very important by individuals from various countries and, thus, illustrate the universal nature of quality of life (Keith et al., 1996; Schalock et al., 2005). Satisfaction and well-being across the life domains listed previously are relevant to all individuals regardless of geographical location; however, the importance of each domain and the individuals' perception about quality of life may vary based on their values, beliefs, and cultural norms (Jenaro et al., 2005). For example, individuals in one country may perceive material well-being as extremely important, whereas individuals in another country may value social inclusion and interpersonal relationships more than other quality-of-life domains. Regardless of the relative importance of material well-being, social inclusion, or interpersonal relationships, these domains contribute to the quality of life of all individuals from the two countries.

The third conceptualization principle describes quality of life as consisting both of *subjective components* and of *objective components*. For example, when assessing a learner's quality of life, it is important to ask questions related to quality-of-life domains, such as opportunities to make choices, to attend leisure and recreational activities with friends, to obtain a job related to their interests and preferences, or to live independently. The purpose of these questions is to identify the learner's perceived satisfaction or well-being across quality-of-life domains (i.e., subjective component). At the same time, it is critical to observe the learner during daily activities in the natural environment to determine whether they actively participate in their community and possess the behaviors needed to function successfully in the current environment (i.e., objective component). For example, in addition to asking a learner with ASD if he or she makes choices throughout the day (i.e., subjective component), it is also important to observe the learner during daily activities in the natural environment and document the number of opportunities for making choices and the type of choices being made (i.e., objective component).

The fourth conceptualization principle states that one's *quality of life is enhanced by self-determination, resources, and social inclusion* in current and future environments (Schalock & Keith, 2016). In general, learners who have the behaviors needed to advocate for themselves, to make choices and decisions regarding their personal and professional life, and to contribute to their community are more likely to be accepted and valued in their group. Consequently, their sense of belonging and satisfaction with life is greater compared to learners who do not possess such behaviors. For example, young adults with ASD who learn to express their preferences and make decisions are more likely to be active participants in educational planning by identifying meaningful postsecondary goals closely aligned with their interests and by advocating for the supports and services needed to achieve those goals. Therefore, these learners will be better equipped to pursue their career and personal goals and enhance their quality of life.

The conceptualization of quality of life has continued to evolve over the past three decades. There is a consensus that quality of life (a) is a multidimensional and universal concept consisting of domains and indicators, (b) includes objective and subjective components, and (c) is greatly enhanced by various factors, such as self-determination, resources and supports, and social inclusion in school and community environments. Understanding what constitutes quality of life is an important first step in designing effective educational programs and delivering interventions and services that have the potential to promote positive and meaningful outcomes across life domains and enhance the personal satisfaction and happiness of learners with ASD.

HISTORICAL PERSPECTIVES ON QUALITY OF LIFE

The concept of quality of life received increased attention in the 1960s and 1970s during the "quality revolution" and was embraced by the field of intellectual and other developmental disabilities in the 1980s (Schalock et al., 2011). The "quality revolution" was a movement characterized by an emphasis on the quality of services provided to individuals and the relevance of the outcomes (Schalock, 2000). In the field of education, the "quality revolution" led to changes in the type and delivery of educational services to learners with disabilities, the selection of socially significant goals closely aligned with learners' interests and preferences, the focus on meaningful and valued outcomes, and the continuous improvement of service-delivery models (Schalock, 2000).

One principle that emerged during the "quality revolution" and represented the basis for the adoption of the quality-of-life concept and its application to learners with disabilities was the principle of normalization. The principle of normalization was first defined by Bengt Nirje in 1969 and continued to evolve over the next two decades. The most recent definition states that *the principle of normalization* refers to "making available to all persons with intellectual or other impairments or disabilities patterns of life and conditions of everyday living that are as close as possible to or indeed the same as the regular circumstances and ways of life of their communities" (Nirje, 1994, p. 19). The principle of normalization reflects several perspectives, including equality and human rights. Equality is achieved when learners with disabilities have access to the same opportunities as learners without disabilities, which allows them to maximize their potential and experience a happy and fulfilling life (Renzaglia et al., 2003). For example, the concept of equality is illustrated when a learner with ASD who acquired the behaviors required for a specific job (e.g., stocking shelves in a grocery store) has the opportunity to perform the job with or without supports alongside his or her coworkers without disabilities.

Human rights refer to moral principles or norms that allow all individuals to live with dignity, equality, and freedom within their community or society regardless of their race, ethnicity, sexual orientation, religion, or ability (Donnelly, 2013). Because all members of a society are entitled to basic human rights, learners with disabilities should have the same rights as learners without disabilities. Several rights may include, but are not limited to, access to meaningful education, valued membership in a group, active participation in the community, and competitive employment (Renzaglia et al., 2003). An example of the human-rights concept is the right of learners with ASD to receive appropriate education in the same educational setting with learners without disabilities to the maximum extent possible (Yell, 2019). Receiving an appropriate education and having the opportunity to learn and interact with learners without disabilities has the potential to promote positive outcomes and increase satisfaction with their life and their sense of belonging.

In the United States, Wolfensberger (1983) proposed the concept of social role valorization (SRV) as an area of change that could promote normalization for learners with disabilities. The most recent definition of *SRV* is "the application of empirical knowledge to the shaping of the current and potential social roles of a party (i.e., person, group, or class)—primarily by means of enhance-ment of the party's competencies and image—so that these are, as much as pos-sible, possibly valued in the eyes of the perceivers" (Wolfensberger & Thomas, 2005). The idea behind the concept of SRV is that individuals are more likely to experience a better quality of life if they assume valued social roles in their community (Osburn, 2006).

In general, learners with disabilities, including learners with ASD, are less likely to assume valued roles in their communities because of characteristics asso-ciated with their condition, such as difficulties with communication and social interaction, repetitive behaviors, restricted interests or activities, and problem behavior. For example, a child with ASD who engages in repetitive behavior, such as rocking or hand flapping, is more like to be perceived as being "weird" by his or her peers and, consequently, be devalued. Historically, learners with disabili-ties who did not assume valued social roles have been treated differently from learners without disabilities and experienced negative consequences, such as peer rejection, abuse and violence, or social exclusion (Osburn, 2006). These negative consequences resulted in lower levels of quality of life (Rodriguez & Thompson, 2015; Wolfe et al., 2019).

The principle of SRV has been extremely relevant for learners with disabili-ties, including learners with ASD, for at least two reasons. One reason for the rel-evance of this principle to learners with ASD is that it produced a shift in attitude toward learners with disabilities and a new way of thinking that was based on acceptance, valued social roles, rights and opportunities, and active participation in the community. Learners with disabilities were no longer perceived as "subhu-mans," "morons," and "idiots" (terms used in the 1960s) but rather as citizens who should have the same rights and opportunities as learners without disabilities and who have the potential to contribute to their community.

One aspect of the principle of SRV is illustrated in the terminology or lan-guage used to describe learners with disabilities. One terminology used to describe learners with disabilities, including those with ASD, is *person-first language* (e.g., learners with autism), a terminology that emerged in the 1970s. Person-first lan-guage emphasizes the importance of referring to the person first and then to their disability and, thus, highlights "the person's unique combinations of strengths, needs, and experiences" (Vivanti, 2020, p. 1). Proponents of person-first lan-guage argue that referring to learners with disabilities by focusing on the person first as an individual and then to their disability reduces stigmatization, promotes a more positive perception and identity for these learners, and is closely aligned with the principles of normalization and SRV (Blaska, 1993; Kenny et al., 2016; Schalock & Verdugo, 2002).

It is important to note that not all communities and learners with disabilities embraced person-first language and advocated for the use of a *disability-first* or *identity-first language* (e.g., autistic learner). Proponents of the identity-first lan-guage advanced the idea that one's diagnosis is an integral part of their identity (Davidson & Henderson, 2010). In the ASD community, identity-first language aligns with the concept of *neurodiversity* (Singer, 1999) in which ASD is perceived as one variation of the human mind that is part of one's identity as opposed to a deficit or impairment that needs to be "fixed" or "cured" (Kenny et al., 2016; Nicolaidis, 2012).

To date, there is a lack of consensus in the literature regarding the most appropriate or acceptable terminology used to refer to learners with ASD. For example, a few researchers report that many learners with ASD and their families embrace identity-first language and the concept of neurodiversity and consider person-first language the least preferred and most offensive terminology (Botha et al., 2021; Bury et al., 2020; Kapp et al., 2012). Other researchers argue that many learners with ASD who require substantial and very substantial levels of support are unable to express their preference for one terminology or another and no assumptions should be made about their preferences (Bagatell, 2010). Furthermore, several researchers have suggested that the identity-first language is embraced by a large percentage of learners with ASD and their families, whereas a large percentage of professionals prefer to use person-first language (Kenny et al., 2016). These researchers proposed the use of both terminologies to respect the diversity of perspectives when referring to learners with ASD. In this book, we will use a combination of person-first language and identity-first language to acknowledge and respect the terminology preference of the scholars who contributed to the book, the learners with ASD and their families, and the practitioners working with this population of learners.

Another reason for the relevance of the principle of SRV to learners with ASD is that it led to changes in the organization and provision of services to learners with disabilities. Specifically, changing one's social and ideological beliefs about learners with disabilities was critical but insufficient for enhancing their competence and promoting independence and successful functioning in current and future environments (Osburn, 2006). To promote positive learner outcomes and enhance their effective functioning in the natural environment, the shift in ideology had to be combined with the delivery of effective education and services (Osburn, 2006). Consequently, there was a shift both in ideology and in the delivery of services from a *medical model* in which learners with disabilities were perceived as sick, unable to learn, and dependent on others for assistance to an *educational model* based on effective and meaningful instruction, empowerment, normalized and typical environments, and individualized supports and services.

Central to the educational model is the concept of inclusion. *Inclusion* is a practice used to promote normalization and it is based on the belief that all learners with and without disabilities should be accepted and welcomed in the society, that diversity is valued, and that all learners can contribute to their communities (Renzaglia et al., 2003). In other words, learners with disabilities should learn, work, and live in the same environments as learners without disabilities, receive instruction on the behaviors needed to function successfully in those environments, and be active participants in their community. For example, a child with ASD who has limited or no socially appropriate communication and does not know how to initiate, maintain, and terminate interactions with social partners should receive instruction in the natural environment where the child is expected to engage in interactions with children without disabilities rather than learning to interact with an adult in a separate room.

Equipping learners with ASD with the behaviors needed to function successfully in the current and future environments will likely promote their competence and a positive image within their community. One critical aspect of promoting competence across quality-of-life domains consists of selecting and teaching behaviors that are socially significant and based on the learner's interests and preferences. *Socially significant behaviors* are those behaviors that are relevant and meaningful to a learner with a disability, are valued by people in his or her environment, and have the potential to enhance his or her quality of life (Baer et al., 1968; Falcomata, 2015). A socially significant behavior for a young adult with ASD working in a fitness center would be to initiate, maintain, and terminate interactions with individuals working out in the fitness center or direct them to another employee for assistance when needed.

The principles of normalization and SRV are critical to understanding the evolution of the concept of quality of life and its applicability to learners with disabilities. These principles rooted in human rights, equality, and valued social roles have contributed both to a change in attitude toward learners with disabilities, including those with ASD, and to a shift from a medical model to an educational model based on effective and high-quality instruction, empowerment, and individualized supports and services. Thus, understanding the principles of normalization and SRV and their applicability to learners with ASD is an important aspect of developing meaningful educational programs and, consequently, promoting a high quality of life.

PROMOTING QUALITY OF LIFE IN LEARNERS WITH ASD

Researchers have demonstrated that learners with ASD experience lower quality of life across the lifespan, including childhood, adolescence, and adulthood, compared to learners without disabilities (Ayres et al., 2018; Kamp-Becker et al., 2011; Tavernor et al., 2013; van Heijst & Geurts, 2015). Despite growing consensus in the field of education that quality of life is an important outcome for learners with ASD and should be a critical component of educational planning and service delivery (Biggs & Carter, 2016; Kober, 2011), many practitioners continue to target intervention outcomes that are unrelated to quality of life and not aligned with the interests, preferences, and values of learners and their families (Kohler, 1999; Pfeiffer et al., 2017). For example, quality-of-life intervention outcomes for a young adult with ASD who is transitioning from high school to adulthood may include goals related to social behaviors required to interact appropriately with employers and coworkers or behaviors related to advocating for himself or herself to obtain the supports needed to successfully perform job responsibilities.

It is critical to develop educational programs that are perceived as meaningful and relevant by learners with ASD and their families and promote the acquisition, maintenance, and generalization of behaviors leading to independence, empowerment, and successful functioning in the natural environment across quality-of-life domains. However, designing meaningful educational programs that promote effective functioning across life domains and an enhanced quality of life in learners with ASD is a very complex process. Effective educational planning requires not only theoretical knowledge and familiarity with the quality-of-life concept and its importance, but it also requires a systematic and collaborative approach in identifying socially valid goals and objectives across quality-of-life domains, using effective approaches to promote quality of life, and assessing outcomes. In this section of the chapter, we will discuss several quality-of-life outcomes that practitioners should consider when developing educational plans and a few aspects related to planning for and assessing quality-of-life outcomes in learners with ASD.

Targeting Quality-of-Life Outcomes

As we mentioned at the beginning of this chapter, quality of life is a multidimensional concept comprised of several domains. Several of the most relevant quality-of-life domains for learners with disabilities, including those with ASD, consist of physical and emotional well-being, social inclusion, interpersonal relationships, and self-determination (Chezan et al., 2021; Cholewicki et al., 2019; Lombardi & Croce, 2016). For transition-age learners with ASD, additional domains may be explored such as personal development, rights, and material well-being. Next, we will describe the quality-of-life domains and outcomes that practitioners should address, at a minimum, during the educational planning process for all learners with ASD regardless of their abilities and co-occurring cognitive deficits.

Physical and Emotional Well-Being

Physical and emotional well-being represent two of the quality-of-life domains. *Physical well-being* has been defined as one's ability to perform activities of daily living such as mobility, eating, or grooming and carry out social roles, whereas *emotional well-being* has been defined as one's satisfaction, happiness, and lack of stress (Schalock & Keith, 2016). Many learners with ASD have associated medical conditions, such as seizures, epilepsy, muscular dystrophy, sleep disorders, gastrointestinal conditions, obesity, or nutritional deficits that negatively impact their physical and emotional well-being and daily functioning and, consequently, their quality of life (Bauman, 2010; Croen et al., 2015; Schieve et al., 2012).

In addition, social communication deficits, repetitive patterns of behavior, and restricted interests and activities experienced by learners with ASD have been shown to produce anxiety, depression, anger, loneliness, stigma, and vulnerability to bullying and cyberbullying for many learners with ASD (Feldman & Crandall, 2006; Mayes et al., 2013; Mazurek & Kanne, 2010; Sreckovic et al., 2014). The negative outcomes listed previously extend beyond social isolation and include low self-esteem, poor academic performance, emotional trauma, and fear for the safety of learners with ASD (Reid & Batten, 2006; Zablotsky et al., 2013) and, subsequently, low levels of emotional well-being and quality of life. For example, an adolescent with ASD who engages in stereotypic behavior (e.g., flapping hands and rocking his body) and has limited functional communication is more likely to be ridiculed and victimized by his peers without disabilities and less likely to make friends and, thus, may experience social isolation, anxiety, loneliness, and peer rejection, which are all detrimental to mental health and quality of life.

On the other hand, learners with ASD who are satisfied with their life and experience happiness are more likely to be active participants and make a significant contribution to society (Noble & McGrath, 2014). Given that learners with ASD are at greater risk for decreased physical and emotional well-being than learners without disabilities, and that decreased physical and emotional well-being are associated with low levels of quality of life, it is critical that practitioners develop educational programs that foster the acquisition of the behaviors needed to minimize the negative effects of physical and emotional challenges in this population of learners while promoting successful functioning in the natural environment and an enhanced well-being. Effective interventions, supports, and services, such as using evidence-based practices to promote social competence, fostering a climate of acceptance of all learners (Lindsay et al., 2014), creating opportunities for social interactions and development of friendships (Carter et al., 2014), and enhancing the quality of student-teacher relationships (Blacher et al., 2014) have the potential to enhance the well-being of learners with ASD and are critical components of effective educational planning.

Material Well-Being

Material well-being is one of the quality-of-life domains that encompasses employment and personal possessions (Schalock, 2004). Employment refers to one's work status (e.g., employed, unemployed) and the type of work the person performs (e.g., competitive, sheltered employment), whereas possessions include financial resources and housing. Although material well-being applies to all learners, it becomes more relevant as learners with ASD transition from adolescence to adulthood. For example, a young child with ASD is less likely to have possessions and seek employment compared to a young adult with ASD who is transitioning from high school to a postsecondary environment. The importance of planning for life after graduation, including employment and housing, is also highlighted by the Individuals with Disabilities Education Improvement Act (IDEIA, 2004), which mandates that all learners with ASD receive transition services and have postsecondary outcomes included in their educational plans beginning with middle school.

Historically, employment and housing have been two of the most difficult aspects of transition to adulthood for learners with ASD (Targett & Smith, 2009). Researchers have shown that few adults with ASD obtain employment and live independently (Howlin et al., 2013; Kirby et al., 2016; Magiati et al., 2014). Precisely, 58% of young adults with ASD in the United States have worked for pay outside their home, and only 21% have obtained full-time employment (Roux et al., 2015). Furthermore, many adults with ASD who obtain employment are hired in positions below their qualification level, work fewer hours, and receive lower salaries than their coworkers without disabilities (Roux et al., 2015; Shattuck, Narendorf et al., 2012).

The social communication and behavioral deficits characteristic to learners with ASD have been associated with difficulties in following rules and instructions, using socially appropriate communicative responses to interact with coworkers and supervisors (Baldwin et al., 2014; Krieger et al., 2012), engaging in conversations in the workplace (Chezan et al., 2020), or working in a team (Richards, 2012) that pose barriers to obtaining and maintaining employment. Furthermore, employers' negative attitudes and biases toward learners with ASD, as well as concerns related to hiring costs, safety issues, and the levels of support an employee with ASD may require on the job, represent additional barriers to employment for learners with ASD (Scott et al., 2019).

In addition to employment, independent living or housing is another area in which learners with ASD encounter barriers. Despite several residential options available to learners with ASD, only approximately 10% of youth and adults with ASD live alone (Billstedt et al., 2005; Wagner et al., 2005). Researchers have found that most youth and adults with ASD continue to live at home with their parents or caregivers after graduation (Cederlund et al., 2008; Hewitt et al., 2017; Wagner et al., 2005). Factors that hinder the transition of learners with ASD from the family home into an independent living situation include low levels of self-determination and problem solving (Minshew et al., 2002; Targett & Smith, 2009; Tsatsanis, 2005), limited self-help skills required for daily activities (Bledsoe et al., 2003; Lee et al., 2007), challenges accessing and navigating the complexity of adult services (Paode, 2020), and low income and unemployment (Schaak et al., 2017).

Difficulties associated with obtaining and maintaining employment and living independently have negative consequences on the material well-being and mental health of learners with ASD and, consequently, their quality of life (Fleming et al., 2013; Wanberg, 2012). Thus, it is critical that practitioners design educational programs that include meaningful transition outcomes to promote the acquisition, generalization, and maintenance of behaviors required for independent living and employment that increase the likelihood of socioeconomic independence and satisfaction with life. Table 1.2 illustrates examples of material well-being quality-of-life outcomes in learners with ASD across the lifespan.

Rights and Personal Development

Rights is a quality-of-life domain that refers to human and legal norms that entitle all people in a society to be treated with respect, dignity, and equality and allow them access to the same opportunities as people without disabilities regardless of their race, ethnicity, sexual orientation, religion, or ability (Donnelly, 2013; Schalock, 2004). For example, a young adult with ASD who has the qualifications to perform a job in a coffee shop has the same right to apply for and be considered for the job as adults without disabilities. If the decision is not to hire the young adult because of their disability rather than the qualifications required for the position, then their rights have been violated. The rights of a young child with ASD are violated when he or she is denied access to the school cafeteria because their stereotypic behaviors distract other children during lunchtime. Rights also refer to the way in which learners with ASD are treated by others in their environment. Learners with ASD have the right to be treated with dignity and respect during interactions with others rather than being labeled as "disabled," "weird," or "retarded."

Personal development is another quality-of-life domain that encompasses all activities in which people engage throughout their life to learn new behaviors, to enhance their competence, and to achieve personal and professional success. Personal development is an important quality-of-life domain because it emphasizes the relevance of education, opportunities, and access to meaningful activities and life experiences in facilitating success and achievements at different stages in life. For example, a preschool child with ASD who attends an inclusive classroom with typical peers has more opportunities to learn and practice socially appropriate communicative behaviors than a preschool child who does not attend school and spends his or her days at home with grandparents.

A young adult with ASD who attends a postsecondary college program for learners with intellectual and other developmental disabilities has numerous opportunities to experience life on a university campus and access academic and employment opportunities that are not available to young adults who do not

Table 1.2.   Examples of Quality-of-Life Outcomes across the Lifespan for Learners with ASD

Quality-of-life domain	Sample quality-of-life outcome		
	Childhood	*Adolescence*	*Adulthood*
Physical well-being	• Teach a child to communicate when they do not feel well	• Teach an adolescent to identify situations when they need assistance to manage health concerns	• Teach an adult to self-manage health concerns by taking their medication
Emotional well-being	• Teach a child to request assistance from an adult when peers bully them	• Teach an adolescent to walk away from a conflictual situation with a peer	• Teach an adult to host a party for neighbors and friends to enhance their self-confidence
Material well-being	• Teach a young child to set up the table for breakfast (i.e., independent living skill)	• Assist an adolescent to identify volunteering opportunities (i.e., employment-related skill)	• Teach an adult to identify apartment rental opportunities and fill out applications
Rights	• Provide instruction on sharing toys during scheduled playtime on the playground	• Teach an adolescent to advocate for receiving instruction in an inclusive classroom	• Assist an adult to identify community clubs aligned with their interests and complete membership applications
Personal development	• Teach a young child to swim so they can join friends at a summer camp	• Assist an adolescent to develop postsecondary goals related to attending a community college after high-school graduation	• Assist an adult to identify and attend a cooking and nutrition course to advance their knowledge related to healthy meals preparation
Social inclusion	• Assign a child the role of score keeper during a game	• Enroll an adolescent in an after-school club at the local library	• Plan opportunities for an adult to attend a monthly social event in the community
Interpersonal relationships	• Teach a child to share toys with peers during play activities and create opportunities for interactions with peers	• Assist an adolescent to identify areas of interests and engage in conversations with peers who share the same interests	• Help an adult to organize an afternoon tea party and invite neighbors
Self-determination	• Teach a child to select preferred leisure activities and provide opportunities for choice making	• Teach an adolescent to identify career interests and advocate for obtaining an internship with a preferred company	• Assist an adult to develop a long-term career plan, identify the supports needed to achieve the planned outcomes, and self-monitor progress

attend such programs. Researchers have demonstrated that young adults with ASD who attend postsecondary programs are more likely to achieve academic success, to enhance their social competence, and to become valued and active members of their community (Griffin et al., 2012; Stodden & Mruzek, 2010). Thus, many learners with ASD and their families consider postsecondary programs a critical avenue for personal development and an enhanced quality of life (Petcu et al., 2015).

Rights and personal development are two critical domains that contribute to one's satisfaction with life. Therefore, it is essential that practitioners who work with learners with ASD are familiar with these domains and their influence on the life of their learners, develop meaningful educational programs that promote success and achievements, and advocate for the rights of learners with ASD and their access to and inclusion in relevant and stimulating activities that have the potential to promote personal development and ensure that learners are treated with dignity and respect. Table 1.2 illustrates examples of rights and personal development quality-of-life outcomes in learners with ASD across the lifespan.

Social Inclusion

Social inclusion refers to participating in activities specific to one's culture in school, work, recreation, and community environments while being a valued member of the society (Keith & Schalock, 2016; Renzaglia et al., 2003). For example, preschool learners with ASD are socially included in the school environment when they play with their peers without disabilities on the playground during recess or when the learners with ASD assist a teacher to pass materials to peers during circle time in the classroom. Another example of social inclusion is a young adult with ASD who goes shopping with his or her friends, watches a movie with neighbors, or works alongside coworkers without disabilities in a grocery store. Assuming valued roles facilitates a sense of acceptance and belonging to one's community, decreases the likelihood of social rejection and isolation, and promotes emotional well-being and quality of life (Knoster & Kincaid, 2005).

Traditionally, learners with ASD have experienced lower levels of social inclusion in school and community environments compared to learners without disabilities and, consequently, lower levels of quality of life. The limited social inclusion of learners with ASD has been attributed to characteristics associated with ASD, including deficits in social communication and social interaction (Laugeson & Ellingsen, 2014; Locke et al., 2010) and restricted and repetitive patterns of behavior, interests, and activities (de Vries & Geurts, 2015; Rodriguez & Thompson, 2015). For example, a young adult with ASD who does not engage in interactions with his coworkers at the grocery store and walks back and forth in the storage room when he has no task to complete is less likely to be invited to join coworkers for lunch break at a local restaurant. If the young adult's pattern of behavior continues over time and no supports are provided to facilitate social interactions and acceptance from coworkers, he will likely experience social isolation and rejection, which may lead to loneliness and depression.

One interesting aspect to consider is that social inclusion may vary based on the gender of the learner with ASD. Specifically, researchers have suggested that females with ASD have lower rates of social inclusion compared to males with ASD, potentially due to the type of social activities attended by males versus females (Arias et al., 2018; Moran et al., 2019). It has been hypothesized that males attend group activities, such as games and sports, that do not require a lot of communication that poses challenges for many learners with ASD; therefore, they are less likely to experience social isolation. On the other hand, females are required to engage in more communicative exchanges with friends and may experience challenges during conversations, which could result in social isolation (Sedgewick et al., 2016; Vine Foggo & Webster, 2017).

It is important to note that the extent to which learners with ASD are socially included is influenced not only by their characteristics (e.g., language and communication abilities, social behaviors, motivation), but also by people in their environment, the opportunities for inclusion and participation in activities, and the interventions and supports needed to acquire the behaviors required for successful social inclusion. For example, a young adult with ASD who enjoys being around same-age peers and receives instruction on initiating, maintaining, and terminating social interactions will not be socially included unless he or she has the opportunity to engage in interactions with peers in the natural environment and peers will be responsive to the young adult's communicative attempts. The simple fact that the learner with ASD is in the physical proximity of a social partner does not promote their social inclusion unless opportunities for cooperative activities and social exchanges are also available during typical routines (Sreckovic et al., 2017). Thus, practitioners should pay increased attention to the individuals and contextual factors that influence a learner's inclusion and acceptance in their environment and plan for social inclusion outcomes that have the potential to promote valued membership and active participation of learners with ASD across school, work, and community settings while making environmental changes that facilitate their social inclusion. Examples of social inclusion quality-of-life outcomes for learners with ASD across the lifespan are provided in Table 1.2.

Interpersonal Relationships

Interpersonal relationships consist of social, communicative, and affective exchanges with social partners in the natural environment and represent one of the quality-of-life domains. Examples of interpersonal relationships include, but are not limited to, interactions with peers and coworkers, friendships, romantic relationships, and social engagement. Interpersonal relationships are critical to the overall functioning and quality of life of learners with ASD across the lifespan. For example, interpersonal relationships such as friendships provide a sense of belonging and self-esteem (Bagwell et al., 1998), offer emotional support and protection from loneliness, facilitate the acquisition of social information processing (Bauminger & Schulman, 2003), and decrease the likelihood of social isolation for children, adolescents, and adults with ASD (Asselt-Goverts et al., 2015; Bauminger et al., 2008; Burgess et al. 2006; Wentzel et al., 2012). In addition, friendships are perceived as one of the most relevant outcomes by parents of learners with ASD who stress the importance of their children having at least one friend they can talk to and spend time with (Knoster & Kincaid, 2005; Petrina et al., 2015).

However, developing meaningful interpersonal relationships represents a challenge for many learners with ASD due to characteristics associated with

ASD. Specifically, many learners with ASD who have deficits in social communication and social interaction experience challenges in interpreting vocal and nonvocal responses, identifying appropriate times to initiate, maintain, or terminate a conversation, and developing and maintaining friendships and romantic relationships (Koegel, R. L., et al., 2012; Spence, 2003). These challenges become more prominent as learners with ASD transition to adulthood, where the complexity of social situations increases (Friedman et al., 2013; Laugeson et al., 2012). For example, adults with ASD have fewer interpersonal relationships than adolescents with ASD (Orsmond et al., 2004; Seltzer et al., 2003). Furthermore, the relationships experienced by adults with ASD are often perceived as less empathic and supportive compared to the relationships perceived by adults without ASD (Baron-Cohen & Wheelwright, 2003).

Considering the relevance and contribution of interpersonal relationships with social partners to the quality of life of learners with ASD or their well-being, it is important for practitioners to develop educational programs that focus not only on academic achievement but also on building meaningful and sustainable relationships. Developing meaningful and sustainable interpersonal relationships is a very complex process that requires careful planning, effective interventions, and responsive environments. For example, a child with ASD who attends classes in a regular education classroom should not only be involved in academic activities required for all learners but should also receive instruction on how to develop friendships with typical learners and be provided with structured opportunities to engage in cooperative activities that are likely to promote collaboration and interactions among learners. Thus, the development of meaningful and sustainable interpersonal relationships is one the most critical components of educational planning and service delivery for learners with ASD that will likely facilitate an enhanced quality of life. Table 1.2 displays examples of interpersonal relationships quality-of-life outcomes in learners with ASD across the lifespan.

Self-Determination

Self-determination has been defined as one's ability to act as a causal agent in his or her life, resulting in an increased quality of life (Wehmeyer, 2005). The premise of self-determination is that people who can make choices and decisions or cause things to happen in their life to achieve an outcome or produce change are self-determined or engage in self-determined behavior (Wehmeyer et al., 2010). For example, a young child with ASD who makes choices regarding the types of activities he or she wants to participate in during leisure time or the types of clothes the child prefers to wear at school engages in self-determined behavior. A young adult with ASD who expresses his interests or preferences for a specific job and then advocates for receiving instruction to acquire the behaviors needed to perform the job displays self-determination. The main components of self-determination are acquired across the lifespan and usually include choice making, decision making, problem solving, goal setting and attainment, self-management, self-monitoring, and self-advocacy (Carter et al., 2009; Wehmeyer et al., 2010).

Traditionally, learners with ASD have demonstrated lower levels of self-determination compared to learners without disabilities (Wehmeyer & Shogren, 2008) and other learners with developmental disabilities (Wagner et al., 2007). Low levels of self-determination in learners with ASD have been attributed to deficits in communication and repetitive patterns of behavior, interests, and activities (Chou et al., 2017). Many learners with ASD have challenges with changes in routines, planning their schedules, setting goals, self-monitoring, self-regulating, and self-advocating (Meltzer, 2018). Consequently, they rely on caregivers and practitioners to make choices and decisions regarding short- and long-term goals. For example, an adolescent with ASD who has limited functional communication and an associated attention deficit hyperactivity disorder (ADHD) and attends an Individualized Education Plan (IEP) meeting with his parents may be unable to advocate for the type of supports he needs to function successfully in his inclusive classes and relies on his parents to identify and ask that individualized supports be provided to their child. Learners with ASD who rely on caregivers and practitioners have limited opportunities for choice making, decision making, and self-advocacy, which leads to low levels of self-determination and independence and, subsequently, decreased quality of life (Cheack-Zamora et al., 2020; Kim, 2019).

Researchers have demonstrated that learners with ASD who engage in self-determined behavior are more likely to experience positive employment and independent living outcomes (Martorell et al., 2008; Shogren et al., 2015), attend recreation and leisure activities (McGuire & Donnell, 2008), participate in social activities in the community, and manage stress (Kim, 2019), which results in an improved quality of life (Lachapelle et al., 2005; Nota et al., 2007). Considering the contribution of self-determination to one's quality of life and the low levels of self-determination in learners with ASD, it is imperative that practitioners develop educational programs that focus on promoting the development of self-determination in this population of learners across the lifespan. It has been suggested that instruction on promoting self-determination should begin in early childhood and then continue through adolescence and adulthood when the complexity of social situations increases (Knoster & Kincaid, 2005). Moreover, social support systems and natural opportunities for engaging in self-determined behavior are needed in addition to effective instruction to facilitate the development of self-determination in learners with ASD. Examples of self-determination quality-of-life outcomes in learners with ASD across the lifespan are provided in Table 1.2.

Using Effective Quality-of-Life Planning

One of the most effective approaches to promoting quality of life is person-centered planning (PCP). *PCP* is a systematic team process that emerged in the mid-1980s and involves learners with disabilities and their families in educational planning (Cohen, 1998; O'Brien et al., 1997; Schall & Wehman, 2009). In PCP, learners with ASD and their family participate in one or more meetings to examine learners' abilities and areas for improvement, their interests, preferences, and aspirations for the future, and goals across quality-of-life domains (Hagner et al., 2014). At the conclusion of the PCP meetings, the team identifies a shared vision for the future of the learner with ASD and creates an action plan to support the shared vision and facilitate the achievement of a high quality of life (Brown et al., 2020). Learners with disabilities, including learners with ASD, who participate in PCP are more likely to gain access to employment (Hagner et al., 2001; Menchetti & Garcia, 2003), be socially included in their communities

(Cloutier et al., 2006; Holburn et al., 2004; Smith et al., 2006), and enhance their self-determination (Held et al., 2004).

PCP is grounded in several assumptions, including the importance of considering the learner first and then his or her disability, identifying the learner's abilities, allowing the learner and his or her family to be active participants and equal members in educational planning, exploring the learner's interests and preferences, and identifying their desired changes across life domains (Mount, 1992). The desired changes across life domains usually translate to goals and objectives across at least five outcomes: (a) making choices and exerting control over one's life, (b) interpersonal relationships, (c) social inclusion, (d) assuming valued roles in the community, and (e) continuing to acquire relevant and meaningful behaviors leading to enhanced personal competence (Brown et al., 2020). A detailed description of the PCP process is provided in Chapter 3.

Assessing Quality-of-Life Outcomes

Assessing one's quality of life has been considered a significant component of intervention implementation and service delivery for learners with ASD (Burgess & Gutstein, 2007; Dardas & Ahmad, 2014). As important as it is to evaluate learners' acquisition of specific target behaviors (e.g., identifying numbers and letters, answering questions, following instructions), it is equally important to assess changes in the quality of life of learners with ASD. As we discussed in this chapter, a key aspect of educational planning for learners with ASD is the identification of goals related to quality-of-life domains that have the potential to improve learners' successful functioning in the natural environment and satisfaction with their life. For example, learners with ASD who have limited friendships and experience social isolation would benefit from effective interventions and services to acquire, generalize, and maintain the behaviors needed to develop and maintain successful interpersonal relationships with social partners and, thus, become valued members of their group. Engaging in socially appropriate interpersonal relationships with social partners is considered a quality-of-life outcome that not only provides a prerequisite for developing friendships but also has the potential to increase satisfaction, happiness, and social inclusion.

Once a practitioner has identified relevant and socially valid quality-of-life outcomes for a learner with ASD and implemented effective interventions to teach the behaviors needed to achieve the predetermined outcomes, the next step is to evaluate the effectiveness of the intervention and its impact on the learner's life. Namely, the practitioner needs to determine if the intervention and services provided to the learner with ASD have produced a change in their life and whether the change was significant enough to enhance the learner's satisfaction or well-being and independent functioning. Questions such as "Does Joe have more friends than before the intervention was implemented?" or "What type of activities does Joe engage in with his friends?" or "Does Joe attend any events in the community with his friends?" or "Does spending time with friends make Joe happy?" should be considered when practitioners evaluate the impact of interventions to promote interpersonal relationships.

To answer these questions and to determine the effectiveness of the intervention and its impact on the learner's life, practitioners have to conduct an assessment. *Assessment* is the process of collecting data to evaluate the effects of an intervention on specific behaviors and to measure a learner's success toward targeted outcomes. Chapter 6 discusses various data-collection methods to evaluate the acquisition, generalization, and maintenance of targeted behaviors and the data-based decision-making process for guiding instructional decisions and for assessing progress toward specific outcomes. In this chapter, we present several quality-of-life measures to evaluate the effects of interventions and services on the quality of life of learners with ASD.

Assessing the quality of life of learners with ASD can be a challenging process for practitioners. At a minimum, practitioners must collect data both on short-term outcomes targeting acquisition of specific behaviors (e.g., greeting a social partner upon arrival to the classroom) and on long-term outcomes targeting changes in the learner's life (e.g., developing friendships). To collect relevant information on the learners' progress toward these outcomes, practitioners should use a combination of subjective and objective data. *Subjective data* consist of one's perceived satisfaction with their functioning across quality-of-life domains and can be collected through interviews and rating scales. One example of gathering subjective data to assess quality of life is asking a learner with ASD or her family questions related to the learner's functioning across quality-of-life domains. Questions such as "What type of choices does Ann make at home?" or "How does Ann let you know that she does not like an activity?" or "Does Ann prefer to play with certain peers?" could be considered when gathering data on a learner's self-determination, which is one of the quality-of-life domains.

Another example of collecting subjective data consists of administering quality-of-life measures, such as self- or proxy-report scales. A self- or proxy-report scale usually consists of several items or questions related to quality-of-life domains and rated on a Likert-type scale that aims to identify the respondent's perceived satisfaction with their or their child's life or well-being. An example of an item that could be included in a proxy-report scale to evaluate a parent's satisfaction with their child's well-being in the interpersonal relationship domain is "My child likes playing with other children." Self-report scales are completed by the learner with ASD whose quality of life is evaluated, whereas proxy-report scales are completed by parents, practitioners, or other stakeholders who know the learner well.

When assessing a learner's quality of life by using self- or proxy-report scales, it is recommended that practitioners use scales that have been designed for learners with ASD. Because learners with ASD have unique characteristics that influence their quality of life, it is preferable to use scales that have been specifically designed for this population of learners and have the potential to be good indicators of quality of life. Scales that do not account for the unique characteristics of learners with ASD may lead to inaccurate data that cannot be used to make informed instructional decisions and measure progress on quality-of-life outcomes.

To date, two scales have been developed and can be used to measure quality-of-life outcomes for learners with ASD. The first scale is the *KidsLife-ASD* scale developed by Gomez and colleagues (2020). *Kidslife-ASD* is a proxy-report scale that consists of 96 items and is intended for learners with ASD ages 4 years to 21 years old. The scale consists of eight domains, including material well-being, physical well-being, emotional well-being, rights, social inclusion, interpersonal relationships, self-determination, and personal development. Researchers have demonstrated that the scale is appropriate for learners with ASD and can be used to assess quality-of-life outcomes, assist with the selection of meaningful outcomes across quality-of-life domains, and guide the educational planning process to ensure the provision of effective interventions and individualized services (Gomez et al., 2020).

The second scale is the *Quality of Life for Children with Autism Spectrum Disorder* (QOLASD-C) developed by Cholewicki and colleagues (2019). QOLASD-C is a parent-proxy report consisting of 16 items and is intended for children ages 5 years to 10 years old. The QOLASD-C scale evaluates quality of life across three domains, including interpersonal relationships, self-determination, and emotional well-being. Researchers have demonstrated that the QOLASD-C is appropriate for evaluating the quality of life of children with ASD and can be used to guide the educational planning and instructional decision-making process (Chezan et al., 2022).

In addition to collecting subjective data to evaluate the quality of life of learners with ASD, practitioners should also gather objective data. One approach to gathering objective data consists of conducting observations during typical activities in the natural environment. During observations in the natural environment, practitioners observe learners with ASD to determine if (a) they have the behaviors needed to function successfully in one or multiple quality-of-life domains, (b) they have the opportunity to engage in preferred activities with peers without disabilities, and (c) people in the environment are responsive to learners with ASD. For example, a practitioner who evaluates the social inclusion of a learner with ASD during physical education instruction may want to first document the type and number of opportunities that the learner has to play baseball with typical peers. Then, the practitioner collects data to assess if the learner has the behaviors needed to play baseball with his or her peers by following instructions, by communicating with peers, and by displaying the required motor behaviors (e.g., running, catching the ball, or throwing the ball). Finally, the practitioner documents whether the learner's peers respond to his or her communicative attempts and provide the supports the learner may need to fully participate in the baseball game.

Thus, using a combination of subjective and objective data is a requirement of conducting a comprehensive assessment of quality of life in learners with ASD. Data collected can be used by practitioners to inform the instructional decision-making process and guide the delivery of interventions and services with the goal of enhancing the learners' satisfaction with their life. It is noteworthy to mention that practitioners may want to use quality-of-life scales in combination with other existing measures to evaluate learners functioning across quality-of-life domains and their progress toward individualized goals and objectives targeted in their educational program.

Promoting quality of life is one of the goals of educational planning and service delivery for learners with ASD. Thus, it is essential that practitioners design and implement educational programs that target quality-of-life outcomes and have the potential to enhance the well-being or satisfaction of learners with ASD. Designing meaningful educational programs that promote quality of life is a multifaceted process that includes components such as targeting quality-of-life outcomes, selecting effective approaches to improve quality of life, and assessing outcomes by using both subjective data and objective data within the context of a collaborative partnership between practitioners, learners with ASD, and their parents or caregivers.

QUALITY OF LIFE AT
ORGANIZATIONAL AND SYSTEM LEVEL

As we discussed in this chapter, quality of life is an important aspect of educational planning and a significant outcome of interventions and service delivery for learners with ASD. Therefore, it is important that practitioners design educational programs to meet the interests, preferences, and values of learners with ASD and their families while targeting long-term quality-of-life outcomes that promote valued roles, a sense of belonging to the community, competence, empowerment, and independence (Watson & Keith, 2002). However, the implications of the quality-of-life concept extend beyond educational planning and individual learner outcomes to organizational and system level.

At the organizational level, a key element is the focus on the quality of services provided to learners with ASD and their families. Specifically, agencies should use a multitude of strategies, including engaging in strategic planning, using evidence-based practices to teach meaningful and relevant behaviors that have the potential to promote independence, social inclusion, and empowerment of learners with ASD, using decision making to guide the selection and implementation of evidence-based practices, and evaluating performance (Gomez & Verdugo, 2016). A comprehensive discussion of strategies to improve the quality of services provided by agencies is beyond the scope of this chapter. Therefore, we will briefly mention only three strategies that can be used across programs and service-delivery providers.

One strategy to enhance the quality of services provided to learners with ASD is to establish measurable and observable program indicators that allow the collection of objective data to assess the impact of interventions and services on learners' quality-of-life outcomes. Indicators such as social inclusion, age-appropriate activities, choices, safe environments, family supports, employment, wellness, nutrition, and ownership can be used to evaluate the quality of services provided to learners with ASD and their impact on promoting an enhanced quality of life (Schalock, 2000). For example, an agency that provides interventions to teach learners with ASD to make choices, offers opportunities for choice making throughout the day, and trains practitioners to respond to and honor the choices made by learners with ASD are better equipped to promote quality of life than agencies where learners with ASD rely on practitioners and have no opportunities for choice making.

A second strategy to enhance the quality of services provided to learners with ASD is to ensure the competency of practitioners delivering interventions and services. One way to promote competency is to provide effective professional development on evidence-based practices to promote quality of life, such as PCP, selection of socially valid goals and objectives, collaboration with and involvement of learners with ASD and their families in educational planning, community-based instruction, assessment, culturally responsive interventions, and natural supports. Several effective professional development strategies are described in detail in Chapter 5.

A third strategy to enhance the quality of services provided to learners with ASD is to use continuous and evidence-based self-assessment to evaluate not only learners' individualized quality-of-life outcomes but also the agency's outcomes or performance. Assessment data on an agency's outcomes can be used to guide organizational changes and to improve the services provided. One assessment method to evaluate an agency's outcomes or performance is the Organization Effectiveness and Efficiency Scale (International Research Consortium on Evidence-Based Practices, 2013). The purpose of the scale is to assess an agency's performance from multiple perspectives, including consumers' satisfaction, growth, financial resources, and the internal processes. The scores obtained are translated into three evidence-based indexes, including an effectiveness index, an efficiency index, and a sustainability index (Van Loon & Van Wijk, 2016). These indexes allow an agency to evaluate the quality of services provided and to identify areas for improvement in the services provided to learners with ASD.

At the system level, change efforts may focus on acknowledging the voices and perspectives of learners with ASD and their advocates, embedding the concept of quality of life as a key component of policy, funding research on quality of life, making recommendations for the delivery of services and improved practices that target an enhanced quality of life, and evaluating the effects and impact of these recommendations on enhancing individualized learner outcomes and the quality of services provided. An example of a system-level change is the collaborative effort led by the South Carolina Act Early Team (SCAET) to improve the quality of life in young children with ASD. The SCAET consists of leaders with decision-making authority from state agencies, institutions of higher education, health care systems, autism organizations, and families. The focus of the SCAET is to improve early identification practices for children under the age of 3 with or at risk for ASD and the delivery of home-based behavioral interventions for children at risk for ASD. Their collaborative effort resulted in policy changes at the state level, training offered to service providers, and modifications in practices implemented by state agencies regarding early identification and delivery of evidence-based interventions for children with or at risk for ASD (Rotholz et al., 2017).

Organizational and system-level changes are critical aspects of implementing evidence-based practices and providing high-quality services to learners with ASD and their families. Focusing on selecting meaningful goals and objectives, providing individualized interventions and services, evaluating both individualized learner outcomes and agency's outcomes or performance, and collecting ongoing self-assessment data are only several strategies that have the potential to enhance educational planning and service-delivery models. Organizational and system-level changes are critical in promoting an enhanced quality of life for learners with ASD as illustrated by their independence, social inclusion, and empowerment.

SUMMARY

The conceptualization and measurement of the quality-of-life concept has continued to evolve over the last several decades. It is important to note that the quality-of-life concept is in its infancy in the field of autism and in the delivery of services to learners with ASD and their families. There is a consensus that quality of life (a) is a multidimensional and universal concept, (b) includes objective and subjective components, and (c) is enhanced by self-determination, resources and supports, and social inclusion. Because learners with ASD have lower quality of life compared with learners with other disabilities and learners without disabilities, it is critical to design educational programs that target quality-of-life outcomes and promote independence, empowerment, social inclusion, and valued membership. Promoting quality of life in learners with ASD is a complex and multifaceted process that has implications at individual, organizational, and system level. As the autism community continues to embrace the concept of quality of life, it is important to incorporate quality-of-life outcomes in educational programs, to develop policies that promote quality of life for learners with ASD, and to evaluate the quality of services provided to these learners and their impact on the well-being or satisfaction with life within the context of social inclusion, responsive environments, and acceptance of diversity.

APPLICATION ACTIVITIES

1. Imagine that you are the leader of an organization that provides interventions and services to children with ASD. One of your responsibilities is to keep practitioners informed about the latest developments in the field of autism and service delivery. Create a presentation to discuss the different terminologies used to refer to learners with ASD and provide a rationale for your selection and use of one terminology.
2. Select one learner with ASD in your classroom or clinic and carefully examine the goals targeted in his or her educational program. How do the goals compare to the following recommendations?

   a. Do the goals reflect the learner's and his or her parents' or caregivers' interests, preferences, and values?
   b. Do the goals focus on quality-of-life outcomes, such as interpersonal relationships, social inclusion, emotional and physical well-being, or self-determination?
   c. Does the learner have opportunities to participate in naturally occurring activities with peers without disabilities in the natural setting?
   d. What methods are used to collect data on the learner's quality-of-life outcomes and his or her well-being or satisfaction with life?

3. Pretend that you are a practitioner providing services to a preschool child with ASD. You are using person-centered planning to select goals that are meaningful to the child and his or her family and are likely to enhance the child's quality of life. Identify at least two goals to facilitate the child's physical and emotional well-being, interpersonal relationships, social inclusion, or self-determination.
4. Use the goals identified in Activity 3 and describe how would you evaluate the child's progress and his or her quality of life.

ADDITIONAL RESOURCES

Autism Society (n.d.). *Quality of life outcomes.* https://www.autism-society.org/about -the-autism-society/guiding-principles/quality-of-life-outcomes/

Bennie, M. (2019, September 26). *Measuring quality of life for ASD: Shifting from diagnosis to happiness.* Autism Awareness Center, Inc. https://autismawarenesscentre.com /measuring-quality-of-life-for-asd-shifting-from-diagnosis-to-happiness/

Community Living BC (2011, May 5). *Quality of Life—Dr. Robert Schalock* [Video]. YouTube. https://www.youtube.com/watch?v=1PorQtVq1Bo

Kapp, S. K. (2018). Social support, well-being, and quality of life among individuals on the autism spectrum. *Pediatrics, 141*(Supplement 4), 362–68. https://doi.org/10.1542 /peds.2016-4300N

International Research Consortium on Evidence-Based Practices (2013). *Organization Effectiveness and Efficiency Scale.* https://sid-inico.usal.es/wp-content/up loads/2018/06/SCALE_Organization_effectiveness_Efficiency_Hard_Copy_with _Cover-10_2103.pdf

Rights Based Social Policy (2015, December 5). *Individual, Organizational, and System Level Alignment—Dr. Robert Schalock* [Video]. YouTube. https://www.youtube.com /watch?v=OQjYOvL8CMA

2

Characteristics of Learners with Autism Spectrum Disorder

Katie Wolfe, Meka N. McCammon, and Aaron R. Check

■ ■ ■

INTRODUCTION AND OVERVIEW

Autism spectrum disorder (ASD) is a complex neurodevelopmental disability characterized by differences in social and communication skills and by restricted and repetitive patterns of behavior (American Psychiatric Association [APA], 2013). Social and communication skills are verbal and nonverbal behaviors that we use to interact with others, such as asking for something we need, making eye contact, and engaging in back-and-forth conversation. Restricted and repetitive patterns of behavior can include engaging in the same vocal or motor movement repeatedly, having an intense interest in a specific topic, and having difficulty with transitions or changes in routines.

Although all learners with ASD must display these two characteristics to receive a diagnosis, ASD is referred to as a "spectrum" because each learner is affected by ASD in different ways and to varying degrees. For example, one learner with ASD may be completely nonverbal, whereas another learner may use verbal communication but have difficulty initiating conversations. Similarly, the learner who is nonverbal may be relatively less impacted by restricted and repetitive patterns of behavior than the learner who is verbal. The broad diversity inherent in ASD is illustrated by the quote, "If you've met one individual with autism, you've met one individual with autism" (Shore, n.d.).

The diagnosis of ASD currently relies on evaluating deficits and delays relative to "typical" patterns of development and behavior. However, we agree with self-advocates and others who have promoted a strengths-based perspective of ASD (Shore, n.d.). As one example, the ability to focus intensely on a narrow topic of interest is necessary for many scientific, technological, and artistic advancements. Rooted in this perspective, we believe that interventions for learners with ASD should build on existing strengths and develop skills to improve quality of life.

Our purpose in this chapter is to provide foundational information about the history and characteristics of ASD. We begin with a historical perspective of ASD by discussing shifts in how the characteristics of ASD have been described and defined over time. Next, we describe the prevalence of ASD and how our understanding of the cause of ASD has evolved over time. Then, we discuss the current diagnostic characteristics in detail and describe the process by which learners are diagnosed with ASD. Finally, we review co-occurring medical conditions and diagnoses that are common among learners with ASD.

HISTORICAL CONTEXT

The features that comprise ASD today were first described formally by a psychiatrist, Leo Kanner, in 1943. Kanner (1943) reported 11 case studies of children who had atypical development before the age of 3 years old and shared similar characteristics based on observations, family interviews, and medical histories. The characteristics that Kanner (1943) described included a perceived preference for aloneness, delays in verbal and nonverbal communication skills, various repetitive behaviors, intensely focused interests, and desire for sameness. Despite these commonalities, Kanner reported that there was significant diversity among the children: three of the children were completely nonverbal, and of the eight who did speak, some only repeated what they heard while others spontaneously produced words and sentences. Kanner used the terms "autism" and "autistic," from the Greek word *autos* meaning "self," to describe the children because of their "inability to relate themselves in the ordinary way to people and situations from the outside world" (p. 242). Prior to Kanner's report, learners with ASD may have been characterized as having schizophrenia or an intellectual disability.

The following year, a pediatrician named Hans Asperger used the term "autistic psychopathology" to describe a group of children with characteristics similar to those identified by Kanner (Asperger, 1944), particularly related to poor nonverbal communication skills (e.g., eye contact, gestures, affect), highly specific and restricted interests, and emotional detachment from others. However, Asperger (1944) noted that the children he observed had strong verbal communication skills, with large vocabularies and appropriate grammar, but difficulties with the nuanced, social aspects of communication such as using varied intonation and engaging in back-and-forth conversation. Asperger's work was published only in German, and awareness of it was relatively restricted to German-speaking countries for many years.

Lorna Wing was a psychiatrist who, like Kanner and Asperger, has contributed significantly to our understanding of ASD. Wing (1981) proposed that autism was characterized by a *triad of impairment*—differences in communication, social skills, and behavioral flexibility—that is still reflected in current diagnostic criteria. She studied the variation among individuals with the characteristics described by Kanner and Asperger and was the first to suggest that autism was a spectrum rather than a single, discrete syndrome (Wing & Gould, 1979). In 1981, Wing also helped bring worldwide attention to Asperger's work when she published a paper in English using the term *Asperger syndrome* to describe the specific constellation of characteristics identified by Asperger (Lyons & Fitzgerald, 2007).

As our understanding of ASD has evolved, so too has the system for classifying and diagnosing individuals with it. *The Diagnostic and Statistical Manual of Mental Disorders* (DSM) provides guidelines for diagnosing mental health and developmental disorders using standard, defined criteria (APA, 2013). Autism first appeared as an independent diagnosis labeled "infantile autism" in the third edition of the DSM (DSM-III; APA, 1980); prior to this edition, "autistic" behaviors fell under the diagnosis of schizophrenia. The diagnostic criteria for infantile autism aligned with Kanner's (1943) descriptions and included an onset before 30 months of age, lack of responsiveness to other people, deficits in language, unusual responses to the environment, and the absence of delusions or hallucinations (Volkmar et al., 1986).

Several significant changes to the diagnosis of autism were introduced in the fourth edition of the DSM (DSM-IV; APA, 1994). First, following Wing's research in the 1980s, the diagnostic criteria for autism were revised to reflect the three areas she identified as characterizing autism: impairment in social interaction, impairment in communication, and restricted, repetitive patterns of behavior. Second, Wing's popularization of Asperger's work also resulted in the inclusion of Asperger syndrome, defined as impairment in social interaction and restricted and repetitive behavior, as a diagnosis for the first time in DSM-IV (APA, 1994). Third, autism and Asperger syndrome were included as two of five *pervasive developmental disorders*, an umbrella term used to group specific diagnoses with similar characteristics. Other pervasive developmental disorders included Rett's syndrome, childhood disintegrative disorder, and pervasive developmental disorder-not otherwise specified (PDD-NOS).

The most recent version of the DSM (DSM-5; APA, 2013) involved another significant change to the classification of autism: the individual diagnoses of autism, Asperger, and PDD-NOS have been removed and replaced with the broader diagnosis of ASD accompanied by severity levels. In addition, social and communication delays are now combined into one diagnostic category. More detail on the current diagnostic criteria for ASD follow in this chapter. Despite shifts and refinements in diagnostic classification, the core features of ASD remain similar to those described by Kanner, Asperger, and Wing, including differences in social and communication skills and restricted and repetitive behaviors.

PREVALENCE

How many learners have ASD? The *prevalence* of a condition is the estimate of the number of people in a group or population who have the condition and is usually indicated by a percent or a proportion of the population. Current prevalence estimates of ASD in the United States suggest that 1 in 54 children, or about 1.9%, have been identified with ASD (Maenner et al., 2020). The prevalence of ASD has steadily increased over time. In 2000, the reported prevalence of ASD was 1 in 149 children, and by 2010, it had risen to 1 in 68 children (Maenner et al., 2020). However, the reason for the increasing prevalence of ASD remains unclear. It could be that there has been an actual increase in the number of children with ASD, or the increase may be due to other factors such as changes to the definition of ASD, increased awareness of ASD, or increased efforts to identify and diagnose children early.

Researchers have identified important differences in prevalence rates of ASD across different groups of people. Boys are four times more likely to be identified with ASD than girls: about 1 in 33 boys were identified with ASD compared to about 1 in 145 girls (Maenner et al., 2020). Similar to the increasing overall prevalence of ASD, researchers do not yet understand the reason for this difference.

Boys may be more likely to develop ASD than girls. Alternatively, the characteristics of ASD may differ in girls and boys. Some research indicates that girls with ASD may be less socially isolated, engage in less repetitive behavior, and have fewer restricted and atypical interests compared to boys with ASD (Dean et al., 2017). Researchers have hypothesized that these differences may allow girls with ASD to better "camouflage" their symptoms, ultimately resulting in the under-identification of girls with ASD (Dworzynski et al., 2012).

Prevalence estimates of ASD also vary by race and ethnicity. Historically, non-Hispanic White children have been identified with ASD at higher rates than members of other racial and ethnic groups (Mandell et al., 2009). This difference has been attributed to greater access to health care and diagnostic services for these children compared to those from other racial and ethnic groups, not to a higher risk for ASD. In recent years, the gap in prevalence rates between non-Hispanic Whites, non-Hispanic Blacks, and Asian Pacific Islanders has closed considerably—prevalence rates of each of these groups was around 1 in 55 (Maenner et al., 2020). However, identification of ASD in Hispanic children has continued to lag, with prevalence estimated at 1 in 65 children. Research suggests that Hispanic families in the United States may encounter obstacles related to the diagnosis of ASD, including language barriers, lack of access to health care, and stigma (Zuckerman et al., 2017). A diagnosis is required to access services designed to support learners with ASD, so it is critical that researchers and policy makers continue to identify ways to reduce racial, ethnic, and socioeconomic disparities in the diagnosis of ASD.

ETIOLOGY

Why do some learners have ASD? The term *etiology* refers to the cause or causes of a condition. Since Kanner described the basic characteristics of autism in 1943, researchers have been trying to understand what causes ASD. A common theory until the late 1960s was that autism was a psychological disorder caused by unaffectionate, unloving parents who failed to connect with their children. The theory suggested that a lack of parental affection caused the child psychological harm, which led them to withdraw from the social world and to display the characteristics of autism. Kanner (1943) noted that "there are very few really warm-hearted fathers and mothers" among the families of the children he described but acknowledged that it was not clear what role this played, if any, in their children's behavior. However, the popularity of Freudian psychology during this time provided fertile ground for the theory to linger for several decades. In 1967, Bruno Bettelheim wrote a book called *The Empty Fortress*, in which he espoused the theory and popularized the term "refrigerator mother" to refer to mothers who, according to his account, were so cold and distant that they caused their children to develop autism.

Also during the 1960s, a psychologist named Bernard Rimland became interested in the causes of autism after his young son began to exhibit the characteristics described by Kanner (1943). He rejected the theory that his parenting behaviors had caused his son's symptoms, and he began reviewing the research related to autism. He found that the evidence supporting the "refrigerator mother" theory was speculative and anecdotal. In his book *Infantile Autism* (1964), Rimland convincingly argued that autism was more likely caused by biological factors, which led to differences in brain development, than by defective parent-child relationships. Rimland's book helped to shift the focus of research on the cause of autism away from parents and toward biology.

Genetic Influences

The most recent research into the cause of ASD suggests that genetic and environmental factors, as well as the interaction between the two, contribute to the development of ASD (Bölte et al., 2019). Research indicates that some learners may have a genetic predisposition to ASD—in other words, their genes may increase the likelihood that they have ASD (Sandin et al., 2017). In families with one child with ASD, the likelihood of having a second child with ASD increases, suggesting that the disorder is hereditary (Sandin et al., 2017). However, genetics are not the sole determinant of ASD. In studies of identical twins, researchers have found that when one twin has ASD, the other twin has ASD between 65% and 90% of the time (Ronald & Hoekstra, 2011). If genes were the only cause of ASD, we would expect that identical twins with the same DNA would either both have, or not have, ASD. There is also not a single "autism gene"—researchers have identified hundreds of genes that are associated with increased likelihood of ASD (Rylaarsdam & Guemez-Gamboa, 2019). Some of these genes are inherited, meaning that the gene is also present in the parents' cells. Some of these genes are *de novo* mutations, meaning that the parents' genetic material changed during fertilization, so the gene is not present in the parents' cells (Iossifov et al., 2014). The presence of de novo mutations may explain why some learners have ASD without any prior occurrences in their family.

Environmental Influences

The environment also appears to play a role in the development of ASD and may include chemical, bacterial, viral, and physical factors that influence a learner's physiology (Bölte et al., 2019), either during the prenatal period or after birth. It is important to recognize that research on the environmental causes of ASD is correlational, not causal. An example of a correlational study is when researchers measure the presence of a particular environmental factor (for example, advanced parental age) and the occurrence of ASD, and look for an association between the factor and the occurrence of ASD over a large sample of individuals. Findings may indicate that parents who are older may be more likely to have a child with ASD (i.e., association between parental age and ASD) than parents who are younger. Although there may be an association between advanced parental age and ASD, this does not mean that advanced parental age caused ASD. There may be other factors that were not measured or accounted for that either caused or contributed to ASD.

Parental age is one environmental factor that has been consistently associated with a higher likelihood of ASD in many studies (Wu et al., 2017). While estimates vary, a large recent study suggested that, compared to men in their 20s, men in their 40s have a 28% higher likelihood of having a child with ASD, and men over 50 years old have a 66% higher likelihood (Sandin et al., 2016). Similarly, women in their 40s are 15% more likely to have a child with ASD than women in their 20s (Sandin et al., 2016). The reason for the link between parental age and ASD is unclear, but one possible explanation is that de novo mutations become more common in sperm and egg cells with age. Researchers have investigated the effects of other potential environmental influences including smoking, alcohol, and medication use during pregnancy, obstetric complications during childbirth, and exposure to environmental toxins such as heavy metals, pollutants, and pesticides. However, except for parental age, researchers have not found a strong and consistent relationship between a specific environmental factor and increased likelihood of ASD.

What About Vaccines?

Vaccines have received significant attention as a potential cause of ASD, based on an article published by Andrew Wakefield and colleagues in a British journal called *The Lancet* in 1998. Wakefield's paper reported on 12 children who had gastrointestinal issues and whose parents stated that they began showing symptoms of ASD soon after receiving the measles, mumps, and rubella (MMR) vaccine. Wakefield and his colleagues hypothesized that the MMR vaccine caused intestinal inflammation, which then caused the development of ASD. However, children typically receive the MMR vaccine around 18–24 months, which is around the same time that language and communication skills tend to grow very quickly and when the social-communication differences in children with ASD can become very apparent.

Despite the small number of children involved and the absence of controlled and objective data to support their hypothesis, Wakefield's theory that vaccines caused ASD received widespread attention and led to fear and distrust of vaccines. Several large epidemiological studies were then published that directly refuted the supposed link between MMR and ASD. In one study, researchers showed that the percentage of children in California who received the MMR vaccine stayed the same each year between 1988 and 1994, but the number of children diagnosed with ASD increased sharply each year (Dales et al., 2001). If the MMR vaccine were causing children to develop ASD, we would expect the number of children diagnosed with ASD to mirror the number of children receiving the MMR vaccine. Instead, rates of ASD increased while rates of MMR vaccination stayed flat. Other similar studies conducted in other states and countries provided strong evidence that the MMR vaccine did not cause ASD.

Shortly after these epidemiological studies were published, almost all of Wakefield's coauthors on the original paper retracted their findings (Murch et al., 2004), admitting that there was not enough data to conclude that the MMR vaccine causes ASD. The journal also learned that Wakefield's research was funded by lawyers who were suing the companies that produce the vaccines, a serious conflict of interest that compromises scientific objectivity and was not disclosed (Horton, 2004). In 2010, the *Lancet* retracted the article based on flaws in the research design as well as ethical concerns. As of 2009, 20 large studies conducted by different researchers in different parts of the world have shown that vaccines do not cause ASD (Gerber & Offit, 2009). However, the belief that vaccines play a role in the development of ASD persists.

Neurological Differences in Learners with ASD

While researchers continue to study the etiology of ASD, there is a consensus that the characteristics of ASD are a result of differences in the structure and function of the brain (Ha et al., 2015). Kanner (1943) noted that the children in his study had a larger head circumference than typically developing children, and that observation has been supported by contemporary empirical research comparing children with and without ASD (Courchesne et al., 2003; Sacco et al., 2015). Studies using neuroimaging have confirmed that this larger head circumference is a result of increased brain volume (Courchesne, 2004), but research has produced conflicting information about whether the overall brain is larger, or if specific areas of the brain are enlarged (Sacco et al., 2015). Interestingly, studies have reported that children who are eventually diagnosed with ASD have average, or even slightly smaller than average, head circumference at birth, with a period of rapid increase between 6 and 14 months that results in a brain volume that is about 10% larger than children without ASD by the age of 2 (Courchesne, 2004). This trajectory of "brain overgrowth" during the critical early childhood period may influence the development of neural circuits that contribute to social and language functioning (Hazlett et al., 2017). Researchers continue to use magnetic resonance imaging (MRI) to study the structural and functional differences in the brains of learners with ASD to gain a better understanding of the underlying nature of the condition and to identify potential biological markers that may assist in diagnosis (Hiremath et al., 2021).

DIAGNOSTIC CHARACTERISTICS

Before we describe the diagnostic characteristics of ASD in detail, it is important to remember that learners with ASD present with a spectrum of symptoms. That is, ASD is a heterogeneous disorder in which some learners are severely limited in their functioning while others may be more mildly affected. Because of the range in severity and ability, everyone with ASD is distinguished by their own characteristics in relation to the specific core symptoms rather than presenting with identical symptoms. For example, deficits in nonverbal communicative behaviors can look different across learners. Someone may present with abnormalities in eye contact and body language while another may have deficits in using and understanding gestures. In other words, not all learners with ASD present with the same behavioral excesses and deficits. *Behavioral excesses* refer to behaviors that occur too frequently, may impinge on learning, and may be harmful to the learner and others such as self-injury and aggression. A *behavioral deficit* is any delay or deficiency in an essential skill that is necessary to support an adequate quality of life and may include daily living skills, social skills, and communicative behaviors. Caregivers are usually the first to notice these excesses and deficits and may do so as early as 15–18 months (Yates & Le Couteur, 2016). These deficits and excesses may begin to affect the child and family's quality of life, often leading to a referral for an evaluation. Given caregivers' unique perspectives, their input is integral to the diagnostic process, particularly for young children.

The DSM-5 (APA, 2013) is a handbook that insurance companies, physicians, and clinical practitioners in the United States use to diagnose behavioral, developmental, and mental disorders based on standardized criteria. The DSM-5 criteria for ASD include two core symptoms: persistent deficits in social communication and social interaction, and restricted and repetitive patterns of behavior (see Table 2.1). Additionally, these characteristics must be present

Table 2.1. DSM-5 Criteria for ASD

Persistent deficits in social communication and social interaction across multiple contexts (must meet all):

   a. Deficits in social-emotional reciprocity
   b. Deficits in nonverbal communicative behaviors
   c. Deficits in developing, maintaining, and understanding relationships

Restricted, repetitive patterns of behavior, interests, or activities (at least 2):

   a. Stereotyped or repetitive motor movements, use of objects, or speech
   b. Insistence on sameness, inflexible adherence to routines, or ritualized patterns of verbal or nonverbal behavior
   c. Highly restricted, fixated interests that are abnormal in intensity or focus
   d. Hyper- or hyporeactivity to sensory input or unusual interest in sensory aspects of the environment

Source: See https://www.cdc.gov/ncbddd/autism/hcp-dsm.html.

in early childhood, cause significant impairment in skills necessary for current functioning, and cannot be attributed to another condition such as intellectual or developmental delay (APA, 2013).

Social Communication and Social Interaction

The first core symptom of ASD is persistent deficits in social communication and social interaction. For many children, the first sign of ASD is a delay in acquiring and using communication skills. *Communication* refers to both verbal and nonverbal methods of sending a message to another person. Early nonverbal communicative behaviors such as eye gaze, vocalizations, and prelinguistic gestures (e.g., waving, pointing, and clapping) develop within the first year of life among neurotypically developing learners. These early nonverbal behaviors not only allow children to express their needs but also set the foundation for establishing and maintaining social interactions. Further, children with ASD often lack or exhibit deficits in joint attention. *Joint attention* is the coordinated shift in attention between two people and an object and may include directing another person's attention to an item of interest or responding to another person's interest in an item, for example by following their eye gaze (Stone et al., 1997; Yates & Le Couteur, 2016). These behaviors are critical to further language and communication development. While most learners with ASD do acquire verbal communication skills, estimates suggest that about a third of those with ASD never develop verbal communication, or develop very minimal verbal communication (i.e., a few words), even after many years of intervention (Tager-Flusberg & Kasari, 2013).

To meet the diagnostic criteria for ASD in the social communication and interaction domain, a learner must present with deficits in social-emotional reciprocity, nonverbal behaviors used for social interaction, and developing, maintaining, and understanding relationships. A deficit in social reciprocity may manifest as difficulty engaging in back-and-forth conversation, sharing interests, or initiating and responding to social interactions. Social reciprocity involves an awareness of the emotions of others, the ability to interpret changes in others' reactions, and responding appropriately by adjusting one's own behavior. Learners lacking social reciprocity are prone to experiencing social isolation due to an inability to sustain appropriate social interactions. Some learners with ASD may have sophisticated verbal repertoires; however, their restricted interests or preoccupations may hinder their ability to participate meaningfully in reciprocal conversations. While conversing they may make statements regarding irrelevant details, abruptly change the topic to their own interests, or even fail to respond to their conversational partner's questions. Social interactions involve not only spoken language but also the use and understanding of nonverbal communication, which is often characteristically deficient among learners with ASD.

The second aspect of the social communication criterion is deficits in nonverbal communication. Nonverbal communication behaviors can take many forms, such as eye contact, body language, or facial expressions. Eye contact may be fleeting during social interactions or coupled with poor awareness of positioning and personal space. For example, one learner may turn their body away or look down as they are interacting with others, while another learner may stand too close or inappropriately touch the person with whom they are interacting. Social relationships also can be impacted by an inability to infer the emotional states of others, interpret facial expressions, and use facial expressions and gestures contextually.

Impairments or deficits in social interaction may affect a learner's ability to develop and understand relationships and adjust one's own behavior in various contexts. For learners who do develop verbal communication, deficits in social interactions largely impact their relationships with others. For example, they may lack an awareness of other's feelings or how their behavior impacts others. Apart from having difficulties engaging in reciprocal conversations and failing to show interest in others' interests, learners with ASD may misinterpret subtle cues, such as tone of voice or facial expression, which may stifle ongoing peer relations despite the learner's interest in developing those relationships.

Restricted, Repetitive Patterns of Behavior, Interests, or Activities

The second core symptom of ASD is the presence of two or more types of restricted and repetitive patterns of behavior (RRB). These patterns are characterized as repetitive vocal or motor behavior, strict adherence to routines or rituals, restricted interests, and hyper- or hyporeactivity to sensory stimuli. While RRB is a diagnostic criterion for ASD, similar to other characteristics of ASD, it can look very different in different learners.

Repetitive Behavior

Repetitive vocal or motor behavior, often referred to as *stereotypy*, is a common characteristic of ASD. Learners with ASD often engage in these repetitious behaviors out of context and with what appears as no discernable purpose. Although these behaviors are not harmful, they can interfere with learning and may be socially stigmatizing. *Vocal stereotypy* is repetitive sounds, words, or even a delayed repetition (echolalia) of previously heard vocal behavior such as saying the script to a favorite show two hours after watching it. *Motor stereotypy* is repetitive movement, such as hand flapping, body rocking, or mouthing objects. While everyone engages in repetitive behaviors that may seem to have no purpose (e.g., tapping a pencil, twirling hair) from time to time, for learners with ASD, these behaviors may occur with a much greater frequency and to an extent that disrupts daily functioning. There are various theories for why these behaviors occur at such a high rate among learners with ASD, including social isolation, impoverished environments, and physiology (Lydon et al., 2013; Rapp & Vollmer, 2005).

Insistence on Sameness

Insistence on sameness was one of the original defining characteristics of autism (Kanner, 1943). This subtype of RRB, along with restricted interests, are often referred to as "higher-level" repetitive behaviors and are more likely to be observed in learners with a higher intelligence quotient (IQ; Turner, 1999). In contrast, "low-level" repetitive behaviors such as repetitive motor movements are more prevalent among learners with a lower IQ (Turner, 1999). An insistence on sameness can be exemplified by requiring a strict adherence to routines or rituals and may manifest in a variety of ways. For example, a learner may repeatedly touch an item, demand that other individuals sit in a specific location, straighten or organize things in a particular manner, or take the same route to a preferred location.

This insistence may dominate the learner's daily life and impede learning and social interactions particularly. Additionally, caregivers and practitioners might mistakenly view the learner as being inflexible or unwilling to accept change. Subsequently, attempts to delay or interrupt these routines may evoke challenging behavior. Insistence on sameness is a primary area of clinical concern. Researchers have reduced the occurrence of ritualistic behavior and the problem behaviors produced by interrupting them through environmental enrichment, teaching coping statements, and functional communication training (Lehmkuhl et al., 2008; Rispoli et al., 2014; Sigafoos & Kerr, 1994). However, children with autism vary in the extent to which they resist interruptions in their rituals; therefore, treatment can be complex and must be individualized.

Restricted Interests

The third subtype of RRB are highly restricted (i.e., limited in variety), fixated interests that are abnormal in intensity or focus. Restricted interests are highly prevalent among learners with ASD. Researchers have found that 88% of learners meeting diagnostic criteria for ASD have some restricted interests (Smith et al., 2009; Turner-Brown et al., 2011). Sometimes these interests are age-appropriate (e.g., a 3-year-old who is interested in Thomas the Tank Engine) but are most often nonsocial in nature. For example, some common areas of restricted interests for learners with ASD include vehicles, electronics, weather, and numbers (e.g., calendars and clocks; South et al., 2005).

Like other forms of RRB, restricted interests can interfere with learning, social development, and daily functioning. Caregivers report their child's restricted interests are one of the most difficult symptoms of ASD to manage (Mercier et al., 2000; South et al., 2005). However, learners with ASD and their families have reported both the negative impact and the positive impact of their restricted interests (Mercier et al., 2000). While others in the environment may find these preoccupations annoying, interests are a source of pleasure, are relaxing, and can increase self-confidence for everyone, including learners with ASD (Attwood, 2003). Caregivers and educators might benefit from a new perspective in which these restricted interests are utilized as a strength and to support deficits in other areas. For example, keen abilities to memorize information and intently focus on a topic can be used to teach rules, facts, and academics. Further, intense interests may be used to identify employment opportunities that the learner will excel at and find rewarding.

Hyper- and Hyporeactivity

In addition to challenges associated with language and communication, learners with ASD may exhibit unusual responses to everyday stimulation. Hyperreactivity to sensory stimulation makes a learner more sensitive to various stimuli such as sound, light, or tactile stimulation. A learner with ASD who is hyperreactive to sound may wear noise-canceling headphones to mask or diminish the level of stimulation they perceive. Everyday activities such as mealtime, grocery shopping, and attending amusement parks may be particularly challenging for learners with ASD and their families. For example, parents of children with sensitivity to color, taste, smell, or texture often report concerns related to nutrition due to the child's restricted intake and food refusal (Cermak et al., 2010; Chistol et al., 2018). Places like the grocery store or amusement parks may be overstimulating for the learner with ASD and, thus, may lead to meltdowns and the need to leave these settings or avoid them altogether. The challenges associated with hyperreactivity may lead to increased stress for caregivers and siblings and prevent the family from enjoying activities together due to an inability to predict and control for the multiple stimuli inherent in the community.

Conversely, when a learner is hyporeactive, they may not readily respond to sources of stimulation. For example, a hyporeactive child may not cry after falling and bumping their head. Whether the learner is hyper- or hyporeactive, caregivers are likely to spend a significant amount of time constantly being on guard, anticipating their child's reactions and behaviors so as to prevent meltdowns and injuries. Furthermore, the symptoms the learner presents with require flexibility from family members; severity will influence the degree to which the family's routines might revolve around the learner with ASD's needs (DeGrace, 2004). Regardless of the purpose or form, the challenge with these restricted, repetitive patterns of behavior, interests, or activities is they may occur at such high rates that it may be difficult to interrupt and may often interfere with skill acquisition or social interaction.

Severity Level

In addition to varying symptom profiles, learners with ASD will also have different prognoses. The long-term outcomes for these learners are in part based on the severity of the symptoms they display. Historically, learners were diagnosed with PDD-NOS, Asperger syndrome, or autism, which distinguished a learner's symptom severity such that a diagnosis of Asperger suggested the learner was "higher" functioning and required less support whereas autism designated more severe symptoms necessitating the greatest level of support (Mehling & Tassé, 2016). The DSM-5 groups these former subtypes into a broader singular disorder, ASD. Further, the DSM-5 includes specifiers for which diagnosticians describe symptom severity into three distinct levels of increasing support that subsequently replace the pejorative terms "low and high functioning" (Bal et al., 2017). The three levels are (1) requiring support, (2) requiring substantial support, and (3) requiring very substantial support (APA, 2013). These levels are assigned based on the findings of comprehensive diagnostic assessments, interviews, and observations that capture the level of support needed to address a learner's deficits in the areas of social communication and interaction, and restricted and repetitive patterns of behavior.

Level 1: Requiring Support

Level 1 or *requiring support* is the least severe classification. Learners with Level 1 ASD are characterized as being vocal with average to high IQ. They often require some behavioral intervention to address deficits in social communication and executive functioning (Didehbani et al., 2016; Lieb & Bohnert, 2017), and may have difficulty making friends. There are noticeable impairments with initiating social interactions, communicating appropriately (i.e., lacking back-and-forth flow of conversation, saying the right thing at the right time), and reading social cues and nonverbal body language. Due to their lack of success communicating, it may appear as though they are disinterested in social interactions, but this may not be the case. Executive functioning, which includes planning, working memory, and self-regulation, is often impacted by deficits in their ability to sustain attention to a task, and inflexibility may limit their ability to move between tasks. Additionally, they may have problems with planning and organizing materials, thus stifling their independence.

Level 2: Requiring Substantial Support

Learners with Level 2 ASD require *substantial support*. Their deficits may be more noticeable and can manifest as problems with verbal and nonverbal communication skills. Vocal speech is often limited to simple sentences, there are limitations in their ability to interpret nonverbal communication, and their own use of nonverbal communication may be odd. They may infrequently respond to others' attempts to socialize. Like learners at Level 1, they may have difficulty sustaining and shifting attention as well as exhibit inflexibilities; however, challenging behaviors are more likely to occur when self-stimulatory behaviors are interrupted or they are required to terminate preferred activities or shift between tasks. A narrow range of interests and restricted and repetitive behaviors significantly hinder their daily functioning.

Level 3: Requiring Very Substantial Support

Level 3 is the most severe form of ASD, and deficits are most obvious. These learners require *very substantial support*. They have severe problems with verbal and nonverbal communication. They are less likely to reciprocate social interactions and may only respond to direct approaches. When they do respond to social initiations, their speech may be unintelligible or limited to a few words and phrases, or they may require the use of augmentative and alternative communication such as sign language, picture exchange, or speech generating devices. Learners requiring very substantial support may engage in higher rates of repetitive behaviors as compared to the other levels, and changes in routines can be especially distressing, causing more severe manifestations of challenging behavior.

Severity level is not fixed, meaning that the amount of support a learner needs in one period of their lives can be changed by the quality of educational or therapeutic services they receive. Given that symptom severity is transient, interventions designed to meet a learner's specific behavioral deficits and excesses related to the core symptoms of autism is crucial. Furthermore, including symptom severity in the diagnostic process, and considering other qualifiers such as cognitive and language abilities, may inform the selection of services and assist with the development of individualized treatment plans, and ultimately influence long-term outcomes. It is also important to recognize that while the DSM specifies one global severity level across all domains, each learner with ASD is likely to benefit from different levels of support across domains. For example, a learner may require very substantial support in the area of social skills, but relatively little support related to restricted behaviors and other areas of adaptive functioning.

Presence of Intellectual Disability

In contrast to ASD, which is defined by deficits in social interaction and communication and restricted, repetitive behaviors, intellectual disability (ID) is a chronic condition that involves impairments in intellectual and adaptive functioning, present prior to age 18 (APA, 2013). While estimates have varied across studies, most recent research suggests that about 30% of learners with ASD also have ID (Thurm et al., 2019).

Intellectual functioning consists of reasoning, problem solving, comprehension, and related skills, and is quantified using IQ tests (Tassé et al., 2016). Although some learners with ASD also have ID, it is critical to remember that a certain level of cognitive functioning is not a diagnostic criterion for ASD. Learners with ASD have a range of cognitive abilities as captured by standardized IQ tests. The most recent Centers for Disease Control and Prevention (CDC) report (Maenner et al., 2020) estimates that 42% of children with ASD have an average or above-average IQ (IQ > 85), while 24% have an IQ that is considered "borderline" (IQ = 71–85), and 33% have an IQ that meets criteria for ID (IQ ≤ 70). Practitioners should also keep in mind that IQ is not a measure of adaptive functioning, and its utility for measuring how a learner navigates day-to-day life is limited. A learner with a lower IQ can attain a high degree of independence in their daily life, and a learner with a higher IQ may be more impaired in terms of everyday activities.

To meet the ID diagnostic criteria, there also must be deficits in at least one of three domains of adaptive functioning (conceptual, social, and practical) that interferes with a learner's ability to meet developmental or sociocultural standards (APA, 2013). The domains of adaptive functioning are needed to complete tasks across environments in everyday life and influence a learner's quality of life. Conceptual skills include basic literacy and understanding constructs such as time and money. Social skills include relating to others, problem solving, and self-advocacy. Practical skills consist of personal care and occupational skills. Deficits in these areas can be identified using norm-referenced standardized tests, interviews, observations, and clinical judgment; however, they only indicate areas of strengths and limitations. The level of support that a learner needs is best determined through ecological assessments that account for the learner's goals, routines, and available support (American Association on Intellectual and Developmental Disabilities [AAIDD], n.d.).

Learners with ASD who also meet the ID diagnostic characteristics are likely to present with more social and communication impairments, higher rates of RRB, or more severe occurrences of self-injury and aggression than learners with

ASD without ID (Cervantes & Matson, 2015). Due to these increased risk factors, learners with ASD and co-occurring ID may require more complex and systematic intervention. Additionally, the increased prevalence of RRB, self-injury, or aggression may limit access to services particularly as learners age (Perry et al., 2013).

THE DIAGNOSTIC PROCESS

In the early years of a child's life, pediatricians and primary health care providers are often the first and most consistent source of information for parents, making it critical that these professionals take an active role in monitoring for and evaluating any number of possible health-related concerns, including developmental delays (Johnson & Meyers, 2007; Lipkin & Macias, 2020). Early identification of developmental disabilities such as ASD is a time-sensitive matter. Earlier identification may result in a caregiver both accessing early intervention services and providing more thorough information for potential etiological research (Barger et al., 2018). In their community report on autism, the CDC's Autism and Developmental Disabilities Monitoring Network (2018) found that although most children eventually diagnosed with ASD exhibited some form of behavior to elicit concern from a caregiver by the age of 3 years, less than half of them received a developmental evaluation by that age, and 30% had not received a formal diagnosis by the age of 8 years.

Given that there are no medical tests or biomarkers for ASD, a diagnosis is derived from direct observation of behavior by extensively trained clinicians, meaning a diagnosis is based on professional judgment (Huerta & Lord, 2012). The following sections will discuss a variety of tools that are utilized in the process of evaluating for a potential diagnosis of ASD, with various levels of expertise required for each tool. Ultimately, the diagnosis must be made by qualified clinicians including, but not limited to, developmental pediatricians, psychologists, or pediatric neurologists.

Surveillance
Surveillance (sometimes referred to as monitoring) is an ongoing and informal process with the purpose of identifying children at risk of eventual diagnoses of developmental delays (Barger at al., 2021; Johnson & Meyers, 2007). Information is collected through interviews to explore family medical histories and discuss parental concerns related to skill development and problem behavior. Interviews and observations may also be conducted to determine if developmental milestones are being achieved at appropriate ages. All information gathered serves to inform parents, caregivers, and practitioners whether more in-depth screening is necessary. Additionally, the information can be used to investigate trends in eligibility for services, such as special education.

Screening
The American Academy of Pediatrics (AAP) recommends general screening take place at ages 9, 18, and 30 months for all children regardless of developmental history or prior surveillance (Hyman et al., 2020). The purpose of *screening* is to quickly identify whether a child is at high risk for a particular disorder. Screening tools are brief—most take less than 10 min—and are usually completed by

parents or caregivers who know the child well. Because diagnostic evaluations are time- and resource-intensive, screening is used to identify individuals who may benefit from a more thorough and costly evaluation. General developmental screening tools are sensitive to language and cognitive delays, and likely to indicate the potential need for an evaluation for ASD (Johnson & Meyers, 2007). The *Ages and Stages Questionnaire*, for example, is a parent questionnaire with age-specific items covering a range of skills across developmental domains that has been increasingly used by physicians in recent years (Lipkin et al., 2017).

The AAP also recommends that all children be screened using ASD-specific screening tools at 18 and 24 months (AAP, 2006). Additional ASD-specific screening may occur earlier if the child is considered high risk—for example, if the child exhibits "red flags" such as failure to respond to their name, lack of eye contact, or delayed language development. There is an assortment of instruments designed specifically for early detection of ASD, focusing on core symptoms related to DSM criteria. For example, the *Pervasive Developmental Disorders Screening Test-II* is a parent report consisting of items with response options of "yes, usually true" or "no, usually not true," designed for children as young as 18 months, and takes approximately 15 min to complete and 5 min to score (Montgomery et al., 2007). Another common screener is the *Modified Checklist for Autism in Toddlers Revised, with Follow-Up* (M-CHAT-R/F; Robins et al., 2009), a parent questionnaire designed for children ages 16 to 30 months that is easy to complete and simple for primary care providers to interpret (Robins et al., 2001). The M-CHAT-R/F includes 20 "yes" or "no" questions (many paired with examples) such as "Does your child point with one finger to ask for something or to get help?" and "If you turn your head to look at something, does your child look around to see what you are looking at?" Scoring takes under 2 min, and for any items answered "no," the screener includes a set of follow-up items with an easy-to-use flowchart for a more in-depth evaluation.

Diagnosis

Results from screening instruments do not constitute a clinical diagnosis; if, however, screening results indicate the individual is at risk for a diagnosis of ASD, they are referred to a qualified clinician for a full diagnostic evaluation. A trained pediatrician, psychiatrist, or psychologist typically completes a diagnostic evaluation by comparing information from the evaluation to the criteria for ASD in the DSM-5. While most learners are diagnosed with ASD during childhood, there are also a significant number of learners who receive their first diagnosis of ASD as an adult (Geurts & Jansen, 2012).

The diagnostic evaluation process is complex and dynamic. The number and variety of assessment tools that are used during the evaluation can vary depending on the learner's symptoms. With no established biomarkers to rely on, a diagnosis must be determined based on clinical and professional judgment. This judgment is informed both by indirect assessment, such as caregiver reports and interviews, and by direct observation or testing.

There are a variety of standardized diagnostic tools available to guide clinicians in evaluating whether a learner has ASD. The *Autism Diagnostic Observation Schedule*, 2nd ed. (ADOS-2) is a semi-structured instrument that assesses social interaction, communication, play, and imaginative use of different materials with excellent diagnostic validity for ASD (Lord et al., 2012). Using this tool, the clinician can select from four modules intended for different levels of expressive language. In sessions up to 30 min in length, the clinician creates situations and observes and records the learner's behavior. For example, one item on the ADOS-2 is evaluating the learner's response to their name. The clinician says the learner's name multiple times and records whether the learner responds by looking at or talking to the clinician. If they do not respond to the clinician, the caregiver is asked to say the learner's name. Observed behaviors are assigned scores, and the clinician subsequently analyzes the scores to generate an overall score that relates to the diagnostic criteria for ASD.

The *Autism Diagnostic Interview Revised* (ADI-R) is an interview given to caregivers that is particularly useful in distinguishing a diagnosis of ASD from other developmental disorders (Rutter et al., 2003; Tadevosyan-Leyfer et al., 2003). The *Childhood Autism Rating Scale*, 2nd ed. (CARS-2) is a clinical rating scale informed by observation of a child with separate scales for individuals with low and high support needs (Schopler et al., 1988). The CARS-2 contains 15 items with rating scales from "1" to "4" and may be administered in a variety of settings by qualified professionals. In comparison to same-age peers, a score of "1" denotes that a behavior occurs within normal limits and a score of "4" denotes that a behavior is abnormal (Vaughan, 2011). The *Gilliam Autism Rating Scale*, 3rd ed. (GARS-3) is a widely used assessment for diagnosing ASD that is particularly useful in estimating severity (Gilliam, 1995). The GARS-3 contains six subscales with a total of 58 items and is designed to be administered to teachers or caregivers by clinicians trained in working with learners with autism (Karren, 2017).

The ADOS-2, CARS-2, and GARS-3 are examples of ASD-specific instruments to assist clinicians in their evaluation. Often, diagnostic evaluation consists of a host of assessments, many of which are not necessarily ASD-specific. These assessments may evaluate IQ, language skills, cognitive skills, or adaptive functioning. For example, the *Wechsler Intelligence Scale for Children* is commonly used to assess cognitive ability in evaluation of learners with ASD (Dale et al., 2021). The decision of which instruments to use varies by clinician preference and experience. The ADOS-2 may produce results sufficient for a diagnosis, or a separate follow-up instrument may be used to support or clarify the results. The authors of the CARS-2, for example, caution that the instrument is not used alone for the purpose of making a diagnosis, but as part of a battery of tools (Vaughan, 2011).

Medical and Educational Diagnoses

Monitoring and surveillance practices as detailed above may reveal the need for more formal screening and subsequent diagnostic evaluation, with all of these practices being completed by qualified professionals (e.g., psychologist or developmental pediatrician). A *medical diagnosis* of ASD is based on comparing the learner's characteristics to the defined criteria in the DSM-5. Once a learner has a medical diagnosis of ASD, they may be eligible for services and supports such as behavioral intervention or speech and language therapy through Medicaid or private health insurance.

School-age children and youth with ASD may also be eligible for special education services; however, a medical diagnosis alone does not qualify a learner for these services. An *educational diagnosis* of autism requires that a learner's characteristics meet the definition of autism in the Individuals with Disabilities Education Improvement Act (IDEIA, 2004) and that the disability adversely impacts learning. IDEIA defines autism as "a developmental disability significantly affecting verbal communication and social interaction, generally evident before age three" (IDEIA, 2004). An educational diagnostic evaluation is typically completed by a school psychologist in cooperation with the family and other school professionals (e.g., special education teacher, speech-language pathologist). Together, this team determines if the learner qualifies for special education and related services according to IDEIA, and which specific support services are appropriate given the learner's needs.

Although medical and educational diagnoses are related, they are separate processes with separate requirements that serve different purposes. Just as a medical diagnosis does not automatically make a learner eligible for special education services, an educational diagnosis is not sufficient for establishing eligibility for supports outside of school. Not all learners with a medical diagnosis of ASD will have an educational diagnosis, and vice versa. In fact, in a study evaluating prevalence of educational and medical diagnoses, Barnard-Brak (2019) found that while the CDC estimated the prevalence of ASD as 1 in 54 children, the prevalence of educational diagnoses in alignment with IDEIA requirements was 1 in 91.

COMMON CO-OCCURRING CONDITIONS

There are a number of medical conditions and psychiatric disorders that are relatively common among learners with ASD. These co-occurring conditions can impact not only the learners' health but also their behavior (Davignon et al., 2018). Studies have found that learners with ASD who have certain medical conditions, such as gastrointestinal issues, sleep disorders, and migraines, have higher rates of challenging behavior and social withdrawal than those without such conditions (e.g., Chaidez et al., 2014). Therefore, practitioners should be aware of conditions that are more prevalent in learners with ASD and should be prepared to rule these out as potential causes of behavior prior to assessing and intervening to change behavior.

Researchers have uncovered several medical conditions that are more prevalent among learners with ASD than among the general population. One common co-occurring condition is epilepsy, a neurological disorder that causes unpredictable seizures that may vary in form and intensity. Recent estimates suggest that about 12% of learners with ASD also have epilepsy (Lukmanji et al., 2019), which is substantially higher than estimated rates of epilepsy in the general population (2.2%; Kohane et al., 2012). Learners with ASD also seem to have a higher likelihood of gastrointestinal issues (11.4%) compared to the general population (4.5%; Kohane et al., 2012). Specific gastrointestinal issues that are more frequent among learners with ASD than those without ASD include abdominal pain, constipation, and diarrhea (Chaidez et al., 2014). Sleep difficulties, including having trouble both falling and staying asleep, are another common co-occurring condition among learners with ASD (Mazzone et al., 2018). Researchers estimate that between 50% and 80% of children with ASD experience sleep difficulties compared to 25% of children without ASD (Mazzone et al., 2018). There is some evidence to suggest that sleep difficulties are more prevalent in children with ASD compared to adolescents or adults (Davignon et al., 2018); however, other studies suggest that sleep difficulties persist throughout the lifespan (Goldman et al., 2012).

Learners with ASD may also have higher rates of certain mental illness than learners without ASD. Mental illnesses are "health conditions involving changes in emotion, thinking or behavior (or a combination of these) . . . that are associated with distress and/or problems functioning in social, work or family activities" (APA, 2018). Bipolar disorder, schizophrenia, obsessive compulsive disorder, generalized anxiety disorder, and depression are all considered mental illnesses. They can be difficult to diagnose in learners with ASD because the instruments used for the general population may not distinguish behaviors associated with the characteristics of ASD from behaviors associated with other psychiatric conditions. In addition, diagnosis of some mental illnesses, like depression, requires self-report of thoughts and emotions. Learners with ASD may have difficulty describing these internal states, which could further complicate the diagnostic process. These challenges may lead to over- or underdiagnosis of comorbid mental illness among learners with ASD.

Given the challenges with accurate diagnosis of mental illness among learners with ASD, it is unsurprising that prevalence estimates of these disorders vary across studies. However, a recent review of 96 individual studies on co-occurring psychiatric disorders in learners with ASD (Lai et al., 2019) indicated that attention-deficit hyperactivity disorder is common in this population (28%), as are anxiety disorders (20%) and depression (11%). All of these prevalence rates are higher than their counterparts in the general population. The studies in this review included learners from childhood through adulthood, and age was associated with different co-occurring conditions. For example, younger age was associated with a higher prevalence of ADHD, whereas older age was associated with a higher prevalence of depression and bipolar disorder (Lai et al., 2019).

The increased prevalence of medical and mental health conditions among learners with ASD highlights the need for an interdisciplinary approach to treatment, which should be integrated and holistic. Learners with ASD benefit from coordinated care from all practitioners—including those from educational, behavioral, medical, and psychiatric disciplines. This means that these practitioners must communicate and work together in the best interests of the learner. The importance of developing strong partnerships with other professionals will be highlighted in subsequent chapters.

SUMMARY

Our understanding of ASD has evolved, and continues to evolve, as researchers conduct more studies and learners with ASD and their families share their experiences. ASD is a complex developmental disability that is defined by differences in social communication and social interaction as well as restricted and repetitive behaviors. Learners with ASD share these two general characteristics, but these characteristics may manifest in different ways and to different degrees in each learner. For this reason, the diagnosis of ASD can be challenging and must be conducted by a highly trained professional. The diversity inherent in learners with ASD also requires that practitioners carefully assess each learner's skills, and collaborate with the learner and their family, to develop meaningful goals and intervention programs.

Although the prevalence of ASD continues to increase, the reason for this increase remains unclear. Rising prevalence rates could be due to increased awareness of ASD; better surveillance, screening, and diagnostic processes; more individuals having ASD; or a combination of these factors. Increasing the numbers of learners with ASD in schools and other settings necessitates that practitioners be prepared to effectively meet the needs of this population through the ethical implementation of evidence-based practices.

APPLICATION ACTIVITIES

1. Develop a timeline illustrating the historical progression of our understanding of ASD, including main events related to (1) describing ASD, (2) diagnosing ASD, and (3) understanding the cause of ASD.
2. Imagine that you are a practitioner, and the parent of a learner with whom you work asks you what causes ASD. How would you briefly summarize the research on the etiology of ASD in a parent-friendly manner?
3. Read the following scenario and identify characteristics that align with each of the core symptoms of ASD. Aubrey is a 5-year-old girl who lives at home with her parents and twin brother. Aubrey's mother reports there were no complications during her pregnancy; the age at which Aubrey met developmental milestones was on target, which suggests motor development should be age appropriate. Aubrey has a brief history of ear infections and antibiotics. She has been on allergy medications (i.e., Singulair and Zyrtec), since 2018. Aubrey has a history of hypersensitivity to sounds such as hair and hand dryers, and public toilets. Her sleep patterns are normal except that she requires physical proximity to others. Aubrey is not on a restricted diet. She eats a wide variety of fruits and vegetables and shows little preference for junk food; however, she refuses to eat any green foods. Aubrey is not toilet trained, which is of high priority since opportunities for assistance at school may be limited. She is independent with the following adaptive skills: using a fork, spoon, and straw; however, some other adaptive skills are not on an age-appropriate level. Grooming and self-care skills are an area in which problem behavior is closely associated. She dresses herself and takes an unusual interest in changing multiple times per day; she has difficulty with buttons, snaps, and tying her shoes. Aubrey's mother is concerned about her language repertoire, indicating that Aubrey speaks in short two-to-three-word phrases but only in response to others' initiations. She does not reciprocate questions to carry on a conversation and often walks away when the topic is not one of her own interests. Aubrey's teacher has concerns that she does not show compassion toward others; specifically, she reported several occurrences of Aubrey laughing when other students cry. Despite these challenges, both Aubrey's parents and teacher reported several positive characteristics. Aubrey has intense focus on animals

and when learning activities have an animal theme, Aubrey quickly acquires concepts. She also enjoys being around other people and shows affection by smiling and hugging.

4. Describe the importance of designating the level of severity when making an ASD diagnosis.

5. Using the free instrument and resources available on https://mchatscreen.com, run a mock M-CHAT-R/F evaluation with a partner, peer, or colleague.

ADDITIONAL RESOURCES

ASD Toddler Initiative. (n.d.). *Early identification of autism spectrum disorder*. https://asdtoddler.fpg.unc.edu/early-identification-autism-spectrum-disorders/early-identification-module-introduction.html

Autism Navigator. (n.d.). *ASD video glossary*. https://autismnavigator.com/asd-video-glossary/

Centers for Disease Control and Prevention. (n.d.). *Autism data visualization tool*. https://www.cdc.gov/ncbddd/autism/data/index.html

National Institutes of Mental Health. (n.d.). *Autism spectrum disorder*. https://www.nimh.nih.gov/health/topics/autism-spectrum-disorders-asd/?utm_source=rss_readersutm_medium

3

Assessment for Instructional Planning

Laura C. Chezan and Erik Drasgow

■ ■ ■

INTRODUCTION AND OVERVIEW

Assessment, the process of collecting information to make an informed decision, represents the cornerstone of instructional planning for learners with disabilities, including those with autism spectrum disorder (ASD). Developing and implementing meaningful educational programs require the collection of objective and accurate data to identify a learner's strengths, areas for improvement, preferences, interests, and current level of performance across academic, communication, social, and behavioral domains. Data collected allow practitioners to identify socially valid outcomes, to select and implement effective and culturally responsive interventions, and to evaluate and monitor learners' progress toward the target outcomes within the context of a balanced curriculum. Thus, assessment plays a significant role in all phases of instructional planning for learners with disabilities, including development, implementation, and evaluation (Root, Wood, et al., 2020).

The importance of assessment to instructional planning has been emphasized in the professional and ethical standards of numerous professional organizations. For example, one of the professional standards for practice in special education requires that all teachers working with learners with disabilities "use assessment to understand the learner and the learning environment for data-based decision making" (Council for Exceptional Children, 2020, p. 2). The Ethics Code for Behavior Analysts emphasizes the need to "select and design assessments that are conceptually consistent with behavioral principles; that are based on scientific evidence; and that best meet the diverse needs, context, and resources of the client and stakeholders" (Behavior Analyst Certification Board, 2020, p. 12). Furthermore, school psychologists are required to systematically collect data to understand learner's abilities and weaknesses, and to evaluate and monitor the effectiveness of interventions (National Association of School Psychologists, 2020a).

For school-age learners with and without disabilities, assessment is mandated by federal laws. For example, the Individuals with Disabilities Education Improvement Act (IDEIA, 2004) states that practitioners who work with learners with disabilities should use a variety of assessments that are (a) valid and reliable; (b) nondiscriminatory regarding a learner's culture, race, or language; and (c) conducted by trained practitioners. Moreover, the Every Student Succeeds Act (ESSA, 2015) highlights the need for assessment and accountability to ensure that all learners, including learners with disabilities, reach proficiency in the key academic areas. The law also states the importance of using valid and reliable assessments that are nondiscriminatory based on a learner's disability, culture, or religion (Root, Wood, et al., 2020).

Because of the crucial role of assessment to instructional planning, it is important that practitioners working with learners with ASD are not only familiar with different types of assessments but are also able to select the assessment that matches the characteristics of the learner and provides reliable and valid data aligned with the purpose for which the assessment is designed. Specifically, assessments are designed for different purposes, such as screening, diagnosis, eligibility, planning, evaluation of interventions and services, and curriculum or program development. For example, a diagnostic assessment is conducted by a pediatrician or licensed psychologist to evaluate and diagnose ASD. An eligibility assessment is conducted by a school multidisciplinary team to determine if a learner is eligible for special education services under the IDEIA (2004). A program development assessment may be conducted by a teacher to identify socially valid outcomes and to assess a learner's performance across curriculum domains. To ensure the collection of relevant data, practitioners should be familiar with and understand that different assessments are designed to be used for different purposes and select the most appropriate assessment when evaluating learners with ASD.

Furthermore, learners with ASD are a heterogeneous population with a wide range of social-communication and behavioral characteristics. For example, one learner with ASD may function academically at the same level as his or her peers without disabilities but have difficulties initiating, maintaining, and terminating social interactions. Another learner with ASD may be nonvocal, require very substantial levels of support with all daily activities, and engage in problem behavior that negatively impacts their learning. Although a practitioner conducts an assessment to identify socially valid outcomes for both learners with ASD, the practitioner will use different types of assessments for each of the two learners to collect accurate data, to select relevant outcomes, and to make data-based instructional decisions.

Thus, conducting appropriate assessments that provide useful and accurate information is the first step in developing meaningful educational programs that are likely to promote positive academic, social, communication, and behavioral outcomes while enhancing the effective functioning and quality of life of learners with ASD. Our purpose in this chapter is to provide an overview of assessment for instructional planning and discuss different types of assessments that can be used by practitioners working with learners with ASD to select and measure individual outcomes. First, we will discuss assessment as it relates to instructional planning. Second, we will describe several aspects related to conducting a meaningful assessment for learners with ASD. Third, we will discuss several assessment methods that can be used with learners with ASD. Fourth, we will present different types of assessments that can be used to develop meaningful educational programs for learners with ASD. Finally, we will emphasize the importance of linking the assessment results to program development, monitoring, and evaluation.

ASSESSMENT AND INSTRUCTIONAL PLANNING

One of the main purposes of assessment is to collect information to guide the instructional planning process. The instructional planning process is comprised of several phases, including program development, progress monitoring, and evaluation of instructional effectiveness. In this section of the chapter, we will briefly discuss how assessment relates to each of the three phases of instructional planning.

Program Development

The first phase of instructional planning is program development. Program development consists of two steps. The first step is the *identification and selection of socially relevant, functional, and chronological age–appropriate behaviors* that are aligned with the preferences, interests, and values of learners with ASD and their families. Further, the selected outcomes should have the potential to promote positive outcomes and enhance learners' quality of life, valued membership in their community, and active participation in inclusive environments. During this component of program development, practitioners conduct a comprehensive assessment to identify "what to teach." To guide the assessment process, practitioners may use questions like "What behaviors will help the learner function successfully in his or her environment?" or "Is this outcome aligned with the learner's interests and preferences?" or "Is this behavior age-appropriate?" or "What are the long-term benefits of learning this behavior?" (Scott et al., 2000).

Because learners with ASD are a heterogeneous population characterized by a wide range of social-communication and behavioral abilities who require different levels of support, the assessment used to inform program development should (a) accurately capture each learner's performance, (b) lead to the identification of individualized outcomes that match the unique characteristics of the learner, and (c) maximize learning in areas that are relevant to the learner's functioning in current and future environments. For example, some learners may benefit from receiving instruction mostly on academic outcomes such as listening and reading comprehension skills, whereas other learners may benefit from receiving instruction mostly on social-communication outcomes such as engaging in socially appropriate interactions with peers and adults. Other learners with ASD may benefit from a more balanced approach that focuses on targeting both academic outcomes and social-communication outcomes. It is important to note that a one-size-fits-all approach to selecting outcomes is not appropriate for learners with ASD and, consequently, practitioners should use assessments that capture the learner's unique strengths, needs, and preferences.

Furthermore, some assessments may not be appropriate for the identification of socially appropriate and functional outcomes or program development in general. For example, norm-referenced assessments that measure the extent to which a learner's score deviates or departs from the average performance of a group of learners with similar demographic characteristics do not provide useful information to assist practitioners with the identification of individualized outcomes (Root, Wood, et al., 2020). Norm-referenced assessments represent standard measures of cognitive performance, academic achievement, or adaptive skills performance and are usually used for different purposes, including screening, diagnosis, and eligibility for special education and related services (Matson, 2007). Norm-referenced assessments have several limitations, including lack of sensitivity and testing constraints, that limit their usefulness for learners with ASD (Akshoomoff, 2006; Akshoomoff et al., 2010; Stahmer & Carter, 2005).

For example, a learner who is not acquiring skills at the expected developmental level will obtain lower standardized scores on norm-referenced assessments over time, which indicates a gap between chronological age and the corresponding skills the child should possess. For learners with ASD who have social-communication and behavior deficits, and who may acquire skills at lower rates than typically developing learners, the scores obtained on norm-referenced assessments will indicate regression or loss of skills even though the learner is actually making progress on the target skills (Bacon et al., 2014). Furthermore, norm-referenced assessments do not allow the evaluation of a learner's performance during typical activities in the natural environment (Groth-Marnat, 2000). Because norm-referenced assessments are not appropriate for selecting and identifying socially valid outcomes and are not good predictors of quality of life for learners with ASD (Burgess & Gutstein, 2007), practitioners should refrain from using these assessments for the purpose of developing educational programs for learners with ASD. Instead, practitioners should consider using other types of assessments to identify target outcomes, including ecological inventories or curriculum-based assessments, which will be described in later sections of this chapter.

The second step of program development is the *selection of evidence-based practices* (EBPs) to teach the target outcomes. During this step, practitioners may use guiding questions to assist with the selection of effective instructional strategies to teach the learner the behaviors or skills needed to achieve the target outcomes. Examples of such questions include "What is the most effective instructional strategy to teach the target behavior?" "When two or more instructional strategies are equally effective, which of the two strategies can be implemented based on available resources?" "Did I consider the learner's preferences and values when selecting this strategy?" A detailed discussion on how to select EBPs to teach learners with ASD is provided in Chapter 4.

Progress Monitoring

The second phase of instructional planning is progress monitoring. *Progress monitoring* consists of systematically collecting, analyzing, and interpreting data to monitor learners' progress toward the target outcomes and to make data-based instructional decisions. For school-age learners with disabilities, progress monitoring is mandated by federal law. Specifically, IDEIA (2004) not only requires educators to monitor a learner's progress toward their individualized education plan (IEP) outcomes, but it also requires them to communicate frequently with the learner's parents or caregivers regarding their child's progress and whether the progress is meaningful or sufficient (Etscheidt, 2006).

Progress monitoring is essential to evaluating the appropriateness and effectiveness of instructional programs to ensure positive learner outcomes and data-based decision making (Orland, 2015; Wilkinson, 2017). Therefore, it is critical that practitioners have a good understanding of how to collect and use data to determine if (a) the learner is making progress toward the target outcomes, (b) the progress is sufficient, and (c) the instructional program needs to be maintained, updated, or changed. For example, based on data collected and the progress made by the learner, practitioners may decide to continue the same intervention, to update the intervention by adding one or more components, to implement the intervention in new settings, to increase the frequency and amount of intervention, or to change the intervention completely.

Because of the critical role of progress monitoring in instructional planning, it is important that practitioners select assessments that capture each learner's performance on the target outcomes, are sensitive to small changes in learners' performance, and are feasible and acceptable for practitioners working with learners with disabilities (Stecker et al., 2008). Furthermore, practitioners need to use progress monitoring consistently throughout the implementation of an intervention and implement the assessment procedures with fidelity. Conducting assessments with fidelity is an important aspect of instructional planning because it leads to the collection of accurate data on learners' progress and allows practitioners to make informed data-based instructional decisions. Chapter 6 provides a detailed description of the data collection process to monitor learners' progress, to evaluate the effectiveness of instruction, and to make instructional decisions.

Evaluation of Instructional Effectiveness

The third phase of instructional planning is evaluation of instructional effectiveness. The *evaluation of instructional effectiveness* consists of an assessment to determine the (a) effectiveness of EBPs on promoting the acquisition, maintenance, and generalization of the target behaviors and quality of life and (b) quality of the program itself on promoting positive learner outcomes. After one or multiple EBPs are selected and implemented to teach a learner the target behaviors, practitioners collect data to monitor the learner's progress and determine if the instructional strategies selected are producing the desired outcomes. When evaluating the effectiveness of EBPs, practitioners may ask questions like "Is there a change in the learner's performance on accurately completing and submitting math assignments?" "Does most-to-least prompting produce an increase in the number of steps of washing hands completed independently by Joe?" "Does reducing the length of the math assignment decrease the number of instances of physical aggression during independent seat work?" Chapter 6 provides a detailed description of data collection procedures and data-based decision making.

In addition to assessing learners' progress toward a target outcome, practitioners also need to gather data to determine the broader impact of instruction on the learner's quality of life and successful functioning in the natural environment (Root, Wood, et al., 2020). For example, a practitioner uses an intervention consisting of prompting and behavior skills training (BST) to teach a young adult with ASD to initiate, maintain, and terminate a conversation with peers in a postsecondary environment. Data collected suggest that the young adult has acquired the behaviors required to engage in conversations with peers after the intervention was introduced and, thus, document the learner's progress toward the outcome and the effectiveness of EBPs. Next, the practitioner conducts an assessment to determine if the intervention also produced a broader effect on the young adult's life by answering questions like "Does the learner engage in more conversations with peers than he engaged in before the intervention was implemented?" "Does the learner seem happier?" "Does the learner perceive that their life has improved after learning the required behaviors to engage in conversations with peers?" (Please refer to Chapter 1 for a more detailed discussion on quality-of-life assessment.)

Another important focus of assessment during this phase of instructional planning is the evaluation of the program quality. The *evaluation of the program quality* within the context of which learners receive instruction consists of collecting data about various aspects of program implementation, including the human and financial resources available, the practitioner-learner ratio, the supports and opportunities provided to learners to achieve the target outcomes, the percentage of learners who achieve their target outcomes, and the supports and training offered to practitioners to implement instruction. Data collected assist an agency or organization to evaluate the quality of services provided to learners and their families and identify areas for improvement to enhance learners' success and practitioners' efficacy and satisfaction with their job. Various assessment instruments have been developed to assist with program evaluation. Several examples include the *Autism Program Quality Indicators* (APQI; Crimmins et al., 2001), the *Program Quality Measurement Tool* (PQMT; Cushing et al., 2009), the *Organization Effectiveness and Efficiency Scale* (International Research Consortium on Evidence-Based Practices, 2013), and the *School-Wide Evaluation Tool* (SET; Sugai et al., 2001).

Assessment is a critical component of instructional planning for learners with ASD. To identify socially valid outcomes and develop meaningful educational programs, practitioners must collect data during each phase of the instructional planning process, including program development, progress monitoring, and evaluation of instructional effectiveness. Data collected assist practitioners to design meaningful educational programs that lead to independence, self-sufficiency, and satisfaction with life for learners with ASD.

CHARACTERISTICS OF ASSESSMENT FOR LEARNERS WITH ASD

Although assessment is usually a straightforward process, conducting an appropriate assessment to identify the strengths, needs, and current level of performance of learners with ASD may be challenging. As we mentioned at the beginning of this chapter, learners with ASD are a heterogeneous population with unique characteristics, a wide range of social-communication and behavioral abilities, and different levels of severity. Therefore, norm-referenced assessments such as intelligence or language tests that focus on evaluating a narrow range of skills and are not sensitive to small changes in a learner's behavior over time do not provide useful information to guide the selection of socially relevant outcomes for learners with ASD (Magiati et al., 2011). The use of inappropriate assessments may lead to an unbalanced curriculum that focuses on one domain (e.g., academic) without considering other relevant domains (e.g., social, behavioral). In this section of the chapter, we will discuss several aspects that practitioners should consider when conducting assessments for the purpose of developing educational programs that have the potential to enhance the quality of life of learners with ASD.

Focus on Meaningful Behaviors

Functional Behaviors

Brown and colleagues (1979) defined a functional behavior as "an action that will be performed by someone else if a person with disabilities does not perform it" (p. 82). In other words, *functional behaviors* are those behaviors that allow learners to function independently and successfully in the natural environment and have the potential to enhance their active participation in the community, self-determination, and satisfaction with life. An example of a functional behavior for a preschool child with ASD may be to return a greeting to the librarian when entering the library. A functional behavior for an adolescent with ASD may be to independently use a cell phone to text their location to his or her parents. An adult with ASD performs a functional behavior when asking an employer to accommodate their needs by providing short breaks every two hours during work.

The focus on functional behavior is critical to educational programs designed to provide instruction on behaviors relevant to the learner's everyday life that promote independence and quality of life. The more functional behaviors learners with ASD have in their behavioral repertoire, the more likely they are to function effectively in their environment and be self-sufficient and valued members of their communities. Functional behaviors are considered *pivotal behaviors* because their acquisition can lead to improvements in other behaviors in the absence of additional instruction (Koegel et al., 1988). For example, a child with ASD who learns to share toys during playtime may acquire additional behaviors such as responding to a peer during the game or asking questions. Moreover, the child may be more likely to spend more time playing with peers, which will offer multiple naturally occurring opportunities for social interactions and for the development of friendships. Researchers have demonstrated that the acquisition of pivotal behaviors leads to self-determination and generalization (Koegel et al., 1999; Najdowski et al., 2014).

Thus, conducting an appropriate assessment that allows practitioners to examine the learners' performance during typical activities in their environment is a critical first step in identifying functional behaviors and developing meaningful educational programs. Practitioners should be aware that functional behaviors are not related only to social, communication, and behavioral outcomes. Functional behaviors can also be embedded within academic outcomes across core content areas. Academic functional behaviors are those behaviors that have long-term benefits and enhance a learner's performance across settings, including home, school, and community (Copeland & McDonnell, 2020). For example, a functional literacy behavior may be teaching adolescents with ASD the names of various products they may want to purchase at a grocery store. A young adult with ASD may learn time management skills by developing and following a schedule during work hours, which represents a functional math behavior. Learning the name of various products and time management skills are behaviors that allow learners to function successfully in the natural environment and reduce their dependence on practitioners or families.

Socially Valid Behaviors

In addition to identifying and targeting behaviors that are functional, practitioners need to ensure that the behaviors included in a learner's educational program are also socially valid. *Socially valid behaviors* are behaviors that align with learners' interests, preferences, and values and are socially relevant for their functioning in the natural environment (Falcomata, 2015). In other words, socially valid behaviors are those behaviors that are rated as important and acceptable by learners with ASD and their families. When identifying socially valid behaviors, practitioners should also consider the immediate benefits the learner will experience because of acquiring the behavior. For example, a nonvocal child who engages in physical aggression to access preferred items will benefit from learning a socially appropriate communicative response (e.g., "toy, please") that will help him or her immediately as opposed to learning a behavior that may help him in the future (e.g., following a schedule).

An important aspect of identifying socially valid behaviors is their relevance to the learner's family priorities and values. Consequently, an appropriate assessment should also involve the learner's family members. For example, for a young adult with ASD who is transitioning to adulthood and whose family would like to prepare him or her to live independently, practitioners may identify and prioritize behaviors such as following a schedule, preparing a meal, housekeeping, and paying bills based on the information provided by family members during the assessment process. Learning such behaviors will likely reduce the young adult's dependence on family members and will alleviate his or her parents' concerns related to the learner's self-sufficiency and successful functioning in the natural environment. Equipping learners with the behaviors needed to be independent and self-sufficient is likely to promote their acceptance and inclusion in the community while providing opportunities for social inclusion and positive relationships.

Chronological Age–Appropriate Behaviors

An important aspect of assessment is the identification of chronological age–appropriate behaviors. *Chronological age–appropriate behaviors* are those behaviors that correspond to the chronological age of a learner and allow them to engage in the same activities as their peers without disabilities. For example, watching Barney daily during breakfast is a chronological age–appropriate behavior for a young child with ASD; however, it is an inappropriate behavior for a 29-year-old man with ASD. In the previous example, teaching the young child to request access to TV to watch Barney during breakfast is an appropriate instructional goal. The same instructional goal would be stigmatizing for the adult with ASD and, therefore, practitioners should consider other behaviors, such as watching a sports channel on TV, going to a baseball game with friends, going out to a restaurant, or purchasing groceries at a local store.

The emphasis on identifying chronological age–appropriate behaviors is one way that the principle of normalization has influenced the field of education. As described in Chapter 1, the principle of normalization highlights the importance of providing the same opportunities to learners with disabilities, including those with ASD, as the ones provided to learners without disabilities while facilitating their inclusion and acceptance into the society. One way to accomplish this goal is by teaching learners with ASD chronological age–appropriate behaviors to the greatest extent possible to minimize the discrepancy between learners with ASD and typical learners, reduce stigmatization, and facilitate their sense of belonging and participation in inclusive environments.

Focus on Natural Environments

Assessments conducted for the purpose of identifying functional, socially valid, and chronological age–appropriate behaviors are conducted in the learner's natural environment. *Natural environment* is the setting or location in which a learner with ASD usually engages in activities throughout the day or will ultimately function in the future. For example, the natural environment of a child with ASD during school hours consists of academic and nonacademic locations in the school. The natural environment of the same child with ASD after school hours may be his or her parents' house and the playground in the neighborhood where the child plays with other children in the afternoon. For a young adult with ASD transitioning to adulthood, the natural environment during school hours may be the hospital cafeteria where the adult completes his or her vocational training.

The purpose of conducting the assessment in the natural environment is to obtain accurate data on a learner's current level of performance in the environments where they usually participate or will ultimately function. Researchers have demonstrated that learners with disabilities, including learners with ASD, have challenges with generalization of behaviors across settings and, thus, they may be unable to perform a learned behavior in an untrained setting (Stokes & Baer, 1977). For example, a speech-language pathologist assesses Joe's behavior of vocally imitating sounds in the speech therapy room (i.e., a contrived environment). The results of the assessment suggest that Joe cannot imitate sounds. However, when the speech-language pathologist observes Joe in his classroom (i.e., natural environment), she notices that Joe vocally imitates the sounds made by his teacher during circle time activities.

In addition to lack of generalization, learners with ASD also can display stimulus overselectivity, which may influence the accuracy and relevance of assessment results. *Stimulus overselectivity* is the tendency of some learners with ASD to focus on irrelevant stimuli instead of on the important aspects of a stimulus (Lovaas et al., 1971). For example, a child who learned to follow a teacher's instructions when the teacher sits on a chair during circle time might not follow the teacher's instructions when he or she stands up next to the child's desk because the child attended to an irrelevant stimulus (i.e., teacher sitting on a chair) as opposed to the relevant stimulus (i.e., instruction being provided). An adolescent with ASD who learned to add three-digit numbers (i.e., relevant stimulus) when displayed in a vertical format might not be able to add the numbers when displayed in a horizontal format (i.e., irrelevant stimulus).

To minimize the effects of stimulus overselectivity and limited generalization on the assessment results, practitioners should evaluate a learner's performance during typical routines in the current and future environments. For example, a practitioner wants to assess the performance of an adolescent with ASD on ordering lunch in the school cafeteria. In this situation, the practitioner should observe and record the adolescent's performance in the school cafeteria when a naturally occurring opportunity for ordering lunch presents itself. If the practitioner assesses the learner's performance in a contrived environment (e.g., an office in the school), the assessment results may not accurately capture the adolescent's performance on ordering lunch and will lead to inappropriate instructional decisions. Assessing learners with ASD in the natural environment enhances the probability of valid assessment results that allow practitioners to capture the learners' accurate performance on target behaviors and develop meaningful educational programs.

Focus on Cultural Responsiveness

Cultural responsiveness refers to a set of educational assessment and instructional practices designed to address the unique needs of learners from culturally and linguistically diverse backgrounds (Miller et al., 2019). The idea behind cultural responsiveness is that cultural variations and differences across learners represent unique strengths that should be considered during the assessment and instructional process and, thus, promote learning and understanding of cultural differences both for practitioners and for learners (Bassey, 2017). Over the last two decades, the importance of cultural responsiveness has been emphasized in the field of education due to the growing number of culturally and linguistically diverse learners (Artiles, 2003; Trainor & Bal, 2014).

Assessment is a component of instructional planning that is greatly influenced by a learner's language and culture. Cultural values and expectations influence the behavior of learners with and without disabilities and, therefore, practitioners should be familiar with the cultural heritage of each learner when conducting assessments, interpreting data, and selecting target behaviors (Norbury & Sparks, 2013). For example, making eye contact with a social partner and pointing with the index finger are considered inappropriate behaviors for a learner in a Chinese family (Zhang et al., 2007). Moreover, facial expressions, proximity, public display of emotions, and pace of conversation may differ across cultures (Norbury & Sparks, 2013; Westling & Fox, 2009). In addition, culturally and linguistically diverse learners and their families may have different expectations and priorities related to the behaviors targeted for intervention. For example, play skills are less valued by Korean American families compared to European American families (Farver & Lee-Shin, 2000).

To obtain valid assessment results that lead to the development of meaningful educational programs for learners with ASD, it is important for practitioners to involve learners and their families in the instructional planning process to ensure that the assessment methods are responsive to their values, preferences, and culture. Involving learners and families in the assessment process is critical, especially when evaluating a learner's level of performance on behaviors related to daily living, social, and transition outcomes, which are greatly influenced by the cultural values and expectations of learners and their families (Greene, 2014). Daily living, social, and transition outcomes are components of quality of life and contribute to a learner's satisfaction with life and successful functioning in the natural environment. One way to ensure that educational programs are meaningful is to use culturally responsive assessment procedures when evaluating a learner's performance in the natural environment and identifying functional, socially valid, and chronological age–appropriate behaviors leading to self-sufficiency, self-determination, and independence.

Multiple Sources of Information

One of the most important aspects of assessment for learners with ASD is the collection of information from multiple sources rather than relying on one source to identify a learner's strengths, needs, and current level of performance. Using multiple sources of information to accurately capture a learner's performance allows practitioners to *triangulate* data and make an informed instructional decision. *Triangulation* is the process of analyzing, comparing, and interpreting data collected from at least three different sources to obtain an accurate representation of the learner's performance on target behaviors (Schall, 2009). Triangulation enhances practitioners' confidence that the influence of various characteristics (e.g., stimulus overselectivity, limited generalization) of learners with ASD on the assessment results is minimized and any discrepancies in the information collected from different sources are resolved.

An example of triangulation is the use of multiple sources of information (e.g., preference assessment inventory, interview with the learner and his or her coworkers, and ecological inventory at the internship site) during a transition assessment for a young adult with ASD. When the young adult completes a preference assessment inventory, he identifies working at the front desk in a fitness center as his preferred job. However, the employment specialist at the school also knows that the young adult has challenges with initiating, maintaining, or terminating conversations with social partners that are sometimes perceived as rude and inappropriate behaviors. The employment specialist decides to expose the young adult to other jobs (e.g., cleaning the equipment in the fitness center, helping a cook to prepare meals in a restaurant, stocking books in a library). She then assesses his performance in each of these jobs using an ecological inventory and interviews with staff at each site. The employment specialist also discusses with the adult's family members to better understand their vision for the young adult with ASD.

By using triangulation, practitioners ensure that the assessment yields accurate and valid results to assist with the identification of functional, socially valid, and chronological age–appropriate behaviors and the development of meaningful educational programs to enhance learners' independence and quality of life. Furthermore, collecting information from different stakeholders (e.g., teachers, parents, peers) allows practitioners to have a better understanding not only of a learner's abilities and needs, but also of others' perceptions and vision for the learner and the resources and supports needed to assist the learner in reaching his or her full potential.

Comprehensive Assessment

A comprehensive assessment is an essential aspect of developing a meaningful educational program for learners with ASD. A *comprehensive assessment* requires the evaluation of a learner's functioning across multiple domains using multiple sources of information and appropriate assessments. Because the main goal of education is to equip learners with the behaviors needed to function successfully in inclusive environments and be active and valued members of their communities, it is important to obtain an accurate representation of the learner's level of performance across quality-of-life domains in addition to academic performance.

A comprehensive assessment yields valid results that allow practitioners to develop a balanced curriculum for learners with ASD. A *balanced curriculum* is an educational program that includes functional, socially valid, and chronological age–appropriate behaviors across domains of human functioning (Najdowski et al., 2014). For example, a balanced curriculum for a preschooler with ASD includes outcomes across domains, such as social, motor, language, adaptive, play, cognition, and academics (Gould et al., 2011). A balanced curriculum for a transition-age learner with ASD may include outcomes across domains, such as academics, cognition, adaptive, social, employability, and community participation (Schall, 2009). Assessing a learner's performance only in one domain (e.g., academic) represents an incomplete assessment that does not provide a good understanding of their strengths and needs.

The number and the specific behaviors included in each of the domains listed previously depend on the results of the comprehensive assessment conducted by a practitioner to identify a learner's strength, needs, current level of performance, interests, and preferences. For example, the educational program of a preschooler with ASD who can count and read sight words but cannot greet peers may have fewer academic outcomes and more functional behaviors related to social, language, and play domains. The educational program of a transition-age learner with ASD who performs academically well but is always late to class or internship and does not initiate interactions with social partners may focus on more functional behaviors related to social, employability, and community participation domains and fewer academic outcomes.

A comprehensive assessment is an essential first step in developing a meaningful and balanced educational program for learners with ASD that has the potential to promote independence and enhance quality of life. A meaningful and balanced educational program is comprised of functional, socially valid, and chronological age–appropriate behaviors across domains of human functioning, including at a minimum language, social, adaptive, and academics. The number and type of outcomes across domains also depend on the needs of learners and on the ASD severity. Figure 3.1 illustrates the variation of outcomes across curriculum domains based on learners' needs. To determine the functionality and social validity of a behavior, practitioners need to consider (a) the long-term effects of behavior acquisition and its impact on the learner's independent functioning in the current and future environments, (b) the opportunities to use the behavior across environments, (c) the likelihood of the skill being maintained over time, and (d) the learner's preferences, interests, and values (Najdowski et al., 2014).

ASSESSMENT METHODS

Several assessment methods can be used to collect information on a learner's current level of performance on specific behaviors related to social, communication, behavioral, and academic outcomes across domains. Each of these methods provides a different type of information and has its own advantages and disadvantages. However, using multiple assessment methods allows practitioners to accurately capture a learner's current level of performance and make data-based informed decisions during instructional planning.

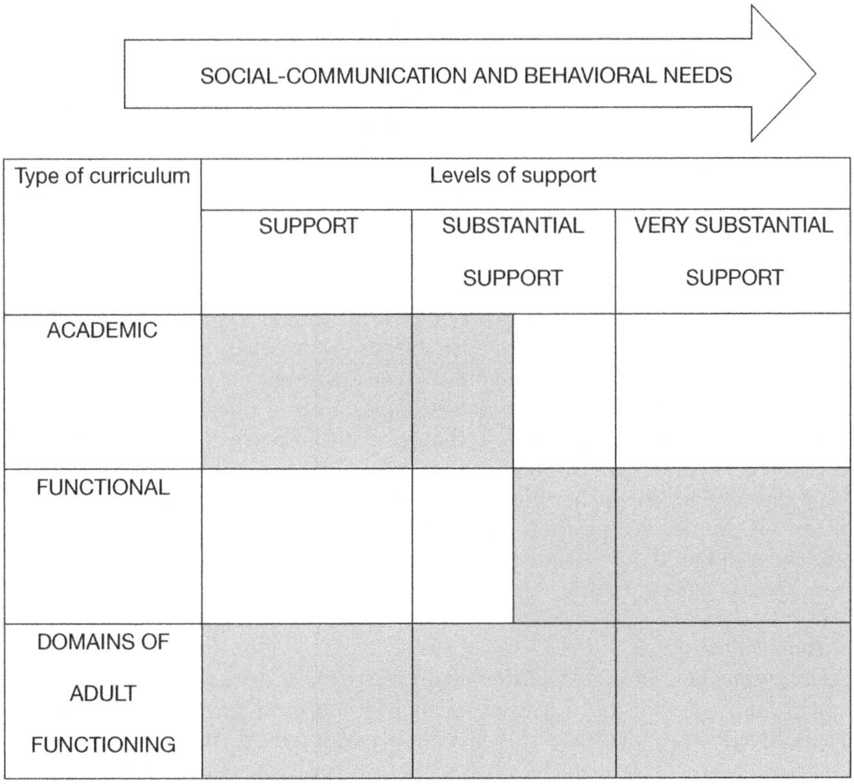
SOCIAL-COMMUNICATION AND BEHAVIORAL NEEDS
Type of curriculum
Levels of support
SUPPORT
SUBSTANTIAL SUPPORT
VERY SUBSTANTIAL SUPPORT
ACADEMIC
FUNCTIONAL
DOMAINS OF ADULT FUNCTIONING

Note. The sections highlighted in grey represent behaviors within specific curriculum domains included in a learner's educational program.

Figure 3.1. Sample matrix of a curriculum based on levels of ASD severity

Indirect Methods: Interviews and Rating Scales

Indirect methods are assessments that allow practitioners to collect information about a learner and their behavior from significant others who know the learner well. Two main indirect methods are usually used: interviews and rating scales.

Interviews

Interviews are discussions with the learner (if appropriate) or with others who know the learner well, including parents or caregivers, friends, educators, and other professionals. Interviews are routinely used during assessment for learners with disabilities, including learners with ASD. Practitioners conduct interviews for different assessment purposes and, consequently, use different types of questions to match the intended purpose of the assessment. For example, a practitioner may conduct a behavioral interview to collect information about the events that trigger and maintain a learner's problem behavior during a functional behavioral assessment. Another practitioner may conduct an interview to gather information about a learner's social interactions with peers and adults during typical activities in his or her environment. Practitioners can also conduct interviews to identify a learner's preferences, as described later in this chapter.

During an interview, a practitioner usually asks open-ended or closed-ended questions. Examples of open-ended questions include "What does your child do when you ask him to complete an academic task?" "What does the problem behavior look like?" "What does your child do when he wants something?" or "Who does your child spend his time with?" Closed-ended questions usually provide the person being interviewed specific options (e.g., yes/no, or agree/disagree). Examples of closed-ended questions or items include "Does your child engage in physical aggression when you interrupt a preferred activity?" followed by two response options (e.g., yes/no or agree/disagree).

One of the advantages of interviews is that it allows practitioners to find out relevant information about a learner's abilities, interests, preferences, problem behaviors, and his or her priorities directly from the learner and their families. Therefore, interview data are likely to reflect a learner's performance during typical activities in their environment from the learner or family members' perspective. The major disadvantage is that people who participate in the interview are asked to recall events, activities, or behaviors displayed by a learner after they have occurred. In addition to being subjective, interview data gathered based on people's recollection of past events or activities may not be accurate and may lead to inappropriate instructional decisions if the interview is the only assessment method used.

Rating Scales

Rating scales consist of items listed on a Likert-type scale (e.g., *never, sometimes, usually, always*) that ask a learner (if appropriate) or a person who knows the learner well to rate the learner's behavior or performance. For example, a practitioner may use a rating scale to assess the severity or frequency of a learner's problem behavior. An example of an item included on such a rating scale could be "My child engages in physical aggression when access to a preferred toy is denied" followed by four response options (e.g., *never, sometimes, usually, always*). Chapter 10 provides an in-depth discussion on rating scales used during functional behavioral assessment. A rating scale can also be used to evaluate the quality of life of a learner with ASD. An example of an item included on a quality-of-life scale may be "My child likes playing with other children" followed by four response options (e.g., *strongly disagree, disagree, agree, strongly agree*).

Although rating scales can be useful in the initial stages of a comprehensive assessment, they also have disadvantages. Their purpose is to collect information about a learner's performance or behavior based on their perception or the perception of people who know the learner well without allowing a practitioner to directly assess the learner's performance on a target behavior. Therefore, the rating scales' scores may capture the intentional or unintentional bias of respondents (Johnson et al., 2008). Practitioners should not use rating scales as the sole method of assessment of a learner's performance on target behaviors to inform instructional planning.

Direct Methods: Naturalistic Observation

Naturalistic observation consists of systematically observing and documenting a learner's behavior or performance during typical activities in the natural environment. This is a *direct assessment method* because it allows practitioners to observe a behavior at the time of its occurrence. Practitioners can conduct direct observations for various purposes. For example, a teacher may observe a middle-school learner with ASD during a visit to the school library to assess his or her current level of performance on checking out a book. Another practitioner may conduct direct observations to document the frequency and type of problem behavior displayed by a high-school learner with ASD during math instruction. Direct observation can also be used to determine whether a young adult with ASD initiates interactions with peers on a university campus as well as the communicative behaviors the young adult uses to approach a peer.

Practitioners can use different instruments to collect data during direct observations depending on the purpose of the observation. For example, a behavior specialist may use antecedent-behavior-consequence (ABC) data collection to record the events that happen immediately before a problem behavior and the events that follow a problem behavior (see Chapter 10 for more information). A teacher may use a task analysis to record a learner's performance on engaging in conversations with social partners during work hours in an employment setting. Regardless of the type of instrument used during direct observation, the purpose of this assessment is to document a learner's performance of the target behavior in real time in the environment where the behavior naturally occurs. It is important to conduct several direct observations across different environments (e.g., playground, classroom, cafeteria) where the behavior occurs, at different times of the day (e.g., morning, afternoon), and in different formats (e.g., one-on-one instruction, small-group instruction) to obtain valid and accurate data (Brown et al., 2020).

One of the main advantages of direct observation is that the documentation of a behavior at the time of its occurrence is generally more accurate than relying on others' reports about what a learner may do (Najdowski et al., 2014). One disadvantage of direct observation is that it could be time consuming, and practitioners may not have the time and resources to conduct multiple observations across settings and at different times of the day. For example, if a learner with ASD engages in low-frequency property destruction (e.g., once, or twice a month), a practitioner may conduct many hours of observation before witnessing an instance of property destruction. In addition, some of the instruments used during direct observations, such as ABC data collection, require training prior to being used to collect data on a learner's behavior.

TYPES OF ASSESSMENTS TO INFORM PROGRAM DEVELOPMENT

As we mentioned at the beginning of this chapter, assessment is designed for different purposes including screening, diagnosis, eligibility, and instructional planning. Different assessment methods are used based on the purpose of the assessment being conducted. For example, a pediatrician or licensed psychologist may use several assessments, such as the *Autism Diagnostic Observation Schedule*, 2nd ed. (ADOS-2; Lord et al., 2012), the *Autism Diagnostic Interview Revised* (ADI-R; Rutter et al., 2003), and the *Peabody Picture Vocabulary Test*, 4th ed. (PPVT-4; Dunn & Dunn, 2007) to determine if a learner has a diagnostic of ASD (please refer to Chapter 6 for additional details). Additional norm-referenced tests may be administered to diagnose ASD, including intelligence scales (e.g., the *Wechsler Intelligence Scale for Children*; Wechsler, 2003) and developmental scales (e.g., *Bayley Scales of Infant Development*; Bayley, 2005). Because norm-referenced assessments do not provide useful information to guide instructional programing for learners with ASD, a comprehensive discussion of such assessments is beyond the scope of this chapter. In this section of the chapter, we will discuss several assessment methods that can be implemented in the natural environment and yield useful data to inform the instructional planning process leading to meaningful educational programs.

Task-Analytic Assessment

Task analysis consists of breaking down a complex activity or behavior into smaller units ordered in the temporal sequence in which they should be performed (Cooper et al., 2020). Many of the daily activities that occur in the natural environment, including school and nonschool settings, require the completion of a predetermined sequence of steps to achieve a desired outcome. For example, working collaboratively with peers during a small-group activity requires a learner to share materials, to take turns, and to engage in interactions with peers. Each of these activities can be broken down in smaller units consisting of fewer or more steps depending on a learner's abilities. Task analysis can be used during both the assessment process and the instructional process for learners with disabilities, including learners with ASD. In this chapter, we will discuss how task analysis can be used as an assessment method to evaluate a learner's performance on specific behaviors, to identify instructional goals, and to monitor progress toward a targeted outcome. Please refer to Chapter 4 for information on how to use task analysis during instruction.

Prior to evaluating a learner's performance on a specific activity, practitioners create a task analysis to be used during the assessment process. It is important to know that task analyses should be individualized based on a learner's age and abilities (Brown et al., 2016) and, thus, a task analysis of a specific skill may be different for different learners (see Chapter 4 for an example). Practitioners can create a task analysis by observing a competent person who can complete the target activity, by completing the activity themselves, or by asking an expert who has experience and expertise and can provide feedback on the appropriateness of a task analysis (Cooper et al., 2020). Table 3.1 illustrates an example of a task analysis for engaging in a conversation with a social partner.

After a task analysis has been created, practitioners conduct an assessment by directly observing the learner and by recording the learner's performance on each step of the task analysis in the environment where the behavior is required. By collecting data on each step of the task analysis, practitioners document which steps of the task analysis a learner completes independently, and for which steps he or she needs assistance. Based on the assessment results, practitioners identify what behaviors to include in the educational program and whether any supports and accommodations are warranted. It is critical that practitioners conduct the assessment in the natural environment where the behavior naturally occurs to obtain an accurate representation of a learner's performance on the targeted activity (Sigafoos & York, 1991).

Table 3.1. Sample Task Analysis for Engaging in a Conversation with a Social Partner

Number	Step of task analysis
1	Walk toward a social partner.
2	Stand at about 1 meter with face and body oriented toward a social partner.
3	Make eye contact with the social partner.
4	Greet the social partner.
5	Wait for a response.
6	Ask a question.
7	Wait for a response.
8	Thank the social partner.
9	End the conversation and walk away.

The assessment session begins when a naturally occurring opportunity presents itself (e.g., an adult entering the room serves as an opportunity for greeting) or when the practitioner asks the learner to perform a specific activity (e.g., "Put on your coat"). Then, the practitioner begins the assessment by observing the learner and allowing him or her a predetermined amount of time (e.g., 3–5 s) to complete each step. If the learner completes the step independently, the practitioner records the behavior and continues to observe the learner. If the learner does not complete the step within the predetermined time, the practitioner assists the learner to complete the step and records the amount of assistance provided. At the end of the assessment session, the practitioner calculates the percentage of steps of the task analysis completed independently by the learner and then selects the steps for which instruction should be provided.

For example, a practitioner assessing a learner's performance using the task analysis for sending an email presented in Table 3.2 selects for instruction only the behaviors that the learner cannot complete independently. Specifically, the

Table 3.2. Sample Task Analysis Assessment Tool for Sending an Email

Number	Step of task analysis	Independent	Prompted VP	GP	PP	FP
1	Type username and password.				+	
2	Log in email.			+		
3	Select new message.		+			
4	Enter the recipient's email address.	+				
5	Type the email title in the Subject line.		+			
6	Type the message.			+		
7	Click Send.		+			
8	Log out.	+				
	Total number (percentage) of steps	2 (25%)		6 (75%)		

Note: VP = verbal prompt; GP = gestural prompt; PP = partial physical; FP = full physical practitioner concludes that the learner can complete independently 2 out of 8 (25%) steps of the task analysis and needs assistance with the remaining 6 out of 8 (75%) steps of the task analysis. Furthermore, the practitioner notices that the level of assistance varies from verbal prompts to partial physical prompts. This information is useful when providing instruction, so that the practitioner provides the minimum level of assistance required to complete a step and, thus, prevents prompt dependence. To obtain valid assessment results, practitioners should conduct a minimum of three assessment sessions prior to providing instruction rather than relying on data collected during a single assessment session.

Ecological Inventory

Ecological inventories are types of informal assessments that consist of a systematic approach to identifying and selecting socially valid, functional, and chronological age–appropriate behaviors for learners with disabilities, including those with ASD (Renzaglia et al., 2003). Ecological inventories are usually used to assess a learner's performance across five domains of adult functioning, including school, home, leisure, community, and employment (Brown et al., 1979). Ecological inventories have also been referred to as a "top-down" approach to instructional planning because the assessment focuses on identifying behaviors that are required for successful participation in the natural environment rather than focusing on behaviors corresponding to a specific developmental level (i.e., "bottom-up approach") (Root, Wood, et al., 2020). Ecological inventories are appropriate assessments when the goal is to develop meaningful educational programs that enhance a learner's independence and quality of life.

Ecological inventories typically consist of five steps (Brown et al., 1979):

1. Identifying the curriculum domain.
2. Identifying the learner's current and future natural environment.
3. Dividing each environment into subenvironments.
4. Identifying the activities performed in each subenvironment.
5. Determining the behaviors required for the performance of activities in each subenvironment.

Curriculum Domains

Although for most learners with ASD all five curriculum domains (i.e., school, home, leisure, community, and employment) are relevant, there may be some variability based on the learner's age, characteristics, and needs. For example, practitioners are less likely to conduct an ecological inventory targeting the employment domain for a preschooler with ASD until the child enters middle school. When using ecological inventories, the assessment focuses on the domains of adult functioning rather than traditional academic domains, because these domains represent the major areas in which a learner will ultimately function and allow practitioners to select instructional goals that emphasize functional behaviors (Brown et al., 2011).

However, it is important to note that practitioners can embed these curriculum domains within the context of academic instruction across content areas, which leads to the development of a balanced curriculum as discussed previously. For example, during shared reading instruction to facilitate the acquisition of listening comprehension (i.e., academic domain), a practitioner can also target behaviors, such as sitting down, listening to the teacher reading a story, and raising a hand to ask a question (i.e., School domain). Another example consists of a situation when during a science experiment to compare different types of soil (i.e., Academic domain), a teacher also targets behaviors, such as washing hands and cleaning up at the conclusion of the experiment (i.e., Home and School domains).

Current and Future Natural Environments

Current and future natural environments represent the settings or locations in which the learner currently lives, learns, or works as well as the settings or locations where the learner will live, learn, or work in the future. Examples of potential current environments for a young child with ASD may be his or her school, the playground, the park in his or her neighborhood, his or her home, the gym where the learner goes with his or her parents in the afternoon, and the clinic where the learner receives behavior-analytic services after school. A potential future environment could be the private middle school in his neighborhood the learner will attend after completing his elementary education. For an adult with ASD, current environments may include their home, the library where the adult works during the day, the community fitness center where the adult works out, and the animal shelter in the neighborhood where the adult volunteers after work. A potential future environment could be the community college where the adult plans to advance his education.

Subenvironments

Subenvironments are physical areas within an environment where different activities take place. Examples of subenvironments in a gym include the front desk, the restroom, the locker room, the snack area, the cycling class area, or the equipment area. In a school, potential subenvironments include the cafeteria, the library, the principal's office, the hallway, the nurse's office, and the playground. Subenvironments are different for different learners with ASD based on their school or living arrangements, their age, and other variables. Therefore, practitioners should use an ecological inventory to identify the subenvironments that represent the living, school, or work arrangements of each learner for whom educational programs are being developed. Ecological inventories will allow practitioners to identify the unique circumstances of each learner and, consequently, design relevant educational programs.

Activities

Several different activities are required for successful participation in each subenvironment. For example, activities that may occur in a school cafeteria include staying in line, ordering lunch, paying for lunch, finding an available seat, eating lunch, engaging in conversations with peers, and cleaning up. Activities that may occur during math instruction include getting materials, following teacher's instructions, taking notes, completing a worksheet, packing up materials, and leaving the classroom when the bell rings. Because a multitude of activities occur within a subenvironment, practitioners need to select those activities that (a) are required for successful participation; (b) occur frequently; (c) are based on the learner's strengths, needs, and interests; and (d) promote the learner's active participation and acceptance as a valued member of their group (Root, Wood, et al., 2020).

Behaviors

Behaviors are the actions that the learner must perform to complete an activity that occurs in a specific subenvironment. Behaviors are identified based on a task analysis as described in this chapter. Once a practitioner develops a task analysis, she or he will then assess the learner's performance by asking them to perform the activity and record the learner's performance on each step of the task analysis. Based on the assessment results, the practitioner identifies instructional goals and continues to use the task analysis during instruction as described in Chapter 4. It is important to note that a task analysis for the same activity (e.g., washing hands) can contain more or fewer steps for different learners based on their abilities and unique characteristics.

Furthermore, a task analysis can be adapted to include collateral skills that may occur during a specific activity. For example, when washing hands in the restroom, a child with ASD may also engage in social interactions with peers present in the restroom. Another example is a task analysis for completing independent seatwork that could also include communicative behaviors, such as requesting assistance. Therefore, it is appropriate to expand a task analysis for a specific behavior by including steps related to communicative behavior, especially for those learners who require language instruction (Sigafoos & York, 1991). Table 3.3 displays an ecological inventory for assessing the social competence of a young child with ASD.

Ecological inventories are a critical component of assessment for learners with ASD because they allow practitioners to identify functional, socially valid, and chronological age–appropriate behaviors that enhance independence and self-sufficiency in the natural environment. Ecological inventories have several advantages. First, ecological inventories allow practitioners to use a team approach and develop collaborative partnerships with learners and their families to identify

Table 3.3. Ecological Inventory for Assessing Social Competence

Environment	Subenvironments	Activities	Behaviors
School	Self-contained classroom	Circle time One-on-one instruction Snack	Greeting Requesting Rejecting Displaying joint attention Taking turns
	Playground	Unstructured play Structured group play	Sharing Taking turns Following instructions Playing with peers
	Library	Story reading	Greeting Displaying joint attention Engaging in conversation Obtaining attention
	Cafeteria	Eating lunch	Greeting Waiting in line Requesting Rejecting Taking turns Engaging in conversation

current and future environments and their relevance to learners. Second, ecological inventories lead to the identification and selection of functional behaviors that enhance the likelihood of successful and active participation in the community. Third, ecological inventories promote generalization and maintenance of newly learned behaviors by providing opportunities for practice in the environment where the behavior should be performed. Finally, ecological inventories are characterized by flexibility and are designed to capture the unique abilities and needs of each learner and, thus, lead to the development of individualized educational programs that are meaningful and relevant for learners and their families.

Discrepancy Analysis

Discrepancy analysis consists of a comparison between a learner's performance on specific behaviors during an ecological inventory and the performance of a learner without disabilities in the same situation. Practitioners can use a discrepancy analysis to identify specific behaviors that need to be addressed to enhance the learner's performance in a specific situation in the natural environment. When conducting a discrepancy analysis, practitioners may ask questions like "What can a learner with ASD do in this situation?" "What behaviors are required in this situation?" "What behaviors do we need to teach the learner so he or she can participate in this activity?" (Root, Wood, et al., 2020).

Consider the example of Sam, a 10-year-old boy with ASD who attends a self-contained classroom for learners with disabilities at a local public school. One of the activities included in Sam's school schedule is to eat lunch with learners without disabilities in the school cafeteria. The ecological inventory conducted by the teacher reveals that Sam does not greet the staff when entering the cafeteria and he forgets to gather his belongings and discard his lunch leftovers after eating. The teacher also conducts a direct observation of Sam's peers without disabilities to identify the skills needed to function effectively during lunch. She notices that all his peers smile and greet the staff, eat their lunch while engaging in conversations with peers, and discard the lunch leftovers before leaving the cafeteria. Next, the teacher compares Sam's performance with the performance of his peers and identifies greeting and discarding lunch leftovers as behaviors that would allow Sam to better participate during lunch in the cafeteria.

Preference Assessments

A preference assessment is the process of systematically collecting data to identify items, people, or activities that are consistently motivating for a learner, their hierarchical preference value, and whether their value changes under different conditions (Cooper et al., 2020). A preference assessment is an important component of instructional planning for at least two reasons. First, practitioners can facilitate a learner's acquisition of target behaviors by providing access to preferred items, activities, and people contingent on the occurrence of the target behaviors (Skinner, 1969). Second, when practitioners design educational programs that incorporate the preferences and interests of learners with ASD, their motivation to engage in instruction and learn new behaviors is greatly enhanced (Iovannone et al., 2003).

Practitioners can use several preference assessment methods. The first method of identifying a learner's preferences consists of interviews. *Interviews* consist of discussions with the learner (if appropriate) or with those who know the learner well. During the interview, a practitioner may ask open-ended questions (e.g., "What do you like to do in your free time?" "What is your favorite food?" "What movie do you like to watch on TV?") or rank-ordering questions (i.e., the learner or the person who participates in the interview is provided a list of preferred items and asked to rank them in order from the most preferred to the least preferred). Researchers have demonstrated that using interviews alone to identify preferences may lead to inaccurate results due to discrepancies between what a learner or significant others report as a preferred item and their motivating value during instruction (Northup, 2000; Whitehouse et al., 2014).

The second method of identifying a learner's preferences is direct observation. *Direct observation* consists of providing the learner access to activities, items, or people and recording the number of times and the amount of time they engage with each activity, item, or person (Cooper et al., 2020). For example, during a 60 min observation session, a practitioner documents that Joe played with the fire truck for 10 min, with the airplane for 45 min, and with the ball for 5 min. Based on these data, the practitioner concludes that the airplane is a preferred item for Joe. Practitioners can conduct direct observations of the learner in a contrived or natural environment. When the observation is conducted in a contrived environment (e.g., a room or office) where predetermined items, activities, or people are available, the assessment is called *contrived observation*. When the practitioner conducts the assessment in the learner's natural environment (e.g., park, playground, library), the assessment is called *naturalistic observation*.

The third method of identifying a learner's preferences is trial-based assessment. *Trial-based assessment* consists of systematically presenting the learner with one, two, or multiple items or activities for a predetermined number of times (Cooper et al., 2020). This method allows practitioners not only to identify preferences but also to rank them along a continuum from high-preference to low-preference items, activities, and people based on a predetermined criterion (e.g., if an item is selected at least 80% of the time, it is classified as a high-preference item) (Carr et al., 2000; Northup, 2000; Paramore & Higbee, 2005).

Several variations of trial-based preference assessment have been described in the literature. The first variation of trial-based preference assessment is single-stimulus presentation. *Single-stimulus presentation* consists of a practitioner providing learner access to one item or activity and recording his or her engagement with the item or activity. An example of a single-stimulus presentation is a situation when a practitioner places a wooden puzzle on the table in front of a young child with ASD while observing the child's engagement with the puzzle. The practitioner records whether the child approached, rejected, or avoided the puzzle, the number of times he displayed the behaviors listed previously, and the amount of time the child played with the puzzle. By analyzing data collected, the practitioner can determine whether the puzzle is a preferred item.

The second variation of trial-based preference assessment is paired-stimulus presentation (Fisher et al., 1996). *Paired-stimulus presentation* consists of a practitioner simultaneously providing a learner access to two items or two activities and recording his or her selection and the learner's engagement with the item or activity selected. An example of a paired-stimulus presentation is a situation in which a practitioner offers a young child with ASD access to two different food items (e.g., grapes and yogurt) and records the child's behavior. If the child consistently selects and consumes grapes, the practitioner concludes that grapes are preferred food. When conducting a paired-stimulus presentation, practitioners should remember that a learner's preferences are relative to the items, activities, or people available during the assessment (Drasgow et al., 2008). Specifically, in the example described previously, although the child consistently selected grapes over yogurt, it does not mean that grapes are highly preferred when other food items (e.g., Skittles, gummy bears) are available.

The third variation of trial-based preference assessment is multiple-stimuli presentation (Fisher et al., 1992). *Multiple-stimuli presentation* consists of a practitioner simultaneously providing the learner access to an array of three or more items or activities and recording his or her selection and the learner's engagement with the item or activity selected. An example of a multiple-stimuli presentation is a situation in which a practitioner offers a learner with ASD access to six different food items (e.g., grapes, carrots, raisins, Skittles, broccoli, and cherries) and records the learner's behavior. If the learner consistently selects and consumes Skittles, raisins, and carrots, the practitioner concludes that these items are preferred food. Furthermore, the practitioner can determine the hierarchical value of the three food items by classifying them as high-preference, moderate-preference, and low-preference based on the percentage of times each food item was selected and consumed.

Practitioners should consider several aspects when conducting preference assessments for learners with ASD. First, preferences are in general variable and may fluctuate over time and, thus, practitioners should conduct preference assessments regularly to capture changes in learners' preferences. Second, preferences are better identified when practitioners use a combination of assessments rather than relying on one assessment. For example, a paired-stimulus presentation combined with interviews and naturalistic observation will yield more valid results than a paired-stimulus presentation alone. Third, practitioners should combine brief preference assessments with preference assessments that are more time consuming but yield more accurate and valid results (Cooper et al., 2020). Fourth, when assessing a learner's preference for food and leisure items, it is recommended that each item category be assessed individually rather than in combination. Researchers have demonstrated that when both food items and leisure items are offered simultaneously in the same assessment, learners with ASD tend to select food items, although leisure items are highly preferred when presented in the absence of food (DeLeon et al., 1997; Pace et al., 1985; Smith et al., 1995). Finally, items and activities included in preference assessments should be valued by learners and their families and enhance their quality of life (Root, Wood, et al., 2020).

A comprehensive assessment is a critical component of program development for learners with ASD. Because one of the purposes of education is to facilitate the acquisition, maintenance, and generalization of behaviors required to function successfully during typical activities in current and future environments, practitioners should use assessments that capture learners' performance in the natural environment. Task analysis and ecological inventories allow practitioners to assess a learner's performance across various activities and domains where learners live, work, play, or learn. Task-analytic assessments and ecological inventories conducted in the natural environment allow practitioners to determine how well a learner meets the requirements of their environment and design instruction that promotes independence, self-sufficiency, and active participation in their community. Furthermore, preference assessments lead to the identification of people, items, and activities that can be embedded in a learner's educational program during typical activities in the natural environment to foster motivation and enhance the acquisition of new behaviors.

Curriculum-Based Assessment

Curriculum-based assessment (CBA) is an assessment method rooted in applied behavior analysis used to inform the instructional planning process, in particular progress monitoring, and consists of direct observation of a learner's performance, usually on academic outcomes (Deno, 1987; Shinn, 2014). CBA allows practitioners to determine a learner's strengths and needs and, thus, provide useful information both for program development and for progress monitoring. CBA does not include standardized assessment procedures and consists of any assessments developed by practitioners to evaluate a learner's performance (Root, Wood, et al., 2020). For example, a teacher who creates a test to evaluate the number of words spelled correctly by a learner with ASD conducts a CBA.

CBA also has been extended beyond academic skills to assess the performance of learners with ASD on other behaviors, such as social skills, language, adapted behavior, and motor skills (Johnson-Martin et al., 2004; Kuo et al., 2019) and to identify events that evoke problem behavior in the classroom (Roberts et al., 2001). For example, a practitioner who develops a task analysis of washing hands to evaluate a learner's performance prior to instruction conducts a CBA. Researchers have suggested that CBA leads to the development of individualized educational programs that address learners' unique functional needs and, consequently, allows the identification of relevant and socially valid instructional goals (Najdowski et al., 2014).

Multiple curricula that include CBA have been developed for learners with ASD. One curriculum is the *Assessment of Basic Language and Learning Skills-Revised* (ABLLS-R; Partington, 2010), a CBA and intervention guide for children with developmental and language delays. ABLLS-R consists of behaviors across 25 domains, including language, adaptive behavior, social interaction, classroom routines, and motor skills. Examples of behavior in the Social Interaction domain include showing interest in the behavior of others, looking at others to start a social interaction, making eye contact, sharing items with others, or initiating greetings. Examples of behaviors in the Classroom Routines domain include following daily routines, working independently on academic and nonacademic activities, getting materials, or raising a hand to ask a question.

Practitioners conduct ABLLS-R by observing and recording a learner's behavior in each domain and by interviewing others who know the learner well and, therefore, emphasize the functional use of various behaviors. Data obtained are used to identify target behaviors, to write IEP goals, and monitor progress. ABLLS-R has been used to assess behavioral interventions for learners with ASD (e.g., Lambert-Lee et al., 2015; Sharma et al., 2010). However, practitioners should know that no empirical studies have been published to date to document the validity of this assessment for instructional planning (Romanczyk et al., 2017).

Another CBA assessment for learners with ASD is the *Verbal Behavior Milestones Assessment and Placement Program* (VB-MAPP; Sundberg, 2014). VB-MAPP consists of five components, including a Milestones Assessment, a Barriers Assessment, a Transition Assessment, task analysis and skills tracking, and placement and IEP goals. The Milestones Assessment assesses 170 learning and language milestones across three levels corresponding to different developmental stages (i.e., Level 1: 0–18 months; Level 2: 18–30 months; and Level 3: 30–48 months). Although the VB-MAPP evaluates social skills and classroom routines, the main purpose of the assessment is to evaluate learners' language behaviors based on function (e.g., requesting, rejecting). The Barriers Assessment evaluates 24 behaviors that may hinder a learner's progress on target behaviors, including failure to generalize, lack of motivation, hyperactivity, and failure to make eye contact or attend to social partners.

The Transitions Assessment evaluates a learner's performance on behaviors required to function in inclusive environments. Examples of such behaviors include working independently on academic tasks; rate of acquisition of new behaviors; generalization and maintenance across settings, materials, and people; adaptability to change; and self-help skills. The task analysis and skills tracking component of VB-MAPP includes approximately 900 behaviors that can be measured to evaluate a learner's progress. The final component, placement and IEP goals, provides guidance on how to write measurable IEP goals based on the assessment results to ensure a balanced curriculum for learners with ASD. Researchers have demonstrated that VB-MAPP has good external validity with *Promoting the Emergence of Advanced Knowledge Relational Training Systems* (PEAK; Dixon et al., 2015), a CBA for learners with ASD. However, additional measurement properties of VB-MAPP have not been published to date.

ABLLS-R and VB-MAPP are only two CBAs that can be used by practitioners providing services to children with ASD to inform the instructional planning process. For older learners with ASD and no co-occurring cognitive deficits, norm-referenced assessments and curriculum-based measurement (CBM) used with typically developing learners may be appropriate. Moreover, the academic performance of learners with ASD and no cognitive deficits on academic content standards is evaluated with *general state standards*, whereas learners with ASD who require substantial and very substantial levels of support are assessed with *alternate achievement standards*. Chapter 9 provides additional information on assessment and instruction on academic skills for learners with ASD.

Curriculum-Based Measurement

CBM consists of a set of formal procedures conducted to assess a learner's progress on academic outcomes, including reading, spelling, writing, and arithmetic (Deno, 1985). These assessment procedures were designed to address the limitations of norm-referenced assessments by allowing practitioners to directly assess a learner's performance on a specific behavior using assessment probes derived from the learner's educational program. For example, Knight and colleagues (2019) conducted a study to examine the effectiveness of CBM on assessing the predictive ability of decoding skills on reading comprehension in 167 children with ASD between the ages of 4 and 7 years. The authors concluded that CBM accurately assessed the performance of children with ASD compared to norm-referenced assessments. Researchers have demonstrated the effectiveness of CBM in assisting teachers to promote positive learner outcomes in elementary grades (Deno, 2003). However, because the focus of CBM is to assess academic performance, this type of assessment may not be appropriate for all learners with ASD, especially for those who require substantial and very substantial levels of support.

LINKING ASSESSMENT TO INTERVENTION

Following the assessment, practitioners must develop educational programs by identifying the behaviors to be included in a learner's program and by writing measurable and observable instructional goals and objectives. For school-age learners, instructional goals and objectives are included in an IEP. Developing an educational program usually consists of two components: prioritizing behaviors identified through a comprehensive assessment and writing instructional goals and objectives.

Prioritizing Behaviors from Assessment

After conducting a comprehensive assessment of a learner's performance across curriculum domains, practitioners may identify numerous behaviors that need to be addressed to promote positive learner outcomes and successful functioning in the natural environment. Prioritizing behaviors allows practitioners to identify the most critical skills that should be addressed first while ensuring the social validity of the behaviors identified. For example, data collected through an ecological inventory reveal the behaviors that a transition-age learner with ASD must receive instruction on, such as engaging in conversations with social partners and using a credit card to purchase groceries at the local store. However, it is important to determine if these behaviors also represent the preferences, interests, and values of the learner and their families.

Prioritization of behaviors occurs within a team approach in which practitioners, learners with ASD, and families work together to identify the strengths, needs, and preferences of learners and prioritize the behaviors to be included in the educational program. One team approach that can be used to prioritize behaviors is person-centered planning (PCP). As described in Chapter 1, PCP is a systematic team process that involves learners with disabilities and their families in the educational planning (Cohen, 1998; O'Brien et al., 1997; Schall & Wehman, 2009). Specifically, learners with ASD and their family participate in one or more meetings to examine learners' abilities and areas for improvement and their interests, preferences, and aspirations for the future, as well as establish instructional priorities across domains of quality-of-life (Hagner et al., 2014). At the conclusion of the PCP meetings, the team identifies a shared vision for the future of the learner with ASD and creates an action plan to support the shared vision and facilitate the achievement of a high quality of life (Brown et al., 2020).

Several PCP processes have been developed to assist with the educational planning process, including *Personal Futures Planning* (PFP; Mount, 2000; Mount & Zwernik, 1988), *Lifestyle Planning* (O'Brien et al., 1990), *Planning Alternative Tomorrows with Hope* (PATH; Pearpoint et al., 1996), *Essential Lifestyle Planning* (Smull, 2005), and *Making Action Plans* (MAPS; Forest & Lusthaus,

1987; Vandercook et al., 1989). Although the PCP processes listed previously may include different items, questions, and procedures, three common themes can be identified across all PCP processes (Knoster & Kincaid, 2005). The first theme, *assessment*, focuses on discussing the learner's history, abilities and areas for improvement, the type of activities available to the learner throughout a typical day across settings, and the strategies needed to support the learner. The second theme is the *vision* and consists of developing a long-term vision for the learner in all life domains that has the potential to promote a high quality of life. The third theme, *planning*, focuses on establishing short- and long-term goals to achieve the desired lifestyle change, identifying barriers that may hinder change, and selecting the supports and opportunities needed to overcome barriers and promote the acquisition, maintenance, and generalization of skills required for successful functioning in the natural environment across life domains.

One of the most widely used PCP processes is MAPS (Vandercook et al., 1989). The learner with ASD, his or her family, friends, and practitioners attend one or two meetings. During MAPS meetings, the participants discuss several questions. The first question is "What is the learner's history?" MAPS participants who know the learner well will describe his or her history, including the most important milestones in the learner's life to provide a better understanding of who the learner is as a person. The second question (i.e., "What is your dream for the learner?") aims to encourage participants to brainstorm their vision for the learner's future or their hopes and aspirations for what the learner may want to do in the future. When participants have difficulties describing the long-term aspirations for the learner, they are encouraged to plan for a shorter period (e.g., 5 years).

The purpose of the third question (i.e., "What is your nightmare for the learner?") is to encourage participants to explore their worries and fears about the learner's future. Sometimes when MAPS is conducted for a young learner with disabilities, this question may be omitted (Snell & Janney, 2000). The fourth question is "Who is the learner?" All MAPS participants are asked to describe the learner using a few words that come to mind when they think of the learner. After all participants have had the opportunity to respond, three words that describe the learner best are identified. The fifth question (i.e., "What are the learner's strengths, gifts, and abilities?") encourages participants to think about the learner's abilities or what he or she can do as well as the things that the learner likes to do. The purpose of this question is to identify and build on the learner's strengths as opposed to focusing on his or her deficits.

The sixth question is "What are the learner's needs?" MAPS participants are first asked to describe the areas and domains in which the learner needs supports or assistance. Once a list of supports across life domains has been created, the participants are encouraged to prioritize the identified needs. The final question (i.e., "What would an ideal day for him or her look like? What can be done to make the ideal happen?") is intended to assist the participants with creating a plan to achieve the desired changes and the supports for meeting the needs identified previously. The outcome of MAPS is the participants' shared vision for the learner and serves as a guide for selecting interventions and providing supports to achieve the desired changes across life domains. Table 3.4 provides an example of MAPS for a transition-age learner with ASD.

Table 3.4. Sample Making Action Plans (MAPS) for Marco

MAPS Question	Response
What is Marco's history?	Marco experienced a normal delivery and birth. He seemed to develop normally during his first 14 months. At approximately 14 months, Marco's parents noticed that he stopped playing and interacting with other children and preferred to engage in solitary play. He also started to display stereotypic behaviors (e.g., body rocking, spinning). Marco was diagnosed with autism spectrum disorder (ASD) a few months later by a licensed psychologist. Marco attended a public school in a self-contained classroom for learners with ASD during his elementary, middle school, and high-school education.
What are your dreams for Marco?	Marco's parents would like for him to attend postsecondary education, live independently in an apartment or small house, have a full-time job, and make friends. Marco's friends who attended the MAPS meeting envisioned him attending a college program on a university campus. Marco's teacher wants him to develop soft skills required in the workplace, including engaging in conversations with social partners, attending social events with friends, and using problem-solving skills when he encounters a challenging situation during daily activities. Recurring themes of the meeting included postsecondary education, independent living, and social relationships.
What are your fears (or nightmare) for Marco?	Marco's parents are worried that he will be alone with no friends after they are not around to look out for him and that he will be taken advantage of by others. They are also afraid that Marco will not be able to manage his finances, including budgeting, paying bills, and troubleshooting when a problem arises, or advocate for himself.
Who is Marco?	MAPS participants generated a list of descriptors to describe Marco, including awesome, smart, perseverant, hardworking, dedicated, charming, likes outdoors, likes cats, likes music, likes pizza, can operate an iPod.
What are Marco's strengths, abilities, and gifts?	Marco's strengths, abilities, and gifts identified by the MAPS participants include perfect attendance at school and internship, being on time, following a schedule, working hard, loving music, operating an iPod, reading, and driving a car.
What are Marco's needs?	Marco's needs identified by the MAPS participants include prompt dependence, problem-solving skills, reading comprehension, reminders to take a bath or shower, help with finances, communicating with peers, coworkers, and supervisors, and lack of self-determination or inability to advocate for himself.

MAPS Question	Response
What would Marco's ideal day look like and what must be done to make it happen?	Marco's ideal day after graduating from high school would be to a. attend a postsecondary program for learners with developmental and other disabilities, b. live in an apartment with a roommate, c. work part-time in the afternoon at a local gym, and d. go out with friends. Based on the information collected during the MAPS meeting, the team will then create a plan to outline specific objectives, supports needed, and people responsible for making this vision possible for Marco.

It is important for practitioners to know that PCP is not necessarily conducted following a comprehensive assessment. There are many instances in practice when practitioners may need to conduct PCP prior to assessment to identify the preferences and interests of a learner and his or her family and to prioritize the domains in which the learner's performance should be assessed first. Moreover, in addition to PCP, practitioners can use additional criteria to prioritize skills by determining their functionality, social validity, and appropriateness. Questions like "Does the behavior reflect the learner's preferences and interests?" "Will the acquisition of this behavior allow the learner to engage in chronological age–appropriate activities?" "Does this behavior promote enhanced independence and social interactions? "Does the behavior allow the learner to participate in inclusive environments?" "Does the behavior represent a priority for the learner and his or her family?" "Will the learner have opportunities to use this behavior in his or her current environment?" The answer to these questions, in addition to the information collected during PCP, will assist practitioners with the prioritization of functional, socially valid, and chronologically age–appropriate activities and the development of meaningful educational programs for learners with ASD.

Writing Measurable and Observable Instructional Objectives

Following the comprehensive assessment and prioritization of behaviors through PCP, practitioners use the information collected to develop meaningful educational programs that promote learners' successful functioning in current and future environments and enhance quality of life. One component of high-quality educational programs consists of measurable and observable objectives that allow practitioners to assess and monitor learners' progress toward target outcomes. An observable and measurable objective consists of four components, namely the conditions under which the behavior should occur, the learner who performs the behavior, the behavior that needs to be performed, and the criterion of performance that must be reached. Please refer to Chapter 6 for additional details on writing observable and measurable objectives. Table 3.5 provides examples of objectives and measurable goals based on a learner's unique needs, current level of performance, and interests.

Table 3.5. Examples of Instructional Objectives Based on Learner's Needs and Current Level of Performance

Needs	Current level of performance	Instructional objective
Stay on task during academic activities	Joe cannot stay on task longer than 5 min during math instruction when instruction is delivered to a large group of students.	During large-group math instruction, Joe will stay on task by taking notes, attending to the teacher, or following instructions given by the teacher for at least 15 min for 4 of 5 consecutive math sessions.
Improve reading comprehension	Tim has good decoding skills, but he has challenges understanding the text read and cannot answer comprehension questions.	After reading a paragraph in a science book at his grade level, Tim will answer correctly five questions related to the content read for 4 of 5 consecutive instructional sessions.
Greet social partners	Lilly does not greet peers and adults, which is sometimes perceived as rude by social partners.	When a peer or an adult enters the room, Lilly will greet the person by waving or saying "Hi. How are you?" or a combination of both within 3 s during 100% of naturally occurring opportunities across 5 consecutive school days.
Ask for preferred items	Tamika hits and bites peers to obtain access to a preferred item.	When a preferred toy is in the possession of one of Tamika's peers during structured or unstructured play activities, she will ask for the toy by saying, "May I please have the toy?" 100% of the naturally occurring opportunities across five consecutive days.
Ask for assistance	When Sam does not know how to complete a task at work, he will walk back and forth in the back room until a coworker or supervisor asks him what he needs.	During scheduled work hours when presented with an unfamiliar task, Sam will ask a coworker or supervisor for clarification or assistance during 100% of the naturally occurring opportunities across three consecutive workdays.
Asking for directions	When Lucy gets lost on campus, she calls her mother, who lives in a different town, to help her.	When Lucy does not know how to locate her destination on a university campus, she will use the Google Maps app on her cell phone to walk to the desired destination during 100% of naturally occurring opportunities across three consecutive days.

SUMMARY

An essential aspect of instructional planning is assessment. Assessment for learners with ASD may be a challenging process due to their unique characteristics. The outcome of a comprehensive assessment is the identification of functional, socially valid, and chronological age–appropriate behaviors that help learners function successfully in the natural environment. Focusing solely on academic behavior without teaching learners the behaviors required in daily life is not sufficient. When developing educational programs, it is important to remember that learners with ASD are a heterogeneous population with a wide range of abilities and needs. Therefore, it is critical to conduct a comprehensive assessment and to prioritize behaviors that are relevant for each learner with ASD across domains within the context of a balanced curriculum. For some learners, a balanced curriculum may be focusing on more academic behaviors and fewer language and social behaviors. For other learners, a balanced curriculum may include more social and language behaviors and fewer academic behaviors. Understanding the characteristics of learners with ASD and selecting the appropriate type of assessments in addition to collecting data from multiple sources of information allow practitioners to develop individualized and meaningful educational programs designed to prepare learners with ASD to live a successful and fulfilling life as active and valued members of their communities.

APPLICATION ACTIVITIES

1. Steve is an 8-year-old boy with ASD and a co-occurring intellectual disability in your classroom or practice. Because Steve has difficulties with putting on his coat before leaving the classroom, he misses the playground activities with his peers during the school day. Develop a task analysis of the behavior of *putting on coat* to assess Steve's performance prior to providing instruction.

2. Pretend that you are an employment specialist who provides vocational instruction to transition-age learners with ASD completing an internship at the local grocery store. Develop an ecological inventory for the work environment by identifying subenvironments, activities, and behaviors required in each subenvironment identified.

3. Select a learner in your classroom or practice and describe your plan to conduct a comprehensive assessment by considering the following questions:

   • What types of assessment do you use to select socially valid, functional, and chronological age–appropriate behaviors?
   • What assessment methods do you use to conduct a meaningful and comprehensive assessment?
   • Have you considered the values, preferences, and culture of the learner and his or her family?
   • How do you use the data collected to inform your instructional planning process?

4. Imagine that you are a teacher working with a middle-school learner with ASD. You conducted a comprehensive assessment and identified numerous behaviors that could be targeted during instruction. Describe how you prior-

itize behaviors using a person-centered planning approach and the questions asked during the meeting.

5. Select one of the learners in your classroom or practice and identify one deficit in each of the following domains: social-communication, behavior, and academic. For each deficit identified, write an observable and measurable instructional objective.

ADDITIONAL RESOURCES

American Speech-Language-Hearing Association. (2021). *Assessing diverse students with autism spectrum disorder.* https://leader.pubs.asha.org/doi/10.1044/leader.FTR2.16 012011.12

Autism Focused Intervention Resources and Modules (AFIRM). (n.d.). *Task analysis.* https://afirm.fpg.unc.edu/task-analysis

Pacer's National Parent Center on Transition and Employment. (2019). *Person-centered planning.* https://www.pacer.org/transition/learning-center/independent-community-living /person-centered.asp

4

Evidence-Based Practice

Finding the Right Treatment That Works

Susan M. Wilczynski, Abby Magnusen,
Shawnna Sundberg, and Ben Seifert

■ ■ ■

INTRODUCTION AND OVERVIEW

The term *evidence-based practice* (EBP) means different things to different professionals, which can create confusion for everyone. EBP has its origins in medicine.
Evidence-based medicine emerged in the 1990s due to concerns that physicians
were not always using the most recent evidence to support the medications, sur-
geries, or other medical interventions they recommended to patients (Guyatt et
al., 1992). However, scientific findings are only one leg of the three-legged stool of
evidence-based medicine. Evidence-based medicine emphasized the role of patient
preference and values as well as clinical judgment in treatment selection (Djulbegovic & Guyatt, 2017).

Many disciplines recognized the need for practitioners to make treatment
recommendations based on current research findings, so the term evidence-based
medicine became EBP. As scholars and professionals across disciplines adopted
the term EBP, many came to describe EBP solely as interventions with consistently strong research support (Slocum et al., 2014; Spencer et al., 2012). To be
consistent with other chapters of this book, we use the term EBP to describe
interventions that have been established to be effective and without adverse side
effects for autistic learners[1] and that are based on multiple studies that have
been published across different research teams. An evidence-based intervention
selection model is like a three-legged stool in which evidence (especially but not
exclusively research studies) serves as a critical leg. The other two legs of the
evidence-based intervention selection model are person-related variables (e.g.,
preferences, values, skill repertoire, tolerance) and contextual factors (e.g., feasibility, cost-effectiveness) that are needed to select the right intervention for
every learner (Wilczynski, 2017).

It is important to understand why science alone is insufficient for selecting
the best interventions for learners before we move on to describe specific EBPs.
Although it is necessary to emphasize the role of scientific findings when selecting
interventions, practitioners who rely solely on research are much more likely to

violate their ethics codes or select ineffective interventions by picking an intervention that has problematic side effects (Wilczynski et al., 2021). For example, educators have an ethical obligation to protect their learners from environmental conditions that could result in harm (National Education Association, 2020). When there are a number of research-supported interventions from which to choose, an educator might pick the intervention that is most convenient or familiar. However, even if the intervention successfully addressed the target behavior, the best intervention has not yet been identified if it has adverse side effects (e.g., higher rates of self-injury, lower rates of engagement, increased stereotypic behavior in other environments such as the home or the community). Similarly, despite the fact an intervention has been deemed "evidence based," it might be destined to be a failure with a specific learner for a variety of reasons. For example, selecting video modeling because it has been listed as an EBP will ultimately be ineffective for a learner who lacks the ability to attend to visual stimuli or the capacity to copy a series of behaviors demonstrated on a video. Blind adherence to only the science leg of the evidence-based treatment selection model could result in an outcome ranging from "phenomenal improvement" to "serious harm to learners."

The evidence-based intervention selection model requires using professional judgment to integrate the best available evidence with person-related and contextual variables until learners are successful (Wilczynski, 2017). The evidence-based intervention selection process begins with asking a series of practical questions (Spencer et al., 2012), and many of these questions are directly connected to social validity. Social validity consists of whether (a) the behavior should be targeted for change; (b) the intervention is acceptable to the learner, parents, and practitioners; and (c) the intervention produced truly meaningful improvements in the learner's life (Kazdin, 1980; Wolf, 1978). Practitioners should first ask themselves if they would develop the same intervention for the behavior if the learner did not have ASD. For example, a non-autistic first grader who occasionally gets out of their seat might simply be told to return to their seat when they wander about the classroom, but the learner with ASD has a behavior intervention plan (BIP) under the exact same conditions. It is ableist to set higher expectations for disabled people than we do for nondisabled people. Next, practitioners should adopt intervention acceptability tools and determine how palatable the intervention is to the learner and the learner's parents before and during intervention implementation (Wilczynski, 2017). If an intervention is not acceptable to all parties, an alternative intervention that has research support should be considered.

A complete discussion of the EB intervention selection model is beyond the scope of this chapter, but we hope readers are motivated to read more materials on this topic (e.g., Wilczynski, Henderson, et al., 2016; Wilczynski, Trammell, et al., 2016; Wilczynski, 2017). In the meantime, we hope to convey that selecting the right intervention for each learner means having knowledge of EBPs, incorporating real-world factors that influence the feasibility of interventions, placing a premium on learner preferences, choices, and tolerance of selected interventions, and collecting meaningful data to determine whether a good intervention has been selected. At the end of this chapter, we provide an application of how practitioners use their professional judgment to combine their knowledge of EBP with person-related and contextual variables until an autistic client has reduced problem behaviors, increased skill acquisition, and is happy with the intervention. To begin the intervention selection process, however, you need to be familiar with interventions that have been demonstrated to produce positive outcomes for autistic learners.

This chapter will begin with suggestions for finding EBPs as well as reviewing key EBPs for autistics. EBPs are categorized as core elements that are basic teaching elements (e.g., reinforcement, prompting, chaining), combining core elements (e.g., modeling and video modeling), and EBP applications at the individual and group levels (e.g., visual supports and token economies). The chapter ends with an application to illustrate the importance of the evidence-based treatment selection model when selecting, retaining, adapting, or rejecting interventions.

FINDING EVIDENCE-BASED PRACTICES

EBPs are identified through systematic reviews or meta-analyses. *Systematic reviews* are a form of literature review that explicitly states and applies comprehensive methods to identify, aggregate, and synthesize research findings in response to a specific need or question relevant to a given field (Page et al., 2021). *Meta-analyses* are studies in which statistical methods are used to quantify the effectiveness of interventions using the size of the outcome and the variability of outcomes across research participants to draw conclusions (Page et al., 2021). Interested readers are encouraged to read more about these methodologies because a large number of decisions are made when conducting systematic reviews or meta-analyses and the decision to label an intervention "evidence-based" is strongly influenced by what appear to be small decisions throughout the process (Wilczynski, 2012).

The Institute for Educational Sciences (IES) as well as the National Professional Development Center for Autism Spectrum Disorder (NPDC-ASD) have conducted or supported the development of systematic reviews or meta-analyses for educational purposes. IES is funded by the U.S. government and serves as a leading force in using science as a foundation for educational practices. IES established the What Works Clearinghouse (https://ies.ed.gov/ncee/wwc/), which provides reviews and meta-analyses for educational interventions to establish whether they are evidence based.

The NPDC-ASD was funded by the U.S. Department of Education via the Office of Special Education Programs between 2007 and 2014 to promote the use of EBP for children and youth. The NPDC-ASD was a collaboration between three universities across the United States and not only resulted in the identification of EBPs for autistic learners, but also, training and support materials that can be accessed today via their website (https://autismpdc.fpg.unc.edu/national-professional-development-center-autism-spectrum-disorder). The NPDC-ASD now refers users to the National Clearinghouse on Autism Evidence & Practice (NCAEP), where practitioners can find the *2020 Evidence-Based Practice Report*, the most recent systematic review focusing on autistic learners that has been published to date (Steinbrenner et al., 2020). The *2020 Evidence-Based Practice Report* reflects the most recent review of educational and behavioral practices for autistic learners and identifies 28 EBPs. Table 4.1 provides a brief definition for 27 of these EBPs (Functional Behavior Assessment is identified as an EBP but is an assessment, and not an intervention). The last column in Table 4.1 identifies *null findings*, which reflect the number of times published

Table 4.1.   Evidence-Based Practices Identified by National Clearinghouse on Autism Evidence & Practice

Evidence-based practices[1]	Definition	Null findings
Antecedent-based interventions	Altering the arrangement of conditions occurring prior to a target behavior to increase the desired behaviors and/or diminish challenging behavior(s).	18.4%
Augmentative and Alternative Communication (AAC)	A nonvocal communication method; often with a program on a device (e.g., iPad) or the use of sign language.	11.4%
Behavioral momentum[2]	The process of delivering a series of easy tasks prior to introducing a more difficult task to increase responding.	0%
Cognitive behavioral/ instructional strategies	A talk therapy that focuses on altering negative self-evaluation by reducing maladaptive thoughts.	4%
Differential reinforcement of alternative, incompatible, or other behavior	The process of providing reinforcement for a target behavior but not for an alternative, incompatible, or other behavior. Differential reinforcement procedures are often combined with extinction.	3.4%
Direct instruction	Using a sequenced and systematic prewritten protocol to teach learners, typically using "I do. We do. You do." formats.	0%
Discrete trial training	Providing a discriminative stimulus (instruction), the opportunity for learner response, a reinforcer for correct responses or error correction for incorrect responses, and a brief break. The process is repeated multiple times per day until mastery.	7.9%
Exercise and movement	Requiring physical movement by means of exercise, mindful movement, and/or gross motor skills.	11.8%
Extinction	No longer reinforcing a behavior. Sometimes called "planned ignoring," when attention is the function of behavior.	7.4%
Functional communication training	Teaching a simple communication skill to ensure needs are met (e.g., request a break or access to activity).	3.1%
Modeling	Demonstrating the correct response resulting in the learner imitating the same, correct response.	6.7%
Music-mediated intervention	Interventions using any type of musical rhythm to support learners acquiring new skills.	2.2%
Naturalistic intervention	Contriving conditions in real-world environments that set the stage for learning through prompting and reinforcement.	1.3%

Evidence-based practices[1]	Definition	Null findings
Parent-implemented intervention	Social, communication, and behavioral interventions led by parents.	6.7%
Peer-based instruction/ intervention	Teaching peers how to engage with learners with ASD through social activities and/or modeling.	4.3%
Prompting	Verbal, gestural, or physical assistance given to a learner to assist them in responding correctly.	4.8%
Reinforcement	A consequence following a behavior that in turn increases the likelihood of the behavior occurring again in the future under the same or similar circumstances.	7%
Response interruption/ redirection	Introducing a prompt or distractor to redirect the learner away from engaging in an interfering behavior.	3.3%
Self-management	Teaching learners how to observe, record, and reinforce their own behaviors.	3.7%
Sensory integration	Intervention targeting a learner's ability to regulate any type of sensory overload they may feel.	25%
Social narratives	Interventions describing social situations and teaching appropriate responding in said situations.	8.7%
Social skills training	Instruction that teaches learners how to engage appropriately and interact successfully with others.	1.3%
Task analysis	Breaking a task down into smaller and manageable steps; skills are taught in a behavioral chain.	NR
Technology-aided instruction and intervention	Instruction that can be taught using various forms of technology to facilitate teaching new skills to learners.	16.6%
Time delay	A procedure in which a discriminative stimulus is followed by a brief pause; the pause often starts at 0 s and is accompanied with the correct answer. Gradually the pause prompts the learner to provide the correct response.	0%
Video modeling	A video recording of a task: the learner watches and then imitates what they saw in the video to complete the task.	3%
Visual supports	A visual display that the learner can reference to learn new skills.	3%

Notes: NR = not reported.

1. The NCAEP also identifies a functional behavior assessment (FBA) as evidence based. However, this is not an intervention. Instead, FBA is an assessment process that should be linked to function-based interventions involving reinforcement.
2. The literature associated with behavioral momentum is on high-probability command sequences.

research *does not* demonstrate a positive outcome for these same interventions. No intervention produces benefit to learners every single time it is applied—not even those identified as EBPs. When selecting among an array of EBPs, knowing which interventions have a larger percentage of null findings reported in the literature may help practitioners make final treatment selection decisions. Practitioners should cautiously use null findings, however, because of publication bias. *Publication bias* reflects the fact that most studies that do not show significant intervention effects are never published. That means there are likely many more instances in which interventions are accurately implemented under real-world conditions that learners do not make significant improvements.

We encourage readers to use the materials (i.e., systematic reviews) provided by NCAEP and NPDC-ASD (e.g., AFIRM training modules) as they focus specifically on interventions for autistic learners. However, the state of evidence changes continuously, so practitioners should rely on the most recent source of credible evidence and on the most recent resources that become available within or outside of IES and NCAEP.

CORE ELEMENTS AND EVIDENCE-BASED PRACTICES

Most EBPs are composed of a number of core elements—that is, behavioral or teaching strategies. These core elements may be used independently but are often combined to create unique interventions that produce benefit for many learners (Slocum et al., 2014). For example, *reinforcement* is a core element that plays a role in virtually all known EBPs. Reinforcement has been applied in hundreds of ways over the decades and aggregating across all studies using reinforcement may mean that interventions that do not share much in common are all called an EBP. Any variation in application of a core element—or the multicomponent interventions that are based on core elements—can produce different levels of benefit or adverse side effects. We argue that each unique intervention should be submitted to rigorous empirical investigation. In addition, core elements were studied in isolation (i.e., not a part of a multicomponent intervention) decades ago when research standards were different than they are today. For example, the use of reinforcement to alter the behavior of autistic people has been studied since 1961 (Ferster, 1961; Ferster & Demyer, 1961) but current published research that includes reinforcement often involve multicomponent interventions (e.g., functional communication training) or drastically different variations of reinforcement (e.g., differential reinforcement, noncontingent reinforcement). For these reasons, we make a distinction between core elements and EBP. We discuss reinforcement and prompting as core elements because these are components of almost every EBP that supports autistic learners. Next, we address how task analysis, a process for breaking a task down into its component parts, can be combined with two EBPs (i.e., chaining and video modeling) as a means of increasing skill acquisition or decreasing problem behaviors. Finally, we describe two commonly used EBPs that are often applied both to individual learners and to whole classrooms.

Core Element: Reinforcement

Reinforcement is the process through which the future likelihood of a behavior is increased. When practitioners want to increase behaviors, they apply reinforcement by focusing on antecedents, behaviors, and consequences (A-B-Cs). Antecedents are the conditions that exist *before* someone demonstrates a behavior and consequences are the conditions that exist *after* someone demonstrates a behavior. For example, a possible antecedent (A) is a fire alarm unexpectedly going off during the school day. The behavior (B) that immediately follows the alarm going off is a learner getting up from their seat and walking quickly and calmly to the nearest exit. The consequence (C) of the learner's behavior of leaving the building is reinforced by avoidance of the smoke and fire as well as potential bodily harm. Reinforcement occurs when consequences following a behavior increase the future chances that behavior will occur again under the same conditions (i.e., antecedents). Although most people think the idea of reinforcement is easy, there are many complex factors that influence whether a behavior will increase under similar conditions in the future (Cooper et al., 2020). We have organized our discussion of reinforcement into seven key areas: antecedents, types of reinforcement, reinforcers, primary reinforcers versus secondary reinforcers, categories of reinforcers, timing, and schedules of reinforcement.

Antecedents

A *discriminative stimulus* or S^D is an antecedent event or change in the environment that signals to the learner that a behavior is likely to be reinforced if it occurs (Cooper et al., 2020). Learners do not need to "know" they are being signaled. Instead, when the S^D occurs prior to behaviors (that receive specific consequences) we all build associations without necessarily having awareness of our behavior changes. If a practitioner tells an autistic learner it was their turn to teach a classmate something new (S^D), that statement could signal that it is a time to discuss their preferred interest. If the practitioner seeks to make a stimulus an S^D, repetition between the S^D—behavior—reinforcement is needed. For example, a reinforcer is delivered every time you introduce the S^D. When learners fail to make progress on new goals, it can be because the S^D is not distinct enough to clearly signal to the learner that a specific behavior will be reinforced or that more repetition is needed.

Motivating operations (MO) are a second type of antecedent and consist of conditions that directly affect behavior and alter the value of reinforcers (see a discussion of reinforcers below; Cooper et al., 2020). For example, if a noise is present—let's say a noise that is quiet enough that the practitioner cannot hear it but it is distracting to the autistic learner—the value of the sticker the practitioner is offering as a reinforcer for correct responding may go way down and the value of any behavior that would eliminate the noise (e.g., throwing the desk so the learner gets sent to the principal's office) may go way up!

Types of Reinforcement

There are two forms of reinforcement. The words *positive* and *negative* are sometimes incorrectly interpreted to mean *good* and *bad*. People making this mistake often impose their own views about what is good or bad on to the learner. For example, the first author of this chapter loves asparagus; however, many readers may not see it as good given asparagus is the least favorite vegetable among U.S. citizens (Fox News, 2019). Similarly, whenever a practitioner says, "I tried reinforcement, but it did not work," the most likely explanation is that they selected a reward they view as good—but their assessment was not accurate from the learner's point of view or that the reward was not good enough to warrant the effort required of the learner to complete the task. Generally, this implementation error can be more easily avoided by using the correct usage of the terms positive and negative reinforcement. When you hear *positive reinforcement*, think of the positive as a *plus sign* (i.e., +). When you hear *negative reinforcement*, think of the negative as a *minus sign* (i.e., –). That is, *positive* refers to adding a stimulus to the learner's environment after they demonstrate a behavior while *negative* refers to removing a stimulus from the learner's environment after they demonstrate a behavior (Cooper et al., 2020). The technical definition for a stimulus is an energy change affecting a living organism through its receptor cells (Michael, 2004). In practice, a stimulus is something that affects the behavior of any living being as a result of their sensory experiences. It does not inherently mean there will be a behavior change in a living organism, but rather, the stimulus has the potential to influence behavior. Examples of stimuli can include practically anything: the wind starting to blow, a ball rolling, or an apple.

Positive reinforcement requires two conditions: (a) a stimulus is provided immediately following a behavior and (b) that behavior is more likely to occur under similar conditions in the future (Cooper et al., 2020). Practitioners intentionally use positive reinforcement when they give a learner an "A" for exceptional work (and it actually increases the likelihood they perform exceptionally in the future). Although practitioners intentionally use positive reinforcement regularly, they sometimes unknowingly use positive reinforcement for behaviors they would like to see reduced or eliminated. For example, a practitioner may reprimand a learner who curses and think this reprimand is a punishment; however, if the learner's cursing continues or escalates, the reprimand is simply a form of attention and the behavior is being reinforced. Remember, the practitioner's intent does not determine if the consequence is reinforcing or punishing; rather, whether the behavior continues or increases determines if the consequence is reinforcing the behavior.

Negative reinforcement also requires two conditions: (a) a stimulus is removed immediately following a behavior and (b) that behavior is more likely to occur under similar conditions in the future (Cooper et al., 2020). For example, Mateo is an autistic learner who pushes a worksheet off his desk whenever his educator places a worksheet on his desk and then walks away. She believes pushing the worksheet off his desk is not being reinforced because she walks back to his desk and replaces the worksheet, standing next to him until he begins working. Yet, Mateo keeps pushing the worksheet off his desk. Mateo is able to avoid (or temporarily escape) a task by pushing the worksheet off the desk. Even when an aversive condition (e.g., having to complete a worksheet) is only avoided or temporarily escaped, negative reinforcement is occurring when the behavior continues or increases.

Reinforcers

Whereas reinforcement is a process, reinforcers are stimuli. A *reinforcer* is a stimulus or consequence that, when presented or removed immediately following a specific behavior (i.e., consequence), increases the likelihood that behavior will occur again in the future (Cooper et al., 2020). The stimulus could be a tangible object, escaping work, attention, or sensory/physiological conditions (e.g., sounds, lighting). For example, consider a learner who is struggling to pay attention during 1:1 worktime. The educator suggests they walk the classroom perimeter and then return to their seat. Once they return to their seat, the educator redelivers the instructions and they successfully complete the task. The educator smiles and tells the learner they are really pleased. We can look at the role of reinforcement and reinforcers from two perspectives—both the educator's perspective and the learner's perspective.

Let's use Table 4.2 to first consider the educator's perspective. *Antecedent*: The educator wanted the learner to successfully complete a task but realized they either needed a break or some physical movement so they could concentrate. *Behavior*: The educator told the learner to walk the perimeter of the classroom. *Consequence*: The reinforcer was that the learner returned to their seat and completed the task. Outcome: The educator's behavior is reinforced because they are more likely to suggest a distracted learner walk the perimeter of the classroom in the future. The entire process is reinforcement, but the reinforcer was learner success.

Now let's use Table 4.2 to look at the same situation from the learner's perspective. *Antecedent*: We are assuming that the practitioner has a good relationship with their learners. The learner just cannot pay attention long enough to correctly complete the task. The practitioner provides the instruction to walk the perimeter of the classroom. *Behavior*: The learner followed the instruction. *Consequence*: The reinforcer was the learner successfully completing the task and

Table 4.2. Temporal Sequence of ABC Educator and Learner Perspective

A *Antecedent*	B ***Educator** Behavior*	C *Consequence*	**Future Outcome** ***Reinforcement***
The educator is ready to move on to a new task but notices their learner's behavior that signals that the learner needs a break.	The educator gave the learner permission to get up from their seat and walk the perimeter of the room.	The learner walked the perimeter of the classroom and then successfully completed task.	Educator is more likely to give the learner a break to walk the perimeter in the future when they notice learner behavior that indicates the need for a break.

A *Antecedent*	B ***Learner** Behavior*	C *Consequence*	**Future Outcome** ***Reinforcement***
The educator gives the learner permission to walk the perimeter of the classroom before a new task is introduced.	The learner walked the perimeter of the room and then completed the task.	The learner received social attention and praise from the educator for completing the task correctly.	The learner is more likely to complete the task after walking the perimeter of the room after they feel the need for a break in the future.

receiving social attention (smile, practitioner saying they are pleased). Outcome: The learner is more likely to follow instructions in the future. The entire process is reinforcement but task completion (which often creates a positive physiological response) and attention were the reinforcers. When two or more people interact, there is value in examining the role of reinforcement and identifying reinforcers from each person's perspective to better understand why people do what they do and how to make situations better.

Primary Versus Secondary Reinforcers

Primary reinforcers are stimuli that serve a biologically important role for human beings (e.g., food, water). When primary reinforcers are repeatedly paired with a neutral stimulus,[2] the neutral stimulus acquires value and becomes a *secondary reinforcer* (a.k.a. conditioned reinforcers; Cooper et al., 2020). For example, when a teacher first meets a new learner, they may comment positively about the learner's Mickey Mouse shirt (e.g., "I love Mickey Mouse. Your shirt is awesome!"). The new teacher was a neutral stimulus but has now been paired with a reinforcer (e.g., positive attention + the teacher = Micky Mouse fan!). Money, clothes, and a host of other stimuli serve as secondary reinforcers. However, too much access to any stimulus lowers its value and eventually results in satiation (i.e., it temporarily stops working as a reinforcer; Cooper et al., 2020). Practitioners who most effectively use reinforcement collect data so they can continue to increase learner behavior (e.g., correctly completing math problems) and avoid satiation. Great practitioners switch reinforcers frequently enough to increase academic and socially appropriate behaviors—and they successfully do this by collecting and using data!

Categories of Reinforcers

The four general categories of consequences are attention, escape/avoid, tangible, and sensory/physiological modulation (i.e., automatic reinforcement in most cases; Cooper et al., 2020). Social attention can be a potent reinforcer when delivered by a parent, teacher, or peer. Although people commonly think of attention as something favorable, reprimands or negative comments can also serve as reinforcers. Escape/avoidance is a reinforcer when actions that lead to "getting out of doing" an aversive task increase in frequency (even if you only temporarily get out of doing the task). Tangible is a class of reinforcers in which specific behaviors mean greater access to "stuff." Tangibles might include but are not limited to edibles, toys, a cell phone, or a car. Automatic reinforcers typically involve altering the way one's body is responding physiologically. It is often referred to as *sensory*, because many autistic learners engage in behaviors to reduce exposure to specific sounds, colors, or other stimuli. But the way one's body wakes up when they drink a cola or the way one's nervous system calms down as a result of meditating can be automatic reinforcers too.

Function-based interventions are selected after conducting a comprehensive assessment that is designed to identify why an individual is engaging in problem behavior (e.g., functional behavior assessment). Function-based interventions should be associated with a support plan that includes client variables and antecedent and consequence strategies, along with teaching techniques that address the function of the target behavior (Pinkelman & Horner, 2017). Practitioners can generate an effective function-based intervention by first examining which of these four general categories most accurately reflect the most common consequence for a target behavior. A practitioner might notice they chastise a learner who is "off-task" and then identify chastisement as a form of attention that is reinforcing the off-task behavior. They then intentionally praise the learner's on-task behavior, so the learner's time on task increases because the consequence for being on task matched the purpose (or function) of being off task. For more information on functional behavior assessment and function-based interventions, see Chapter 10.

When identifying reinforcers, it is important to remember that no matter how well we know a learner, we are often lousy at guessing which stimuli will alter their behavior. The only way to know whether the stimulus a practitioner is adding or removing following a specific behavior actually serves as a reinforcer is to measure whether the behavior increases. The same stimulus could serve as a reinforcer or as a punisher[3] under different conditions. For example, peer attention could serve as a reinforcer (e.g., the learner says something funny, and classmates laugh *with* them) or as a punisher (e.g., the learner says something not intended to be funny and classmates laugh *at* them). Practitioners must be aware that reinforcers are individual in nature—what reinforces one person's behavior may punish the exact same behavior for another person. This means that practitioners cannot assume that a stimulus will be a reinforcer for a particular learner, and instead must assess that learner's preferences and observe whether the stimulus increases a behavior when it is delivered as a consequence following demonstration of the target behavior.

Timing

It is crucial to deliver reinforcers immediately after a target or desired behavior occurs, or a different behavior could be unintentionally increased (i.e., reinforced; Cooper et al., 2020). Consider two children who argue frequently on the playground. One of these children offers a ball to the other so the practitioner wants to reinforce this behavior. She says, "Check out how you two are playing together!" Unfortunately, by the time she makes this statement, the second child throws the ball and hits the first child in the nose. Although the statement is no longer "praise," it is social attention, and this statement might just increase the likelihood the second child will throw a ball at other children in the future to get the practitioner's attention!

Schedules of Reinforcement

Effective reinforcement-based interventions consider how frequently the reinforcer is delivered. Readers interested in a complex discussion about schedules of reinforcement are encouraged to consult Cooper and colleagues (2020). For the purposes of this chapter, we want to discuss how to develop and then sustain improvements as separate steps of intervention. When first teaching a skill or seeking to decrease a behavior, providing very consistent consequences by delivering a reinforcer every time the behavior occurs will alter a learner's behavior most successfully. This is called *continuous reinforcement*. For example, an educator may give a learner a sticker every time that they turn in their homework, regardless of whether the answers are correct. The educator's intent is to reinforce the behavior of returning homework. Later, they can alter the target behavior (i.e., stickers for correct performance at a specified criterion). Over time, a practitioner can gradually deliver the reinforcer less frequently—for example, every other time the behavior occurs. This is called *intermittent reinforcement*. Based on the preceding scenario, the educator would be using intermittent reinforcement if they gave the learner a sticker every other time they turn in their homework. However, if reinforcers are provided too infrequently at first, a skill may not develop, or a problem behavior may not decrease. People sometimes think an intervention was not successful because "the problem behavior came back," but the real issue is that reinforcers were not delivered frequently enough.

Consider Akeno, an autistic learner who hates difficult schoolwork. When given difficult assignments, Akeno requests help some of the time and kicks the seat in front of him at other times. Akeno goes to timeout every time he kicks a desk, which means he escapes or avoids difficult schoolwork every single time he kicks a desk. When Akeno asks for help, Ms. Sanchez comes to help him once out of every four times he asks because she also must respond to other learners. Her suggestions sometimes help Akeno complete the work, but it does not always translate to academic success. The schedule of reinforcement for kicking desks is *rich* because it always allows Akeno to avoid difficult schoolwork. The schedule of reinforcement for requesting help is leaner because Ms. Sanchez does not always provide actionable support. We can easily predict Akeno will continue to kick desks when presented with difficult schoolwork based on the two schedules of reinforcement. Even though Ms. Sanchez was reinforcing Akeno's requests for help, she more reliably provided reinforcement for kicking the desk, so this behavior came to predominate.

Summary and Other Essential Information

Reinforcement explicitly plays a key role in most EBPs identified through the NCAEP, even when the term *reinforcement* does not appear in the title. For example, antecedent-based interventions involve alterations of the environment prior to the occurrence of a target behavior. However, the purpose of making these changes is to ensure that the learner can access reinforcers for acceptable academic, social, or behavioral conduct. In fact, most social scientists would consider *noncontingent reinforcement* (i.e., delivering reinforcers on a fixed-time schedule irrespective of whether problem behavior occurs) an antecedent-based intervention because it occurs before the behavior (Coy & Kostewicz, 2020). In addition, differential reinforcement of alternative, incompatible, or other behaviors are listed separately from reinforcement as an EBP in the NCAEP's *2020 Evidence-Based Practice Report*. To best understand the importance of reinforcement as a core element, we encourage practitioners to look for the role it plays in all interventions.

Core Element: Prompting

Reinforcement can only be accessed when a target behavior occurs. What happens if the learner cannot perform the target behavior independently? Parents are often a learner's first educator, and they naturally use prompts such as taking their child's hand when crossing the street or sounding out initial letters as their child learns their first sight words. *Prompting* occurs when instruction is supplemented with a cue and the cue increases the likelihood a learner will respond accurately. There are two forms of prompting: response prompting and stimulus prompting (Cengher et al., 2018). See Table 4.3 for common prompting strategies.

Table 4.3. Common Prompting Strategies from Most to Least Intrusive: Advantages and Disadvantages

Response prompting strategy	Advantages	Disadvantages	Example (brushing hair)
Full physical Learner is guided hand-over-hand through the entire response.	• Errorless • Minimal vocal language used • Easiest to fade	• Used even when not needed • Often implemented without permission • Increased susceptibility for abuse • Most intrusive	Instructor physically guiding the learner's hand and to pick up hairbrush.
Partial physical Learner is guided with partial physical assistance through some or all of the response.	• Allows for independent responding	• Higher possibility that learner will make an error • Used even when not needed • Often implemented without permission • Increased susceptibility for abuse	Instructor touching the learner's elbow and guiding their arm toward hairbrush.
Positional Materials are presented in a position of closer proximity to the learner to make the correct response more apparent.	• Minimally intrusive	• Can lead to faulty stimulus control (i.e., learner response based on position and not features of the intended stimulus)	Instructor placing the hairbrush physically closer to the learner than any other object in the area and telling them to pick up the brush.
Visual Learner is provided with a picture, textual, or other visual cue.	• Learner can often use independently • Minimal vocal language used • Less intrusive	• Assumes learner is a visual learner	A picture or written schedule identifying all of the hair brushing steps; the learner using this list to complete the task.
Verbal Learner is presented with a word, sentence, or specific verbal cue that often includes the correct response.	• Convenient • Less intrusive	• Difficult to fade • Used when not needed or inadvertently so practitioners are unaware that the learner has not mastered the skill	Instructor telling the learner to pick up hairbrush and the learner then picking up the hairbrush.
Gestural Learner is provided a cue by pointing or gesturing.	• Minimally intrusive	• Used inadvertently so practitioners are unaware that the learner has not mastered the skill	Instructor pointing to the hairbrush while telling the learner to pick up the hairbrush.
Time Delay A prompt is not provided until a specific amount of time has passed.	• Allows time for independent response	• Higher possibility for learner to make an error • Prerequisite of waiting for designated time	Pointing to the hairbrush 2 s after the learner has not responded to the demand of "Brush your hair."

Within stimulus prompting strategy	Advantages	Disadvantages	Example (Putting clothes on a hanger)
Stimulus shaping A relevant feature of the stimulus is modified to increase the likelihood of correct responding.	• Faster skill acquisition	• Requires more preparation • May require a level of technological expertise	Coloring the "start" button green and fading the green color to neutral over time.
Stimulus fading An irrelevant feature of the stimulus is modified to increase the likelihood of correct responding.	• Faster skill acquisition	• Requires more preparation • May require a level of technological expertise	Putting an arrow sticker pointing to the "start" button taking little parts of the sticker off over time.

Response Prompting

Response prompting occurs when a cue is added to the environment to increase the likelihood of correct responding. For example, when the teacher tells the learner to line up at the door and simultaneously points to the door, pointing to the door serves as a response prompt. Response prompts are commonly used because they are convenient and occur naturally between people and across situations. There are many different kinds of response prompts that are associated with different advantages and disadvantages; Table 4.3 includes descriptions and considerations for using each type of prompt. Increasingly, professionals are recognizing the need to reduce prompts with high levels of intrusiveness.

Intrusiveness of Prompts

All prompts involve higher levels of engagement with learners, but some prompts involve much more intensive physical/sensory involvement than others. A *prompting hierarchy* describes response prompts based on the level of intrusiveness the prompt introduces to the practitioner-learner interaction (see Table 4.4). There are many reasons to avoid more intrusive prompts, such as full physical guidance, unless it is absolutely unavoidable. The first reason is that efficiency of skill acquisition varies across learners, with some learners benefiting more from a least-to-most intrusive method (LTM). An *LTM* method of prompting consists of beginning with a minimally intrusive prompt (e.g., gesture) and then increasing the level of prompt (e.g., partial physical prompt) if the learner cannot successfully respond with a less intrusive prompt (Gil et al., 2019). A second and perhaps more important reason to provide less intrusive prompts is the experience of trauma that some learners have reported, particularly as a result of more intrusive prompts like full physical prompting (Sandoval-Norton & Shkedy, 2019). In addition, there is a higher risk of injury whenever practitioners physically manipulate or come in contact with another person's body.

The third reason, perhaps even more important, is the message using highly intrusive prompts sends to disabled learners. Whenever a learner does not have control over who touches them and when they are touched, the learner loses agency over their body. Disabled learners are at significantly higher risk for abuse than nondisabled learners and intrusive prompting may be connected to this risk (Wilczynski et al., 2015). For example, when a person in authority has control over when, where, and how a disabled learner is touched, disabled learners may learn that they cannot say "no" to touch, making them easier targets for predators. Further, by modeling that one person can take control of another person's body without permission, practitioners potentially send confusing messages that could result in autistic learners engaging in sexually predatory behavior. Practitioners should assume it is almost always avoidable, and may want to consider *hand under hand* physical prompting if they deem it cannot be avoided. Hand under hand makes it easier for the learner to remove consent for being touched by withdrawing their hand whenever they choose. At a minimum, consent or assent should be obtained when highly intrusive prompts are used.

Despite the fact the LTM prompting is advisable, there are some learners who may not be able to benefit from this method efficiently and effectively; most-to-least (MTL) prompting should be considered under these conditions. The *MTL* method is an errorless prompting technique where more intrusive prompts are

Table 4.4. Assessing Preferred Prompting Method When Using Response Prompting

This form was developed based on assessment methods proposed by Schnell et al. (2020) but emphasizing the need to use less intrusive prompts and assess adverse side effects. If other response prompts are assessed, always test the two least intrusive prompts first.

Instructions: Randomize the order in which you present each prompt level being assessed; then follow Steps 1–7. Material required: at least 40 picture cards the learner has not mastered. On a separate piece of paper, record all adverse side effects to report at Step 6. Adverse side effects include, but are not restricted to, reductions in smiling or increases in crying, work refusal, self-injury, aggression, and destruction of property.

Step #	Step direction	What you should do after each step using the type of prompt below:		
		Model	Partial physical[1]	Full physical[1]
1	**0 s prompt delay** Place 3 cards on the table and say, "touch the _____." Record adverse side effects below.	Using your finger, immediately touch the correct card.	Immediately take the learner's hand and direct their hand over the correct card.	Immediately take the learner's hand and put it on the correct card.
2	Once the learner has two consecutive correct responses	Move on to a **2 s prompt delay**		
3	**2 s prompt delay** Place three cards on the table and say, "Touch the _____."	Wait 2 s and then touch the correct card.	Wait 2 s and then take the learner's hand and direct their hand over the correct card.	Wait 2 s and then take the learner's hand and put it on the correct card.
4a	Once the learner has two consecutive correct responses	The prompt assessment is over; go to Step 5.		
4b	After at least four trials the learner is scoring 50% or less on any given prompt level	Go back to Step 1 for that prompt level.		
5	Write down how many trials it took to meet mastery criterion in 2 s Prompt Delay condition. Circle that option.			
6	Identify the adverse side effects associated with each prompting method at any point during the assessment.			
7a	If the method that produced the fastest acquisition did not have adverse side effects, use that method with this learner when developing similar skills.			
7b	If the method that produced the fastest acquisition resulted in adverse side effects, the alternative did not produce side effects, and learning occurred with the alternate method, use the alternate method with this learner when developing similar skills.			
7c	If neither modeling nor partial physical prompting resulted in learning after a significant number of trials, compare partial physical with full physical prompts if adverse side effects did not occur during assessment.[2]			

1. Remember to obtain assent prior to using prompting procedures that involve physically touching any learner.
2. Critical Note: If modeling and partial physical prompts both result in adverse side effects, it suggests either (a) the task is too difficult or (b) the learning history has been coercive, and pairing should occur before the assessment is attempted again.

delivered at the outset of instruction and then faded to less intrusive prompts as instruction continues to ultimately give the learner an opportunity to respond independently (Halbur et al., 2020). For example, when instructing a learner to push in their chair, the teacher would first give the instruction immediately followed by a full physical prompt. Assuming the learner pushed in the chair when the full physical prompt was delivered, the teacher delivers the instruction and immediately provides a partial physical prompt (like placing the learner's hand on back of the chair) on the next attempt. On the third attempt, the teacher would use a gestural prompt (pointing at the chair) after they deliver the instruction to push in the chair. Lastly, the teacher would not deliver any prompt but only deliver the instruction to push in the chair. Given variability in learner response to LTM and MTL, assessments to identify learner-specific prompting and prompt-fading methods can be highly beneficial. Table 4.4 provides a brief overview of the assessment procedures for comparing three common forms of prompts (model, partial physical, and full physical) adapted from Schnell and colleagues (2020). Included in this process is how to incorporate time delay to fade any of these three prompts. Given the role of time delay in this assessment, we describe how to make best use of Table 4.4 at the conclusion of the time-delay section.

Time-Delay Prompts

Time delay is a unique form of response prompting. A *time-delay prompt* is when a discriminative stimulus is delivered and then a pause (i.e., brief interval of time passes) serves to cue the learner that they should be responding. Initially, the practitioner may have to provide the "answer" at the end of the pause but over time, the learner begins responding independently. Consider the case of Jaime, an autistic preschooler whose educator wants Jaime to learn that speaking can lead to fun and exciting opportunities. There is a door in the preschool classroom that leads directly to the playground, which includes a swing set that Jaime adores. For several days, the educator stands in front of the door with their hand on the door-knob and says, "Open door" and Jaime, who has learned to repeat words his educator says, repeats, "Open door." After several days of this repetition, Jaime and his educator stand before the door, the educator's hand is on the doorknob, and the educator pauses and looks at Jaime. Jaime says, "Open door," because he has come to associate these conditions with this phrase—and with then accessing the reinforcer of playing on the swings. In this case, the pause served as the prompt.

A time-delay prompt allows a learner the opportunity to complete a task independently. There are two kinds of time-delay prompts: constant and progressive. A *constant time-delay prompt* is when the length of the pause (as a cue) is delivered on a consistent schedule (e.g., 2 s). The educator delivers the "answer" if the learner does not respond independently. Although they are easy to implement, constant time-delay prompts have a higher chance of creating prompt dependency. *Prompt dependency* is when a learner waits for other people to take some action before they start responding. Prompt dependency can be easier to avoid with a progressive time-delay prompt. A *progressive time-delay prompt* is also when the pause serves as a prompt, but the "answer" is delivered on a schedule that increases in small increments (e.g., 0 s, 2 s, 4 s). How quickly you progress to longer pauses varies depending on the learner's response. Learners have to progressively wait longer before they are able to access a reinforcer if they fail to respond. If you have successfully identified potent reinforcers, learners avoid a longer pause and access reinforcers when they begin responding independently rather than waiting to get the prompt (O'Neill et al., 2018).

Time-delay prompts can be used to develop a wide variety of skills and have been used for teaching autistic learners to verbally respond (Meleshkevich et al., 2020), use sign language (Silbaugh & Falcomata, 2019), use social skills through peer mediation (Lorah et al., 2019), and read functional sight words (Swain et al., 2015). For example, one study involved three autistic boys (5–9 years old) who had documented delays both in social communication and in play skills (Liber et al., 2008). They were taught a variety of social skills using a graduated time-delay method. (A graduated time delay is sometimes also called a progressive time delay.) They learned to use a peer's name, turn their face and body toward their peer, and communicate with the peer using a statement, request, or question. Beginning with a 0-s time-delay prompt before prompting the social-communicative actions and then increasing to a 2-s time delay (and additional progressive time delays), all three participants were able to successfully learn these skills and generalize some skills as well to different environments and peers (Liber et al., 2008).

Time-delay prompts are often used individually but can also be used in a group without making learners feel singled out with a prompt. For example, an educator may give the whole class instruction to line up. Rather than singling a learner out (i.e., "Timmy, you need to line up," the educator can implement the time delay by pausing for 5 s before verbally prompting Timmy to line up. Gradually, the pause can be increased to 10 s before verbally prompting Timmy, until Timmy joins the rest of the class independently.

The purpose of Table 4.4 is for practitioners to compare different prompt levels so the least intrusive prompt that the learner prefers and that yields skill acquisition is selected whenever working on similar tasks to the ones used during testing. Although Schnell and colleagues (2020) compared three prompting procedures, we suggest initially assessing only modeling prompts (see Modeling section) and partial physical prompts as a means of intentionally limiting the intrusiveness of the selected prompt. To begin the prompting comparisons, rotate trials between model and partial physical prompts using a 0-s time delay. Once the learner responds correctly two consecutive times in either condition, fade the delivery of that prompt for 2 s after the initial demand is placed. Once the learner has responded correctly for two consecutive sessions without modeling or partial physical prompts, they have met mastery criteria.

Whichever prompt level is mastered first in the 2-s condition *and* results in no adverse side effects will be the preferred prompt level to use with the learner when teaching similar tasks. A separate assessment may be necessary when tasks are significantly different; different prompting procedures may be needed based on the complexity of the skill and distractions in the environment. In contrast, practitioners should select the alternative prompting method when the method that produced the fastest mastery is associated with adverse side effects and (a) the alternative prompting method produced learning and (b) had no adverse side effects. If learning occurs with neither modeling nor partial physical prompting, it would be prudent to assess the full physical prompt if the previously assessed prompting methods were not associated with adverse side effects and the learner has given permission prior to completing the assessment.

Should the learner demonstrate adverse side effects across both prompting methods, the task may be too difficult, or pairing between the practitioner and preferred stimuli may be needed. If both methods produce adverse side effects, this may be due to a negative learning history in general, and the practitioner may need to build rapport with the learner or any instructions/prompting can be expected to evoke adverse side effects. This learning history must be changed by teaching the learner to associate the practitioner with positive experiences; then the assessment can resume. Finally, we selected these three prompting methods because these were identified in Schnell and colleagues (2020); however, we would encourage practitioners to assess responding based on multiple less-intrusive prompts if feasible.

Stimulus Prompting

Stimulus prompting requires practitioners to manipulate the appearance of instructional materials to cue correct responding. There are two forms of stimulus prompting: within and extra stimulus prompting. *Within stimulus prompting* involves modifying the stimulus to increase the likelihood of correct responding. For example, a child learning the letter *s* might be shown a snake in the shape of the letter *s* to help the child remember the *s* sound at the beginning of the word snake. Initially, the snake *s* might have prominent features (snake's head and tail, scaly skin) but across instructional interactions, these features would fade until only the letter *s* remained. *Extra stimulus prompting* involves adding to the stimulus materials to cue correct responding. For example, if the background of the correct answer was red and all incorrect responses were white, the red background would serve as an extra stimulus prompt. This extra stimulus prompt could be faded by gradually making the background change from red to dark pink to light pink to white. Importantly, it is necessary to alter the appearance of instructional materials across instructional interactions with a learner until the materials appear as they do in the natural environment.

More than twice as much research has been conducted on response prompting than stimulus prompting, even though stimulus prompting teaches learners more efficiently (Cengher et al., 2018). That is, learners are likely to take less time and fewer instructional attempts (i.e., trials to criterion) when stimulus prompts are used. Why? Stimulus prompting is not as readily available as a gesture or a physical prompt under real-world conditions. Further, stimulus prompting requires greater planning across all instructional interactions. As technology improves, stimulus prompting is increasingly a viable option (Lorah et al., 2014) and should be explored to the maximum extent possible given its clear benefits over response prompting.

Prompt Fading

Irrespective of the prompting method used, practitioners need to effectively fade prompts if they want learners to independently use academic and social skills (Sam & AFIRM Team, 2015). *Prompt fading* is the act of reducing and eliminating prompts as quickly as possible while maintaining accurate performance (Dietz & Malone, 1985). Although prompts can be necessary to help learners acquire new skills, prompt dependency can occur if prompts are not faded as soon as the learner can perform the task either independently or with a less intrusive prompt.

It is hard to remember exactly what level of prompting to use for each skill with each learner given the large number of learners practitioners often serve. Practitioners can most effectively fade prompts in way that yields the best learner outcomes and minimizes any unwanted side effects by collecting data on the level of prompting used with a given learner and using those data to guide future decisions. Consider the example of Katia, an autistic learner who calls out a response without raising her hand. Mr. Biaglin decided to use a response prompt whenever he believed Katia might know the answer (e.g., "What is 5 + 4? Katia, raise your hand if you know the answer."). He was initially pleased when Katia started answering questions only after raising her hand and being called on. Mr. Biaglin kept this intervention in place for 3 weeks to ensure Katia understood his expectations. When Mr. Biaglin stopped prompting her, Katia neither raised her hand nor called out answers. Katia was clearly prompt dependent, so Mr. Biaglin cleverly told Katia to raise her hand when she saw other learners raising their hands if she knew the answer. Initially, Mr. Biaglin called on Katia every time she raised her hand. By the second day, Mr. Biaglin started calling on Katia intermittently when she raised her hand. Katia started responding like other learners. Prompt dependency is not always this easy to address and not all learners alter their behaviors this quickly—so it is best to fade prompts quickly!

Task Analysis

Although task analysis is identified as an EBP by the National Professional Development Center for autism spectrum disorder,[4] we do not characterize task analysis as a core element or an EBP because it is not a method for teaching skills, reducing behaviors, or altering the environment in a way that supports learners. Instead, *task analysis* is the act of breaking an activity down to its component parts, ordering them in the sequence in which they must be performed to correctly complete an activity (Moore & Quintero, 2018). Tasks can typically be broken down into larger chunks or very small pieces. A task analysis can be completed for any type of skill or behavior that has multiple components. The depth of the analysis and number of steps included will depend on what skills the learner already possesses, the rate at which the learner acquires new skills, and the complexity of the skill. For example, the task of washing one's hands could be broken down as a 9-step process or a 4-step process (see Table 4.5). Chaining is the most common method for teaching tasks once they have been task analyzed. We will discuss this method next. However, a task analysis can be very helpful prior to modeling or creating a video model as well. Modeling will be described after chaining.

EBP—Combining Core Elements: Chaining

Perhaps the most common EBP practitioners use after completing a task analysis is chaining. *Chaining* involves using one of the three methods (described below) for teaching the sequence of steps identified in a task analysis as a behavioral chain. A *behavioral chain* is when each step of a task is completed in a specific sequence, with each step serving as a discriminative stimulus for the next step when the task has been fully mastered. The three methods used for teaching a chain of behaviors are backward chaining, forward chaining, and total task presentation. When creating a task analysis and then implementing a backward or forward chaining or a total task presentation intervention, there are several considerations (adapted

Table 4.5. Steps in Writing a Task Analysis and an Example

| | Steps in writing a task analysis | |
Number	Step	Examples (if applicable)
Step 1	Identify the target skill	Cleaning a mirror
Step 2	Identify the prerequisite skills	
Step 3	Identify the materials needed	Paper towel, glass cleaner
Step 4	Break down skills into components	
Step 5	Confirm task is completely analyzed	
Step 6	Identify which chaining method to use	Forward chaining, backward chaining, total-task presentation
Step 7	Identify possible prompts to be used	Full physical, partial physical, model, gestural
Step 8	Select the recording method to collect data	Task analysis data sheet
Step 9	Implement the intervention	

9-step hand-washing task analysis	4-step hand-washing task analysis
1. Turn on water	1. Wet hands
2. Wet hands	2. Rub soap on hands for 20 s
3. Get soap	3. Rinse and dry off hands
4. Rub soap on hands for 20 seconds	4. Turn off water using paper towel and throw paper towel in the trash.
5. Rinse hands	
6. Get paper towel	
7. Dry hands	
8. Turn off water using paper towel	
9. Throw paper towel in the trash	

from Szidon & Franzone, 2009) to ensure the process is complete, comprehensive, and appropriate for the individual learner.

Backward chaining begins with the last step (which feels backward). "Throw paper towel in the trash" might be the last behavior in a task analysis for hand-washing. Prompting and reinforcement are delivered to ensure fluent performance of the terminal step. Practitioners have two choices on how to address the previous steps in backward chaining. First, practitioners might complete all except the last step themselves and provide prompts with reinforcement to support autistic learners' completion of this terminal component of the task. Once they have mastered this last step, practitioners simply teach each preceding step until learners have mastered the first step. Second, learners can be given full physical prompts to complete the initial steps in the sequence. The repetition of full physical prompts may be helpful for some learners who require numerous attempts before approximating the steps. However, there is an extremely high level of intrusion with full physical prompts, which often sends the message to learners that they do not have full agency over their own bodies.

Given the high risk for abuse disabled people face (Wilczynski et al., 2015), it seems inadvisable to take this approach unless absolutely necessary. In addition, higher levels of physical prompting increase the physical interaction between the practitioner and learner, thus increasing the risk for injury. Finally, using full physical prompts for a protracted period increases the risk of prompt dependency. Having stated these firm reasons to avoid full physical prompting of initial steps when backward chaining, we acknowledge that some learners benefit from the repetition and that, in limited cases, it may aid skill acquisition. In addition, some tasks will require learner involvement (e.g., rubbing hands together while washing hands), so physical prompting may be necessary. However, practitioners should obtain consent or attempt assent before touching learners—even when highly intrusive prompts are deemed necessary.

Forward chaining involves teaching the first step identified in the task analysis until it is mastered and then teaching subsequent steps one at a time until the learner completes the task independently. Let's use teaching a learner to tie their shoes as an example of forward chaining. The educator has the learner attempt the first step and provide prompts if needed (e.g., holding one lace in each hand) independently and then finishes tying the shoe for them. On the first occasion in which the educator tells the learner to tie their shoes after they have mastered the first step, the learner then completes the first step independently and attempts the second step with prompts (as needed). The educator then completes the rest of the shoe-tying steps for them. The educator continues to add the subsequent step after each previous step has been mastered. The skill is mastered once the learner can tie their shoes independently. You move forward one step at a time! Practitioners provide prompts and reinforcement for correct performance of this first step in the chain. As with backward chaining, practitioners must weigh their decision about whether to prompt subsequent steps in the chain and should seek to eliminate or minimize intrusive prompting.

The third way to teach steps in a behavioral chain is through *total task presentation*. When using total task presentation, practitioners present the entire complex task (e.g., steps A–H) and prompt any step in the sequence requiring assistance. The skill is considered mastered once the learner can complete all the steps in the chain independently and in the correct order (Cooper et al., 2020). This method is most effective if a learner already has many of the steps in their behavioral repertoire (but just cannot complete them in the correct order), has a well-developed imitative repertoire, and when teaching tasks in the natural environment because behaviors are taught in a natural order. Total task presentation is also the preferred chaining method when teaching moderate-to-severe learners (Test et al., 1990).

Some learners will be unable to complete one or more steps of the task independently. For example, an autistic learner with limited fine motor skills may be permanently interdependent on others when performing the task of putting on a coat because fastening zippers and buttons are both too difficult to perform. The criterion for "correct performance" will need to be amended to reflect only those items the learner completes independently (McGreevy et al., 2014). However, it is common for learners to make a mistake by skipping a step or performing a step incorrectly even when they are physically able to complete the task. Using the task analysis for hand washing (see Table 4.5), a learner who is told to "rinse your hands" might simply rub their hands together under the faucet but fail to turn on the water. This is not a "flaw" in the learner or the teaching method! It only means that the previous step (i.e., rub soap on hands for 20 s) is not yet a strong enough discriminative stimulus for all aspects of the next step in the behavioral chain (i.e., "rinse your hands"). It might be necessary to add a prompt (e.g., gesture to turn the handle on the faucet) a number of times before this connection is made. Practitioners should simply redeliver the instruction and provide a prompt to evoke the correct response. The prompt level depends on a number of factors—Which prompts have worked in the past? or What type of learner-specific prompts have been evaluated to be effective for the individual learner (See Table 4.3)?

Chaining is not limited to daily living skills. For example, practitioners have taught autistic children how to play with toys appropriately (Stahmer et al., 2013), share objects with others (DeQuinzio et al., 2008), and play social games (Kourassanis et al., 2015). Practitioners have also used chaining to address social activities (e.g., social interaction with peers when playing games or cooking) by providing a written task analysis of the skills needed to complete the social task and using chaining until the social interactions occur independently. Many autistic learners are able to self-monitor their own performance in the context of social activities such as game playing and cooking social scenarios (Parker & Kamps, 2011).

EBP—Combining Core Elements: Modeling and Video Modeling

All children learn through observing behaviors modeled by peers and adults. Many preschoolers naturally imitate by pretending to text on a toy phone, blurting out a curse word, or "fighting" with swords like the characters on television. It would be naive to assume all modeling involves behaviors we would hope to be imitated. A group of eighth grade learners are standing in the hall during the passing period and making hand gestures behind the back of their physical education (PE) teacher as she walks past. An autistic learner who interprets these gestures as an appropriate greeting, walks into the PE class, and greets his educator with this gesture may be surprised at her response!

Practitioners can use modeling of skills to their advantage in the classroom. They can model behaviors ranging from the correct pronunciation of a word, to forming a letter when writing on paper, to completing the steps of a dance routine. As an EBP, *modeling* involves intentionally providing an example of the correct way to perform a task with the goal of the learner accurately performing the same task (Abadir et al., 2021). Completing a task analysis prior to modeling means that the practitioner can be certain each step will be accurately modeled in a manner that yields the intended outcome (e.g., the packaging of materials for vocational training, the making of a sandwich for daily living skills).

With the ease of access to technology, *video modeling* may be an easy and cost-effective way to model new skills. Video modeling is a process in which an educator uses recorded video to demonstrate or model a skill or skills for a learner. Individuals who play a central role in developing successful videos to be used for the purposes of modeling may involve an adult, peers, and/or the target learner. Editing allows a learner who has not mastered each step of a task, confuses the sequence of the steps, or simply lacks fluency, to serve as their own model. Videos can be edited to provide texts or other enhancements to support better learner outcomes (Alzyoudi et al., 2015), and the same video model could be used for multiple learners who are working on the same skill.

Modeling has been demonstrated to successfully teach autistic children functional living skills (Hong et al., 2016), abduction avoidance skills (Abadir et al.,

2021), play skills (Lee et al., 2017), social engagement (Ho et al., 2019), and empathy (Schrandt et al., 2009). It can also free up practitioner time because rather than having to model a skill repeatedly until a learner masters the task, the practitioner can ensure the learner views the same task being accurately implemented repeatedly until the learner has mastered the task (Wilczynski et al., 2011).

EBP—Individual and Group Applications: Token Economy

We collectively agree that uniquely designed paper holds a specific value and can be exchanged for goods and services. The value of money results from the pairing of the paper with the goods and services we desire. Similarly, a *token economy* is a reinforcement-based intervention in which learners earn tokens (i.e., conditioned reinforcers) and then exchange their tokens for reinforcers (Cihon et al., 2019). Tokens are the equivalent of money. Practitioners can select different forms of tokens (e.g., distinctly designed paper, chips, points) and deliver these tokens immediately after learners demonstrate specific behaviors (e.g., on-task behavior, prosocial behaviors). These tokens are accumulated, and educators offer a menu of "goods" (e.g., iPad, favorite toy) or "services" (e.g., a break from work, line leader, dance party).

When first implementing a token economy with a learner, a single token is immediately delivered after correct performance of a task and then exchanged for goods or services. By consistently obtaining goods and services for accurate performance, the token becomes a secondary reinforcer. The schedule of reinforcement is slowly leaned (i.e., the number of tokens needed to purchase items off the menu is increased). Eventually, most learners earn a large number of tokens that are exchanged one to two times per day or even once per week if the learner can continue performing well with such delayed access to reinforcers from the "store." The frequency of exchange should be individualized based on the learner's continued improvement. Token economies can be especially beneficial in school settings because they are structured and can be generalized and easy to dispense and accumulate (Tarbox et al., 2006).

Researchers have provided some practical suggestions for the use of token economies. For example, practitioners may want to incorporate a learner's special interest into the token economy (e.g., tokens with Spider-Man on them). Although limited data are available, preliminary data suggest having the token represent the special interest may increase on-task behavior and decrease problem behavior (Carnett et al., 2014). Similarly, practitioners have sometimes noted that some learners stop appropriate responding once they know they have earned enough tokens to purchase the goods or services they desire. Based on data involving young autistic children (ages 4–6), the store can simply adopt a "flexible earning requirement" in which the learners are not informed of exactly what the cost of the goods or services will be until the time of purchase. Although they did not know what the "magic number" of tokens would be to make their purchases, all children had increased commenting, which was the target behavior (Cihon et al., 2019).

Like all EBPs, token economies may not always be the best fit for a given learner. For example, tokens may not serve as potent reinforcers for all learners (Fiske et al., 2020). In addition, when tasks require a lot of responses to complete, the schedule may signal that a significant delay can be anticipated before gaining access to reinforcers from the store, which could actually suppress performance (Gadaire et al., 2021). An unfortunate disadvantage of token economies is that they are easy to implement. As a result, token economies become so commonly used that they are applied with learners who will work without external reinforcers, or they are applied identically for all learners, without consideration of the skills within the learner's repertoire or the needed schedule of reinforcement (i.e., how often tokens are delivered; how often the store is visited). Practitioners will always want to collect meaningful data to determine if their selected EBPs are having the intended outcome.

EBP—Individual and Group Applications: Visual Supports

Visual supports are a group of interventions that involve visual display of information that increases the likelihood a learner can demonstrate a target skill or display acceptable behavior without the use of additional prompts. Visual supports might include, but are not restricted to, creating visual schedules, using scripts, or, as described in the prompting section, providing visual cues. One of the advantages of visual prompts is that they are often easier to fade than verbal prompts (West, 2008). Visual schedules are often used to help learners follow a routine; however, the stimulus used for visual schedules can vary dramatically. An autistic learner with very limited expressive or receptive speech skills might require objects that represent specific activities. For example, a "Hot Wheels" car might represent the need to travel from one location to another or a toy building that looks like a school could be used to convey that the learner will be taking the car from home to the school. Often, visual schedules involve photos or drawings but may also involve words or smartphone applications. As always, practitioners should develop the intervention based on the learner's repertoire of skills. There is an endless variety of ways that visuals can be used in the classroom. An educator may wear a ring of visual pictures on a lanyard for quick access to convey to their learners it is time to "wait," "stop," "go," "sit down," or "raise hand."

Scripts involve a written description of the roles one or more people play under specific circumstances; they include statements by people under these conditions. Scripts have been used primarily to increase communication by autistic learners. For example, four transition-aged autistic learners were taught to identify and describe a problem and request assistance during vocational training (Dotto-Fojut et al., 2011). Scripts have even successfully been used to increase communication as a peer-mediated intervention; however, generalization of the skills was not evidenced (Ganz et al., 2012).

Scripts are often presented in a written format, which is why they are often included as a "visual support." However, scripts may also be presented in an audio format (Gallant et al., 2016; Wójcik et al., 2020). Whether written or audio scripts are provided, scripts will need to be faded because they are a type of prompt and all prompts should be faded as quickly as possible (Wichnick-Gillis et al., 2019). In addition, practitioners need to reinforce all spontaneous communications that are appropriate and relevant to the environment. For example, if a script was developed for a learner to request a bathroom break but they approached the practitioner and asked for a break to go to the school nurse, the practitioner should reinforce this request and not redirect them to their script!

Despite the popular belief that autistic learners are all "visual learners," not all autistic learners will benefit from visual supports. For example, learners who cannot attend to visual stimuli long enough to build an association between an object (e.g., car) and activity (e.g., leaving the house and going somewhere else) will not initially benefit from object-based visual schedules. Similarly, blind/low-vision autistic learners should receive consultation from a specialist to determine the specific needs of these learners to ensure that they are able to access the visual supports or are given an alternative support that matches their needs.

Visual boundaries are often described as a visual support (Sam et al., 2019), but we were unable to find any research supporting their use. *Visual boundaries* involve demarcating spaces that are available/unavailable or safe/unsafe. For example, different-colored tape could be applied to the floor to indicate spaces in which an autistic learner is free to move (e.g., the "free play" part of the classroom might have blue tape at its perimeter) and those that are restricted (e.g., leaving the building can only happen when accompanied by an adult for a very young learner). Although there is no clear research using this method, some scholars argue it contains enough features that are consistent with EBP that involve visual supports that it should be deemed evidence based. We disagree with the conclusion but would still encourage any practitioner or parent to consider adopting the strategy despite the paucity of evidence supporting its use given its potential for increasing safety and the low likelihood for significant adverse side effects. This is an example of why professional judgment should always drive treatment selection!

THE EVIDENCE-BASED INTERVENTION SELECTION MODEL: REMINDER AND APPLICATION

As we stated at the beginning of this chapter, the evidence-based intervention selection model involves using one's professional judgment to bring research findings, local data, learner factors, and contextual variables together to select the right intervention for each learner. Practitioners face two common risks when they select interventions. First, they may not individualize interventions sufficiently and risk that the intervention will (a) not change behavior, (b) be culturally insensitive, and/or (c) not adequately meet the needs of their learners. Second, practitioners may individualize interventions but use components that lack research support. In many cases, interventions that lack research support will result in the situation of getting worse for learners and practitioners alike. Managing these risks highlights why professional judgment is essential to the evidence-based intervention selection process. These risks can be reduced by collecting frequent and meaningful data to quickly determine whether learners are benefiting from an intervention.

An exhaustive discussion of all factors resulting in sound professional judgment are beyond the scope of this chapter. However, practitioners need to know the range of factors that should influence the individualized intervention selected for each of their learners. In Table 4.6, we briefly review the person-related factors such as learner characteristics, values, and preferences as well as real-world contextual variables (e.g., resource constraints, limited environmental supports, and the need to build capacity) that should influence the intervention selection process. We

Table 4.6.   Person-Related Factors and Contextual Variables: How to Incorporate Professional Judgment

How to incorporate professional judgment	Definitions	Examples
Person-related factors (e.g., learner characteristics, values, and preferences)		
Repertoire	Skills a learner needs to benefit from an intervention.	A learner must be able to: 1. Develop an association between a token and a reinforcer to benefit from a token economy. 2. Pay attention to a video to benefit from video modeling.
Health	A learner's physical or mental health condition that may include, but is not restricted to, medication usage, pain, feeling unwell physically or mentally.	1. A medication makes a learner irritable so they cannot tolerate intrusive prompts. 2. A learner has a headache so fewer demands are placed, easier tasks are approached, and the schedule of reinforcement is rich. 3. The learner with ASD experiences a lot of anxiety in anticipation of the visual schedule, showing a transition will occur but did not experience this level of anxiety without this visual support.
Preferences	A learner liking one intervention compared to other options.	1. Completing a preference assessment to identify potent reinforcers. 2. Using interventions that automatically involve choice (e.g., token economy). 3. Explaining the intervention options to a learner with ASD and asking which they like better.
Tolerance	A learner's capacity to endure intervention without negative side effects.	1. The intervention "reduced" a problem behavior but led to higher rates of crying. 2. The intervention increased a targeted skill but now the learner engages in high rates of stereotypic behavior.

How to incorporate professional judgment	Definitions	Examples
Values	A learner's regard for something as important or culturally meaningful.	1. A learner with ASD self-advocates for agency over their own body so intrusive prompts are not appropriate. 2. A practitioner only uses examples of heterosexual "couples" when teaching social skills with middle- or high-school learners, despite the fact that more learners with ASD are on the LGBTQIA+ spectrum.
Contextual variables		
Resource constraints	Limited financial resources or access to needed materials.	1. An intervention might be preferred by all parties; however, the costs are prohibitive and other interventions are likely to produce positive learner outcomes without negative side effects. 2. An intervention requires the school staff to purchase materials and the items are on back order so are not readily available.
Environmental supports	Staffing needed to implement interventions with a high degree of accuracy and climate in the workplace.	1. A practitioner does not have enough trained paraprofessionals who can implement the intervention correctly. 2. Administrators adopt different interventions for the school so frequently that educators are not supported in advocating for a different intervention for their learner.
Capacity needs	The length of time it takes to develop skills and hire staff to implement an intervention accurately.	Staff have not implemented the intervention previously and require training. Trainers are not immediately available, and coaching is needed after initial training.

(continued)

Table 4.6. *Continued*

How to incorporate professional judgment	*Definitions*	*Examples*
Social validity and ethics		
Intervention acceptability	The extent to which the learner, practitioner, and legal guardians find the intervention palatable.	1. A learner believes the visual supports offered single them out and make them look unable to communicate using words like their classmates. 2. A practitioner believes physical prompts are abusive because they can be traumatizing and so they will not implement interventions using this element.
Meaningfulness of learner outcomes	The degree to which the intervention has yielded socially important and useful improvements in the learner's life.	1. A constant time delay prompt was used because it was less complicated, but the learner has become prompt dependent and cannot perform the task independently. 2. The intervention was fairly labor intensive; therefore it could be implemented in the school where multiple paraprofessionals were available but did not lead to meaningful improvement in skills that were applied across home and community because these resources were unavailable there.
Code of Ethics	Acting consistent with the ethical codes of one's profession. For example, https://www.nea.org/resource-library/code-ethics-educators	A research-supported punishment procedure is palatable to a practitioner but does not maintain the dignity of the learner with ASD.

also introduce how social validity and ethical obligations should influence decision making. Referencing the table while considering the application below will emphasize why professional judgment is crucial in selecting the right intervention.

Background

Maisie is in sixth grade at Harris Middle School, in a suburb of a mid-sized city in the United States. The school district found Maisie eligible for special education services in the category of autism spectrum disorder and speech and language impairment at 3 years of age and her eligibility has been reverified since that time. She has continuously received consultation for speech services to work on her communication skills. Maisie currently communicates that she is overwhelmed through multiple means including verbally (e.g., "I can't deal with this"), increased levels of some stereotypy (i.e., hand flapping, pacing the room), and through behavioral outbursts (i.e., screaming, throwing objects, pushing/scratching people).

A BIP was developed in kindergarten to address behavioral outbursts. Several interventions were incorporated into Maisie's schooling based on the functional behavioral assessment (FBA; see Chapter 10). First, a visual schedule was implemented because the FBA showed Maisie was much more likely to have intense outbursts when unpredictable events occurred. Maisie worked with the resource educator to make most of her own pictures for her visual schedule in her last two years. Second, functional communication training was used to teach Maisie to request breaks whenever hand flapping and pacing occurred. Breaks were provided in the classroom or in the resource room based on Maisie's preference at the moment. Other forms of stereotypy (i.e., a quiet hum and finger posturing) were more likely to occur when Maisie appeared happy and did not occur prior to outbursts, so these forms of stereotypic behavior were not addressed. Third, Maisie was most engaged in learning when adults delivered higher rates of quiet attention. When Maisie was told she was "doing a great job completing her work" or that her educator "liked how well she was playing near other children" using a quiet tone, her appropriate behaviors continued or improved further. Maisie seemed startled by louder noises so her educators neither corrected nor delivered praise using a louder voice. The BIP included educators and the principals delivering reinforcement in the form of quiet praise at higher rates on any days in which schedule changes were anticipated (e.g., a shortened schedule, a fire drill).

Maisie had behavioral outbursts a few times per year in elementary school, but her educators reported they occurred only on days when the BIP was implemented with less accuracy. For example, one of the substitute educators provided prompts to request a break when any form of stereotypy occurred, which meant she was expected to take more breaks. When the plan was implemented accurately the outbursts remitted.

Maisie transitioned to sixth grade in a new middle school. All of the learners and educators were adjusting to the new environment and Maisie was assigned a resource educator who was unable to attend Maisie's case conference meeting the previous year because she was hired in the month before classes started in the fall. Maisie's sixth grade schedule included four core academic periods, two electives, and one "Behavior Skills Development" class that she attended with other learners with IEPs. Her resource educator checked in at random intervals throughout the day but did not notice that Maisie was not provided her visual schedule. In addition, the resource educator was not present when Maisie requested a break and her general education educator told her that expectations were different in middle school and that she could take a break along with the other learners during lunch.

In her third week of school, the guidance counselor adjusted Maisie's schedule due to mistakenly putting Maisie in a class that was far below her academic level. Maisie began screaming and pushing past educators to get to her original classroom when she learned this at the beginning of the school day. The principal emphatically and repeatedly told Maisie he would not tolerate this kind of behavior in his school and then suspended her for aggression toward educators and disruption of the learning environment. He did not take time to determine what caused the behavior. Maisie's parents reported that she was agitated and did not want to return to school. The resource educator came and asked Maisie to go with her to the resource room to talk about how she was feeling when Maisie returned to school from the suspension. Maisie refused to leave her home room and once again escalated to the point that she knocked over a desk and threatened to hit the educator with her chair. Other learners in the room were evacuated and the principal was called. Maisie was suspended from school for a second time.

After her second suspension, Maisie's parents requested that a review of the BIP occur and that new supports be put into place now that Maisie is in a new setting and is exhibiting problem behaviors. In addition, they are concerned that Maisie is not being included in any conversations about her schooling; they want her to be able to self-advocate. Although the school personnel have seen Maisie when she is most distressed, they know Maisie can participate in decisions about her own educational experience if given the opportunity and during a time when she has not been triggered. Maisie's parents have stated that the educators, guidance counselor, and principal did not follow the IEP and have shared that they are currently consulting with a special education advocate to determine next steps. They point to previous evaluations showing Maisie exhibits above-average cognitive skills and high levels of academic achievement. They also want the school to address Maisie's interactions with peers. Maisie struggles to initiate and maintain conversations and friendships with peers, but does have an interest in friendships. She tends to gravitate to adults in social situations rather than learners her own age. Although this has been helpful to educators in the past, Maisie now expresses interest in peers and told her parents she "feels awkward that my classmates have seen me at my worst."

Step 1: Questions to Initiate the Evidence-Based Treatment Selection Process

The first step in selecting an evidence-based treatment is to generate questions that will focus and guide the team in the process. Given the preceding information, Maisie's team may develop the following guiding questions:

1. Does Maisie need a new FBA/BIP to address the behavioral outbursts Maisie has had since entering middle school?
2. What intervention(s) may be needed to reduce behavioral outbursts?

3. What intervention(s) may be needed to increase Maisie's appropriate engagement with educators and learners at the school?
4. Are interventions needed to help Maisie participate in her own intervention development?

Step 2—Part 1: Best Available Evidence

The school has excellent sources of evidence to consider for Maisie. First, the NCAEP and NPD-ASD identify a large number of EBPs that should be prioritized as good options. Second, the elementary school provided years of documented response to the implemented interventions—which is also a source of evidence. In fact, the elementary school provided especially strong evidence that the interventions worked because their data show Maisie had behavioral outbursts when there was inaccurate implementation of multicomponent interventions (reinforcement in the form of praise using a quiet voice, a visual schedule, and the use of breaks when requested).

The results of the FBA are quite old, so a new FBA needed to be conducted. Both interview and observation were critical parts of the FBA, each providing evidence to guide intervention selection. Through the interview, Maisie's parents reported behavioral outbursts were consistently preceded by statements of protest (e.g., "We are not supposed to be doing that!") and increased hand-flapping and pacing. Although Maisie has been in middle school for only a short time, one of her educators noted this same pattern. This information allowed the observation portion of the FBA to include these two precursor behaviors and not just behavioral outbursts. No intensive behavioral outbursts were observed during the FBA; however, the A-B-C data showed verbal protests and targeted stereotypic behavior were structurally related to changes in Maisie's schedule as identified on her visual schedule. This pattern suggested that the existing interventions identified on the BIP may still be highly useful in reducing behavioral outbursts and increasing appropriate ways to engage with others in the school.

Step 2—Part 2: Person-Related Variables

Learner Repertoire, Preference, and Tolerance of Interventions

Maisie's ability to communicate through multiple means (i.e., verbally, increased levels of hand flapping and pacing, and behavioral outbursts) shows she can be persistent in advocating her preferences. However, Maisie does not yet know how to self-advocate regarding intervention preferences or when triggering conditions are present. Historically, Maisie has shown no adverse effects (i.e., she tolerates the interventions well).

Learner Values and Preferences

Maisie told the guidance counselor she loved going to elementary school but does not like the unexpected changes in middle school. She acknowledged being overwhelmed because there are many transitions throughout the day and there are no familiar educators or staff members there. She is terrified of the principal and has drawn numerous pictures of him yelling at her and throwing her out of school. Maisie wishes her new educators listened to her like the ones at her old school. She does not like her visual schedule any longer because it uses pictures, and she worries that makes her look like a baby. Maisie still likes when her educators provide quiet praise because she hates loud noises, and she does not want other children noticing when she gets the educator's attention. Maisie liked the resource room in elementary school because she got to sit in an area of the resource room that contained her pictures.

Parental Values and Preferences

Maisie's mother is a womanist and believes in dismantling ableism. She wants Maisie to self-advocate for specific interventions. Both parents stated a preference for unintrusive, positive interventions but believe these should be faded quickly so Maisie can learn to respond under the same conditions as other learners. Her parents advocate both for independence and for interdependence (i.e., when people may be dependent on each other some of the time) as best meets Maisie's needs.

Step 2—Part 3: Contextual Variables

Resource Constraints

The principal felt all previous interventions reflected a good investment and that the school had been ill-prepared for Maisie's outbursts due to her consistent success in elementary school. He preferred using paraprofessionals as little as possible in middle school so learners can become more independent, but recognized they were sometimes valuable.

Environmental Supports

Maisie's resource educator has requested a behavioral coach because she has limited experience implementing EBPs; the coach does not have availability until the following month. The entire school staff provides reinforcement for desired behaviors at a very low rate and the climate is that learners should just "behave appropriately." The principal has been in this role for more than 20 years, describes himself as "drawing a hard line" when it comes to problem behaviors, and often relies on punishment. He did acknowledge mistakes were made in Maisie's transition, endorsed continued use of previously implemented interventions, and approved the use of a behavioral coach for the resource educator.

Step 3: Professional Judgment

Practitioner Values and Preferences

Maisie's educators all agreed the interventions on her previous BIP appeared reasonable. Although they did not appreciate her outbursts, they each noted discomfort with punishment for Maisie and that suspensions would just create problems.

Speech-Language Pathologist and School Counselor Values and Preferences

The speech-language pathologist (SLP) only recently met Maisie. She found previous interventions acceptable but argued to change to a text-based visual schedule given Maisie's reading skills and concerns about being different from her classmates. The SLP and the school counselor run a peer-mediated intervention program, which she believes could help Maisie address interacting more with peers and her feelings of awkwardness around her peers due to her behavioral outbursts.

Step 4: Intervention Selection

Maisie, her parents, the advocate, and involved school personnel attended a meeting to select interventions for Maisie. Maisie was invited to share how she felt about her middle school experience and then her parents expressed their concerns. Maisie reported she was "stressed out" about middle school and that she does not like the school principal because he "just kicks her out instead of listening to her." Maisie's parents were also concerned that the suspensions were reactive and that the first suspension should have triggered an FBA and this meeting. Based on the best available evidence, person-related variables, and contextual variables, all agreed that modifying the visual schedule to include text instead of pictures made sense. Maisie asked if she could use a phone instead of the front of her binder for her visual schedule. Her parents agreed to get her a phone for this purpose. The educator (with SLP consultation) will teach Maisie how to use the app.

All agreed the educators should honor requested breaks to the resource room. The resource educator agreed to post some of Maisie's pictures in part of the room and Maisie agreed the pictures would not be of the principal yelling at her. The advocate suggested a paraprofessional to prompt Maisie to request a break when she started hand flapping or pacing. Maisie objected because she did not want to stand out from her classmates. The principal suggested they could reevaluate the need for a paraprofessional every two weeks. Maisie said the paraprofessional would not be necessary for more than two weeks. All agreed that delivering praise using a quiet voice should be continued. The principal asked Maisie if he could praise her in a quiet voice and she told him "not yet." They agreed that he would ask again after a month and he would honor her decision either way.

Maisie liked the idea of having peers work with her in middle school. Two peers, at least one of whom always shared a class with Maisie, would be taught how to support Maisie with transitions using vernacular used by same-aged peers (e.g., "It's time we head to math now."). Maisie offered to help these peers in other ways (e.g., reading, drawing). Both peers share a lunch with Maisie so all of them would be taught effective strategies for engaging each other in conversation. For example, all learners could be taught to spend some time identifying and then talking about their favorite topics, with all learners getting a chance to talk and listen.

Step 5: Intervention Implementation and Data Collection

Data were collected on hand flapping, pacing, verbal protests, and behavioral outbursts following implementation of the multicomponent intervention. Hand flapping, pacing, and verbal protests occurred somewhat frequently in the first days after accurate intervention implementation. The paraprofessional regularly prompted Maisie to ask for a break on the first day and only a few times on the second day. By day three, these behaviors occurred infrequently, and Maisie requested breaks independently and the paraprofessional support was unnecessary—proving Maisie right: she did not need the paraprofessional for more than 2 weeks.

Social validity data were collected using the Intervention Rating Profile for educators (Tarnowski & Simonian, 1992), the Children's Intervention Rating Profile (Witt & Elliot, 1985) for Maisie, and the Behavior Intervention Rating Scale (Elliott & Von Brock, 1991) for Maisie's parents. Maisie created and used her own social validity intervention satisfaction scale, with 1 indicating very dissatisfied and 5 indicating very satisfied. All respondents reported finding the interventions acceptable and Maisie reported a four or higher on intervention satisfaction for 95% of school days. Days with lower satisfaction ratings occurred on days educators provided lower rates of quiet praise. Maisie's highest ratings for the interventions was the text-based visual schedule because "I love having my own phone!"

Step 6: Reevaluation

Data suggested no additional alterations to the intervention would be necessary. A month after the meeting, the principal asked if he could quietly praise Maisie. She decided she was not yet ready for that but suggested he could record a voice memo on her phone so she could listen to it if he silently gave her a "thumbs up" sign. For a person who often relied on punishment, he was tickled by the compromise.

Maisie's educators worked in accordance with their ethical code by individualizing interventions, using EBPs, and putting Maisie's needs first. They also established a healthy relationship with Maisie, supporting her development of self-advocacy skills, which were respected by the principal. The peer-mediated intervention resulted in interpersonal relationships that were a priority to Maisie. All of these ethical and socially valid decisions were made in a cost-effective and time-efficient manner that did not overwhelm Maisie, her family, or the school system.

SUMMARY

The evidence-based treatment selection model is essential for making best decisions about which intervention to apply for any individual learner because it requires using professional judgment to incorporate the best available evidence with client and contextual variables that influence the likelihood an intervention will produce the intended outcome while avoiding adverse side effects. Whether applying a core element (e.g., reinforcement) or combining core elements (e.g., video modeling), educators must attend not only to the acquisition of meaningful skills and the reduction of behaviors that lower the learner's quality of life, but also to assess and minimize any adverse side effects. EBPs can be applied both at the individual level and at the group level, so educators are encouraged to select interventions that support learners with the minimal level of intrusiveness that leads to benefits.

APPLICATION ACTIVITIES

1. Use the evidence-based treatment selection model on a new or current case with a learner. If you do not currently have an autistic learner on your caseload, create a profile and then attempt to apply the evidence-based treatment selection model to the case.
2. Think of a common procedure that you use. Identify autistic learners for whom the intervention would not be appropriate. Is there a way to adapt the treatment to make it appropriate?
3. Think of a time that you needed to provide prompts for yourself to learn new material. What prompting strategy did you use? How did you fade those prompts? Were you successful in learning the new material?

4. Create a task analysis for an everyday activity such as washing your hands, cooking a meal, or doing the dishes. Give your list to someone else and have them complete the task *exactly as written*. Was your task analysis complete? Do you need to add more steps or break the steps down in more detail? Did the person interpret something very literally and end up confused or doing the wrong thing?

5. Imagine that you are in a room and a person who is much larger than you comes in and gives you an instruction. You do not want to follow the instruction, so you say, "no." The person comes to you and physically forces you to complete the task. While you resist, they say, "You are just a student. You do not know that I am doing this for your own good." How do you feel about this interaction? How would you feel if you had this experience daily? If you are upset, are you upset by the words, the physical coercion, or both? How does this alter your future choices when selecting from an array of interventions?

ADDITIONAL RESOURCES

Autism Focused Intervention Resources and Modules (AFIRM): https://afirm.fpg.unc.edu/afirm-modules

National Clearinghouse on Autism Evidence and Practice: https://ncaep.fpg.unc.edu/

Prompting: Introduction and Practice: https://afirm.fpg.unc.edu/node/2601

Use of Evidence-Based Practices: https://researchautism.org/use-of-evidence-based-practices/

Wilczynski, Henderson, et al. (2016). Evidence-based practice, culture, and young children with autism spectrum disorder. *Perspectives in Early Childhood Psychology and Education*, 1(2), 141–60.

NOTES

1. The authors adopt identity-first language because autistic self-advocates often prefer this term. Autistic self-advocates have reported that the language of "individual with ASD" seems like autistic features are separate from the "real person" instead of being central to their identity. The authors are all anti-ableist and believe honoring autistics' preferences is important to dismantling discriminatory practices against autistics and other disabled people.

2. The process of pairing begins with establishing a positive relationship between an item and something that is already reinforcing. Eventually the new item may be used as a reinforcer without the original primary reinforcer.

3. A punisher is a stimulus that when delivered after a behavior decreases the likelihood the behavior will occur under similar conditions in the future.

4. A careful review of the National Professional Development Center for Autism Spectrum Disorder module on task analysis shows that it combines task analysis with chaining. We separate these because it is technically more accurate to do so and because task analysis can serve as the foundation for other interventions (e.g., modeling) as well.

5

Implementation of Evidence-Based Practices

Rose A. Mason, Emily Gregori, Jennifer Elaine Smith, Amanda Austin, and Hannah Crosley

■ ■ ■

INTRODUCTION AND OVERVIEW

Ample research exists identifying evidence-based practices (EBPs) that have been shown to lead to positive outcomes for learners with autism spectrum disorder (ASD; Council for Exceptional Children, 2014; Horner & Kratochwill, 2012; Steinbrenner et al., 2020). However, these interventions are of little to no value if they are not delivered frequently and with a high degree of *implementation fidelity* or the extent that an intervention is implemented as it was intended. In fact, frequent exposure to well-delivered EBPs is crucial for learners with ASD to make progress on academic, social, and behavioral goals (Browder et al., 2014; Odom et al., 2013). Given this, it is imperative that all practitioners charged with carrying out treatment plans or individualized education plans (IEPs) are proficient at implementing relevant EBPs with fidelity.

Teachers are tasked with providing comprehensive instructional programming across academic, behavioral, employment, functional, and social domains. However, teachers do not provide instructional programming in isolation. Often, teachers work with other practitioners (e.g., paraeducators, parents, speech-language pathologists, or Board Certified Behavior Analysts [BCBAs]) to deliver the most effective and comprehensive instructional programming. For example, BCBAs *are also responsible for collaborating with teachers and other practitioners both in schools and in other settings to deliver interventions to learners with ASD.* Unfortunately, some practitioners may have little to no training or experience in implementing EBPs for learners with ASD. Ensuring EBPs are implemented frequently and across settings necessitates that all partners are well versed in each learner's treatment plan or IEP and are prepared to carry out the instructional strategies with the utmost level of implementation fidelity. Given the variation that may exist in individual treatment plans as well as varying degrees of training in execution of specific EBPs, it is highly likely that many practitioners will require some degree of professional development (PD). As the teacher is charged with ensuring learners achieve adequate educational progress, they will also be tasked with training other practitioners to implement EBPs with fidelity. Learning to implement EBPs with high levels of implementation fidelity requires explicit training. Just as for learners with disabilities, there are evidence-based interventions to train stakeholders to implement effective instructional strategies.

EFFECTIVE PROFESSIONAL DEVELOPMENT

Although most schools, agencies, and organizations provide some degree of PD to their staff, this training is typically delivered in a large-group format with a one-size-fits-all approach. This type of training is beneficial in that it provides foundational knowledge; however, providing training in a large-group format is not specific to individual learner needs and does not typically facilitate cooperation and teamwork among practitioners. Additionally, content is rarely differentiated based on the trainees' prior training, experience, or skill level. Also, large group training approaches are not the most effective for ensuring translation of EBPs into practice (Fixsen et al., 2005).

Effective PD, on the other hand, requires follow-up with ongoing modeling, observations, and feedback (Conroy et al., 2015; Hemmeter et al., 2016; Range et al., 2011). This type of training allows for differentiation based on the current knowledge and skill level of the trainee as well as variations in learner needs and educational contexts (Brock & Carter, 2013). Implementing this type of continual training increases the likelihood that all practitioners will implement EBPs with fidelity, even those with little to no preemployment training, such as paraeducators (Brock & Carter, 2013; Rispoli et al., 2011). Additionally, ongoing PD facilitates maintenance and generalization (Reinke et al., 2012).

For teachers and BCBAs, incorporating the components of effective PD to train other stakeholders can be daunting, particularly when they also must provide educational and behavioral programming for learners. Fortunately, several strategies exist that incorporate the components of effective PD and are also feasible for teachers and BCBAs to implement. These strategies, which will be reviewed in the remainder of this chapter, provide efficient options for ensuring all instructional personnel are skilled in delivering EBPs. Most of these strategies are best conceptualized within a coaching model and, thus, for the remainder of this chapter, *coach* will refer to the teacher or BCBA and *coachee* will refer to the practitioner with whom they are working.

COACHING

Coaching is an adult learning strategy employed to teach new skills and improve current performance (Rush & Shelden, 2008) while providing ongoing support to improve implementation fidelity of EBPs. Although several models of coaching exist in the PD literature, most are predicated on a partnership in which a coach facilitates strengthening the aptitude and competence of the coachee (National Center for Quality Teaching and Learning [NCQTL], 2014). The process provides a model for delivering job-embedded PD that can be ongoing and individualized to the needs of the coachees and the learners with whom they are working.

Practice-based coaching (PBC) is a specific, empirically supported model of coaching that can efficiently and effectively increase instructional personnel's use

Table 5.1. Components of Practice-Based Coaching

Coaching component	Definition
Needs assessment	A process used to identify needs or gaps between an individual's current skillset and the desired conditions
Developing shared goals	Specific, observable, and measurable behaviors that the coachee wishes to improve
The action plan	A written form that documents the supports, materials, and resources a coachee needs to meet his or her goal
Focused observation	A time for the coach to observe the coachee implement the EBP during ongoing routines
Reflection and feedback	Written or verbal statements describing the coachee's progress on their implementation of the EBP

of EBPs. As such, it is an ideal fit for teachers to support other stakeholders' use of EBPs (Conroy et al., 2015; Hemmeter et al., 2016; Metz et al., 2013). With PBC, the coachee partners with a content area specialist, the coach, to improve their implementation of EBP and, in turn, improves learner outcomes through a cyclical process. The primary components of PBC, as defined in Table 5.1, include (1) needs assessment; (2) developing shared goals; (3) action plan development; (4) focused observation; and (5) reflection and feedback. However, prior to beginning the process of PBC, a strong "collaborative partnership" must be established (Snyder et al., 2015).

Collaborative Partnership

The collaborative partnership is predicated on a common purpose—*ensuring optimal learner outcomes*. This partnership is not a hierarchical relationship, where one person tells the other what to do; both partners bring their knowledge and expertise, contributing to shared decision making. This necessitates establishing rapport and trust through collaborative decision making and building upon each other's strengths, as well as reciprocal communication.

Rapport and Trust

Building rapport and trust requires that both the coach and the coachee have a shared understanding of the goals of coaching and acknowledge each partner's areas of expertise to facilitate building rapport and trust. This requires listening to each other's perspectives. Further, demonstrating the value of each partner's input by taking time to brainstorm ideas together is also important. Additionally, it is critical that the coach recognizes the strengths of the coachee by conveying appreciation for his or her role and acknowledging what they do well. Also, the coach should take time to discuss challenges, incorporating the coachee's ideas for addressing these challenges to support positive learner outcomes.

Reciprocal Communication

Establishing a collaborative partnership requires a concerted effort to engage in reciprocal communication. This necessitates the coach asking open-ended questions. Open-ended questions are those that allow for freedom of response and elaboration rather than a "yes/no" response. Examples include

- "Tell me what is going well."
- "Tell me how you feel about the augmentative and alternative communication training."
- "What parts of the behavior intervention plan do you think are going well?"

Open-ended questions allow the coachee to share his or her views prior to the coach sharing their own views. Everyone will bring individual perspectives and experiences to the partnership. These experiences and perspectives must be acknowledged to build a positive coach/coachee relationship.

Needs Assessment

The coaching cycle begins by identifying the purpose or focus of coaching, specifically identifying the target skill that the coachee wishes to improve. *Needs assessment* is a process used to identify needs or gaps between an individual's current skillset and the desired outcomes (e.g., fidelity, frequency, quality). A needs assessment outlines an individual's current performance and specific areas for growth that will lead to the desired outcome (Snyder & Wolfe, 2008). The results from this assessment inform goals, and the goals drive the action plan, which will ultimately lead to improved coachee performance. The needs assessment process is critical to the coaching partnership because it facilitates the organization and delivery of coaching as it keeps the focus on specific skills and practices.

Implementing a Needs Assessment

Implementation of a needs assessment has three steps. The first step is to identify the strengths and needs of the coachee. The second step consists of selecting the skill or practice the coachee will examine or target. The third step is to complete the needs assessment.

Identify Strengths and Needs. To begin the needs assessment process, the coach and the coachee need to determine which target skills or practices will be the focus of the coaching partnership. The skills or practices targeted for the needs assessment should be linked to learner outcomes. This means that the coachee should prioritize skills and practices that will lead to improved learner outcomes. It is important to remember that the skills addressed in the needs assessment will be the focus of the coaching process and, therefore, these skills or practices should be of high priority to the coachee and the learners they serve.

Determine the Focus. A needs assessment should be organized into a written document that outlines multiple target skills or practices. As stated earlier, these practices should be linked to improved learner outcomes. The coach should discuss these practices with the coachee and determine the focus of the assessment, such as specific classroom routines and activities, subject areas, or target learners. The structure and organization of a needs assessment can be individualized based on the needs and preferences of the coach and the coachee. However, the needs assessment must outline (a) a list of skills to be addressed during coaching and (b) criteria for assessing the coachee's knowledge, comfort, or desire to learn the skill. Table 5.2 displays a sample needs assessment from the ParaImpact project. The column on the far left lists a series of data collection skills. The subsequent columns ask the coachee to rate their knowledge, confidence, and preference for implementing the target skill. The coach should orient

Table 5.2. Sample Needs Assessment from ParaImpact

Target skill: Data collection	How much do you know about this practice?					How confident are you using this practice?					Would you like to use this practice more often?
	None	Some		A lot		Not at all	Somewhat		Very		
Identify appropriate student learning goal/objective in verbal or written form (worksheet, board, data sheet)	1	2	3	4	5	1	2	3	4	5	Yes No
Record data systematically to measure student progress	1	2	3	4	5	1	2	3	4	5	Yes No
Demonstrate reliability (total agreement or percentage agreement) of data collected	1	2	3	4	5	1	2	3	4	5	Yes No

the coachee to the needs assessment and (a) describe the purpose of the needs assessment, (b) define the terms and skills listed in the needs assessment, and (c) ask the coachee if he or she has any questions. Once the coachee understands the practices as they are written on the needs assessment, the coachee should complete the needs assessment form.

Complete the Needs Assessment. The coach and the coachee should each complete the needs assessment. In the needs assessment, both the coach and the coachee will be asked to rate their **knowledge** of specific skills or practices with the numbers 1 to 5, indicating a range between *no knowledge* (1) and *a lot of knowledge* (5). They will also rate how well they **implement** a practice with the numbers 1 (*not at all*) to 5 (*very*). This item indicates self-efficacy, which is how confident or competent a coachee feels about implementing a certain skill or practice. Last, the coach and coachee will identify if they feel the coachee needs to implement each practice **more often**. This item is rated as *yes* or *no*. The needs assessment should also include a notes section so that the coach and coachee can record other important thoughts or ideas.

A needs assessment is an individualized approach for identifying strengths and needs, which means that the coachee should select the skills and practices that are most important or relevant to them and have the potential to improve learners' outcomes. The coach's role in the needs assessment process is to guide the coachee in identifying their specific strengths and needs in a nonjudgmental manner. It is important to maintain a strength-based approach for building rapport and trust during the needs assessment process. Throughout the needs assessment process, the coach's role is not that of an evaluator but rather a facilitator. This means that the coach will guide the coachee to make decisions about their strengths and needs, but ultimately, the skills or practices selected for intervention are chosen by the coachee.

Developing Shared Goals

Following the needs assessment, as discussed earlier in this chapter, the next step is developing shared goals. The goal, which will be based on the priorities of the coachee, is pivotal; it establishes the focus for all observations and coaching sessions. The role of the coach is to help the coachee develop the goal through self-assessment and reflection. It is crucial to remember that the coach is not a leader in this process, but rather a partner. Utilizing the data from the assessment, the coach assists the coachee in narrowing the focus to one practice. The cyclical process of PBC will allow for choosing different goals later, after initial goals are met.

Similar to writing goals for a learner's IEP or treatment plan, goals established as part of PBC need to be *specific, observable, and measurable* behaviors. Table 5.3 provides examples and nonexamples of well-written goals. Additionally, goals must be *achievable* within a predetermined timeframe (e.g., 2–3 weeks). The coach and the coachee may have to work together to break down the goal into smaller goals. Goals must be specific and feasible, which require the coach and coachee to consider (a) the learner with whom the coachee is working, (b) how frequently the EBP is implemented, and (c) how frequently the coach will observe the coachee implementing the EBP.

Table 5.3. Examples and Nonexamples of Shared Goals

Checklist for Goals:

- Based on the coachee's self-identified strengths, needs, and priorities
- Specific, observable, and measurable
- Achievable—can be accomplished in 2–3 weeks

Nonexamples	Examples
❏ I will have materials ready and tell learners what we are doing.	❏ Prior to the beginning reading lessons, I will tell learners what activity they will do and why for 4 consecutive reading lessons during the upcoming week.
❏ I will implement most-to-least prompting with Susan during reading.	❏ I will implement most-to-least prompting with 85% fidelity for 3 out of 4 opportunities during math instruction over 3 consecutive days.

The Action Plan

The *action plan* is the step-by-step guide to achieving the goal set both by the coach and by the coachee. This document will serve as a checklist of steps that both the coach and the coachee will need to take to accomplish the goal within the established timeframe (Snyder et al., 2015). Similar to the goal, the steps must describe specific and observable behaviors. The plan should also specify who is responsible for completing each step, including the role of each partner in achieving the agreed-upon goal and the timeline for the completion of each step.

In addition to specifying the steps, the action plan should also include any resources needed to complete the steps. For instance, the coachee might indicate that a visual support or video model would be helpful in achieving the goal. In this case, one step might be for the coach to create the resource. Keep in mind that a new goal and action plan will not be created in every coaching session; however, it is important to complete a minimum of one step between each session. This will increase the likelihood of accomplishing the goal within a reasonable timeframe.

Focused Observation

The purpose of the focused observation is for the coach to collect data about the coachee's implementation fidelity of the specified components of the EBP, so the coach is able to offer feedback and support to facilitate goal attainment. The focused observation occurs at a time agreed upon by both partners during the action-planning phase. Additionally, the observation should occur during the context that was also agreed upon. For example, if the partners agreed the observation would occur during the reading lesson with sixth graders, the coach would conduct the observation during reading rather than another time unless both partners agree to modifications to the plan. This is particularly important to remember if the coach and coachee work closely together in the same classroom, a situation that is likely to occur when the coachee is a paraeducator. Although there might be multiple times to conduct the observation, it is imperative that the coach adhere to the agreed-upon plan. This will continue to cultivate trust and respect, whereas deviations from the plan are likely to erode trust and respect.

The "focused" part of this observation is imperative. The focused observation is driven by the coachee's goal; thus, the coach must only observe practices directly connected to this agreed-upon goal. For instance, Mrs. Florez (coach) and Mr. McKinney (coachee) agreed on the following goal for Mr. McKinney: *I will implement most-to-least prompting with 85% fidelity for 3 out of 4 opportunities during math instruction over 3 consecutive days.* During her focused observation, Mrs. Florez took data on Mr. McKinney's implementation fidelity of most-to-least prompting during math instruction. Data consisted of whether each step of prompting was completed correctly and notes specifically detailing how Mr. McKinney implemented the steps. Mrs. Florez did not attend to other aspects of his instruction, such as how the instructional environment was set up or implementation fidelity of reinforcement procedures. Maintaining focus on the targeted practice as defined by the goal will ensure the coach has adequate information to facilitate reflection and feedback, the next stage of the PBC model.

Reflection and Feedback

After the focused observation, the coach and coachee will meet for a coaching meeting during which the *reflection and feedback* component will take place. This meeting, which will likely take no longer than 20 min, is an opportunity for the coach to provide supportive and constructive feedback regarding the implementation of the instructional practice—specifically focused on progress toward the agreed-upon goal (Snyder et al., 2015). During this time, the coach and coachee will review data collected during the focused observation and ascertain progress toward achievement of the goal. It is important that the coach begins each session with a focus on the positive aspects of EBP implementation and uses open-ended questions and prompts to facilitate and encourage reflection. Each session should include the following:

1. **Reflective Conversation**—an opportunity for the coachee to contemplate and discuss strengths and challenges implementing the target practice during the observation
2. **Supportive Feedback**—the acknowledgement of progress toward the goal or successful implementation of the target practice
3. **Constructive Feedback**—guidance to assist the coachee to improve or enrich implementation of the target practice
4. **Materials and Resources**—coach and coachee discuss additional resources and materials needed to support accomplishing the agreed-upon goal

The coachee may choose additional strategies (see Table 5.4) that they think would be useful in achieving the agreed-upon goal. It is unlikely that all of these strategies will be utilized, but they should be considered when creating or revising the action plan. This is a great opportunity for the coachee to choose preferred strategies.

The feedback provided during this session should be guided by the information collected during the focused observation. Supportive feedback aims to focus on successes and will enhance the coachee's confidence regarding their abil-

Table 5.4. Additional Strategies to Augment Practice-Based Coaching

Additional strategies can be implemented to augment coaching beyond the essential strategies. These strategies should be utilized to support goal attainment in those situations when they are preferred by the coachee. Some of these strategies can be implemented while conducting the focused observation, while others can be implemented during the coaching meeting. When choosing these strategies to include in the coaching plan, be sure to consider the coachee's preferences, provide choice, and consider the setting, feasibility, and usefulness of the strategy.

Additional strategies for coaching meeting	Additional strategies for focused observation
Graphic feedback—graphed observational data (it is recommended this be included at least every 2–3 sessions)	In vivo modeling—during the focused observation the coach models implementation of the target EBP
Observation video—brief video clip of the coachee engaged in implementation of 1–2 steps of the target instructional practice	Verbal or gestural support—coach provides side-by-side prompts to support the coachee's implementation of the EBP
Video modeling—video exemplar of target skill	Environmental modification—rearrange the teaching area or provide instructional materials (e.g., task analysis, visual reminder, preparation of lesson materials)
Role play—coach and coachee take turns playing role of child and interventionist and practice the target skill	
Problem-solving discussions—identify problems, possible solutions, and action plan	

ity to implement new EBPs. Constructive feedback aims to provide the coachee with information, as obtained from the focused observation, about their needs. Constructive feedback must be *behavior specific*, that is, focused on what the coach observed the coachee saying or doing. Feedback that is not behavior specific is not helpful; it does not inform the coachee exactly what is being said or done. Examples of non-behavior-specific feedback are: "You are amazing," "You are kind," or "That was impatient." An example of behavior-specific feedback is "You implemented the reinforcement procedure correctly when you provided the high-five immediately after George matched the printed word dog to the picture of the dog." In addition to providing behavior-specific feedback, the feedback must be *informed by the data gathered during the focused observation*. Data-based feedback is objective and, thus, seemingly nonpersonal. For instance, saying, "During color identification trials with an array of 5, Johnny chose the wrong color 20 times. For those errors, you implemented a gestural prompt for 30% of the opportunities" is behavior specific and based on data. Constructive feedback is objective and measurable. During the reflection and feedback meeting, the coach and coachee should also think about any additional resources or materials that are needed to support successful implementation of the target instructional practice. The following case study illustrates a PBC example.

CASE STUDY: MR. GONZALEZ

Mr. Gonzalez is a student teacher in an elementary special education classroom that provides instruction to learners with autism and substantial level of support in third, fourth, and fifth grade. He is struggling with classroom management during transition times. In one instance, Mr. Gonzalez announces that the class is finished with the whole group reading instruction and then he tells learners to move to their next activity, which is small group reading centers. Learners are assigned to specific reading centers that they rotate through every 20 min. While learners are transitioning, Mr. Gonzalez tries to ensure that they are moving toward the correct centers by calling out each learner's name and pointing where they need to go. The classroom becomes extremely noisy while multiple learners are moving to their centers and Mr. Gonzalez announces names. This results in learners becoming confused and selecting either the closest center to them or a center that is their preferred choice. Although transitions should only take between 2 and 3 min, currently the transitions between activities often last around 10 min. This results in a loss of instructional or learning time for the learners in the classroom.

Application: Mr. Gonzalez and his coach (the cooperating teacher in the classroom) plan to meet to discuss how to make transitions run timelier and more smoothly. How might using PBC benefit Mr. Gonzalez? What specific areas of improvement could Mr. Gonzalez and his coach discuss? What might be a goal that Mr. Gonzalez could set for himself?

BEHAVIOR SKILLS TRAINING

Behavioral skills training (BST) is an evidence-based training package used to teach new skills. BST has been shown to be effective for training general educators, special educators, related-service providers, and parents to implement EBPs (Davenport et al., 2019; Gregori et al., 2021; Hogan et al., 2015; Rosales et al., 2009). Implementing BST requires a coach with expertise in the EBP targeted for training and a coachee. The coach can be a classroom teacher, a related-service provider, school psychologist, behavior analyst, or any other practitioner with the relevant skills and training. The coachee is the individual learning a new skill and can include paraeducators, teachers, parents, and related-service providers. BST is the most commonly used method to teach new skills and has been shown to improve coachee implementation of many EBPs (Kirkpatrick et al., 2019). Although variations exist, the general BST model includes instructions, modeling, rehearsal, and performance feedback (See Table 5.5; Ward-Horner & Sturmey, 2012). BST can be used as a standalone training program or can be embedded into instructional coaching. When combined with PBC, BST should be used after the coachee has identified their goals and before the first focused observation. Additional supports and training supports can be added, if needed, during the reflection and feedback meeting. How BST is used will depend on the needs and preferences of the coachee.

Table 5.5.   Components of Behavioral Skills Training (BST)

BST component	Definition
Instructions	Coach provides a verbal and written description of the target skill and its implementation.
Modeling	Coach demonstrates how to implement the target skill while the coachee observes and asks questions.
Rehearsal	Coach and coachee practice implementing the target skill.
Performance feedback	Coach provides supportive and corrective feedback on the coachee's implementation of the target skill until the mastery criterion is reached.

Preparing to Implement Behavior Skills Training

Training Format

BST can be implemented individually or in small groups. Individual BST involves one or two coaches to implement the training, and one coachee. Conversely, small-group BST includes one to two coaches and multiple coachees. Choosing the appropriate BST format requires consideration of multiple factors. First, the coach should consider the *complexity of the target skill*. If the target skill is complex and may require intensive training or feedback, individual BST may be more appropriate. Second, the coach needs to consider the number of coachees that need to learn the target skill. If more than one coachee requires training, it would be more efficient to provide BST in a group format. Both individual BST and small-group BST have been shown to lead to improvements in coachee implementation fidelity of a variety of skills, such as functional analysis and differential reinforcement (Flynn et al., 2016; Gregori et al., 2020; Jenkins & Reed, 2016; Kunnavatana et al., 2013). The coach should select the format that is most appropriate based on the goals and context of the training.

Logistics

After the coach selects the appropriate training format, they should determine where and when BST will occur. It is important for the coach to select a setting and time to implement BST when distractions can be limited. For example, implementing BST in an empty classroom before school may result in fewer interruptions and distractions than implementing BST in a classroom full of learners in the middle of the school day. The duration of BST will vary based on the number of coachees participating in the training and the complexity of the target skill. The duration of BST will generally be longer if it is conducted in groups or if the target skill is complex. In general, BST can be implemented in 30 to 90 min.

Developing a Mastery Criterion

The purpose of BST is to improve coachee implementation fidelity of specific skills. Therefore, it is important to establish a *mastery criterion* before BST is implemented. A mastery criterion dictates the *level of performance* the coach expects the coachee to reach after training. The level of performance typically refers to the number of correct responses that the coachee engages in, compared to the number of incorrect responses the coachee makes. This is often reflected as a percentage that is calculated by dividing the number of correct responses by the total number of responses and multiplying the quotient by 100. For example, if a coachee implements an EBP that contains five steps and only implements one step correctly, their implementation fidelity would be 20%. Conversely, if a coachee implements an EBP that contains 10 steps, and they implement eight correctly, their implementation fidelity would be 80%. It is generally recommended to set the mastery criterion at 100%. A mastery criterion of 100% indicates that each step of the target skill or intervention has equal importance. A mastery criterion can be set below 100% if the critical steps of the target intervention or skill have been identified and other steps are less important.

Implementing Behavior Skills Training

Instructions

The first component of BST involves the coach providing both a *verbal description* and a *written description* for how to implement the target skill. First, the coach should provide the coachee with a written description of the target skill. Written instructions should include a high level of detail and should list all of the relevant steps of the target skill in observable and measurable behaviors. Using a task analysis can help ensure that the coach addresses all of the critical steps of the target skill. *Task analysis* is a systematic process for breaking down a complex skill into its individual parts (Cooper et al., 2020). While task analysis is commonly used for learners, it can also be used to improve a coachee's use of target skills. In the context of training, a task analysis involves listing each step of the EBP that the coachee is expected to implement (see Table 5.6).

To develop the task analysis, the coach should observe an experienced coachee implement the target skill and record his or her behaviors using a checklist. The coach should then evaluate the task analysis to confirm that no necessary steps have been omitted. When developing a written task analysis, the coach should ensure that the document is free from jargon, so the text of the task analysis does not interfere with the coachee's understanding of the target skill. The task analysis the coach develops will also be used to collect data on the coachee's behavior once BST has ended, so it is helpful to create columns on the task analysis where the coach can record the coachee's behavior. Structuring the task analysis in this way can also be used to help the coachee monitor and record his or her own behavior.

Table 5.6. Sample Task Analysis for Implementing Most-to-Least Prompting

Most-to-least prompting	Correct	Incorrect
1. Provide the relevant instructional cue, or a signal to the learner that the lesson will begin (e.g., "It's time to review our animal flashcards").		
2. Give the learner 5–10 s to respond.		
3. Provide praise if the learner responds correctly (e.g., "Great job saying 'dog.' You are right, this is a dog!").		
4. If the learner does not respond or makes an incorrect response, provide a prompt at the appropriate prompt level.		

Modeling

After the coach has provided written and verbal instructions, they should demonstrate, or model, how to implement the target skill. During the demonstration, the coach should model each step of the EBP as it is described in the task analysis. The coach can model the target skill *live* or provide the coachee with a *video model*. Live modeling involves demonstration of the target skill in real time. Live modeling is most effective when there are two coaches present to demonstrate the skill. During the live model, one coach will play the role of the learner, and the other coach will play the role of the coachee. The demonstration should be scripted and practiced before the live model. Adherence to the script is critical to ensure accuracy and fluency during the demonstration. If a second coach is not available for a live model, the coach can have the coachee act as the learner during the demonstration. If the coachee is involved in the demonstration, it is important that the coach provide the coachee with detailed instructions and a script, so they know exactly what they are supposed to do during the demonstration.

Live modeling has been used to train teachers, direct care staff, and parents to implement a variety of educational and behavioral interventions and assessments (Gregori et al., 2020; Gregori et al., 2021; Kirkpatrick et al., 2019). Video modeling is an effective alternative to live modeling that does not require the presence of two coaches or the involvement of the coachee in the demonstration. Video modeling involves the coach prerecording a video demonstration of the target skill. The demonstration should adhere to the same guidelines described above. During the training, the coach will play the video model for the coachee. One of the benefits of video modeling is that the coachee can replay the video until they feel comfortable with the procedure. Video modeling has also been shown to improve coach implementation of many evidence-based assessments and interventions (Rispoli et al., 2016).

Rehearsal

After the live or video demonstration, the coachee should practice, or rehearse, implementing the target skill. The rehearsal should be structured in a similar manner to the live model, except the coachee will implement the target skill, and the coach will play the role of the learner. During the rehearsal, the coachee should implement the target skill, with the coach acting as the learner. It is important that the coachee rehearse the target skill under various simulated scenarios. For example, the coachee should rehearse the target skill using ideal scenarios (e.g., the learner makes no errors, or the learner engages in no challenging behavior) and using nonideal scenarios (e.g., the learner makes multiple errors or engages in high levels of challenging behavior). Rehearsing the target skill with only ideal scenarios may prevent the generalization of skills into the natural environment (Gregori et al., 2020). It is helpful to develop scripts for the coach to follow when they play the role of the learner. This will ensure accuracy and consistency throughout the rehearsal portion of the training. If a coach is conducting a group BST, it is critical that each coachee have an opportunity to rehearse the target skill. If multiple coachees attend the BST, the coach should allocate sufficient time for rehearsal.

Performance Feedback

As the coachee rehearses, the coach should provide performance feedback. Specifically, the coach should provide *supportive* and *corrective* feedback. *Supportive feedback* in BST involves acknowledging the steps of the target skill that the coachee implemented correctly. The coach should be specific when providing supportive feedback so that the coachee knows exactly what they did correctly. For example, a coach might say, "Great job providing praise after the learner used his picture board to communicate." If the coachee makes an implementation error during the rehearsal, the coach should provide specific corrective feedback. *Specific corrective feedback* consists of the coach acknowledging the error that the coachee made. For example, a coach could say, "Remember, if the learner makes a request using her picture board, you should provide praise." Corrective feedback may also include providing a brief model or reviewing the written instructions. Performance feedback can be provided in vivo while the coachee is practicing the target skill or after the rehearsal is complete. The coach and the coachee should continue this rehearsal and feedback cycle until the coachee meets the mastery criterion. Performance feedback is a critical component of BST. In fact, multiple research studies have shown that BST is more effective when a performance feedback component is added (LaBrot et al., 2020; Ward-Horner & Sturmey, 2012).

Follow-up Observations

After BST is complete, the coachee can begin implementing the target skill during ongoing routines with learners (if applicable). However, it is critical that the coach conduct follow-up observations to ensure that the target skills learned during BST have generalized to the natural environment. During follow-up observations, the coach should record the coachee's behavior using the task analysis described earlier. The coach should carefully review the data to make sure that the coachee's implementation fidelity is still at the mastery criterion. If levels of implementation fidelity fall below the mastery criterion, the coach should provide booster training.

Booster Training

It is not uncommon for levels of implementation fidelity to drop below mastery once BST has ended. Often, the simulated training setting makes it difficult for the target skills to generalize to the natural environment (Gregori et al., 2021; Himle et al., 2004). In cases where implementation fidelity falls below the mastery criterion, the coach should provide additional, or booster training. *Booster training* involves providing a portion of BST again. For example, the coach might model the target skill again and then have the coachee engage in brief rehearsal. The coach may also provide the coachee with supplemental supports. Regardless of the supports provided, booster training should continue until the coachee reaches the mastery criterion.

ADDITIONAL TRAINING PROCEDURES

Just like the learners we serve, practitioners require different levels of support to acquire important knowledge and skills. It is not uncommon for interventionists to need additional supports to implement target skills or interventions with high levels of implementation fidelity in addition to BST and coaching. Therefore, teachers need to be equipped with a variety of tools for supporting other practitioners' use and implementation fidelity of target skills. Self-monitoring and in vivo coaching are two interventions that have been shown to effectively supplement BST and coaching and have been shown to lead to improvements in teacher implementation of target skills (Ennis et al., 2020; Gerow et al., 2018; Gregori et al., 2021; Gregori et al., 2020).

Self-Monitoring

Self-monitoring is a process in which an individual observes and records their own behavior (Cooper et al., 2020). In the context of coachee training, self-monitoring involves the coachee using a self-monitoring sheet or task analysis to record the number of steps that they implemented correctly related to the target skill. The coach and the coachee then analyze those recordings to evaluate their performance (Cooper et al., 2020; Rispoli et al., 2017). Self-monitoring is a low-cost intervention that has been shown to improve practitioners' use of a number of instructional and behavioral practices (Gregori et al., 2021; Rispoli et al., 2017).

Steps for Implementation

Step 1. The first step in implementing self-monitoring is to develop the *self-monitoring sheet*. The self-monitoring sheet should be written as an intervention checklist or task analysis. The task analysis should list each step of the target skill that the coachee is expected to implement (see the example in Table 5.7). As described previously in this chapter, the task analysis should include all relevant steps of the target skill and should be free of jargon that may interfere with the coachee's understanding of the target skill. Next to each step of the target skill, there should be columns with space for the coachee to record their performance.

Step 2. After the self-monitoring sheet has been developed, the coachee should implement the target skill during ongoing routines. It is important that the coachee have access to the self-monitoring sheet while they implement the intervention. The self-monitoring sheet will serve as a prompt and will help remind the coachee of the steps of the target skill that they should implement. Before implementation, the coachee should determine if they will record their behavior in vivo or after they have finished implementing the target skill. In vivo recording

Table 5.7. Sample Self-Monitoring Sheet

Target skill: Most-to-least verbal prompting

Mastery criterion: Implement 100% of steps correctly

	Did I remember?		
	Yes	*No*	*N/A*
1. Provide the relevant instructional cue.	+		
2. Give the learner 5–10 s to respond.		+	
3. Provide praise if the learner responds correctly.	+		
4. If the learner does not respond, provide a prompt at the appropriate prompt level.	+		
Number of steps implemented correctly		3	
Percentage of steps implemented correctly		75%	

involves the coachee recording their behavior as they implement the target skill. In vivo recording allows the coachee to record their behavior in the moment, which can enhance the accuracy of the observation. The coachee can also record their behavior after they have finished implementing the target skill (i.e., delayed recording). This approach relies on the coachee remembering how they implemented the target skill and, therefore, may be less accurate than in vivo recording. However, delayed recording may be a more feasible approach to self-monitoring, particularly if the coachee is working directly with learners.

Step 3. After the coachee has recorded their behavior, they should analyze the data to measure their progress toward the mastery criterion. Analysis should begin by calculating the percentage of steps of the target skill that the coachee implemented correctly. Next, the coachee should compare their score against the mastery criterion. This will allow the coachee to determine if they have reached the mastery criterion. After the coachee has analyzed the recordings, they should meet with the coach to review their performance. During these meetings, the coachee and coach should review the self-monitoring sheets to determine if the coachee reached the mastery criterion. If mastery was reached, the coach should help the coachee identify supports to maintain their performance. If mastery was not reached, the coach should assist the coachee in identifying areas for improvement and supplemental supports or materials. The coachee should continue self-monitoring until they have reached the mastery criterion.

In Vivo Coaching

In vivo coaching is a procedure used to provide in-the-moment support to a coachee as they implement a target skill. Specifically, coaches will provide in-the-moment prompts to facilitate the coachee's use of specific skills and provide feedback based on their performance. In vivo coaching has been used to increase practitioners' fidelity of academic and behavioral interventions across a variety of applied settings (Ennis et al., 2020; Gerow et al., 2018; Gregori et al., 2020; Kleinert et al., 2017).

Implementing In Vivo Coaching

To implement in vivo coaching, the coach should observe the coachee implement the target skill in the typical setting and during ongoing routines. If the coachee plans to implement the target skill with learners, he or she must ensure that the in vivo coaching will not be disruptive to the learning environment. During implementation, the coach should stand near the coachee. As the coachee implements the target skill, the coach should provide a continuum of supports, including verbal prompts, live modeling, and supportive and corrective feedback. The type of support provided during the coaching session should be selected based on the coachee's needs and preferences and with consideration of the implementation setting (e.g., classroom).

Considerations for Implementation

While in vivo coaching is an effective method for increasing practitioners' implementation fidelity, several considerations should be made before it is implemented in a classroom or other applied setting. First, in vivo coaching relies on the presence of the coach while the coachee implements the target skill, which makes this practice resource intensive. The coachee should ensure that the school, organization, or agency has the resources to support the use of in vivo coaching. Second, while providing in vivo support may improve interventionist behavior, the use of live prompting and feedback may be distracting to others in the environment. Therefore, the coachee should consider whether in vivo coaching will disrupt ongoing instructional activities or interfere with learner engagement with instructional programming. Issues associated with in vivo coaching, including resource intensiveness and intrusiveness, can be addressed by providing in vivo support remotely using bug-in-ear (BIE) devices as described in the next section. Third, providing in-the-moment support may interfere with the coachee's ability to generalize the target skill or perform the target skill in the absence of the coach providing the support. To address this issue, the coach should develop a plan for systematically reducing or fading the amount of support provided to the coachee. The process of fading support should continue until the coachee can implement the target skill to the mastery criterion without in vivo support from the coach.

TECHNOLOGY TO ENHANCE DELIVERY OF TRAINING

Telepractice

Although coaching is known to be an effective method for teaching professionals to implement EBPs, schools may face barriers that limit access to consultants and coaches. For example, rural school districts may have difficulty securing in-person consultation from outside experts due to the distance, time, and cost required for traveling to and between schools (Bice-Urbach & Kratochwill, 2016; McDaniel & Bloomfield, 2020). In some cases, district-based service providers (e.g., school psychologists, speech-language pathologists, BCBAs, social workers, occupational therapists) may have large caseloads or cases that span multiple school sites, rendering frequent training, coaching, and consultative meetings difficult or impossible (Bice-Urbach & Kratochwill, 2016; Feldman & Kratochwill, 2003; Green et al., 2019). *Telepractice* is an umbrella term that encompasses a variety of delivery modalities, including synchronous (e.g., video and audio conferencing), asynchronous (e.g., online modules), or a combination of the two for a hybrid model (Rispoli & Machalicek, 2020; Snodgrass et al., 2017). Telepractice has recently received increased attention in education (Bice-Urbach et al., 2018). It can be a cost-effective method of training that allows the trainee to access materials from multiple sites with flexible access options (Rios et al., 2020), permits repeated engagement with the content (Fairburn & Cooper, 2011), and enhances the level of confidence using the intervention (Kobak et al., 2013). Consequently, it is a promising alternative to in-person PD and is a valuable way of disseminating EBP expertise to school professionals (Fairburn & Cooper, 2011).

Online Modules

Online modules are a commonly used strategy for training staff in the school setting (Douglas et al., 2013). One option for decreasing the amount of personnel time needed to deliver initial instruction to school staff is using online instructional modules (Mason et al., 2017). This training strategy can be offered to teachers and paraeducators in a cost-effective and efficient manner outside of the school day. Online modules offer the user control over the learning sequence and the pace of instruction (McCulloch & Noonan, 2013). Typically, online modules include the following components: PowerPoint slides with narration, embedded video models for introduced concepts, practice questions that target content knowledge, and activities to apply the knowledge to applicable situations (Douglas et al., 2013). Through self-paced modules, the user gains content knowledge that can be applied in the workplace.

APPLICATION

Think back to the case study about Mr. Gonzalez. What technology (or technologies) could be used to help Mr. Gonzalez implement and reflect upon transition times in the classroom?

Granpeesheh and colleagues (2010) investigated the use of an online training tool in the field of applied behavior analysis (ABA). The study examined the effectiveness of online modules to teach ABA content knowledge on treatments for learners with ASD with a group of newly hired service providers. The online modules presented the information through text, voice-over narration, and videos. Performance of participants who received e-learning training was compared to the performance of a group who received traditional in-person training. Results showed that knowledge of ABA principles and procedures increased significantly for both groups. This suggests that e-learning tools, such as online modules, may be similarly successful as traditional in-person training for teaching knowledge and concepts (Granpeesheh et al., 2010). Similar to traditional in-person training, follow-up training procedures such as BST and coaching will be necessary to maximize effectiveness and ensure accurate implementation.

Telecoaching

One method for offering coaching remotely is to use a telecoaching model, where coaches and natural implementers (e.g., teachers, paraeducators, related-service providers) communicate through online videoconferencing platforms, mimicking a traditional face-to-face coaching model (Frieder et al., 2009). Coaches observe the classroom through a live webcam video feed or a video recording, and then meet later via videoconferencing for the coach to deliver affirmative or corrective performance feedback. This model of telecoaching involves delayed feedback, which requires the implementer to recall their performance of a skill some time after it has occurred. Though research has shown that delayed feedback may still improve performance of new implementers, some school-based personnel may benefit from more immediate feedback (Scheeler et al., 2018; Solomon et al., 2012).

Bug-in-Ear Coaching

One evidence-based method for integrating technology and immediate performance feedback is to use bug-in-ear (BIE) coaching (Schaefer & Ottley, 2018). BIE coaching (also referred to as "eCoaching") provides feedback to the implementer through a wireless earpiece while the consultant or coach observes from the same room at a distance (Scheeler et al., 2006) or remotely through an online videoconferencing platform (Regan & Weiss, 2020). This allows the coach to provide prompting and immediate performance feedback to the implementer without being next to the implementer. Another benefit of using BIE coaching is that coaching can be provided discreetly to prevent interruption and distraction in the classroom, which may occur when providing traditional side-by-side in-person coaching (O'Reilly et al., 1994). Practitioners who have received BIE coaching report the method to be feasible, acceptable, and successful at improving teaching strategies and learner outcomes (Grygas Coogle et al., 2018; Grygas Coogle et al., 2015; Ottley et al., 2015; Randolph et al., 2020).

BIE coaching has been used effectively to train preservice teachers, special education teachers, general education teachers, and paraeducators to implement a variety of EBPs with learners with disabilities (Schaefer & Ottley, 2018). Preservice teachers have learned via BIE coaching to successfully teach communication strategies to young children with disabilities during small group rotations in an inclusive preschool classroom (Grygas Coogle et al., 2015) and increase the number of accurate and complete teaching trials presented during instructional small groups (McKinney & Vasquez, 2014; Scheeler et al., 2006; Scheeler & Lee, 2002). BIE coaching has been demonstrated as an effective mechanism for teaching general education teachers to utilize a self-monitoring strategy with learners engaging in off-task behavior (Owens et al., 2020) and increase opportunities for learners to respond and teachers to deliver feedback within a secondary science classroom (Garland & Dieker, 2019). Special education teachers have learned to implement a reading comprehension strategy (Cheek et al., 2019) and increase opportunities to respond (Randolph et al., 2020) by BIE coaching. Additionally, studies have shown BIE coaching as a useful tool for teaching classroom paraeducators to use motivation within the learner's natural context to respond correctly (Rosenberg et al., 2020) and deliver behavior-specific praise (Scheeler et al., 2018).

Video Feedback

Video feedback is a training strategy that can be used to enhance the skills and knowledge of teachers (LeBlanc et al., 2005). Several researchers have shown that using video feedback has positive effects on teachers' use of stimulating behavior, sensitive responsivity, and verbal stimulation (van Vondel et al., 2018). During a video feedback session, the coachee records a video of themselves demonstrating the specific skills for the coach to provide feedback on their performance (Suhrheinrich & Chan, 2017). After recording the video, the coachee and coach watch the video together. The coachee's strengths and areas for improvement are identified and discussed. When providing constructive feedback, the coach should implement a 3:1 positivity ratio (Fredrickson, 2004). Therefore, during the feedback session, the coach should include three skills that the coachee performed well for every identified area of improvement. Based on the coachee's performance, the coachee and coach can collaborate on developing personal learning goals. Once the learning goals are identified, the coachee can practice the specific skills to prepare for the next video feedback session (Suhrheinrich & Chan, 2017). Within the field of education, the use of video feedback to instruct teachers has been well documented for more than 25 years (Tripp & Rich, 2012).

To improve upon teaching practices, teachers may also use microteaching. *Microteaching* consists of the teacher recording a video of themself demonstrating specific skills or instructional practices and then later the video is analyzed with peers. Microteaching offers teachers the opportunity to reflect on their lesson and receive constructive feedback. Research supports video feedback, including microteaching, as a useful strategy for school administrators to improve their teacher evaluation methods, and for teachers to make meaningful changes to teaching practices (Tripp & Rich, 2012).

Considerations for Telepractice

Telepractice is a viable evidence-based alternative to traditional in-person coaching methods; however, special considerations for successful and ethical use of these strategies are needed. Video recording or livestreaming of classrooms may need written informed consent for not only the target learners and staff, but other learners and school-based personnel who may be present and within visual and audible range of the web camera (Frieder et al. 2009; Grygas Coogle et al., 2018; Grygas Coogle et al., 2015). Additionally, coaches must ensure the videoconferencing platform, internet network, and storage location of files are all password protected compliant with the Health Insurance Portability and Accountability Act (HIPAA; 2002) and Family Educational Rights and Privacy Act (FERPA; 2001). Furthermore, the purchase of special equipment, such as wireless earbuds with Bluetooth capabilities, web cameras that can be controlled remotely, or an attachable fisheye lens to see the entire classroom, may be needed (Randolph et al., 2020; Randolph & Duffy, 2019).

Zoder-Martell and colleagues (2020) also recommend two additional technologies for telecoaching, which include a Swivl (https://www.swivl.com/) and a telepresence robot. The Swivl is a mount for a tablet that can rotate 360 degrees and automatically follow anyone who is wearing a transmitter. The transmitter also includes a microphone to improve audio quality, which may be a benefit in contrast to the quality of sound that is likely to be distanced or muffled from using a regular webcam. The Swivl can be used for live videoconferencing or to record sessions to watch later (Zoder-Martell et al., 2020). The other equipment mentioned by Zoder-Martell and colleagues (2020) is a telepresence robot, which can physically move around a classroom or school building while being controlled remotely by an observer or consultant. While these telepresence robots are more costly, they offer a unique ability to provide a remote observer an opportunity to provide coaching across multiple environments. Telecoaching conducted via live observation feed over the internet also will need a strong wireless internet connection along with a plan for reconnecting in the event the internet connectivity is lost (Randolph et al., 2020; Scheeler et al., 2012); it is recommended to test the video and audio setup prior to beginning true coaching sessions, to ensure that the technology is functioning properly. Technology-enhanced coaching is a practical and effective method for specialists and consultants to conduct observations and provide performance feedback in real time to school-based teams.

CONSIDERATIONS FOR TRAINING OTHER PRACTITIONERS

Collaboration to determine educational objectives and ensure maintenance and generalization across settings is essential. As previously mentioned, the educational team will include general education and special education teachers as well as parents. In addition, related-service providers with expertise in a variety of areas such as speech and communication, physical therapy, occupational therapy, and psychology may be involved.

Teachers

Collaboration between a general education teacher and a special education teacher is an important practice for the success of learners with disabilities, including those with ASD (Thornton et al., 2015). This means that effective training and competency in strategies and curricula for all teachers is necessary for learner success. Use of PBC is one strategy to support this collaboration. Building upon the strengths of each teacher, both the general education teacher and the special education teacher could take turns in the coach role and the coachee role.

General education teachers might have greater specific content or curricular knowledge that a special education teacher wants to improve upon. Therefore, in this instance, the general education teacher would serve in the coach role and the special education teacher would serve in the coachee role. Strategies such as online modules or self-monitoring might be considered for this purpose. For example, the special education teacher might elect to develop their knowledge of a specific curriculum that is being used in the classroom in which they co-teach.

On the other hand, special education teachers might have targeted strategies for working with learners with disabilities that the general education teacher wants to improve upon. For this circumstance, the coach (in this case the special education teacher) and the coachee (the general education teacher) might meet to select a strategy the general education teacher wants to develop. During this meeting, the coach and coachee can discuss what strategies they might want to use. The coach and coachee might consider strategies such as in vivo coaching or video feedback.

Paraeducators

Given the rise in enrollment of learners with special needs and the scarcity of licensed special education teachers (Robinson, 2011), the U.S. Bureau of Labor Statistics (2017) projects the number of paraeducators working in schools will continue to increase. Thus, it is highly likely that all teachers will work with at least one paraeducator regularly. As paraeducators provide instruction to learners under the supervision of the teacher, it is imperative that supervising teachers have training in effective strategies to provide ongoing PD to paraeducators under their supervision.

As a teacher, it is important to understand that paraeducators often join the education workforce with varying levels of education, experience, and training. Education requirements for becoming a paraeducator are minimal, with federal law requiring only 2 years of postsecondary education as well as evidence of competence in basic academics (Individuals with Disability Education Improvement Act, 2004), with requirements varying across states. Further, formal training is often limited to large-group PD provided by the local education agency. Paraeducators report that training is often limited to what they learn on the job and note that observation and feedback would be helpful (Mason et al., 2021). Thus, as the training of paraeducators will most likely occur in the classroom, teachers will need a plan for implementing this training. Further, the teacher and paraeducator will likely work more closely together than they do with other related-service personnel. This will require a high level of synergy and teamwork with shared goals (Kratz et al., 2014). The strategies described in this chapter are particularly conducive to the training of paraeducators, given the varying level of experience and education. PBC, for instance, allows for individualization and fosters opportunities for development of a collaborative partnership focused on learner outcomes.

In addition to ongoing training with observation and feedback, licensed teachers must ensure that assigned tasks are appropriate for the paraeducator. The role of paraeducators is not clearly defined, yet they should not be tasked with planning curriculum, choosing instructional methods and materials, or assuming primary teaching responsibilities. Licensed teachers are responsible for overseeing and supervising paraeducators who work with their learners. This includes assessing skills and determining appropriate educational objectives, designing curriculum, choosing the most appropriate EBPs to address target skills, delivering primary instruction, and ensuring the educational progress of learners. The paraeducator can assist with preparing materials as designed by the teacher, assisting with monitoring of learners, and engaging in other supportive tasks as assigned by the licensed teacher. Paraeducators may also supplement the instruction provided by the licensed teacher, such as reteaching and repeated practice (Carter et al., 2009; Mason et al. 2020), facilitating group practice, and assisting with delivery of accommodations such as reading questions aloud or monitoring during extended time. The teacher must supervise this instruction to ensure the paraeducator is implementing the chosen EBPs with a high degree of fidelity (Capizzi & Da Fonte, 2012).

Related-Service Providers

Learners with ASD will need coordinated programming to address their educational, behavioral, adaptive, social, and health care needs. Because learners with ASD have diverse needs that cannot be addressed by a single practitioner, they will often receive support from related-service providers. *Related-service providers* are professionals who provide support based on specialized training and knowledge. It is common for learners with ASD to receive support from related-service providers, including speech and language pathologists, physical therapists, occupational therapists, social workers, BCBAs, school psychologists, and medical professionals (e.g., nurses, pediatricians); learners with higher support needs usually receive more intensive supports from multiple related-service providers to achieve their IEP goals and objectives. The unique expertise of each related-service provider is critical in ensuring that the goals and objectives listed in the learners' IEP are achieved. Therefore, it is necessary that teachers be prepared to work collaboratively with these practitioners. Please refer to Chapter 13 for a detailed description of collaborative partnerships with other practitioners.

Working with related-service providers can enhance a learner's educational experience. However, teachers should be prepared for potential challenges to multidisciplinary collaboration and be equipped with tools to address those challenges. While teachers and related-service providers have unique strengths and skillsets, oftentimes they hold different professional or educational philosophies, which may pose challenges for service design and delivery (Giangreco et al., 1997). When philosophical disagreements arise, it is important for the teacher and related-service provider to discuss the disagreement and determine how the unique strengths of each practitioner can be used to strengthen the learner's educational programming. It may also be helpful during the initial goal-planning meeting for the teacher and related-service provider to document their shared goals for the learner and describe how providing services will enhance their educational outcomes (Gregori et al., 2021). Identifying these shared goals can help teachers and related-service providers resolve disagreements more quickly while keeping the focus on the learner.

Parents

Parents are essential members of the education team. One of the main goals of a comprehensive instructional programming is to teach learners new skills to help them function independently across settings, including school, home, and the community. Generalizing skills across these settings often requires additional training. Because teachers cannot spend 24 hours a day with learners, it is important that they train parents to implement effective interventions in home and community-based settings. Training parents to implement EBPs can lead to improved learner outcomes, increased parent well-being, improved parent-child relationships, and increased parent implementation fidelity of EBPs (Akemoglu et al., 2020; Bekhet et al., 2012; Liu et al., 2020; McConachie & Diggle, 2007; Nevill et al., 2018; Tarver et al., 2019).

While parent training has a number of benefits, teachers should be aware of the complexities of working with families and should understand how to effectively collaborate with families with diverse needs and backgrounds. First, while educators have expertise in educational pedagogy and EBP, it is important to remember that *parents are the expert on their child and the needs of their family*. Therefore, teachers should not begin parent training before discussing whether the training program meets the needs of that family. Understanding the values and needs of families can be done by developing a relationship with each family. Educators should ensure that they have consistent and ongoing contact with the families of each learner in their class. Second, it is important to remember that parents often manage numerous family, career, and personal obligations. Teachers should be sensitive to the time and logistical challenges that parent training might present to a family and should select training formats and procedures that are most feasible for a family. For example, if a family does not have a car and can only meet for training in the evening, the teacher may want to use telecoaching to provide training. Using this technology-based training will remove the transportation barrier the family faces in accessing training. Please refer to Chapter 12 for a detailed description of developing collaborative relationships with parents.

SUMMARY

In this chapter, we have focused on evidence-based training strategies that can be employed to ensure all practitioners are well-versed in the delivery of EBPs for learners with ASD. Access to EBPs delivered with a high degree of fidelity is imperative for maximizing outcomes for learners with ASD. This entails collaboration with all practitioners responsible for the educational progress of the learner to ensure EBPs are accurately delivered across settings. Given the varying backgrounds of team members, it is likely that some may not be familiar with the chosen strategies.

The evidence-based training strategies described in this chapter are particularly conducive to provision of ongoing PD. Both for PBC and for BST, the teacher takes on the role of the coach, collaborating with the coachee to assess needs, establish goals, develop a plan, observe and collect data, and then deliver feedback to acknowledge progress and problem-solve identified challenges. Additional strategies, such as in vivo coaching and self-monitoring, can be implemented either on their own or to enhance coaching. Further, technology-enhanced strategies, including video feedback and online modules, can be implemented to support ongoing training efforts.

Perhaps one of the most important aspects to remember is that the educational team is there to ensure optimal outcomes for learners with ASD and their families. This necessitates working together and learning together. One must value each partner's role and areas of expertise and how these will contribute to ensuring the best possible programming for learners with ASD.

APPLICATION ACTIVITIES

1. Download the Home Companion Guide for any of the AFIRM training modules found at https://afirm.fpg.unc.edu/afirm-modules for a specific EBP. With a peer, role play development of an action plan for coaching a parent to implement an EBP at home.
2. Choose an EBP as identified by the National Professional Development Center on Autism Spectrum Disorders (https://autismpdc.fpg.unc.edu/national-pro fessional-development-center-autism-spectrum-disorder). After reviewing the procedures for implementing the EBP, create a list of your strengths and needs as it relates to implementing the identified EBP. What type of training would be most helpful for addressing your needs? What resources would be helpful?
3. Discuss the need for professional development and support for paraeducators, considering variability in education and experience. In what ways would implementation of PBC or BST be helpful? What are potential challenges and what are options for addressing these challenges?

ADDITIONAL RESOURCES

Autism Focused Intervention Resources and Modules. https://afirm.fpg.unc.edu/afirm -modules

National Center for Pyramid Model Innovations https://challengingbehavior.cbcs.usf.edu /Implementation/coach.html

National Clearinghouse on Autism Evidence and Practice. https://ncaep.fpg.unc.edu/

National Professional Development Center on Autism Spectrum Disorder. https://autismpdc .fpg.unc.edu/national-professional-development-center-autism-spectrum-disorder

Paraprofessionals: What you need to know. https://www.understood.org/articles/en/para professionals-what-you-need-to-know

6

Progress Monitoring and Data-Based Decision Making

Katie Wolfe, Meka N. McCammon, and Aaron R. Check

■ ■ ■

INTRODUCTION AND OVERVIEW

Systematically collecting, analyzing, and interpreting data to inform decision making when providing services is essential to maximizing learner progress. Even when a practitioner thoughtfully selects an evidence-based practice (EBP) that matches the context and the preferences, values, and characteristics of the learner, they cannot assume that the EBP will be effective. Practitioners must collect data on learner performance and review the data in an ongoing manner to evaluate whether the learner is making progress. If data indicate that the learner is not acquiring a particular skill and the EBP is implemented with fidelity, the practitioner can respond to the data by modifying the EBP and continuing to monitor the learner's progress to see if the modification is effective. By continually collecting, analyzing, and using data to inform instruction, practitioners can maximize the effectiveness and efficiency of their instruction and enhance learner outcomes (Browder et al., 2005; Fuchs et al., 1984; Stecker & Fuchs, 2000).

Within school settings, data-based decision making has both legal implications and best practice implications. As a component of best practice, the ongoing collection of meaningful data serves two purposes. First, it provides accountability and serves as evidence of the effectiveness of instruction. Second, it guides instructional decision making by helping the practitioner determine when to modify, continue, or terminate an instructional strategy (Gischlar et al., 2009; Yell et al., 2005). As an issue of legality, educators are required to attend to the provisions of the Individuals with Disabilities Education Improvement Act (IDEIA, 2004). The IDEIA requires that the Individualized Education Plan (IEP) include measurable annual goals and that the educator engage in ongoing progress monitoring of each goal. Meetings to inform parents of a learner's progress must take place at a minimum every 9 weeks. Failure to do so puts an educational agency at risk of not providing a free, appropriate public education (Yell, 2019).

Data-based decision making is required by the ethical codes and standards of many professions whose practitioners work with learners with autism spectrum disorder (ASD). The Council for Exceptional Children (CEC) Ethical Standards require that special educators commit to "Using evidence, instructional data, research, and professional knowledge to inform practice" (CEC, 2010). The Behavior Analyst Certification Board (BACB) considers data-based decision making a requisite skill for selecting and implementing interventions in Items H-7 and H-8 within their *Task List for Behavior Analysts* (BACB, 2017). Additionally, the BACB's updated *Ethics Code for Behavior Analysts* (BACB, 2020) addresses data-based decision making in Items 2.17, *Collecting and Using Data* and 2.18, *Continual Evaluation of the Behavior-Change Intervention*.

Although there is evidence that practitioners consider data collection and data-based decision making to be an important part of the education process (Ruble et al., 2018; Sandall et al., 2004), non-data-based decisions made using intuition and casual observation continue to be used by practitioners to make instructional decisions (Grigg et al., 1989). Practitioners report a variety of barriers to data-based decision making, including lack of resources and time, and difficulty with data management (Ruble et al., 2018). Our primary purpose in this chapter is to describe user-friendly methods for collecting, graphing, and analyzing learner data to inform instructional decision making across a variety of settings. We provide tools and supports that we hope will streamline the process of data-based decision making for busy practitioners. First, we will describe how to operationally define behavior. Next, we will describe methods for collecting data on a behavior. Then, we will describe how to write a clear and measurable objective that serves as a benchmark for evaluating progress. Finally, we will describe how to graph data, how to analyze graphed data, and how to make instructional decisions based on graphed data.

COLLECTING DATA

Data-based decision making involves a four-step cycle including collecting data, displaying data, interpreting data, and implementing a data-based decision. As practitioners, we have a responsibility to use data to inform our instruction so learners benefit from evidence-based approaches. Collecting data on a behavior or skill is essential for monitoring progress, identifying areas of need, and determining whether instruction or interventions are effective and necessary. In contrast to judgment or intuition, data are objective. They provide practitioners with a numerical quantity that summarizes a learner's performance relative to the interventions being implemented. Collecting data is a multistep process that involves identifying the behavior to measure, defining the behavior, developing a data collection method, determining when to collect data, training others to collect data, collecting the data, and developing an observable and measurable objective.

Identifying the Behavior or Skill

The first step in collecting data is to identify the behavior or skill to be changed. This is often referred to as the *target behavior*. The behavior should be positive, meaning that it describes what the learner should do as opposed to what they should not do. For example, if a learner is frequently out of their seat, related target behaviors that are positive include task completion or on-task behavior. The behavior or skill should also be of social importance. In other words, it should be targeted for change because it has immediate and long-term benefits for the learner. It may address a behavioral deficit (desirable behaviors that are low fre-

Table 6.1. Examples and Nonexamples of Target Behaviors

Example	Nonexample
Requesting	Defiant
Kicking	Calm
Reading	Unmotivated
Raising hand	Hyperactive

quency or short duration) or a behavioral excess (desirable behaviors that occur too often). Sometimes, behavioral deficits are skills the learner has not yet learned, or they have previously learned but are not using in the appropriate social context. Similarly, behavioral excesses such as crying may occur because the learner has not yet learned a more appropriate behavior and subsequently interferes with the learner's access to other environments. Finally, the target behavior should be an observable action that specifies what the learner does. Emotions, intentions, and states of being, such as being frustrated, wanting to hurt a peer, or being stubborn are not observable behaviors. In contrast, kicking, writing, and raising one's hand specify behaviors that can be observed and measured. Refer to Table 6.1 for additional examples and nonexamples of target behaviors.

Operationally Defining the Behavior or Skill

After the behavior of interest has been identified, it must be operationally defined. An *operational definition* is a clear, objective, and complete description of the behavior. It specifies exactly what the behavior does and does not look like. The operational definition includes objective language referring only to observable and measurable characteristics to eliminate ambiguity. Delineating the boundaries of what the behavior does and does not include ensures that multiple observers can consistently agree on the occurrence or nonoccurrence of the behavior of interest. Without a clear definition, what constitutes an occurrence of the behavior may be left to the interpretation of the observer. As a result, different people who collect data may have different views and opinions about what the behavior looks like and may collect data differently based on their own opinion. In this case, the data would not accurately reflect the learner's performance.

An operational definition is considered clear, objective, and complete when anyone can read it and know exactly what to look for. For example, if two practitioners are asked to record the number of times a learner calls out, but they do not have a well-written operational definition of calling out, it is likely that their data will differ. However, if calling out is defined as "The learner makes on- or off-topic verbal statements without permission while the teacher is providing instruction," then it is clear to both observers what constitutes calling out. Having a well-written operational definition makes data collection and progress monitoring easier and more accurate (see Table 6.2 for examples).

Selecting a Data Collection Method to Record Real-Time Data

Data are the source of information practitioners need to accurately monitor learners' progress and assess whether interventions are effective. The third step in preparing to collect data is selecting a data-collection method so that the

Table 6.2.   Examples of Poorly Defined and Clearly Defined Operational Definitions

Target behavior	Poorly defined	Clearly defined
Requesting	Asking for what is wanted or needed.	Using at least a three-word phrase that includes a subject, verb, and a noun with an intelligible articulation that specifies what is wanted or needed.
Kicking	Extension of the leg toward objects or people.	Extension of the leg with contact between the learner's foot and objects or any part of another person's body that may or may not result in damage or injury. It does not include contact with balls or instances in which the foot does not contact objects or people.
Raising hand	Putting one's hand in the air.	Extending the arm vertically in the air at or above the shoulder level, remaining seated, and quietly following a teacher's question until called on.

target behavior can be recorded in real time. Measurement is the process of quantifying observed instances of a behavior. Measurement provides the means for communicating a learner's progress in a clear and consistent manner in terms of whether and how much the behavior changes over time. Measuring behavior allows practitioners to determine whether an intervention is needed and informs whether existing interventions warrant continuation, modification, or termination. Various types of data can be collected on any behavior. The method should be implemented consistently and provide the most useful information about the behavior being measured.

Continuous Data-Collection Methods
Continuous data-collection methods involve measuring or recording every occurrence of a behavior. When using continuous data-collection methods, the observer either counts each instance of the behavior or the specific amount of time a behavior occurs. These methods should be used when having a complete record of the behavior is necessary. There are five continuous data-collection methods that are practical for use in applied settings: frequency, rate, per opportunity, duration, and latency.

Frequency. *Frequency* is the number of times a behavior occurred. When measuring frequency, the observer counts the number of times a behavior occurs during a specified observation period (e.g., 30 min, Friday, during independent work time). When the behavior can occur at any time, or there is no maximum number of opportunities, it is necessary to always specify the observation period and keep it constant so that comparisons can be made. For instance, a practitioner might want to know how many times a learner requests help during a 20-min independent work period. Each time they record this behavior, they should record data for a 20-min observation period. When it is impractical to record the behavior across a consistent observational period, *rate* should be used instead of frequency.

Another important consideration when collecting frequency data is to specify if the behavior can only occur a limited number of times. For example, stating that Monique completed five worksheets this week is meaningless if we do not know how many worksheets she was given. Completing five out of six (83%) worksheets certainly tells a much different story than completing five out of 20 (25%) worksheets. When the behavior is not free to occur (i.e., there are a specific number of opportunities), *per opportunity data* should be used instead of frequency.

There are several convenient ways to collect frequency data including using golf counters, beads, or marking tallies on a piece of masking tape on one's pants. These methods offer practitioners a convenient and portable method of collecting data immediately upon observing its occurrence without interrupting instruction. Regardless of which of these methods are used to quickly record data, the data must always be transferred to a paper or electronic datasheet as quickly as possible. Frequency recording requires constant, vigilant observation; therefore, it should only be used for behaviors that have a clear beginning and end, occur slowly enough that each instance can be observed, and are brief in duration. For example, initiating social interactions, taking bites of food, or hitting a peer are all behaviors that would be appropriate for frequency measurement. When behaviors have a clear beginning and end, it is easy to detect each occurrence. For example, it might be unclear to determine when body rocking starts and ends, whereas it is easy to count the number of clothing items folded. The major advantages of frequency recording are that it is easy to use and the observer only needs a well-written definition and the recording tool (i.e., golf counter, or pencil and paper). Frequency data for a session or observation period are summarized by simply counting the number of occurrences in that session.

Rate. *Rate* is derived from the ratio of frequency and observation time. It is often reported as responses per minute, but rate per hour or day may be meaningful for some behaviors. For instance, if a practitioner is interested in reading fluency, then collecting data on the rate of words read correctly per minute would be appropriate. In contrast, when a behavior such as biting peers is free to occur at any point in time, then summarizing the data as bites per day may give the practitioner a better sense of whether biting is improving or worsening over time. Rate is an appropriate measure to use when the observation time varies from day to day. To use rate, the observer records the frequency of the behavior during each observation period as well as the duration of the observation period. Rate data for a session or observation period is summarized by dividing the number of times the behavior occurred by the length of the observation period. For example, if Nathaniel read 24 words correctly in 2 min, this would be described as 12 words per minute.

Per Opportunity. *Per opportunity recording* involves measuring how often a target behavior occurs when the learner is given the opportunity and is generally reported as a percentage. Following each opportunity, the observer indicates a yes or no, or plus or minus, if the behavior of interest occurs. This type of measurement requires that the observer first define what sets the occasion for an opportunity. For example, if a learner has a goal to respond to the teacher's greetings, then an opportunity occurs when the teacher says, "Hello, Abigail." When the observer sees an opportunity for the behavior to occur, they watch the learner so they can record data on their response. Often, a per-opportunity datasheet has columns for each day and rows for each opportunity. In the intersecting cell, the observer can record data on the learner's response to each opportunity. Per opportunity data for each session or observation period is summarized by dividing the number of opportunities in which the behavior occurred by the total number of opportunities in the session and multiplying by 100.

An advantage of per opportunity data is that if the practitioner can control when the learner has an opportunity to respond or engage in the target behavior, then the practitioner is better equipped to allocate resources toward data collection. Additionally, the use of per opportunity measurement reduces the demands for continuous observation given that the observer's attention is only necessary immediately following each opportunity for the learner to respond. Some other behaviors that can be measured using per opportunity data include steps in a hand-washing task analysis, questions answered correctly, and responding to peers' requests. Most importantly, per opportunity recording can allow practitioners to compare performance from day to day even when the number of opportunities that learner has to engage in a behavior varies.

Duration. *Duration recording* is used to monitor how long a behavior occurred. Duration recording requires that the behavior have a discrete beginning and end. This means that it must be clear when the observer should start and stop the timer to measure the duration of the event. Ideally, the observer should begin the timer as soon as the behavior begins. For example, a caregiver interested in how long it takes her son to put all his toys away might start the timer when her son picks up an item from the floor and end the timer when the last toy has been put in the designated location. A practitioner might find it helpful to use duration recording when they are interested in decreasing behaviors that occur for long periods of time, such as a learner being out of their seat. Alternatively, duration data can be used when the behavior of interest is not occurring long enough, such as increasing the duration for which a teenager cycles on a stationary bike.

Duration data for a session or observation period can be summarized in several ways. *Total duration* is computed by simply adding the duration of all occurrences within an observation period. For example, consider a learner who was out of his seat 3 times, for 3 min, 7 min, and then 5 min. The total duration is 15 min. The *percentage of time observed* is the percent of the observation period in which the behavior occurred. It is computed by adding the duration of all occurrences and dividing by the duration of the observation period. Using the previous example, if the learner was out of his seat for 15 total min of a 40-min math class, the duration percentage is 37.5%. The *average duration per occurrence* is calculated by summing the duration of all occurrences (3 min + 7 min + 5 min) and dividing the total by the frequency of occurrences (15 min/ 3 occurrences = 5 min/occurrence).

Latency. *Latency* is a variation of duration recording in which the time between some event, prompt, or environmental cue and the onset of the behavior of interest is measured. Latency measures how long it takes the learner to start engaging in the target behavior when given the opportunity. It may be important to measure how long it takes a learner to arrive to class after the bell has rung. In this case, the timer would start immediately after the bell rings and stop when the learner walks into the classroom. Practitioners may consider latency when the goal is to decrease the amount of time it takes for a learner to start engaging in the target behavior. Alternatively, it may be desirable to increase the amount of time between an environmental cue and the occurrence of inappropriate behavior, such as the time between when a toothbrush enters the mouth and when the learner turns away. Short latencies indicate that the learner is responding to the cue quickly, whereas long latencies suggest that it takes the learner a longer amount of time to initiate the behavior after the cue is presented.

If there are multiple occurrences of the behavior during each session or observation period, latency data can be summarized by calculating the average latency per occurrence. If a learner is often late to class, and attends seven class periods per day, each educator may record latency to class after the bell rings. The seven latencies would be summed and divided by 7 to calculate the average latency for the day.

Discontinuous Data-Collection Methods

When using discontinuous data-collection methods, only a sample of the behavior is captured; some instances may not be recorded. Interval recording procedures are discontinuous measurements. They involve breaking the observation period into brief intervals and recording whether the behavior occurs during the interval or at a specific point in time. At the end of the observation period, the data are summarized in terms of the percentage of intervals in which the behavior occurred.

In general, interval recording may be an alternative to latency or duration recording particularly because it provides an approximation or estimation for how often the behavior occurs. Interval recording offers a few important benefits over continuous data-collection methods. First, they require less effort than frequency recording because the observer does not have to observe and record each instance of the behavior. Second, they can be used when the observer needs to engage in other activities or observe multiple behaviors or learners at the same time. Third, interval recording is appropriate for behaviors that occur at a high frequency and are short in duration, or those that do not have a clear beginning and end such as crying, tapping a pencil, and on- or off-task behavior. Some caution should be taken when using interval recording. It is less accurate than duration recording and may overestimate or underestimate the occurrence of behavior. Although discontinuous data-collection methods yield less accurate data than continuous data-collection methods, interval recording may be more feasible in busy environments where practitioners have many competing responsibilities. There are three types of interval recording methods: whole interval, partial interval, and momentary time sampling.

Whole Interval Recording. *Whole interval recording* involves observing for the occurrence of the target behavior and indicating with a plus or minus whether the behavior occurred during the entire interval. Whole interval recording is ideal for high-rate behaviors, those that do not have a clear beginning and end, or those that are likely to continue across intervals, and are best for behaviors we want to increase. The practitioner must first determine the length of the observation. Perhaps an educator's schedule only permits him or her to observe the learner for the first 10 min of each session. The observation period is then broken down into smaller equal intervals. For example, the 10-min observational period may be broken into 10 equal 1-min intervals. If the educator is interested in a learner's on-task behavior in math, reading, science, and art, he or she would observe during the first 10 min of each period, and after each 1-min interval the educator would record a plus if the learner was on task for the entire minute and a minus if at any point the learner was off task. At the end of the day, once all four observations have been completed, the educator summarizes the data by counting the number of intervals he or she recorded as a plus (the learner was on task the entire minute) and dividing it by the total number of intervals (40; 10 1-minute intervals for the four class periods). If the educator recorded 30 plus signs, then the learner was on task for 75% of the observation period, or approximately 30 min.

When using interval recording methods, the observer should use a stopwatch or app to keep track of the intervals. This will keep the intervals consistent and alert the observer of when the interval has ended, and when to mark on the data-sheet. This method can be particularly challenging because it requires attending to the learner, managing a timing device, and recording data. Therefore, whole interval recording should be selected when another practitioner is either work-ing with the learner or is available to collect data while the primary practitioner works with the learner. As previously noted, some caution should be taken when using interval recording. Whole interval recording may underestimate the occur-rence of behavior because if it does not last the entire interval, it is not recorded as happening. Shorter intervals will produce more accurate data.

Partial Interval Recording. *Partial interval recording* is similar to whole inter-val recording in that brief observation periods are identified and then broken into small intervals. The difference is that the observer indicates a plus or a minus if the target behavior occurs at any point during each interval. Like whole interval recording, after the observation period has ended, the observer counts the number of intervals in which the behavior was observed and derives a percentage of inter-vals by dividing the number of intervals with an occurrence by the total number of intervals. For example, an educator may want to measure a specific form of motor stereotypy (e.g., jumping) a learner engages in during the beginning of a writing task. It might be less valuable to know how long jumping occurs, thus partial interval recording can be used. The educator would break down the 5-min observation period into 20 equal 30-s intervals. The educator would observe for jumping during each interval. If the learner jumps after 10 s within the first inter-val, the educator records an occurrence and can discontinue observing for the remaining 20 s because the frequency or duration of jumps is irrelevant. Just as with whole interval recording, the educator summarizes the data by counting the number of intervals he recorded as a plus (the learner jumped at some point during the interval) and dividing it by the total number of intervals (20 30-s inter-vals for the first 5 min of the writing task). If the educator recorded 15 plus signs, then the learner jumped at least once in 75% of the intervals.

Partial interval recording documents whether behavior occurred or not but will not provide information about how many times a behavior occurs within the interval. This procedure tends to produce a slight overestimation of the duration of the target behavior, particularly as the length of the intervals increase, and should therefore be used when the goal is to reduce behavior, or when an estimate of rate of responding is desired. One advantage of this measurement, however, is that the observer may allocate their attention elsewhere after the first instance of the behavior during each interval then return their attention to the learner when alerted that the interval has ended.

Momentary Time Sampling. *Momentary time sampling* (MTS) involves recording an occurrence if the target response occurs at a predetermined moment. Like the other interval methods, MTS involves identifying the length of the observation period, then breaking it down into smaller equal intervals. To measure the occurrence of the target behavior, the observer attends to the learner and records whether the behavior is occurring at the end of the interval. MTS is advantageous in classrooms and other similar settings where the practitioner has many demands on their attention because the observer does not need to be attending to the learner's behavior all the time—only at the end of the interval. In other words, MTS is minimally intrusive as compared to the other sampling methods because the observation time is modest enough so as not to interfere with instructional activities. Although MTS can underestimate the frequency of the behavior and overestimate the duration, it may be a viable substitute for duration recording when using small intervals (Gardenier et al., 2004). For instance, MTS can underestimate behavior if it occurs throughout an interval but stops right before the end of the interval because this interval would be scored as a nonoccurrence. Just as with the other two interval recording methods, data are summarized according to the percent of intervals in which the observer recorded an occurrence of the target behavior. At the end of the observation period, count all the occurrences and divide by total intervals observed to get the percentage of intervals in which behavior occurred. A teacher might use MTS to estimate a learner's engagement with a manipulative activity (e.g., blocks) during a 10-min free play session. The teacher might break the free play session into 10 1-min intervals. At the end of each 1-min interval the teacher would observe the learner and record whether he or she was engaged with the blocks at that moment. When the free play session ends, the teacher summarizes the data by summing the total intervals in which the learner was engaged with the blocks when the interval ended and dividing by the total number of intervals and multiplying by 100. Not only does this provide the teacher with an estimate of how long the learner engaged with blocks during free play, but also this method of data collection allows the teacher to allocate their attention to other learners or tasks during each interval while only needing to observe the target learner when the intervals end.

Which Data-Collection Method to Use?

Descriptions of all the data-collection methods and examples are displayed in Table 6.3. Selecting an appropriate method for measuring behavior is a critical component for behavior change because this system must be appropriate for the behavior, must measure the aspect of the behavior that is desirable to change, and must align with the mastery criterion in your objective, which is discussed later in this chapter. The appropriateness of a data collection method refers to whether it matches the characteristics of the behavior. For example, using frequency requires that the practitioner can identify discrete occurrences of a behavior (e.g., hitting a peer). A behavior that does not have a clear beginning and end, such as "on-task behavior," would be difficult to measure using frequency and an interval method may be more appropriate. Practitioners may also want to change a particular aspect of a given behavior. For example, it might be important to increase or

Table 6.3. Overview of Data-Collection Methods

Method	Description	Example
Frequency	The number of times the behavior occurs within an observation period	The number of requests made
Rate	The ratio of the number of times the behavior occurs divided by the length of the observation period	The number of single digit addition facts answered correctly per minute
Per opportunity	The percent of correct or independent responses out of total opportunities	The percentage of questions answered correctly when called on
Duration	The time that passes between when the behavior starts and ends	The time it takes a learner to walk to class from the playground
Latency	The time that elapses between when a cue is provided and the individual begins to respond	The time it takes to begin placing supplies into one's bookbag after being asked
Whole interval	Whether the behavior of interest occurred for an entire predetermined interval	The percentage of 30-s intervals a learner is on task in a 10-min observation
Partial interval	Whether the behavior of interest occurred at any point during a predetermined interval	The percentage of intervals in which calling out occurs at any time
Momentary time sampling	Whether the behavior of interest occurred at the end of a predetermined interval	The percentage of intervals in which a learner is interacting with a peer when the interval ends

decrease the number of times a learner gets out of their seat during instruction. In this case, a frequency or rate measure should be used (e.g., number of times out of seat). Alternatively, it may be more important to know how long the learner is out of their seat each time. In this case, a duration measure would capture the aspect of the behavior that is of interest to the practitioner.

Determining When to Collect Data

The fourth step in planning to collect data is to determine when data collection will occur. The time will depend on the target behavior, how frequently it occurs, and available resources. It is best to collect data when and where the target behavior is likely to occur. For example, if hitting peers only occurs during physical education instruction, then observing the learner at lunch or during math instruction may not provide enough information about how often the learner hits their peers. Once the times for data collection have been established, it is important to adhere to that schedule consistently so that data are representative of the learner's performance. If data are not collected consistently, and immediately following the behavior, then the accuracy of the data is compromised.

Developing a Data Collection Sheet

The last step in planning to collect data is to develop a data collection sheet, which is a form that is used to record data on the target behavior in real time. At a minimum, data collection sheets should include the learner's name, the operational definition of the target behavior, instructions for the observer, the date (and time, if appropriate) that data were collected, data codes if needed (e.g., +/−), and a space for the observer to collect the data. The space for recording data will look different depending on the data-collection method. For example, a frequency data collection sheet may simply include a table with multiple rows where the observer enters the date and tallies occurrences of the behavior on that date in a corresponding row. A partial interval data collection sheet, on the other hand, would need to have a space for the observer to record data in each interval within a recording session (see Figures 6.1 and 6.2 for examples of datasheets).

SAMPLE FREQUENCY DATASHEET

Learner Name: Tameika

Operational Definition. Raising hand is defined as Tameika extending her arm vertically in the air and remaining seated and quiet following a teacher's question until called on. Do not count an occurrence of raising hand if Tameika extends her arm into the air but also vocalizes or calls out prior to the teacher calling on her.

Instructions

1. Conduct your observation during the 20-min large group reading instruction.
2. Enter the date of your observation in the first column.
3. In the second column, make a tally mark each time Tameika raises her hand according to the operational definition above.
4. At the end of the session, count the number of tally marks and enter that number in the third column.

Date	Tally Occurrences	Total Occurrences
9/15	IIII	4

Figure 6.1.

SAMPLE INTERVAL DATASHEET

Learner Name: Marcus

Operational Definition. Attending to class discussion is defined as Marcus looking at the speaker or relevant materials (board, book). This does not include looking out the window or looking in his desk.

Instructions

1. Conduct your observation during class discussions.
2. Enter the date of your observation in the first column.
3. When the discussion begins, start your timer.
4. Use whole interval recording to measure the behavior.
5. During each 1-min interval, observe Marcus. If he attends to class discussion according to the operational definition above **for the entire minute**, mark a +.
6. If at any time within the interval he is not attending, mark a −.
7. Continue for the remaining intervals.
8. At the end of the session, count the number of + codes, divide by 10, and enter that number in the column labeled "Percentage of Intervals."

Date	Intervals										Percentage of intervals (number of + ÷ 10)
	0–1 min	1–2 min	2–3 min	3–4 min	4–5 min	5–6 min	6–7 min	7–8 min	8–9 min	9–10 min	

Figure 6.2.

Training Others Who May Collect Data

After the target behavior has been identified and defined, an appropriate measure has been developed, the timing of data collection has been determined, and a data collection sheet has been generated, the next step is to train practitioners who will be responsible for collecting data on the learner's target behavior. Training others to reliably collect data is essential because instructional decisions are made based on those data. Ideally, training should consist of some didactic instruction that informs the practitioner why data collection is important, what behavior is being measured and how it is defined, and the specifics on how to use the datasheet. Once these formal instructions have been provided, the trainer should demonstrate how to observe and measure the target behavior using the datasheet.

Trainees should then be given an opportunity to rehearse or practice using the datasheet while receiving corrective feedback until they demonstrate mastery.

Collecting Baseline Data

Baseline should always serve as the starting point for instruction. Baseline is the phase (or brief period) in which the behavior is measured before an intervention is introduced. Baseline data justify the need for an intervention and provide a reference point against which the effect of the intervention can be evaluated. Baseline data indicate the learner's current level of performance. The purpose of gathering baseline data is to inform the mastery criterion in an instructional objective and to provide a point of comparison so the practitioner can evaluate whether performance on the target behavior changed when the intervention is being implemented. Without baseline data, it would be difficult to determine whether the behavior changes over time and if those changes occurred only when the intervention was being implemented. Baseline data collection should be systematic and informed; that is, the same measurement should be used during the specified observation period by all trained observers. This consistency in measurement and observation time is imperative so that any changes that occur in the data over time reflect actual changes in learner performance, and not changes in how the data were collected. Baseline data directly informs the objective, which serves as a roadmap for how the intervention should affect learner performance.

Developing an Objective

An *objective* is a statement that serves as a benchmark for comparing a learner's current and past performance. Objectives can be written for social, academic, or behavioral skills that are targeted for increase or decrease. Well-written objectives serve as goal posts for practitioners to evaluate the effectiveness of their interventions and to monitor whether learners are making adequate progress toward their goals.

Objectives should contain four components. First, the objective indicates the condition in which the behavior should occur. The condition should be as specific as possible and indicate when the target behavior should occur. For example, when an adult or peer says hello to Tyler. Second, the learner who must engage in the target behavior under the specified condition must be clearly specified. In the case of the example condition above, Tyler is the learner whose behavior is of interest. Third, the objective must indicate the specific target behavior the learner is expected to engage in. The target behavior should be objective and must identify the specific action the learner must perform; however, a full operational definition need not be included within the objective. For example, the target behavior portion may state that Tyler will look at the speaker and say hello.

The fourth and final component of an objective is the criterion of performance that must be reached. For instance, Tyler's objective might specify the following criterion: independently in a minimum of 80% of opportunities across five consecutive days. The criterion indicates how well and for how long the learner should perform at that level. The mastery criterion should be informed by the learner's baseline performance (i.e., the current level of performance), and should align with how data are collected. The complete objective would be "When an adult or peer says hello to Tyler, he will look at the speaker and say hello independently in a minimum of 80% of opportunities across 5 consecutive days." Alignment with the data collection system is critical to evaluating whether the learner has met the objective. If per opportunity is used to measure steps completed in a morning routine, then the mastery criterion must specify the percent of steps that must be completed for mastery (e.g., 90% of steps). A mastery criterion based on duration of completing the morning routine (e.g., in less than 15 min) would not align with the data collection system and this mismatch would prevent the practitioner from evaluating learner progress.

The importance of the behavior also helps inform the mastery criterion. Health, safety, reading, and math skills may be best at 100% because they are imperative for the learner's overall development and also support other academic skills. Whereas skills such as on-task behavior, hand raising, or some social skills may not require that the learner always perform correctly. Practitioners should also consider the appropriateness of the mastery criterion and should specify the number of consecutive sessions or days the learner must engage in the behavior at the predetermined performance requirement. It is not realistic to expect a first grader to never call out during an entire day, so a mastery criterion of 0 call outs per day is not appropriate, but perhaps fewer than 5 is both meaningful and reasonable.

A complete objective that considers the importance and appropriateness of the skill might be, "When conversing with a peer at lunchtime, Tessa will make at least three on-topic statements across 3 consecutive days." The condition is conversing with a peer at lunch, the learner is identified as Tessa, the behavior is making on-topic statements, and the criterion indicates that the observer will be recording the frequency of those statements. Additionally, the mastery criterion for on-topic statements is three and Tessa has to maintain this level of performance across 3 consecutive days.

GRAPHING DATA

Data are a collection of measured behavior and are used to guide decisions about whether to continue, discontinue, or change an intervention. However, because it is difficult to identify patterns in raw data (Table 6.4), it can be helpful to display these numbers on a graph (Figure 6.3). Graphs offer several advantages over raw data, both for monitoring progress and for communicating with others. Graphs can make changes in the learner's performance over time more evident, allowing practitioners to respond more quickly when the instruction needs to be changed or adjusted. Graphs can also make it easier to communicate with the learner and other stakeholders, including parents and caregivers, other service providers, and administrators, about progress toward individual objectives.

Parts of a Line Graph
A *line graph* is the most common type of graph used to depict learner performance over time, and it has several basic components. First, the *horizontal axis or x-axis*, is the straight horizontal line that represents the passage of time such as days, weeks, or months. Next, the *vertical axis or y-axis* is the straight vertical line that represents a range of values (e.g., frequency, rate, or duration) for the behavior being measured. In the example graph of a learner's biting behavior (Figure 6.3),

Table 6.4. Example of Raw Data

Day	Frequency of biting
1	4
2	9
3	1
4	11
5	3
6	7
7	10
8	6
9	5
10	13
11	9
12	8
13	6
14	5
15	5
16	4

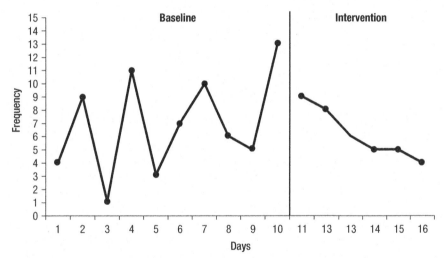

Figure 6.3. Sample graph

the y-axis shows a range between 0 and 15. This indicates the frequency of bites per day. The x- and y-axes will both have *axis labels*. The axis labels give us information about the unit of time and the measurement method used to collect data on the target behavior.

Each graph should have a title. Often, this includes the learner's name and a brief description of the objective or behavior that is being measured, for example "David's Frequency of Biting per Day." The *phase change line* is a vertical line drawn upward from the x-axis that shows the point in time in which the phases of the intervention changed (i.e., right before the intervention starts).

There is typically a phase change line between the baseline phase, which shows the learner's performance before the intervention begins, and the intervention phase, which shows the learner's performance while the intervention is being implemented. Headings to the left and right of the phase change line are called *phase labels*. These are brief descriptions that identify which phase was in effect when the data were collected. Each *data point* represents the performance of the behavior at some point in time. In Figure 6.3, for example, data indicate that the behavior of biting occurred 9 times in Day 2. The final feature of the graph is the *data path*; it is the line that connects successive data points within a phase. It is important to note that data points should not be connected across phase lines. For instance, in Figure 6.3 the data points on Days 10 and 11 are not connected due to a change from the baseline to intervention phase. When data points are only connected within a phase, we are better able to visually analyze the data and detect changes in the level of the behavior.

Creating Line Graphs

Graphs are a visual display of measured behavior, and by graphing data practitioners can quickly evaluate progress and make data-based decisions. They are relatively simple to create using Microsoft Excel® or Google Sheets and can be continually updated to allow for ongoing data display and analysis. We developed two brief video models for creating line graphs both in Excel and in Google Sheets that can be accessed by clicking the following links:

> https://www.youtube.com/embed/kSWGcdITOrU
> https://www.youtube.com/embed/7Vx7FqUIs2Q

ANALYZING DATA

After creating a graph of the learner's performance on a particular skill or behavior, it is important to use that graph to monitor the learner's progress toward the objective to inform instructional decisions. Before describing the steps of data-based decision making in detail, it is important to be familiar with basic features of the data in a line graph: level, trend, and variability. The *level* of performance is its average height on the y-axis. The level indicates how often, on average, the behavior is occurring. To estimate the level, imagine a line parallel to the x-axis with approximately half the data points above it and half below it. See Figure 6.4 for examples of level. The *trend* of the performance is the direction of change in performance over time. It displays whether the learner's performance is improving, worsening, or staying the same—and how quickly it is changing. A steep trend indicates a quick change in the target behavior, whereas a shallow trend indicates a slow change in the target behavior. To estimate the trend, imagine a line following the general trajectory of the data path over time. See Figure 6.5 for examples of trend. The *variability* of performance is how much the individual data points deviate or "bounce" around the estimated trend line. The variability is an indication of how predictable or unpredictable the learner's performance is on any given day. Variability is generally described as being low, moderate, or high. See Figure 6.6 for examples of variability.

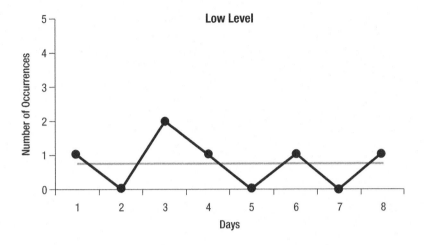

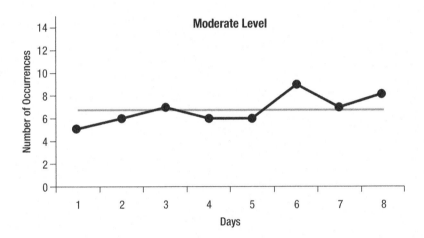

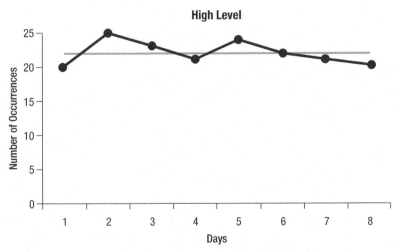

Figure 6.4. Graphs with low, moderate, and high level

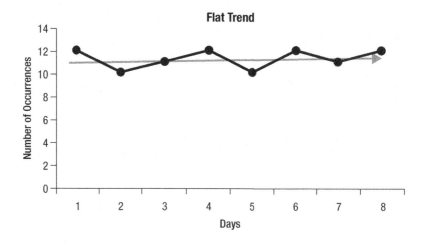

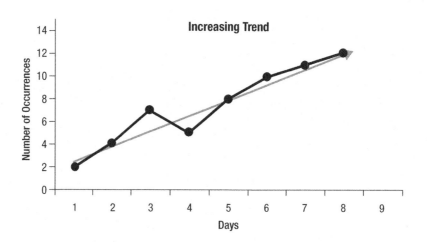

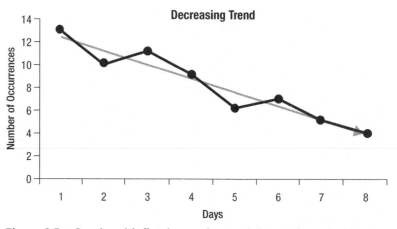

Figure 6.5.   Graphs with flat, increasing, and decreasing trends

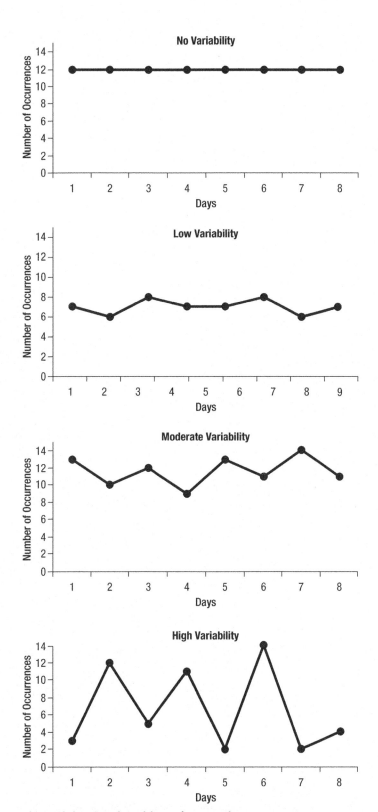

Figure 6.6.   Graphs with no, low, moderate, and high variability

MAKING DATA-BASED DECISIONS

Data-based decision making is a three-step cycle that includes (1) identifying the pattern of the learner's performance, (2) making an instructional decision, and (3) implementing the instructional decision. The steps in this cycle should be repeated until the learner masters the objective. We have included a decision-making model (Wolfe et al., 2021; Figure 6.7) to assist in carrying out Steps 1 and 2 of the data-based decision-making process.

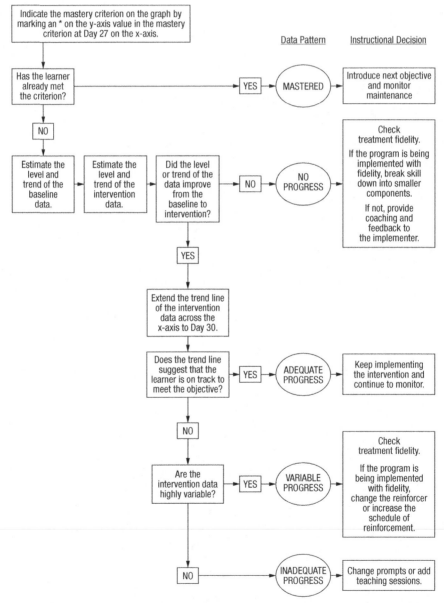

Figure 6.7. Data-based decision-making model (Wolfe et al., 2021)

Patterns of Performance and Corresponding Decisions

The first step of data-based decision making involves identifying the pattern of performance. The pattern of performance refers to the progress that the learner is making toward the objective, based on the graph, and informs the instructional decision. Five common patterns include (1) no progress, (2) slow progress, (3) variable progress, (4) adequate progress, and (5) mastery (Browder et al., 2011). To identify the pattern of performance, it is necessary to evaluate the level, trend, and variability of the data in baseline and intervention, and compare the learner's performance to the mastery criterion in the objective. The following sections include a description of what each pattern means, what it looks like, and potential instructional decisions aligned with each pattern.

Mastery

A learner has reached *mastery* when they perform the skill at the level required in the objective and maintain performance at that level for the required duration of time. On the graph, this means there are sufficient data points at or above the mastery criterion to demonstrate that the learner can consistently perform the skill or behavior at the required level. For example, suppose that an objective specifies that a learner needs to engage in back-and-forth conversation for an average of at least 5 min for 3 consecutive days. Data displayed in Figure 6.8 show that the learner engaged in the required average duration of conversations each day for at least 3 consecutive days and, thus, suggests that the learner mastered the behavior according to this objective.

When an objective is mastered and the learner is performing the skill independently, subsequent instructional decisions will involve discontinuing or fading the intervention. Valuable instructional time must not be used teaching a skill the learner can already perform. However, plan to monitor whether the learner maintains and generalizes performance of the mastered skill. To monitor maintenance

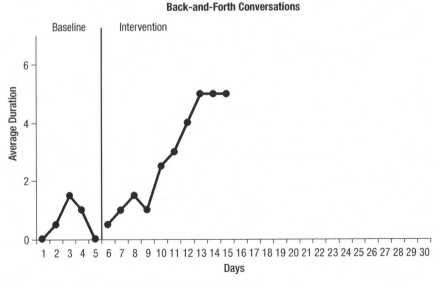

Figure 6.8. Sample graph depicting mastery

over time, assess the skill periodically even though it is no longer being taught to determine if the learner continues performing the skill without specific practice or intervention. To monitor generalization, assess the skill in situations or with materials that are different from those in which the skill was originally taught.

Take, for example, a handwashing program taught to mastery using a sink located in the back of the classroom, following a consistently presented instruction by the educator to "Wash your hands." Possible variations to assess for generalization may include different educators presenting the instruction, varying the specific wording of the instruction, asking the learner to wash hands at different sink locations throughout the school, or determining if the learner washes hands without a specific instruction (i.e., in response to recognizing hands are dirty). If the learner does not generalize the behavior, additional instruction devoted to teaching more variations may be needed. Successful performance of the behavior in various conditions indicates generalization and the ability to devote instructional time elsewhere.

No Progress

At the other end of the spectrum, *no progress* means the learner's performance has not improved consistently during the intervention. When data displayed on the graph show the level or trend of performance in intervention is the same as it was in baseline, or has worsened, the learner is not making progress (see Figure 6.9). If the pattern of performance is no progress, instructional decisions will depend on how long the intervention has been implemented.

If it has been fewer than 2 weeks since initiating the intervention, an appropriate decision may be to continue without changes and reevaluate after consistently implementing for 2 weeks (Browder et al., 2011). If the intervention has been delivered for at least 2 weeks, an appropriate decision may be to evaluate treatment fidelity to determine if the intervention is not working, or if it just has not been implemented correctly (Wolfe et al., 2021). As discussed in Chapter 5, treatment fidelity refers to whether an intervention or instructional procedure is implemented as intended. Some common treatment fidelity errors may include the practitioner not delivering the correct prompt, delivering a reinforcer for an incorrect response, or not delivering a reinforcer for a correct response. If data collected on treatment fidelity indicate that the intervention has not been implemented correctly, an appropriate instructional decision may be to (1) provide training and coaching to the practitioner to improve fidelity and (2) continue to monitor the implementation of the intervention.

If, on the other hand, treatment fidelity data indicate the intervention has been implemented correctly and the learner is still not making progress, an appropriate instructional decision should focus on simplifying the skill (Browder et al., 2011). This may include teaching a necessary prerequisite skill, breaking the skill down into smaller steps, or teaching one step of a task analysis at time. For example, if a learner is not making progress on an objective related to making a peanut butter and jelly sandwich with a visual task analysis, instruction could focus on teaching just two steps of that skill (taking out the bread and opening the peanut butter jar) until those are mastered and then adding two more.

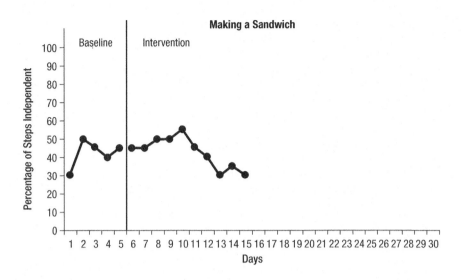

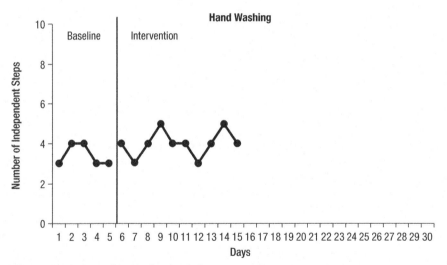

Figure 6.9. Sample graphs depicting no progress

Types of Progress

The data patterns of mastery and no progress are fairly easy to visualize on the graph. If the learner's performance has improved but has not yet met the objective, it can be a little more difficult to judge if that progress is large enough or happening quickly enough for them to meet the objective during the timeframe. To determine what type of progress the learner is making, it is necessary to estimate the trend of behavior during the intervention and extend it forward in time to evaluate if the learner will meet the mastery criterion based on the trajectory of their current performance. The following steps can help determine what type of progress a learner is making toward an objective.

1. Draw a star on the graph at the intersection of the level of performance required for mastery (on the y-axis) and the date by which the learner has to attain that level (on the x-axis). For example, if the mastery criterion in the objective is "for at least 15 min for 5 consecutive days" and the learner is to master this objective in 6 weeks, draw a star at 15 min on the y-axis and 6 weeks from the beginning of the intervention on the x-axis.
2. Estimate the trend of the intervention data and extend that line forward in time across the graph. This will show the projected behavior change over time if intervention were continued. To project the trend line over time, create your graph as described earlier in this chapter.
3. If the projected behavior change line reaches the mastery star, then the learner is making *adequate progress* (see Figure 6.10).

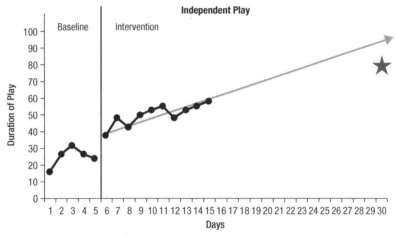

Figure 6.10.   Sample graph depicting adequate progress

4. If the projected behavior change line *does not* reach the mastery star

   a. and the data are consistent from day to day, then the learner is making *inadequate progress* (see Figure 6.11).

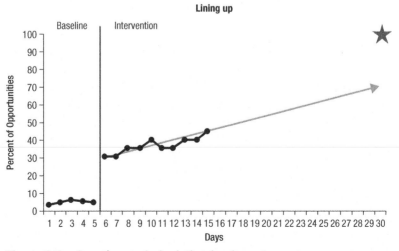

Figure 6.11.   Sample graph depicting inadequate progress

b. or the data are fluctuating from day to day, then the learner is making *variable progress* (see Figure 6.12).

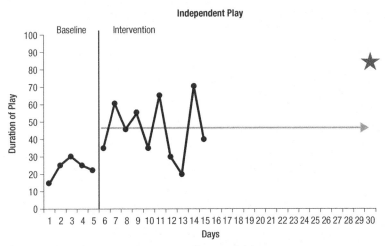

Figure 6.12. Sample graph depicting variable progress

Adequate Progress. *Adequate progress* means that the learner's performance appears to be on track to meet the mastery criterion within the time frame. When the learner is making adequate progress, this suggests the intervention is working, and no changes are necessary. The appropriate instructional decision should be to keep implementing the intervention in the same way and continue to monitor the data at least every week. It is important to remember that even though the learner is making adequate progress at this time, their performance may change, and different instructional decisions may be required in the future.

Inadequate Progress. Sometimes, a learner's performance improves during intervention, but the improvement is not large enough or happening quickly enough for them to meet the objective during the timeframe. This is *inadequate progress*, identified on the graph if the projected behavior change line does not reach the mastery star. Inadequate progress suggests that the intervention is somewhat effective but may need a "boost" to help the learner acquire the skill more quickly or master a particular step within the skill. Subsequent instructional decisions should involve changing some element of intervention, but the change will vary depending on the situation. For example, the learner's performance may be improving during intervention, but just not quickly enough to meet the objective—in other words, it may have a shallow trend (see Figure 6.11). In this case, an appropriate instructional decision may be to keep intervention procedures the same but increase the number of instructional sessions to give the learner more opportunities to practice the skill. An instruction presented by a teacher such as "Line up at the door" may naturally occur a limited number of opportunities each day; it may be necessary for the educator to contrive additional opportunities for the learner to respond to this instruction to achieve mastery in a timely manner.

Another type of inadequate progress is when the learner's performance initially increases and then plateaus, or levels off (see Figure 6.13). This data pattern

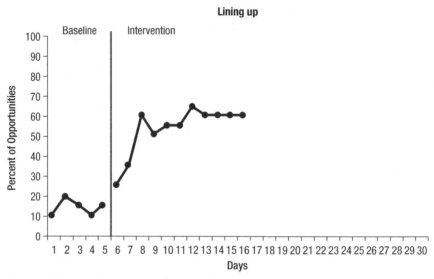

Figure 6.13. **Inadequate progress with plateau**

indicates that while there was some initial improvement following intervention, the learner is not currently improving. In this case, instructional decisions may involve changing the prompt or reinforcer to increase independent responding. To determine how to change the prompt, examine the raw data to look for patterns in the learner's responses. The raw data may indicate the learner has a high number of incorrect responses, even though the practitioner is prompting the correct response. This suggests the need to change the intervention to provide a more intrusive prompt. For example, an adult learner at a group care facility has recently started participating in dinner setup. When handed a set of plates and given an instruction to "set the table," the practitioner also gestured toward the placemats on the table. However, even with this prompt the learner engaged in an incorrect response, setting the stack of plates on the edge of the table and walking away. In subsequent instructional opportunities, the practitioner now provides a physical prompt, guiding the learner as they place a plate on each available placemat. Alternatively, the raw data may indicate the learner has a high number of prompted responses. This suggests the need to change intervention to fade the prompt, either by providing a less intrusive prompt or increasing the delay before the prompt. For example, an intervention to teach a learner to request using sign language may initially require hand-over-hand prompting, but the practitioner must fade the physical prompt or use time delay to allow the learner to respond independently.

There may be a specific step or part of the skill that the learner is consistently performing incorrectly or waiting for a prompt. If a consistent error is identified that is preventing the learner from meeting the objective, it is appropriate to change the intervention only for that specific step or part of the skill. Consider teaching a learner to restock shelves for their employment at the local drug store. This task requires a sequence of steps, any of which may be difficult for a learner to complete independently. If, for example, the learner can independently complete most steps (gathers all required materials, locates the item to be restocked), but has difficulty counting or determining how many items are necessary to fully restock, the practitioner might use a more intrusive prompt only for that specific step.

Inadequate progress that plateaus over time may also indicate the need to assess the type and frequency of the reinforcement that is delivered for engaging in the target response. If a learner's performance is no longer improving, it may indicate that the reinforcer that is being delivered is (a) no longer highly preferred, (b) not being delivered immediately enough, or (c) not being delivered often enough to strengthen the behavior. In this case, the reinforcer may need to be changed to increase motivation, or it may need to be delivered closer in time to the behavior or on a more frequent basis. For example, consider a practitioner who is working on teaching a young child to greet others. The practitioner is delivering a verbal prompt (e.g., "say hi"), which is effective for this learner because they can imitate vocalizations. However, the practitioner is delivering praise as a consequence (e.g., "great job!"), which is not highly preferred for the child and does not function as a reinforcer. Although the child's performance initially increased, the practitioner needs to deliver a more highly preferred reinforcer (e.g., a thumb up) to continue to strengthen the behavior.

Variable Progress. The final pattern of progress that may arise when examining a learner's graph is variable progress. *Variable progress* means that the learner's performance is fluctuating or inconsistent from day to day (see Figure 6.13). The performance is better than it was during baseline on some days, but on other days it may be similar to baseline. This data pattern suggests the intervention itself may be effective, but it may not be implemented consistently and correctly from day to day, which may result in the learner's progress being inconsistent. In this case, instructional decisions will involve checking for treatment fidelity to see if the intervention is being implemented correctly every time it is implemented. Similar to the instructional decision for no progress, if treatment fidelity is low, then it is necessary to take steps to improve it (for example, by retraining or coaching the implementer) before making any changes to the intervention.

If treatment fidelity data indicate that the intervention is being implemented consistently and correctly, then variable progress may be due to a lack of motivation. Perhaps the reinforcer for correct responses is not valuable, immediate, or frequent enough to support improved and consistent performance every day. In this case, an instructional decision should involve changing something about the reinforcer. One option is to change the reinforcer, selecting a different item, activity, or interaction to deliver for correct responses, based on the learner's preferences and knowledge of what the learner has recently accessed during the day. In general, an item or activity the learner has not had access to for an extended period will be more valuable than one with which they have just engaged. For example, when implementing the intervention immediately after physical education class, access to the trampoline may not be as valuable a reinforcer as it would have been if the intervention were implemented after a long period in which the learner was sitting at a desk. Present the learner with a menu of reinforcers from which they can choose immediately before implementing the intervention each day. This may increase the likelihood that a reinforcer being used is valuable in the moment.

Changing aspects of the reinforcer delivery is an additional option. When teaching a new skill, it is important to reinforce every correct response to build an association between the correct response and the reinforcer. Reinforcement that occurs less frequently—for example, every other response—may lead to variable progress. Changing the intervention to reinforce every correct response may produce more consistent correct responses. In addition to changing the frequency of reinforcers, consider when the reinforcer is delivered in relation to the correct response. Reinforcers are most effective when delivered immediately, within 1 s to 3 s. Delays in delivering the reinforcer may lead to variability in how the learner responds, so it is important to ensure that the reinforcer is always delivered within a few seconds of a correct response.

Implementing Data-Based Decision Making

The decision-making model in Figure 6.7 is intended to support the use of learner data to inform the decisions that practitioners make as they monitor progress toward objectives. The following section includes a description of logistics and additional considerations for implementing data-based decision making, including how frequently to monitor progress, how to indicate instructional decisions, and the ongoing nature of data-based decision making.

Upon collecting and graphing learner performance data on a particular objective, the frequency with which instructional decisions are made will depend on how often the intervention is implemented and how often data are collected. Practitioners may review graphs as frequently as every time data are collected, or less frequently as on a weekly basis; the critical element is to ensure that the intervention has been given sufficient time to work before making changes. A general rule of thumb is to wait until there are at least 3–5 data points, allowing a trend in the learner's performance to become evident; a trend cannot be visible with only 1 or 2 data points. If data are collected once per week, wait at least 3–5 weeks before making an instructional decision. An important exception can be made when collecting data on an infrequent but dangerous behavior. In this case, an instructional decision may need to be made sooner to protect the safety of the learner and others in the environment. Alternatively, if data are collected on an objective multiple times per week, 2 weeks of data likely contain enough data points to see a trend and make an instructional decision. Some learners with ASD require more practice opportunities to acquire new skills, and so the specific frequency with which practitioners monitor progress and make instructional decisions will also depend on knowledge of the learner. It is critical to collect enough data points to make a decision and to allow enough time for the intervention to work, but not to wait too long to evaluate progress and change a potentially ineffective intervention.

Once a decision has been made, it is important to indicate the decision on the graph by drawing a phase change line and writing the decision above the new phase. For example, if a practitioner evaluates a graph and the learner is not making progress, perhaps his decision was to check treatment fidelity. He found that the intervention was not implemented as intended, so he retrained the implementers. He inserted a phase change line on the graph to separate the data paths with a text box containing "retrained staff" placed above the data in the new phase. The phase change line indicating the instructional decision now allows him to evaluate the effect of this decision on the learner's performance as data continue to be collected.

Importantly, data-based decision making is not a one-and-done event—instead, it is an ongoing process that continues until the learner meets the mastery criterion. After practitioners make a decision, indicate it on the graph, and implement it for a sufficient amount of time, they should continue to engage in the data-based decision-making process by identifying the pattern of performance and making and implementing a corresponding instructional decision. Continuing with the previous example, the first instructional decision was that the learner was not making progress due to the treatment not being implemented correctly, and the practitioner retrained the implementers. Now, upon looking at the data in the phase labeled "retrained staff," he determines that the learner is making inadequate progress—certainly an improvement from no progress but not sufficient to meet the objective. He makes another instructional decision to increase the prompt level from a gestural prompt to a physical prompt. He inserts another phase change line with a text box labeled "physical prompt" above the new phase, trains the implementer on the new prompting procedures, and continues collecting data and monitoring progress.

CASE STUDY

Millie is a 9-year-old female with a diagnosis of ASD. She is currently in a general education classroom and receives weekly services with both an occupational therapist and a speech-language pathologist. Her teacher, Mrs. Brice, is concerned with what seems to be a recent increase in classroom interruptions, particularly during large-group instruction time. Millie will call out answers and questions during class, interrupting Mrs. Brice during instruction as well as her fellow learners as they participate.

During her annual IEP meeting, the team agrees on a new goal to replace calling out with appropriately raising her hand. *Calling out* was defined as "any vocalization emitted without being called on" and *raising hand* was defined as "extending Millie's arm vertically in the air, remaining seated and quiet following a teacher's question until called on." Raising hand did not include when Millie extended her arm into the air but also vocalized prior to the teacher calling on her.

Given that both behaviors have a clear beginning and end, and tend to last short durations of time, Mrs. Brice decided to use frequency recording. However, the group instruction periods varied in length, so Mrs. Brice recorded the duration of each instructional period and converted the behaviors into a rate per minute by dividing the number of behaviors by the number of minutes. She created a line graph in Microsoft Excel® to display the data.

Mrs. Brice collected data for a week on both behaviors to establish a baseline (Figure 6.14). Considering baseline levels, she developed objectives with the goal of replacing calling out with hand raising. During baseline, Millie did not raise her hand at all, and called out an average of .25 times per minute (approximately 4 times in a 15-min lesson). Mrs. Brice decided to set the goal for raising her hand at this rate. Her specific objectives are below. Can you identify all four components of objectives that were discussed earlier in the chapter?

(continued)

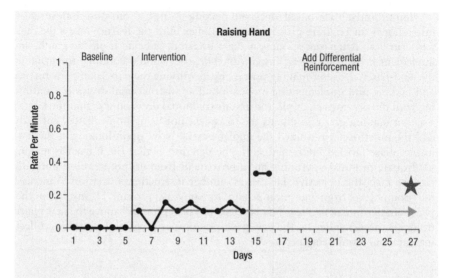

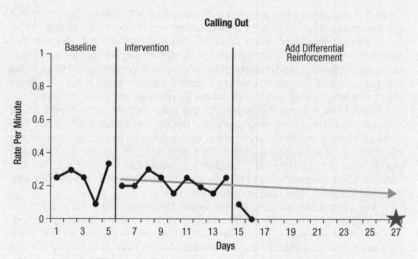

Figure 6.14. Millie's data for hand raising (top) and calling out (bottom)

1. During large-group instruction, Millie will raise her hand at a rate of at least .25 times per minute for 3 consecutive days.
2. During large-group instruction, Millie will call out 0 times per minute for 3 consecutive days.

To teach the skill of raising her hand, Mrs. Brice moved Millie's seat closer to the teacher's desk in front of the class and placed a visual on Millie's desk reminding her to raise her hand when she had a question or wanted to participate. If Millie called out during class, Mrs. Brice would point to or reference the visual reminder on her desk.

Data were collected and entered in Excel at the end of each day, and Mrs. Brice conducted a visual analysis of the graphed data. After 5 days of intervention, there was a clear level change in Millie's hand raising. Calling out remained at the same level as baseline, although there did appear to be a decreasing trend. For these reasons, Mrs. Brice decided to continue the intervention for a second week. Upon completion of the second week, Mrs. Brice drew trend lines and projected them forward in time to see if Millie was making adequate progress to meet her objective. Based on these trend lines, it was clear there was not sufficient change in level or trend for either behavior, indicating inadequate progress toward Millie's objective. Given this lack of progress, Mrs. Brice adjusted her intervention to include a differential reinforcement component. She gave Millie a token each time she raised her hand and continued to redirect her to the visual reminder when she called out. Mrs. Brice added a phase line to her graph, implemented the differential reinforcement intervention, and continued to take data and monitor progress daily.

SUMMARY

One of the most important aspects of implementing EBPs with learners with ASD is collecting data on their performance and analyzing it to monitor progress and make data-based instructional decisions. Directly observing and collecting numerical data in real time provides an objective picture of the learner's performance toward their short-term objectives and long-term goals. However, data are only the means to an end. It is critical that practitioners use the data that they collect to inform their instruction. Keeping close contact with learner data enables practitioners to make changes in a timely manner if the data indicate that an EBP is not working. Data-based decision making is an iterative and recurring process that continues until a learner has demonstrated maintenance and generalization of a skill. True mastery of the skill occurs when the learner can use the skill over time, across environments, and in naturally occurring situations.

APPLICATION ACTIVITIES

1. Select a behavior that you can observe over a period of 1–2 weeks. It may be a pet's, roommate's, friend's, or partner's behavior. Write an operational definition of the behavior that is clear, complete, and objective.
2. Select a data collection system that is appropriate for the behavior you defined in #1. Record data on the behavior for at least 5 days. You may record data throughout the entire day, or only at specific times of the day. Create a graph of your data using the graphing conventions described in this chapter.
3. Look at your graph from #2. How would you describe the level, trend, and variability of the data pattern?

ADDITIONAL RESOURCES

Kansas Technical Assistance System Network. (n.d.). *Data collection video series.* https://www.ksdetasn.org/resources/1704 (click "download file" to access a Word document with links to several data collection videos).

Wakeman, S. (2010a). *Data-based decisions: Modules addressing special education and teacher education (MAST).* East Carolina University. https://mast.ecu.edu/Data%20Collection/Data-based%20Decisions/index.html.

Wakeman, S. (2010b). *Data collection: An introduction. Modules addressing special education and teacher education (MAST).* East Carolina University. https://mast.ecu.edu/Data Collection/Data Collection/index.html.

7

Ethics and Evidence-Based Practice

An Important Partnership for Meaningful Outcomes

Ilene S. Schwartz, Elizabeth M. Kelly, and Kaitlin Greeny

■ ■ ■

INTRODUCTION AND OVERVIEW

What does it mean to be an ethical practitioner? There is no easy answer to this question. Many professionals believe that adherence to a set of rules (i.e., an ethics code) automatically makes them an ethical practitioner, while others believe that they are engaging in ethical behavior if the decisions they make result in positive learner outcomes. Still others may see themselves as ethical when they adhere to their professional ethical codes and their intentions are good, even if the outcomes of their actions do not always result in good outcomes for their learners and other stakeholders. As we will see in this chapter, ethical decision making is complex and becoming an ethical practitioner requires ongoing effort. Being an ethical practitioner is about the journey, not the destination. There are many considerations practitioners must be aware of as they strive to make good decisions and maintain an ethical practice.

To maintain an ethical practice as practitioners move through the process of identifying, recommending, and implementing evidence-based practices (EBPs), they must consider how to ensure that their decisions are informed by ethics. When practitioners consider ethics, they might be considering their own morals and values, the professional ethical codes of their own field, and the professional ethical codes of related fields that they may be collaborating with. Practitioners, professionals, and paraprofessionals from multiple disciplines working with learners with autism spectrum disorder (ASD) and their families frequently make decisions in practice that involve ethics and it is important that those practitioners have the appropriate information to ensure that they are making well-informed decisions. In this chapter, we will discuss a brief history of ethics and basic ethical considerations for professionals working with learners with ASD and related disabilities. We will also discuss how EBPs and ethics intersect and how ethical issues can impact the selection of EBPs used in practice. Finally, we will present a model for ethical problem solving and decision making and provide a case study to illustrate the model.

BRIEF HISTORY OF ETHICS

There are multiple approaches to ethical decision making and these approaches have roots in different ethical theories. Two of the most widely known theories are deontology and utilitarianism. These ethical theories focus on the behaviors or actions of an individual and it is helpful to have a basic understanding of them before we discuss ethical decision making in the context of being a practitioner.

Deontology, or rule-based ethics, is characterized by adherence to a set of moral rules or duties (Alexander & Moore, 2020). In other words, when individuals make ethical decisions rooted in a deontological approach, the result is less important than the means by which the decision is made. Deontology is about what rules and duties we ought to follow, regardless of the consequences. A benefit to this approach is that it sets up a system based on fairness, consistency, and moral equality across all individuals. Critics of this approach argue that when we make ethical decisions according to universal rules, we minimize the role that human judgment plays in ethical decision making and may not allow for important contextual considerations. An often-cited example of this critique centers around the universal Christian rule "Thou shall not bear false witness against thy neighbor" (also commonly found in other religions; for example, the Buddhist precept "Refrain from false speech"). This universal rule simply states that people should not lie. But imagine a Christian family living in World War II–era Germany and hiding a Jewish family in the attic when a Nazi officer comes knocking at the door, asking the family if they know where any Jewish families are hiding. Nearly all of us would agree the most ethical response in that context is to lie. This example emphasizes that it may be necessary for us to consider the outcomes of our decisions just as much as the rules we live by. An example relevant to learners with ASD may be related to intervention hours. In 2001, the National Resource Council recommended that all children diagnosed with ASD receive 25 hours of intensive intervention (National Research Council, 2001). Practitioners applying that recommendation without consideration of additional contextual variables (e.g., financial strain on a family, emotional and mental capacity, family or cultural preferences) would likely be using a more deontological approach to service delivery.

Utilitarianism, or ends-based ethics, is based on the idea that ethical behavior should be judged by the outcome of a decision or action (Driver, 2014). To put it simply, we are ethical when we make decisions that result in the greatest good for the greatest number of people. The benefit of this approach is that it is democratic and objective. Critics of this approach argue that it is impossible to foresee the consequences of everyone's behavior; therefore, we cannot anticipate the "goodness" of our actions before the outcome is known. Even if the outcome could be known, there are other problems with exclusively using this approach. This approach may ignore basic individual rights to serve the greater good. For example, a medical professional using this approach alone may ethically justify the death of a child in medical research if the result saves hundreds of lives. Again, many of us would agree (as would organizations designed to protect the rights of research participants [e.g., the U.S. Office for Human Research Protections]) that in this example, the ends would not justify the means. An example relevant to learners with ASD is commonly found in school classrooms.

In general, there is a public consensus that educators should provide *all* of their learners with the greatest educational benefit possible and that they should make instructional decisions based on the potential outcomes of their learners. However, there are times when the learning needs of an individual learner (with or without ASD) is in conflict with the learning needs of the rest of the class. When an educator makes a decision about academic or behavioral instruction based on the greatest good for the greatest number of learners, they are using a utilitarian approach to their decision making. (For helpful information on how to avoid sacrificing one learner's needs for the greater group, consider looking into universal design for learning or UDL.)

PROFESSIONAL ETHICS

Educating learners, those with and without disabilities, requires practitioners from several different disciplines to work together for the benefit of learners and their families. Therefore, practitioners working in the field of education may abide by many different professional codes of ethics. For example, Board Certified Behavior Analysts® (BCBAs®), including the authors,[1] abide by the *Ethics Code for Behavior Analysts* (2020). Another code of ethics often discussed in education is the Council for Exceptional Children (CEC) *Professional Ethical Principles and Standards*, which applies to the behavior of special education teachers (2015). Other practitioners working in education, such as speech-language pathologists and occupational therapists, also have their professional organizations and their own code of ethics. Ethical principles and codes serve different functions among different professions. It is important to be informed as to the ethics of your own field, how those ethics are promoted or enforced, and how your ethical obligations influence collaboration and teaming with professionals from other disciplines (Fiedler & Van Haren, 2009).

Throughout the process of collaborating with families and other professionals, practitioners often need to identify and rely upon ethical principles to guide their practice. Ethical principles are different from ethical codes in that they are "broad statements that help individuals transform conceptual and philosophical beliefs into ethical behavior" (Kelly et al., 2020, p. 492). While it is necessary to be fluent with the professional ethical codes of one's own field, it is important to be able to discuss ethical issues with colleagues from other disciplines. By identifying ethical principles, practitioners may find common ground with other professionals who abide by different codes of ethics. Ethical principles help professionals consider the context of an ethical situation along with a person's own philosophical beliefs and values to determine ethical solutions (Kelly et al., 2020).

The ethical principles that we have identified that guide the mission of our organization include beneficence, inclusion, professional excellence, self-determination, and social justice (See Table 7.1). By identifying ethical principles, practitioners can find commonalities among professional ethics codes and use the principles as a basis for ethical decision making. For example, the specific standards in a special educator's code of ethics may differ from the standards on a behavior analyst's code of ethics, but both disciplines likely prioritize the principles beneficence and professional excellence. These common values can support ethical and productive professional collaboration across different fields.

Table 7.1. Sample Ethical Principles from an Applied Behavior Analysis Organization

Principle	Description
Beneficence	Behavior analysts have a responsibility to engage in practices that maximize their clients' well-being and avoid those that cause harm. We understand that behavior-analytic services are most likely to benefit our clients when they are provided in the context of a trusting and compassionate relationship. Where conflicts of interest arise between consumers of behavior analysis, we prioritize outcomes for the most vulnerable clients.
Inclusion	Behavior analysts have a responsibility to provide clients of all backgrounds and abilities access to and authentic participation in meaningful activities that promote relationships, a sense of community, and an improved quality of life.
Professional excellence	Behavior analysts have a responsibility to be honest and transparent. We engage in ongoing professional development and analyze our own practices. Professional excellence requires respectful and effective collaboration with individuals from other disciplines, while maintaining a commitment to data-based decision making. Analyzing evidence from different methodologies is encouraged as a way of collaborating with others and improving practice.
Self-determination	Behavior analysts respect clients' rights and promote client dignity, privacy, and autonomy. We assist clients in setting and achieving their own goals, developing their own agency, and making decisions about their own lives.
Social justice	Behavior analysts have a responsibility to attend to injustice where they see it, avoid perpetuating inequitable systems, and advocate for change to produce equitable systems. We are uniquely qualified to identify controlling and contextual variables that contribute to inequitable educational and service-delivery systems and develop solutions to supplant them.

Ethics clearly come into play in all facets of using EBPs, so it is critical that educators and practitioners be fluent with the ethical codes of their profession and practice what Kidder refers to as "Ethical Fitness®" (Kidder, 2005). *Ethical fitness* refers to practicing ethical decision making and "getting in shape to tackle the tough ethical dilemmas as they arise" (Kidder, 2005, p. 157). To make ethical decisions throughout the process of identifying, choosing, and implementing EBPs, practitioners must practice ethical fitness often. Ethics are a part of every aspect of education and throughout this chapter we will further explore ethical fitness and using ethical principles to guide decision making.

EVIDENCE-BASED PRACTICES

The advent of EBPs has helped to codify and improve the services that consumers receive across many different fields, ranging from medicine to education to interventions for learners with ASD. There are multiple definitions of EBP (e.g., Slocum et al., 2014; Smith, 2013). In general, EBP involves practices that attempt to use replicated, quality research outcomes to make decisions about what intervention strategies should be used with learners. While some consider EBP a procedure or set of procedures built upon a base of validated research, many professional organizations (e.g., American Psychological Association [APA], 2005; American Speech-Language-Hearing Association [ASHA], 2005) consider EBP to be a decision-making process about the best intervention procedure to use with learners based on research, practitioner experience, learner preferences, learner characteristics, and learner values.

Most EBP definitions from across disciplines share common elements. They all agree that the research upon which the recommended practice is based must be robust and replicable. They agree that the individual characteristics both of the practitioner and of the learner should be considered when selecting an EBP. The clinical experience and competence of the practitioner is also an important component that should be factored into identifying an EBP. We propose two additional elements that should be considered when selecting and evaluating EBPs: effectiveness in the moment and consideration of intersectional identities.

Effectiveness in the Moment

One advantage of the increased attention to EBP is that there are now many lists of scientifically validated treatments, recommended practices, or high leverage practices for learners with ASD, in early childhood special education, in teaching literacy, and in many other areas that impact the lives of people with ASD and other disabilities (e.g., Division for Early Childhood, 2014; McLeskey et al., 2017; Steinbrenner et al., 2020). Although these lists are helpful, they are decontextualized. They provide intervention strategies and practices that have been judged to meet an agreed-upon research criterion, but they do not provide information about how to match interventions with learners, providers, or contexts. Most importantly, they do not provide information about evaluating the effectiveness of the EBP to teach a specific skill to a specific learner in a specific context at a specific moment in that learner's skill acquisition history.

The identification of EBPs is actuarial. They are developed by compiling research results and determining that, more often than not, a specific intervention is effective. That makes EBP a good starting point but does not provide adequate information to determine if an EBP is effective for the specific learner, on a specific task, at a specific point in that learner's skill acquisition history. Practitioners working with learners with ASD are held to a higher level of accountability. First, they are required to write educational plans for learners that are appropriately ambitious (Yell & Bateman, 2017) and must be able to document the causal relation between implementing an intervention and observing a concomitant change in behavior.

We recommend that ethical practitioners working with learners with ASD consider EBPs starting points from where they evaluate and document the effects of treatment. If a practitioner implements an EBP and observes the anticipated change in behavior, fantastic. They can add this example to their professional experience about the effectiveness of the practice. If, however, an EBP is implemented with fidelity and does not result in a positive change in behavior, it is incumbent upon the practitioner to change the intervention as discussed in

Chapter 6. The change may be in the intensity of the intervention or the type of reinforcers being used, or perhaps an entirely different intervention strategy is necessary. The important lesson is that an instructional strategy cannot be said to be evidence based for an individual learner until we have collected data to demonstrate its effectiveness in this specific situation, with this specific behavior, in this specific context. To be accountable to learners and to practice ethically, practitioners need to conduct these treatment evaluations one learner at a time.

Intersectionality

Kimberle Crenshaw (1989) coined the term intersectionality more than 30 years ago to describe how different parts of a person's identity overlapped and how these overlapping or intersecting identities formed a unique whole that could not be separated. Intersectionality requires us to understand how individuals are impacted by systems based on all parts of their intersecting identities. Although the original discussion of intersectionality focused on race, class, and gender, this concept has been expanded to describe multiple aspects of a person's life including issues of ability, nationality, and religion.

When selecting EBPs to be used with learners with ASD, it is essential that practitioners consider the intersectional identities that make up the person with whom they are working. Practitioners never work with a learner with ASD, they work with a Black, English-speaking learner with ASD who lives with a wealthy family including parents and siblings who include her in all aspects of family and community life. Or they may be working with a nonspeaking young male learner with intellectual and developmental disabilities (IDD) who recently immigrated from Honduras with his single Spanish-speaking mother, who is now living in a large, multigenerational home. Understanding the different identities that learners bring with them to school helps practitioners be more mindful when selecting interventions to meet their needs. Learner ability and its concomitant areas of strength and need do not occur in isolation. Learner ability and educational needs must be contextualized in the intersectionality of their lives, and the effectiveness of all EBPs must address the uniqueness of learners' stories and behavior.

It would be ideal to have EBPs backed up by research that reflected the diversity of our learners and the contexts in which they live and learn. The reality, however, is that the majority of research in special education has been conducted on White, English-speaking children (West et al., 2016). This is yet another reason that it is important to consider EBPs as a starting point for selecting interventions for learners. Although it is important for researchers to broaden the diversity of participants and settings in which they work, research will never reflect all of the unique learners with whom practitioners work. Part of practicing ethically is to embrace the intersectionality of the learners with whom we work and use strong analytic tools to evaluate how different EBPs affect their behavior and overall quality of life.

The first step to using EBPs involves identifying which practices fit the criteria for EBP. Practitioners also have the job of ensuring that this decision is individualized to each specific learner's goals and context. When identifying an EBP, ethics immediately come into play. Ethical practitioners are committed to identifying potential interventions and teaching strategies for a particular goal by examining the available evidence and analyzing it in the context of the situation. It is the responsibility of practitioners to be familiar with evidence supporting different EBPs and to ensure that they have the training necessary to implement that EBP. They must also consider if the EBP is appropriate for the current context. Before implementing an intervention, the educational team members should consider questions such as "Do our team members have the training and resources necessary to implement this intervention with fidelity?"; "Will this practice fit into the social context of the school?"; "How does this practice address the intersectional identities of the learner and family?" A practice being considered "evidence based" does not necessarily mean that it should be on a list of ideas for strategies for teaching a specific learner; however, practitioners must be aware of the evidence base for any intervention that they are considering.

After we have identified potential EBPs, the practitioner moves into choosing an EBP. When choosing an EBP for a specific learner or group of learners, the first step is identifying the goal or behavior. Many interventions lead to an outcome of either increasing a new behavior or decreasing a behavior of concern. Our goal in choosing an EBP is to consider the intersection of the best available evidence, individual outcomes, and the best environmental and contextual fit (e.g., Moes & Frea, 2000). The contextual fit of an intervention influences the fidelity of implementation and effectiveness of the intervention (McLaughlin et al., 2011). Given the importance of contextual fit and evidence, choosing an intervention is not always a straightforward process. It involves analyzing the evidence, the learner's goals, and the environment.

When implementing our chosen EBP, ethics come into play in many ways. EBPs often involve specific steps or have been demonstrated effective in an environment that might be different from the current situation. As a result, EBPs should be implemented with fidelity, along with a data collection system to monitor its level of effectiveness. It is important for practitioners to create a plan for monitoring implementation fidelity and progress monitoring. If a specific intervention is not successful for a particular learner or the environment, changes should be made using evidence from the available literature and student data.

BASIC ETHICAL CONSIDERATIONS

All practitioners must adhere to basic ethical guidelines regarding competency, confidentiality, and accountability. Multiple disciplines similarly approach these three basic ethical considerations. Therefore, educators, behavior analysts, speech-language pathologists, and other practitioners serving learners with ASD are expected to have a basic understanding of what it means to be a competent practitioner who is accountable to others and maintains the confidentiality of their learners, their learners' families, and their colleagues.

Competency

Practitioners are expected to practice within their scope of competence. Scope of competence is "the range of professional activities of the individual practitioner that are performed at a level that is deemed proficient" (Brodhead et al., 2018, p. 57). Competency may apply to specific populations (e.g., learners with ASD) and cultures (e.g., learners who identify as transgender, learners who speak Spanish), assessments and evaluations, EBPs, and training/coaching/mentorship. For example, a special education teacher who only has experience teaching young children with ASD may not have the competency to teach sixth grade learners with learning disabilities without additional training, supervision, or consultation. A serious negative outcome when practitioners practice outside of their scope of competence is they may waste precious resources and time and cause harm to learners by implementing ineffective and inappropriate practices. For example, a BCBA who conducts an assessment they are not yet competent to deliver may misidentify important skills to work on with their learner with ASD (Brodhead et al., 2018). Ethical practitioners who want to practice in a new area outside their scope of competence should do so after obtaining appropriate professional development through continuing education opportunities; mentorship, training, coaching, or consultation; and review of the scientific literature.

Practitioners must also be mentally and physically competent to practice. That means they have the mental and physical capacity to perform their work at a level that benefits learners. If practitioners are experiencing a life event that prevents them from acting in the best interest of their learners, they must consider ways to resolve that situation. Practitioners who regularly collaborate with colleagues to serve learners with ASD likely have more access to professional support when a life event prevents them from competently practicing due to a sudden physical or mental illness.

Confidentiality

Whether practitioners work in a school, clinic, home, hospital, or other setting, the confidentiality of the learner and family must be respected and protected. Confidentiality occurs when practitioners protect sensitive learner information from being disclosed without the learner's or family's knowledge. Confidentiality is a promise practitioners make to learners and their families and must be upheld. Practitioners may sometimes have trouble maintaining confidentiality when, in an effort to help, well-meaning colleagues ask about confidential learner information. Other times, confidentiality may be threatened when practitioners let important learner information "slip" during casual conversations with fellow practitioners, families, or friends.

Respecting the privacy of the learners and families with whom practitioners work, however, is an ethical and legal obligation (Family Educational Rights and Privacy Act, 1974; Health Insurance Portability and Accountability Act, 2004). There are a few exceptions under which practitioners can disclose personal information about learners without their explicit consent. The most obvious exception is when a learner's life is threatened, or the learner threatens the life of someone else. There may be other expectations depending on federal or state laws, and the professional rules under which a particular practitioner operates. For example, in most helping professions, practitioners are considered "mandated reporters" who have a duty to report learner neglect or abuse to local authorities.

Maintaining confidentiality does not prohibit practitioners from discussing challenging cases or ethical dilemmas with trusted colleagues, but it does require them to be considerate and careful about the information they share. For example, practitioners should never share identifiable personal information, including photographs or video recordings, without explicit permission from families or the learners themselves. Practitioners should also be very judicious about where conversations about learners occur. Practitioners should engage in professional conversations that take place in professional settings. Discussing the behaviors of a learner in a busy classroom or in a crowded coffee shop, even if their name is not used, is not appropriate. One never knows when a learner's sibling, neighbor, or grandparent could be sitting at a nearby table.

Accountability

Practitioners are accountable to others for their professional behavior. Professional accountability is not about compliance with rigid standards or rules. It is a commitment that practitioners make to themselves and others to take responsibility for their professional actions, no matter the consequences. Practitioners are accountable to learners, colleagues, and professional communities. They are responsible for the individual decisions they make about learners and their progress, the work they engage in alongside their colleagues, and how they represent their profession.

Accountability to Learners

Practitioners are accountable for their learners' progress. This does not mean that practitioners' work should be judged solely on prespecified learner performance criteria. Rather, they should make decisions about learner progress based on the best evidence available, effectiveness in the moment, practitioner experience, and learner preferences. Being accountable to learners also means advocating for learners' best interests, listening to learners, and helping them advocate for themselves. Practitioners should always, to the greatest extent possible, include learners' voices in decisions about their services and encourage learner self-determination. Being accountable also includes evaluating the effects of your actions. If the decision a practitioner makes results in positive outcomes, the practitioner should help the learner and family work to make those changes sustainable. If a practitioner learns that the decision they made is not benefiting the learner, they take responsibility and change their behavior to better meet the needs of learners and their families.

Accountability to Colleagues

Being accountable to colleagues means being a good team member. Practitioners serving learners with ASD almost always collaborate with professionals from other disciplines to provide a menu of necessary services. Collaborating across disciplines and services can sometimes be difficult but practitioners must be willing to work together for the benefit of the learners they serve. Accountability means that you are open to new ideas that are in the best interest of the learner, despite possible discomfort with new areas of learning. Each profession has a different body of scientifically validated research with which they are familiar, and each practitioner brings a different strength to the menu of necessary services. Practitioners must contribute their expertise across service teams while respecting the contributions of others. For example, a BCBA who is unfamiliar with an intervention recommended by a learner's occupational therapist may contribute by developing a useful data collection system to assess the effectiveness of the intervention.

Accountability to colleagues also means that members of a profession should hold themselves and each other responsible. Sometimes practitioners commit obvious ethical violations. It is important that when a practitioner sees a colleague commit an ethical violation, whether knowingly or unknowingly, that practitioner take corrective action. For example, if a teacher witnesses a BCBA colleague implementing an aversive procedure to decrease nonharmful learner behavior without first recommending reinforcement, it is the teacher's responsibility to address the issue. That may mean having a difficult conversation with the colleague or the colleague's supervisor. For more egregious ethical violations, practitioners may also need to make a report to a licensing or certification board, or take some other uncomfortable but necessary action, to correct the issue and prevent future ethical violations from occurring. All practitioners must also be accountable to themselves, meaning that they admit to their mistakes and correct them. It also means that they do their best to avoid ethical errors by practicing their ethical fitness. Practitioners can do this by carefully and thoroughly working through tough ethical dilemmas when they encounter them. When practitioners are accountable to themselves and others, they demonstrate integrity and professional excellence.

AN ETHICAL DECISION-MAKING MODEL

Decision-making models are helpful for guiding problem solving around difficult professional dilemmas, including dilemmas around choosing and implementing EBPs. Many different ethical decision-making models can be found throughout the professional literature in education, psychology, and social work (e.g., McAuliffe & Chenoweth, 2008) to guide practitioners. Most of these ethical decision-making models are broadly relevant to any ethical dilemma that a practitioner may encounter. Below, we present an adapted, multistep ethical decision-making model from the field of behavior analysis (Rosenberg & Schwartz, 2019), along with case scenarios to help practitioners identify and problem-solve dilemmas common to recommending, implementing, and evaluating EBPs (see Figure 7.1 for a flowchart of the ethical decision-making process).

Step 1: Clarify the Problem

An important first step in ethical decision making is for the practitioner to pinpoint exactly what dilemma they are facing. Oftentimes, practitioners believe they have encountered an ethical dilemma when faced with a "right" versus "wrong" issue. For example, practitioners may identify an ethical issue when they observe colleagues misrepresenting their credentials, intentionally misreporting data, or engaging in unsavory hiring practices. While these are all concerning practices that should be addressed, they represent instances of "right" versus "wrong" dilemmas. For example, it is "right" for practitioners to represent their credentials truthfully and "wrong" to misrepresent them. When a colleague misrepresents their credentials, the practitioner needs to address it, even though it may lead to a difficult or uncomfortable conversation.

True ethical dilemmas, on the other hand, are those predicaments in which practitioners are presented with choices where two "right" values are pitted against each other. According to noted ethicist Rushworth Kidder, we are often presented with true ethical dilemmas when we encounter choices that pit truth against loyalty, individualism against community, short-term outcomes against long-term

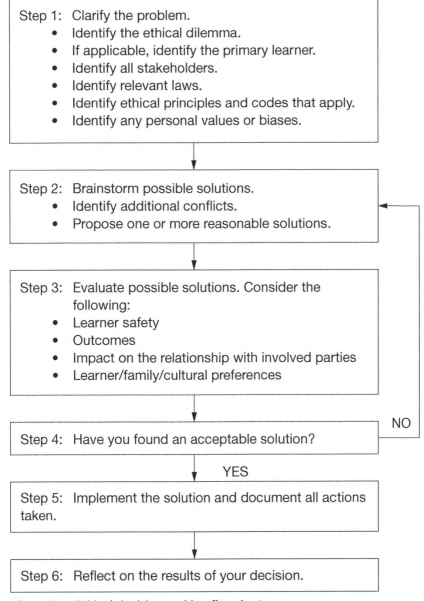

Figure 7.1. Ethical decision-making flowchart

outcomes, or justice against mercy (Kidder, 2009). Identifying the ethical dilemma is arguably the most important step in ethical decision making because it influences each successive step in the problem-solving process. We share the following case study to illustrate an example of putting the ethical decision-making process into action with a "right" versus "right" ethical dilemma.

CASE STUDY

Kendra is a kindergarten teacher at a local elementary school. She is currently in her second year of teaching and is working with experienced educators who have been assigned to be her mentors. She has 20 students in her classroom. Sami, one of Kendra's students, has autism spectrum disorder and qualifies for special education. Kendra consults with Sami's special education teacher and the paraprofessional in her classroom regarding Sami's learning goals. Sami enjoys school and has many friends in his class. He participates in all group activities and his favorite parts of the day are free-choice time and recess. Sami struggles with one-on-one work time and does not always complete his assignments. He gets off task easily and engages his peers in conversation. Kendra is concerned about Sami's off-task behavior because it interferes both with his learning and with the learning of his peers.

She brought this concern to her two mentor teachers for guidance. Joel is a first grade teacher and Talley teaches second grade. Joel and Talley both agreed that Kendra should keep Sami in from recess. Kendra knew that other teachers in the building keep students in from recess to finish their work, but she is concerned that keeping Sami in from recess would affect his learning in other areas. Sami, like all young children, benefits from academic learning breaks, physical activity, and opportunities to engage with his friends socially. She also knew from her training that this would be considered a "punishment" procedure. She knew that there may be other less restrictive, reinforcement-based strategies that she could try first, but she also wanted to respect the advice of her mentors. Kendra asked Joel and Talley if they had any other ideas, but they continued to tell her that keeping Sami in from recess to complete his work is the best option. Kendra then tried to decide what she should do next.

Step 1: Clarify the Problem

Kendra acknowledged that her ethical radar was triggered. She identified that she was experiencing an ethical dilemma in which there may be two "right" options. It was "right" for her to respect and honor the advice of her experienced mentors and it was also "right" for her to consider less restrictive strategies that would not prevent Sami's participation in recess.

Once the dilemma is identified, the practitioner must then identify the primary learner who is most impacted by the dilemma and any other relevant stakeholders impacted by the dilemma. In a school, the person at the center of a dilemma is often a particular learner. Other relevant stakeholders may be the family of the primary learner, other learners in the classroom, or school staff and administration. Next, the practitioner must identify relevant laws, ethical principles, and codes applicable to the dilemma. For example, the practitioner must consider whether the ethical dilemma involves facts that legally mandate them to report to law enforcement or child protective services. If so, the practitioner is obligated to report.

The practitioner must also consider the ethical professional principles and codes under which they operate. For example, social workers must adhere to the National Association of Social Workers *Code of Ethics* (2017), school psychologists must adhere to the National Association of School Psychologists *Principles for Professional Ethics* (2020b), and special educators may adhere to the Council for Exceptional Children *Code of Ethics and Practice Standards* (CEC, 2015). Finally, the practitioner must have the self-awareness to identify any personal values or biases that may affect the decision-making process (Mattison, 2000). We all have our own social learning histories that impact our personal values, preferences, and biases. One of the most challenging steps of ethical decision making is recognizing and reflecting on how those values, preferences, and biases affect ethical decisions. Practitioners must acknowledge when their personal values conflict with the values of their learners and stakeholders and take measured steps to resolve that conflict.

Kendra identified that Sami was the focus of this dilemma. She also identified that it was important to include other stakeholders in this decision, such as Sami's family, his special education teacher, and the paraprofessional in her classroom. Kendra identified that if she were to implement a new intervention, all these people should be involved in the process.

When identifying relevant laws, ethical principles, and codes, Kendra determined that it was important to consider the school district policies regarding recess time. In Kendra's school district, recess is not a required part of the day for learners. Although policies don't prohibit keeping learners in from recess, Kendra knew that physical activity is important for young children. She also studied applied behavior analysis (ABA) in her program and knew that the ABA ethical code has information about using punishment procedures. Kendra evaluated the *Ethics Code for Behavior Analysts* (Behavior Analyst Certification Board [BACB], 2020). The code described that the use of punishment, such as removing recess time, should not be used prior to using less intrusive strategies. It also describes the importance of assessment and evaluating the effects of strategies implemented.

Kendra then considered her own personal values and biases that may affect her decision making. She identified that she is still new to the teaching profession and was worried about making the wrong decision. She recognized that she was not always confident and that this could get in the way of her decision making. She also had previously gone to her mentor teachers for advice and been grateful for their support. She did not want to hurt anyone's feelings by not taking their advice. Kendra also recognized that she has had many positive experiences in her student teaching with using reinforcement-based plans before implementing punishment procedures, such as removing recess. She wanted to consider both the rationale of her mentor teachers and her own experiences with other strategies.

Step 2: Brainstorm Possible Solutions

The next step in the ethical decision-making process is for the practitioner to identify any conflicts that rose to the surface as they were clarifying the problem. For example, if the practitioner has identified that the ethical dilemma is a "right" versus "right" dilemma, already there is a situation in which two ethical values or principles are in conflict. These "true ethical dilemmas often arise when ethical principles seem to require a person to do two (or more) actions, but the person cannot do both (or all) of the actions" (Rosenberg & Schwartz, 2019, pp. 475–476). Similarly, professional ethical codes often conflict with each other, making "easy" decisions difficult in a practitioner's effort to adhere to their professional ethical responsibilities. Sometimes, professional ethical codes conflict with the cultural values of the learners and stakeholders involved. In each case, a conflict arises that must be acknowledged and addressed to the extent possible as the practitioner moves through the ethical decision-making process.

After identifying and addressing conflicts, the next step is to propose one or more reasonable solutions. It is often easiest to get started with this step by considering initial solutions based on their alignment with laws and professional ethical codes of conduct. However, practitioners may also brainstorm possible solutions that are not addressed by their profession's code of ethics or practice standards. If the practitioner has identified a "right" versus "right" dilemma, it is very likely that they will propose at least two solutions at this stage to identify and address the dilemma's inherent value conflict. This step is also an opportunity to consider possible ethical solutions that may be in opposition to the practitioner's own learning history, values, and biases. Consulting with a trusted colleague or friend at this stage regarding the dilemma and possible solutions is recommended for a few reasons. First, colleague feedback may help mitigate the impact of the practitioner's personal biases on the ethical decision-making process. Second, a colleague may provide valuable insight into the dilemma that was not initially present. Sometimes, we are so entrenched in our ethical dilemma that it is difficult to see all the factors affecting it. Trusted colleagues and friends can help analyze ethical dilemmas and possible solutions, so practitioners can move forward in the ethical decision-making process, evaluating those solutions with clarity. But remember, practitioners must always maintain learner confidentiality when they solicit feedback from coaches and colleagues.

Step 2: Brainstorm Possible Solutions

When clarifying her ethical dilemma, Kendra realized that she had several different options and that she was struggling to make a choice. She decided to speak with Omar, a friend who she met while in her teacher preparation program. She explained her "right" versus "right" decision, while ensuring that she didn't share Sami's name or personal information. She explained her concerns that keeping Sami in from recess might not be the right intervention and there were other things that she wanted to try. She also explained her concerns about her personal relationships with her mentors and that she worried about disregarding their advice. Omar reminded her that they learned about many different reinforcement-based procedures in their program that have an evidence base. He also explained that her mentor teachers were sharing advice based on their own experiences and that they would likely want her to use her own knowledge and ideas to make the decision that will be best for her learner. After speaking with Omar, Kendra brainstormed a few possible solutions:

- Implement the strategy of keeping Sami in during recess to complete unfinished work, as suggested by Kendra's mentor teachers.
- Implement a positive reinforcement system for completing work.
- Implement a visual schedule as an antecedent strategy.

Step 3: Evaluate Possible Solutions

Step 3 in the ethical decision-making process is to evaluate each proposed solution, considering four different factors: learner and stakeholder safety; learner outcomes; learner, family, and cultural preferences; and the impact that the solution will have on the practitioner's relationship with all involved parties. Learner and stakeholder safety should always be prioritized in the development of proposed ethical solutions. For example, when identifying and recommending an EBP to teach skills that involve the safety of the primary learner (e.g., crossing the road, riding the bus, cooking with a hot stove), an EBP should be chosen that maximizes learner safety and goals should be set using criteria that ensure the learner can perform the skill safely before supports are faded. Stakeholder safety must also be considered. This is especially relevant in cases where learners engage in aggressive behaviors that put themselves or others at risk of harm.

The next step in evaluating proposed solutions is to consider the primary learner outcome for each proposed solution. This is in alignment with utilitarianism, or end-based thinking, in which the possible outcome of each solution is considered. While it is important to evaluate the outcome of solutions on all involved parties, this step gives the practitioner the opportunity to consider what is in the best interest of the primary learner and the ethical value of beneficence or maximizing benefit to the client; a professional value found in most helping professions (e.g., APA, 2017; BACB, 2020; CEC, 2015).

Finally, practitioners must consider learner, family, and cultural preferences and the impact that the proposed solutions will have on their relationship with all involved parties. All learners belong to family and cultural groups with shared norms, beliefs, preferences, and learning histories. Practitioners must be aware of learners' cultural identities (as well as their own; see Step 1: Clarify the Problem) when considering ethical solutions so they can make decisions that align with learner culture and family preferences. This not only increases the likelihood that learners and their families will receive a greater benefit from the practitioner's ethical decision, but it also helps the practitioner avoid making professional ethical decisions in direct conflict with learner and family cultural practices that negatively impact their relationship. Making ethical decisions about EBPs without consideration of student and family cultural variables may result in barriers to EBP implementation and harm to the learner (Beaulieu et al., 2019).

Step 3: Evaluate the Solutions

Kendra evaluated each of the possible solutions, while considering Sami's safety and the safety of those around him, outcomes for Sami related to his learning goals, Sami's family and cultural preferences, and the impact the solution would have on her relationship with Sami, Sami's family, Sami's school team, and mentor teachers.

Solution 1. Implement the strategy of keeping Sami in during recess to complete unfinished work, as suggested by Kendra's mentor teachers.

When Kendra considered solution number one, she identified that keeping Sami in from recess would not interfere with Sami's safety, but it would interfere with his opportunity to engage in physical and social play with his peers. She identified that Sami has learning goals related to social skills and that recess is a primary time for him to practice those skills. It was also important for her to consider Sami's learning goals around work completion. While keeping Sami in from recess might help target his work completion goal, it would simultaneously interfere with his social goals. Kendra reached out to Sami's family to discuss her concerns and they shared their values around outside play and being physically active. They requested that Sami get as much time to play outdoors as possible. In considering her relationship with Sami and other stakeholders, Kendra identified that Sami would not like staying in from recess and that this solution could impact her relationship with Sami and his family.

Solution 2. Implement a positive reinforcement system for completing work.

When Kendra considered solution number two, she identified that implementing a positive reinforcement system for work completion would not interfere with Sami's safety. When considering Sami's learning goals, Kendra was not sure if a positive reinforcement system would be sufficient to help Sami because it often appeared that he didn't always understand the directions or forgot what the class was supposed to be working on. She did think that positive reinforcement would be helpful to increase Sami's work completion and knew that positive reinforcement is an EBP, but wanted to consider other strategies as well. Kendra considered that Sami's family would likely have supported this plan because it did not involve Sami missing recess. This plan may also have had a positive impact on Kendra's relationship with Sami. She would still be concerned about a negative impact on her relationship with her mentor teachers if she did not take their advice to keep Sami in from recess.

Solution 3. Implement a visual schedule as an antecedent strategy.

When Kendra considered solution number three, she identified that implementing a visual schedule would not interfere with Sami's safety. She also thought that it could be helpful for Sami in remembering what he should be working on and knew that visual supports have a strong evidence base. Sami's family would also likely support this plan because Sami would still be able to engage in outside play and would be able to see on his schedule when that is going to happen. It might have been motivating for Sami to complete his work if he could see that recess was happening afterward. This solution may have positively impacted Kendra's relationship with the paraprofessional in her classroom and Sami's general education teacher long term because the visual schedule could be a tool that he used across different activities throughout the day, helping him stay on task in his work with other teachers as well.

Step 4: Propose an Acceptable Solution

After careful consideration of the factors in Step 3, the practitioner should identify whether an acceptable solution has presented itself. They might consider the following questions to make a careful decision about the final solution: Is there a solution that continues to present itself over and over to me because it feels like the "best" option? Is the solution consistent with one or more of my profession's ethical values and codes? Does the acceptable solution maximize learner safety and limit harm more than other solutions? Is the solution aligned with my learner's cultural identities and family preferences? If the practitioner answers "yes" to many of these questions, then an acceptable solution has likely been identified. The practitioner's final steps, then, are to implement the solution and reflect upon the results of the decision. If the practitioner has trouble identifying an acceptable solution at this step, we recommend moving back to Step 2 and moving through the decision-making process again.

Step 4: Propose an Acceptable Solution

Kendra found herself continuing to come back to possible solutions two and three and decided to consider combining the two solutions. Using positive reinforcement in conjunction with a visual schedule would allow Kendra to use EBPs to target Sami's goal around work completion and allow Sami to play outside during recess. These solutions seemed to be a better fit than solution one (keeping Sami in from recess) because they incorporated teaching Sami new skills that will help him with work completion and allowed him to go to recess and engage in physical activity during the school day. This solution was also more aligned with Kendra's values and philosophy about teaching than the one that used a punishment procedure as the first intervention. Combining solutions two and three maximized the learning time for Sami during the school day and were more in line with the values of Sami's family.

Step 5: Implement the Solution and Document All Actions Taken

Once an acceptable solution has been proposed, the practitioner should implement the plan with fidelity and document the steps taken throughout the decision-making process. To implement the solution with fidelity, the practitioner must make a plan for how to implement the solution (much like creating a teaching lesson plan or a behavior plan) and then follow those steps as intended. If the practitioner has already documented steps throughout the decision-making process, drawing up a plan for implementing the solution should be relatively easy. During this step in the process, practitioners might consider if there are additional resources to seek out and the best way to involve all of the stakeholders identified in previous steps. Documentation of the decision steps and the solution are both integral to following the ethical decision-making process. Documentation allows the practitioner to easily share their decision-making process with others and guides later reflection.

Step 5: Implement the Solution and Document All Actions Taken
Kendra decided to combine solutions two and three and implement a visual schedule with positive reinforcement. To implement this solution, she first identified how she would go about implementing this plan. The first step involved speaking with Sami and his family to explain the proposed solution and gain their input. The second step was to get feedback on the plan with Sami's school team, including his general education teacher and the paraprofessional. Third, Kendra explained her plan to her mentor teachers. Finally, Kendra wrote out the plan, created the visual schedule, and determined a reinforcement system for Sami. To evaluate the effects of the plan, Kendra knew that she would need data on Sami's work completion, so she also identified a data collection system to use. Kendra documented these steps and reflected on them after the plan had been implemented for a few days.

Step 6: Reflect upon the Results of the Decision

The final step of the ethical decision-making process is to reflect upon the results of the decision. When engaged in this step of the process, practitioners might consider whether the solution was successful, whether there are additional steps that need to be taken, and what was learned throughout the process that could guide future ethical decision making (Rosenberg & Schwartz, 2019). This reflection may take place by gathering and monitoring new information as the solution is implemented, reviewing documentation generated throughout the ethical decision-making process, or consulting with a trusted colleague again. This step is important in determining whether the current ethical dilemma has been solved, if the solution needs any adjustments, or if an entirely new course of action is necessary. Reflection also helps practitioners build and maintain "ethical fitness" to improve their ability to make confident and competent ethical decisions going forward.

Step 6: Reflect upon the Results of the Decision
After completing the steps that Kendra identified to implement the solution to her ethical dilemma, Kendra spent time analyzing the data on Sami's work completion and reflecting on the results of her decision. She reviewed her notes and the data that Sami's school team gathered on his work completion. Overall, Kendra was happy with the decision that she made during the ethical decision-making process. Sami reported that his work is easier now that his schedule reminds him what work he needs to get done. Sami was making progress on his goal and his family was happy with the plan that was being implemented. They have even started using a visual schedule at home, which they reported was going very well. Sami's school team also expressed their support of the plan and found it helpful across different activities throughout the school day. When Kendra spoke with her mentor teachers, they were impressed that she had considered her learner's unique needs and used a structured process to make her decision. They even offered some simple classroom-friendly ideas for collecting data on work completion!

Kendra learned that it is important to consider the advice of her mentor teachers, but that she also needed to consider the individual needs of her learner and analyze practices that are evidence based, when trying to decide about student programming. Kendra is now even more equipped to make ethical decisions going forward!

SUMMARY

Working with learners with ASD is a complex and rewarding undertaking. Learners with ASD are individuals who present with unique strengths and areas of need and who bring with them personal histories including culture, gender, interests, and learning histories. Practitioners who have the opportunity to work with learners with ASD, therefore, have the responsibility of being prepared to meet learners where they are and to help them achieve their ambitious goals through the ethical application of high-quality instruction and EBPs.

Understanding ethics is an important component of being prepared to work with learners with ASD and other disabilities. Embedding ethics into one's work is an active practice. Ethics are not clear cut; they are difficult and sometimes murky. They are not the right vs. wrong decisions—those are easy. Ethics are the right vs. right decisions. Practitioners need to become and remain ethically fit to do the difficult work of identifying ethical behavior and resolving ethical dilemmas. Ethical fitness is the practice of engaging in regular ethical workouts, that is, having a regularly scheduled time when trusted colleagues and mentors discuss ethics, dilemmas they are facing in their practice, and how their own disciplinary ethical code addresses them. As part of one's ethical fitness regime, it is important to have a process to use when faced with an ethical dilemma. Decision-making processes must be systematic and transparent. Adopting a decision-making process is helpful both when making decisions about evaluating ethical dilemmas and when selecting and evaluating EBPs with learners.

Working with learners with ASD and their families provides practitioners with opportunities to meet interesting, diverse, and remarkable individuals. It is important that practitioners greet every learner as an individual and consider the whole learner, all parts of an identity that a learner brings to school when identifying and assessing behavior, selecting interventions, and evaluating the effectiveness and acceptability of those interventions. In this chapter, we discuss the importance of ethical decision making when selecting, implementing, and evaluating EBPs. As ethical practitioners, we must always keep an eye on outcomes. Do learners have goals that are appropriately ambitious? Are the programs being implemented resulting in meaningful outcomes for the learners? That is the true measure of ethical practice, teaching skills and behaviors that result in an improved the quality of life of learners with ASD and their families.

APPLICATION ACTIVITIES

1. Reflect on the following questions after reading the chapter:

   a. Describe two common philosophical approaches. How do these approaches inform ethical decision making?

b. What are three basic ethical considerations? Identify a time when you may have observed a colleague violate one or more ethical considerations. What did you do at the time of the violation? What would you do differently after reading this chapter?

2. Different disciplines have different ways of evaluating empirical data and different standards for what constitutes an evidence-based practice. How might you collaborate with members of an interdisciplinary team to determine if a practice is being recommended is evidence based?

3. Use the following case scenario to work through a "right versus right" ethical dilemma about recommending an EBP for a learner with ASD:

You are working as a teacher in a special education program at an elementary school in your community. Taylor, one of your students, is in first grade. She enjoys going to school and making new friends. She loves to play outside and likes activities that involve music and movement. You are concerned because Taylor has recently started hitting her peers when they are nearby. Taylor previously engaged in behaviors like this but stopped last year when she began using a new token system. Taylor's family and other teachers are worried about this behavior because it involves the safety of Taylor and her friends. You decide to call a meeting with Taylor's interdisciplinary team, which consists of yourself, a general education teacher, an occupational therapist (OT), and the school psychologist. During the team meeting, Taylor's OT suggests using a weighted vest to intervene with Taylor's hitting behavior and promote self-regulation. The rest of the team agrees that this sounds like a good next step. This suggestion triggers your ethical radar. While you want to be collaborative and open to the team's ideas, you also know that weighted vests are not currently an evidence-based practice for the purposed outcome of decreasing challenging behavior. You aren't sure whether to go along with the team's ideas or raise your concerns about the effectiveness of the weighted vest in decreasing Taylor's hitting.

ADDITIONAL RESOURCES

Consider taking an implicit bias test on Harvard's Project Implicit website to help you identify your own biases prior to engaging in the ethical decision-making process. https://implicit.harvard.edu/implicit/takeatest.html

Consider viewing the Behavior Analyst Certification Board Ethics Resource webpage for a list of ethics-related toolkits, podcasts, and more. https://www.bacb.com/ethics-infor mation/ethics-resources/

Consider reading *How Good People Make Tough Choices* by Rushworth Kidder (2009).

Consider reading *Practical Ethics for Effective Treatment of Autism Spectrum Disorder* by Brodhead, Cox, & Quigley (2018).

NOTE

1. We all identify as White, monolinguistic, cisgender women trained in special education and applied behavior analysis (ABA). We are all deeply committed to teaching future practitioners about ethical issues.

8

Evidence-Based Practices to Enhance Social Competence

Jeff Sigafoos, Amarie Carnett, Mark F. O'Reilly,
and Giulio E. Lancioni

■ ■ ■

INTRODUCTION AND OVERVIEW

Educational efforts are often directed at developing learners' social competence, which has been defined as "the ability to engage in meaningful interactions with others" (Junge et al., 2020, p. 1). Goodman and colleagues (2015) noted that social competence objectives are an increasingly prominent component of contemporary early childhood education. McCay and Keyes (2001) highlighted the continuing relevance of social competence instruction in the primary or elementary school years. Moving on to the higher grades of middle and secondary or high school, Stichter and colleagues (2016) expressed the need for, and potential value of, enhancing adolescents' social competence through school-based programming. Beyond the confines of school, many adults are also likely to benefit from developing greater social competence (Kusché et al., 2020). The development and enhancement of social competence could thus be seen as a relevant intervention goal across the lifespan.

Several reasons have been given for intervening to enhance social competence among children, adolescents, and adults. Han and Kemple (2006), for example, argued that developing social competence is critical for becoming "a successful social member of human society" (p. 241). McLaughlin and colleagues (2017) viewed social competence as "one of the most significant areas of early learning and development" (p. 21). They further suggested that social skills (a key component of social competence) can facilitate learning and promote positive peer relations. Both of these potential benefits could have long-term positive impacts on a person's overall well-being and quality of life. Supporting this view, Segrin and Taylor (2007) discovered that social skills were positively correlated with greater psychological well-being (e.g., happiness and quality of life) in their study of a large sample ($N = 703$) of adults. Collectively, the reasons listed previously provide a compelling rationale for incorporating social skills instruction into educational curricula.

The need for systematic efforts to enhance social competence by teaching specific social skills would seem particularly compelling for learners with autism

189

spectrum disorder (ASD). This is because learners with ASD are likely to have difficulty with social-communicative interactions (Mells Yavuz et al., 2019). Indeed, social-communication impairment is one of the two core deficits that define ASD, the other being repetitive behaviors and a restricted range of interests (American Psychiatric Association, 2013).

The range of social functioning difficulties associated with ASD is extensive (Frye, 2018; Mells Yavuz et al., 2019). Learners with ASD are likely to have considerable difficulty with making and keeping friends, initiating and maintaining social interactions, and forming emotionally satisfying social relationships with others (Frye, 2018; Mells Yavuz et al., 2019). Intervention is clearly indicated for such learners to offset the potential negative impacts of impaired social functioning on their happiness, quality of life, learning, and ability to effectively interact with family and friends and more generally participate in society. But how can practitioners help learners with ASD develop greater social-communication skills?

This chapter seeks to answer this question by reviewing evidence-based practices for teaching a number of key or foundational social-communication skills to learners with ASD. First, we aim to delineate key social-communication skills that contribute to social competence. Second, we review intervention studies that have evaluated procedures for teaching several specific types of social-communication skills to learners with ASD. The specific social-communication skills covered in this chapter are (a) requesting and rejecting, (b) gaining attention, (c) greeting behavior, (d) conversational skills, (e) joint attention, and (f) peer interaction skills. The overall aim of this chapter is to inform educational practitioners of evidence-based practices that have been developed for teaching a variety of important social-communication skills to learners with ASD. Information of this type is intended to assist practitioners in the implementation of evidence-based instructional strategies for enhancing the social competence of learners with ASD.

DEFINING SOCIAL COMPETENCE

Social competence can be broadly conceptualized as a domain of adaptive behavior functioning that covers the extent to which one is successful or effective in relating to and interacting socially with others. This domain also encompasses "a person's age-appropriate knowledge and skills for functioning peacefully and creatively in his or her own community or social environment" (Orpinas & Horne, 2006, p. 108). In line with this conceptualization, social competence involves successfully getting along with others, forming and maintaining peer relationships, and adapting to varying social situations (Orpinas, 2010; Semrud-Clikeman, 2007). Social competence is often manifest through a range of social skills.

SOCIAL SKILLS

Social skills are learned behaviors that facilitate successful social interaction (Little et al., 2017). Social skills enable one to interact with others in a meaningful way (Greenspan, 1981). A person could therefore be seen as more socially competent when he or she has acquired specific social skills that facilitate success in getting along with others, forming and maintaining friendly peer relationships, and adapting to varying social situations. Put another way, achieving a high degree of social competence may depend to some extent on the successful acquisition, generalization, and maintenance of an array of specific social skills.

Many of the component skills that underpin social competence involve the use of communication behavior and, thus, could be classified as social-communication skills (Sigafoos et al., 2008). Examples of social-communication skills include (a) requesting and rejecting, (b) appropriately gaining attention, (c) participating in culturally and contextually relevant greeting rituals, (d) engaging in conversation, (e) establishing joint attention, and (f) interacting with peers. Social-communication skills of these types are ubiquitous features of everyday social interactions. They also happen to be areas where learners with ASD often show considerable difficulty (Chesnut et al., 2017; Loukusa et al., 2018). Unlike typically developing children, who appear to learn such skills rather incidentally, learners with ASD often seem to require explicit, deliberate, and structured teaching programs to develop effective social-communication skills. Consequently, interventions aimed at promoting the acquisition, generalization, and maintenance of social-communication skills are likely to be a major educational priority for many learners with ASD. Fortunately, educational practitioners can draw upon a considerable amount of research that has demonstrated effective instructional procedures for teaching social skills to learners with ASD (Radley et al., 2020). The next sections of this chapter will review strategies that have demonstrated successful acquisition, generalization, and maintenance of several specific social-communication skills.

FOUNDATIONAL SOCIAL-COMMUNICATION SKILLS

Requesting and Rejecting

Requesting and rejecting are foundational skills crucial to the development of social competence. Requesting and rejecting skills are also functional in the sense of being of considerable benefit to the child (Sigafoos, 2021), and they are also among the first uses or functions in children's communication development (Salley et al., 2020), including among children with ASD (Paparella et al., 2011). The ability to request preferred objects, activities, and assistance and reject nonpreferred objects and activities, for example, enables learners to express their wants and needs, indicate preferences, and exert some degree of control or self-determination over the environment, including others in the environment. Requesting and rejecting enable learners to access reinforcement and avoid aversive stimuli, respectively. Teaching foundational requesting and rejecting skills could thus be seen as an important educational priority for learners with ASD, given that many learners with ASD lack effective and socially appropriate requesting and rejecting skills.

Teaching Requesting Skills

A considerable amount of intervention research has investigated procedures for teaching requesting skills to learners with ASD. Most of this research has focused on teaching learners to request access to preferred objects or activities (Carnett et al., 2017; Drasgow et al., 2009). But there are also studies on teaching other types of requesting skills, such as requesting help or assistance, requesting an alternative when offered an incorrect or undesired item, and requesting a break from a learning task (Reichle & Wacker, 2017). Overall, this research has led to a number of evidence-based instructional strategies for teaching requesting skills to learners with ASD. Requesting (and rejecting) skills can occur using spoken words and sentences or via some type of augmentative and alternative communication (AAC) system. AAC could include the use of gestures, manual signs, and various aided systems, such as exchanging picture cards or selecting symbols on an electronic speech-generating device (Reichle et al., 2016).

One well-researched and widely used program for teaching aided (i.e., picture-based) requesting is the Picture-Exchange Communication System (PECS; Bondy & Frost, 2001). PECS is a manualized communication skills training program that is indicated for use with learners who are considered nonverbal, minimally verbal, or as having complex communication needs. These terms essentially refer to learners for whom speech and language is not sufficiently well developed to meet their everyday communication needs (Keen, Meadan, et al., 2016; Koegel et al., 2020). In the PECS program, learners are initially taught to exchange a picture of an object (e.g., a picture card with a drawing of a preferred toy on it) to obtain access to the corresponding preferred object or activity (e.g., to obtain access to the preferred toy). For learners who are minimally verbal, the exchange of picture cards thus provides them with a functional and socially acceptable means of requesting access to preferred objects and activities.

Alsayedhassan and colleagues (2020), for example, taught two parents to use the PECS protocol with their children with ASD. Both children were described as "nonverbal" or having "very limited expressive language" (p. 32). The intervention began by first undertaking an assessment to identify preferred objects (e.g., preferred food items and toys). The aim of the intervention was to teach the children to request preferred objects by exchanging photographs of the objects. Parents were trained to implement the PECS protocol via written and verbal instructions, modeling the procedures, and practicing while receiving feedback from the researchers. After gaining proficiency on the implementation steps, parents conducted the PECS training with the children. The children were first offered a preferred item and given 10 s to make a request by exchanging the corresponding photograph. If the child did not make a request within 10 s, the parent used hand-over-hand guidance to physically prompt the child to make the exchange. Once the exchange was made, the child received the requested item as reinforcement. After learning this initial exchange, children were then taught to seek out and approach the parent. In a third phase, the children were taught to discriminate between two preferred items.

In a multiple baseline across participants design, the researchers showed that both children learned to make discriminated requests with 100% accuracy when the parents implemented each phase of the PECS protocol. These results are consistent with the conclusions of a recent review of 25 studies, which indicated that the PECS program, as well as other AAC interventions, "show favorable outcomes for encouraging social-communication behavior" for children with ASD (Mahoney et al., 2018, p. 1). Given that consistency between home and school is important for promoting generalization and maintenance of social-communication skills, this study also points to a practical set of methods (i.e., instruction, modeling, practice, and feedback) that teachers could use to support parents (and perhaps also teaching assistants, peers, and other educational support staff) with the implementation of social-communication interventions.

Cheung and colleagues (2020) described another intervention approach for teaching requesting skills to children with ASD that appears particularly well suited for use within various classroom instructional activities. This study involved three (6- to 8-year-old) learners with ASD who attended a private school in Hong Kong. The intervention focused on teaching the learners to make unprompted spoken requests (e.g., "I want [object]." "I want [x quantity] [of object]") in response to communication temptations or evocative events created by the teacher (e.g., the teacher not providing enough materials or guidance for the learner to be able to complete an assigned task). A unique aspect of the study was that these communicative temptations were embedded into small-group instructional sessions within vocational learning tasks (e.g., preparing an order in a simulated fast-food restaurant) and within mathematics lessons (e.g., answering questions about a survey).

The teaching procedures involved embedding communicative opportunities or temptations within the learning activity, waiting 5 s for the learner to respond, and providing reinforcement (e.g., providing the correct number of materials or giving additional guidance) for correct responses. If the learner did not respond correctly within 5 s, then the teacher used a flexible prompt fading procedure to recruit a correct response. Flexible prompt fading consisted of presenting a hierarchy of prompts (e.g., presenting written text, then modeling one word of the response, and then using a full verbal model of the correct response) to assist the learner in producing the correct spoken request.

The effects of the intervention on the percentage of correct responses to the communicative opportunities were evaluated in a multiple baseline across participants design. The results showed that all three children reached 100% correct responding on the communication targets after only a few (3 to 5) days of intervention. These skills were also maintained. It is important to note, however, that maintenance was assessed at only one point in time, 5 days postintervention. Interestingly, the learners also showed improvement from 60% to 100% correct with respect to performance of the academic tasks in which the communication opportunities had been embedded. This suggests that embedding communication training into academic tasks not only promoted acquisition of educationally relevant requesting skills, but it also did not seem to hinder the children's academic learning in relation to those tasks. This study illustrates how communication intervention aimed at teaching requesting skills could be effectively incorporated into small-group instruction of vocational and academic (mathematics) tasks.

In contrast to the use of manualized treatments such as PECS, researchers have also evaluated intervention packages that bring together a number of different instructional tactics. Along these lines, Wójcik and colleagues (2020) evaluated an intervention package that combined the behavior chain interruption strategy (Carnett et al., 2017), audio scripting, and sufficient exemplar training. The behavior chain interruption strategy involved briefly interrupting a preferred activity by withholding a needed item to create the opportunity (motivation and need) for requesting continuation of the activity. Audio scripting was used as a response prompting strategy and was applied if correct requesting did not occur in response to the interruption itself. Audio scripting involved playing a recording of the correct requesting response (e.g., "I don't have [name of missing materials].") for the learner to imitate. Use of sufficient exemplars was intended to promote generalization and involved teaching the learners to request a range of different [missing] items (e.g., various toys, toothbrush, and book) within three different activities (i.e., play, self-help, and academic tasks).

The study involved three (4- to 6-year-old) boys with ASD who were taught to express requests for missing items using short sentences (e.g., "I don't have the toothbrush."). With these procedures, all three children learned to make the targeted requests and showed generalization to new communication partners. A novel aspect of the study was the inclusion of assessment probes to ascertain whether the learners would make requests even when this was unnecessary—that is, when there were no missing items. The results suggest that the learners did not overgeneralize the use of their newly acquired requesting responses in that requests did not occur unless there was an item missing and thus when there was in fact a need to make a request. This study provides a useful example of how a teacher could assemble an intervention program by combining a number of previously researched instructional tactics. This study also provides an excellent example of how instruction to teach requests for missing items can be integrated into the regular primary school curriculum.

Teaching Rejecting Skills

Compared to studies on teaching requesting, there are relatively fewer studies on teaching rejecting skills to learners with ASD. Sigafoos and colleagues (2004) summarized seven studies that demonstrated successful instructional procedures for teaching rejecting skills to learners with ASD and other developmental disabilities. Two specific rejecting skills were taught across these seven studies, specifically rejecting nonpreferred objects and rejecting wrong items. The instructional approaches used for teaching these rejecting skills were similar across the seven studies and generally included several steps. First, the learner was offered a nonpreferred or wrong item. Second, the learner had a certain amount of time (e.g., generally up to 10 s) to produce the targeted rejecting response, which could be saying, signing, or selecting a graphic symbol to indicate "No, thanks." Third, if the targeted rejecting response did not occur within that time, the teacher delivered some type of response prompt (e.g., modeling the correct response or physically assisting the learner to make the response). Fourth, contingent upon the occurrence of the targeted rejecting response, whether prompted or not, the nonpreferred or wrong item was removed. The removal of the nonpreferred or wrong item was assumed to function as an effective type of reinforcement for the rejecting response. Alternatively, when presented with a nonpreferred or incorrect item, the learner could be taught (using an appropriate response prompt) to indicate "No" and then request an alternative (e.g., "No, thanks. I want [name of object] instead.").

Groskreutz and colleagues (2014) provided an interesting example of teaching a rejecting response to two (7- to 9-year-old) boys with ASD. The aim of the study was to teach the participants to use a manual sign ("Stop") to escape from a range of nonpreferred stimuli. Nonpreferred stimuli included a variety of irritants, such as the noise of a vacuum cleaner or alarm clock. The intervention occurred in the learners' respective classroom and consisted of presenting a specific nonpreferred stimulus and then prompting the learner to produce the manual sign for "Stop." The prompting procedure included progressive time delay and graduated guidance. That is, the instructor waited increasing periods of time for the response to occur (3 to 5 s). If the sign did not occur within this time, then the instructor used the least amount of physical guidance necessary to assist the learner in making the sign. Once the sign occurred, the nonpreferred stimulus was removed for 30 s. Thus, the reinforcement for producing the manual sign was the resulting cessation of the nonpreferred stimulus.

A number of different nonpreferred stimuli were used in training as a way of programming for generalization (i.e., use of the Train Sufficient Exemplars strategy; Stokes & Baer, 1977). With these procedures, both boys learned to independently produce the rejecting response when nonpreferred stimuli were impinging on the environment. Furthermore, the response generalized to nontraining contexts. Another interesting outcome from this study was that various forms of problem behavior previously exhibited by the learners in the presence of nonpreferred stimuli (e.g., crying, ear covering, and throwing items) decreased as the boys learned to use the manual sign to reject. This suggests that the new rejecting response effectively replaced some of these learners' problem behaviors. Given that many learners with ASD seem to react negatively to various nonpreferred stimuli, such as loud noises, the present study illustrates a promising approach for replacing the learners' negative reactions with a more proactive way to indicate displeasure, that is, using a socially acceptable form of rejecting.

In summary, requesting and rejecting are foundational communication skills that are necessary to learn so that the person can express their wants and needs in ways that are socially appropriate. A range of requesting and rejecting skills is likely to be an intervention priority, such as requesting preferred objects, requesting assistance, and rejecting nonpreferred objects and activities. Data from a large number of studies have demonstrated the acquisition, generalization, and maintenance of requesting and rejecting skills by learners with ASD. Effective instructional strategies generally include (a) creating opportunities for requesting or rejecting, (b) prompting the targeted response, and (c) reinforcing the response by providing the requested event or removing the rejected stimulus. Over time, independent responding can be achieved by gradually fading out the use of response prompts by delaying these for longer and longer periods and using lessening amounts of prompting. Using this general instructional paradigm, learners with ASD have been successfully taught to engage in requests (or reject items) using words, sentences, and manual signs, and by exchanging pictures or selecting graphic symbols on a speech-generating device.

Teaching Attention-Gaining Skills

The ability to recruit attention effectively is an important aspect of social competence (Alber & Heward, 2001). It is an area of social-communicative functioning that appears challenging for many learners with ASD. In particular, children with ASD may experience difficulty in the acquisition, generalization, and maintenance of socially appropriate attention-gaining skills. In support of this claim, Bourque and Goldstein (2020) reported on six preschool children with ASD who were being taught to use a speech-generating device with peers. The children learned to make requests and comments but showed minimal progress in learning to gain peers' attention. In the absence of such skills, many learners with ASD are likely to rely on difficult-to-interpret prelinguistic gestures to recruit attention (Keen, Meadan, et al., 2016). Examples of prelinguistic gestures could include looking at or moving toward another person, moving one's body in an animated manner or vocalizing in the presence of another person, or simply making eye contact. Others may develop challenging behavior, such as aggression or self-injury, to gain attention (Love et al., 2009). Intervention to teach socially appropriate attention-gaining skills is therefore likely to be indicated for many learners with ASD.

There are several specific purposes and potential benefits of teaching socially appropriate attention-gaining skills. Acquisition of such skills may help to replace idiosyncratic or problematic forms of behavior that are maintained by the resulting attention from parents, teachers, or peers (see Chapter 10). In addition, when a learner with ASD acquires culturally appropriate, socially appropriate, and age-appropriate attention-gaining skills, it is possible that their success in engaging socially with others—and their overall social status—might also improve. Effective and appropriate attention-gaining skills will also likely be of direct benefit to learners who enjoy social interaction because the resulting attention will be naturally reinforcing for them. In other cases, gaining a listener's attention is a prerequisite for entering into additional social-communicative exchanges.

With respect to soliciting reinforcing attention or social interaction, Sigafoos and Meikle (1996) evaluated a set of instructional procedures for teaching two 8-year-old boys with ASD to recruit attention. The study was conducted in the classroom by the children's teacher. Prior to intervention both boys used challenging behavior (e.g., aggression, self-injury, and disruption) to gain attention. To address this lack of socially appropriate attention-gaining skills, one boy was taught to lightly tap the teacher's hand, whereas the other boy (who had some imitative speech) was taught to call out the teacher's name.

Teaching occurred over a series of 10-minute sessions. Sessions were scheduled into the classroom routine two times each day and from 3 to 5 days each week. Within each session, the teacher created four opportunities for the children to recruit attention. She did this by sitting nearby but not attending to the child. After creating each opportunity, the teacher initially waited 1 s before prompting each child to use their respective targeted attention-gaining response (i.e., either tapping the teacher's hand or calling her name). As soon as the child produced the attention-gaining response, the teacher acknowledged the child's attempt ("*Yes, you asked for me.*") and gave him contingent attention for the next 60 s. If the child did not produce the attention-getting response, the teacher prompted the child to make the response. To prompt the hand-tapping gesture, the teacher used graduated guidance, which involved providing the least amount of physical guidance necessary to evoke the correct response (Miltenberger, 2011). To prompt the other child, the teacher provided an imitative model ("*Say Beth.*").

After this initial phase, when prompting occurred after a 1-s delay, the delay interval was increased to 3 s, a procedure known as *progressive time delay*. The increase in the wait time from 1 to 3 s was intended as a way of fading out the need for prompting by giving the children more time to produce an independent response. With the 3-s delay in place, both boys learned to independently make their respective attention-getting responses within about 18 sessions, that is within about 72 teaching opportunities. Interestingly, as the intervention progressed, challenging behavior decreased, suggesting that the children's challenging behavior had, in fact, been replaced by the newly taught attention-gaining skills. The children also showed fairly good maintenance of their newly acquired attention-gaining skills after 1 month. Overall, the results of this study suggest that an intervention package—consisting of progressive time delay, response prompting, and contingent attention or social interaction—was successful in teaching two boys with ASD to gain their teacher's attention using socially acceptable communication responses. The progression from a 1- to a 3-s time delay could be seen as a type of errorless instructional format (Mueller et al., 2007).

In addition to this errorless strategy, the instructional package also included (a) creating the need for communication by withholding attention, (b) using response prompts that were individualized to each learner's targeted response form (i.e., graduated guidance for the tapping response and verbal modeling for the spoken name-calling response), and (c) delivering contingent teacher attention to reinforce the children's use of their new attention-gaining response forms. All of these instructional components (i.e., creating opportunities, progressive time delay, response prompting, and contingent reinforcement) are well-established instructional strategies for teaching learners with ASD and other developmental disabilities (Brown et al., 2019).

In the Sigafoos and Meikle (1996) study, contingent teacher attention appeared to be sufficiently reinforcing to ensure acquisition and maintenance of the new attention-gaining responses. In some cases, however, social interaction or gaining attention might not be sufficiently reinforcing to maintain socially appropriate attention-getting responses. In this case, one might teach children to first recruit a listener's attention so that they can then engage in another communicative interaction—which then results in a reinforcing consequence, such as requesting access to a preferred object.

To this end, Cipani (1990) described an intervention for teaching attention-gaining behavior to a 7-year-old boy and a 10-year-old girl. The intervention for both participants occurred in their classroom for children with significant cognitive disabilities. The aim of the intervention was to teach the children to tap the arm of the teacher or call her name to recruit her attention. Once the children had recruited the teacher's attention in this way, they could make a request for a needed but missing item using spoken-word requests. Instructional opportunities were conducted in the context of a morning snack routine. The children were given a bowl (for cereal) with one of several needed items missing (e.g., either the spoon, the cereal, or the milk). The teacher then walked away, and the children were given time (specifically 15 s) to gain the teacher's attention and then make a request for the needed but missing item. If the child did not initiate an attention-getting response within 15 s, a least-to-most prompting system was implemented to evoke the attention-getting response. Once that occurred, the teacher responded by saying, "*Yes, what do you want?*" and waiting for the child to make the correct request for the missing item. Once this request occurred, the teacher gave the child the missing item. With these procedures, both children reached a high level of proficiency in using the attention-getting response before making the request for the needed/missing item.

This is an important achievement; it is often critical to ensure that one has the attention of a listener before attempting to engage that listener in communication. It is also critical for children to learn to recruit listener attention in ways that are socially appropriate, such as by tapping the listener on the arm or calling their name. While this study showed successful acquisition of the attention-getting response, the two participants did not have an ASD diagnosis. However, there is no particular reason that these same instructional tactics would not be equally applicable to children with ASD. Indeed, the least-to-most prompting procedure used in this study has also been widely used in teaching a range of adaptive skills to learners with ASD and to children with a range of other developmental disabilities (MacDuff et al., 2001). The study is also limited by the lack of generalization and maintenance checks.

A third illustrative study by Soenksen and Alper (2006) explored the effects of a novel set of instructional tactics for teaching a young child to gain the attention of peers. The participant was a 5-year-old boy diagnosed with hyperlexia (advanced reading skills, but with limited comprehension). The child also met the eligibility criteria for special education services under the ASD category. A Social Story™ intervention (Gray & Garand, 1993) approach was used. This involved presenting visual and verbal cues in a 4-page storybook format. Page 1, for example, contained a picture of two friends standing side by side with an accompanying written script that read: *When I want to talk to a friend, I first get their attention.*

Intervention sessions included the target child and a varying set of four peers without disability, half of whom were familiar with the story. During sessions, the child and his peers were given copies of the story, and the researcher also read the story aloud while the target child and the peers who were familiar with the story read along. Following these story-reading sessions, the target child was observed in various classroom settings, and the frequency with which he used the attention-gaining skills was recorded. The data showed an increase in the child's use of appropriate attention-gaining responses (i.e., looking at and calling peers by name) when the intervention was implemented. Gains were highest during recess and choice times, with relatively little change during math lessons.

Generally, the Social Stories™ approach could be conceptualized as a type of script that is intended to prompt or guide behavior once it is learned. It is a widely used strategy for teaching a range of social skills to learners with ASD, but the quality of the evidence supporting this approach, and similar narrative or bibliotherapy approaches, has been questioned (Leaf et al., 2020). Social Stories™ and similar approaches are probably best suited to learners with more advanced language and comprehension skills, that is, those who require support. However, as suggested by the results reported by Soenksen and Alper (2006), it is possible that repeated readings of a well-crafted social story could improve a child's comprehension or at least help the child recall story elements and translate these into the corresponding social behavior. Once those social behaviors occurred, they might then be strengthened and maintained (reinforced) by the resulting positive reactions of social partners.

In summary, the ability to gain the attention of others is often a first and necessary step for initiating a social-communication interaction. Some learners with ASD are likely to require intervention to acquire, generalize, and maintain socially appropriate attention-gaining skills. Several instructional approaches have demonstrated success in teaching appropriate attention-gaining skills to learners with ASD. One approach that would seem suited toward learners with more limited repertoires involves creating discrete opportunities where the attention of another person is required and then prompting the learner to produce the attention-gaining response. Once the response occurs, the partner would then attend to the person and engage in further social interactions, such as by then creating an opportunity for the learner to make a request. For learners with more developed repertoires, teachers could make use of the Social Stories™ to support the learning of appropriate attention-gaining skills. Social Stories™ could be seen as a type of script that is rehearsed with the learner and which, once learned, is intended to remind the person what to do in social situations.

Teaching Greeting Skills

Greeting rituals are a ubiquitous feature of human social encounters (Ferguson, 1976). Individuals who lack appropriate greeting skills are likely to be viewed as less socially competent (Han & Kemple, 2006). Unfortunately, the acquisition of appropriate greeting skills appears difficult for many learners with ASD (Capps et al., 1998). Hobson and Lee (1998), for example, compared the greeting rituals of 24 adolescents and young adults with ASD to those of 24 similarly aged individuals with intellectual disability. They found that, when introduced to an unfamiliar adult, participants with ASD were less likely to spontaneously greet (and bid farewell to) the adult. Limited skills with respect to greeting rituals could negatively impact on a person's social image, ability to make friends, and ability to successfully enter positive social interactions both with familiar people and with unfamiliar people (Gantman et al., 2012). It would therefore seem critical to assist these learners with gaining competence in the performance of greeting rituals. One educational approach to developing social competence in this area might be to directly set out to teach culturally, age-appropriate, and contextually relevant greeting behaviors.

Along these lines, Reichow and Sabornie (2009) described a controlled case study using an ABAB withdrawal design. The study was aimed at teaching a consistent and acceptable greeting ritual to an 11-year-old boy with autism (George). Specifically, George was taught to recognize when the performance of a greeting was appropriate and to then engage in any one of several acceptable forms of verbal greeting (e.g., saying *Hi*, *Hello*, or *Good morning*). The study was conducted in George's school environment during 5-min sessions in which there were opportunities to greet three different adults and five different peers. Prior to intervention, George never initiated an acceptable greeting in response to any such opportunities.

The intervention involved creating a 4-page Social Story™. The story included written and pictorial instructions outlining (a) when to greet someone, (b) why greeting is important, (c) acceptable forms of greeting, (d) how to initiate a greeting, and (e) what to expect when you greet someone. As part of the intervention, George was instructed to read the story at the beginning of the school day. George read the story in a resource room and then moved to his regular classroom, where there were multiple opportunities for initiating greetings. This relatively simple intervention appeared to be successful. Specifically, George started initiating greetings both to adults and to peers during about 50% of the opportunities.

A major strength of the study was that the authors employed an ABAB withdrawal design, which provided a convincing demonstration that the Social Story™ intervention was most likely responsible for the increase in George's greeting initiations. However, when the story element of the intervention was withdrawn following the initial intervention phase, George failed to initiate greetings. This reversal of the intervention effect suggested that George was depending on the story to prompt his greeting behavior. To address this issue, the researchers modified their intervention to incorporate a fading procedure to gradually eliminate George's reliance on the scripted social story. Eliminating instructional prompts is obviously desirable and necessary to promote greater independence, but doing so abruptly may cause deterioration in performance. In such situations, teachers should seek to more gradually reduce or fade out prompts and instructional cues so that children do not become overly dependent on these. To this end, Cengher and colleagues (2018) reviewed evidence-based strategies for fading prompts that teachers could draw upon during instruction.

Kagohara and colleagues (2013) also used a Social Story™ intervention to teach greeting behavior. An innovative aspect of this study was that the overall intervention program included a video-based modeling procedure. The study involved two 10-year-old children, one girl and one boy. Both children had been diagnosed with Asperger syndrome or high-functioning autism and attention-deficit, hyperactivity disorder. The children had some basic conversational skills but rarely initiated greetings. The Social Story™ procedure involved having the children read through a story that (a) explained that when two people meet for the first time each day, they should greet each other, (b) gave examples of appropriate greeting responses (e.g., *Hello. Hi.*), (c) explained that it was polite to greet people, and (d) indicated that people like being greeted.

The video modeling procedure involved having the children watch a video of two cartoon characters greeting each other and engaging in a brief conversation (e.g., Student 1: *Hi, how are you?* Student 2: *I'm fine. Thank you.*). Following an initial baseline phase in which neither the Social Story™ nor the video modeling procedures were used, the children first received the Social Story™ intervention and then the video modeling intervention. During all phases of the study, observers recorded whether the children made a short greeting (e.g., *Hi.*) or engaged in a longer greeting or conversation (e.g., *Hello. How are you?*) when meeting a teacher or other adult. During baseline, the two children never initiated any type of greeting or conversation. When the Social Story™ was implemented, both children showed an increase in their use of short initial greetings (e.g., *Hi.*). Use of longer greetings and conversational responses increased only when the video modeling procedure was added. These preliminary results suggest that the addition of video modeling may enhance the effects of a Social Story™ intervention.

In line with these findings, Litras and colleagues (2010) combined video modeling with Social Stories™ to teach three social-communication skills to a 3-year-old child with ASD. This child learned to initiate a greeting, invite a communication partner to play, and respond appropriately to their partner's utterances. The results were encouraging in that all three of these social-communication skills increased after four to six intervention sessions. The skills were also maintained at a 3-week follow-up during which the intervention procedures were no longer applied. Generalization across settings was also documented.

Collectively, these two studies by Kagohara and colleagues (2013) and Litras and colleagues (2010) support the use of an intervention package that combines Social Stories™ with video modeling. While such a combined instructional package could thus be seen as promising, it is important to note that both studies are limited due to their small number of participants. In addition, Kagohara and colleagues (2013) failed to assess for generalization. Another limitation of the Kagohara and colleagues (2013) study was that one child, Peter, showed limited maintenance of the greeting response during follow-up sessions. The authors noted that this child did not seem to enjoy social interaction as much as the other child, which could account for his limited maintenance. This suggests that for some children, there may be value in providing additional reinforcement when social interaction alone does not function as an effective type of reinforcement. Of course, over time, teachers would want to fade out the need for any such contrived reinforcers so that greeting behavior is eventually maintained by the natural positive social feedback received from the person being greeted.

In another illustrative study, Kern and colleagues (2007) used a novel song-based intervention to establish a greeting routine in two 3-year-old boys with ASD and limited speech. The intervention was implemented in their child-care program. A song-based intervention was developed to teach the children to independently participate in a five-step morning greeting routine. The five steps were (a) entering the classroom, (b) greeting a teacher or peer by either saying *Hello* or handing over a response card with the printed word "Hello" on it, (c) greeting a second person, (d) waving or saying *Goodbye* to their caregiver, and (d) initiating appropriate toy play.

The song-based intervention involved having the teacher sing an individualized greeting song to each child as he entered the classroom. The songs' lyrics specified the five steps of the morning greeting routine, and the teacher paced the song so that each lyric was sung at the time that the corresponding step was to be executed by the child. With this intervention, both children showed an increase in the number of independently performed steps from about 40% correct in baseline to 100% correct by the end of the intervention program. However, one child required a procedural adaptation that involved eliminating the requirement to say goodbye to his caregiver. This adaptation was made because the child cried when the caregiver left. As such, a modification was implemented, which involved having the caregiver make a discreet exit to cause less stress for the child. The song-based intervention used in this study could be conceptualized as a type of Social Story™ intervention with the twist that the script was sung to, rather than read to, the children.

Overall, these illustrative studies on teaching greeting responses provide some support for using Social Story™, video modeling, and song-based intervention procedures. This is consistent with the fact that these three instructional approaches have been widely used in teaching a range of adaptive skills to learners with ASD and other developmental disabilities (Bellini & Akullian, 2007; James et al., 2015; Reynhout & Carter, 2006). Possibly, the use of music, songs, and song-based Social Story™ intervention might be useful for some children with ASD, given that song lyrics may represent an effective mnemonic aid (Werner, 2018). Familiar songs might also help to reduce stress and increase a child's interest in social interaction (Cirelli & Trehub, 2020).

However, there remain questions regarding the wholesale applicability of these approaches for learners with more severe ASD symptoms or with more significant cognitive disabilities (e.g., learners requiring substantial or very substantial levels of support). Compared to more direct response prompting procedures, Social Stories™, songs, and video modeling interventions would seem to involve a more symbolic learning process. Success with such approaches may therefore depend to some extent on the person being able to comprehend stories and lyrics and attend to video models. The learner's level of comprehension and attending should be assessed prior to the use of such interventions. For learners who may have comprehension or attention difficulties, there may be a need to undertake initial pretraining or include additional intervention procedures to address such difficulties (Plavnick, 2013).

In summary, the ability to greet others appropriately is a mark of social competence. Some learners with ASD may have difficulty learning greeting rituals incidentally through their everyday interactions with others and may therefore benefit from a more structured intervention to explicitly and directly teach specific greeting skills. To this end, practitioners can draw upon a number of evidence-based strategies for teaching greeting skills to learners with ASD. One teaching approach involves the implementation of a generic systematic instructional approach, which involves (a) creating structured opportunities for engaging in greetings, (b) cueing or prompting the learner to make the greeting response if the response does not occur independently, (c) being responsive to (i.e., reinforcing) the learner's greeting response, and (d) gradually fading out the cues and prompts to promote self-initiated greeting behavior. In addition to this generic instructional approach, success in teaching greeting skills to learners with ASD has also been achieved using Social Stories™, video modeling, and song-based intervention procedures.

Teaching Conversational Skills

As noted by Sng and colleagues (2018), good conversational skills are central to social interaction. Unfortunately, socially interacting with others in appropriate and meaningful ways is one of the major areas of difficulty associated with ASD (American Psychiatric Association, 2013). In light of this, the development of effective and socially and age-appropriate conversational skills will likely be an important educational priority for many learners with ASD. Fortunately, many studies demonstrate successful procedures for teaching a range of conversational skills to individuals with ASD.

Hood and colleagues (2017), for example, developed a successful instructional program for teaching a number of discrete conversational skills to three learners with ASD, aged 8, 15, and 16 years. The conversational skills targets included (a) making two topic-relevant comments during a conversational episode, (b) shifting the topic of conversation when the listener appeared bored, (c) asking questions, and (d) listening or not interrupting when the other person is talking. The instructional program involved a number of procedural steps based on a more general behavior-analytic teaching process. Briefly, during one-to-one, discrete-trial training sessions, the trainer first described the conditions under which the learner was to respond and then explained what would be considered an acceptable response for the learner to make (e.g., *When your partner looks bored, such as by yawning or looking around the room, then you should change the topic of conversation.*). The trainer then modeled the described scenario during a role play with another adult. The trainer modeled both correct responses and incorrect responses and then asked the learners whether what they had just seen was correct or incorrect. Multiple opportunities to practice correct responses with reinforcement (e.g., praise) were then arranged.

The results of this program were generally positive in that all learners acquired at least 15 out of the 16 targeted skills. Moreover, the newly acquired skills generalized to novel communication partners, both adults and peers. In addition, the skills were maintained at 1 to 3 months follow-up. However, in addition to the discrete trial or role-play intervention, several learners were provided with an additional textual or written prompt to evoke more correct responses. Furthermore, two learners showed limited gains from the initial role-play intervention and, therefore, additional reinforcement contingencies (e.g., earning free time for correct responses) were introduced for them.

The study highlights the importance of modifying one's teaching procedures in light of a learner's responsiveness (or lack thereof). The underlying approach could be seen as involving flexible use of structured role-playing, verbal explanations, role play or modeling, and practice with feedback. The study also highlights the fact that some learners may require additional cues or prompts and individualized reinforcements to develop and maintain the performance of targeted conversational skills. Indeed, this study illustrates the value of individualized adaptations. When such adaptations were made to the instructional procedures, then all learners in this study successfully acquired an impressively large number of diverse conversational skills.

In another relevant study, Chezan and colleagues (2020) set out to teach self-initiation of conversations to three young adults (18 to 22 years of age) with ASD and moderate intellectual disability. The participants attended two centers in which they had opportunities to socially interact with peers/coworkers. Participants were taught to follow an 8-step sequence that included (a) approaching another person, (b) greeting that person, (c) waiting for a response, (d) making a statement or asking a question, (e) waiting for a response, and (f) terminating the conversation in an appropriate way (e.g., *See you later.*). To teach this conversational sequence, the researchers implemented an intervention package that included Behavior Skills Training (BST) and Covert Audio Coaching (CAC). BST involves a number of evidence-based teaching strategies, specifically providing verbal instruction, modeling correct responses, and arranging multiple practice opportunities with feedback and reinforcement. CAC involves providing on-the-spot feedback to learners in real time through a bug-in-ear auditory system. With these procedures in place, all three participants showed acquisition of the targeted conversational skills and two participants also showed increased self-initiation. The gains made were retained during follow-up sessions that occurred 2 to 6 weeks postintervention.

In addition to these objective gains, the participants reported the intervention to be helpful, although one person did not like wearing the bug-in-ear device. Teachers also reported that the intervention was useful and easy to implement but could be time consuming. The overall results of this study were positive and could also be seen as largely acceptable to the recipients and teachers involved. The study, therefore, provides a useful and highly practical example for applying two well-established instructional techniques (i.e., BST and CAC) in the service of teaching an extended conversational sequence to young adults with ASD and moderate intellectual disability.

In another BST-based study, Sevlever and colleagues (2015) evaluated a variation of the BST procedures for teaching conversational skills to four (7- to 11-year-old) children on the autism spectrum. The variation, known as the teaching interaction procedure (TIP), involved applying the core BST procedures (i.e., verbal instruction, modeling, practice, and feedback) in a small-group format. Five general types of conversational skills were targeted, specifically (a) establishing eye contact with the communication partner, (b) beginning a conversation, (c) sustaining the conversation by asking questions, (d) listening to others and using appropriate gestures to indicate comprehension, and (e) ending a conversation. These skills, and the overall conversational sequence targeted, were quite similar to those targeted both by Hood and colleagues (2017) and by Chezan and colleagues (2020).

Instructional sessions lasted 10 to 15 min and involved the use of verbal instruction, modeling, and practice opportunities with feedback. Sessions were conducted in the context of a role-play scenario. During sessions, teachers also used more standard response prompts to evoke correct responses and reinforced these responses with praise and tokens. Following sessions, the children were instructed to engage in conversational exchanges with the staff or peers, and their performance of the skills was recorded. The results indicated improvement in the children's conversational skills, although the magnitude of the intervention effect was somewhat difficult to determine because many children showed improvement during the initial baseline phase, that is, prior to implementation of the full intervention package. Overall, however, the mean level of performance on each of the five targeted conversational skills increased from about 10% to 50% when intervention was completed. These skills also generalized to novel conversational partners. Overall, this study offers some evidence to support the use of a group-based version of BST for teaching conversational skills to children with ASD. Interventions that can be successful in a group format would seem highly practical for classroom settings and, thus, may be quite appealing to teachers.

The wider literature on teaching conversational skills to learners with ASD has consistently demonstrated the success of the specific instructional procedures reviewed in this chapter, specifically Social Stories™, video modeling, BST, and various combinations and refinements of these strategies (Scattone, 2007). These procedures appear to work consistently well when applied under more controlled research conditions, but perhaps less so when applied under real-world, whole-classroom conditions. White, Keonig, and colleagues (2007), for example, reviewed 14 studies on the effectiveness of group-based social skills interventions. They found support for the use of these types of systematic teaching procedures in general but noted the need for additional studies involving group-based formats. A useful starting point might thus be for teachers to replicate the TIP approach using the Sevlever and colleagues (2015) study as a guide.

In summary, the ability to initiate and engage in sustained conversations is important for the development of meaningful relationships with, getting along with, and enjoying meaningful interactions with others. Engaging in conversation is a complex process and learners with ASD may need instruction on a number of specific conversational skills, such as how to initiate a conversation, respond to questions, stay on topic, and engage in conversational turn-taking. Success in teaching these types of conversational skills to learners with ASD has been accomplished using three main tactics or approaches, specifically Social Stories™, video modeling, and application of generic systematic instructional tactics associated with the general BST approach.

Teaching Joint Attention and Peer Interaction Skills

The ability to engage with peers is a critical element for continued development of social-communication skills. In young children these social relationships may begin with episodes of shared attention (i.e., joint attention). *Joint attention* has been defined in the literature as involving the coordinated, reciprocal focus of two individuals on an object. Joint attention typically occurs in the context of daily social interactions (Sullivan et al., 2015). For example, when playing, a child might point to an object of interest while looking at their friend or respond to a friend's pointing gesture. Skills that are contingent on the development of social engagement are necessary for social-communication development and may be specifically targeted for the development of social communication (Sullivan et al., 2015). Furthermore, research indicates that when underdevelopment of joint engagement persists in children with ASD, later complex social skills (e.g., imitation, play, and pragmatics) might also be underdeveloped (Hansen et al., 2019; Toth et al., 2006). As such, this is often a targeted area of intervention for learners with ASD and developmental disabilities.

For example, Hansen and colleagues (2019) utilized what might be considered a naturalistic approach for teaching peer-mediated joint attention skills to young children with ASD. Joint attention refers to two individuals engaging in reciprocal social interactions and jointly attending and directing each other's attention to some aspect of the environment. For example, a child might aim to direct an adult's attention to a preferred toy that is out of reach by alternating his or her gaze from the adult to the toy and back again. The Hansen and colleagues study aimed to evaluate the impact of a joint attention intervention on the response to joint attention among seven preschool-aged children (six boys) with ASD. Response to joint attention was defined as the target child shifting his or her gaze from a preferred item to the social partner. The joint attention intervention in this study involved using a least-to-most prompting procedure to teach the target children to first look at the preferred item and then look back at the partner. Adults served as the main interventionists, but there were also sessions with a peer serving as the child's social partner. The prompting hierarchy involved the following sequence of prompts: (a) gaze shift, (b) gaze shift and point, (c) partial physical prompt, and (d) full physical prompt. Results of the intervention showed increases in joint attention responses as a result of peer-mediated opportunities and social responses of the peers. There are several positive aspects to this study. First, the use of natural change agents, such as peers, to teach a social skill may help to create learning opportunities that generalize within social environments. Second, the use of naturalistic environments, such as preschool classrooms, may also help to promote better generalizability of social skills.

As social interactions continue to progress, it is important to provide learning opportunities to target specific social-communication targets, such as requesting. Several studies have investigated the use of peers to help teach various types of requesting. For example, Paden and colleagues (2012) evaluated the effects of differential reinforcement increase in peer-directed requests for children with ASD who communicated using PECS (Bondy & Frost, 2001). For this study, two children were paired up as communication partners during preferred leisure activities. During teaching sessions, the children sat at a table together with an array of five picture symbols (three highly preferred and two nonrelated pictures that served as distracting items), and a therapist was present. If a request was made to the therapist, the child was prompted to make their request to the peer using the least intrusive prompt necessary. Peer responses following a request (e.g., taking the picture card and providing the corresponding item) were also prompted using the system of least prompts. During the intervention phase, both participants learned to engage in peer-directed requests and listener responses. These results indicate that children who use alternative communication modalities, such as PECS, may benefit from interventions that address teaching initiation of communication with peers.

More recently, research has utilized peer-mediated interventions to teach listener responses. For example, Lorah and colleagues (2014) taught six children with autism to engage with peers by requesting play materials and by responding as a listener to a peer's request for play materials using systematic instruction. During the teaching sessions that targeted speaker initiation to a peer, a 5-s delay was provided to allow the children time to respond. This was followed by the use of the least intrusive prompt needed to ensure the occurrence of the appropriate request (e.g., *I want puzzle.*). During the listener teaching sessions, following a peer's request, if the child did not engage in the targeted listener response (e.g., providing access to a requested toy) after 5 s, the least intrusive prompt was used to prompt the targeted behavior. Further, generalization to a novel peer was assessed after acquisition both of speaker responses (requesting item) and of listener responses (delivering requested item) had occurred. Although each child acquired the targeted speaker and listener responses, the results of tests for generalization to novel peers were mixed. Only one participant generalized both their speaker response and their listener response. This study highlights that there may be a need to directly teach both types of social-communication roles (speaker and listener roles) and to do so with multiple peer dyads.

In summary, there is growing interest in teaching joint attention and peer interaction skills to learners with ASD. Joint attention could be seen as a component of most social-communicative interactions and peer interaction is crucial to promoting positive interactions with one's social group. These are also areas of development where many learners with ASD seem to have some difficulty. Supporting the development of joint attention and peer interaction has been accomplished through the application of systematic instructional tactics or the general BST teaching approach. As illustrated by the studies reviewed in this section, these instructional tactics can be implemented in naturalistic contexts, which helps to promote generalization and maintenance.

SUMMARY

Achieving a reasonable level of social competence is important for participation in nearly all aspects of life. Unfortunately, ASD is associated with social impairments that can hinder participation, learning, and the ability to express a range of social-communication functions. Fortunately, there are many studies demonstrating successful procedures for teaching social skills to learners with ASD (Radley et al., 2020), including studies on teaching foundational social-communication skills, such as requesting and rejecting, recruiting attention, greeting others, conversational engagement, establishing joint attention, and interacting with peers. The illustrative studies reviewed in this chapter would seem to offer some guidance to practitioners regarding the general instructional procedures that are likely to be successful in teaching these types of social-communication skills to learners with ASD.

As indicated by the material reviewed in this chapter, practitioners can draw upon a number of well-established (evidence-based) instructional practices that have demonstrated success for teaching social-communication skills to learners with ASD (Brown et al., 2019), such as the use of a range of response prompting and prompt fading techniques. Consistent and structured use of these strategies is collectively known as systematic instruction. In addition to the generic application of systematic instructional strategies, practitioners can make use of a number of more specific named procedures, such as (a) BST, (c) CAC, (d) video modeling, and (e) Social Stories™. These practices can be varied, combined, and modified to suit the learner's unique circumstances. Well-established learning principles (e.g., reinforcement, chaining, shaping, and fading) underpin all of these types of evidence-based instructional practices (Madden et al., 2013). The application of these learning principles has a long history of demonstrated success in teaching learners with ASD and other developmental disabilities (Lang & Sturmey, 2021; Sturmey & Didden, 2014).

The intervention procedures employed across the studies covered in this chapter could be seen as components within an overall more general instructional approach. That more general approach involves the systematic yet flexible delivery of instructional procedures that have been selected for their suitability to a given learner's unique needs, characteristics, and circumstances. Table 8.1 outlines some of the components that such a generic instructional approach might include when teaching social-communication skills to learners with ASD. Based on the research reviewed in this chapter, practitioners who can skillfully implement these component steps with flexibility and consistency are likely to be more successful in teaching social-communication skills that will enhance the overall social competence of learners with ASD.

Table 8.1. Components of a Generic Instructional Approach for Teaching Social-Communication Skills to Learners with ASD

Component	Description
Define target behavior	Define the skill you aim to teach in observable and measurable terms. For example, gaining attention might be defined as the learner calling out the teacher's name. Initiating a conversation might be defined as the learner approaching a peer and asking an appropriate question, such as "What did you do over the weekend?" Starting with an objective definition of the target skill is important; this clarifies exactly what skill is being taught and facilitates accurate recording of whether the learner is in fact gaining proficiency as a result of the intervention.
Create opportunities	Once the skill has been defined, the next step is to figure ways to create or capture opportunities for teaching the target skill. For example, opportunities to teach requests for help may arise during the day whenever the learner is struggling with a task. Opportunities to teach greeting behavior may similarly arise the first time a learner encounters a familiar person each day. Practitioners can also create structured opportunities to increase the number of learning opportunities that the learner receives each day. Learners with autism spectrum disorder (ASD) may benefit from increased teaching opportunities.
Implement time delay and response prompting	When a social-communication opportunity arises, the practitioner should wait for increasing amounts of time— 3 s, 5 s, and 10 s—to give the learner a chance to respond. If the targeted response does not occur within the allocated wait time, then the practitioner should provide a response prompt to recruit the correct response. Response prompts should be selected based on the types of cues or prompts that the learner is most likely to respond to. Commonly used prompts include verbal instruction, modeling, pointing, and use of physical assistance. Over successive opportunities, the use of prompts should be gradually eliminated or faded by waiting longer before delivering a prompt and by giving less and less of the prompt. Importantly, if using Social Stories™ or video modeling, then prior to experiencing a teaching opportunity, the practitioner would rehearse the script or show the video to the learner. Social Stories™ and video modeling can be seen as a type of antecedent prompt that is given prior to or at the beginning of an opportunity as a way of priming the learner to respond. The overall aim of promoting is to increase the probability that the target skill will occur during each opportunity so that it can then be reinforced.

Component	Description
Provide reinforcement	Once the target skill has occurred during the opportunity, then reinforcement should occur. The appropriate type of reinforcement will depend on the function of the response the learner has made. For example, if the learner has requested a preferred toy, then the appropriate reinforcer would be to provide access to the requested toy. If the learner has instead used a speech-generating device to initiate a conversation with a peer, the natural reinforcer would be for the peer to respond conversationally to that initiation. Generally, practitioners should aim to ensure natural reinforcement is provided consistently for the learner's newly acquired social-communication skills. However, some learners may also need some additional contrived reinforcement, such as praise and tangible rewards, to strengthen the target response. Ultimately, the goal is to eventually fade out these contrived reinforcers.
Program for generalization and maintenance	Finally, as part of overall intervention effort, practitioners should aim to program for generalization and maintenance of the targeted social-communication skills. This programming might consist of incorporating naturally maintaining contingencies, such as ensuring there is ongoing social interaction when the learner initiated a greeting or conversation and ensuring the learner who requests help does then actually receive help. Additional strategies to promote generalization include using a variety of people materials and settings during intervention (i.e., teach with multiple exemplars).

CASE STUDY

Katie Wolfe and Laura C. Chezan

Background

Marisol is a 3-year-old girl who has just been diagnosed with autism spectrum disorder (ASD). Her parents have enrolled her in an inclusive early childhood education classroom in their local school district, where she has peers with and without disabilities. She also participates in 1:1 intervention based on applied behavior analysis (ABA) in the afternoon at home and in the community 3 days per week. Marisol loves unicorns and fairies and enjoys coloring and doing puzzles. She does not currently produce any verbal sounds other than "ma" and "ba," and primarily relies on gestures (e.g., pointing, reaching) to get her wants and needs met. She is beginning to engage in challenging behaviors, such as hitting, when her family is unable to identify what she wants.

The Board Certified Behavior Analyst (BCBA°) who is overseeing her home-based intervention program wants to determine how to best help Marisol gain requesting skills that will enable her to access more preferred items. Marisol's parents have identified this as a priority, especially since her challenging behaviors have increased.

(continued)

Step 1: Questions to Initiate the Evidence-Based Treatment Selection Process

The BCBA begins the evidence-based treatment selection process by generating questions to guide the team through the process. The questions she develops include:

1. What modality of requesting (verbal, Picture Exchange Communication Systems [PECS], sign language) is most appropriate for Marisol?
2. What interventions can be used to teach Marisol to request using the target modality?

Step 2—Part 1: Best Available Evidence

The BCBA uses the questions from Step 1 to guide her search for evidence regarding what modality to teach Marisol and what interventions to use to teach that modality. She reviews information from the IRIS Center and the National Professional Development Center on ASD and finds that interventions targeting verbal language, PECS, and sign language have all been effective for young learners with ASD. However, she notices that the children who have been successful with verbal language interventions have usually had a larger repertoire of sounds than Marisol currently does when they started the intervention. The BCBA also researches potential interventions to teach requesting and finds that discrete trial teaching and naturalistic intervention were identified as evidence-based practices (EBPs) for teaching communication (Steinbrenner et al., 2020; Wong et al., 2015). Discrete trial teaching is an adult-directed instruction that typically occurs at a desk or table and involves the rapid presentation of learning trials on various instructional targets. Naturalistic intervention is a child-directed instruction that capitalizes on the child's interests and is embedded within naturally occurring routines and activities.

Step 2—Part 2: Person-Related Variables

The BCBA considers the learner's repertoire in relation to the three potential modalities. Marisol does not currently produce sounds, so trying to teach her to use words to request items may be challenging. She does have strong fine motor skills that might make her a good candidate for sign language, and she can associate objects with their pictures so PECS may also be effective. Although Marisol cannot directly express her preferences, she pushes the interventionist's hand away when they attempt physical prompting. She can imitate other people's motor behavior. The main goal of Marisol's parents is for her to be able to let them know what she wants and needs using vocal language. Her parents were worried that others in the community would not understand sign language. Both parents would prefer an intervention that they can use throughout the day during regular activities like bath time and mealtime.

Step 2—Part 3: Contextual Variables (Resource Constraints, Environmental Supports)

Marisol has 1:1 ABA-based intervention three times a week after school. The interventionist would have the time and capability to implement either discrete trial training or naturalistic intervention during that time. However, the family has two other young children, and it would be challenging for them to conduct discrete trial training at a separate table for extended periods of time. They could, however, use naturalistic intervention embedded during ongoing routines and activities within the home.

Step 3: Professional Judgment
The BCBA considers the advantages and disadvantages of the three modalities (see Table 8.2) and the two interventions (see Table 8.3).

Table 8.2. Advantages and Disadvantages of Potential Communication Modalities for Marisol

Communication modality	Advantages	Disadvantages
Vocal communication	• Easily understood by communication partners • No additional materials needed	• Marisol does not have prerequisite skills • May take longer for Marisol to acquire
Sign language	• No additional materials needed • Marisol has strong fine motor skills	• Communication partners may not understand Marisol's signs • Number of signs may be more limited
Picture exchange communication system (PECS)	• Pictures are easily understood by most communication partners • Marisol has strong picture-object correspondence skills	• Need to have PECS book available at all times • Communication may be limited to the pictures available in the PECS book

Table 8.3. Advantages and Disadvantages of Potential Communication Interventions for Marisol

Intervention	Advantages	Disadvantages
Discrete trial training	• Predictable instructional format • Conducted in a distraction-free environment • Many trials conducted in a short period of time	• Skills may not generalize to natural situations • Parents cannot implement given other demands on their time • Adult-directed instruction may produce some challenging behavior
Naturalistic instruction	• Skills more likely to generalize because they are taught in natural contexts • Parents can implement during ongoing activities • Child-directed instruction capitalizes on motivation and may be more enjoyable for Marisol	• May require more planning to ensure that instructional opportunities are provided during play and other ongoing activities

(continued)

She has more experience teaching young children to use verbal language or sign language to communicate their wants and needs compared to PECS but is concerned that Marisol does not have the prerequisite skills to quickly acquire verbal communication skills. Marisol's parents have a strong preference for PECS compared to sign language, because others in the community could understand the pictures. The BCBA would prefer to use naturalistic intervention instead of discrete trial training to promote generalization and to better enable the parents to work with Marisol outside of the scheduled sessions.

Step 4: Intervention Selection

With the family's input, the BCBA decides to teach Marisol to use PECS to request items and activities using naturalistic intervention. Even though all three modalities were supported by research, Marisol's skills aligned with the prerequisite skills for picture exchange, which would allow her to learn to request more quickly. Although the parents want Marisol to communicate vocally, they understand the urgency of selecting a modality she can acquire quickly. The BCBA also lets them know that they will continue to work to develop her vocal communication, and that research suggests that PECS does not impede the development of vocal communication. The BCBA has less experience teaching this modality than sign language or verbal language, but she did learn about it during her master's program and has committed to attending a continuing education event to learn more. The team also selected naturalistic intervention, so that opportunities to teach Marisol could be included throughout the day during activities.

Step 5: Intervention Implementation and Data Collection

The BCBA trains the interventionists and parents to implement naturalistic intervention with Marisol to teach her to use PECS to request items and activities. Data are collected every day and the BCBA analyzes and graphs it once a week to evaluate Marisol's progress. She also checks treatment fidelity once per week to ensure that the interventionists are implementing the intervention correctly.

Step 6: Reevaluation

After 4 weeks, Marisol has acquired six requests and can independently use PECS to ask for these items. The team agrees to continue working on building her repertoire by adding more pictures and ensuring that her pictures are available across all environments (home, school, and community). Marisol has also begun to produce the initial sounds for some of the items that she is requesting with PECS. The team plans to continue monitoring her progress with the goal of teaching her to comment on her environment after she has a strong requesting repertoire.

APPLICATION ACTIVITIES

1. Create a Social Story. Based on the guidelines for developing an effective Social Stories™ intervention (see https://www.autismparentingmagazine.com/social-stories-for-autistic-children/), develop a Social Story™ script for an adolescent with ASD who has difficulty making friends with peers. What specific social skills might the learner need to learn, and what would be the content of the corresponding Social Stories? How would you go about implementing this intervention with the learner and peers? How would you evaluate whether the intervention was effective?

2. Develop a Video Model. Based on the guidelines for using video modeling (see https://autismclassroomresources.com/video-modeling-what-is-it-and-why-use-i/), create an instructional video for teaching a child with ASD how to appropriately enter a peer playgroup. Which type of video modeling approach (i.e., basic, self, point-of-view, or video prompting) would be best suited to this situation? How often would you show the video to the child? Based on the review by Bellini and Akullian (2007), what if any additional instructional procedures might be used in conjunction with video modeling?

3. Replicate a Successful Intervention. Select one of the intervention studies reviewed in this chapter, preferably one that addresses a situation similar to one that you are facing as a practitioner. For example, perhaps one of your learners with ASD lacks the appropriate communication skills for recruiting attention or fails to appropriately greet others. Read the original study and attempt to implement those same intervention procedures. What problems did you experience in your efforts to use the intervention? What additional information, training, or resources would have been helpful in your effort to use this intervention?

ADDITIONAL RESOURCES

Systematic Reviews

Qi, C., Barton, E., Collier, M., Lin, Y., & Montoya, C. (2018). A systematic review of effects of Social Stories™ interventions for individuals with autism spectrum disorder. *Focus on Autism and Other Developmental Disabilities*, 33(1), 25–34. https://doi.org/10.1177/1088357615613516

Wang, P., & Spillane, A. (2009), Evidence-based social skills interventions for children with autism: A meta-analysis. *Education and Training in Developmental Disabilities*, 44(3), 318–42. https://www.jstor.org/stable/24233478

Books

Leaf, J. B. (Ed.) (2017). *Handbook of social skills and autism spectrum disorder*. Springer.

Matson, J. L. (Ed.) (2017). *Handbook of social behavior and skills in children*. Springer.

Websites

Autism Classroom: News and Resources. https://autismclassroomresources.com/video-modeling-what-is-it-and-why-use-i/

Autism Parenting Magazine. https://www.autismparentingmagazine.com/social-stories-for-autistic-children/

9

Evidence-Based Practices to Teach Academic Skills

Veronica P. Fleury, Jenny R. Root, Kelly Whalon,
Emily Stover, and Alice Williams

■ ■ ■

INTRODUCTION AND OVERVIEW

The terms *academic achievement* or *academic performance* are used to describe the extent to which practitioners have successfully taught their learners to reach established educational goals. Numerous benchmarks are used as evidence of academic achievement, including graduation rates and proportion of learners who achieve grade-level proficiency in content areas. The percentage of learners with autism spectrum disorder (ASD) who meet grade-level expectations on state assessments is not readily available; however, we may get a sense of academic achievement by looking at graduation rates. During the 2017–2018 school year, approximately 72% of learners with ASD served under the Individuals with Disabilities Education Improvement Act (IDEIA, 2004) graduated from high school with a regular diploma, 18% graduated with an alternative certificate, and roughly 10% of learners either dropped out or aged out of the education system (National Center for Education Statistics, 2020). Learners with ASD are more frequently being included in general education settings and will be expected to master core curricular content areas (Barnett et al., 2018; Cihak et al., 2016). In this chapter, we describe what is known about academic performance of learners with ASD with a specific focus on reading and mathematics. We then present empirically supported strategies to teach academic content-related skills to allow learners to achieve their optimal academic outcomes. We preface this chapter by highlighting a few important considerations.

CONSIDERATIONS FOR TEACHING ACADEMIC SKILLS

First, **academic difficulties are not a diagnostic characteristic of ASD**. Intellectual disability was once thought to be a comorbid condition associated with ASD (Evans, 2013). Our understanding of ASD and its associated characteristics has since evolved. Current research estimates that 31% of children with ASD have an intellectual disability (intelligence quotient [IQ] < 70) and 25% are in the borderline range (IQ = 71–85; Christenson et al., 2016). Though academic difficulties are not a benchmark characteristic of ASD, many learners with ASD will have difficulty participating in, and learning from, many traditional learning activities due to behavioral excesses and deficits that are characteristic of the disorder. The relationship between social functioning, problem behaviors, and academic performance is well established in typically developing populations (Elliott, 1990) and appears to hold true in studies involving children with ASD.

The role of executive functioning (EF) in ASD has received attention from the research community. EF is a term used to describe a number of cognitive tasks, specifically the ability to maintain focus on tasks, switch between tasks, inhibit impulsive responding, and mentally retain and use information. Recent studies including learners with ASD highlight that EFs are more strongly associated with school readiness than IQ (Blair & Razza, 2007) and serve as predictors of literacy and numeracy scores in preschool through high school (Assouline et al., 2012; Clark et al., 2010). The outward expression of disrupted EF processes is increased levels of distractibility, impulsivity, forgetfulness, and poor focus. Youths with ASD and their families confirm that these behaviors often impede learners' ability to fully participate in school activities and express the need for strategies that support EF skills (Tamm et al., 2020).

Second, **academic skill performance varies** widely across the ASD population. ASD represents a spectrum marked by great heterogeneity. Although learners with ASD share common behavioral characteristics—deficits in social communication and persistent restrictive behaviors, mannerisms, and rituals—the extent to which any particular learner demonstrates these behaviors varies. Reflective of ASD's heterogeneous nature, academic profiles of learners with ASD are considerably variable. Some studies suggest that learners with ASD do not perform differently from typically developing peers in math or literacy (May et al., 2013) while others report discrepancy in performance (Keen, Webster, et al., 2016). These discrepancies may be explained by examining who is included in the study sample and what academic constructs are measured.

Cain and colleagues (2019) assessed academic achievement in two groups of learners with ASD between the ages of 3 and 17: twice exceptional (2e) learners who qualified for gifted programs and scored > 90th percentile on any Woodcock Johnson III (WJ-III; Schrank et al., 2001) subtest; and learners with ASD who did not score above the 90th percentile on the standardized test. As expected, the 2e learners had stronger academic performance than the comparison group of learners with ASD from a young age. Over time, the 2e learners slightly increased their scores, while comparison learners slightly decreased their scores, in relation to their peers. The highest average scores were in the letter-word identification followed by calculations, passage comprehension, and applied problems. The subtests in which learners with ASD often perform well—letter-word identification and calculations—largely rely on rote memory skills (i.e., code-focused tasks). In comparison, learners with ASD often have difficulty with tasks that require them to apply knowledge in a deeper way or think flexibly, as is demanded in passage comprehension tasks and applied problems (i.e., meaning-focused tasks).

Third, much of the research used to describe academic profiles is **based on a subsample of learners with ASD**. Studies that provide descriptive information about academic performance commonly rely on formal, standardized measures (e.g., WJ-III) to allow researchers to draw conclusions about how learners' performance compares to a normed sample. These instruments require the assessor follow a standardized administration protocol; changing the administration by repeating prompts, rewording questions, or providing additional scaffolding or support violates standardization. This has implications for who can be evaluated using standardized instruments. Learners are required to have sufficient cognitive and language abilities to sustain attention during the testing period, comprehend directions, and respond to assessment items consistent with the standardized protocol. For this reason, several studies that rely on standardized instruments to assess achievement include only learners with ASD without intellectual delay, or an IQ > 70 (Cain et al., 2019; Estes et al., 2011; May et al., 2013). We highlight this because *selection bias*, systematically including or excluding participants based on a set of characteristics, can artificially influence study results in a positive or negative way (Durand & Rost, 2005). Understanding who is in the study sample is important because it informs the extent to which we can generalize study findings to the broader population.

Take, for example, the Cain and colleagues (2019) study, which revealed that learners with ASD performed better on *code-focused tasks* needed to decode words in text compared to *meaning-focused tasks* required to comprehend text. It would be inaccurate for us to interpret this to mean that all learners with ASD have strengths in code-focused skills and weaknesses in meaning-focused skills given that the researchers only included learners with ASD who had an IQ > 70 in their study sample. Learners with an intellectual disability, defined as IQ < 70, were not eligible to participate in the study. Recall that approximately one-third of the ASD population has an intellectual disability (Christenson et al., 2016). It would be inappropriate to infer that the findings apply to this population because they are not represented in the study sample. Indeed, some learners with ASD may demonstrate weakness in only meaning-focused skills (i.e., vocabulary, ability to retell stories, inference making), as the Cain and colleagues study suggests; however, other learners with ASD may demonstrate difficulties in only code-focused skills (i.e., phonological awareness, alphabet knowledge) or weaknesses both in code-focused skills and in meaning-focused skills.

Fourth, we have chosen to focus this chapter primarily on **academic instruction related to reading and mathematics**. We acknowledge that academic achievement reflects learners' proficiency in a broad range of content areas. The traditional core academic content areas taught in U.S. public schools are English language arts, mathematics, science, and social studies (or history and civics). Our decision to narrow our focus to reading and mathematics is primarily based on the assumption that foundational proficiency in these areas is essential to academic success broadly and has applications to other specific content areas. A learner who lacks fundamental decoding and reading comprehension skills will not perform well in other subject areas. Likewise, learners who have difficulty with basic calculations and mathematical application will have difficulty in science courses.

Our second rationale for focusing on reading and mathematics instruction is that the field has research to guide our instruction in these areas. The majority of intervention research for learners with ASD addresses outcomes that reflect the core behavioral characteristics of ASD, specifically strategies to improve social and communication skills. The next most commonly studied outcome is challenging behavior (Steinbrenner et al., 2020). Interventions to support academic outcomes for this population are relatively less abundant, although the field is growing. Within this subset of the literature, reading (Chiang & Lin, 2007; Finnegan & Mazin, 2016) and mathematics instruction (Barnett & Cleary, 2015; Gevarter et al., 2016; King et al., 2016) are more commonly addressed than other content areas.

Academic skill instruction is critical to supporting quality standard of living for learners with ASD. Competency in reading, writing, and mathematics has important implications for school success, but also extends to independence in home, work, and community settings. The ability to gather and share information, communicate with employers and the community, participate in simple mathematical transactions such as purchasing a meal at a restaurant, or choosing which bus to take to get home are all impacted by a learner's prior academic exposure. According to the National Longitudinal Transition Study-2 (NLTS-2; Newman et al., 2009), only 33% of adults with ASD reported employment (the second lowest of the 12 disability categories listed) and 42% reported making less than minimum wage. Academic skills are also needed to connect learners to their friends and family through posting on social media, texting, tweeting, and emailing. When asked about making friends, only 43% of young adults with ASD reported being able to make friends with the same ease as their peers (NLTS-2; Newman et al., 2009). Explicit instruction in academic skills for learners with ASD can lead to improved postsecondary outcomes for learners with a variety of support needs (Fleury et al., 2014).

Practitioners should support broad academic outcomes such as reading, writing, and mathematics to ensure that they are generalizable to a variety of situations. For instance, proficient readers should be able to read and comprehend, for a variety of purposes such as for obtaining knowledge on a topic, reading for leisure, following written directions, or following a bus schedule or recipe. Compare this to instruction that is focused on narrow splinter skills (i.e., reading and responding to social media communication). Though learners can be taught to acquire focused skills, we need to question whether this is a meaningful skill, and whether this skill can be generalized to other critical areas. Skills that are generalizable and can be maintained over time potentially make a large impact on learners' overall quality of life.

DESCRIPTION OF ACADEMIC ACHIEVEMENT

Reading Achievement

The purpose of reading is to comprehend text (Rayner et al., 2001). One highly supported theory (e.g., Catts, 2018; Kim, 2017; Nation, 2019), the Simple View of Reading (SVR), defines reading comprehension (RC) as the product of two discrete skills: (1) decoding and (2) listening comprehension or RC = Decoding × Listening Comprehension (Gough & Tunmer, 1986). *Decoding* refers to the processes and skills necessary to decipher the alphabetic code. *Listening comprehension* involves the application of foundational and complex language skills (e.g., vocabulary, syntax, narrative) to generate a clear mental representation of text (Cain & Barnes, 2017; Kendeou, 2020). The SVR provides a useful framework for understanding differences in reading achievement; these component skills are essential to RC (Snow, 2018). Early indicators of decoding and listening comprehension are

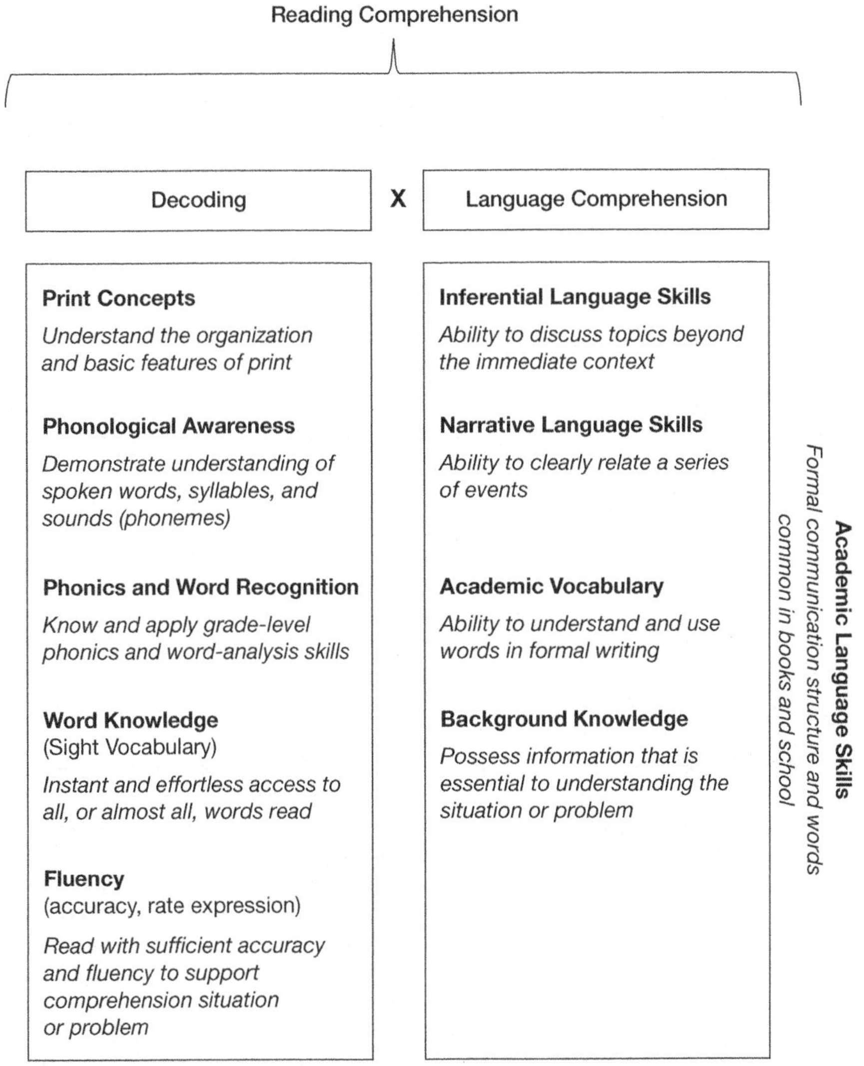

Reading Comprehension

Decoding	**X**	Language Comprehension

Print Concepts

Understand the organization and basic features of print

Phonological Awareness

Demonstrate understanding of spoken words, syllables, and sounds (phonemes)

Phonics and Word Recognition

Know and apply grade-level phonics and word-analysis skills

Word Knowledge
(Sight Vocabulary)

Instant and effortless access to all, or almost all, words read

Fluency
(accuracy, rate expression)

Read with sufficient accuracy and fluency to support comprehension situation or problem

Inferential Language Skills

Ability to discuss topics beyond the immediate context

Narrative Language Skills

Ability to clearly relate a series of events

Academic Vocabulary

Ability to understand and use words in formal writing

Background Knowledge

Possess information that is essential to understanding the situation or problem

Academic Language Skills
Formal communication structure and words common in books and school

Figure 9.1. The simple view of reading framework (Gough & Tunmer, 1986)

highly predictive of future RC (e.g., Language and Reading Research Consortium [LARRC] & Chiu, 2018; National Early Literacy Panel [NELP], 2008). Although termed the SVR, the authors have acknowledged that the development and application of these processes is far from simple (Hoover & Gough, 1990). The component skills of the SVR framework are depicted in Figure 9.1.

Simple View of Reading and Autism Spectrum Disorder

Studies examining the reading skills of children and youth with ASD have established three reading profiles consistent with the SVR: (1) average to above-average scores on all reading measures (i.e., average readers); (2) average to above-average scores on measures of word recognition, and scores at least one standard deviation below the mean on comprehension measures (i.e., specific comprehension deficit); and (3) scores below average both on word recognition and on comprehension measures (e.g., Henderson et al., 2014; Huemer & Mann, 2010; Jones et al., 2009; McIntyre, Solari, & Gonzales, 2017; Nation et al., 2006; Solari et al., 2019). The profile associated with dyslexia (i.e., scores in the average/above range on language comprehension and below average on word recognition; Catts et al., 2012) has not emerged in the literature on learners with ASD.

The proportion of learners with ASD with profiles indicative of a specific comprehension deficit (e.g., about one third) exceeds that of typically developing learners (Huemer & Mann, 2010; Jones et al., 2009; Lucas & Norbury, 2014; McIntyre, Solari, & Gonzales, 2017; McIntyre, Solari, Grimm, et al., 2017; Nation et al., 2006) and learners with ADHD (McIntyre, Solari, Grimm, et al., 2017). Although word recognition is often deemed a strength for learners with ASD, recent studies have shown a more sizable portion of learners with ASD (34–47%) struggle both with word recognition and with RC (McIntyre, Solari, & Gonzales, 2017; Solari et al., 2019). Participant selection criteria in many of these reading development studies required an IQ score of 70 or higher, indicating that many learners with ASD are likely to underperform on reading measures (e.g., Brown et al., 2013; McIntyre, Solari, & Gonzales, 2017; Solari et al., 2019). The considerably small percentage of learners (approximately 30%) achieving scores consistent with the average reader profile further underscores that school-age children with ASD are at high risk for reading failure (e.g., McIntyre, Solari, & Gonzales, 2017; McIntyre, Solari, Grimm, et al., 2017; Nation et al., 2006; Solari et al., 2019).

Word Recognition. Some studies have reported more than 40% of learners with ASD performed poorly on word recognition measures (Gabig, 2010; Henderson et al., 2014; Nation et al., 2006; Ricketts et al., 2013; Solari et al., 2019). To effectively decode, children apply their knowledge of sound-letter relationships to map sounds to corresponding letters and blend those sounds together to read words. As children practice applying the alphabetic principle, they expand their *orthographic skills*, the ability to identify patterns of specific letters as words. This allows learners to readily recognize parts of words and eventually whole words and, thus, enable quick processing and enhance comprehension. Word recognition is also supported by pairing decoding skills with knowledge of word meanings (morphological and semantic knowledge; Nation & Castles, 2017). Over time, children rely increasingly less on phonetic decoding and begin to chunk larger units of sound or meaning (Kamhi & Catts, 2012). This progression to automatic word reading is dependent on experience reading text (Nation & Castles, 2017).

Although studies have not specifically investigated how learners with ASD develop word recognition skills, there is evidence of inconsistent performance on word recognition measures. Several studies include word identification and nonword reading measures to provide a more comprehensive understanding of word recognition skills. Nonword measures assess one's ability to apply knowledge of the alphabetic principle to decode novel words. In some of these studies, learners with ASD have scored in the average to above average range both on word measures and on nonword measures (e.g., Cronin, 2014; Jones et al., 2009; Ricketts et al., 2016); yet, other studies report a subset of learners who score better on word than nonword measures, suggesting some learners with ASD may not reliably apply decoding skills (Gabig, 2010; Henderson et al., 2014; McIntyre, Solari, & Gonzales, 2017; McIntyre, Solari, Grimm, et al., 2017; Nation et al., 2006; Newman et al., 2007; White et al., 2006). In addition, correlations between scores on word reading and nonword reading are reportedly lower for children with ASD than typically developing children indicating poor alignment between these skills (Henderson et al., 2014; Nation et al., 2006). Similar to their typically developing peers, low scores on measures of nonword reading are linked to poor performance on measures of phonological processing (Jacobs & Richdale, 2013; McIntyre, Solari, Grimm, et al., 2017) and syntax/grammar (Jacobs & Richdale, 2013).

Preliminary evidence also shows that some learners with ASD will encounter difficulty reading irregular words in connected text. Unlike typically developing learners, they may fail to link decoding skills with context to identify irregular words (Henderson et al., 2014; Norbury & Nation, 2011). Challenges related to word reading are also evident on measures of reading fluency with some learners with ASD unable to read sentences (Lucas & Norbury, 2014) or connected text (McIntyre, Solari, Grimm, et al., 2017; Solari et al., 2017) fluently.

Listening Comprehension. Studies investigating the reading development of school-age children with ASD have reported that more than half of their participants scored at least 1 standard deviation below the mean on measures of RC (e.g., McIntyre, Solari, Grimm, et al., 2017; Nation et al., 2006). Moreover, when children with ASD improve their RC, their gains remain depressed in comparison to typically developing learners, and on measures of listening comprehension their growth peaks while typically developing learners continue to advance (Grimm et al., 2018).

Effective comprehension is dependent on the reader's ability to form a clear and coherent mental model of text. Developing a mental model requires the same processes used when listening to text read aloud or reading independently. That is, the reader applies their understanding of words, sentences, and discourse to build a representative mental model (Cain & Barnes, 2017). This process is flexible as text content evolves and readers refine their mental models by integrating prior knowledge, by generating relevant inferences and discarding irrelevant ones (Pearson & Cervetti, 2017). The low scores of learners with ASD on measures of RC are linked to poor vocabulary, syntax, and higher-order oral language skills (e.g., Brown et al., 2013; Jacobs & Richdale, 2013; McIntyre, Solari, Grimm, et al., 2017; Nation et al., 2006; Norbury & Nation, 2011; Ricketts et al., 2013).

Measures of vocabulary that require children to define words are more predictive of comprehension than labeling alone (NELP, 2008). These measures reflect depth of vocabulary knowledge; they require understanding of word meanings (Oakhill et al., 2015). While some young children with ASD learn to identify words receptively (e.g., pointing to a picture representing a word from an array of four; Westerveld et al., 2017), they often score poorly on measures of definitional vocabulary (e.g., "What is _____? What is it used for/what does it do?"; Dynia et al., 2014; Dynia et al., 2017; Fleury & Lease, 2018). Similarly, the scores of school-age children with ASD on measures of receptive vocabulary are reportedly inconsistent with other measures that ask learners to define words (McIntyre et al., 2020; Solari et al., 2019). Performance of learners with ASD on assessments that require depth of vocabulary knowledge are associated with scores on inference and narrative measures (McIntyre et al., 2020).

The influence of higher-order language skills (i.e., inference generation, story retelling, sentence completion) on the RC of children with ASD is substantial (McIntyre, Solari, Grimm, et al., 2017). After adding higher-order language processing to their model, it was the only significant predictor of RC (McIntyre, Solari, Grimm, et al., 2017). Inference making appears to be particularly challenging for learners with ASD (Lucas & Norbury, 2015; McIntyre, Solari, Grimm, et al., 2017) with emerging evidence suggesting that scores on inference measures may even decline over time (McIntyre et al., 2020). Some learners with ASD make appropriate local inferences but have greater difficulty integrating and inferring information to form a full mental model of text (Tirado & Saldaña, 2016). Inference making appears to be partially influenced by language development. That is, learners with ASD and structural language difficulties perform similarly to learners with language impairment on measures of inferencing than learners with ASD and no language impairment; however, learners with ASD and no language impairment score lower than typically developing learners (Lucas & Norbury, 2015).

Impact of Social Communication. Social interactions can support access to and engagement in literacy activities (RAND, 2002). Consequently, social skills have an impact on vocabulary and RC (Sparapani et al., 2018). This effect appears to be reciprocal with social skills, vocabulary, and RC influencing each other (Sparapani et al., 2018). Specific to learners with ASD, higher scores on measures of autism symptomology are associated with lower scores on RC measures (e.g., Jones et al., 2009; McIntyre, Solari, & Gonzales, 2017; McIntyre, Solari, Grimm, et al., 2017; Norbury & Nation, 2011; Ricketts et al., 2013). Studies have also identified a predictive relationship between theory of mind (ToM; inferring the mental states of others) and RC in learners with ASD (McIntyre et al., 2018; Ricketts et al., 2013). McIntyre and colleagues (2018) found that both ToM and oral language were unique predictors of RC in children with ASD, whereas word reading and oral language, but not ToM, were significant predictors for typically developing peers (McIntyre et al., 2018). This may partially explain why children with ASD are more likely to struggle comprehending text that requires social knowledge or understanding (Brown et al., 2013); these texts require the reader to make casual connections between actions or events and subsequent character feelings, emotions, and motivations (Guajardo & Cartwright, 2016).

Importance of Comprehensive Reading Instruction

Because of the heterogeneity associated with ASD, reading instruction must be comprehensive to include skills associated with word recognition (e.g., phonemic awareness, phonics, fluency) and comprehension (e.g., vocabulary, inference making, language comprehension, narrative understanding). Understanding that several learners with ASD will have difficulty developing word recognition and higher-order language skills (e.g., depth of vocabulary knowledge; inference generation) reinforces the need to intentionally select a comprehensive reading program that specifically and systematically teaches these skills. These skills emerge in the preschool years, suggesting that comprehensive literacy instruction (e.g., phonological awareness; language comprehension) should begin early (Kahn &

Justice, 2020). A quality comprehensive curriculum is designed to address the skills or precursor skills (preschool years) necessary for decoding, fluency, and comprehension in a targeted way that is guided by ongoing progress monitoring (Foorman et al., 2011).

Very few studies have investigated the benefits of comprehensive reading programs for learners with ASD, but emerging results are promising (e.g., Arciuli & Bailey, 2019; Arciuli & Bailey, 2021; Whalon, 2018; Whalon et al., 2009). Moreover, reviews of reading research demonstrate that children and youth with ASD do benefit from instruction that is consistent with scientifically based reading research in phonemic awareness, phonics, fluency, vocabulary, and comprehension (e.g., Arciuli & Bailey, 2019; Chiang & Lin, 2007; El Zein et al., 2016; Finnegan & Mazin, 2016; Whalon et al., 2009). Although identifying or designing a high-quality comprehensive program may be sufficient for some learners with ASD, others will require greater levels of intensity in one or more areas of reading (Whalon, 2018). Continuous progress monitoring will be required to select instructional goals and adjust instruction to ensure appropriate levels of instructional intensity (Arciuli & Bailey, 2021; Whalon, 2018).

In summary, reading interventions for all learners with ASD should be grounded in scientifically based reading instruction. Many learners with ASD will better access instruction with the addition of individualized focused intervention strategies to support their participation in learning activities (Arciuli & Bailey, 2019; Chiang & Lin, 2007; El Zein et al., 2016; Finnegan & Mazin, 2016; Whalon et al., 2009).

Mathematics Achievement

As a spectrum disorder that includes learners with and without a comorbid intellectual disability and above-average cognitive ability, it should be unsurprising that there is not a clear or agreed-upon mathematics achievement profile of learners with ASD. A conservative generalization is that the mathematical profile of learners with ASD is uneven (Jones et al., 2009) and compared to typically developing learners, learners with ASD are up to five times more likely to exhibit a mathematics disability (Mayes & Calhoun, 2003; Oswald et al., 2016). Large-scale assessments have found underachievement relative to cognitive ability (Charman et al., 2011). Strengths in rote memory and procedural tasks may mask some learners' true understanding of operations during early elementary years, suggesting a complexity and heterogeneity in the mathematical profile of learners with ASD (Wei, Christiano, et al., 2014). The theory of weak central coherence suggests that learners with ASD are likely to have strengths in processes requiring attention to detail, such as mathematics procedures (Happe & Frith, 2006). However, as they progress into middle grades, learners with ASD may face unique challenges making connections between concepts, applying mathematical procedures flexibly in unique contexts, and reasoning abstractly (Barnett & Cleary, 2015).

While learners with ASD will vary in their support needs in the area of mathematics, Cox and colleagues (2020) identified potential barriers related to characteristics associated with ASD and identified in the mathematics literature that will impact their academic instructional needs. Student-level characteristics include EF, weak central coherence, communication and reasoning, and ToM. In addition, past learning experiences influence the learner's preparedness to participate in mathematical learning opportunities. Level of literacy, level of numeracy, and past expectations were three factors identified by Cox and colleagues that will need to be considered in mathematics instruction for learners with ASD. Mathematics instruction that overemphasized functional skills such as time and money may leave learners without prerequisite or facilitating skills to make progress in mathematics (Cowan & Powell, 2014). As a developmental disability, ASD impacts the timing and rate of development. Some learners may need additional time and supplementary instruction to develop foundational skills.

Number sense and problem solving are critical components of mathematics instruction for all learners. Number sense is a broad term that refers to explicit number knowledge (Whitacre et al., 2017). Early number sense ability is predictive of future mathematical achievement but varies between learners based on their experiences (Jordan & Levine, 2009). Although number sense is a strong predictor of later success in mathematics for young children with ASD (Titeca et al., 2014), simply gaining number sense is not enough to become mathematically proficient. It lays the foundation for understanding operations learners need to make mathematical judgements required in more complex problem solving (McIntosh et al., 1992).

Problem solving is the cornerstone of mathematical learning, according to the National Council of Teachers of Mathematics (NCTM, 2000). Problem solving experiences in school settings are typically structured in the format of word problems, with stories presenting situations requiring a mathematical solution. Yet without a strong foundation of number sense, learners will struggle with reasoning and having a productive disposition about their ability to solve mathematical problems (Baroody et al., 2006). As such, Saunders and colleagues (2019) put forward a conceptual model for teaching mathematics that places continuous emphasis on building early numeracy skills (e.g., number sense) and mathematical problem solving throughout grade levels and domains of mathematics.

Number Sense

Number sense is key to meaningful access to and participation in mathematics (NCTM, 2000). Skills under the umbrella of number sense, such as rote counting, number identification, one-to-one correspondence, set making, estimation, and patterning are primarily emphasized in early elementary grades. Learners who struggle in mathematics in later grades often lacked opportunities to acquire critical number sense skills (Berch & Mazzocco, 2007), which has important implications for the early learning targets of learners with ASD. Three reasons learners fail to develop number sense are (1) lack of experience or exposure, (2) poor prior instruction, and (3) slow developmental progression (Sarama & Clements, 2009). To be successful, learners need explicit instruction in number sense skills the same way they need structured opportunities to gain early literacy skills like phonemic awareness and listening comprehension when becoming readers (Gersten & Chard, 1999). Some children acquire early number sense through conversations and play activities (Sarama & Clements, 2009) but many require specific instruction to develop them (Andrews & Sayers, 2015). Given that children with disabilities enter kindergarten with less number sense than typically developing peers and demonstrate less growth than those without disabilities (Hojnoski et al., 2018), attention to growth in number sense is warranted.

Emerging research indicates that the counting skills of learners with ASD are likely similar to typically developing learners, but they do not develop or rely on subitizing (Gagnon et al., 2004). *Subitizing* is the ability to rapidly or immediately comprehend the magnitude of small numbers (i.e., knowing there are three dots without having to count the dots; Clements, 1999). In other words, learners with ASD focus on individual items when counting as opposed to the composition or pattern of the picture as a whole. Counting and subitizing are predictive of future mathematical abilities for learners with ASD and typically developing learners, with subitizing being the most predictive skill for learners with ASD (Titeca et al., 2014). This may be because skills such as subitizing are often not an explicit learning target in preschool or primary grades, but rather learned through observation of materials and behaviors of other people (Sarama & Clements, 2009). Given difficulties with observational learning and social communication, mathematics skills that are expected to be learned intuitively or implicitly are likely to be more difficult for learners with ASD to acquire (Titeca et al., 2015). It is clear that learners with ASD need explicit instructional opportunities to learn foundational number sense skills to make progress in mathematics (Clements & Sarama, 2015; Henning & Intepe, 2021; Jimenez & Kemmery, 2013; Nguyen et al., 2016; Root et al., 2020)

Problem Solving

Word problem solving is a strong school-age predictor of employment and wages in adulthood (Batty et al., 2010). The ability to apply mathematical skills and knowledge to a given situation requires a deep and robust knowledge of problem-solving procedures (Star, 2005) that are deployed based on rapidly and accurately perceiving the mathematical structure of the situation at hand based on prior experience with similar problems (Van Dooren et al., 2010). Further, proficiency in problem solving requires strong metacognitive skills; learners must plan, check, monitor, and evaluate performance (e.g., Montague, 1997). Expert problem solvers demonstrate the ability to distinguish relevant information from irrelevant (contextual details) and knowledge of problem-solving procedures for a given class of problems and metacognitive skills to check their work (Schoenfeld & Herrmann, 1982). That is, successful problem solvers combine conceptual and procedural knowledge to solve real-world problems.

Conceptual knowledge reflects knowledge about the relationships or foundational ideas of a topic, combining the two skills of comprehending the problem and modeling the problem (Eisenhart et al., 1993; Rittle-Johnson & Schneider, 2015). *Procedural knowledge* is demonstrated by fluency in the use of rules and procedures in carrying out mathematical processes and the symbols used to represent mathematics (Rittle-Johnson, 2017). A learner would use conceptual knowledge to distinguish between word problems that require combining quantities to find a total from those that require finding the difference between two quantities. For example, the following problem is classified as a *change* problem and requires finding the difference between two quantities: "Hazel is a waitress at a restaurant. She had 7 drinks on her tray. Then she tripped and spilled 2 drinks. How many drinks does she still have left on her tray?" Procedural knowledge is then needed to use manipulatives, representations (e.g., drawings, tally marks), or mental math to carry out the subtraction procedures and arrive at a solution.

Word problem solving draws on a combination of language comprehension and mathematical problem-solving processes (Fuchs et al., 2020). According to original theories of Kintsch and colleagues (Cummins et al., 1988; Kintsch & Greeno, 1985), individuals first construct a representation of the ideas that are directly expressed in a text. Next, problem solvers supplement that information with inferences based on their own knowledge, including relations among quantities. Finally, problem solvers use knowledge about schemas to formalize relations among quantities and formalize a plan to apply solution strategies. This process draws heavily on working memory as the problem solver must store and sequentially update information in memory as they process segments of the word problem (Fuchs et al., 2019).

Mathematics learning difficulties are related to the combination of disrupted function of the central executive, which includes attentional control and poor inhibition of irrelevant associations, and difficulties with information representation and manipulation in the language system (Geary & Hoard, 2005). EF is a critical factor in math performance (Zentall, 2007) and is required for planning, organizing, switching cognitive sets, and working memory, areas in which learners with ASD often have executive dysfunctions (Hill, 2004). Language plays an important role in problem solving because it is required for text comprehension (Catts et al., 2005). In samples of typically developing children, language is more strongly related to word problem solving skill development than arithmetic (Fuchs et al., 2008; 2016). Two forms of language comprehension are involved in word problem solving: general language comprehension and word problem–specific language comprehension (Fuchs et al., 2020). Further, participation in mathematical discourse relies on expressive language abilities. The ability to communicate one's own mathematical ideas is likely to be difficult for learners with ASD with social communication deficits. Learners with ASD will need instruction that connects procedural and conceptual understanding while considering communication and language needs, going beyond computation to support comprehension and mathematical vocabulary (Bae et al., 2015).

CONSIDERATIONS FOR DESIGNING INSTRUCTION

Three critical assumptions when selecting instructional targets include (a) all learners can learn, (b) communicative competence is integral to achievement, and (c) assessment and instruction must be responsive to learners' language, cultural heritage, and disability (Root et al., 2019). Donnellan's (1984) criterion of the least dangerous assumption can guide the assessment and planning process by ensuring the focus is on gathering information on the supports and skills learners need to have as optimal a life as possible. The assumption that all learners can learn motivates educators to conduct assessments and use data as the mode for determining what learners with ASD have learned and might best be taught.

Determining What to Teach
The foundational skills required of RC and mathematics are the same for all learners. In other words, the process for learning how to read or understand

mathematical concepts is not different for learners with ASD compared to their typically developing peers. For this reason, all learners should be taught foundational skills consistent with current research. As we established earlier in the chapter, however, many learners with ASD may have more difficulty acquiring specific content-related skills compared to their typically developing peers. This will require that educators be able to individualize their instruction based on the specific needs of their learner (more on this later). An essential question that practitioners must initially decide is "what do I teach?" Fortunately, there are resources available that can guide practitioners' selection of academic skills. One such resource is practice guides for teaching foundational reading and early mathematics published by the U.S. Department of Education's What Works Clearinghouse (WWC; see additional resource section). These recommendations are based on current research of reading and mathematics development and are applicable for learners with ASD.

In terms of reading, the WWC recommends that educators focus their instruction on the following skills that form the foundation for reading development:

1. Teach learners academic language skills, including the use of inferential and narrative language, and vocabulary knowledge.
2. Develop awareness of the segments of sound in speech and how they link to letters.
3. Teach learners to decode words, analyze word parts, and write and recognize words.
4. Ensure that each learner reads connected text every day to support reading accuracy, fluency, and comprehension.

Examples of foundational reading learning goals aligned with these recommendations can be found in Table 9.1.

Similarly, the WWC published a practice guide based on mathematics research. The following are evidence-based recommendations for early mathematics skills:

1. Teach number and operations using a developmental progression.
2. Teach geometry, patterns, measurement, and data analysis using a developmental progression.
3. Teach learners to view and describe their world mathematically.

Examples of early mathematics learning goals aligned with these recommendations can be found in Table 9.2.

State Content Standards: General & Alternate Achievement

Every state adopts educational standards that outline learning goals that learners should achieve at each grade level. State content standards should align with research recommendations, such as those published by the WWC. Teachers are expected to align their instruction and assess their learners' progress toward these goals. School-age learners with ASD can access, and therefore be assessed on, two types of academic content standards. Learners with less extensive academic

Table 9.1. Examples of Common Core State Standards (CCSS) Aligned with What Works Clearinghouse (WWC) Foundational Reading Skills Recommendations

WWC Recommendation: Teach students academic language skills, including the use of inferential and narrative language, and vocabulary knowledge.
CCSS.ELA-LITERACY.RL.1.1 Ask and answer questions about key details in a text.
CCSS.ELA-LITERACY.RL.1.2 Retell stories, including key details, and demonstrate understanding of their central message or lesson.
CCSS.ELA-LITERACY.RL.2.9 Compare and contrast two or more versions of the same story (e.g., Cinderella stories) by different authors or from different cultures.
WWC Recommendation: Develop awareness of the segments of sound in speech and how they link to letters.
CCSS.ELA-LITERACY.RF.K.2.A Recognize and produce rhyming words.
CCSS.ELA-LITERACY.RF.K.3.A Demonstrate basic knowledge of one-to-one letter-sound correspondences by producing the primary sound or many of the most frequent sounds for each consonant.
CCSS.ELA-LITERACY.RF.K.2.E Add or substitute individual sounds (phonemes) in simple, one-syllable words to make new words.
WWC Recommendation: Teach students to decode words, analyze word parts, and write and recognize words.
CCSS.ELA-LITERACY.RF.K.3.B Associate the long and short sounds with the common spellings (graphemes) for the five major vowels.
CCSS.ELA-LITERACY.RF.K.3.C Read common high-frequency words by sight (e.g., *the, of, to, you, she, my, is, are, do, does*).
WWC Recommendation: Ensure that each student reads connected text every day to support reading accuracy, fluency, and comprehension.
CCSS.ELA-LITERACY.RF.K.4 Read emergent-reader texts with purpose and understanding.
CCSS.ELA-LITERACY.RF.1.4.B Read grade-level text orally with accuracy, appropriate rate, and expression on successive readings.

Note: A comprehensive list and description of Common Core State Standards can be found online at http://www.corestandards.org/

Table 9.2.   Examples of Common Core State Standards (CCSS) Aligned with What Works Clearinghouse (WWC) Early Mathematics Recommendations

WWC Recommendation: Teach number and operations using a developmental progression.
CCSS.MATH.CONTENT.K.CC.A.1 Count to 100 by ones and by tens.
CCSS.MATH.CONTENT.K.CC.B.4 Understand the relationship between numbers and quantities; connect counting to cardinality.
CCSS.MATH.CONTENT.K.OA.A.1 Represent addition and subtraction with objects, fingers, mental images, drawings, sounds (e.g., claps), acting out situations, verbal explanations, expressions, or equations.
WWC Recommendation: Teach geometry, patterns, measurement, and data analysis using a developmental progression.
CCSS.MATH.CONTENT.K.G.A.2 Correctly name shapes regardless of their orientations or overall size.
CCSS.MATH.CONTENT.K.MD.B.3 Classify objects into given categories; count the numbers of objects in each category and sort the categories by count.
CCSS.MATH.CONTENT.K.MD.A.1 Describe measurable attributes of objects, such as length or weight. Describe several measurable attributes of a single object.
WWC Recommendation: Teach children to view and describe their world mathematically.
CCSS.MATH.CONTENT.K.MD.A.2 Directly compare two objects with a measurable attribute in common, to see which object has "more of"/"less of" the attribute, and describe the difference. *For example, directly compare the heights of two children and describe one child as taller/shorter.*
CCSS.MATH.CONTENT.K.G.A.1 Describe objects in the environment using names of shapes, and describe the relative positions of these objects using terms such as *above, below, beside, in front of, behind,* and *next to.*

Note: A comprehensive list and description of Common Core State Standards can be found online at http://www.corestandards.org/

support needs who do not have a comorbid cognitive impairment access general state standards. Learners with ASD may have accommodations on their individualized education programs (IEPs) related to these formal summative assessments, but they are expected to be taught and make progress on the same state standards as typically developing peers, referred to as general achievement standards. Learners with ASD who have more extensive support needs and a comorbid cognitive impairment (e.g., learners who require substantial and very substantial levels of support) may instead access alternate achievement standards and, therefore, take alternate assessments.

Alternate assessments based on alternate achievement standards (AA-AAS) are assessments of academic content used for accountability purposes required by the IDEIA (2004) for learners with "significant cognitive disabilities," as determined by each state's eligibility criteria (National Center on Educational Outcomes, 2016). Federal mandates for states to assess learner progress in math and reading in Grades 3–8 and in high school also apply to learners with disabilities, including ASD. The most recent national data available show 27% of the learners who participated in their state's AA-AAS were eligible for special education under the category of autism in 2015 (National Center and State Collaborative [NCSC], 2016). Approximately half of the learners who receive special education services under the category of autism take their state's AA-AAS (Newman et al., 2007). These assessments are based on the same grade-level content standards, but they have different achievement standards (NCSC, 2016).

State content standards define what content will be taught and, therefore, assessed in each grade both on general assessments and on alternate assessments. Alternate achievement standards define how well learners need to perform to be considered proficient (NCSC, 2016). Table 9.3 provides an example of the same

Table 9.3. Example of General and Alternate Achievement Standards in Reading and Mathematics

Content and grade level	General achievement standard	Alternate achievement standard
Third grade reading	Describe the relationship between a series of historical events, scientific ideas or concepts, or steps in technical procedures in a text, using language that pertains to time, sequence, and cause/effect.	Identify the sequence of events in an informational text.
Eighth grade reading	Determine the meaning of words and phrases as they are used in a text, including figurative, connotative, and technical meanings; analyze the impact of specific word choices on meaning and tone, including analogies or allusions to other texts.	Identify and interpret an analogy within a text.
Second grade mathematics	Solve one- and two-step word problems involving dollar bills (singles, fives, tens, twenties, and hundreds) or coins (quarters, dimes, nickels, and pennies) using $ and ¢ symbols appropriately.	Solve word problems using dollar bills, quarters, dimes, nickels, or pennies up to $50.
Seventh grade mathematics	Solve real-world and mathematical problems involving area, volume, and surface area of two- and three-dimensional objects composed of triangles, quadrilaterals, polygons, cubes, and right prisms.	Solve one-step, real-world measurement problems involving area, volume, or surface area of two- and three-dimensional objects.

content and different achievement standards in reading and mathematics at the elementary and secondary level. The determination of whether a learner participates in the standard assessment (and therefore is expected to make progress on the general achievement standards) or in the AA-AAS (and therefore be expected to make progress on alternate achievement standards) is made by the IEP team.

While state standards, published guidelines, and commercially available curricula give starting points for selecting instructional targets, additional considerations can help in prioritizing skills. Instruction should be designed to target prioritized standards and address IEP goals, which are not intended to encompass everything that should be taught to a learner or cover every standard in a grade level (Saunders, 2020). The relationship between high-quality instruction, curriculum, and assessments can be viewed as a triangular relationship that indicates alignment (Courtade & Browder, 2016). True alignment occurs when the general curriculum or grade-level standards are used, instruction on these standards is based on sound research and evidence-based practices, and the learner is being prepared for the general assessment or their state's alternate assessment (Saunders, 2020).

Follow the 3 P's

The 3 P's (prioritize, pinpoint, progress monitor) can be followed to help select what to teach to ensure learners with ASD are making progress in academic learning targets (Saunders, 2020). Skills can be **prioritized** by determining which are pivotal to making progress in the domain and being prepared for what will come next. General education teachers are experts in content areas and can provide important insight during this process. To have meaningful access to the general curriculum, learners with ASD need ongoing instruction at their level in pivotal foundational reading and mathematics skills, as well as targeted instruction on grade-level content. Foundational skill knowledge should not be a barrier (or a deterrent) from simultaneously teaching grade-level content (Root et al., 2019).

Next, selected standards can be **pinpointed**, as they are often complex and encompass multiple skills and concepts (Saunders, 2020). Often the standard will need to be narrowed down or broken into component skills. For example, in the seventh-grade mathematics example in Table 9.3, a learner with ASD who accesses the general achievement standard may focus on one formula at a time (e.g., area of two-dimensional objects) before moving onto an additional formula (surface area of three-dimensional objects). For a learner with ASD who is accessing the alternate achievement standards, instruction on foundational mathematics skills (e.g., counting with one-to-one correspondence) can be embedded within instruction on this grade-level standard by counting how many square tiles fit inside a given quadrilateral.

Selecting instructional targets is not an annual or static process but should be revisited and evaluated based on data from **progress monitoring** (Saunders, 2020). Data should be used to determine learners' strengths and needs in reading and mathematics as well as to assess progress to adjust instruction (Cox et al., 2020). A capacity-building view of assessment posits the assessments as tools for increasing learner capacity to learn and achieve, in contrast to a deficit view in which assessments are seen as mechanisms for identifying deficiencies (Browder et al., 2015). Assessments can be powerful tools for promoting learner competence and academic success if they are selected, administered, and interpreted correctly. An important consideration for learners with ASD is that many standardized or formal assessments are already biased against their specific learning characteristics. For example, comprehension tests that require independent reading of traditional (unsupported) text may be difficult for learners who benefit from assistive technology such as text-to-speech. Similarly, learners who do not use vocal speech may face challenges demonstrating what they know when tests require vocal speech as a response mode. Obtaining accurate data on learner needs is crucial to selecting academic instructional targets.

Address Stages of Learning

Instruction needs to provide an appropriate level of challenge, which occurs when the tasks' difficulty and learners' performance are aligned (Burns et al., 2008). This can also be thought of as the "Goldilocks rule." Learners need to experience success contingent upon effort. As previously discussed, assessment data should be used to determine learner instructional targets. Instructional approaches should vary depending on which stage of learning (e.g., acquisition, fluency, maintenance, generalization) learners are in for that particular skill (Shurr et al., 2019). There is an interactive relationship between these stages; each stage is dependent on the others (Kubina & Wolfe, 2005). Table 9.4 provides examples of how academic goals build across the stages of learning.

The initial and most basic stage of learning is *acquisition*, which Collins (2012) describes as the ability to do something that could not previously be done with some degree of accuracy. Shurr and colleagues (2019) quantify performance in this stage as less than 60% accuracy, with low-to-moderate levels of initiation.

Table 9.4. **Instructional Goals Across Stages of Learning**

Acquisition	Fluency	Maintenance	Generalization
Given 10 or more objects, the learner will make sets of 2–5 objects with verbal prompting.	Given 10 or more objects, the learner will make sets of 2–5 objects independently within 1 min.	Given 10 or more objects, the learner will make sets of 2–5 objects independently within 1 min on biweekly probes.	Given 10 or more classroom supplies, the learner will gather supplies for 2–5 classmates within 1 min.
After reading or listening to a text read aloud, the learner will identify the main character when given an array of three choices that include one near and one far distractor.	After reading or listening to a text read aloud, the learner will identify the main character when given an array of three choices that include two near distractors.	After reading or listening to a text read aloud, the learner will identify the main character when given an array of three choices that include two near distractors.	After watching a film, the learner will identify the main character.

Burns and colleagues (2008) characterize this stage as low accuracy and subsequent dysfluency. To support acquiring new behaviors and skills, learners with ASD will need high levels of support and reinforcement and cannot be expected to perform consistently or flexibly. Errorless learning strategies such as constant time delay, simultaneous prompting, and modeling are appropriate for academic skills that are in the acquisition phase (Wood et al., 2018). The goal of errorless learning is to prevent learners from making mistakes that they will need to eventually "unlearn" (Collins, 2012). Learners with ASD will need frequent opportunities to produce the correct response with mastery-oriented feedback. Providing ample opportunities to rehearse skills in combination with explicit reinforcement for correct responding improves learners' engagement, acquisition, and retention of the target skill (Burns et al., 2008).

As learners meet the criterion for acquisition, instructional strategies should shift to focus on supporting both accuracy and efficiency to facilitate fluency, the second stage of learning. Learners must achieve automaticity (automatic retrieval) and fluency (accurate and fast retrieval) of academic skills for them to be useful (Wood et al., 2018). Some have described this stage as an indication of initial "mastery"; the goal at this stage is for learners to apply the target skill with accuracy and a rate that is appropriate for the context (Haring & Eaton, 1978). Take, for example, a learner who requires 5 min to calculate a percentage of a whole number. While his calculation is accurate, the time he requires to reach the correct response may prevent him from using this skill to figure the tip on a restaurant bill.

Shurr and colleagues (2019) operationalized *fluency* phase as greater than 60% accuracy combined with the ability to initiate and consistently perform the skill with minimal support. The appropriate rate can be determined by considering the age-appropriate speed for the skill, expectations in different situations, and how technology can assist the learner to increase fluency (Shurr et al., 2019). In academic learning targets, fluency is most associated with reading (e.g., oral reading fluency). In fact, oral reading fluency is a strong predictor of RC (National Reading Panel, 2000). In mathematics, fluency allows learners to compose and decompose numbers, use computation methods flexibly, and express confidence in their understanding of numbers (Parrish, 2014). Two instructional variables that support fluency are trial format and reinforcement (Collins, 2012). Learners will need multiple opportunities to practice skills to gain automaticity and reinforcement that is contingent on behavior at a desired level or rate.

The third stage of learning is sometimes seen as a component of the other levels of learning (Haring & Eaton, 1978), but Shurr and colleagues (2019) emphasize the importance of viewing maintenance as its own stage when assessing and planning instruction, especially for learners with ASD. *Maintenance* is the ability to perform a response over time without reteaching (Collins, 2012). Learners with ASD who maintain academic learning skills demonstrate self-initiation, independence, accuracy, and consistency but do not necessarily apply the skill to new settings or under different conditions than those under which they were taught. Maintenance of skills can be promoted through periodic review of previously learned content, careful integration of mastered skills into future instruction, and multiple opportunities for skill practice after fluency has been achieved (e.g., overlearning; Shurr et al., 2019). As learners have the opportunity to practice mastered skills, instructional supports and reinforcement should match or be faded from those used during the fluency phase. In other words, control and responsibility for skill performance should shift as much as possible to the learner with ASD. Periodic monitoring of learner progress determines whether learners have maintained skills over time and whether any skills or steps continue to need support (Shurr et al., 2019).

Although generalization is the final stage of learning, it can and should be considered when planning all other stages (Collins, 2012). Academic instruction will have the most value when learners with ASD are able to consistently demonstrate skills or concepts with different people, in different places, or with different materials. Shurr and colleagues (2019) position *generalization* as the primary purpose of learning because it means the learner is able to predictably complete a skill accurately, independently, and consistently over time when given materials or cues that differ from those used in instruction. Instructional procedures used in the acquisition stage may be appropriate (e.g., constant time delay, modeling). Alternatively, it may be that learners need explicit discrimination training using a multiple exemplar approach to assist with concept formation or correct overgeneralization (Steinbrenner et al., 2020; Wood et al., 2018). Using multiple exemplars, or various examples of the stimuli or responses to stimuli during instruction, promotes generalization as it teaches learners to attend to the relevant features of the concept and disregard the irrelevant features. Similar to maintenance, generalization probes should be used to identify specific skills or steps to target for additional instruction.

EVIDENCE-BASED PRACTICES TO TEACH READING AND MATHEMATICS SKILLS

Effective instruction for learners with ASD requires that practitioners are planful and systematic about their instruction. Learners with ASD benefit most from instruction that has clear expectations and explicit consequences. In this section, we discuss practices that practitioners can embed within learning activities to accomplish this. Multiple strategies have been used to teach content-related skills for learners with ASD (Fleury et al., 2014; Steinbrenner et al., 2020), which we summarize in Table 9.5. For the purpose of this chapter, however, we will limit our discussion to five specific evidence-based strategies: prompting, time delay, visual supports, task analysis, and explicit or direct instruction. These were selected because each strategy has a robust research base to support its effectiveness and has been successfully used to teach skills across academic domains to learners who represent a range of ability levels.

Prompting

A traditional learning trial according to a behavioral learning perspective includes three key elements: the discriminative stimulus (S^D), the target behavior, and the consequence. The S^D sets the occasion for a learner to demonstrate a specific behavior. Consider the following example. Upon seeing a multiplication problem, learners are expected to answer the problem. The teacher reviews their work and provides a grade based on the accuracy of their responses. In this example, the math problem serves as the S^D, which sets the occasion for a specific behavior (i.e., answer the problem). The consequence serves as feedback for the accuracy of the

Table 9.5. Strategies to Teach Content Area Skills

Instructional strategy	English language arts						Math			
	Phonemic awareness	Phonics	Fluency	Vocabulary	Comprehension	Writing	Counting & cardinality	Numbers & operations	Operations & algebraic thinking	Geometry & measurement
Prompting	X	X	X	X	X	X	X	X	X	X
Visual Supports	X	X	X	X		X	X	X	X	X
Reinforcement	X	X	X	X	X		X	X	X	X
Cognitive Behavioral Strategies	X	X	X	X		X	X	X	X	X
Discrete Trial Training	X	X	X	X	X		X	X		
Technology Aided Instruction					X	X	X	X	X	X
Time Delay	X	X	X	X	X	X	X	X	X	X
Video Modeling					X	X	X	X	X	X
Direct Instruction	X	X	X	X		X	X	X	X	X
Task Analysis	X	X	X	X	X	X	X	X	X	X
Multiple Exemplars	X	X	X	X		X	X	X	X	X
Graphic Organizers				X	X	X		X	X	X
Model-Lead-Test	X	X	X	X	X	X	X	X	X	X

behavioral response and influences the likelihood that the learner will demonstrate the behavior in the future. The consequence can only be delivered, however, if the target behavior is demonstrated. Practitioners can teach their learners to demonstrate the target response—in this case, providing the correct answer—through prompting. Prompts are delivered after the S^D to provide additional support for the learner to produce the desired behavioral response. Prompting assumes different forms including visual, verbal, gestural, model, or physical assistance. The type of prompt an educator selects depends on the target behavior and learner.

Rameriez and colleagues (2014) conducted a study to teach adolescents with ASD to calculate the duration of time that elapsed when conducting activities. They created a task analysis for solving equations for elapsed time that involved three steps: (1) setting up a vertical subtraction problem, (2) subtracting the start time from the end time, and (3) writing the answer. For each step of the task analysis, the teacher prompted the learner if they did not initiate the step independently. In this study, the teacher completed the problem along with the learner, using her own paper. The teacher used a model prompt, which involved her writing out the correct step. The learner referred to the model and completed the corresponding step. This procedure was repeated until all steps of the task analysis were completed.

Prompting has also been used to teach sentence writing to elementary learners with ASD and learners with moderate intellectual disabilities (Pennington et al., 2018). This study included three learners who were taught to write several types of sentences. Learners were provided a picture and given the direction to "Write a sentence about _____." If the learners did not initiate the target response, the teacher prompted them using a printed model (e.g., "I see a fish."). If this prompt did not elicit the target response, the teacher introduced a more intrusive level of prompting by presenting a word bank and physically prompting the learner to select an appropriate response to complete the sentence.

Time Delay

It is important for practitioners to systematically fade any prompts that are used initially in their instruction to prevent learners from becoming prompt dependent. The goal is for learners to independently demonstrate the skill in the presence of the natural S^D, not the instructional prompt. This is also referred to as *stimulus control*. One method for systematically fading prompts is called *time delay*. When using time delay, the practitioner withholds the delivery of the prompt to allow the learner the opportunity to respond independently. There are two types of time delay procedures (Touchette, 1971). In *progressive time delay* (PTD), the controlling prompt is provided in slowly increasing intervals, beginning with 0 s in initial instruction and then increasing incrementally (e.g., 2 s, 4 s, 6 s). In *constant time delay* (CTD) the controlling prompt is provided after a set (or constant) delay interval, beginning with 0 s during initial instruction and a consistent number of seconds during subsequent trials (e.g., 4 s). Both CTD and PTD must begin instruction with the 0 s delay rounds, meaning that there is 0 s between the presentation of the stimulus and the delivery of the prompt, which is what makes the procedure considered "errorless"; learners should be emitting the correct response on initial learning trials as they are imitating the controlling or model prompt.

Time delay was used to teach five elementary learners with ASD and/or moderate intellectual disability number identification (Jimenez & Kemmery, 2013). During initial teaching trials, the teacher verbally prompted the correct response immediately after showing the number (e.g., 0 s delay) and then had the learner repeat the name. Once the learner consistently responded, the teacher began fading the verbal prompt using time delay at 5-s intervals. This involved presenting the number (S^D) and waiting 5 s for the learner to name the number. If no response was provided after 5 s, the teacher would verbally prompt the learner.

Visual Supports

Visual supports are widely used for learners with ASD. They are particularly beneficial to learners with ASD because of their concrete nature. Moreover, they minimize reliance on oral language comprehension skills that are required when following verbal directions. Visual supports can be used in a variety of ways and across activities, such as providing the learner with information regarding the steps of a task or behaviors that are expected in an activity or setting (Steinbrenner et al., 2020). They are often used in conjunction with other evidence-based practices such as prompting, task analysis, and explicit instruction that are described in this chapter. Visual supports are provided in the form of visual schedules, graphic organizers, and visual cues.

Bethune and Wood (2013) studied the effects of wh-question graphic organizers on RC for three elementary learners with ASD. The graphic organizer consisted of four columns, each labeled with the following wh-questions: who (person), where (place), what (place), and what (thing). Learners sorted words into the corresponding categories on the graphic organizer. Once the words were sorted into the correct category, the teacher read a short passage and asked the learners to reread the passage aloud. The teacher asked eight wh-questions and prompted the learners to use the graphic organizer to assist in answering the questions. All three learners demonstrated a positive change in ability to answer comprehension questions after the implementation of the graphic organizer.

In another study, Browder and her colleagues (2017) used an electronic story-mapping procedure to improve comprehension of narrative text for elementary school learners with ASD. This single case design study included three elementary school learners with ASD who participated in the AA-AAS. The intervention procedures included the use of CTD to answer questions about story elements. In addition, teachers used a system of least prompts to teach content vocabulary and graphic organizers to support learners' story comprehension. The results demonstrated a functional relation between the intervention and improved understanding of story elements. In addition, learners' use of graphic organizers improved correct responding to comprehension questions.

Task Analysis

Many academic skills are comprised of multiple steps that, when executed in sequence, lead to the correct response. Many learners with ASD will benefit from breaking down, and being explicitly taught, smaller skills that make up the larger task. Task analysis is a procedure that involves taking a larger task comprised of multiple steps, breaking it down into smaller achievable steps, and systematically teaching each step. In a study conducted by Cox and coauthors (2020), task analysis was used to assist learners to solve proportion word problems. Two middle-school learners in general education math classes were provided with explicit instruction on the use of a task analysis to solve word problems during an intervention that took place after school hours. The teacher provided explicit instruction in the use of the task analysis that showed the relationship between quantities in problems and used systematic prompting and feedback. During the intervention, the teacher modeled how to follow the steps of the task analysis to solve one problem in two ways and explain the answer, led the learner in guided practice through solving a second problem, and tested the learner's ability to solve the problem and explain their answer through independent practice. Both learners correctly solved proportional word problems using multiple strategies and explained their mathematical reasoning more consistently and at a higher rate during intervention and maintenance stages with the use of a task analysis and schematic diagrams.

Explicit Instruction

Explicit instruction is a structured approach to teaching that involves scripted lessons, utilizes teacher and learner interaction through dialogue in a choral and independent manner, and provides systematic and explicit error correction to increase mastery and generalization (Steinbrenner et al., 2020). Explicit instruction is traditionally implemented in small groups, with lessons delivered at a rapid pace to maintain learner engagement. The teacher evokes learners' responses through defined prompts, and explicit procedures are used for error correction or non-responses (Steinbrenner et al., 2020). Through explicit instruction (e.g., model-lead-test and multiple exemplars) the teacher designs instruction in a sequential manner so that the learner is able to obtain mastery of the critical skills prior to moving on to more complex skills (Pennington et al. 2019). During model-lead-test, the teacher models the task, then completes the task along with the learner, and then tests the learner by having them complete the task independently.

Language for Learning (McGraw Hill, 2008) is a commercially available curriculum that uses a direct, explicit instruction approach to teach early language and literacy skills. A key feature of Direct Instruction curriculum is the use of scripted interactions and cued responding. A common concern with explicit instruction is the extent to which a learner's skills generalize to more natural educational conditions. Wolfe and her colleagues (2018) evaluated the extent to which learners' skills acquired through the *Language for Learning* curriculum generalized to untrained stimuli, specifically instructional stimuli, educational staff, and books that were not part of the original study. Two children, ages 4 and 7 years old, participated in the curriculum as prescribed. The results were variable, with one child demonstrating generalized behaviors to untrained stimuli while the other child generalized language skills with other educational staff.

Explicit instruction has also been successfully applied to teach math problem solving for learners with ASD. Root and her colleagues (2018) evaluated the use of modified based schema instruction (MSBI) on problem solving that requires algebraic reasoning. The MSBI procedure involved the following: (a) reading problems aloud to increase accessibility for learners; (b) graphic organizers to increase the conceptual understanding of problems presented; and (c) explicit instruction of task analysis in conjunction with systematic prompting as needed for error correction. Middle school–aged learners with ASD were taught to discriminate between, and solve, "missing whole" and "missing part" problems. Ultimately, Root and colleagues (2018) established a functional relation between MSBI and improved problem solving, and student learning maintained over time.

SUMMARY

Academic skills profiles vary across the population and within individual learners. It is essential, albeit challenging, for practitioners to provide instruction to meet the varied academic needs of their learners with ASD. In this chapter, we provide an overview of what is known about academic performance of learners with ASD in regard to reading and mathematics. We referred to the extant literature to describe the nature of difficulties that learners may have in acquiring and using reading and mathematics skills to inform potential instructional targets aligned with general education and alternate achievement standards. Fortunately, the research on academic interventions has grown across the last decade to reveal a number of evidence-based practices that practitioners can use to teach a range of skills across content areas. The information presented in this chapter serves as an initial guide for practitioners who want to know *what* to teach in addition to *how* to teach academic content to learners with ASD who present heterogeneous support needs.

CASE STUDY

Katie Wolfe and Laura C. Chezan

Background

Ahmad is a 9-year-old with ASD who loves playing outside and doing art. He attends his local neighborhood school where he spends most of his day in the general education classroom with his peers. During reading, his special education teacher comes into the classroom to provide Ahmad with additional instruction on comprehension skills. Although Ahmad is able to decode many grade-level words, and is able to define many words in isolation, he has difficulty identifying the basic elements of narratives. One of his IEP goals is to identify the main character, the setting, and the problem in a short story after reading it.

Step 1: Question to Initiate the Evidence-Based Treatment Selection Process

What interventions may be effective for teaching Ahmad to identify the basic elements of stories he has read?

Step 2—Part 1: Best Available Evidence

Ahmad's special education teacher uses his question from Step 1 to guide his search for evidence for interventions he can use to teach reading comprehension skills, and specifically the identification of story elements (i.e., main characters, settings, and problem) to learners with ASD. He searches the What Works Clearinghouse database, the National Clearinghouse on Autism Evidence and Practice, and the IRIS Center. He also searches practitioner journals including *Teaching Exceptional Children*. Although the special education teacher does not find one singular evidence-based practice (EBP) specifically for teaching story elements, he finds that both direct instruction (for example, the corrective reading program) and graphic organizers have research support for teaching general reading comprehension skills to learners with ASD.

Step 2—Part 2: Person-Related Variables

As Ahmad's special education teacher considers the best approach to teach him how to identify story elements, he takes into account Ahmad's preferences. Ahmad enjoys art and is very creative, so he may prefer graphic organizers to direct instruction. When the teacher asks Ahmad about his preferences, he indicates that he would like to use the graphic organizers to support him in learning this new skill.

Step 2—Part 3: Contextual Variables (Resource Constraints, Environmental Supports)

Ahmad's special education teacher plans to implement the intervention in the general education classroom during reading. The teacher and other learners will be present in the room, and the implementation of the scripted, structured direct instruction curriculum may be stigmatizing for

(continued)

Ahmad. However, it is possible that other learners in the classroom could benefit from additional instruction on reading comprehension and the special education teacher could implement the intervention with multiple learners in a group format. The direct instruction curriculum is also packaged, scripted, and ready to go, requiring minimal teacher preparation time. The graphic organizers, on the other hand, would require the teacher to select a story, create a corresponding graphic organizer, and design instructional strategies to teach Ahmad how to use the graphic organizer.

Step 3: Professional Judgment

Ahmad's special education teacher considers the advantages and disadvantages of the two intervention strategies (see Table 9.6). Although the graphic organizers would require more planning time, Ahmad's special education teacher sees the value in teaching Ahmad to use a tool that he could create independently for any novel story that he reads. He also wants to select an intervention that is likely to be engaging and motivating for Ahmad, and given Ahmad's interest in art, graphic organizers are likely to be preferred. In addition, graphic organizers are widely used in schools, providing evidence of their social validity.

Table 9.6. Advantages and Disadvantages of Potential Interventions for Ahmad

Intervention	Advantages	Disadvantages
Direct instruction	• Scripted • Minimal teacher preparation • Can be implemented in a small group format	• May not generalize to novel stories • May be less preferred • May include many other skills that Ahmad has mastered
Graphic organizers	• Applicability across stories and subjects • Use across settings indicates social validity • Preferred by Ahmad	• Requires more teacher time to prepare • Teacher must design instruction on how to use

Step 4: Intervention Selection

The special education teacher decides to use graphic organizers, along with prompts, to teach Ahmad to identify the basic elements of a narrative. While the direct instruction curricula may have been easier for him to implement, the teacher ultimately decided that Ahmad's interest in the graphic organizer and its long-term benefits for Ahmad were worth the extra time.

Step 5: Intervention Implementation and Data Collection

The special education teacher selects initial stories and develops related graphic organizers. He also plans to use direct and indirect verbal prompts to teach Ahmad to identify the story elements and use the graphic organizer. The teacher collects data twice a week on Ahmad's accurate identification of the story elements. He graphs the data weekly to evaluate progress.

Step 6: Reevaluation

After 4 weeks, Ahmad can accurately identify the main character and the setting, but is having difficulty identifying the beginning, middle, and end of the story. The special education teacher reviews Ahmad's completed graphic organizers and notices that he often recalls the events but is not sequencing them correctly. He decides to add a supplemental instructional program designed to teach sequencing of events using activities that are familiar to Ahmad, such as brushing teeth, to bolster this skill.

APPLICATION ACTIVITIES

1. Review your state's grade-level standards for a given content area. Create corresponding alternate achievement standards that align with each general achievement standard.
2. Write behavioral objectives aligned with grade-level standards that reflect different stages of learning: acquisition, fluency, maintenance, and generalization.
3. Select a narrative or expository text and create a graphic organizer that would be used to support their comprehension of the selected text. Discuss how the text or graphic organizer can be adapted to accommodate learners with extensive support needs.

ADDITIONAL RESOURCES

Autism Focused Intervention Resources & Modules (AFIRM). https://afirm.fpg.unc.edu/afirm-modules

Bouck, E. C., Root, J., & Jimenez, B. (2020). *Mathematics Education and Students with Autism, Intellectual Disability, and Other Developmental Disabilities*. Division on Autism and Developmental Disabilities.

Carnahan, C., & Williamson, P. (2010). *Quality Literacy Instruction for Students with Autism Spectrum Disorders*. AAPC Publishing.

Designing from the Ground Floor: Alternate Assessment on Alternate Achievement Standards. https://osepideasthatwork.org/designing-ground-floor-alternate-assessment-alternate-achievement-standards

U.S. Department of Education, What Works Clearinghouse Practice Guides:

  1. *Foundational Skills to Support Reading for Understanding in Kindergarten through Third Grade*. https://ies.ed.gov/ncee/wwc/practiceguide/21
  2. *Teaching Math to Young Children Practice Guide*. https://ies.ed.gov/ncee/wwc/Docs/PracticeGuide/wwc_empg_summary_020714.pdf

10

Evidence-Based Practices to Address Problem Behavior

Mandy Rispoli, Catharine Lory,
Eric Shannon, and Charissa Voorhis

■ ■ ■

INTRODUCTION AND OVERVIEW

Problem behaviors may take many forms such as crying, tantrum, aggression, property destruction, or even self-injury, and can range in intensity and severity. Problem behavior may lead to many negative short- and long-term outcomes including loss of instructional time, peer rejection, teacher rejection, and fewer opportunities for inclusion in educational and community settings (Horner et al., 1999). As discussed in Gur (2018), learners with problem behavior have been shown to have a lower quality of life due to reliance on others to complete tasks, lack of social interaction opportunities, and difficulties in accessing appropriate health care. Problem behavior is a leading predictor for student placement in more restrictive and self-contained educational environments (Koegel, L., et al., 2012), which may further reduce access to the general education curriculum and to social opportunities (Wehmeyer et al., 2020). It is estimated that 94% of children with autism spectrum disorder (ASD) engage in problem behavior (Matson & LoVullo, 2008). While problem behavior is a typical part of child development, it tends to persist well beyond the early childhood years for learners with ASD (Green et al., 2005; Murphy et al., 2005) and occurs at a higher rate in ASD than in other developmental disabilities (Richards et al., 2012).

A variety of factors may increase the risk for problem behavior including an individual's learning history, their recent access to reinforcement, or skill deficits. Deficits in social-communication skills greatly increase the risk of challenging behavior (e.g., Sigafoos, 2000). One hypothesis for this relation between communication skills and problem behavior is that problem behavior serves a communicative purpose. When an individual presents with deficits in social-communication behaviors, this increases the likelihood that they may turn to other behaviors to get their message across. For example, if a young child does not want to get in their car seat, but lacks the communication skills to say, "I don't want to go in the car right now," they may communicate this message by screaming, crying, or arching their back. Viewing problem behavior as communication may explain the high prevalence of problem behavior for

243

learners with ASD, for whom social-communication deficits are a core diagnostic feature (American Psychiatric Association, 2013).

The principles of operant conditioning can help us to understand why problem behaviors occur. Within operant conditioning, behaviors that come into contact with desired consequences are more likely to occur in the future through the process of reinforcement, while behaviors that lead to aversive or undesired outcomes are less likely to occur in the future through the process of punishment. Therefore, when problem behaviors continue to occur over time, we hypothesize that the behavior is contacting reinforcement. The link between the problem behavior and the desired outcome leads the individual to engage in the problem behavior in the future to obtain the same desired consequence.

There are three broad categories of reinforcement that may influence behavior: social positive reinforcement, social negative reinforcement, and automatic reinforcement. In social positive reinforcement, the "positive" refers to the addition of something to the environment, such as an object, activity, or social attention. For example, a learner may call out during group instruction, which results in the teacher walking over to the learner and reminding them that one of the classroom rules is to be quiet during class. If the learner continues to call out during group instruction and the teacher continues to provide attention, the calling out behavior is likely communicating, "I want attention," and is therefore maintained by access to social positive reinforcement.

In social negative reinforcement, the "negative" refers to the removal of something aversive from the environment. Behaviors maintained by social negative reinforcement communicate a desire to escape or avoid something. For instance, a teacher may assign a difficult task to a learner. The learner then shouts and refuses to complete the task. In this case, the learner's behavior of shouting and noncompliance communicates "I don't want to do this!" and the removal of the task functions as social negative reinforcement. In educational settings, behaviors maintained by negative reinforcement often occur to escape or to avoid task demands or transitions to undesired locations or activities (Anderson et al., 2015).

Unlike socially reinforced behaviors, behaviors that are maintained by automatic reinforcement are not dependent on the behaviors of others in the environment. Automatic reinforcement occurs when the behavior produces the reinforcer immediately through its impact on the environment. Behaviors that are automatically maintained often occur in the absence of other environmental stimulation and are likely to be repetitive in nature. We all engage in automatically maintained behaviors from time to time. For example, we may tap our pen against our desk, or twirl our hair around a finger. Learners with ASD also engage in repetitive or restrictive behaviors, which have been identified as a core diagnostic feature of ASD (American Psychiatric Association, 2013). Oftentimes these behaviors take the form of repetitive motor movements or vocalizations (e.g., hand flapping, body rocking, repetitive speech) or strict adherence to ritualized behaviors or routines (American Psychiatric Association, 2013). When such behaviors occur at a rate or intensity that interferes with learning limits or social opportunities, or causes risk or injury to the learner, they may warrant intervention.

When a learner engages in problem behavior, stakeholders such as teachers, providers, and caregivers may be eager to begin intervention to reduce this behavior as quickly as possible. However, the key to an effective intervention is to understand why the behavior is happening in the first place. Identifying the communicative function of a specific problem behavior and the source of reinforcement that is maintaining that behavior allows us to hypothesize the behavior's operant function. The process of gathering and analyzing information to identify variables that trigger and maintain problem behaviors is known as a functional behavior assessment (FBA). Research shows that interventions that are based on results of FBAs are more efficient and effective than interventions that are not linked to the communicative function of behavior (Dunlap et al., 2018; Koegel, L., et al., 2012).

Throughout this chapter we will discuss the FBA process and how to use this process to identify function-based interventions. This chapter is designed to provide guidance for assessing, preventing, and addressing problem behavior. We begin with an overview of the FBA process and then offer guidance for conducting each component of the FBA. Next, we discuss how to interpret FBA data and use those data to build function-based interventions for determining which behaviors to target and how to collect meaningful data on them through observations and also indirect assessments. Finally, we will touch on how to evaluate an intervention's effectiveness and how to create a plan to fade the reinforcement delivered to the learner.

FUNCTIONAL BEHAVIOR ASSESSMENT

Assessment is simply a means of gathering information to inform decisions. The goal of an FBA is to place the problem behavior in context of antecedents (events or variables that precede and trigger a behavior) and consequences (events or variables that maintain or reinforce a behavior) to identify the operating function of that behavior. By examining patterns of antecedents and consequences in relation to the problem behavior, we can better understand the circumstances under which problem behavior is likely to occur. This information can assist in identifying the communicative purpose, or function, of problem behavior, which enables the design of efficient and effective behavior support plans (O'Neill et al., 2015).

Consider an example of a young adult who yells and attempts to run from their group home. As part of the FBA, information is gathered to identify *antecedents*, or the events that precede screaming and running away. During the FBA process it becomes clear that the young adult screams and attempts to run out of the group home when it is time to put their tablet away and go to the day program. In this scenario, the removal of preferred activities is the antecedent variable that occasions problem behavior. Knowing this antecedent, we can begin to hypothesize what the young adult is communicating: "I don't want to put away my tablet!" or "I want to keep playing my video game!" or "I don't want to do something different!"

Identifying antecedents for problem behavior is an important component of an FBA, but we need more information before we can identify a behavior's function. We also need to identify what occurs after the problem behavior by examining its consequences. A *consequence* is simply an event that follows a behavior and influences whether the behavior will recur. Applying the principles of operant conditioning, we can identify variables that serve to reinforce, or maintain, the problem behavior. The FBA may show that when a teacher tells the class to clean up (antecedent), the focus child screams and runs, which results in the teacher providing the child with continued access to preferred materials (consequence). This continued access to preferred materials functions as positive reinforcement for screaming and running; positive, because something is added to the environment (access to toys) and reinforcement because this consequence strengthens the behavior so that it is likely to occur again in the future.

Identifying antecedents, consequences, and the operant function of a problem behavior is a multicomponent team-based process. It is critical for multiple stakeholders to have active and meaningful involvement in the FBA process. This includes the learner's family; teachers; individuals with expertise in problem behavior, such as Board Certified Behavior Analysts or licensed school psychologists; and as appropriate, the learner themselves (Benazzi et al., 2006). Members of the FBA team work together to gather information, synthesize this information, and generate hypotheses about the function of the problem behavior.

An FBA is not a singular assessment, but rather a collection of assessments in which results are synthesized to identify the purpose of a specific behavior. This collection of assessments includes indirect assessments, descriptive assessments, and, in some cases, experimental functional analysis. Figure 10.1 illustrates the FBA process. We begin by bringing the team together to identify the target behavior of concern. Next, we conduct indirect assessments to hear from multiple stakeholders familiar with the focus individual and their behavior. These results help us select times and environments to directly observe the problem behavior in the natural context to identify antecedents and consequences. We synthesize the results from indirect assessments and descriptive assessments to develop a

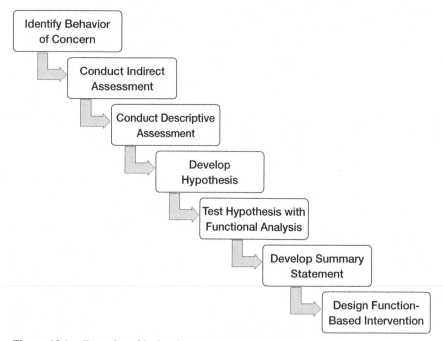

Figure 10.1. Functional behavior assessment process

hypothesis for the function of the behavior. The team may then test this hypothesis through an experimental functional analysis, which involves the systematic manipulation of antecedents and consequences to examine their influence on the problem behavior (Iwata & Dozier, 2008).

Identifying Target Behavior

When you are working with a learner who engages in problem behavior, how do you decide which behaviors to target, and if the learner engages in multiple problem behaviors, which one to target first? The team can begin by analyzing the social significance of the behaviors. Target behaviors should be chosen because they will benefit the quality of life for the learner both in the short term and in the long term (Lerman et al., 2013). Cooper and colleagues (2020) suggest guidelines for selecting and prioritizing target behaviors by asking questions that address the frequency, severity, and potential harm of the problem behavior, whether replacing the problem behavior will result in positive outcomes (e.g., skill acquisition, independent functioning, natural reinforcement contingencies) that outweigh current outcomes, the cost of intervention, and the likelihood of success in changing the problem behavior using existing resources.

Operationalizing Target Behavior

Once the team has agreed on what target behavior to address and has established the social significance for addressing this behavior, the team begins to describe this behavior in a clearly observable and measurable way. This measurable description of the target behavior is called an operational definition. To review operational definitions, please refer back to Chapter 6 for more information and examples. To operationalize a target behavior, the team must be able to define the form or *topography* of the behavior. For example, if a child is throwing a tantrum, the team could describe the behavior topographically by saying exactly what is happening during the tantrum: the child lies on the floor and cries and yells while throwing anything in their reach. This type of description does not tell us *why* a behavior is occurring, it simply tells us what the behavior looks like. An operational definition of the target behavior is essential to ensuring that the rest of the FBA process is focused on this specific behavior of concern.

Indirect Assessment

Once the team has agreed upon an operational definition of the target behavior, they may move to the indirect assessment phase of the FBA. *Indirect assessment* is a means of gathering others' perspectives on the history of the problem behavior, the contexts within which the behavior is likely to occur, and the potential sources of reinforcement that may maintain that behavior. Indirect assessments allow teams to obtain information about a problem behavior from those who are typically present in the learner's natural settings, such as caregivers and teachers. These individuals can often provide valuable information about situations that evoke problem behavior, the frequency, intensity, and history of problem behavior, what interventions have been attempted in the past and the success of those interventions, and how others in the environment respond to that problem behavior. Indirect assessments may be administered in the form of interviews, rating scales, or surveys.

Interviews

The purpose of conducting a behavioral interview is to obtain information about the possible antecedents and consequences of a problem behavior and narrow down situations (i.e., when, where, with whom) that are most suitable for descriptive assessment of the behavior. In a behavioral interview, the interviewer asks a caregiver, educator, or direct care staff a set of questions to obtain relevant background information of the learner with ASD (e.g., age, language and communication skills, typical school or home routines), the problem behavior, people or events in the environment that influence the occurrence of the problem behavior, and interventions that have been implemented before or are currently in place. Behavioral interviews may be structured with a predetermined list of questions or prompts (e.g., Functional Assessment Interview; O'Neill et al., 2015) or semi-structured with opportunities for follow-up questions based on the interviewee's responses (e.g., Open-Ended Functional Assessment Interview; Hanley, 2012). Examples of interview questions or prompts may include "Describe the child's language abilities." "What does the problem behavior look like?" "When are the behaviors most and least likely to occur?" "How does the learner react if you stop playing with them?" "How do you or others typically respond to the behavior when it occurs?"

It is recommended that interventionists conduct behavioral interviews with individuals who have daily or frequent opportunities to observe the learner who engages in problem behavior. If the interventionist intends to address the problem behavior across multiple settings (e.g., home and school, instructional time with teacher, and recess with paraprofessionals), the interview may be conducted with multiple people who are typically present in the target settings. Information gathered on the antecedents and consequences of a problem behavior can be used to guide when, where, and which type of descriptive assessment should be conducted in the subsequent phase of the FBA process. Information related to a learner's language abilities, skill repertoire, and preferences may be gathered and used to inform the development of interventions.

Rating Scales/Surveys

People who know the learner well and who have witnessed the occurrences of the target problem behavior may be asked to complete a rating scale or survey as part of the indirect assessment process. There are a number of validated rating scales for assessing problem behavior such as the Motivational Assessment Scale (Durand & Crimmins, 1988), the Questions About Behavioral Functions (Matson et al., 2012), and the Functional Analysis Screening Tool (Iwata et al., 2013). In addition to the information that can be obtained through interviews, rating scales may capture information on how frequently a problem behavior occurs over a specific window of time, how severe the behavior is, common situations in which the problem behavior occurs, and likely consequences that maintain or reinforce the problem behavior. As with interviews, rating scales and surveys completed by caregivers, educators, or other service providers may not present the most objective or accurate information about a behavior. Indeed, research has shown that the reliability, which is the consistency of responses across different people, may be low for rating scales and surveys that assess problem behavior (Tyrer et al., 2016). Nevertheless, these indirect assessments offer a quick and simple method of beginning conversations with respondents with knowledge of the learner and their behavior and can inform whether additional indirect assessments should be conducted.

While indirect assessment results can lead to promising identification of environmental factors that may influence the target behavior, the FBA process should not stop here. Indirect assessment results are critical for guiding the next phase of the FBA process. This next phase, referred to as descriptive assessment, allows the team to observe the behavior within the typical contexts in which it is likely to occur.

Descriptive Assessment

Once the team has obtained information regarding the context in which problem behavior is likely to occur, the descriptive assessment phase of the FBA process may begin. *Descriptive assessment* involves the repeated direct observation of the problem behavior within typical contexts to identify potential antecedents and reinforcers for the behavior. Descriptive assessments are also known as direct observation, or antecedent-behavior-consequence (ABC) data collection. Within this process, an observer records instances of problem behavior and documents the antecedents that preceded that behavior and the consequences that occurred directly following that behavior. Descriptive assessment data collection continues until clear patterns emerge with respect to antecedents and consequences that appear to be associated with the problem behavior. These observations are typically conducted by someone outside of the instructional setting, such as by a school psychologist or behavior analyst. In some cases, a teacher conducts the descriptive assessment while another staff member delivers instruction. Descriptive assessment recording forms for data collection are usually organized into three sections: antecedents, behaviors, and consequences. Within this structure, there are two primary systems for gathering descriptive assessment data: narrative data collection and selection-based data collection.

Narrative Antecedent-Behavior-Consequence Data Collection

In narrative ABC data collection, open-ended recording forms are used to record antecedents that precede the target problem behavior and consequences that occur following the target problem behavior. Narrative ABC data collection allows the observer to record antecedent and consequence events exactly as they were observed and to provide detailed information about the environmental factors that may affect the target behavior. For example, the observer may see the learner engaging in the target behavior of aggression toward peers. The observer could write down "learner pushed a peer's shoulder" and then record the antecedent and consequence for that instance of behavior. The observer may write under antecedent, "peer started building blocks on floor across the play area" or "teacher gave verbal instructions to clean up toys." Under the consequence section next to that behavior occurrence, the observer may record, "learner took blocks and peer cried" or "teacher gave verbal reprimand and told learner to apologize to peer."

Narrative ABC data collection is recommended for assessing problem behaviors that occur less frequently, as it requires more time to write down narrative observations of events. The flexibility of being able to record exactly what is observed is useful in cases where the antecedents and consequences of the problem behavior seem fairly unpredictable or tend to vary greatly, perhaps because the respondents involved in the indirect assessment have limited knowledge about the problem behavior.

Selection-Based Antecedent-Behavior-Consequence Data Collection

In selection-based ABC data collection, every occurrence of the target behavior is recorded as well. However, the antecedents and consequences are selected from a list of preidentified events based on the data collected through indirect assessment. Further, the consequences are typically classified based on function. The menu of antecedents and consequences can either be prefilled to be used across learners or can be developed by the FBA team based on indirect assessment results. For example, if indirect assessment results showed that a learner leaves an assigned seat when (a) classwork is assigned, (b) a peer initiates a conversation, or (c) the teacher attends to other students, these three events may be listed on a selection-based ABC form as potential antecedents. If the indirect assessment indicates the consequences for the out-of-seat behavior include (a) time away from assigned classwork, (b) social interaction with peers, and (c) verbal reprimand from the teacher, these events may be prefilled as potential consequences. The selection-based ABC data-collection process requires less time for recording and, thus, is highly applicable and feasible for problem behaviors that occur frequently. However, selection-based ABC data recording forms are typically generic in nature and may not fit the idiosyncratic variables that influence the focus learner's problem behavior.

Blended Antecedent-Behavior-Consequence Data Collection

Several tools have been developed for recording descriptive assessment data that blend a variety of data collection and data analysis procedures. For example, the Functional Assessment Observation Form (O'Neill et al., 2015) allows for simultaneous narrative and selection-based ABC data collection while also incorporating a scatterplot of the results. A *scatterplot* is a visual display of data that captures time-based patterns and facilitates the identification of frequent antecedents and consequences of the problem behavior within or across time frames. When selecting the most appropriate tool for collecting descriptive data, the team should consider the observation setting, the frequency and topography of problem behavior, the required training for the observer, and the utility of the data that could be collected from each tool toward developing a hypothesis about the function of the problem behavior.

In some cases, it may be challenging to identify a single function of the learner's problem behavior based on the analysis of indirect and descriptive assessment data. In other cases, relying on observed correlations between antecedents, consequences, and behaviors may lead to inaccurate identification of the function. In either of these situations, it may be helpful to conduct a functional analysis of the problem behavior. FBA teams may find value in conducting a functional analysis to confirm the hypothesized function based on the indirect and descriptive assessment result.

Functional Analysis of Problem Behavior

A *functional analysis* involves the systematic manipulation of antecedents and consequences to examine if there is a functional relation to the problem behavior. Functional analysis can provide a useful tool for systematically testing the hypothesized function of the problem behavior. Within a functional analysis the learner is exposed to different social conditions simulating social positive reinforcement, social negative reinforcement, and a control condition to test for automatic reinforcement. Within each social condition, antecedents and consequences are systematically manipulated to evaluate whether they evoke and reinforce problem behavior. Common conditions in a functional analysis include the attention condition to determine if the target behavior is reinforced by attention, the tangible condition to assess whether the target behavior is reinforced by access to tangibles, and the escape condition to assess whether the target behavior is reinforced by escape or avoidance of a stimulus. In addition to these conditions, a functional analysis may also include an alone condition. The alone condition assesses whether the target behavior is maintained by nonsocial sources of reinforcement (i.e., automatic reinforcement). Finally, every functional analysis includes a control condition (Beavers et al., 2013). The levels of problem behavior across each condition are compared and the condition with the highest levels of problem behavior is interpreted as indicating the function of that behavior.

Many functional analysis models and variations may be useful in FBA. Some of these models include a traditional experimental functional analysis (Iwata, Dorsey, et al., 1982/1994) that compares multiple social conditions against a control condition; a pairwise functional analysis (Iwata, Duncan, et al., 1994), in which only one social condition is conducted and compared to a control condition; a brief functional analysis (Cooper et al., 1990), in which single probes of different social conditions are assessed; and a trial-based functional analysis (Sigafoos & Saggers, 1995), in which the assessment is embedded into brief trials conducted within the learner's typical routines and environments. The FBA team should explore each of these functional analysis models and determine which model would be the best approach for a given case. It is important to note that functional analysis of problem behavior requires extensive training (e.g., McCahill et al., 2014) and should only be conducted in strict accordance with ethical guidelines (Behavior Analyst Certification Board, 2020).

Interpreting FBA Results and Developing a Summary Statement

Indirect and descriptive assessments are essential tools within the FBA process. Yet, it is what we do with the data collected from those assessments that enables us to draw conclusions about the function of problem behavior. In other words, data are only useful when they inform decisions. FBA data should enable the team to identify the function of the problem behavior and should inform the design of the behavior support plan. To make these decisions, the team must analyze and interpret FBA data to develop a succinct summary of antecedents, behaviors, and consequences.

Pages of descriptive assessment data can sometimes be overwhelming and difficult to interpret. By graphing the descriptive assessment results, it becomes easier to identify patterns and to draw preliminary conclusions about antecedents that evoke problem behavior and consequences that reinforce problem behavior. To graph descriptive data, convert the data into simple frequency counts of each antecedent that precedes problem behavior and the frequency of each consequence that follows problem behavior. Figure 10.2 provides an example of a graph of descriptive data for antecedent events. FBA teams may also find it useful to graph other contextual variables that may influence problem behavior such as setting, time of day, or other idiosyncratic variables that pertain to the unique case. Once

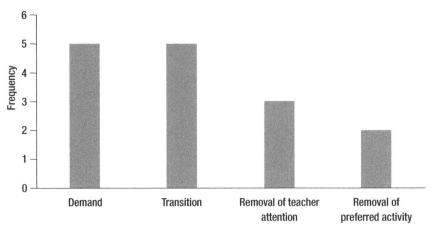

Figure 10.2. Graphing ABC data

the data are graphed, teams can identify which antecedent(s) and consequence(s) occurred most frequently with respect to the problem behavior. Should the team decide to conduct a functional analysis of the problem behavior, the result should also be graphed in a line graph so that patterns of responding within each social condition over time can be observed.

Once the team is comfortable with the accuracy and thoroughness of the FBA data, a summary statement is developed. A *summary statement* is a concise statement consisting of one to three sentences that synthesize all data gathered during the FBA (O'Neill et al., 2015). A summary statement functions to place the problem behavior in the context of antecedents and consequences. The summary statement should have these elements: individual, concise summary of antecedent(s), operationalized definition of target problem behavior, and concise summary of consequences. It is helpful to follow this summary with a clear statement of the hypothesized operant function of the problem behavior. Here are some examples:

> "When Luke [*learner*] is getting little attention during large-group instruction [*antecedent*], he is likely to shout and throw objects at peers [*target problem behavior*] to get peer attention [*consequence*]. It appears Luke's shouting out and throwing objects is maintained by positive reinforcement in the form of access to peer attention."

> "When Maya [*learner*] has had less than four hours of sleep the night before [*contextual variable*] and her job coach asks her to do independent assembly jobs at work [*antecedent*], she is likely to tear up materials and hit her job coach [*target problem behavior*] to escape from the task demands [*consequence*]. It appears Maya's problem behavior is maintained by negative reinforcement in the form of escape from task demands."

An FBA is a process comprised of multiple steps and assessments including identifying and operationalizing the target behavior, conducting indirect assessments, conducting descriptive assessments, and developing and, in some cases, testing hypotheses. Training in each of these components is critical to conducting a high-quality FBA. The FBA culminates in a concise and thorough summary statement. Summary statements synthesize FBA data and serve as a critical link between the FBA and the function-based intervention development process.

FUNCTION-BASED INTERVENTION

A function-based intervention is an intervention derived from FBA results that focuses on the identified function(s) of the target behavior. A function-based intervention is a detailed, individualized support plan with the goal of decreasing or eliminating problem behavior and improving appropriate behaviors and skills. Function-based interventions built from high-quality FBAs have been shown to reduce problem behavior and increase appropriate social communicative behaviors (e.g., Cook et al., 2012, Rispoli, Ganz, et al., 2013; Watkins et al., 2019). By understanding the communicative function of a learner's problem behavior, teams can work to modify the environment to prevent problem behavior, to teach appropriate behaviors to replace problem behavior, and to provide consequences that reinforce appropriate behavior. Table 10.1 presents examples of how two function-based interventions could be adapted for different communicative functions of problem behavior.

Table 10.1. Adapting Function-Based Interventions for Different Behavioral Functions

Function	Functional communication training	Noncontingent reinforcement
Positive Social Reinforcement	Use functionally equivalent communicative response to request access to a preferred item, activity, or person. For example, instead of lying on the ground and crying to access screen time, exchange a picture card that reads, "I want screen please."	Allow access to highly preferred item, person, or activity without the learner needing to engage in a specific behavior. For example, if the learner's problem behavior is maintained by attention and occurs about every 10 min, provide "free" attention every 9 min.
Negative Social Reinforcement	Use functionally equivalent communicative response to avoid an unwanted object, person, or activity. For example, instead of throwing objects when told to clean up, the learner could sign "more" to gain more time with their preferred activity.	Allow the learner to escape from a task, item, or person at predetermined times. For example, if a learner elopes from their work on average every 45 min, provide them a structured break every 40 min.
Automatic Reinforcement	Use functionally equivalent communicative response to request an opportunity to obtain automatic reinforcement instead of having a tantrum when repetitive behaviors are interrupted. For example, a learner who likes waving paper in front of their eyes could be taught to request "Paper time" instead of having a tantrum.	Allow the learner access to a matched stimulation that approximates the automatic reinforcement. For example, if a learner sings loudly during work tasks, provide free access to music while they work.

Function-based interventions should consist of (a) evidence-based antecedent interventions for preventing problem behavior, (b) evidence-based teaching interventions for supporting acquisition of appropriate behavior, and (c) evidence-based consequence interventions to maximize reinforcement for appropriate behavior and to minimize or eliminate reinforcement for problem behavior. Antecedent interventions focus on preventing problem behavior before it occurs. Antecedent interventions are derived from the information gathered in the FBA to decrease motivation to engage in problem behavior. For example, if the FBA identified that unstructured classroom transitions tend to evoke problem behavior, then the antecedent intervention may be to increase the structure and decrease the duration of transitions. Teaching interventions are also informed directly from the FBA and focus on instruction and support to help the learner engage in appropriate behavior instead of problem behavior. Teaching interventions can focus on teaching a new behavior that serves the same function as the problem behavior. Alternatively, teaching interventions may also focus on shoring up social, academic, or employment skills. Finally, consequence interventions involve increasing access to reinforcement for appropriate behaviors and decreasing access to reinforcement for problem behavior.

In the remainder of this chapter, we present an overview of selected function-based intervention strategies. These interventions are organized according to function (social positive reinforcement, social negative reinforcement, and automatic reinforcement). Within each function, we identify strategies that can be used as antecedent interventions to prevent problem behavior, strategies that serve to teach new responses and behaviors, and consequence strategies that can be used to strengthen appropriate behaviors and to reduce problem behaviors. In best practice, teams will design behavior support plans that include antecedent, teaching, and consequence strategies.

SOCIAL POSITIVE REINFORCEMENT

Socially mediated positive reinforcement occurs when a learner's behavior is maintained by the addition of something to the environment that increases the likelihood of similar behaviors occurring in the future (Cooper et al., 2020). Usually, social positive reinforcement is categorized as providing access to attention, an activity, or a tangible object. Team members can modify the environment to increase the likelihood that learners will engage in appropriate behavior to access reinforcement, teach the use of such appropriate behavior, and alter consequences to ensure appropriate behavior is properly reinforced. Proactive, function-based support for learners with ASD should be individualized for the learner, environment, and context (Sugai & Simonsen, 2020).

Antecedent Strategies

Antecedent strategies involve modifying the instructional environment to promote appropriate communication and activity engagement, which in turn reduces the likelihood of a learner engaging in problem behavior to avoid these activities. We will highlight four antecedent strategies for problem behavior maintained by social positive reinforcement. These include modifying the physical environment, noncontingent reinforcement, visual supports, and priming.

Physical environment modifications alter the space to decrease problem behavior and increase appropriate behavior. Some aspect of the environment (a stimulus) occasions behavior to occur, including but not limited to adult directives or the presence of materials, an adult, or peers (Hardy & McLeod, 2020; Conroy et al., 2007). Modifying aspects of the environment can increase the likelihood that prosocial behaviors that access reinforcement occur. For example, a middle-school teacher may position her desk near a learner who frequently yells out to access her attention and, thus, makes it easier for the learner to properly obtain the teacher's attention.

Another way to reduce motivation to engage in problem behavior is to provide the learner with access to the reinforcer before they engage in problem behavior. That is, if a learner engages in problem behavior to access her teacher's attention, the teacher can provide her with attention before she has an opportunity to engage in problem behavior. This is called *noncontingent reinforcement*. In this intervention, reinforcement refers to the delivery of the same reinforcer that maintains problem behavior, and noncontingent means the learner gets it for free—they do not have to engage in a specific response to access this reinforcement. Within noncontingent reinforcement, the need to engage in problem behavior is eliminated because the reinforcer is provided on a predetermined schedule (Fritz et al., 2017). For example, if a learner attempts to access the attention of his favorite custodian, a noncontingent reinforcement intervention could involve the two of them walking together between every class. If a young child routinely has tantrums because she wants to go to the park, her family can incorporate morning walks to the park as part of their normal routine. As with other function-based intervention strategies, noncontingent reinforcement requires proactive planning, identifying the function of the learner's problem behavior, and delivering the reinforcer before problem behavior occurs.

A common antecedent intervention for behavior maintained by positive reinforcement for learners with ASD is the use of visual supports. *Visual supports* may include pictures, words, or other stimuli that remind the learner to engage in contextually appropriate behaviors. For example, a teacher might leave a small picture of a hand to remind a learner to raise her hand when she wants the teacher's attention. Similarly, a high school resource room teacher may list on the whiteboard the steps for writing a paragraph for his learners who are working for a computer break.

Another antecedent strategy for behaviors maintained by social positive reinforcement is priming. *Priming* is the process of previewing a scenario that is about to occur and reminding the learner what the expectations are for that context (Gengoux, 2015). Priming, followed by rehearsal or practicing those desired behaviors, can increase the learner's engagement in the desired behavior and reduce their engagement in the problem behavior. For example, before going to lunch, a paraprofessional might remind his learner that children who wait in line receive their lunch first. The paraprofessional is being proactive and priming the learner's behavior of waiting in line to access a preferred activity (lunch). In another example, the teacher may provide a verbal reminder to the learner that when she blows the whistle, the learner should line up to go inside from recess. The teacher and student could also rehearse this behavior immediately before the teacher signals the end of recess.

Teaching Strategies

While antecedent strategies focus on altering the environment to prevent problem behavior and increase the likelihood that learners engage in appropriate behavior, teaching strategies provide learners with the skills needed to perform those prosocial behaviors. For learners who lack social interaction skills and require supplementary support to access attention from peers, *social skills instruction* can be an approach to teach complex social interactions. The process involves explicit teaching and role playing of skills such as giving a compliment, maintaining a conversation, reading body language, or handling bullying or teasing (White et al., 2010). The use of *video modeling* has also been effective in increasing the social skills of children, adolescents, and adults with ASD (Bellini & Akullian, 2007; Mason et al., 2012). Using this strategy, the learner could watch a video of an individual asking peers to change the game being played during recess. After watching the video, the focus learner would practice the skill in a role play situation. This strategy is particularly useful because the learner can see a real-life example as a guide, practice the skill in a controlled environment, and generalize the skill to their own social situation. Video modeling has even been successful with teaching social skills to preschoolers with ASD (Delano, 2007; Wilson, 2013).

One of the most researched and effective interventions for addressing problem behavior maintained by social positive reinforcement is *functional communication training* (FCT; Carr & Durand, 1985). FCT is considered an evidence-based practice by the National Clearinghouse on Autism Evidence and Practice (Steinbrenner et al., 2020). Chezan and colleagues (2018) found large effects sizes when FCT was informed by the results of an FBA and when FCT was implemented for behaviors maintained by social positive or social negative reinforcement.

FCT involves teaching a new communicative response that serves the same function as the problem behavior and providing function-based differential reinforcement to the learner for engaging in the new communicative response (Durand & Moskowitz, 2015; Machalicek et al., 2007). FCT involves a three-step process: (1) conducting an FBA to identify the reinforcer maintaining problem behavior; (2) selecting a communicative response that matches the function of the problem behavior and that the learner is capable of performing; and (3) developing and implementing systematic instruction to teach the new communication response (Carnett et al., 2019; Schmidt et al., 2014).

For example, an adolescent with ASD may hit his instructor to access a puzzle piece. The FBA reveals that his hitting is maintained by social positive reinforcement in the form of accessing desired or preferred materials. The team identifies that exchanging a picture card to request the puzzle piece would match the function of his problem behavior and be within his skill set. The team then systematically teaches him to select the picture card and hand it to his instructor when he wants a puzzle piece. When he hands the card, he is immediately provided with access to the puzzle along with behavior-specific praise, such as "You want the puzzle! Thanks for letting me know by handing me the card."

Consequence Strategies

Consequence strategies involve delivering reinforcement for appropriate behavior and minimizing the delivery of reinforcement for problem behavior. With respect to problem behavior maintained by social positive reinforcement, the goal of consequence strategies is to provide immediate and high-quality positive reinforcement for appropriate behavior and to withhold or minimize positive reinforcement for problem behavior.

Differential reinforcement is one of the most effective strategies for managing problem behavior. In *differential reinforcement*, the interventionist no longer reinforces the problem behavior or provides only minimal reinforcement following problem behavior and provides high-quality reinforcement for the appropriate behavior (Cooper et al., 2020). Within function-based interventions, differential reinforcement provides contingent access to the same reinforcer that maintains the target problem behavior. So, for behavior maintained by social positive reinforcement in the form of access to adult attention, the team may design a behavior support plan that involves delivering high-quality immediate adult attention for appropriate behavior and limited or low-quality attention for problem behavior. The high-quality attention will function to reinforce, or increase, the appropriate behavior, while the reduced or eliminated attention for problem behavior will result in a decrease of that behavior (Weston et al., 2018).

Consequence strategies also seek to reduce or remove reinforcement for problem behavior (Durand & Moskowitz, 2015). The process of eliminating reinforcement for responses that previously contacted reinforcement is called *extinction*. If a learner routinely yells to get his teacher's attention during independent work time, implementing extinction would require the teacher to withhold attention after the outbursts occur. It is critical that if a team decides to place a target problem behavior on extinction, they also systematically teach and provide reinforcement for appropriate behavior. In other words, teams should focus on teaching new skills to replace problem behavior while also working to reduce problem behavior. If extinction is not used consistently across different contexts and interventionists, the problem behavior may increase.

For example, a special education teacher may no longer provide attention when a learner engages in problem behavior and the behavior may be decreasing. Yet, the general education teacher does provide attention to the learner for his problem behavior. This lack of consistency in implementing extinction will reduce the effectiveness of the behavior support plan. In fact, occasional reinforcement can increase a behavior more than consistent reinforcement (Cooper et al., 2020). For these reasons, it is vital that, when using extinction, all stakeholders are consistent and persistent in withholding the reinforcer for problem behavior, and interventions are being implemented to teach replacement behavior (Vollmer et al., 2015).

SOCIAL NEGATIVE REINFORCEMENT

Socially negative reinforcement refers to the removal of a nonpreferred or aversive stimulus from the environment contingent on the occurrence of a specific behavior. In other words, engaging in a problem behavior results in escape from specific events that may be aversive to the learner (e.g., difficult instructional activities, unwanted social engagement with other individuals). Research has shown that social negative reinforcement is one of the most common functions of problem behavior in learners with ASD and developmental disabilities in educational settings (Anderson et al., 2015). Fortunately, there is a large evidence base of interventions that can reduce problem behavior maintained by social negative reinforcement for learners with ASD.

Antecedent Strategies

Antecedent strategies that address social negative reinforcement are designed to reduce the motivation for a learner to escape from events. It is important to use individualized assessment to identify specific variables that motivate a learner to engage in escape-maintained problem behavior. These variables may be related to the difficulty of instructional activities, preference for mode of receiving instructional content, availability of tools to engage with assigned tasks, or capacity to follow verbal instructions. After identifying the variables that influence the motivation for problem behavior, the team can alter the environment to eliminate or reduce the influence of those antecedents on the target behavior. In this chapter, we present three antecedent strategies for problem behavior maintained by social negative reinforcement. These include choice, instructional modifications, embedding preferred interests, and visual supports.

Providing choice-making opportunities is an antecedent intervention that can effectively reduce escape-maintained problem behavior and increase appropriate activity engagement among children and adults with ASD (Smeltzer et al., 2009; Watanabe & Sturmey, 2003). Choice-making interventions can be classified as across-activity choice or within-activity choice. *Across-activity choice* involves presenting two or more activities and allowing the learner to select the one they want to complete. For example, a child could choose whether to play in the block center or the water table. *Within-activity choice* involves presenting two or more methods of completing a predetermined activity. For example, within-activity choice could include learner choice of whether to type an assignment or complete the assignment using pen and paper. Rispoli, Lang, and colleagues (2013) compared the effects of within- and across-activities choice among young children with ASD and demonstrated that both types of choice were similarly effective in reducing escape-maintained problem behavior.

When learners are not interested in the tasks they are asked to complete, they are less motivated to complete the task. To reduce the motivation to escape, practitioners may consider modifying a task by reducing its length or difficulty (McComas et al., 2002). Providing instructional tools that aid in completing academic tasks (e.g., math manipulatives, number lines, calculators) can be a simple antecedent intervention to increase a learner's motivation to engage with a task and decrease their motivation to engage in problem behavior (McComas et al., 2002).

In addition to providing choice and modifying instructional tasks, *visual supports* can also effectively reduce problem behavior maintained by social negative reinforcement in learners with ASD across all school ages (Hume et al., 2021; Wong et al., 2015). Visual supports may be especially helpful for changing the behavior of learners with ASD due to their relative strengths in processing visual information (Knight et al., 2014). Furthermore, breaking down the steps of an activity visually is likely to eliminate the motivation to escape due to task complexity because the learner would have a clear understanding of what the steps are for completing a task. A visual activity schedule is comprised of a series of photographs or picture symbols that represent different activities (e.g., math, reading, lunch) or steps within an activity (e.g., steps for washing hands). To implement a visual activity schedule effectively, practitioners should ensure that the learner knows what each picture represents on the activity schedule. Based on individual needs, practitioners may need to conduct some training (i.e., matching each picture with the task that it represents) prior to using the visual activity schedule (Machalicek et al., 2009).

Capitalizing on a strengths-based approach, the behavior support team may build from the restricted interests that form a core diagnostic feature of ASD. By embedding preferred or restricted interests into nonpreferred activities, motivation for escape may decrease and activity participation and completion may increase. For example, a caregiver may provide their child with a toothbrush with the child's favorite superhero on it to increase compliance during tooth brushing. A teacher may design reading comprehension lessons around the learner's favorite topic. A practitioner may promote social interaction by anchoring the interaction to the student with ASD's favorite board game. Embedding preferred interests as an antecedent intervention for learners with ASD has empirical support from early childhood (Dunst et al., 2012) through adulthood. Ninci and colleagues (2017) reviewed the research literature and found that embedding preferred interests into vocational activities for adults with developmental disabilities decreased problem behavior and increased indicators of happiness.

Teaching Strategies

In addition to reducing motivation to engage in problem behavior maintained by negative reinforcement, it is also essential to focus on teaching skills that reduce the value of escape or skills that provide the learner with a more socially appropriate means of requesting negative reinforcement. Skills that reduce the value of escape may include those skills that are necessary to complete the task or activity the learner finds aversive (Hagan-Burke et al., 2015). For example, a learner may engage in problem behavior when it is their turn to read a passage aloud to the class. In such a case, teaching reading decoding and reading fluency skills may prove to be the most effective "behavioral" intervention. By teaching prerequisite skills, academic skills, or other behaviors required to complete the task, the task becomes less difficult and, therefore, less aversive.

While teaching skills required to complete a task or activity successfully is critical, the behavior support team may also implement FCT to teach a socially appropriate, efficient response that matches the function of problem behavior. FCT with respect to social negative reinforcement often takes the form of requesting a break, appropriately declining to participate in an activity, or requesting assistance. The response form of this new communication behavior may vary and could include vocalizations, picture card exchange, a specific gesture, or activation of a speech-generating device. For example, a learner may be taught to exchange a picture card to request a break from a nonpreferred activity, or to raise their hand and request assistance with a difficult task. Selecting a response form for the new communication behavior should involve examining the learner's preferences for different communication modes and the learner's skill sets (Falcomata et al., 2017).

Consequence Strategies

As with behavior maintained by social positive reinforcement, consequence strategies for behaviors maintained by social negative reinforcement seek to maximize reinforcement for appropriate behavior and minimize reinforcement for problem behavior. When behaviors are maintained by social negative reinforcement, reinforcement includes removal of the aversive stimulus, as is the case with FCT. That is, when the learner engages in appropriate behavior, negative reinforcement can be provided. For example, if a teacher sees the learner working independently and completing math problems, instead of engaging in problem behavior, he may provide negative reinforcement by reducing the assignment length. For example, "Because you are working quietly and carefully, you only need to complete the odd numbered problems."

Even though the problem behavior is maintained by negative reinforcement, the team may also elect to positively reinforce appropriate behavior to shift the learner's behavior toward appropriate behavior and away from problem behavior. This is often achieved through differential reinforcement. Systems of differential reinforcement have been shown to be effective with learners with ASD (Steinbrenner et al., 2020). One such system is called a token economy. A *token economy* is a system of delivering reinforcement for appropriate behavior. The learner earns a small tangible item or digital point for engaging in appropriate behavior. Once the learner has acquired a predetermined number of tokens, they are able to exchange those tokens for a backup reinforcer. Maggin and colleagues (2011) identified five essential elements of a token economy including (1) selecting the target appropriate behavior(s), (2) selecting a token to use within the system, (3) creating a list of backup reinforcers for the learner to select from, (4) developing a clear procedure for exchanging tokens for backup reinforcers, and (5) fading the token economy system.

Token economies lend themselves to educational and workplace environments because of the built-in delay to reinforcement, unobtrusive nature of supports, and brief, consistent access to reinforcement in a way that does not interfere with task engagement or work productivity (Maggin et al., 2011). They can also be customized to meet the unique needs of learners including the rate at which tokens are delivered, the quantity of tokens required to exchange for a backup reinforcer, and the menu of back up reinforcers from which the learner can choose. Carnett and colleagues (2014) evaluated a token economy that was built using the perseverative interest of a boy with ASD. They found that the tokens that were based on the child's restricted interest were more effective at increasing task engagement and decreasing problem behavior than generic tokens.

AUTOMATIC REINFORCEMENT

Learners with ASD often engage in behaviors that are stereotypic, such as repeating words or phrases from a song or dialogue, or vocalizing sounds that do not constitute functional speech, or making rhythmic body movements. Research has found that automatic reinforcement is the most prevalent function of stereotypic behaviors, which can be determined through a functional assessment (Beavers et al., 2013). When a learner continues to engage in a problem behavior that does not produce a socially mediated consequence, it suggests that the behavior is producing its own consequence, which continues to evoke future occurrence of the same behavior. This means that even when there are no social consequences provided, such as access to attention, items, or activities, behaviors that are maintained by automatic reinforcement would persist. Because the consequences of behaviors maintained by automatic reinforcement do not involve things or people in the external environment, it might be challenging for the practitioner to control and alter the consequence produced by the problem behavior. Fortunately, research has demonstrated that there are effective ways to reduce problem behavior maintained by automatic reinforcement through these approaches: (a) decreasing the motivation to engage in the problem behavior through antecedent manipulation and (b) teaching and reinforcing a replacement behavior or activity that is incompatible with (i.e., cannot occur at the same time as) the problem behavior.

Antecedent Strategies

After determining through an FBA that a problem behavior is most likely maintained by automatic reinforcement, the team should conclude, from notes and data collected during the FBA, if the problem behavior produces auditory, visual, tactile, or kinetic (i.e., motor) stimulation. Then, the team may design an intervention that involves delivering a similar form of stimulation regardless of the occurrence of the problem behavior, so that the learner has access to a matched stimulation (i.e., *noncontingent matched stimulation*) without having to engage in the problem behavior. Freely accessible matched stimulation reduces the learner's motivation to engage in the problem behavior.

Noncontingent access to music or other auditory stimulation is a type of matched stimulation intervention that has demonstrated relatively strong effects in reducing problem behaviors maintained by auditory stimulation (Lanovaz & Argumedes, 2009; Lanovaz et al., 2014; Love et al., 2012; Rapp, 2004; Saylor et al., 2012). Providing noncontingent access means that the matched stimulation is delivered on a predetermined schedule (e.g., every 30 s, every 5 min, continuously for 10 min every hour, continuously throughout an entire session) regardless of whether the problem behavior has occurred. A few factors should be taken into consideration when implementing noncontingent matched stimulation, including (a) the learner's preference for the matched stimulation, (b) how often the matched stimulation should be delivered, and (c) how problem behavior should be addressed when it occurs.

Research suggests that compared to less preferred stimuli, using more preferred stimuli for matched stimulation may produce more significant reductions in stereotypic behavior maintained by automatic reinforcement (Lanovaz et al., 2012; Vollmer et al., 1994). For example, if music were selected as the matched stimulation for addressing stereotypic vocalizations, the practitioner may consider identifying the learner's highly preferred genre or artists to determine the type of music to use as matched stimulation (Lanovaz et al., 2012). If toys that produce sounds have been identified as items of matched stimulation, the practitioner may consider assessing the learner's preference for toys (Rapp et al., 2013). However, it should be noted that the presence of some toys or objects may evoke more problem behavior in some learners with ASD. Hence, intervention effects should be closely monitored through systematic data collection to ensure that the selected items function as matched stimulation without evoking more problem behavior.

The schedule of delivering the matched stimulation may be determined based on how often the problem behavior occurs. If the behavior occurs at an average of two times per minute, it would be recommended to deliver the matched reinforcer *two times or more* per minute, to ensure that the learner has an opportunity to access the matched stimulation before they engage in the problem behavior each time. When the matched stimulation is delivered intermittently on a specific schedule instead of continuously throughout a session, access to the matched stimulation may be withheld briefly when an occurrence of the problem behavior coincides with the predetermined time of access. In cases where the problem behavior interferes significantly with important instructional routines or other appropriate behaviors, the practitioner may consider delaying the delivery of the matched stimulation (e.g., 5–10 s) when a problem behavior occurs at the same time that the matched stimulation is supposed to be delivered.

Teaching Strategies

Differential reinforcement of alternative behaviors is an intervention that can effectively reduce problem behavior maintained by automatic reinforcement. Alternative behaviors may be in the form of functional communication, typical play behaviors, or other prosocial behaviors (e.g., Lang et al., 2014; Lang et al., 2020; Potter et al., 2013). While the reinforcement of these prosocial behaviors may not directly address the automatic reinforcement function of the problem behavior, it increases the repertoire of prosocial behaviors in learners with ASD, which has been shown to produce an overall decrease in problem behavior maintained by nonsocial functions (Lang et al., 2020; Ledbetter-Cho et al., 2017).

FCT is a teaching strategy that is not only effective for problem behavior maintained by social reinforcement, but also effective for addressing problem behavior maintained by automatic reinforcement in learners with ASD (Akers et al., 2020). For example, Falcomata and colleagues (2010) implemented FCT with a 5-year-old boy with autism and minimal verbal repertoire whose problem behavior was in the form of running away from a supervised area to repeatedly open and close a door (i.e., elopement to access door play). The boy was taught to touch a card to communicate that he wanted to play with a door. If the boy touched the given card instead of eloping, he would be allowed to play with a door for 30 s. After the boy demonstrated consistent card touches and no occurrence of elopement, the reinforcement of playing with a door was gradually delayed to 10 min after each card touch (i.e., 2 s, 5 s, 10 s, 20 s, 40 s, 80 s, 160 s, 320 s, 600 s). Teaching the boy to engage in functional communication (i.e., card touch) that was less effortful than the problem behavior (i.e., elopement) successfully eliminated the problem behavior. The gradual delay of reinforcement taught the boy to tolerate a duration of time when door play was not permitted. This delay fading procedure would allow the boy to participate in instructional or other prosocial activities without reverting to problem behavior when a card touch does not result in immediate access to door play.

Consequence Strategies

Response interruption and redirection is a multicomponent intervention that has strong evidence of effectiveness for reducing problem behavior such as repetitive vocalizations and motor movements (Ahearn et al., 2007; Cassella et al., 2011;

Martinez et al., 2016). The intervention consists of the following major components: (a) verbally or physically disrupting or blocking the occurrence of a problem behavior, (b) presenting a few consecutive tasks that require the learner to engage in a vocal or motor behavior that is incompatible (i.e., cannot occur at the same time) with the problem behavior, and (c) praising the completion of these tasks. This intervention is beneficial because it teaches functional speech (e.g., answering questions) or physical movements (e.g., clapping, pointing to an object) and may be embedded into natural instructional routines. However, the implementation of response interruption and redirection typically requires one-on-one attention from the practitioner to interrupt and redirect the target problem behavior, which may limit the feasibility of implementation in group settings (Wang et al., 2020). Current literature also suggests that although the immediate effects of response interruption and redirection on problem behavior may be strong, the reduction in problem behavior may not be maintained over time unless the intervention is implemented for a duration of 20 min or more (Sivaraman & Rapp, 2020). Hence, the team should consider the availability of personnel who can serve as an interventionist and the instructional context prior to adopting response interruption and redirection as an intervention.

A substantial proportion of learners with ASD may engage in problem behavior that leads to physical injury or harm (e.g., skin picking, head hitting, self-restraint), and such behaviors are often termed self-injurious behavior. When self-injurious behavior is maintained by social reinforcement, it may be reduced by teaching and reinforcing a functionally equivalent replacement behavior that requires less response effort than the self-injurious behavior. However, research has shown that about a quarter of the time, self-injurious behaviors occur to produce automatic reinforcement (i.e., sensory stimulation; Iwata, Pace, et al., 1994; Hagopian et al., 2015). In such cases, it may be challenging for practitioners to control the reinforcement produced from the behavior. Hence, blocking the self-injurious behavior or masking the sensory stimulation produced by the self-injurious behavior (e.g., using gloves to mask the sensory effect of scratching) may sometimes be necessary to immediately reduce the problem behavior to protect the safety of the learner (Hagopian et al., 2015). However, practitioners should note that less restrictive and reinforcement-based interventions are strongly recommended prior to considering more restrictive, punishment-based procedures (Akers et al., 2020; Lang et al., 2010; Matson et al., 2008; Wang et al., 2020). Practitioners should also consider the possibility that for some self-injurious behaviors or severe problem behaviors, a combination of antecedent and consequence strategies or a combination both of reinforcement procedures and of punishment procedures (e.g., response interruption and redirection) may be needed to reduce the problem behavior more effectively.

MULTIPLY MAINTAINED PROBLEM BEHAVIOR

Although we have presented interventions according to separate functions of problem behavior, it is critical to note that in some cases, a learner may present with problem behavior that is maintained by multiple sources of reinforcement (Love et al., 2009). In such cases, selecting comprehensive intervention plans that include strategies both for positive reinforcement and for negative reinforcement may be important. This may include teaching multiple replacement communication behaviors, one for each function of problem behavior. Other solutions may include combining reinforcement for appropriate behavior. For example, if a learner's problem behavior is maintained both by social positive reinforcement in the form of access to preferred objects and by social negative reinforcement in the form of escape from tasks, then the team may elect to provide the learner with access to preferred objects during breaks from tasks (Rispoli, Ganz, et al., 2013). Ultimately, regardless of whether the problem behavior is maintained by a single function or multiple functions, the results of an FBA are essential for informing the design and implementation of behavior support plans.

EVALUATING INTERVENTION EFFECTIVENESS

Interventions require constant evaluation to determine their effectiveness. Rather than relying on perceptions and anecdotal reports, all well-informed decisions for behavior change must be based on data (Bruhn et al., 2020). Attending to the data allows the team to make the proper decisions to stop, alter, or continue current practices, and results in improved treatment outcomes (Gould et al., 2019). Behavioral intervention data primarily falls under two categories: behavior data and fidelity data.

Accessing accurate behavior data allows the team to properly evaluate the effectiveness of interventions, adapt those interventions accordingly, and improve learner performance (Demchak & Sutter, 2019). Data collection systems can vary depending on the learner, context, and behavioral topography. During the assessment and progress monitoring phase of intervention, team members may take data to determine the frequency, rate, or latency of problem behavior or replacement behavior. In addition, interval data may inform decision makers what percentage of the time a particular behavior is occurring. As with other types of target behaviors, it is essential that practitioners graph, interpret, and use the data to inform instructional decisions, as discussed in Chapter 6.

Although tracking a learner's behavior is essential, collecting fidelity data on the intervention itself is just as important. Fidelity refers to the accuracy with which the intervention is implemented. Programs that fail to assess implementation fidelity properly cannot interpret intervention results accurately and may not be adhering to evidence-based practices (DiGennaro Reed et al., 2014). Unsurprisingly, high levels of intervention fidelity have been directly related to more positive outcomes for those participating in the interventions (Flannery et al., 2014; Mandell et al., 2013; Wilder et al., 2006). Effective program fidelity measurement involves identifying and specifying the particular fidelity criteria, having multiple observers measure fidelity, and assessing the reliability and validity of those results (Mowbray et al., 2003).

FADING INTERVENTIONS

Interventions to treat problem behavior are used to support learners as they acquire communication, social, and other essential skills. However, in most situations, these supports are not designed to be relied upon indefinitely. Ideally, as learners acquire appropriate behavior, interventions are slowly withdrawn until some level of independence is achieved, a process called fading or thinning. Analyzing data to make decisions regarding behavioral supports, dosage, and generalization ensures that programs are individualized to meet specific needs (Fuchs et al., 2018).

Fading supports will look different depending upon the intervention and learner and may involve reducing the level of supports at the antecedent or consequence level. For learners who require high levels of prompting for learning, it is vital to fade prompts from most-to-least intrusive. Using this strategy, teams slowly decrease prompts after consistent and repeated demonstrations that the learner is successful with the current level of support (Schnell et al., 2020). For example, a teacher may use a partial physical prompt to assist a kindergartner pressing a speech-generating app to request assistance. Then, once the learner is responding with that prompt level, the teacher may move to a gestural prompt by pointing to the speech-generating app icon.

Practitioners can also fade consequences. When an intervention is novel, it is common practice to provide high levels of reinforcement for every correct response or appropriate behavior. However, as the learner acquires the appropriate behavior, this level of reinforcement is no longer needed. For example, when first teaching a new communication response to request a break during instruction to replace problem behavior, the team may provide immediate access to that function-based reinforcer after every occurrence of the new response. This could result in the learner asking and receiving a break at an almost constant rate. To address this, the team may slowly and systematically fade the intervention by either slowly reducing the quantity of reinforcement (shorter and shorter breaks) or increasing the number of correct responses until reinforcement is provided (e.g., "First complete five problems, then you can ask for a break."). Such fading procedures have been used to increase communication and social skills while decreasing problem behavior such as aggression (Kelley et al., 2011; Slocum et al., 2018).

SUMMARY

Throughout this chapter we have reviewed evidence-based practices to help assess, prevent, and reduce problem behavior. The FBA involves a process of completing many assessments including collecting indirect and direct data (see Figure 10.1) to ultimately determine the best interventions to use in a behavior support plan. The FBA places the target behavior in the context of antecedents and consequences to identify the function (automatic reinforcement, social negative reinforcement, or social positive reinforcement) that drives the development of the behavior support plan. A behavior support plan should include individualized evidence-based antecedent, teaching, and consequence strategies that match the communicative function of the problem behavior.

Once the function-based intervention is in place, it is important to remember to monitor intervention effectiveness and whether the interventions are being implemented with fidelity through data collection. The team could choose the best intervention, but if it is not being implemented with fidelity it is not likely to have the effect you had hoped for. Also, your goal should be that every intervention is ultimately faded out while the targeted behavior maintains the appropriate level, so you need to have a fading plan in place. Training in each of these aspects is critical so that you can provide the most effective interventions for those you serve.

CASE STUDY
Laura C. Chezan and Katie Wolfe

Background

Paul is a 12-year-old boy who has a diagnosis of autism spectrum disorder (ASD). He attends a self-contained classroom for learners with disabilities at a local public school. There are four other learners, two paraprofessionals, and one special education teacher in Paul's classroom. Paul requires substantial levels of support to complete academic tasks. He prefers to be by himself, but occasionally he interacts with peers when prompted. Paul lives at home with his parents and younger sibling. He enjoys walking, listening to music, and playing with small objects (e.g., marbles, blocks). Paul likes snacks, such as Goldfish, cookies, and Skittles.

Paul has started engaging in problem behavior 5 months into the school year. His problem behavior consists of verbal and physical aggression toward peers and his teacher and property destruction. These behaviors occur 4–5 times per day especially during reading and math instruction, transitions from preferred activities to nonpreferred activities, and group activities. Several interventions have been implemented including time-out from reinforcement and extinction. Furthermore, Paul's psychiatrist prescribed several medications over the last 2 months to address his physical aggression and property destruction.

Because Paul has continued to engage in problem behavior at a higher frequency and intensity over the last month, his teacher requested the assistance of the school psychologist to address Paul's problem behavior. The school psychologist and the teacher collaborate to conduct a functional behavior assessment (FBA) to identify the function or purpose of Paul's problem behavior. The FBA consists of several steps. First, the school psychologist meets with Paul's teacher and paraprofessionals to inquire about the behaviors that pose a concern and asks them to describe how the behaviors look. The teacher, paraprofessionals, and school psychologist identify and define the following behaviors: (a) physical aggression defined as kicking, biting, and pushing peers and staff; (b) verbal aggression defined as cursing and yelling; and (c) property destruction defined as throwing items on the floor or against the walls and hitting walls.

Second, the school psychologist and the teacher agree that an indirect assessment would help to gather more information about Paul's problem behavior both at school and at home. They decide to conduct an interview with Paul's parents to determine whether he displays these behaviors at home and under what conditions. Because the teacher has a close relationship with Paul's mother, she agrees to conduct the interview using the Functional Assessment Interview (O'Neill et al., 2015) after receiving training from the school psychologist on how to best use the interview to collect relevant information. The school psychologist uses the same interview with the paraprofessionals who work with Paul during school hours. Third, the school psychologist administers the Questions About Behavior Functions (Matson et al., 2012) to Paul's teacher and paraprofessionals to collect additional information about Paul's behavior. Fourth, the school psychologist trains the teacher to conduct direct observations during typical activities in the classroom to identify potential antecedents and consequences that evoke and maintain Paul's problem behavior. The school psychologist and the teacher agree that the Functional Assessment Observation Form (FAOF; O'Neill et al., 2015) would be easier to use than narrative ABC recoding. The teacher uses the FAOF for approximately 2 weeks to record environmental variables that contribute to Paul's problem behavior and the frequency of his problem behavior during school hours. Finally, the school psychologist and the teacher meet to analyze and interpret the FBA results. They develop the following summary statement:

"When Paul is asked to complete an academic task during reading or math instruction or he is asked to transition from a preferred to a nonpreferred activity, he is likely to engage in verbal and physical aggression and property destruction to escape from task demands or nonpreferred activities. It is likely that Paul's problem behavior is maintained by negative reinforcement in the form of escape from task demands or nonpreferred activities."

Step 1: Questions to Initiate Evidence-Based Treatment Selection Process

At the conclusion of the FBA, the school psychologist and teacher begin the evidence-based treatment selection process by generating questions to guide the selection process. These questions are:

1. What socially appropriate replacement behavior is most appropriate for Paul to learn to request a break or assistance when presented with a task demand or a nonpreferred activity?
2. What antecedent, teaching, and consequence interventions can be used to prevent the occurrence of Paul's problem behavior, teach him a socially appropriate replacement behavior, and maximize reinforcement for appropriate behavior while minimizing reinforcement for problem behavior?

Step 2—Part 1: Best Available Evidence

Based on the FBA results indicating that Paul's problem behavior is likely maintained by negative reinforcement in the form of escape from task demands and nonpreferred activities, the school psychologist and teacher conduct a review of evidence-based practices (EBPs) that address that function and have been shown to be effective in teaching appropriate behaviors and reducing problem behavior in learners with ASD. They review several sources, including the IRIS Center, the Center on Positive Behavior Interventions and Supports, and the National Professional Development Center on Autism Spectrum Disorder. The school psychologist and the teacher find that antecedent interventions (e.g., providing choices, Premack Principle or performing a less desirable behavior prior to obtaining access to a more desirable behavior), teaching interventions (e.g., video modeling, FCT), and consequence interventions (e.g., differential reinforcement, token economy) have been identified as EBPs for teaching appropriate behaviors and reducing problem behavior for learners with ASD.

(continued)

Step 2—Part 2: Person-Related Variables

The school psychologist and teacher consider Paul's abilities or behavioral repertoire and his preferences that may influence the acquisition of the socially appropriate replacement behavior. Because Paul has good language skills, they decide to teach a verbal response (e.g., "May I have a break, please?" and "May I complete a different activity first?") as the replacement behaviors. The teacher interviews Paul's mother about his preferences and interests to identify items and activities that seem motivating for Paul. Next, the teacher conducts a preference assessment in the classroom and compiles a list of preferred items and activities that can be used during the intervention.

Step 2—Part 3: Contextual Variables (Resource Constraints, Environmental Supports)

The school psychologist discusses with the teacher and paraprofessionals the acceptability and feasibility of the potential interventions that can be used to address Paul's problem behavior. Table 10.2 lists advantages and disadvantages identified for each intervention by the team.

Table 10.2. Advantages and Disadvantages of Antecedent, Teaching, and Consequence Strategies for Paul's Behavior Support Plan

	Type of intervention	Advantages	Disadvantages
Antecedent Interventions	Providing choices	• Easy-to-use intervention • Can be used during 1:1 and group work	• Peers may request the same choices • Paul may select only one preferred activity when presented with choices
	Premack Principle	• Easy-to-use intervention • Increases motivation for nonpreferred activities	• May be perceived as "bribe" by some practitioners
Teaching Interventions	Video modeling	• Visual representation of appropriate behavior • Peers can serve as role models • Can be used across settings	• Time, resources, and experience needed to create the video • Can be disruptive to peers during instruction

	Type of intervention	Advantages	Disadvantages
	Functional Communication Training	• Easy to use with minimal training • Can be used across settings and practitioners	• May be difficult to withhold reinforcement when problem behavior occurs • Paul may request a break or assistance often
Consequence interventions	Differential reinforcement	• Easy to use with minimal training • No materials or other resources required • Can be used across settings and practitioners	• May be difficult for some practitioners to withhold reinforcement when problem behavior occurs • May lead to an increase in problem behavior if not implemented correctly
	Token economy	• Easy to use • Can be used across settings and practitioners • Can be used with an individual or a group	• Time and resources needed to create the token economy • Requires time to teach Paul how it works

Step 3: Professional Judgement

After discussing the advantages and disadvantages of each potential intervention with the school psychologist, the teacher feels comfortable using the two antecedent interventions (i.e., providing choices and Premack Principle) identified to prevent the occurrence of Paul's problem behavior. However, she would prefer to use FCT rather than video modeling because she does not feel prepared to create a good video model and does not have the time and resources needed. Furthermore, she thinks that differential reinforcement may work better than a token economy because it has the potential to promote generalization of behavior by providing access to naturally reinforcing contingencies as opposed to a token economy that relies on tokens and artificial reinforcers and raises concerns about the maintenance of the behavior.

(continued)

Step 4: Intervention Selection

After requesting feedback from Paul's teacher, paraprofessionals, and parents and considering Paul's abilities and preferences, the school psychologist and the teacher conclude that providing choices and the Premack Principle should be embedded in daily activities when Paul is presented with a task demand or nonpreferred activity to increase his motivation to engage in the task. Next, they agree that the teacher uses FCT training to teach Paul to request a break or assistance when presented with an academic task or request a different activity when presented with a nonpreferred task. The school psychologist instructs the teacher and the paraprofessionals that they immediately provide Paul with assistance or a break when he uses the replacement behavior and continue to present the task demand or nonpreferred activity when he engages in problem behavior (i.e., differential reinforcement). The school psychologist also tells them that they may have to use verbal prompts (e.g., "Say, I need a break." or "Can you help me, please?") to teach Paul to learn the replacement behavior when the intervention is first implemented.

Step 5: Intervention Implementation and Data Collection

The school psychologist and the teacher develop an intervention protocol listing the step-by-step procedures required to implement each antecedent, teaching, and consequence intervention. The school psychologist trains the teacher and paraprofessionals how to implement the interventions and collect data. The teacher uses datasheets to document Paul's behavior after the interventions are implemented. Data are collected every day during typical activities in the classroom and represented on a graph to determine his progress. The school psychologist also collected fidelity of implementation data once per week to determine if the interventions are implemented as intended.

Step 6: Reevaluation

Two weeks after the interventions have been implemented, the school psychologist meets with the teacher, paraprofessionals, and parents to evaluate Paul's progress. Data indicate that the frequency of Paul's problem behavior decreased from 4–5 times per day to 2–3 times per day and he uses the replacement behaviors more consistently across school settings. The team agrees to continue the same interventions and meet again after one month to determine his progress and create a plan to fade the interventions if he continues to show progress.

APPLICATION ACTIVITIES

1. Pick a TV show character to observe and then choose a behavior they exhibit that you believe should be targeted for change. Write an operational definition for the chosen behavior and then collect data using an ABC data collection chart. Based on the data you collected, what is your hypothesis for a potential function of this behavior? Why did you choose that function? Which other character would you choose to complete an indirect assessment with and why?

2. Based on indirect and direct assessments, you hypothesize that a 6-year-old child engages in physical aggression (e.g., kicking, biting, hitting) to access adult attention. Which of the following settings would be appropriate for testing your hypothesis and why? (1) family mealtime (2) play time with siblings (3) reading time before bed. What other factors should you consider (e.g., safety, family routines)?
3. A learner you are observing routinely yells at the paraprofessional during computer lab to escape from difficult computer tasks. What intervention(s) could you implement to increase prosocial behavior and decrease aggression? Why?

ADDITIONAL RESOURCES

Center on Positive Behavior Interventions & Supports. (n.d.). *Home*. https://www.pbis.org/

Intervention Central. (n.d.). *Behavioral Interventions*. https://www.interventioncentral.org/behavioral-intervention-modification

The IRIS Center. (2009). *Functional behavioral assessment: Identifying the reasons for problem behavior and developing a behavior plan*. https://iris.peabody.vanderbilt.edu/module/fba

National Center on Intensive Intervention. (n.d.). *Home*. https://intensiveintervention.org/

11

Evidence-Based Practices for Secondary Transition Planning and Supports for Youth with Autism Spectrum Disorder

Anthony J. Plotner, Valerie L. Mazzotti,
Stephen M. Kwiatek, Wen-hsuan Chang,
Aaron R. Check, Abigail Mojica, and Charles Walters

■ ■ ■

INTRODUCTION AND OVERVIEW

The transition into adulthood is one that many learners and families look forward to with anticipation; it is the beginning of a new chapter in their life. Preparation for this transition is at the core of secondary education, leaving many learners equipped to pursue their various adulthood or long-term goals and aspirations. Unfortunately for learners with disabilities and their families, this time is often riddled with uncertainty and concern because these learners are frequently ill equipped for the transition to postschool settings (Wehman et al., 2014). Reliance on support from a variety of professionals is critical, but guidance for those professionals is currently inadequate. Studies and literature regarding outcomes for adults with autism spectrum disorder (ASD) are incredibly limited; tend to focus on postsecondary education, employment, and community living; and most often explore outcomes of younger adults in their 20s and 30s (Fombonne, 2012; Howlin & Moss, 2012; Levy & Perry, 2011; Roux et al., 2013; Shattuck, Narendorf, et al., 2012; Taylor & Seltzer, 2011).

Data from the National Longitudinal Transition Study-2 (NLTS-2) found that only 55% of all learners with disabilities were employed in 2009 (Shattuck, Narendorf, et al., 2012). The percentages were even lower for learners with more significant disabilities: 39.4% of learners with multiple disabilities, 37.2% of learners with ASD, and only 33% of learners with intellectual disabilities were employed one year after exiting high school (Newman et al., 2009; Snell & Brown, 2011). Employment is often influenced by education, and not only impacts an individual's financial independence, but also plays a role in an individual's ability to live independently (Collier et al., 2017). In a study exploring the perspectives of both youth with ASD and their parents, Sosnowy and colleagues (2018) found that the participants viewed postsecondary outcomes as far more complex and integrated than simply whether the learner attended college or gained employment. These outcomes were means to bolster a sense of self-worth and broaden opportunities for the learner as they progressed through adulthood.

This chapter will focus on a variety of topics related to the inherent need for supporting learners with ASD in the transition to adulthood. We will discuss (a) transition-focused legislation, (b) secondary transition and the importance of transition planning for learners with ASD, (c) secondary transition frameworks and practices, and (d) evidence-based practices and predictors of postschool success for secondary learners with ASD. Finally, we conclude this chapter with practical applications to help ensure practitioners can support the needs of learners with ASD as they transition into adulthood. We hope to convey in this chapter the importance of transition planning, services, and supports for secondary learners with ASD. Effective transition planning and providing services and supports for learners with ASD in high school may have a positive impact on these learners' postschool outcomes, including quality of life across all community living experiences (Trainor et al., 2020).

LEGISLATION SUPPORTING
TRANSITION-AGE YOUTH WITH DISABILITIES

Poor postschool outcomes for learners with ASD demonstrated in the growing, but still limited, literature make evident the need for quality transition services for these youth. To understand where we are currently, it is important to understand how transition services have evolved over the years. The Education of All Handicapped Children Act of 1975 (EAHCA), P. L. 94-142, mandated a free appropriate public education (FAPE) for all qualified learners with disabilities and provided federal funding to all states that complied with the act. Prior to EAHCA, learners with disabilities were frequently excluded from public schools or found their educational needs largely unmet as a result of limited resources at the district and state levels (Yell, 2019). It is estimated that nearly 1.8 million learners with disabilities were excluded from education prior to the act; public schools have since progressed to the inclusion and service of over 7.5 million learners with disabilities (Individuals with Disabilities Education Improvement Act [IDEIA], 2004).

In 1990, EAHCA was renamed the Individuals with Disabilities Education Act (IDEA), P. L. 101-476. The purpose of IDEA was to

> ensure that all children with disabilities have available to them a free appropriate public education that emphasizes special education and related services designed to meet their unique needs and prepare them for future education, employment, and independent living, to ensure that the rights of children with disabilities and parents of such children are protected, to assist state, localities, educational service agencies, and federal agencies to provide for the education of all children with disabilities (IDEA, 20 U.S.C. 1400(d)).

One of the additions to IDEA in 1990 was the requirement to address the transition needs of learners with disabilities by the age of 16, although several states have mandated those services begin sooner (e.g., transition services begin at age 13 in South Carolina; Yell, 2019). As a result, transition services were incorporated into the individualized education program (IEP) of learners with disabilities. Transition services are defined as

> A coordinated set of activities for a student, defined with an outcome-oriented process, which promotes movement from school to post school activities, including post-secondary education, vocational training, integrated employment (including supported employment), continuing and adult education, adult services, independent living, or community participation (20 U. S. C. 1401(19)).

In addition to mandating and defining transition services, the 1990 amendments required a learner's interests, preferences, and needs inform the development of their transition services and learners take an active role in the transition planning process (Kohler & Field, 2003).

In 2004, the IDEIA was reauthorized by congress and signed into law by President George W. Bush. One of the amendments made to the act was the requirement for the inclusion of appropriate measurable postsecondary goals based on relevant transition assessments. Teachers are required to develop postschool goals for employment, postsecondary education or training, and independent living when appropriate (IDEIA, 2004; Yell, 2019). The recently reauthorized Workforce Innovation and Opportunity Act of 2014 (WIOA) uses terminology similar to IDEIA to define transition services. This act, however, stipulates guidelines for adult service providers who assist young adults with disabilities transitioning into postschool educational and employment settings (Povenmire-Kirk et al., 2018; WIOA, 2014). For example, to improve the accountability of vocational rehabilitation service providers in the delivery of services and in their collaboration with school districts, WIOA mandates that vocational rehabilitation provide pre-employment transition services to learners with disabilities beginning at the age of 14. Moreover, these service providers are required to set aside 15% of funding to achieve these efforts (Collier et al., 2017).

SECONDARY TRANSITION AND WORKING WITH LEARNERS WITH AUTISM SPECTRUM DISORDER

Approximately 1 in 54 children are diagnosed with autism, and the prevalence of this diagnosis is steadily increasing (Maenner et al., 2020). Early recognition and intervention are becoming the norm, and many children are now diagnosed and eligible for services well before the age of 5. Despite the many high-quality interventions that currently exist for children with autism, early intervention efforts have not been correlated to success in adulthood; many leave school unprepared for work, college, and community living (Howlin & Moss, 2012; Wehman et al., 2014). Specifically, research has consistently found that adults with ASD experience high rates of unemployment and low rates of college attendance (Taylor & Seltzer, 2011); remain living at home with parents; and struggle to develop friendships and relationships (Levy & Perry, 2011). Postschool outcomes are often even less favorable for those with problem behaviors, ritualistic behaviors, poor language development, and lower socioeconomic status (Howlin & Moss, 2012). The increasing rates of autism reported by the Centers for Disease Control and Prevention (CDC), coupled with a system ill equipped to support adults with ASD, is indicative of a need to focus on transition services (Friedman et al., 2013).

Autism is one of 13 disability categories recognized by the IDEA (1990), a federally mandated law. A learner with a diagnosis of autism is eligible to receive the programs and services provided by the law, such as an IEP. In 1990, IDEA required transition services be included in the educational programming of transition-age youth, and in 2004, amendments to the act further stipulated that transition services include measurable goals developed from transition assessments (Yell, 2019). Unfortunately, IDEIA (2004) mandates are not being reliably met (Friedman et al., 2013), as evidenced by poor postschool outcomes.

However, beyond the need for compliance with legislation is the importance of improved postschool outcomes for the benefit of the person's quality of life. It is important to note that quality of life and the concept of success have varying definitions and criteria. Until the early 2000s, the literature commonly categorized measures of success as "poor" or "good" and rarely were these terms clearly defined or consistently measured. However, in the past 20 years, there has been a shift to address these limitations by adding more rigorous and quantifiable definitions of success. The focus has become integration of person and the environment (Henninger & Taylor, 2012). In their review of studies on quality of life of individuals with ASD, Chiang and Wineman (2014) found, in addition to postsecondary education and employment, factors such as behavior problems, social communication skills, and adaptive skills impacted quality of life. Their review found less than desirable results: most of the participants in the studies did not report having good quality of life. Bishop-Fitzpatrick and colleagues (2016) reported similar findings in their sample of participants, stating most were unemployed, did not live independently, and did not regularly socialize with friends and family. Most of the participants were, however, physically healthy and living in good neighborhoods.

Quality of life for parents of children with autism is also a concern; they are at an increased risk for stress, psychological distress, depression, and increased levels of physical and mental health issues (Howlin & Moss, 2012). Additionally, there are financial demands that can take a toll on a family's financial well-being both directly (e.g., out-of-pocket costs for interventions) and indirectly (e.g., one parent giving up work to stay at home with the child; Friedman et al., 2013). Similarly, the quality of life of typically developing siblings can also be impacted; they often show more social isolation, difficulties with peer relationships, behavioral problems, and greater concern for the future.

SECONDARY TRANSITION FRAMEWORKS AND PRACTICES

Transition-focused education emphasizes the principles of normalization and individualization as central tenets of the field of special education, by equipping learners with the skills necessary to achieve their desired postschool outcomes in the least restrictive environment. To achieve this end, it is critical that practitioners (e.g., educators, transition specialists) implement effective transition practices. Effective transition practices are those that have been documented in the literature to have a positive impact on learners' postschool outcomes. These practices occur both at the program level and at the individual level and can be organized into five categories: student-focused planning, student development, interagency and interdisciplinary collaboration, family involvement, and program

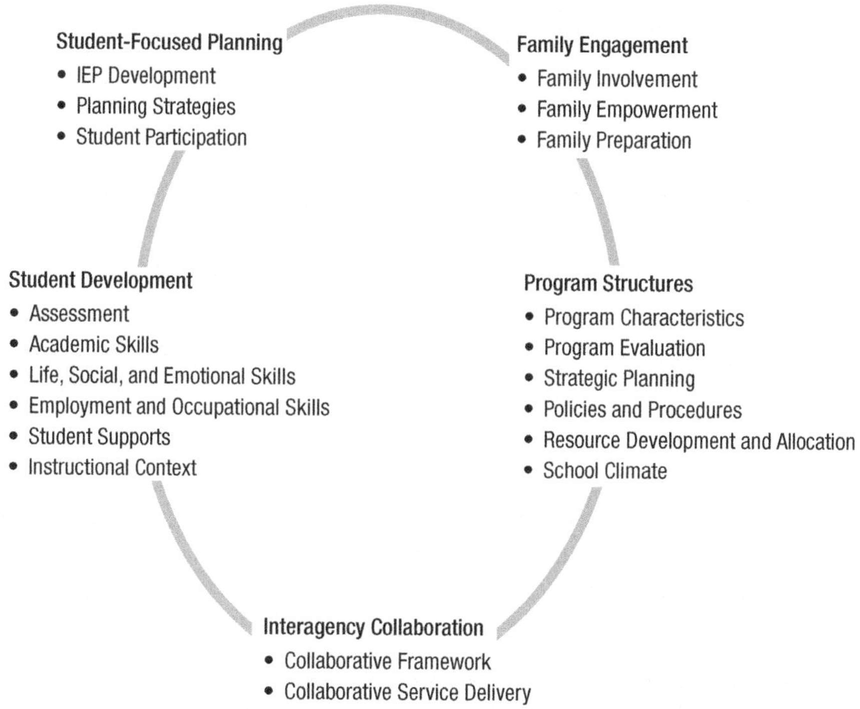

Student-Focused Planning
- IEP Development
- Planning Strategies
- Student Participation

Family Engagement
- Family Involvement
- Family Empowerment
- Family Preparation

Student Development
- Assessment
- Academic Skills
- Life, Social, and Emotional Skills
- Employment and Occupational Skills
- Student Supports
- Instructional Context

Program Structures
- Program Characteristics
- Program Evaluation
- Strategic Planning
- Policies and Procedures
- Resource Development and Allocation
- School Climate

Interagency Collaboration
- Collaborative Framework
- Collaborative Service Delivery

Figure 11.1.   Taxonomy for transition programming 2.0

structures and attributes (Kohler et al., 2016). Figure 11.1 shows Kohler's Taxonomy for Transition Programming 2.0.

First, student-focused planning empowers a learner to become the driving force behind educational decisions pertaining to their future. As such, goals are developed based on learners' preferences, interests, and needs. Moreover, the learner engages in progress monitoring and reflection to inform future action (Griffin et al., 2013; Johnson et al., 2020; Kohler & Field, 2003; Kohler et al., 2016). We use Jeffrey, an 11th grade learner with ASD, to illustrate the application of the concepts discussed throughout this section. For example, one of Jeffrey's IEP goals might be: When given a quiz or test, Jeffrey will advocate for his IEP accommodation of extended time in each of his seven classes for 4 out of 5 trials across three consecutive opportunities.

Similarly, the category of student development emphasizes the learner. Here the focus is on developing a learner's knowledge and skillset and providing opportunities for the application of these in school-based, work-based, and community-based settings. For example, another one of Jeffrey's IEP goals may be: During his shift at the local pet spa, Jeffrey will greet each customer with the work-required greeting of "Welcome to Pet Paradise. How may I help you and your pet today?" for 5 out of 5 trials for 3 consecutive weeks.

Given the reality that many learners receive a variety of supports and services (Ruble & McGrew, 2007), interagency collaboration is essential to achieve cohesion and continuation in the supports and services a learner receives (Whittenburg et al., 2018). Effective collaboration helps to ensure that learners access the breadth and depth of transition services and supports that they need. Common collaborative partners of special education practitioners may include organizations with disability-specific missions. Such organizations may include local offices of vocational rehabilitation, developmental disability service providers, parent training and information centers, and centers for independent living. Many states and locales also benefit from the presence of other organizations with missions specific to the support of youth and adults with ASD and their families.

Collaborative partners need not be limited to organizations with disability-based missions, however. Other organizations like American Job Centers, whose prospective clientele extends to the whole of the community, may also have a range of services that may benefit learners. Further, collaborative partnerships with entities like for-profit employers may also provide a host of mutually beneficial possibilities. Effectively leveraging collaborative partnership to maximize the postschool outcomes of learners involves a landscape that can be complicated to navigate for practitioners. Implementing aspects of community resource mapping processes like the environmental scan (Crane & Mooney, 2005) may be a beneficial starting place for practitioners to ensure they understand the context of interagency service provision in their communities.

With a clear understanding of that context and partnerships that may benefit learners, practitioners may attend to the task of building collaborative partnerships. In so doing, it is important to delineate roles and responsibilities of each agency and communicate strategies and collaborative actions clearly. For example, Jeffrey's case manager developed a goal tracking sheet for his job at Pet Paradise and shared it with Jeffrey's manager. Jeffrey's manager, a community member with whom Jeffrey's case manager had a long history of establishing work-based learning experiences, agreed to track data each day Jeffrey worked. By having Jeffrey's manager so involved with Jeffrey's performance evaluation, she recognized he was a quality worker and offered him permanent employment. Such examples of collaborative partnerships with mutual benefit for all involved abound. Nevertheless, barriers to achieving collaboration are also numerous, including ineffective use of time during planning meetings, intimidating language, and complex procedures (Kohler & Field, 2003).

Family engagement is also key to positive learner outcomes; family expectations and support play a critical role in supporting the development of self-determined behavior (Curtiss et al., 2020; Grigal & Neubert, 2004; Odom et al., 2021). Moreover, family engagement is positively correlated to school attendance (Falbo et al., 2001) and high-school graduation or completion (e.g., Doren et al., 2012; Newman, 2005). Strategies for improved family engagement include access to informational materials, joint training opportunities for all stakeholders, support groups, resource fairs, networking opportunities, and a single knowledgeable contact.

Finally, program structures are also critical, providing the framework within which transition practices and teams operate. Program philosophy, policies and evaluation, strategic planning, human resource development, and resource allocation all serve as a foundation upon which school personnel effectively deliver transition services to the benefit of the learner (Lindstrom et al., 2011; Wehman, 2013). An example of program structure to support Jeffrey in the transition planning process is that Jeffrey's school district wants to evaluate the quality of career development it has provided to its learners to prepare them for post-school employment. Therefore, the district used the Predictor Implementation School/District Self-Assessment (PISA; https://transitionta.org/pisa-self-assessment/) to evaluate the degree of implementation of career development. Upon examination of the evidence of implementation of each of the career development predictors (i.e., career awareness, career technical education, occupational courses, paid employment/work experience, work study), the district found they needed to enhance their opportunities for paid employment/work experience and work-study experiences.

Unfortunately, despite legislation and the identification of best practices in the literature, learners with disabilities continue to experience poorer postschool outcomes than their typically developing peers. This may be due to a variety of factors including a lack of educational programming and instruction on self-determination, a lack of consistency in the implementation of best practices, focus on compliance, and limited use of basic transition elements such as transition teams (Kohler & Field, 2003; Plotner et al., 2020). For widespread systemic change to occur, organizations must closely examine their learners' outcomes and align their transition services with those identified in the literature as best practice.

DESCRIPTION OF SECONDARY TRANSITION EVIDENCE-BASED PRACTICES AND PREDICTORS FOR LEARNERS WITH ASD

Learners with ASD face persistent disparities in education, employment, and community living outcomes before and after graduation from high school (Lipscomb et al., 2017; Newman et al., 2011). IDEIA (2004) mandates learners with disabilities, including learners with ASD, receive transition services in high school to prepare them for postschool life. More recently, the Every Student Succeeds Act (ESSA) of 2015 has reaffirmed the importance of preparing all learners for adult life (i.e., college, careers) and requires teachers to use evidence-based practices (EBPs) to do so. To identify effective practices, researchers have worked diligently to identify secondary transition EBPs to determine what works, for whom, and under what conditions (Rowe et al., 2021; Test, Fowler, et al., 2009). In addition to EBPs, transition researchers have also identified evidence-based in-school predictors of positive postschool outcomes for youth with disabilities (Mazzotti et al., 2016, 2021; Test, Mazzotti, et al., 2009).

The predictors should be considered at the *macro level*. The predictors are transition program characteristics or in-school experiences that learners with disabilities receive in high school. Based on the research, one can assume if transition programs align with the predictors of postschool success (e.g., career awareness, community experiences, inclusion in general education), youth with disabilities will be more likely to experience positive postschool outcomes. Test, Mazzotti, and colleagues (2009) identified 16 promising and research-based predictors of postschool success. Building on this work, Mazzotti and colleagues (2016) identified four new predictors of postschool success (i.e., goal setting, parent expectations, travel skills, youth autonomy/decision making). Most recently, Mazzotti and colleagues (2021) identified three new predictors of postschool success (i.e., psychological empowerment, self-realization, and technology skills) and additional evidence for 14 preexisting predictors. Among the identified predictors, career technical education (CTE; previously vocational education) was the first predictor that had enough evidence to support CTE as an evidence-based predictor of postschool success (Mazzotti et al., 2021).

Several research-based predictors have also emerged from the literature, many of which support postschool success across multiple domains (i.e., education, employment, and independent living). For example, in addition to being an evidence-based predictor for employment, CTE is also a research-based predictor for postschool success in education. Two research-based predictors that promote success across all three postschool domains are inclusion in general education and goal setting. Paid work experiences, programs of study, self-advocacy/self-determination, and youth autonomy/decision making are research-based predictors for postschool success in education and employment. Additional research-based predictors for employment include parent expectations, learner support, and work-study opportunities. Research-based predictors for success in independent living specifically include self-care/independent living skills (Mazzotti et al., 2021). There are also several promising practices that promote positive postschool outcomes in education, employment, and independent living; however, there is still a need for further exploration of these predictors. Figure 11.2 provides a list of the predictors by postschool outcome area.

In addition to the predictors, prior literature has identified a range of secondary transition EBPs (i.e., demonstrates a strong record of success for improving outcomes, uses rigorous research designs, and adheres to indicators of quality research) and research-based practices (RBPs; i.e., demonstrates a sufficient record of success for improving outcomes, uses rigorous research designs, and *may* adhere to indicators of quality research; www.transitionta.org). The EBPs and RBPs should be considered at the *micro level*. These practices (e.g., community-based instruction, Project SEARCH, video modeling) support and promote learner skill development in class, school, or community. Test, Fowler, and colleagues (2009) identified 32 EBPs for teaching learners with disabilities transition skills (e.g., providing community-based instruction, teaching purchasing using the *one more than* strategy, teaching self-determination skills). As an update to this work, Rowe and colleagues (2021) expanded on these transition EBPs to help the field better understand what works, for whom, and under what conditions. Rowe and colleagues identified 9 new EBPs and 22 RBPs for over 45 transition skills (e.g., EnvisionIT to teach technology skills, Project SEARCH to teach transition skills).

An EBP that facilitates inclusion in general education, a predictor of postschool success across all domains (i.e., education, employment, independent living), is the EnvisionIT curriculum. This online curriculum integrates instructional content in reading, writing, and technology for learners at risk and with disabilities. EBPs that support self-determined behavior, a predictor of postschool success both for education and for employment, include the Take Charge Curriculum, the Self-Determined Learning Model of Instruction (SDLMI), and student-led IEP meetings. Two RBPs that support self-determination, self-advocacy, and goal setting are Communicating Interagency Relationships and Collaborative Linkages for Exceptional Students (CIRCLES) and *Whose Future Is It Anyway?* Plus

Predictors/Outcomes	Education	Employment	Independent Living
• Career Awareness	Promising	Promising	
• Career Technical Education (was Vocational Education)	Research-based	Evidence-based	
• Community Experiences		Promising	
• Exit Exam Requirements/High School Diploma Status		Promising	
• Goal-Setting	Research-based	Research-based	Research-based
• Inclusion in General Education	Research-based	Research-based	Research-based
• Interagency Collaboration	Promising	Promising	
• Occupational Courses	Promising	Promising	
• Paid Employment/Work Experience	Research-based	Research-based	Promising
• Parent Expectations	Promising	Research-based	
• Parental Involvement		Promising	
• Program of Study	Research-based	Research-based	
• Psychological Empowerment (new)	Promising	Promising	Promising
• Self-Advocacy/Self-Determination	Research-based	Research-based	Promising
• Self-Care/Independent Living	Promising	Promising	Research-based
• Self-Realization (new)		Promising	Promising
• Social Skills	Promising	Promising	
• Student Support	Promising	Research-based	Promising
• Technology Skills (new)		Promising	
• Transition Program	Research-based	Promising	
• Travel Skills		Promising	
• Work Study		Research-based	
• Youth Autonomy/Decision-Making	Research-based	Research-based	Promising

Figure 11.2.   Predictors of postschool success by outcome area

Rocket Reader. For the domain of independent living, several RBPs support the development of self-care and independent living skills (e.g., basic finance/purchasing skills, social skills, food preparation). These RBPs include peer-assisted instruction and support, simulation, video modeling, Working at Gaining Employment (WAGES), and one-more-than strategy. Table 11.1 provides the EBPs and RBPs to support secondary learners with ASD skill development aligned with the in-school predictors of postschool success.

Table 11.1. EBPs and RBPs for Secondary Learners with ASD

Predictor(s)	Practice	Target skills	# of SwASD	Definition	Level
• Inclusion in general education • Program of study • Transition program	EnvisionIT Curriculum	Information Technology Skills	17	"*EnvisionIT* is an online curriculum focused on informational technology that integrates instruction in reading, writing, and technology content for students at risk for and with disabilities" (Rowe et al., 2021, p. 33).	EBP
• Career awareness • Paid work/work experience • Program of study • Self-advocacy/self-determination • Social skills • Transition program • Work study	Project SEARCH	Employment status, hours worked, benefits, adaptive behavior	63	Project SEARCH is a high-school program school-to-work transition model, which includes rotating internships for a school year; experiences combining real-life work; employment and independent living skills training; assistance with vocational placement through active collaboration with employers, school systems, and vocational rehabilitation; and entire school days spent in the workplace (Wehman et al., 2013).	EBP
• Goal setting • Self-advocacy/self-determination	Self-Determined Learning Model of Instruction	Self-determination skills	18	"The *Self-Determined Learning Model of Instruction* (SDLMI) is a curriculum that teaches students to engage in self-directed and self-regulated learning" (Rowe et al., 2021, p. 36).	EBP
• Goal setting • Self-advocacy/self-determination • Transition program • Youth autonomy/decision making	Self-Directed IEP	Learner involvement in IEP meetings and self-determination skills	11	"The Self-Directed IEP (SD IEP) lesson package is divided into four instructional units, including students leading meeting, reporting interests, reporting skills, and reporting options. It is a multimedia package designed to teach students the skills needed to manage their own IEP meetings" (Rowe et al., 2021, p. 36).	EBP
• Goal setting/self-advocacy/ self-determination • Transition program • Youth autonomy/decision-making	Take Charge Curriculum	Self-determination skills, knowledge and engagement in educational planning and persistence in school	8	"An integrated self-determination promotion approach that includes student coaching, mentorship, peer support, and parent support (Powers et al., 1998)" (Rowe et al., 2021, p. 36).	EBP

• Program of study • Self-advocacy/self-determination • Social skills transition program	Video Modeling	Home maintenance skills	6	Video modeling is "a form of response prompting (i.e., a stimuli that later functions as extra cue" Rowe et al., 2019). "Video modeling involves a video recording of a multistep task in which an individual will watch and will then be allowed an opportunity to imitate the steps in the task" (Rowe et al., 2021, p. 36).	EBP
• Self-advocacy/self-determination • Youth autonomy/decision making	Communicating Interagency Relationships and Collaborative Linkages for Exceptional Students (CIRCLES)	Self-determination skills as measured by the American Institute for Research Self-Determination Scale and participation in the IEP	79	"Communicating Interagency Relationships and Collaborative Linkages for Exceptional Students (CIRCLES) to increase self-determination. CIRCLES is a multilevel intervention that includes interagency collaboration and teaming as a key component to ensure positive postschool outcomes for students with disabilities (Rowe et al., 2019)" (Rowe et al., 2021, p. 37).	RBP
• Program of study • Transition program • Social skills	Community-based instruction	Purchasing skills, social behaviors, and safety skills	4	"Community-based instruction is teaching functional skills in the community where target skills naturally occur" (Brown et al., 1983). "Video modeling is a form of video response prompting. Response prompting is defined as a stimuli that later functions as extra cues and reminders for desired behavior (Cooper et al. 2020)" (Rowe et al., 2021, p. 36).	RBP
• Social skills	Multimodal Anxiety and Social Skills Intervention (MASSI)	Social responsiveness	30	Multimodal Anxiety and Social Skills Intervention (MASSI) is "a curriculum that incorporates traditional verbal explanation and examples, visual supports, writing and drawing activities, among other approaches (e.g., drama, tactile reminders) to address anxiety symptoms and social skill deficits" (Rowe et al., 2021, p. 37).	RBP

(continued)

Table 11.1. *Continued*

Predictor(s)	Practice	Target skills	# of SwASD	Definition	Level
• Self-care/Independent living	One-More-Than Strategy	Purchasing	4	"The One-More-Than Strategy is a rounding up strategy that teaches individuals to give 'one more' dollar than the amount requested (e.g., if the requested amount is $3.29, the individual gives $4.00 and waits to receive change; Denny & Test, 1995). The strategy is also referred to as 'next dollar', 'counting on,' or 'dollar more' strategy" (Rowe et al., 2021, p. 34).	RBP
• Community experiences • Program of study • Self-care/independent living • Transition program • Travel skills	Peer-assisted instruction/ support	Social interactions	46	"Peer-assisted instruction and support (aka; peer tutoring, peer mediated instruction) has been defined as having students of the same age delivering academic of functional skills instruction to each other or work together as partners or in small groups to complete assignments" (Rowe et al., 2021, p. 37).	RBP
• Community experiences • Program of study • Self-care/independent living • Social skills • Transition program • Travel skills	Simulation	Basic finance	1	"Simulation is defined as using materials and situations in the classroom that approximate the natural stimulus conditions and response topographies associated with the performance of functional skills in community settings (Bates et al., 2001)" (Rowe et al., 2021, p. 37).	RBP
• Community experiences • Program of study • Self-care/independent living skills • Social skills transition program • Travel skills	Video Modeling	Interviewing skills	15	Video modeling is "a form of response prompting (i.e., a stimuli that later functions as extra cue; Rowe et al., 2021). Video modeling involves a video recording of a multistep task in which an individual will watch and will then be allowed an opportunity to imitate the steps in the task" (Rowe et al., 2021, p. 36).	RBP

Skills	Intervention	Topic	# SwASD	Description	Type
• Self-care/independent living • Paid employment/work experience	Video Modeling	Food preparation	6	Video modeling is "a form of response prompting (i.e., a stimuli that later functions as extra cue; Rowe et al., 2019). Video modeling involves a video recording of a multistep task in which an individual will watch and will then be allowed an opportunity to imitate the steps in the task" (Rowe et al., 2021, p. 36).	RBP
• Self-care/independent living	Video Modeling	Leisure skills (e.g., darts, basketball, origami, puzzles, entertaining guests)	5	Video modeling is "a form of response prompting (i.e., a stimuli that later functions as extra cue; Rowe et al., 2021). Video modeling involves a video recording of a multistep task in which an individual will watch and will then be allowed an opportunity to imitate the steps in the task" (Rowe et al., 2021, p. 36).	RBP
• Goal setting • Self-advocacy/self-determination • Transition program • Youth autonomy/decision making	*Whose Future Is It Anyway?* Plus, Rocket Reader	Self-determination skills	7	"*Whose Future Is It?* is a published curriculum that teaches students how to be involved in the IEP process " (Rowe et al., 2021, p. 38).	RBP
• Community experiences • Program of study • Self-care/independent living • Social skills • Transition program • Paid employment/work experience	Working at Gaining Employment Skills (WAGES)	Social skills and occupational skills	16	"Working at Gaining Employment Skills to teach social and occupational skills. Working at Gaining Employment Skills (WAGES) is a job-related social skills curriculum focused on teaching self-regulation, teamwork, communication, and problem solving" (Rowe et al., 2021, p. 38).	RBP

Note: # of SwASD = numbers of learners with ASD; ASD = autism spectrum disorder; EBP = evidence-based practices; RBP = research-based practice; Information derived from Mazzotti et al. (2021) and Rowe et al. (2021).

CONSIDERATIONS FOR PRACTICAL APPLICATION OF SECONDARY EBPS, RBPS, AND PREDICTORS

Practitioners who teach learners with ASD should be guided by research in conjunction with their own expertise and take into consideration learners' and parents' input and values when implementing EBPs (Cook & Cook, 2013; Harn et al., 2013). If sufficient research is not available for teaching specific skills, they should consider using promising practices (e.g., graduated sequence of instruction and graphic organizers to teach math, mnemonics to teach social studies vocabulary) and take caution if specific practices have not been established through research. Ongoing data-based decision making informed by learner performance is critical regardless of the level of evidence that supports a particular intervention. However, if practitioners make the determination that promising or unestablished practices are the best fit for their learners with ASD, they should attend even more closely to learner performance data to evaluate the effectiveness of the practice. It is also important to ensure there is leadership support (e.g., administrators, local/state-level agencies) and collaboration between stakeholders to promote the use of EBPs for learners with ASD. Clearly communicating about the use of each practice (e.g., definitions of EBPs and RBPs, settings, time, numbers of learners, materials) among stakeholders may promote the fidelity and validity of using these practices. Table 11.2 includes a list of secondary transition resources to support implementation of EBPs for learners with ASD.

It is important to understand how to implement these EBPs for learners with ASD. Therefore, we have included Figures 11.3 through 11.6 to provide research-to-practice lesson plans that practitioners can use to implement the EBPs and RBPs discussed in this chapter. These research-to-practice lesson plans include the SDLMI to teach goal setting and problem solving, the one-more-than strategy to teach purchasing, video modeling to teach food-preparation skills, and the self-directed IEP to teach IEP participation.

As practitioners support learners with ASD with approaches grounded in science, it is also important to consider how best to objectively evaluate learner outcomes over time. The IDEIA (2004) mandates that state education agencies (SEAs) report annually (a) on outcome measures for learners with IEPs like the rate of graduation (known as Indicator 1) and (b) the rate of engagement in employment or postsecondary education within one year of high-school exit (known as Indicator 14). While these types of data may be helpful for policy makers at the state or district level, they may not be packaged in a way that is particularly helpful for those providing direct support to learners. Fortunately, creating and implementing metrics to track learner outcomes over time is something that practitioners can take on with minimal effort.

For instance, a special education teacher might create a simple spreadsheet to start tracking learner employment outcomes at the time of high-school exit. That teacher could track anything from the frequency with which learners are employed at the time of high-school exit to wages, the number of hours they work per week, or the industries in which they are employed. Such data become particularly valuable over time as practitioners identify trends in outcomes that may be indicative of gaps in services or supports, disparities between certain subgroups of learners, or particularly effective approaches to the provision of transition ser-

Table 11.2. Secondary Transition Resources to Support Implementation of EBPs

Resource	Description of resource	Link to resource
National Technical Assistance Center on Transition's (NTACT) Lesson Plan Starters	NTACT's Lesson Plan Starters are developed based on high-quality research and provide pertinent information for implementing effective practices across settings (e.g., community, self-contained classrooms, general education classrooms) and content (e.g., academic skills, employment skills, life skills).	https://transitionta.org /lesson-starters/
Predictor Implementation School/District Self-Assessment (PISA)	The PISA can be used by teachers, administrators, or transition professionals to assess the quality of transition programs or classroom practices that are related to improved postschool outcomes. Also, the PISA offers suggestions on how to prepare learners for adult life.	https://transitionta.org /pisa-self-assessment/
Communicating Interagency Relationships and Collaborative Linkages for Exceptional Students (CIRCLES)	CIRCLES is the only research-based practice identified by Rowe et al. (2021). Free resources and guidance can be found on the CIRCLES website.	https://circles.charlotte.edu/
Transition Coalition Do It Yourself (DIY) Resources	These DIY resources are supported by research and cover multiple topics (e.g., response prompting, video modeling). All resources support teacher and transition professional skill development.	https://transitioncoalition .org/diy/
NTACT:C Social Media	NTACT:C shared new information and resources through weekly News Blast (NB), Facebook, Twitter, TeachersPayTeachers (TPT), Pinterest, and Medium blog.	https://transitionta.org/
Secondary Transition ASD Resources (STAR)	The STAR is a large collection of 42 research-based practices to support learners with ASD.	https://transitioncoalition .org/blog/tc-materials /secondary-transition -autism-spectrum -disorders-resources-star/
Secondary Practices, Predictors, and Postsecondary Outcomes for Individuals with Autism Spectrum Disorder: Annotated Bibliography	Within this annotated bibliography, high-quality research supporting learners with ASD is highlighted and summarized.	https://transitionta.org /autism-spectrum -disorder-ab/

RESEARCH to PRACTICE LESSON PLAN STARTER

Using the SDLMI to Teach Goal Setting and Problem-Solving

Objective: The purpose of SDLMI is to help students set goals, make a plan for achieving them, and adjust their plan as needed.

Setting and Materials:

Settings: General Education Classroom
Materials: None

Teaching Procedures
Content Taught

Self-Determined Learning Model of Instruction (SDLMI) is an instructional process that includes the following:

- Instructional Phase 1: What is My Goal? Student Questions
- Instructional Phase 2: What is My Plan? Student Questions
- Instructional Phase 3: What Have I learned? Student Questions
- Teacher Objectives for each Instructional Phase

Teaching Procedures

1. Make appropriate changes to the wording of student questions, based on needs of students.
2. Refer to the teacher objectives to ensure the problem-solving intent of the questions remain intact. For example, changing student question 1 from "What do I want to learn?" to "What is my goal?" changes the nature of the question.
3. Provide students with visual copy of questions for Phase 1.
4. Read the questions with or to the students.
5. Discuss what the questions mean. Possibly rephrase questions if students struggle with the wording.
6. Direct students to choose a goal they want to work towards. This could be an academic or functional goal, possibly an IEP goal.
7. Direct students to answer the student questions in Phase 1 based on what goal they selected to work toward.
8. Once students identify a goal, identify possible goal outcomes for each goal using a 5-point scale ranging from the most unfavorable possible outcome to the most favorable possible outcome (see example of Goal Attainment Scaling form in evaluation section below).
9. Provide students with visual copy of questions for Phase 2.
10. Read the questions with or to the students.
11. Discuss what the questions mean. Possibly rephrase questions if students struggle with the wording.

Figure 11.3.   Research-to-practice lesson plan starter: SDLMI

12. Direct students to answer the student questions in Phase 2 based on what goal they selected to work toward.
13. Provide students with visual copy of questions for Phase 3.
14. Read the questions with or to the students.
15. Discuss what the questions mean. Possibly rephrase questions if students struggle with the wording.
16. Direct students to answer the student questions in Phase 3 based on how they answered the questions in Phase 2.
17. When instruction has been completed on all three phases, continue collecting progress data on the goal students selected to work toward.
18. Complete the GAS scoring form to determine improvement or attainment of goal.

Instructional Phase 1 for Self-Determined Learning Model of Instruction

Set a Goal: Problem for Student to Solve: What is my Goal?	
Student Questions	Teacher Objectives
1) What do I want to learn?	• Enable students to identify specific strengths and instructional needs. • Enable students to communicate preferences, interests, beliefs, and values. • Teach students to prioritize needs.
2) What do I know about it now?	• Enable students to identify their current status in relation to the instructional need. • Assist students to gather information about opportunities and barriers in their environments.
3) What must change for me to learn what I don't know?	• Enable students to decide if action will be focused toward capacity building, modifying the environment, or both. • Support students to choose a need to address from prioritized list.
4) What can I do to make this happen?	• Teach students to state a goal and identify criteria for achieving goal.

Instructional Phase 2 for Self-Determination Learning Model of Instruction

Take Action: Problem for Students to Solve: What is my Plan?	
Student Questions	Teacher Objectives
5) What can I do to learn what I don't know?	• Enable student to self-evaluate current status and self-identified goal status.
6) What could keep me from taking action?	• Enable student to determine plan of action to bridge gap between self-evaluated current status and self-identified goal status.
7) What can I do	• Collaborate with student to identify most appropriate

(continued)

to remove these barriers?	instructional strategies. • Teach student needed student-directed learning strategies. • Support student to implement student-directed learning strategies. • Provide mutually agreed upon teacher-directed instruction.
8) When will I take action?	• Enable student to determine schedule for action plan. • Enable student to implement action plan. • Enable student to self-monitor progress.

Instructional Phase 3 for Self-Determined Learning Model of Instruction

Adjust Goal or Plan: Problem for Student to Solve: What have I Learned?	
Student Questions	Teacher Objectives
9) What actions have I taken?	• Enable student to self-evaluate progress toward goal achievement.
10) What barriers have been removed?	• Collaborate with student to compare progress with desired outcomes.
11) What has changed about what I don't know?	• Support student to reevaluate goal if progress is insufficient. • Assist student to decide if goal remains the same or changes. • Collaborate with student to identify if action plan is adequate or inadequate given revised or retained goal. • Assist student to change action plan if necessary.
12) Do I know what I want to know?	• Enable student to decide if progress is adequate, inadequate, or if goal has been achieved.

Evaluation

Results of GAS scores and/or compare pre/post-tests of AIR Self-Determination Scale or Arc Self-Determination Scale.

Blank GAS Scoring Form

Goal Attainment Scaling Goals			
Goals	Goal 1:	Goal 2:	Goal 3:
Time Line			
Level of Attainment			
Much less progress than expected (-2)			
Somewhat less progress than expected (-1)			
Expected level of			

Figure 11.3. *Continued*

progress (0)			
Somewhat more progress than expected (+1)			
Much more progress than expected (+2)			
Comments:			

Lesson Plan Based on:

Wehmeyer, M. L., & Palmer, S. B. (2000). Promoting causal agency: The self-determined learning model of instruction. *Exceptional Children, 66*(4), 439-453. https://doi.org/10.1177/001440290006600401

Coffe, G. & Ray-Subramanian, C.E., (2009). Goal attainment scaling: a progress monitoring tool for behavioral interventions. *School Psychology Forum, 3*(1), 1-12.

The contents of this Lesson Plan Starter were developed under a grant (H326E200003) from the Department of Education. However, those contents do not necessarily represent the policy of the Department of Education, and you should not assume endorsement by the Federal Government.

IDEAs
that Work

U.S. Office of Special
Education Programs

Lesson Starter
Using One-More-Than Strategy to Teach Purchasing Skills
(Research-Based Practice)

Objective: To teach students to use the one-more-than strategy to make independent purchases.

Setting and Materials

Setting: Resource classroom, school bookstore, community (i.e., local department store)
Materials:
1. Three sets of 15 flashcards with differing price amounts listed
   a. Set 1: $5.00 to $9.99
   b. Set 2: $10.00 to $14.99
   c. Set 3: $15.00 to $20.00
2. Real money
   a. One-dollar bill (5)
   b. Five-dollar bill (2)
   c. 10-dollar bill (1)
   d. 20-dollar bill (1)

Content Taught

The one-more-than strategy (also called the "counting on" or "next dollar" strategy) is a technique used to teach students to purchase items using one more dollar than requested. Students are given 10 of 15 possible prices of dollar and cents amounts and taught how to make independent purchases by counting one more dollar bill within simulated and community settings. For example, with amounts from $5.00-$9.99, students will begin with a five-dollar bill, and then, use one-dollar bills to "count-on from there, six, seven...". For amounts from $10.00-$14.99, students will begin with a 10-dollar bill, and then, use one-dollar bills to "count on from there eleven, twelve...". For amounts from $15.00-$20.00, students will begin with a 10-dollar bill and a five-dollar bill, and then, use one \-dollar bills to "count-on from there, 16, 17...".

Teaching Procedures

Within the classroom (simulated):
1. Tell the students they will be learning a method they can use for going to the store to buy things.
2. Explain to the students they will practice making purchases by going through a list of prices and pretending you are the cashier, and they are buying something.
3. State the price to the student while showing them the randomly selected flashcard from Set 1 first.

Figure 11.4. Research-to-Practice lesson plan starter: One-More-Than strategy

4. Use verbal descriptions and modeling to introduce the one-more-than strategy. For example, for amounts from $5.00-$9.99, begin with a five-dollar bill and show the five-dollar bill to the student and say "five dollars" and "count-on from there, six, seven..." as you count one-dollar bills.
5. Give money to the student and deliver an instructional prompt for the student to make a purchase.
6. Provide verbal praise if the student makes an independent purchase.
7. If the student makes an error, use least-to-most hierarchy prompting by giving:
    a. verbal prompt (e.g., Do you see the number on the bill?")
    b. gesture (e.g., pointing to number on the bill)
    c. gesture plus verbal explanation (e.g., pointing to the number on the bill andproviding a verbal explanation
    d. modeling plus verbal explanation (e.g., pointing to the number on the bill,providing a verbal explanation, and demonstrating the correct response
    e. physical assistance plus verbal explanation (e.g., holding the student's wrist,pointing to the number on the bill, providing a verbal explanation, and physically assisting the student to the correct response).

Within the community (generalization):
8. At the end of the simulated classroom training, have the students purchase items in various amounts under $20.00 within the school (e.g., school bookstore) and within the local community. Allow at least a 10-min delay between purchasing opportunities.
9. Deliver descriptive verbal praise for independent purchases within the community and use least-to-most prompting (see above hierarchy) until the student can correctly make the purchase independently.

Evaluation

Students should independently make purchases using the one-more-than strategy at 100% accuracy over three consecutive sessions.

Lesson Plan Based on:

Cihak, D. F., & Grim, J. (2008). Teaching students with autism spectrum disorder and moderate intellectual disabilities to use counting-on strategies to enhance independent purchasing skills. *Research in Autism Spectrum Disorders, 2*(4), 716–727. https://doi.org/10.1016/j.rasd.2008.02.006

The contents of this Lesson Plan Starter were developed under a grant (H326E200003) from the Department of Education. However, those contents do not necessarily represent the policy of the Department of Education, and you should not assume endorsement by the Federal Government.

2

(*continued*)

This product is public domain. Authorization to reproduce it in whole or in part is granted. While permission to reprint this publication is not necessary, the citation should be:

National Technical Assistance Center on Transition: The Collaborative (2021). *Research to practice lesson starter: Using One-More-Than Strategy to teach purchasing skills.* University of North Carolina at Charlotte.

U.S. Office of Special
Education Programs

Figure 11.4. *Continued*

RESEARCH to PRACTICE LESSON PLAN STARTER

Using Self-Directed IEP to Teach Participation in the IEP

Objective: The purpose of Self-Directed IEP is to help students to participate in IEP meetings through the use of the Choicemaker multimedia package that includes the Self-Directed IEP.

Setting and Materials:

Settings: Self-contained high school classroom.

Materials: Choicemaker Self-Directed IEP Multimedia Package (Includes teacher's manual, student workbook, two videos). To obtain SD-IEP, call Sopris West Inc. at 1-800-547-6747. Cost: $120

Content Taught

Four instructional units including:

Instructional Unit 1: Leading Meeting
Step 1: Begin Meeting by Stating a Purpose
Step 2: Introduce Everyone
Step 3: Review Past Goals and Performance

Instructional Unit 2: Reporting Interests
Step 5: State Your School and Transition Goals

Instructional Unit 3: Reporting Skills
Step 5: State Your School and Transition Goals

Instructional Unit 4: Reporting Options
Step 9: Summarize Your Goals
Step 10: Close Meeting by Thanking Everyone

Teaching Procedures

1. Within each step a format is followed:

a) Review of prior steps, as needed.
b) Preview lesson content and instruction on new vocabulary used.
c) Videotape material provides model and sample situations used for
d) guided practice.
e) Workbook activities (teacher reads aloud, writes on overhead, and leads class discussion in place of workbook activities when needed) used to practice each step.
f) Teacher demonstrates and students practice for real IEP meetings.
g) Brief student skill evaluation.
h) Ask students to relate skills to other situations, wrap up.
i) Picture prompts for steps 1, 2, & 3 for students with limited reading, writing and cognitive skills.

Evaluation

1. **Five Mock IEP Meetings**. After each instrumental unit is completed, a mock IEP meeting is held.

Figure 11.5. Research-to-Practice lesson plan starter: Self-directed IEP   (*continued*)

2. Student performance in Mock and Real IEP meetings is measured using a task checklist.

Lesson Plan Based on:

Allen, S., Smith, A., Test, D., Flowers, C., & Wood, W. (2002). The effects of self-directed. IEP on student participation in IEP meetings. *Career Development for Exceptional Individuals,24*(2), 107-120. https://doi.org/10.1177/08857288010400202

The contents of this Lesson Plan Starter were developed under a grant (H326E200003) from the Department of Education. However, those contents do not necessarily represent the policy of the Department of Education, and you should not assume endorsement by the Federal Government.

U.S. Office of Special
Education Programs

Figure 11.5. *Continued*

RESEARCH to PRACTICE LESSON PLAN STARTER

Using Video Modeling to Teach Food Preparation Skills:
Making Spaghetti
(Research-Based Practice)

Objective: To evaluate the effectiveness of an iPad as a prompting device for teaching how to make spaghetti to young adults with disabilities.

Setting and Materials

Settings: Two apartments in a living facility
Materials: iPad, task analysis, spoon, pot, hot mitts, measuring cup, strainer, spaghetti, cheese, sauce, pot

Content Taught

Using a task analysis, students will be taught how to properly make spaghetti.

Teaching Procedures

- Create a video using a video model to show the steps for the making spaghetti task on an iPad (see Kellems et al., 2016 below).
- Use the iPad video to teach each step of the task analysis.
- Prompt students to turn on the iPad and watch the corresponding video (e.g., making spaghetti).
- Allow students to choose whether they would like to watch a video for all steps or just the steps they need extra support learning.
- Guide students to complete the steps in the task analysis to ensure the home maintenance task is complete.
- If the student does not begin the step within 5 seconds of viewing the video, verbally prompt the student to "do what they had viewed in the video."

Task Analysis: Making Spaghetti
1. Wash hands
2. Get spoon
3. Get pot
4. Get hot mitts
5. Get measuring cup
6. Get strainer
7. Get spaghetti
8. Get parmesan cheese
9. Get sauce
10. Fill pot with four cups of water
11. Turn to HIGH

Figure 11.6. Research-to-Practice lesson plan starter: Video modeling *(continued)*

12. Wait until water boils
13. Add noodles to pot
14. Set timer to 9 min
15. Stir noodles
16. Put on mitts
17. Drain noodles
18. Measure one cup of sauce
19. Put sauce on noodles
20. Put spaghetti on plate

Evaluation

Students performance is evaluated by calculating a percentage of the steps the student completed independently. A step is considered completed independently if the student began the task within 5 seconds and completed it correctly. If a student scores 80% for three consecutive sessions they can move on to the next home maintenance skill.

Lesson Plan Based on:

Kellems, R. O., Rickard, T. H., Okray, D. A., Sauer-Sagiv, L., & Washburn, B. (2018). iPad® video prompting to teach young adults with disabilities independent living skills: A maintenance study. *Career Development and Transition for Exceptional Individuals*, *41*(3), 175–184. https://doi.org/10.1177/2165143417719078

For Developing a Video Model:

Kellems, R. O., Mourra, K., Morgan, R. L., Riesen, T., Glasgow, M., & Huddleston, R. (2016). Video modeling and prompting in practice: Teaching cooking skills. *Career Development and Transition for Exceptional Individuals*, *39*(3), 185-190. https://doi.org/10.1177/2165143416651718

The contents of this Lesson Plan Starter were developed under a grant (H326E200003) from the Department of Education. However, those contents do not necessarily represent the policy of the Department of Education, and you should not assume endorsement by the Federal Government.

IDEAs that Work
U.S. Office of Special
Education Programs

Figure 11.6. *Continued*

vices. Moreover, such data can ensure that collaborative partnerships between practitioners are objective and data driven. For example, a school-level transition specialist might start collecting data about the rate with which secondary learners with disabilities are connected to outside organizations and recognize that learners with ASD tend to not be connected with adult disability service providers. This finding could then serve both as a conversation starter with collaborative partners and as a baseline before intervening to improve the rate with which learners with ASD are connected to the services they provide.

SUMMARY

Over the years, legislation such as the EAHCA of 1975, the IDEIA of 2004, and the ESSA of 2015 have strived to provide learners with disabilities access to environments, opportunities, services, and supports related to education, employment, and independent living. However, access alone is not enough, as evidenced by current postschool outcomes for youth with disabilities, including youth with ASD, who continue to experience higher rates of unemployment and lower rates of enrollment in postsecondary education than their peers without disabilities. For youth and young adults with ASD who engage in problem behavior or ritualistic behaviors, or have limited expressive and receptive communication skills, these outcomes are even less favorable (Howlin & Moss, 2012). The quality of life of family members is also a continued concern; research has found that parents and siblings of learners with ASD are more likely to experience stress, psychological distress, depression, increased levels of physical or mental health issues, and social isolation (Howlin & Moss, 2012). To improve the quality of life for youth and young adults with ASD and their families, it is critical that effective transition services and practices, with a documented positive impact on learner postschool outcomes, are implemented.

Kohler's Taxonomy 2.0 for transition programming organizes effective transition practices into the following five categories: student-focused planning, student development, interagency and interdisciplinary collaboration, family involvement, and program structures and attributes (Kohler et al., 2016). At the individual level, there is an emphasis on the learner, who is empowered to lead discussions about their future by voicing their preferences and interests. The Taxonomy 2.0 further acknowledges the role families play in fostering self-determined behavior in their children. Programmatically, there is an emphasis on program structure (i.e., philosophy, policies, evaluation) and cohesion and collaboration between programs and services (i.e., schools, adult service providers).

Beyond legislative efforts and the best practices identified in the literature, there is still a need for widespread systemic change. For this to occur, organizations need to examine their learner outcomes closely and align their transition services with those identified in the literature as best practice. Research has identified in-school predictors (i.e., program characteristics) associated with postschool success, along with the EBPs and RBPs that can be implemented to develop and refine the skills associated with a given predictor (Mazzotti et al., 2016, 2021; Test, Mazzotti et al., 2009). As identified in Table 11.1, a number of predictors and practices have been shown effective for youth with ASD. The EBPs and RBPs are the specific practices directly used with learners. For example, self-determination/self-advocacy are predictors of postschool success; to develop the skills associated with this predictor (i.e., self-determined behaviors), an EBP that can be implemented by transition professionals is the SDLMI. Recently, Rowe and colleagues (2021) identified nine new EBPs and 22 RBPs for more than 45 transition skills (e.g., EnvisionIT to teach technology skills, Project SEARCH to teach transition skills).

As the prevalence of ASD continues to steadily rise, it is critical that EBPs and RBPs be implemented to equip a growing number of youths with ASD with the skills and knowledge necessary to successfully transition to postschool settings. As one of 13 disability categories recognized under IDEIA (2004), ASD learners may have the benefit of access to specialized and individualized supports and services during their K–12 education; however, greater efforts must be made to improve their postschool outcomes. This can be achieved by aligning predictors of postschool success with EBPs and RBPs and implementing those programs and practices with fidelity.

CASE STUDY

Laura C. Chezan and Katie Wolfe

Background

Andrew is an 18-year-old young man with autism spectrum disorder (ASD). He attends a local public school where he receives special education and related services under the autism category of the Individuals with Disabilities Improvement Act (IDEIA) of 2004. Andrew reads at a 7th grade level but has difficulties with reading comprehension. He can complete several independent living tasks (e.g., grooming, making his bed, housekeeping) but relies on his parents to prepare his meals. Andrew's strengths include being on time, having perfect attendance to school and community-based instruction, and navigating the internet and various applications on his computer. He likes listening to music, working out, riding his bike, and hiking.

His teacher uses a person-centered planning (PCP) approach to identify and prioritize Andrew's short- and long-term transition goals. Andrew, his family, his teacher, the transition specialist, and a vocational rehabilitation counselor attend the PCP meeting to determine how to best support Andrew and his family's vision for transition to adulthood. Andrew and his parents identified the transition from the family house into an apartment as a priority for Andrew. The team decided that teaching Andrew food-preparation skills is an important transition goal that is likely to support his vision to live independently after graduation from high school. Furthermore, food preparation has been identified in the literature as a predictor of successful independent living.

Step 1: Questions to Initiate the Evidence-Based Treatment Selection Process

Andrew's teacher begins the evidence-based treatment selection process by generating questions to guide the PCP team through the process. She asks the following questions:

1. What interventions may be effective for teaching Andrew food-preparation skills?
2. What supports are needed to decrease Andrew's reliance on his parents to prepare meals?

Step 2—Part 1: Best Available Evidence

The teacher and the transition specialist conduct a review of evidence-based practices (EBPs) that have been effective in teaching independent living skills to youth and adults with ASD. They review several sources, including the National Technical Assistance Center on Transition, the Zarrow Center for Learning Enrichment, and the National Professional Development Center on Autism Spectrum Disorder. The teacher and the transition specialist find that video modeling and prompting have been demonstrated effective in teaching a wide range of independent living skills, including food-preparation skills, to learners with ASD. Video modeling consists of asking a learner to watch a video recording of the steps needed to complete a target behavior and then providing the opportunity to perform the behavior. Prompting consists of providing a predetermined amount of assistance to a learner to complete a task or activity and it is usually used in combination with reinforcement.

Step 2—Part 2: Person-Related Variables

The teacher and the transition specialist consider Andrew's abilities and preferences that may influence the acquisition of food-preparation skills. Andrew can read at a 7th grade level, can imitate motor behavior, and can maintain his attention for at least 20 min. In addition, he knows how to use a computer and is very good at navigating the internet and various applications. Because Andrew has the prerequisite skills needed to watch a video model and has good technology skills, video modeling can be an effective intervention. He also responds well to verbal prompts and can follow instructions and, thus, prompting may also be effective. Andrew's parents prefer an intervention that can be implemented throughout the day at the time when a naturally occurring opportunity to prepare a meal arises. Furthermore, they would like an intervention that is likely to decrease Andrew's reliance on them to prepare his meals.

Step 2—Part 3: Contextual Variables (Resource Constraints, Environmental Supports)

The teacher discusses with the transition specialist, Andrew, and his parents, the acceptability and feasibility of the potential interventions that can be used to teach Andrew food-preparation skills. Andrew receives transition services 3 times per week at school. The transition specialist could implement either video modeling or prompting to teach food-preparation skills. However, Andrew will have only one daily opportunity 3 times per week to receive instruction in school. Parents would be able to provide additional instruction at home using either prompting or video modeling, but they prefer to limit prompting their son. Furthermore, during the PCP meeting, the vocational rehabilitation counselor stated that the agency could assist with the technology needed to create and use video modeling.

(continued)

Step 3: Professional Judgment

The teacher and the transition specialist consider the advantages and disadvantages of the two interventions (see Table 11.3).

Table 11.3. Advantages and Disadvantages of Potential Interventions for Andrew

Intervention	Advantages	Disadvantages
Video modeling	• Visual model of target behavior • Andrew or peers can serve as models • Can be used across settings • Provides multiple practice opportunities	• Time, resources, and experience needed to create the video • Can be disruptive to peers during instruction • Requires prerequisite skills (e.g., imitation, sustained attention to watch the video) • Need to teach Andrew how to play and watch the video independently to decrease reliance on others
Prompting	• Easy to use with minimal training • Does not require many resources • Decreases the likelihood of errors	• May promote prompt dependency if prompts are not faded • Requires the practitioner to be present during the intervention and identify the appropriate time to deliver the controlling prompt

After discussing the advantages and disadvantages of each potential intervention with the teacher, the transition specialist feels comfortable using both interventions (i.e., video modeling and prompting) to teach Andrew food-preparation skills. However, she would prefer to use video modeling rather than prompting because she agrees with Andrew's parents than he needs to decrease his reliance on others. In addition, Andrew could watch the video independently at times when the transition specialist is not present or is busy attending to competing responsibilities. Furthermore, she believes that video modeling can be used across settings and will promote generalization and maintenance of skills.

Step 4: Intervention Selection

With Andrew and his parent's input, the teacher and the transition specialist decide to teach Andrew food-preparation skills using video modeling. Even though both interventions were supported by research, Andrew's technology skills and his ability to read, imitate models, and sustain attention would allow him to acquire the skill quickly. Furthermore, the teacher and the transition specialist work with Andrew and his family to develop a routine for implementing video modeling at home when an opportunity for preparing a meal occurs throughout the day. Implementing the intervention at home would provide him multiple practice opportunities and promote generalization across settings.

Step 5: Intervention Implementation and Data Collection
Because the teacher has received training on how to create and implement video modeling during her teacher education training, she assists the transition specialist with the development of the video modeling intervention. They develop a teaching procedure to show Andrew how to play and watch the recording independently prior to each meal preparation. The transition specialist uses a data sheet to collect Andrew's performance on food-preparation skills when the intervention is implemented at school. She also trains Andrew's parents to collect data on his performance when the intervention is implemented at home. The transition specialist and Andrew's parents provide data to his teacher to visually represent it on a graph.

Step 6: Reevaluation
Two weeks after the intervention has been implemented, the PCP team meets to evaluate Andrew's progress. Data reveal that video modeling has been effective in promoting the acquisition of food-preparation skills. Andrew' parents report that he can play and watch the video independently. He occasionally asks for assistance with troubleshooting issues, such as rewatching a step, locating an ingredient, or turning on the stove. The team agrees to continue the same intervention and meet again after one month to determine his progress and create a plan to fade the intervention if he continues to show progress.

APPLICATION ACTIVITIES

1. Complete the Evidence-Based Practices Do It Yourself (EBP-DIY) on the Transition Coalition website (https://transitioncoalition.org/diy/). This is a great way to learn how to implement EBPs and RBPs to support transition skill development for youth with ASD. There are currently three EBP-DIYs: Response prompting, SDLMI, and video modeling. These EBP-DIYs provide (a) an opportunity to watch an expert implement the practice, (b) access to materials and resources, and (c) the "how-tos" to implement the EBPs on your own.

2. Use the Predictor Implementation School/District Self-Assessment (PISA) to develop, evaluate, and improve transition programs, practices, and services for secondary youth with ASD (https://transitionta.org/pisa-self-assessment/). The PISA is intended to provide schools, districts, or other stakeholders in secondary transition with a framework for determining the degree to which their program is implementing effective transition practices likely to lead to more positive postschool outcomes for students with disabilities.

3. Complete modules on the National Professional Development Center on Autism Spectrum Disorder website (https://autismpdc.fpg.unc.edu/evidence-based-practices). These modules can be used to support secondary skill development for youth with ASD.

ADDITIONAL RESOURCES

Kansas University Center on Developmental Disabilities (n.d.). https://kucdd.ku.edu/
Kansas University, Self-Determination Resources (n.d.). https://selfdetermination.ku.edu/
National Technical Assistance Center on Transition: The Collaborative (NTACT; n.d.). https://transitionta.org/topics/effective-practices/
Zarrow Center for Learning Enrichment (n.d.). https://www.ou.edu/education/centers-and-partnerships/zarrow

12

Collaborative Partnerships

Parents and Families

Hedda Meadan and Jamie N. Pearson

■ ■ ■

INTRODUCTION AND OVERVIEW

Parents and families can be involved and can engage in their children's education in different ways across the child's life. There is clear evidence that family engagement leads to positive outcomes for learners with and without autism, their parents, and their families. Family engagement and effective family-practitioner collaboration are critical to support the needs of learners with autism and their families. Building a solid partnership with parents and families involves consistent communication, persistent involvement, and trust. The purpose of this chapter is to discuss the importance of collaborating and partnering with families of learners with autism and to describe strategies to facilitate effective partnerships. The chapter first describes the theoretical contexts that ground family involvement and engagement. Then, this chapter highlights (a) ways parents and families can be involved and engaged in their children's education and specialized services, (b) factors that could influence involvement and engagement, and (c) the outcomes of involvement and engagement. Finally, we describe strategies for building effective family-practitioner partnerships, enhancing family involvement and engagement, and evaluating family partnerships.

*   *   *

Shay is a happy boy who will turn 5 years old in a couple of months. He loves to play with Legos, do puzzles, and listen to music. He was diagnosed with autism when he was 3 years old and has delays in social-communication and motor skills. He receives speech therapy and physical therapy during the week in the school setting. Shay has a younger sister who is almost 3 years old, and they both live in a three-bedroom apartment with their mother, Miriam, and their maternal grandparents, Joe and Marisela. Shay is currently enrolled in the school district's early childhood education program and will transition into a kindergarten classroom in the fall.

Shay's mother, Miriam, is busy working two jobs, leaving every morning at 7:00 a.m. and coming back home around 8:00 p.m. The grandparents, Joe and Marisela, are taking care of Shay's younger sister during the day, along with Shay when he comes home from the early childhood program at 1:00 p.m. Shay has very limited verbal communication, so the early childhood teachers and therapists are using a communication notebook to share information about Shay's day with his family. Because Joe and Marisela are home during the day, they are the ones who communicate most frequently with Shay's teachers and therapists. Marisela can understand English, but is not fluent in speaking, reading, and writing English, so Joe reviews the communication notebook that Shay brings every day from school, reads the notes about Shay's day, and adds comments and questions.

Recently, Miriam was notified about the upcoming individualized education program (IEP) meeting for Shay and was told by the early childhood teachers that they will need to discuss and make a decision about Shay's kindergarten placement in the fall. Although Shay has made a lot of progress while in the early childhood program, he still needs support in expressing his wants and needs in socially appropriate ways and with fine motor tasks. Because Joe and Marisela are very involved in Shay's life, Miriam hopes they can help in making the decision about the kindergarten placement for Shay. Miriam has many questions about the transition process from early childhood to the school programs, the different kindergarten placement options, and the expectations in kindergarten. She wants to find a program that will support Shay's development and she is very nervous about the upcoming IEP meeting. Miriam is not sure what to do, who to talk with, and where she can get more information and support. She wants to be involved and engaged in Shay's schooling and education, but also knows that she has very limited time and energy to do much more than what she is currently doing. She hopes both of her children will be healthy and happy, have friends, and be successful in life.

* * *

FAMILY INVOLVEMENT AND ENGAGEMENT

Parents are "children's first and most important teachers, advocates, and nurturers" (U.S. HHS & ED, 2016, p. 1) and their participation in their children's education and treatment can lead to social and academic development and success (Jeynes, 2017; Sheridan et al., 2019). More specifically, among learners with autism, parent involvement and engagement can lead to more effective intervention implementation, positive parent-practitioner relationships, and positive learner outcomes (Azad & Mandell, 2016; Mapp & Kuttner, 2013; Topor et al., 2010). Parents of learners with autism report higher satisfaction with school services when they are more actively involved (Zablotsky et al., 2012). When parents are not involved in their child's schooling, however, practitioners report barriers to positive learner outcomes (Henderson & Mapp, 2002; Olmstead, 2013). Researchers and practitioners (e.g., teachers, therapists, early interventionists) have been using different terms to describe parents' participation in their children's education and treatment. In this section, we define and describe terms related to family engagement in education.

Parent involvement in education was defined as "the resources that parents invest in a child's learning experience" (Calzada et al., 2015, p. 872). Based on Epstein's (2001) theoretical framework, there are three primary forms of parent involvement: home-based involvement (e.g., reading to the child at home, helping with homework), school-based involvement (e.g., participating in school activities, communicating with teachers), and home-school conferencing (Manz et al., 2004). Types of parent involvement include providing parenting skills and knowledge to parents, communicating with parents, involving families as volunteers, supporting parents and children learning at home, including parents in educational decision making, and collaborating with the community (Epstein & Salinas, 2004; Epstein et al., 2002).

Parent engagement was defined as "the systematic inclusion of families in activities and programs that promote children's development, learning, and wellness, including in the planning, development, and evaluation of such activities, programs, and systems" (U.S. HHS & ED, 2016, p. 1). Although parent involvement and parent engagement are used by many as interchangeable terms, Ferlazzo (2011) states that "One of the dictionary definitions of *involve* is 'to enfold or envelope,' whereas one of the meanings of *engage* is 'to come together and interlock.' Thus, involvement implies *doing to*; in contrast, engagement implies *doing with*" (p. 1). In addition to the terms involvement and engagement, researchers and practitioners use *partnering* with parents and families and describe it as "A relationship in which families and professionals agree to build on each other's expertise and resources, as appropriate, for the purpose of making and implementing decisions that will directly benefit students and indirectly benefit other family members and professionals" (Turnbull et al., 2011, p. 137).

The U.S. Departments of Health and Human Services (HHS) and Education (ED) developed a policy statement on family engagement titled *From the Early Years to the Early Grades* and emphasized the need to "promote a vision for family engagement that is consistent across systems and programs, and can set the stage for families' involvement in their children's development and education at all ages" (U.S. HHS & ED, 2016, p. 8). Parents and families can be involved and engaged in their children's education in different ways across the child's life (e.g., during early intervention, transition to school, and transition to adulthood), and there is clear evidence that these could lead to positive outcomes for learners with and without disabilities, their parents, and their families (e.g., Burrell & Borrego, 2012).

Parents, Caregivers, and Families

For learners with disabilities, the Individuals with Disabilities Improvement Education Act (IDEIA, 2004) requires that parents be included in the educational decision-making process. Schools must obtain parental consent for evaluation and programmatic changes, inform parents of progress toward individualized education program (IEP) goals, and invite parents to attend and participate in IEP meetings. The law clarifies that the term *parent* is used in a broad way. In section 602(23) of IDEIA, the term *parent* includes natural, adoptive, and foster parents, guardians, and individuals acting in the role of parent. Furthermore, some researchers have been using the term *caregivers* instead of *parents* to include other guardians and people who take care of a child, such as grandparents, aunts, uncles, and older siblings. Finally, the term *family* was described to include "children, youth, and parents as identified in IDEIA, adult siblings, grandparents, extended family members, and non-related adults that act in the role of a family member" (Office of Special Education Programs [OSEP], 2020, p. 3).

Given the changes in the family structure and composition in the United States since the last century, using broad terms to describe caregivers and families is important. For example, based on the U.S. Census Bureau's annual *America's Families and Living Arrangements* (2020), from 1960 to 2020, the proportion of children under 18 living with two married parents decreased steadily from 88% to 70%. During the same period, the proportion of children living in mother-only families increased from 8% to 23%, and the proportion of children living in father-only families increased from 1% to 6%. In addition, in 2017, the proportion of children living with their grandparents was 7%, and about 5% of children were living without either parent. Instead, they lived with a relative or nonrelative adult (U.S. Census Bureau, 2020). These data reflect some of the changes in family structure and emphasize the need to consider different types of caregivers and families when partnering with families.

Parents and Families from Diverse Backgrounds

In addition to the changes in the family structure and composition in the United States, there have been significant and rapid racial and ethnic changes over the past decade. The largest growth has been in the Hispanic/Latino and Asian American populations. Moreover, it is predicted that the non-Hispanic White population will no longer account for the majority in the U.S. population by 2045 (Vespa et al., 2018). In addition, the multiracial population in the United States, those who identify with two or more races, is also increasing with the rise in interracial caregivers. The children in these families are forming a new generation that identifies with multiple racial groups (Mather et al., 2019). Fung and colleagues (2018) emphasize that different cultures provide diverse sub-contexts in which children develop and socialize. Values and norms influence caregivers' beliefs about child-rearing goals and practices. Caregivers from different racial/ethnic or religious backgrounds often face distinct challenges associated with their histories or immigration status, may hold different child-rearing values, and may engage in different parenting practices (Fung et al., 2018). To partner with marginalized and minoritized caregivers and families, practitioners must understand the context in which children grow up, and the values, norms, and parenting practices of the caregivers and families with whom they work.

To address the need to work with all families, different professional organizations developed standards and recommended practices to support partnership with and engagement of marginalized and minoritized families of children with disabilities. For example, the Council for Exceptional Children (CEC) have specific standards for professional practice (2015), including those to guide collaboration with families from diverse backgrounds (e.g., "Use culturally appropriate communication with parents and families that is respectful and accurately understood" and "Actively seek and use the knowledge of parents and individuals with exceptionalities when planning, conducting, and evaluating special education services and empower them as partners in the educational process"). The Division of

Early Childhood within CEC described recommended practices including specific practices for working with families (2014). The family practices include ongoing activities that (a) promote the active participation of families in decision making related to their child (e.g., assessment, planning, intervention); (b) lead to the development of a service plan (e.g., a set of goals for the family and child and the services and supports to achieve those goals); and (c) support families in achieving the goals they hold for their child and the other family members.

Although there are clear changes in the structure and composition of families in the United States and specific standards and recommended practices for how to work with marginalized and minoritized families with learners with disabilities, a recent survey study ($N = 1500$) conducted by the CEC's Pioneers Division titled *The State of the Special Education Profession* revealed that only a small percentage of special education teachers rated themselves as having high levels of confidence in engaging families from backgrounds different from their own. For example, only 37% of special education teachers felt confident when working with families who differ from them by ethnicity or race, and only 22% of special education teachers felt confident when working with families who spoke a different language (Fowler et al., 2019). When teachers and practitioners face challenges and experience low confidence when working with racially, ethnically, and linguistically diverse learners and their families, the services and practices used to partner with and engage families could be impacted; therefore, there is a clear need to train future practitioners on how to partner with and engage all families.

Grounding Family Involvement and Engagement in Theory

Family engagement and effective family-practitioner collaboration are critical to support the needs of learners with autism (Burrell & Borrego, 2012). Building a solid partnership with caregivers involves consistent communication, persistent involvement, and trust (Curtiss et al., 2016; Turnbull et al., 2011). Therefore, it is important to consider the theoretical contexts that ground family involvement and engagement with practitioners, including the family systems theory, ecological systems theory, and sociocultural theory.

Family Systems Theory

The family systems theory (FST; Kerr & Bowen, 1988) views the family as a system of interrelated and interdependent individuals. Turnbull and colleagues (2011) recommended that the family system be examined as a whole. To understand and support a learner with autism, practitioners must understand their family's patterns of interaction. Turnbull and colleagues (2011) describe four major subsystems within the family: (a) the marital subsystem that includes interactions between spouses or significant others who function as marital partners; (b) the parental subsystem that includes interactions between parents and their children; (c) the sibling subsystem that includes interactions among brothers and sisters; and (d) the extended family subsystem that includes interactions among members of the nuclear family and other relatives. There are bidirectional relationships among all subsystems within the family and, therefore, the development of a child with autism is related to and influenced by all family members and by the interactions among the systems.

Ecological Systems Theory

Bronfenbrenner's ecological systems theory (1979), a psychological theory of human development, explains how individuals interact with their environment, including how each environment plays a role in the growth and development of the individual. The ecological systems theory suggests that individuals are intertwined with different ecosystems that start as the most intimate settings (e.g., home environment), and broadening into larger, more expansive settings such as schools and workplaces. The model organizes stages of development into five categories, or ecosystems: (a) microsystem, (b) mesosystem, (c) exosystem, (d) macrosystem, and (e) chronosystem. Each system interacts with the other and affects the individual development of the person (Bronfenbrenner, 1986). When working with families with learners with autism, it is important to consider all subsystems that could impact the learner and their family.

Sociocultural Theory

Sociocultural approaches are based on three concepts: (1) human activities take place in their cultural context, (2) human activities are mediated by language and other symbol systems, and (3) human activities can be best understood when investigated in their historical development (John-Steiner & Mahn, 1996). The sociocultural theory emphasizes the notion that child learning and development is shaped by the culture and contexts in which they live and learn (Vygotsky, 1978). For children with autism, two contexts in which they spend their time are home and school. An evident disconnect between these two contexts could negatively impact learners with autism and their families, whereas a collaborative relationship between the two could positively impact the learner's development and learning.

Families with Children with Autism

As described earlier, family involvement and engagement in the education and treatment of learners with autism and other disabilities is encouraged by educators and practitioners, supported by researchers, and required by the U.S. law (Bruder, 2010; IDEIA, 2004). High levels of family involvement and high satisfaction with school services are significantly related to increased learner achievement (Jeynes, 2003; Sheldon & Epstein, 2005). Yet, many caregivers report barriers to involvement and collaboration with the schools (e.g., Hammond et al., 2008; Wang et al., 2004). When caregivers are not involved, students with disabilities are more likely to have poor educational programming (Fish, 2008). In addition, when caregivers are not satisfied with services, they are more likely to have poor family-school partnerships and experience increased stress (Burke & Hodapp, 2014). Caregivers who are dissatisfied with school services are also more likely to have a poorer family quality of life (Summers et al., 2007).

Turnbull and colleagues (2011) describe eight major roles that caregivers of learners with disabilities play over time, including (a) the source or cause of their child's disability, (b) organization members, (c) service developers, (d) recipients of professionals' decisions, (e) teachers, (f) advocates, (g) educational decision makers, and (h) partners with professionals. Although service delivery practices in the past followed a medical model in which the practitioners were the experts who worked directly with the child with disabilities, current practices emphasize family involvement and engagement in their children's education and treatment. Caregivers of learners with autism can be involved and engaged in different ways and in different phases of an educational plan or treatment. For example, caregivers can be involved and engaged during (a) the assessment phase (e.g., sharing information about the child and the family and help with data collection), (b) the intervention development and educational planning phase (e.g., developing goals and expectations), and (c) the implementation phase (e.g., implementing evidence-based strategies; Campbell & Kozloff, 2007; Chung & Meadan, 2021; McDuffie et al., 2013). In addition, when caregivers are involved and engaged through caregivers' education, training, coaching, and caregiver-implemented interventions, children with autism have more opportunities to practice, improve, and generalize their skills in the natural environments (Burrell & Borrego, 2012; Meadan et al., 2016).

Many learners with autism engage in behaviors (e.g., limited social-communication skills, challenging behavior) that could impact their family members and their family unit (Meadan et al., 2010) and researchers emphasize that caregiver involvement and engagement are especially important in the education and treatment of learners with autism (Burrell & Borrego, 2012; Garbacz et al., 2016; Liao et al., 2020). For example, one of the primary characteristics of autism is support needs related to social-communication skills. Caregivers' involvement and engagement can facilitate successful integration of language and communication interventions in the home with their children with autism (Meadan et al., 2016). Caregivers are key communication partners because they can provide various opportunities during everyday routines and activities and within the learner's natural environments.

Kaiser and Roberts (2013) describe three specific roles caregivers can have in supporting their child's communication development. "The roles fit along a continuum from most similar to typical parenting roles to most like a systematic interventionist teaching specific language skills" (p. 98). Caregivers can take on the role of (a) communication partner by enriching the communication environment and being responsive to their child's communication acts, (b) co-interventionist and work with the practitioners while implementing interventions or evidence-based strategies, or (c) the primary interventionist and implement a systematic teaching strategy. Caregivers can take on different roles, depending on the needs of the child and their own skills, preferences, and resources. Kaiser and Roberts (2013) argue that regardless of the role caregivers take, education and support from practitioners are important.

When caregivers and families are involved and engage in the education and treatment of their children with autism, there are positive impacts on children's development, family members' well-being, and caregiver-child interaction (Burrell & Borrego, 2012). Garbacz and colleagues (2016) described the factors that could influence family involvement and parent-teacher relationships, including child characteristics, maternal education, sources of support, and satisfaction with services. In their study of factors that influence involvement of caregivers of children with autism, Garbacz and colleagues found that both child variables and family variables significantly predicted family involvement and the parent-teacher relationship. They reported that caregivers of children with autism with higher developmental risk reported less family involvement and poorer relationships with their child's teacher. Additionally, family histories accessing services predicted family involvement and parent-teacher relationships. The researchers emphasized the importance of involving and engaging caregivers of children with autism and call for additional research in this area. In addition, given the data that show that the United States becomes increasingly ethnically and racially diverse, there is a clear need to identify practices that will encourage and predict involvement and engagement of families with learners with autism from diverse backgrounds. However, racially/ethnically diverse populations remain underrepresented in autism research (Harris et al., 2020), and there is limited information about best practices for intervention with racially and ethnically diverse learners with autism, particularly among Black and Latino populations (Wong et al., 2015).

Strategies for Building Effective Family-Practitioner Partnerships

Although mandated and incredibly valuable, family-practitioner partnerships often encounter challenges and barriers. As a result, researchers have developed models that help to facilitate effective partnerships (e.g., Blue-Banning et al., 2004; Sheridan & Wheeler, 2017). Across these models, components include strategies such as family-school/practitioners' collaboration, communication, and problem solving to support and build partnerships. These strategies are consistent with Turnbull and colleagues' (2011) seven principles of family-practitioner partnerships. These seven principles include communication, professional competence, respect, commitment, equality, advocacy, and trust (see Figure 12.1). Turnbull and colleagues suggest that trust is the core principle that keeps the other six principles grounded. In this section, we will explore each of the seven principles of partnerships.

Communication

Establishing clear modes of communication between families and practitioners can be challenging. Communication can be even more challenging for families and practitioners who do not speak the same native language, and/or who do not share the same cultural norms, customs, and values (Fowler et al., 2019). Some families report feelings of anxiety and a lack of support in school environments, which makes them hesitant to communicate with practitioners (Burke & Goldman, 2018). These barriers to effective communication and partnership often persist when educational systems fail to intentionally and effectively engage families of learners with disabilities and their communities. In an effort to overcome these barriers to effective communication, Turnbull and colleagues (2011) prescribe components of effective communication as one of their seven principles of family-practitioner partnerships.

According to Turnbull and colleagues (2011), "effective communication requires that we pay careful attention both to the quality and to the quantity of our communication" (p. 139). Quality family-practitioner communication should be positive, clear, and respectful. Quantity in family-practitioner communication is a measure of how often practitioners and families communicate, and the extent to which they use each other's time effectively. In an effort to engage in effective communication with families of learners with autism, practitioners should employ five key actions: be friendly, listen, be clear, be honest, and provide and coordinate information (Blue-Banning et al., 2004; Turnbull et al., 2011).

Be Friendly. The first key action for effective communication is to be friendly (Turnbull et al., 2011). In some cases, practitioners misunderstand the intentionality

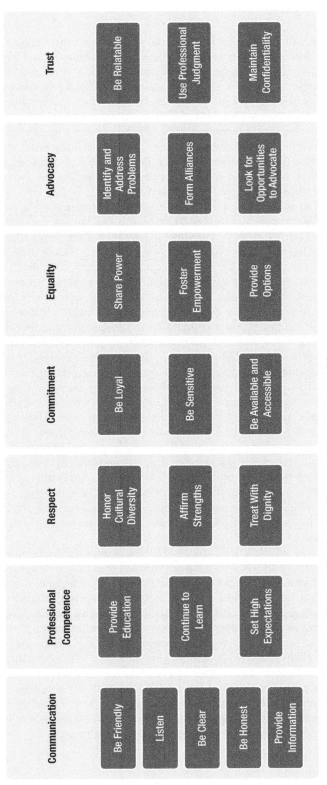

Figure 12.1. Strategies for building effective family-practitioner partnerships

and importance of establishing friendly relationships with caregivers of learners with autism. Although practitioners often think that a professional and businesslike approach is the most effective method of communication, caregivers might perceive these interactions as demeaning and patronizing. Instead, practitioners should engage with families using a sense of "personal touch." That is, practitioners should foster a space that is comfortable and welcoming for families. Mannerisms and tone of the conversation should be similar to the way one would engage with someone over a cup of coffee. While practitioners have a professional responsibility to meet the needs of their learners with autism, they also want to ensure that they are personable and that they create a space where caregivers feel comfortable enough to share information about their child and their family.

Listen. The second key action for effective communication according to Turnbull and colleagues is to listen. "Listening is the language of acceptance" (Turnbull et al., 2011, p. 139). Families of learners with autism and other disabilities often feel that their voices are not being heard. This is especially true among Black caregivers of learners with autism. Pearson and Meadan (2018) found that Black caregivers of learners with autism experienced tension and frustration related to communicating with school-based practitioners and health care professionals about their child's and their family's needs. Black caregivers recommended that practitioners really listen to the caregivers so that things are not overlooked: "I recommend that educators, healthcare professionals, and other service providers really listen to the parents. I think everybody is so busy and time is so limited that, you know, things fall between the cracks" (Pearson & Meadan, 2018, p. 28). To overcome these types of communication barriers, Turnbull and colleagues suggest that practitioners work to hear and understand family members' perspectives first, before sharing their own perspectives; they describe this as listening mode. Another way to think about listening with intention to truly understand is called empathic listening (Covey, 1991). Turnbull and colleagues posit that when practitioners listen empathetically, they are making an effort to understand the other person's experience, and not to agree or disagree. Therefore, practitioners should listen without making judgments, and try to relate to families' experiences, differences, and values. Engaging in purposeful, intentional, and empathic listening is a key strategy for establishing effective communication with families of learners with autism.

Be Clear. The third key action for establishing clear communication with families of learners with autism is to be clear (Turnbull et al., 2011). Unless they have a background in the field, or extensive experience, caregivers can be overwhelmed by the acronyms and technical jargon that special education practitioners use. To better support families' understanding of their child's present level of performance, areas of needed support, and special education services, for example, practitioners should listen (the second key action) to the terminology that the families use to help gauge the best way to communicate with them. If the family has extensive background and familiarity with special education services and terminology, the practitioners might communicate with them using more complex terms. If, however, the family has less familiarity with the terminology, or if they are communicating in a language other than their native language, it is important to be mindful of this and use language that is accessible to them.

Be Honest. The fourth key action for establishing clear communication with families of learners with autism is to be honest. In other words, practitioners need to be direct, but also tactful (Turnbull et al., 2011). Special education practitioners may find themselves in a situation where they need to share news that might be difficult for family members to understand and accept. In these situations, it is important for practitioners to deliver information honestly, while also being sensitive to how the family might receive this information. Another element of honest communication is admitting when you do not know the answer to a question. Even seasoned special educators encounter questions to which they do not know the answer; when these instances arise, the best response is an honest one. In other words, practitioners can inform the family member that they don't know the answer to their question at the moment, but that they will gather the information they need and follow up with them.

Provide and Coordinate Information. The fifth and final key action for establishing clear communication with families of learners with autism is providing and coordinating information. Families of learners with autism are often seeking information; they want to know more about the services the learner receives or future services for which they are eligible (Turnbull et al., 2011). Sometimes parents want to hear from others who have similar needs and experiences. To support families in gathering the information they need, special education practitioners should not only support families by sharing information about available interventions, for example, but also help them coordinate their next steps.

Providing and coordinating information is especially important for racially, ethnically, and linguistically diverse families of learners with autism. Research has shown that minority families often face more barriers to accessing services and interventions than do White families (Blanchett et al., 2009; Pearson & Meadan, 2018). These systemic barriers often result in families of color facing inadequate services for their children, such as untimely access to early intervention (Pearson & Meadan, 2018). Caregivers truly want to learn more about how to support their children and address their support needs. For example, in their study with Black parents of children with autism, Pearson and Meadan (2018) interviewed a mother who shared the following:

> For me, the biggest thing is to help me to understand or help me to help him; not the generic class, but maybe what your particular child might need. More parent education as far as, how to navigate these systems. (Pearson & Meadan, 2018, p. 29)

Professional Competence

The second principle of partnerships is professional competence. Turnbull and colleagues (2011) outline three characteristics that describe professionally competent practitioners. Special education practitioners who have professional competence should know how to provide an appropriate education; continue to learn; and set high expectations.

Provide an Appropriate Education. IDEIA (2004) mandates that schools provide a free and appropriate education for students with disabilities who receive special education services. Moreover, IDEIA describes *appropriate* as "an education that offers an equal opportunity to learn." From caregivers' perspectives, however, an appropriate education begins with a competent practitioner who can recognize their child as an individual and plan a curriculum and delivery method that build on the child's strengths (Turnbull et al., 2011). To provide an appropriate education, special educators should master the content provided in their training programs and then apply that knowledge to individualize the instruction to meet the needs of each of their learner.

Continue to Learn. Special education practitioners must remember that they are lifelong learners. It is important to build on current knowledge and strengths (Turnbull et al., 2011). In some states, teachers are required to renew their teaching certificates periodically to demonstrate their continued mastery of the curriculum and instruction. Practitioners also have more informal opportunities to engage in learning activities. Each time practitioners interact with families, they are presented with a learning opportunity. Practitioners should practice communication and partnership skills and reflect on processes and outcomes. These applied experiences with families often help to solidify content from training programs, and they serve as a learning opportunity that can strengthen practitioners' confidence and competence.

Set High Expectations. A common barrier to delivering effective education to learners with disabilities is that both families and educators sometimes have low expectations for the learner (Turnbull et al., 2011). Therefore, the third exercise of professional competence is to set high expectations. In many cases, when families first learn about their child's disability, they may fear what the future might be for their child and their family. To support children and families who are working through these emotions, practitioners should encourage a perspective of "great expectations." In other words, help children and families find a positive, self-enhancing outlook that creates a foundation for great expectations. When practitioners model (and believe in!) this practice for learners and families, they too will find value in setting high expectations for themselves.

Respect

The third principle of partnerships is respect. In partnerships between families and practitioners, respect means that each party regards the other with esteem through both their actions and their words (Blue-Banning et al., 2004; Turnbull et al., 2011). In an effort to establish a respectful partnership with families of learners with autism, practitioners need to honor cultural diversity, affirm strengths, and treat learners and their families with dignity.

Honor Cultural Diversity. As noted earlier in this chapter, the racial and ethnic diversity of children in the United States is rapidly shifting (U.S. Census Bureau, 2020), and special education practitioners must be prepared to partner with and engage diverse families (CEC, 2015). Many policies and practices in special education emerged from dominant, mainstream cultures and they do not always reflect the values held by minority cultures (Kalyanpur & Harry, 2012). Moreover, the population of special education practitioners in the United States does not reflect the diversity of the learners they teach or the families they support (Scott & Alexander, 2019). Therefore, given the disparities both in access and in outcomes among racially, ethnically, and linguistically diverse families of individuals with autism, it is critical for practitioners to foster culturally responsive partnerships with their families (West et al., 2016). Diverse learners come from diverse families who bring specific cultural practices and beliefs that represent who they are. Therefore, practitioners must honor the cultural and ethnic diversity of learners with autism and their families by making a concerted effort to understand the family's cultural beliefs and practices (Turnbull et al., 2011).

Affirm Strengths. The field of special education is based on a medical model that often leads to deficit views of learners with disabilities (Harry, 1992). For learners with autism, these deficit views may arise in health care settings, home settings, or in school-based settings. As a result, families may grow accustomed to a focus on their child's weaknesses, as opposed to their strengths. This deficit approach not only impacts the special education services provided to learners and their families (Kirby, 2017), but it also impacts the quality of partnerships between practitioners and families (Turnbull et al., 2011). When practitioners focus on learner weaknesses as opposed to strengths, families experience feelings of frustration and sadness, and they often become defensive. Instead of highlighting learners' areas of need, practitioners should emphasize learner strengths and positive outcomes. In addition, practitioners should affirm the families' strengths and let them know that you value what they do to support their child (Turnbull et al., 2011).

Treat Learners with Autism and Their Families with Dignity. The third component of respect is to treat learners with autism and their families with dignity. Practitioners treating learners with autism and their families with dignity shows that you value them, and that they are worthy. Treating families with dignity demonstrates the ability to regard an individual as a person, and not as a disability or as a label (Turnbull et al., 2011). Another valuable approach to treating learners and their families with dignity is to engage with family members knowing that they are decision makers. In other words, practitioners should avoid condescending attitudes and partner with families in ways that makes them feel valued.

Commitment

The next principle of family-practitioner partnership is commitment. "Commitment occurs when professionals consider their relationship with a child and family to be more than an obligation incurred through work. It occurs when they feel loyal and are sensitive in working with the child and the family" (Turnbull et al., 2011, p. 147). Practitioners who support learners with autism and their families can demonstrate their sense of commitment to families by being sensitive to their emotional needs, being available and accessible, and going "above and beyond."

Practitioners can be sensitive to the needs of families by engaging in empathetic listening and connecting them to other families who have shared experiences and emotional needs (Turnbull et al., 2011). Connecting families can be especially beneficial for those who come from historically marginalized communities. For example, Black parents of learners with autism experience more positive outcomes when they are connected to other families who have shared backgrounds and cultural experiences (Pearson & Meadan, 2021). Practitioners who are available and accessible to families make a concerted effort to arrange their schedules to be able to better reach their families. Families report higher levels of satisfaction with practitioners who are available during "off hours"—times when parents are available before or after work. Finally, caregivers often describe practitioners who go "above and beyond" as effective partners. For example, practitioners who take the time to engage with families in community settings are viewed as those who go above and beyond. For some practitioners, going "above and beyond" challenges the boundaries of professionalism. However, when practitioners make an effort to build closer and friendlier relationships with learners with autism and their families, particularly those who come from marginalized backgrounds, it demonstrates a commitment to meeting their needs; that commitment reflects a critical principle that helps to facilitate effective partnerships between families and practitioners (Turnbull et al., 2011).

Equality

When families and practitioners feel that they each have the same power to shape and influence the learner's education, then they have achieved equality (Turnbull et al., 2011). Practitioners who establish equality in their partnerships with families of learners with autism should share power, foster empowerment, and provide options. When families experience shared power and empowerment and are provided with options, it helps to create an environment for equality. It is also important to note, however, that learners with autism and their families are also entitled to *equitable* supports. While equality is associated with sameness in treatment and access, equity is associated with fairness and justice (Espinoza, 2007). Ultimately, families should have both equal and equitable access to special education services to support learners with autism.

Share Power. Families of learners with autism and other disabilities have feelings of anger when they feel that practitioners approach them from a place of power. This is called a "power-over" relationship. In power-over relationships, learners and families experience the consequences of practitioners' decisions. For example, the practitioner might describe their intended IEP goal, with no room for family input or shared decision making. These vertical or hierarchical types of power-over dynamics can lead to anger and tension between parents and practitioners, ultimately resulting in ineffective collaboration (Turnbull et al., 2011). In shared-power partnerships, however, practitioners and family members all contribute their knowledge and resources to work toward a common goal. This type of group synergy helps to create even more shared power and strengthened partnerships.

Foster Empowerment. One of the most significant ways to build families' capacity to partner, engage, and support their child with autism is to help them feel more empowered. Family empowerment has been described as central to improving services for learners with autism and their families (Pearson et al., 2019). Findings suggest that strong family-school partnerships may positively impact family empowerment (Whitley et al., 2011). Therefore, practitioners who strive to establish equality in the families they support should also work to foster empowerment. When families are empowered, they take action to get what they want and need and know the steps they need to take to solve the problems they face (Turnbull et al., 2011). Empowerment requires persistence and sustained effort over time. In families who experience low empowerment, family members might feel stuck when they face challenges, or they may not have the motivation or capacity to solve the problem. Therefore, practitioners can be an agent of empowerment for families by demonstrating how the team (caregivers, student, practitioner) can take action to achieve the goals for the learner. In addition, practitioners need to feel empowered themselves. Having a partnership where all members feel empowered leads to strengthened outcomes for the learner and the family. Empowered practitioners have the capacity to be consistent in supporting families and helping them strengthen and exercise their own empowerment.

Provide Options. The third strategy in equal partnerships is to provide options. During challenging and often tense situations, it is important for practitioners to be flexible and creative. Sometimes challenges require novel solutions—ones that haven't been tried before. Practitioners who strive for equality can do so by embracing the challenges they face and engaging in creative problem solving to address them. Presenting multiple solutions to families supports the notion of equality so that families do not feel forced into a single alternative (Turnbull et al., 2011).

Advocacy

The next principle of effective partnerships is advocacy. "Advocacy refers to speaking out and taking action in pursuit of a cause" (Turnbull et al., 2011, p. 151). When practitioners advocate on behalf of a learner or their family, it demonstrates a commitment to them, and thus, leads to strengthened partnerships. Practitioners who are strong advocates should work to (a) prevent problems, (b) look for opportunities to advocate, (c) identify and document problems, (d) form alliances, and (e) seek win-win solutions. Practitioners who are advocates work proactively to prevent problems, and when they do arise, advocating practitioners address those problems head-on, instead of passing them along to someone else. Advocating practitioners should also look for opportunities to advocate. When practitioners position themselves to identify instances of injustice against learners with autism and their families, they are creating opportunities to empathize with families and engage in joint advocacy to address the concerns. Once practitioners identify instances of injustice, they have an obligation to document the problem by providing a clear description of the issue, and evidence that supports the extent of the problem. For example, practitioners should observe the behavior of people who may be contributing to the problem, as well as those who contribute to the solution. These data help to build stronger cases for advocates to address the challenges that learners with autism and their families face.

Trust

The final principle of effective family-practitioner partnerships is trust. Trust is defined as "having confidence in someone else's reliability, judgment, word, and action to care for and not harm the entrusted person" (Turnbull et al., 2011, p. 153). You might also think of rapport as a component of trust. Similar to trust, rapport involves a sincere interest in the families that practitioners support. For example, findings suggest that positive rapport between speech-language pathologists and parents of learners with disabilities such as autism leads to increased positive outcomes for families (Akamoglu et al., 2018).

There are four specific practices that help practitioners develop trust in their partnerships with families: being reliable, using sound judgment, maintaining confidentiality, and trusting oneself. Caregivers of children with disabilities depend on practitioners to stick to their word. Practitioners who do what they said they would do are viewed as reliable. Reliable practitioners are well organized, and they make efforts to carefully schedule both their tasks and time. Practitioners also establish trust with families by using sound judgment. Many practitioners have to make in-the-moment judgment calls related to instruction, discipline, and safety, for example. Families will be able to better trust those practitioners whose judgment calls are sound. Being able to make sound judgments requires that practitioners are competent and well equipped to support the needs of the students in their classrooms (Turnbull et al., 2011).

*   *   *

Miriam has taken off part of the morning from her first job to join her parents, Joe and Marisela, for Shay's IEP meeting. Miriam is still very nervous about what to expect from this meeting, and she is feeling a little intimidated about all of the people who are there. To begin the meeting, Mrs. Thompson, Shay's case manager, welcomes and introduces everyone in the meeting. Mrs. Thompson is familiar with Shay's family and has worked hard to engage them by using effective partnership strategies. Because Mrs. Thompson communicates with Shay's grandparents regularly, she knows that their family speaks Spanish in the home, and has made sure to include a Spanish interpreter, Ms. Yvette, in the IEP meeting. Mrs. Thompson knows that having the interpreter will allow for more clear communication, and also honor the family's cultural diversity. Mrs. Thompson begins by explaining the purpose of the IEP meeting, and then she asks Miriam, Joe, and Marisela to share their hopes and goals for Shay. Joe shares with the team how helping to raise Shay, his first grandson, has been one of the greatest joys of his life. Joe tells the team that he has learned much about how Shay is doing from the daily communication logs, and he hopes that is something that will continue once Shay goes to kindergarten. Joe has noticed that Shay is starting to pick up on more words, and he knows that Shay will get better every day. Mrs. Thompson is happy to hear that Joe demonstrates a sense of pride and empowerment about how Shay is doing; she has worked hard to engage in shared power with her families and affirm their strengths and her learners' strengths. Marisela, a bit more reserved, shares with a warm smile that Shay is a smart and capable boy, and "mi príncipe." When it's her turn, Miriam thanks Mrs. Thompson for being such a kind teacher and communicating with their family regularly. Holding back tears, Miriam shares how much it means to her that her parents can help her raise her children and that without them, she doesn't know what she would do. Miriam's hopes for Shay are that he will be able to communicate his needs and wants and that he will start to make friends—she is very worried that Shay will be picked on once he moves into kindergarten in the fall.

*   *   *

Strategies to Enhance Family Involvement and Engagement

One way to improve outcomes for learners with autism is by purposefully involving and engaging families in their child's school and treatment experiences. Family-practitioner partnerships can lead to more effective implementation of evidence-based practices, positive caregiver-educator relationships, and positive outcomes for learners with autism (Azad & Mandell, 2016; Mapp & Kuttner, 2013; Topor et al., 2010). In this section, we identify three strategies that practitioners can employ to enhance involvement among families of learners with autism. These strategies include cultural reciprocity, family-centered practices, and family capacity building.

Cultural Reciprocity

Earlier in this chapter we highlighted the importance of honoring cultural diversity to build effective partnerships with learners with autism and their families. In this section, we emphasize the importance of not only honoring families' cultural diversity, but also engaging in cultural reciprocity. Cultural reciprocity is described as a means of promoting stronger empowerment among both families and practitioners (shared power). The first step of cultural reciprocity is to engage introspective identification of one's own values and beliefs. The second step of cultural reciprocity is for practitioners to identify similarities and differences between their own values and the values of the families they serve. Third, practitioners should explicitly discuss those values with their families and respect their cultural differences (Kalyanpur & Harry 2012; Pearson et al., 2019). When practitioners are able to identify and understand cultural similarities and differences, they foster an environment for respect, rapport, and trust among families of children with autism.

Family-Centered Practices

The term *family-centered* is defined as a type of help-giving practice that involves adherence to principles and values in which practitioners treat families with dignity and respect, share information so caregivers can make informed decisions, acknowledge and build on family member strengths, actively engage family members in obtaining resources and support, and respond to each family's changing life circumstances (Dunst, 2002; Dunst & Espe-Sherwindt, 2016). Family-centered service delivery is focused on identifying families' unique priorities and needs and providing families with the necessary knowledge and resources to make decisions related to service provision (i.e., build family capacity; Dunst, 2002). Researchers have reported that using family-centered practices leads to positive outcomes for children, caregivers, and families, including self-efficacy beliefs, caregivers' sense of confidence and competence, and caregiver and family well-being (Dunst et al., 2007; Mas et al., 2019). Implementing family-centered practices is especially important among historically marginalized families; doing so emphasizes families' strengths and highlights their agency in decision making, which can more effectively facilitate service provision for historically marginalized families (Pearson et al., 2019). In an effort to combat decreased family engagement, Dunst and Espe-Sherwindt (2016) explain that family-centered practices include two types of practices: relational practices and participatory practices. Relational practices emphasize the use of relationship-building strategies, active and reflective listening, and acknowledging practitioner beliefs about family member strengths and capabilities. Participatory practices emphasize informed family choice and decision making, active family member involvement in achieving desired goals and outcomes, and practitioner use of capacity-building help-giving practices. When true family-centered services are provided, families' ratings of positive child behaviors increase (Trivette et al., 2010).

Family Capacity Building

One way to improve child outcomes is by purposefully involving and engaging families in their child's school experiences. Families of children with autism can benefit from capacity-building strategies such as advocacy training and caregiver education, training, and coaching. Advocacy training is one way to support caregivers of students with disabilities who may face barriers while navigating the special education system (Burke, 2013). Advocacy training prepares families to access appropriate education services for their children. Research in special education advocacy training is limited and it is still unclear what content areas should be taught, what experiences individuals should undergo, and what maintenance is needed after training takes place. There is a need for more research on effective caregiver-school collaboration models in special education (Burke, 2013). Burke states, "by having a line of research about special education advocacy, research can better inform us about the content that is necessary for trainings, the efficacy of special education training, and the implications of parent-school collaboration on the family" (p. 233).

Capacity Building Among Marginalized Families. The importance of building and supporting cultural capital in historically marginalized families, including those living in poverty, has been highlighted by researchers (e.g., Harry, 2008; Pearson & Meadan, 2018; Trainor, 2010). Researchers have identified cultural issues that strain partnerships between marginalized families and educators: (a) cross-cultural differences in views of disabilities, (b) deficit views of families of color, (c) cultural conflicts in setting goals, and (d) differential understanding of families' roles in the education system. Many of these cultural issues are addressed by the community-based parent-advocacy training program Fostering Advocacy, Communication, Empowerment, and Supports (FACES). FACES is an 18-hour parent-training and advocacy intervention driven by (a) minority families' need for community resources to increase knowledge of special education rights (Burke & Goldman, 2018) and advocacy strategies (Burke, 2013; Mueller & Carranza, 2011; Pearson & Meadan, 2018). FACES is designed to empower and educate families to better advocate for the needs of Black children with autism. Findings from the FACES intervention indicate that the program leads to increased knowledge of autism, increased family empowerment, and strengthened advocacy efforts in Black families of children with autism (Pearson & Meadan, 2021). Specifically, Black caregivers spoke to the importance of engaging in effective communication with practitioners. A previous FACES participant shared how critical it is for her to partner with her son's educator to ensure that his goals are met:

> In order to effectively get to those goals, I have to have solid communication and trust, which can only be built through that solid communication with the other people who are in his life. The teachers won't be replaced; the social workers won't be replaced, so communicating, setting my expectations, and understanding theirs, is what is most important for my son. (Pearson & Meadan, 2021)

Implementing Evidence-Based Practices with Families

Adopting and implementing evidence-based practices (EBPs) improves outcomes for learners with autism (Johnson et al., 2018; Steinbrenner et al., 2020).

Although families of learners with autism have reported a desire to learn more about the EBPs used in schools to support their children (Pituch et al., 2011), they do not always receive effective supports to do so. Therefore, in an effort to best support learner outcomes, families and practitioners should engage in collaborative partnerships that can facilitate the effective implementation of EBPs for learners with autism. In this section, we describe two methods of partnership to facilitate the use of EBPs among families: training and coaching, and comprehensive partnerships.

Training and Coaching

One way to facilitate the effective implementation of EBPs is through training, coaching, and consultation interventions with families. There are various models of intervention to support the effective implementation of EBPs by families (e.g., Internet-based Parent Implemented Communication System [iPiCS]; Meadan et al., 2016; Conjoint Behavioral Consultation [CBC]; Sheridan & Kratochwill, 2007; Sheridan et al., 2013; Collaborative Model for Promoting Competence and Success [COMPASS]; Ruble & Dalrymple, 2002). Among caregivers, there are a number of studies that have produced promising caregiver outcomes following caregiver training and coaching. Examples of positive outcomes include high levels of acceptability, successful implementation of EBPs with fidelity, increased knowledge, and high levels of caregiver engagement (Boisvert & Hall, 2014; Ingersoll & Berger, 2015; Meadan & Daczewitz, 2015; Meadan et al., 2016). Among learners with autism, previous caregiver-implemented interventions have demonstrated positive outcomes such as increased communication skills, reduced challenging behaviors, and improved adaptive behavior skills (Ingersoll et al., 2016; Kuravackel et al., 2018; Meadan et al., 2016). These findings suggest that caregiver training and coaching can lead to improved learner outcomes. In addition, caregiver-implemented interventions for learners with autism are recognized as EBPs (Steinbrenner et al., 2020).

Comprehensive Partnerships

Throughout this chapter we have identified strategies for building effective family-practitioner partnerships, strategies to enhance family involvement, and tools to support the implementation of EBPs among families. Effective caregiver-practitioner partnerships are a valuable and critical approach to addressing the needs of learners with autism. The prevalence of autism and the increasing diversity of learners in U.S. schools highlights the need for sustainable, culturally responsive family-practitioner partnerships that can build agency among families and support the implementation of EBPs to strengthen outcomes among learners with autism. Comprehensive partnerships should encompass a combination of strategies such as clear and honest communication, respect for cultural diversity, knowledge building, and shared power. Moreover, families require capacity-building supports such as empowerment strategies. Practitioners require professional development opportunities that expose them to interventions and resources they can adopt in their partnerships with families. When families and practitioners engage in multiple modes and strategies for partnership, they establish comprehensive partnerships, which have the greatest potential to strengthen outcomes among learners with autism.

* * *

Following Shay's IEP meeting, Miriam, Joe, and Marisela feel a little better about Shay moving on to kindergarten. Mrs. Thompson has made them feel like equal partners in making decisions about Shay's kindergarten placement. Miriam is still worried about how Shay will socialize, but the team has explained the types of support that will be in place for Shay. Mrs. Thompson also connected Shay's family with an empowerment program and a support group in their community to facilitate their ongoing empowerment and advocacy for Shay. Miriam, Joe, and Marisela tell Mrs. Thompson how much they have appreciated her kindness and partnership—they are very hopeful that Shay's new case manager will be a good partner for their family, just like Mrs. Thompson.

* * *

Evaluating Partnerships with Families

Educators like Mrs. Thompson are tasked with partnering with families in an effort to best meet the needs of learners with autism like Shay. In addition to employing strategies to build effective partnerships, enhancing family engagement, and implementing EBPs with families, educators must be sure to evaluate the extent to which their strategies are meeting families' needs. Educators can evaluate their partnerships with families by asking themselves the following questions (adapted from DEC recommended practices; 2014):

- Have I spent time learning about the family's culture, background, and previous experiences?
- Have I worked with the family to identify their concerns and priorities?
- Have I presented and helped with evaluating the pros and cons of different options for addressing the family's concerns and priorities?
- Have I worked with the family to develop a plan to access and utilize the resources and supports for the learner with autism?
- Have I supported the family with identifying next steps for implementing their plan?
- Does the family understand which professionals will be involved in each step of the action plan?
- Does the family have all of the resources they need to move forward with implementing the action plan?
- Does the family communicate with me to express questions, concerns, or achievements?

When evaluating the strength of family-practitioner partnerships for learners with autism, the answer to each of these questions should be *yes*. However, if at any point an answer is *no* to any of these evaluation questions, practitioners should spend time gathering and sharing information and addressing family concerns.

SUMMARY

Cultural reciprocity, family-centered practices, family capacity building, and caregiver-implemented interventions reflect four important strategies that practitioners can adopt and employ to strengthen family-practitioner partnerships. In addition, practitioners must evaluate how well their partnership is addressing the families' needs. When practitioners implement (and evaluate) strategies that empower and engage families, they are better able to build effective family-practitioner partnerships. These partnerships create an environment that fosters opportunities for implementation of EBPs in addressing the needs of learners with autism. While caregivers are their children's first and most important teachers, positive caregiver-practitioner partnerships have the potential to enhance caregivers' capacity to implement EBPs, and ultimately, to strengthen outcomes among learners with autism.

APPLICATION ACTIVITIES

1. You learned in this chapter about the importance of affirming family strengths when engaging in partnerships. What strengths do the families you work with have? How do you affirm their strengths? How might you reflect the strengths of the families you support?
2. Now that you are familiar with the strategies for effective family-practitioner partnerships, what strategies do you already have in place? What strategies will you adopt to better meet the needs of learners with autism and their families?
3. In this chapter you learned about the disparate experiences of historically marginalized learners with autism and their families. How might you employ partnership strategies to specifically address the needs of marginalized families you serve?
4. *Critical Reflection.* How does your background and experiences shape your interactions with the families you serve? What are three areas of growth for you as a practitioner to better meet your families' needs?
5. What might comprehensive family-practitioner partnerships look like for you? What additional resources do you need to build a comprehensive partnership with your families?

ADDITIONAL RESOURCES

Autism Focused Intervention Resources and Modules (AFIRM). https://afirm.fpg.unc.edu/afirm-modules

Early Childhood Technical Assistance Center: resources on family engagement. https://ectacenter.org/topics/familyeng/familyeng.asp

IRIS Center—Family Engagement. https://iris.peabody.vanderbilt.edu/module/fam/

U.S. Department of Education—Family and Community Engagement. https://www.ed.gov/parent-and-family-engagement

13

Collaborative Partnerships

How and Why to
Foster Professional Collaborations

Jennifer M. Asmus, Lindsay M. McCary,
and Taylor P. Dorlack

■ ■ ■

INTRODUCTION AND OVERVIEW

As discussed in Chapter 2, autism spectrum disorder (ASD) is a complex condition in that it impacts several areas of functioning, including social, behavioral, mental health, and academic performance. High rates of co-occurring medical and mental health problems necessitate care from multiple professionals across settings and increased collaboration among professionals. Medical comorbidities experienced by learners with ASD include epilepsy, gastrointestinal issues, sleep problems, and feeding disorders (Kohane et al., 2012). Learners with ASD are also much more likely to have psychiatric conditions such as attention disorders, mood disorders, and disruptive behavior disorders than their peers without autism (Gurney et al., 2006). These co-occurring conditions often lead to increased need for professional collaboration due to higher risks of negative social, behavioral, medical, educational, and psychiatric outcomes (Neuhaus et al., 2018). Therefore, professional collaboration is key in best meeting the needs of learners with ASD.

Professional collaboration occurs when professionals from different areas of expertise provide comprehensive services by working with learners with ASD, their families, and communities to deliver high-quality services across settings (Gilbert et al., 2010). Characteristics of strong teams include providing clarity of roles and responsibilities, optimizing individual professional skills, and improving the provision and coordination of care through teamwork (Bridges et al., 2011). Professional collaboration for learners with ASD occurs both within the school building and across systems, given the complexity of the condition and the different ways in which learners can be classified with ASD (as discussed in Chapter 2).

In this chapter, we will discuss the importance of interprofessional collaboration for learners with ASD. We will highlight the roles of the different professionals involved in collaboration, including both school-based professionals and community-based professionals, the problem-solving framework, and the process and skills needed for successful professional collaborations. We will conclude with case studies to highlight the importance of collaboration. However, it should be noted that this chapter does not differentiate the varied impact that children from minoritized families experience in terms of ASD diagnosis, needs, and considerations. In fact, the most recent *Autism and Developmental Disabilities Monitoring* report provides evidence that although data indicate that the prevalence of ASD is similar across all ethnicities, disparities in ASD identification are in fact moderated by race/ethnicity (Maenner et al., 2020). Therefore, the potential that families from diverse racial and ethnic backgrounds may have unique experiences and barriers when engaging their learner with ASD in successfully accessing interprofessional collaboration is of significant concern (Cascio et al., 2021; Čolić et al., 2021; Kim et al., 2020).

Although outside the scope of this chapter, Chapter 12 discussed considerations for understanding and partnering with families from diverse backgrounds. In addition, we strongly recommend resources, readings, and texts specific to the minoritized family experience such as *The Resistance, Persistence and Resilience of Black Families Raising Children with Autism* (Drame et al., 2020); "Padres en Accion: A Parent Education Program for Latino Parents of Children with ASD" (Magaña et al., 2018); "Cultural Experiences of Arab American Caregivers Raising Children with Autism Spectrum Disorder" (Habayeb et al., 2020); or "The Parenting Experiences and Needs of Asian Primary Caregivers of Children with Autism: A Meta-Synthesis" (Shorey et al., 2019) among others, both for families and for professionals to consider, address, and improve interdisciplinary and professional collaborations. There is a considerable amount of both work and education that is needed to remove potential barriers and stressors for minoritized families. This begins with recognition, understanding, and ongoing education by professionals in order to lead to more culturally relevant ASD diagnosis and treatment practices (Ozonoff et al., 2005) that will ultimately benefit learners and their families.

THE PROFESSIONAL AS AN EXPERT FOR PROBLEM SOLVING IN THE SCHOOL SETTING

It would be no surprise to find that schools are of vital importance to families of a child with ASD; school services often are the most readily available to learners with ASD and can also serve as the means through which services within the community are obtained (White, Scahill, et al., 2007). In the United States, 6.4 million, or 10% of all public-school learners in the 2017–2018 school year, ages 6–21, received special education services, with learners served under the ASD category being one of only two categories that increased in percentage of the population reported (by 0.5 of a percentage point). In total, learners with ASD make up 11% of those 6.4 million (708,877) learners (U.S. Department of Education, 2020). School professionals support diverse learners, improve school- and district-wide accountability, strengthen family-school partnerships, and are critical to helping these learners achieve optimal learning, social, and behavioral outcomes. However, as the number of learners with ASD continues to grow, so do the special education service needs, which with diminishing resources pose a serious challenge to meeting the support needs of learners with ASD (Yeargin-Allsopp et al., 2003). Therefore creative, strategic, and effective ways to meet those needs will be required of school personnel.

We know that special education services for learners with ASD can differ by age, disability severity, and demographic characteristics. Bitterman and colleagues (2008) found that children with ASD received not only more services but also more intensive services than children with other kinds of disabilities. Wei, Wagner, and colleagues (2014) analyzed national datasets to examine types of school-aged special education services and supports for learners with ASD. Their analysis revealed that speech-language therapy was the most common special education service elementary school learners with ASD received (85% of IEP files reviewed). However, there were differences in the types of services available based on age and setting. For example, elementary learners with ASD were more likely to receive adaptive physical education, specialized computer software or hardware, and transportation, but less likely to receive academic supports. In comparison, secondary school learners were less likely to receive speech-language therapy, occupational therapy, or behavior management plans; however, they were more likely to receive mental health services than those with ASD in the elementary school setting.

The primary roles of school professionals with specialized training, such as school psychologists, speech-language pathologists, occupational and physical therapists, school counselors, and social workers involve (1) assessment, (2) treatment, and (3) consultation (Fagan & Wise, 2007). Of critical importance, school professionals are instrumental in consulting with parents, teachers, and other professionals within and outside the school setting to devise strategies to improve conditions and outcomes for learners generally and for learners with ASD in particular. Use of evidence-based practice (EBP) is paramount to successful collaboration (see Chapter 4).

PERSPECTIVES ON THE ROLE THE PROFESSIONAL PLAYS IN SERVICE PROVISION OUTSIDE OF THE SCHOOL SETTING

ASD is a complex neurodevelopmental condition requiring comprehensive intervention programming and support. Professionals play a critical role in effectively communicating and collaborating with interdisciplinary service providers in the greater community. While actual receipt of community-based services may differ by chronological age, grade level, nature and severity of impairment, demographic background, and individual and family preferences (Bitterman et al., 2008; McConachie & Robinson, 2006; Shattuck et al., 2011; Thomas et al., 2007), families of children and adolescents with ASD regularly pursue and participate in a wide range of services provided by various professionals (Dymond et al., 2007; Goin-Kochel et al., 2007). Thus, effective collaboration between school-based and community-based providers is key to the promotion of positive developmental and behavioral outcomes for learners with ASD.

HISTORICAL PERSPECTIVE ON PROFESSIONALS AS SUPPORTS FOR LEARNERS WITH ASD

Schools function at the forefront in identifying learners with social, behavioral, and emotional needs. With the passage of the No Child Left Behind Act (2001) and the Response-to-Intervention (RtI) and Positive Behavior Support movements, schools focus on meeting academic, behavioral, and emotional needs of all learners even more than in the past. How might practitioners best meet the adaptive, social, behavioral, and academic needs of learners with ASD in the school setting while addressing time, knowledge, and resource challenges? Use of a problem-solving framework situated within problem-solving teams is advocated as an evidence-based approach for supporting and identifying effective education and support for learners with ASD.

Emergence and Evolution of a Problem-Solving Framework of EBP

A problem-solving framework is foundational to evidence-based practices (EBPs) in schools (Kratochwill et al., 2014; Sanetti & Collier-Meek, 2019) and appropriate for use within a multitiered RtI and positive behavior support framework (PBS; Burns et al., 2005; National Association of State Directors of Special Education, 2005). In practice, the problem-solving process is typically limited to developing intensive, individualized interventions (i.e., Tier 3 interventions) for learners with more significant behavioral and academic concerns, especially those who are unresponsive to supplemental interventions (i.e., Tier 2). However, initial concerns at a Tier 1 level are also often brought to a problem-solving team for guidance (Dowd-Eagle & Eagle, 2014).

Many problem-solving consultation models can be considered extensions of behavioral and instructional consultation models that follow structured and multistage procedures for intervention formation (i.e., behavioral consultation [Bergan & Kratochwill, 1990; Kratochwill et al., 2014], conjoint behavioral consultation [Sheridan & Kratochwill, 2008], and instructional consultation [Rosenfield & Gravois, 1996]). Similar to a problem-solving framework or model, these approaches foster collaboration among team members, which is a critical element; schools are important not only for fostering academic achievement but also for their role in social, emotional, and behavioral development. To best meet those needs, the ability to collaborate effectively with professionals to develop, evaluate, and effectively disseminate interventions with integrity is paramount (Costello et al., 2004).

School-based problem solving typically refers to an indirect service delivery model used to develop interventions for learners who are struggling academically or behaviorally in the regular education setting (Gutkin & Curtis, 1999). Within this model, teachers consult with a multidisciplinary team of educators (i.e., school psychologist, administrators, and other members of the problem-solving team [PST]) for intervention assistance, in comparison to (a) not intervening in hopes that the difficulty will decrease or go away, or (b) directly referring the learner for a comprehensive evaluation to determine eligibility for special educations services. Collaboratively, the team defines and analyzes the referral concerns and develops an intervention and progress monitoring plan. This model provides a mechanism to deliver EBPs to more learners through the PST's interaction with the teacher than would be reached through a more traditional service-delivery model (Kratochwill, 2008).

Problem-solving procedures within the problem-solving framework are typically carried out in four phases answering critical questions at each stage: (1) *problem identification* (Is there a problem? What is the problem?), (2) *problem analysis* (What factors contribute to the occurrence of the problem? What is the hypothesized cause of the behavior?), (3) **plan implementation** (What can be done to improve the problem? How will we monitor implementation integrity and progress?), and (4) **plan evaluation** (Did our EBP work?; Sheridan et al., 1996; Sheridan & Kratochwill, 2008). An additional preliminary stage of relationship building has been included in some models of problem-solving consultation (e.g., Kratochwill et al., 1995); this stage is especially critical for PSTs working with general and special education teachers, who will implement the intervention. Rather than taking a predetermined progression, the stages of the problem-solving model are meant to be dynamic and focus on the objectives of strengthening the consultative relationship, developing consultation skills, and facilitating ongoing communication between the consultant(s) (PST) and consultee(s) (teacher; Kratochwill et al., 2014; Sheridan & Kratochwill, 2008).

Establishing a Collaborative Relationship

This step is not a formal part of the problem-solving model because it refers to a stage before the actual problem solving begins. However, establishing a collaborative relationship will assist with the problem-solving process and can increase its effectiveness (Sheridan & Kratochwill, 2008). Critical components of this stage include establishing a sense of trust, building rapport and mutual respect, and clarifying responsibilities (Allen & Graden, 2002), with an emphasis on "cooperative partnership" striving to work jointly on an equal basis through recognition that needs and expertise among professionals will be unequal (Zins & Erchul, 2002). In schools, it is critical that leaders assisting in working through the problem-solving steps (e.g., principal, school psychologist, other staff member) establish collaborative working relationships with the other team members (Benishek et al., 2016; Rosenfield et al., 2018).

Problem Identification

The collection of information to define the problem(s) in observable and measurable terms is the primary objective of the *problem identification* phase. Objective data are collected and presented by the referring teacher, who assists the team in identifying the discrepancy between what the learner is expected to do and what he or she is doing (Albers et al., 2005). This can be permanent products, such as homework or in-class assignments, or behavior counts (e.g., how many times did the learner get up from their seat or shout out in class in 1 hour across 3 different days). The team can then determine if additional data need to be collected to best understand the problem (Sanetti & Collier-Meek, 2019). If the problem is behavioral, a functional behavioral assessment (FBA) is warranted to better understand the relationship between the learner's behavior and the environment. To develop a full understanding of the problem, data should be collected from multiple sources (e.g., parents, teachers, learners) and in multiple formats (e.g., interview, standardized assessments, observations) and ideally across settings (e.g., home, school, community). Therefore, parents or community service providers can be called upon to add data for consideration in the problem-solving process. It is also critical in this phase to determine an outcome goal to aim for in terms of changes to expect. Using data to establish where the learner's skill or behavior is before intervention (termed *baseline*) is critical to set a realistic goal and a timeline in which to meet that goal.

Problem Analysis

This stage is focused on examining the data that have been collected to identify contributing factors to the problem (Albers et al., 2005) to select interventions through identification of changes in instruction, curriculum, and/or the environment that would result in better learner outcomes. Data are instrumental to identify environmental factors rather than learner characteristics that cannot be changed or modified (Bollman et al., 2007). For example, rather than determining that a learner's inability to master basic math facts is the result of their neuro-developmental disability or lack of home support, focus is directed on how to increase learner motivation, provide additional practice opportunities, revise the curriculum to meet the learner's skill level, or increase levels of explicit instruction with immediate feedback to address this issue. While it does not mean that factors including diagnostic features of a learner or home support difficulties do not exist, it is more efficient to spend the limited time school professionals have focused on identification and control of factors and resources the school can more easily change or manage that will lead to actual change for the learner.

In the **problem identification** phase, data would be gathered about environmental antecedents and consequences that appear to contribute to the problem behavior (Zins & Erchul, 2002). In the **problem analysis** phase, those antecedents and consequences are examined to determine where and what is controllable or alterable. Through the use of an FBA in the *problem identification* phase, antecedent setting events such as hunger, lack of sleep, or an earlier event, such as being teased on the bus, that impacts behavior in the classroom may be a focus of the problem analysis phase. These can be addressed in different ways, such as having breakfast served at school, allowing a child to rest the first hour of school, or providing a seat change to be near the bus driver. However, all of these require objective data to identify where and when the problem is occurring. One of the most common pitfalls in the *problem analysis* phase occurs when insufficient or unrelated data have been collected that do not inform intervention planning, focusing on internal (e.g., the learner is angry) rather external variables (e.g., when the learner is given work above their instructional level, they use inappropriate language that results in being sent to the office, which results in escape from work completion), and forming hypotheses that are not supported by data (Allen & Graden, 2002). Therefore, while data collection may seem time consuming, it will actually save time in the long run by focusing on the reasons and factors responsible for difficulties so that an appropriate intervention can be selected, which is a second critical feature of the *problem analysis* phase.

After analyzing the data and developing hypotheses about factors that are causing and maintaining the problem, the next step is to select an EBP to address the identified problem. EBPs are encouraged for selection because positive learner outcomes are more likely to occur if the proposed strategies are supported by quality research (Forman & Burke, 2008). To assist educators in determining the quality of an intervention's evidence base, there are several resources to identify appropriate interventions. The American Psychological Association's Division 16 School Psychology Task Force published a comprehensive coding system (*Procedural and Coding Manual for Review of Evidence-Based Interventions*; Kratochwill & Stoiber, 2002) to evaluate evidence regarding an intervention's effectiveness. To minimize the research-to-practice gap and promote the use of interventions that are evidence based in clinical and school settings, several federal agencies and international organizations have also developed lists of EBPs addressing a variety of social-emotional, academic, and behavioral problems (e.g., What Works Clearinghouse, Promising Practices Network, National Standards Project) and a recent update to practices specific to ASD, *Evidence-Based Practices for Children, Youth, and Young Adults with Autism* (Steinbrenner et al., 2020). While EBPs have their own set of challenges (e.g., validity and reliability of evidence ratings and the transportability of research to "real-world" settings; Hunsley, 2007), many education scholars, from numerous professional areas, fully recommend using an EBP approach.

A final step prior to plan implementation is to carefully review all intervention procedures to be sure every aspect of the intervention is clear. One way to do this is to develop a written step-by-step summary of how to implement the intervention, including information about how to evaluate if the intervention is being implemented correctly (***treatment integrity***) and how ongoing progress will be monitored (***treatment monitoring***). Critical elements of this plan include identifying and training the person responsible for each intervention procedure, specifying the settings in which the intervention will occur, outlining specific dates for the formal review of progress, and highlighting how and when that progress and evaluation of the integrity of the intervention will be established (Allen & Graden, 2002).

Plan Implementation

During this third phase of the problem-solving process, the intervention is implemented. As previously indicated, it is very important to ensure that the practitioner who will be implementing the intervention clearly understands each step of the plan and has or is trained to have the skills to implement the intervention with integrity (Albers et al., 2005; Gresham, 1989). ***Treatment integrity*** is the formal name for this and is a primary concern for the plan implementation phase. To promote treatment integrity, the team should look for ways to support the practitioner or team of practitioners implementing the intervention (e.g., classroom teacher and paraprofessional). For example, it is important that a staff person who identified or selected the intervention (e.g., school psychologist) stays in regular contact with those implementing the intervention to (a) reinforce plan implementation, (b) help with the collection of progress monitoring data, and (c) problem-solve when issues arise (Zins & Erchul, 2002). Planning for and conducting systematic assessment of treatment integrity can be accomplished by using a treatment plan or intervention integrity checklist, where each component of the intervention is included in a checklist format. The practitioner can frequently refer to this intervention checklist to be sure they are implementing each component of treatment, which is a critical part of plan implementation (Fein & Dunn, 2007). When this stage is done well, and data continue to be collected and shared with the team, this allows the team and teacher to draw more valid and objective conclusions about the effectiveness of the intervention.

A second critical part of *plan implementation* is systematic (planned) regular progress monitoring (Albers et al., 2005). A variety of methods and measures can be used to monitor intervention, but ideally the same method of data collection used in baseline is used to inform our understanding of the prevalence of the behavior, after sufficient time in intervention, to determine how much has or has not changed after the intervention was implemented. Monitoring should be done consistently and at interval lengths that are short enough to allow for realization that things are or are not working, but not so short that it interferes with classroom functioning (Horner et al., 2010). Measurement should be approached in such a way that is planned and deliberate (Vannest et al., 2013) and focused on ongoing feedback both throughout the course of intervention or treatment, often referred to as formative assessment, and at the end of treatment, known as summative assessment (Kratochwill et al., 2004). This is most often built into everyday teaching practices and times. For example, collecting information on the frequency of out-of-seat behavior during 20-min intervals three times per day 2 to 3 days per week. Progress monitoring data can also include frequency counts (e.g., targeted behavior, homework turned in, spelling words correctly), A-B-C charts (reporting the antecedents, behaviors, and consequences that occur when targeted skills are monitored), goal attainment scales (GASs; provides a way to monitor parent and teacher reports of treatment progress, usually on a scale from –2 to +2), checklists, rating scales, and test or quiz scores. A simple checklist of target skills (e.g., raises hand to answer, uses materials appropriately, responds to name when called) can be used to determine if a variety of skills have been mastered such as academic (read sight words correctly), behavioral (waited turn to talk), mobility (used wheelchair independently), communication (used communication device to request more snack), and safety (used a seat belt on the bus; Brown et al., 2020). All this information can assist the teacher and PST in selecting initial data collection and treatment monitoring data that are appropriate and most useful for the targeted skill(s).

Ideally the team, or selected members of the team (e.g., school psychologist and teacher), should schedule or hold a time during regular meetings when data on progress monitoring are shared so that others are aware of how the intervention is going throughout the plan implementation phase. Finally, it is recommended that predetermined decision rules are followed prior to making changes in the intervention such as at least 10% change in behavior in Week 1, 20% behavior change in Week 3, and 80% behavior change at the end of intervention in Week 8, so that team members can objectively decide if adjustments to the intervention are needed or if there is a need to re-examine the issue by repeating prior problem-solving phases if targeted goals are not being met (see additional information about data-based decision making in Chapter 6).

Plan Evaluation

The primary objective of the *plan evaluation* phase is to determine if the identified goals have been met. This usually and ideally requires a formal evaluation meeting, but the focus is on determining whether each goal has been achieved, through examining the data collected throughout the problem-solving process to determine if a discrepancy between the learner's current performance and desired and targeted level of performance remains following the implementation of the intervention. This is evaluated by examining the differences between baseline (data collected before intervention) and postintervention performance (data after the intervention has been in place for several weeks) that determine the overall intervention effect (Tilly, 2008).

Optimally an additional component, to be discussed later in this chapter, is to conduct a postintervention acceptability evaluation (e.g., how difficult was the intervention to implement, was the time required to implement reasonable, was this intervention viewed to be effective), filled out by important stakeholders such as interventionists and parents, that can further assist the team in evaluating outcomes (Kratochwill et al., 2002). Treatment integrity data and the overall quality of the data collected throughout the intervention is also analyzed and considered in this phase as part of evaluating intervention effectiveness. A final indicator of effectiveness is to evaluate and collect data on the extent to which the learner has generalized newly acquired skills across environments, people, and time (e.g., intervention was focused on math class to decrease out-of-seat behavior, collect data in math class but also during reading, specials, and after-school program). A summary of the phases of the problem-solving framework and examples of implementation can be found in Table 13.1.

PSTs AND A PROBLEM-SOLVING MODEL OF EBP

School PSTs have become the centerpiece of implementation of interventions in schools, and, as the name implies, they are designed to solve problems related to social, adaptive, behavioral, and academic challenges that learners experience at school. PSTs are "committees" that revolve around a core group of school professionals (e.g., school psychologist, social worker, administrator, grade-level team leads) and draw in other school practitioners (e.g., general education or special education teacher) when a specific learner is referred. These individuals meet, in addition to other instructional responsibilities, to work with practitioners seeking assistance (usually teachers) by providing indirect service and developing an intervention that the persons requesting help ultimately implement. In fact, PSTs are commonplace across schools in the United States and are utilized both for general education learners and for special education learners (Algozzine et al., 2016; Blankenship et al., 2010; Boudett et al., 2006a, 2006b; Boudett & Steele, 2007; Chenoweth, 2010; Coburn & Turner, 2012; Leithwood, 2010; Murnane et al., 2005; Steele & Boudett, 2008a, 2008b).

Continued use of PSTs has been driven largely by legislative conceptual frameworks that emphasize data-based decision making (Algozzine et al., 2016), with the understanding that group problem solving will produce better outcomes than each team member acting alone (e.g., individual consultation with the teacher). There is an abundance of literature, mostly from the 1980s and 1990s when PSTs were a focus of research, that provided guidance and recommendations as to how the problem-solving model can be applied for use by PSTs (Algozzine et al., 2016; Bransford & Stein, 1993; Carroll & Johnson, 1990; Gilbert, 1978; Jorgensen et al., 1981; Marsh et al., 2010; McNamara et al., 2008; Ysseldyke et al., 2006). Algozzine and colleagues (2016) identified several important takeaways specific to the PST and the problem-solving process. They indicated that the phases for effective problem solving remain consistent across time, context, and authors who have studied PSTs and that just telling or giving teams the steps for the problem-solving process does not guarantee they will effectively use them. The challenges they have encountered with PSTs included that there is often ineffective use of problem-solving practices within school-

Table 13.1. Overview of Problem-Solving Phases and Examples

Phase	Summary of phase	Example of phase implementation
———	Relationship building— a preliminary phase	Create a team that has expertise across areas with core members who lead the team, often 2–9 individuals. Administrative support, time to meet, and evidence-based team training are critical. Assign key roles of timekeeper, facilitator, note taker, and data presenter (data are sent to and then reviewed by this person).
1	Problem identification phase • Is there a problem? • What is the problem? • Data collection is critical. • What is an appropriate goal or change to expect and by when?	• Identify aggression and noncompliance during academic subjects in first grade for Josh. • Define the behaviors and collect counts of aggression and noncompliance for 15 min each during math and reading on T, Th, and Fri. • Most often after noncompliance behavior was ignored but after aggression, Josh was removed from his desk (time-out or sent to office).
2	Problem analysis phase • What factors contribute to the occurrence of the problem? • What is the hypothesized cause of the behavior? • Examine the data to inform selection of evidence-based practice. • Develop a written plan for intervention steps, training, and monitoring (treatment integrity and progress monitoring).	• Aggression occurred 4–7 times, noncompliance 8–10 times across math and reading observations. • Hypothesis was tasks were too hard and Josh was trying to escape/get out of the tasks. • Goal for 0 aggression and 2 or less noncompliance occurrences within 2 months. • Differential reinforcement of communication selected as intervention with training and steps clarified with paraprofessional using a task analysis checklist. • Integrity check by school psychologist 1–2x/week; review data at beginning of each PST meeting.
3	Plan implementation phase • What can be done to improve the problem? • Plan for regular review of implementation integrity and progress monitoring data review to inform decisions.	• Paraprofessional trained to follow intervention checklist steps. • Implemented alternating during math or reading each day. • Data counts on aggression and noncompliance sent to school psychologist daily for review. • Problem solving after integrity checks.
4	Plan evaluation phase • Did our evidence-based practice (EBP) work (was goal or change identified met for the child)? • Was the intervention viewed as acceptable?	• Aggression reduced to 0 occurrences by Week 6. • Noncompliance at 2 occurrences or less during Week 7. • Intervention successful. • Collected acceptability survey from teacher, paraprofessional, and parent. • Check in and share intervention and outcome with family throughout the process.

based PSTs, and that there is a lack of or inconsistent collection and use of data and EBP in assessment and intervention selection.

School PSTs are well placed to utilize a problem-solving model to reach solutions to learner behavioral and academic issues including for learners with ASD. PSTs have been shown to be effective in achieving learner academic and behavioral success in general education classrooms (Chalfant & Pysh, 1989; Dowd-Eagle & Eagle, 2014; Flugum & Reschly, 1994; Fuchs et al., 1990; Graden et al., 1985; Rosenfield & Gravois, 1996; Rosenfield et al., 2018). Referrals are typically made to the team for learners with serious behavioral and academic problems, and the team will confer with the learners' teacher(s), parents, and any other involved practitioners to plan and implement classroom interventions to resolve the learning and behavior problem. The team consultation literature has consistently shown that the PST process is most effective with the use of problem-solving strategies, data-based decision making, and the implementation of EBPs (Dowd-Eagle & Eagle, 2014; Flugum & Reschly, 1994; Jayanthi & Friend, 1992; Meyers et al., 1996; Rosenfield, 1992; Rosenfield et al., 2018). PSTs have been central to the increased implementation of EBPs with the RtI and positive behavior support movement (Kratochwill, 2006; Reschly & Bergstrom, 2009).

Recent research on PSTs has utilized team-initiated problem solving as a larger part of schoolwide positive behavior intervention and supports (Algozzine et al., 2016; Horner et al., 2017; Todd et al., 2017). These innovative and creative researchers have made progress with methods to improve PST functioning. For example, Bradshaw and colleagues (2010) evaluated 21 elementary schools in Maryland over a 5-year period that committed to two summer days and two in-school training days every year to problem-solving practices, as well as twice-monthly PST meetings. As a result, participating schools reduced the number of office discipline referrals and learner suspensions during that period. While frequent and regular PSTs are critical, what occurs during those PST meetings and follow-up outside of those meetings, by adhering to the problem-solving phases, is critical. Although PSTs will adopt differing models of problem solving, the underlying components need to be consistent across methods (Fuchs et al., 2003).

Expanding Adoption and Implementation of a Problem-Solving Model

The problem-solving process is ideal to address problems and concerns for learners with ASD, whether the issue is academic, adaptive, social, or behavioral in nature. When applied properly, the problem-solving process can lead to a set of data and analyses that will guide intervention selection. There is an additional advantage to the use of the problem-solving process: it allows specialists in the community and school professionals to address the needs of many more learners than they could typically serve through direct treatment models (Kratochwill, 2008). Remediation and prevention are primary goals of the problem-solving process (Gutkin & Curtis, 1999). There is an expectation that when a teacher engages in the problem-solving process, their efforts will result in improved learner performance. Thus, a primary objective of the problem-solving process is the remediation of skill or performance deficits exhibited by the learner. Similarly, at the systems level, PSTs strive to strengthen district-, school-, or class-wide services to improve learner outcomes (Kratochwill, 2008).

In addition, problem solving can be conceptualized as a preventive model. For example, a teacher who learns new techniques to remediate academic or behavioral difficulties through engaging in the problem-solving process, especially with careful attention to plan implementation, treatment integrity, and treatment monitoring, is likely to generalize the skills learned to address similar concerns with other learners in the future. Thus, through the problem-solving process, the system and practitioners' ability to prevent or address certain problems may improve (Kratochwill, 2008). In addition, the development, implementation, and monitoring of effective, prereferral interventions in general and special education classrooms prevent schools from providing unnecessary intensive and expensive services to learners who could be treated earlier and more efficiently (Burns & Symington, 2002; Sanetti & Collier-Meek, 2019).

A beneficial aspect of the problem-solving process is the facilitation and development of collaborative team relationships. Having team members support each other on an equal level with a common goal to develop and implement effective interventions to improve outcomes for a learner or group of learners is an implicit aspect of the approach (Burns et al., 2005). Through development of strong collaborative relationships, teams may experience less resistance among team members during the process, benefit from improved treatment integrity when it is actively planned for, and benefit from improved outcomes for learners overall (Kratochwill, 2008). The problem-solving process enables teams to establish a sense of shared responsibility that strives to prevent any one member from feeling burdened with responsibility for more than they can accomplish. This can be addressed by identifying key roles each team member will serve, such as time-keeper, data reporter, minute taker, and meeting facilitator (Kratochwill, 2008; Newton et al., 2012).

It should be noted that systematic problem-solving approaches rely on and are based in behavioral theory because they emphasize the lawfulness of behavior, interactions between learners and their environments, and the ability to alter environmental factors to affect desired behavior change (Sugai & Horner, 2006). The behavioral theory has behind it decades of support to utilize experimental approaches in measurement of problems, analysis of factors that influence the occurrence of behavior, and systematic assessment and intervention practices that lead to meaningful outcome changes (Zins & Erchul, 2002). Problem solving was first described in the behavioral consultation literature by Bergan (1977), Bergan and Kratochwill (1990), and Tharp and Wetzel (1969), but has stood the test of time with decades of research support utilizing behavioral assessment techniques such as FBA that lead to effective understanding of the referring problem and selection of an appropriate EBP. PSTs commonly employ these evidence-based strategies to improve the academic and behavioral functioning of learners (Dowd-Eagle & Eagle, 2014).

SETTING THE COURSE FOR
EFFECTIVE PROFESSIONAL COLLABORATION

Planning for Meaningful Collaboration in Schools

Effective collaboration among school professionals working with learners with ASD as well as family members improves learner outcomes, facilitates transitions, and strengthens relationships (Emmons & Zager, 2018). Effective collaboration requires commitment, communication, strong leadership from administration, understanding the cultural climate, adequate resources, and preplanning. There need to be shared priorities by school professionals, family members, and learners. Please refer to Chapter 12 for details on skills needed to establish successful collaborations.

Collaboration is a conceptual construct in which shared respect and responsibility are paramount. Collaborative teaming is a dynamic process that involves consultation among professionals from a variety of disciplines and involves shared planning, decision making, and interaction (Kelly & Tincani, 2013). This process is cyclical, in that it involves ongoing information flow and feedback emphasizing the importance of effective communication (Ellsworth, 2020).

Collaboration Within the School Setting

Within the school setting, there are a variety of professionals involved in the education of learners with ASD. Regular education and special education teachers, school psychologists, related service providers, administrators, and behavioral support personnel may all be involved in the planning and implementation of a learner's educational programming. Collaboration within the school setting is important during the assessment process, the initial determination of eligibility for services, and in the intervention process.

Assessment. Collaboration during the assessment process, or determination for special education eligibility, is considered best practice for ASD. Collaboration allows for multiple perspectives about a learner's areas of growth and areas of strength, to best inform educational planning. During the assessment process, one effective form of collaboration that builds on and supports the problem-solving model, is the comprehensive developmental approach (Klin et al., 2005). This is an interdisciplinary model for assessing learners for ASD that is useful both for medical evaluation and for educational evaluation.

The **comprehensive developmental approach** provides a framework to incorporate assessment findings from multiple domains of functioning across disciplines. This model requires a team that is cohesive and functioning well, such as the PST, to allow for optimal assessment integration including discussion and reconciliation of disparate findings. Important to this model, and relevant to requirements of the Individuals with Disabilities Education Improvement Act (IDEIA, 2004), this model includes the parent or caregiver as part of the assessment process. Also important for educational planning, the comprehensive developmental approach emphasizes the assessment of *functional adjustment* for learners with or suspected of ASD.

Intervention. Collaboration and teamwork during intervention within the school is equally important. Despite the challenges that can occur when working as part of a team, Sylvester and colleagues (2017) strongly support a team approach to intervention. Broadly, the benefits of teamwork include multiple perspectives of the team members, opportunities for cross-disciplinary work, and the potential for systems-based approaches. Limitations, or costs, associated with collaboration include the time and effort required to create an integrated team. There may also be perceived territorial boundaries that can create conflict when breached. To work effectively, teams can engage in six steps. They can (1) set goals, (2) choose methodologies, (3) co-treat or co-teach, (4) evaluate treatment progress, (5) modify methodologies, and (6) make collaborative dismissal decisions. All of these elements are also accounted for in the problem-solving model previously described.

Effective teams set goals that are strengths based and that promote socially valid outcomes (Wilkinson, 2017). Goals are based on assessment data that directly inform methodologies. A focus on methodologies that enhance skill acquisition should be evidence based and user friendly (Ogletree et al., 2019). When co-treating or co-teaching, teams can employ passive consultation, observation, more active co-treatment, or co-teaching strategies. Within a school setting, there may be some natural discipline pairings, such as physical and occupational therapy, or speech-language pathology and special education. Evaluation of treatment progress is ongoing and includes evaluating integrity of intervention implementation and data. Based on evaluation, teams can modify methodologies as appropriate, and use data to make dismissal decisions. Dismissal decisions may be from a related service, a particular intervention, or special education services overall.

Common professionals who collaborate when designing and implementing school-based interventions for learners with ASD include school psychologists, speech-language pathologists, occupational therapists, social workers, general education teachers, special education teachers, behavioral support personnel, and administrators. We will highlight just a few of these professionals in this chapter. A brief overview of different school professionals and their roles is included in Table 13.2.

School Psychologists. School psychologists are members of interdisciplinary school-based teams who support the academic, social, emotional, and behavioral success of children and adolescents through application of evidence-based assessment and intervention approaches (National Association of School Psychologists, 2020c). Specific to service provision for learners with ASD, school psychologists engage in a variety of activities. Regarding assessment, school psychologists are responsible for evaluating the cognitive, academic, social-emotional, behavioral, and autism symptom–specific profiles of children and adolescents for whom a referral is made. Through the assessment process, these professionals conduct diagnostic interviews with families and school personnel to gather detailed information about referral concerns, administer psychoeducational diagnostic assessment measures and interpret normative data, engage in FBA activities to examine and determine the function of challenging behaviors, write comprehensive evaluation reports to inform intervention recommendations, and participate as part of interdisciplinary school teams to determine special education eligibility.

Regarding intervention, school psychologists provide a variety of evidence-based individual and group-based services to support learners with ASD in gaining social communication and adaptive living skills, engaging in functional and appropriate behaviors, and utilizing self-regulation and coping strategies. Data-based decision making is utilized throughout intervention implementation to determine treatment goals and objectives, monitor treatment integrity and targeted outcomes, and evaluate intervention progress and success (Shaw, 2011). School psychologists also collaborate with educational professionals, caregivers, families, and community-based professionals to ensure that all children and adolescents thrive within the school, home, and community settings (National Association of School Psychologists, 2020c).

Table 13.2. Descriptions of School Professional Staff and Roles to Assist Learners with ASD

School-based professionals involved in supporting students with autism spectrum disorder (ASD)	Professional roles and responsibilities
School psychologists	• Conduct diagnostic interviews and psychological assessments to determine special education eligibility within interdisciplinary teams. • Engage in functional behavior assessment activities to hypothesize functions of behavior. • Provide and evaluate individual and group-based psychological interventions to support skill development.
Speech language pathologists	• Conduct speech and language assessments within interdisciplinary teams to clarify special education eligibility. • Design, implement, and progress monitor interventions to support language and communication skill development.
Occupational therapists	• Collaboratively assess occupational skills and determine special education eligibility. • Implement and evaluate interventions supporting academic, adaptive, and daily living outcomes.
Physical therapists	• Conduct and interpret gross motor skill evaluations within interdisciplinary school teams. • Provide and progress monitor therapeutic interventions to promote physical skill development.
School social workers	• Implement interventions for learners with mental health, behavioral health, and academic concerns. • Connect learners, families, and school professionals with resources in the community.
General education and special education teachers	• Design and provide academic, vocational, social-emotional, and behavioral supports to learners within the general and special education environments. • Collaboratively participate as members of special education evaluation, eligibility, and program planning teams.
Special education paraprofessionals	• Provide one-on-one programming and support to learners receiving special education services.
Behavioral support personnel	• Engage in efforts to support positive behaviors and prevent challenging behaviors. • Respond to and address learner challenging behaviors when they occur.
School nurses	• Engage in case management, collaborative communication, and direct care to assist learner's physical health status and help families remove health-related barriers to learning.
School administrators	• Oversee and allocate funding for service provision within school-based settings.

Speech-Language Pathologists. Speech-language pathologists (SLPs) serve a variety of roles on the interdisciplinary school team. According to the American Speech-Language-Hearing Association (ASHA; 2010), SLPs have integral roles in education that include prevention, assessment, intervention, program design, data collection and analysis, and compliance. The work of the SLP is done in partnership with other professionals to best meet learners' needs. When providing services to support a learner's instructional program, SLPs work with general education teachers, reading specialists, literacy coaches, special education teachers, and other related-service providers. SLPs often serve a prevention role when they work on PSTs and help with developing interventions within the problem-solving framework. Furthermore, SLPs are often involved in the assessment process for eligibility, especially for learners with ASD. Their assessments are conducted in collaboration with other team members to help identify learners with communication disorders and to inform instruction and intervention. Intervention is a frequent role SLPs serve in schools because speech-language therapy is one of the most common special education services received by learners with ASD (Wei, Wagner, et al., 2014). The EBP implemented by SLPs may include a focus on language, sound production, and social communication skills. SLPs, like all educators, are accountable for learner outcomes. That necessitates the use of data-based decision making, including gathering and interpreting data both on the individual level and on the program level (ASHA, 2010).

Occupational Therapists. School-based occupational therapists (OTs) help support a learner's ability to participate in daily school activities or "occupations." They help learners fulfill their maximum potential by supporting academic achievement and promoting positive behaviors necessary for learning (American Occupational Therapy Association, 2020). School-based OTs help learners by supporting both academic outcomes and nonacademic outcomes, including social skills, academic skills, behavior difficulties, recreational activities (recess), self-help skills, and transportation. OTs are very skilled at helping learners access the environment, with a focus on learners' strengths. Within a school team, OTs collaborate with a variety of partners including learners, parents, educators, related service providers, and administrators. OTs can be involved in the assessment process when determining eligibility for special education services. When occupational therapy is identified by the team as a necessary service, OTs collaborate with other professionals on the development of IEP goals and the services, supports, modifications, and accommodations that are required. OTs provide school-based intervention when the IEP team determines a learner will benefit from these services (Frolek Clark & Chandler, 2014).

Social Workers. School social work is a specialized area of practice within the broad field of the social work discipline (School Social Work Association of America, 2020). School social workers bring unique knowledge and skills to the school system and the learner services team. They are trained mental health providers who can assist with mental health concerns, behavioral concerns, and academic concerns. They do this through consultation with teachers, parents, and administrators, as well as related service professionals. School social workers are well suited to provide individual and group counseling within the school. School social workers are also able to provide consultation to staff regarding cultural, societal, economic, or other factors affecting a learner's academic performance and behavior. They can participate as a member of the PST and the evaluation team when assessing learners for eligibility for special education services.

General Education and Special Education Teachers. General and special education teachers are critical to the interdisciplinary school team. While some children and adolescents with ASD receive educational and intervention services through the general education setting, others may require more intensive and individualized accommodations or modifications through special education to appropriately access the academic curriculum (Flannery & Wisner-Carlson, 2020; Wong et al., 2015). Individually and collaboratively, teachers are responsible for providing academic and vocational instruction, supporting positive and adaptive behaviors, and encouraging healthy social-emotional development of all learners in the classroom. They actively participate as members of PSTs, collaboratively engage in the evaluation, eligibility determination, goal development, and service planning process for special education, and consult with families and professionals across the school environment (Flannery & Wisner-Carlson, 2020).

Collaboration Outside the School Setting

Outside of the school setting and within the greater community, there are a wide array of professionals involved in providing clinical services and supports to children and adolescents with ASD. Pediatric medical providers, outpatient therapy providers, and behavioral service providers may all be involved in screening, diagnostic evaluation, treatment planning, and intervention implementation efforts. Understanding of and effective collaboration with community-based providers is critical to the promotion of positive developmental, learning, and behavioral outcomes for learners with ASD, especially given the complex and frequently comorbid nature of the neurodevelopmental disorder (Neuhaus et al., 2018).

Identification and Assessment. Interdisciplinary collaboration throughout the identification and diagnostic evaluation process is considered best practice for ASD, and the comprehensive developmental approach (described previously) is key to gathering and incorporating information across disciplines and stakeholders. A comprehensive identification process for ASD includes universal developmental and ASD surveillance and screening, developmental and ASD screening when concerns are raised during the surveillance process, and clinical diagnostic evaluation when there is a concerning screening result. Diagnostic evaluation should assess developmental concerns related to ASD, confirm or rule out other diagnoses, and identify targeted areas for linking assessment findings to intervention (Gardner et al., 2016). Effective collaboration across all steps of the identification process is critical to the delivery of appropriate services and supports for learners with ASD and their families. See Chapter 2 for more information on ASD diagnostic characteristics.

Intervention. Following receipt of an ASD diagnosis, professionals who are involved in the diagnostic evaluation process develop detailed intervention recommendations and assist children, adolescents, and families in navigating therapeutic services that may be available within the greater community. These providers also help learners and families in understanding supports that may be available within the school system, communicating information from the diagnostic evaluation process to professionals on the school-based team, offering evidence-based treatment recommendations, and requesting initiation of special education evaluation as warranted. To ensure that treatment services are appropriately provided to learners with ASD, intervention planning and program implementation must be linked to findings from the assessment process, individualized to the unique strengths and challenges of the child or adolescent with ASD, and provided in a collaborative manner (Gardner et al., 2016; Volkmar et al., 2014).

While a variety of professionals may be involved in service provision for learners with ASD in the community, pediatric medical providers, outpatient therapy providers, and behavioral service providers commonly offer community-based services and supports to children, adolescents, and families. However, it is important to note that engagement with services depends heavily on the strengths and challenges that are identified for the learner with ASD, the assignment of any co-occurring medical or psychiatric diagnoses, and the preferences and priorities of each learner and family.

Pediatric Medical Providers. Many learners with ASD have medical comorbidities, including the presence of epilepsy and seizure disorders, gastrointestinal issues, sleep challenges, feeding disorders, hyperactivity and impulsivity, and attentional difficulties (Hyman et al., 2020; Van Steensel et al., 2011; Vargason et al., 2019). Learners with ASD are also more likely to need greater acute and emergency medical care, utilize greater medication management services, and require interdisciplinary collaboration for the purposes of medical monitoring and treatment than same-aged learners within the general population (Deavenport-Saman et al., 2015; Neuhaus et al., 2018). Thus, an understanding of the role that primary medical care providers, specialty medical care providers, registered dieticians, and nutritionists play in service provision for learners with ASD is key to effective and holistic collaboration.

Outpatient Therapy Providers. In addition to receiving treatment and consultation for a wide array of medical needs, children and adolescents with ASD regularly participate in various outpatient therapeutic services. Given that learners with ASD are at an increased risk for developing anxiety, mood, and other psychiatric disorders, psychological treatment and counseling interventions are often warranted (Hyman et al., 2020) and may be provided by a range of community-based professionals, including licensed psychologists, professional counselors, and clinical social workers. Many learners with ASD also exhibit a range of speech, social communication, fine motor, gross motor, and coordination challenges and require the therapeutic support of speech-language pathologists, occupational therapists, and physical therapists (Hyman et al., 2020; U.S. Department of Health and Human Services, National Institutes of Health, and National Institute on Deafness and Other Communication Disorders, 2014).

Behavioral Service Providers. Children and adolescents with ASD often present with a range of challenging behaviors, which may include self-injury (head banging, self-biting), physical or verbal aggression toward others (hitting, kicking, swearing), elopement, property destruction, noncompliance, toileting difficulties, and tantrum-like behaviors. While some outpatient therapeutic services may assist in targeting the development of functional communication and adaptive skill capabilities, learners with ASD frequently receive applied behavior analytic (ABA) or behaviorally oriented treatment services to promote the acquisition of functional skills and behaviors, increase the likelihood of desirable or socially appropriate behaviors, and decrease the likelihood of those that are more problematic or difficult in nature (Hyman et al., 2020). These types of supports can be provided both in home settings and in clinical settings, and service providers typically include Board Certified Behavior Analysts (BCBAs) or others who work alongside or under the supervision of a BCBA, including Board Certified Assistant Behavior Analysts (BCaBAs) and Registered Behavior Technicians (RBTs).

Process for Collaboration. Learners with ASD and their families interact with a multitude of community-based providers through the receipt of identification, diagnostic assessment, and treatment services. Thus, it is critical that school-based professionals be able to accurately conceptualize the various roles, service delivery modalities, and supports offered by these providers. Such understanding can assist in promoting effective, focused, and evidence-based collaboration between school and community-based providers and enhancing coordination of care for children and adolescents with ASD and their families.

Evaluating Impact and Acceptability of Collaboration

Whether at school or within the community, it is critical for providers of services for children and adolescents with ASD to conduct ongoing evaluation of EBPs to understand both short- and long-term success of the intervention. While it is common for school professionals or parents to verbally report that things seem to be going well (or not), utilizing objective data that are shared to inform statements about the status of intervention is imperative to fairly evaluating whether the outcome is best serving learners' needs. We reviewed that, at the time of problem analysis, a target goal should be identified, or learner performance comparison identified as the target for intervention. Once this goal is close to being reached, a final data point can be collected to confirm the success achieved. The team can then celebrate the hard work and consistent effort that led to learner improvement.

A final aspect of consideration for every completed intervention that is critical to treatment success is to collect information on *treatment acceptability* (Cooper et al., 2020). *Treatment acceptability* is defined as the degree to which an individual considers the procedure to be fair, appropriate, reasonable, and unobtrusive (Risley, 2005), and includes factors related to treatment integrity, including (a) difficulty of treatment, (b) time intensiveness of treatment, (c) number of individuals required for treatment implementation, (d) degree of resources required for treatment, and (e) acceptability of treatment by the person(s) implementing the treatment (Gresham, 1989). Intervention integrity and acceptability increase when there is evidence of the treatment's effectiveness (Cooper et al., 2020). Therefore, a PST trained to utilize student behavioral data and implement EBPs is more likely to find the intervention effective and acceptable, leading to an increase in treatment integrity.

Strategies and Considerations for Impact and Acceptability

Recall that treatment integrity, by definition, is the degree to which practitioners (in schools, typically classroom teachers) implement treatment with accuracy and consistency (Sanetti & Kratochwill, 2014). Treatment integrity is central to the PST process because the efficacy of the recommended and adopted treatment is dependent on the treatment being implemented as planned. Cordray and Pion (2006) emphasize that treatment effects can only be considered relative to the degree to which the treatment was delivered as intended. Therefore, while collecting progress monitoring data, if a learner is determined to not respond to intervention, the intervention can only be deemed ineffective if there is objective evidence of intervention integrity. Thus, progress monitoring and treatment integrity are dependent on each other to accurately interpret the data that are being collected. A final check is to determine how acceptable all aspects of intervention identification, selection, training, and implementation were to those who were a critical part of implementing the intervention.

There are several useful acceptability measures that can be used or modified to assess how willing and able practitioners were to implement the intervention and what they thought about it overall. One example is the *Treatment Acceptability Rating Form-Revised* (TARF-R; Reimers et al., 1992). This measure was developed to evaluate the degree to which parents, teachers, and professionals find the identified intervention acceptable and beneficial. It is a rating scale comprising questions that best represent the acceptability of interventions and asks a series of questions that assess perceptions of intervention acceptability, willingness to conduct intervention procedures, and negative side effects of intervention procedures (e.g., disruption to classroom routine). There are 20 questions that are answered indicating a range of responses on a scale of 1 to 7. For example, in response to the question, "How acceptable do you find the treatment to be regarding your concerns about this child?" ratings range from (1) not at all acceptable to (7) very acceptable.

The *Intervention Rating Profile* (IRP-15) also uses a Likert-type scale from 1 (strongly disagree) to 6 (strongly agree) developed to directly assess teachers' perceptions of classroom interventions (Martens et al., 1985). Sample questions include "I would suggest the use of this intervention to other teachers" and "This intervention is reasonable for the behavior problem identified." While treatment acceptability is a subjective assessment, by utilizing or modifying one of the mentioned rating scales, the process can be made more systematic by asking the same questions across interventionists (e.g., teacher, special educator, paraprofessional, parent) and across different learners. Teacher-created checklists can also be used if using a published checklist is not feasible. It is important to ask for and consider individuals' perceptions of the intervention and the PST process in general to inform the practice, communication, training, selection, and implementation of interventions for children with ASD.

SUMMARY

This chapter has focused on defining roles and identifying ways in which school and community professionals work in collaboration and support to meet the needs of children and adolescents with ASD and their families. A problem-solving process was described that has been a guiding framework of successful school PSTs for decades to address in a systematic, objective, and consistent manner a multitude of behaviors and academic concerns faced by school-aged children and adolescents with ASD. The supports and services provided within and outside of the school setting to children and adolescents with ASD are critical to development and set the stage for skill development, social interaction, adaptive behavior, learning, and quality of life for years to come. As highlighted, collaboration, communication, and objective and planned assessment, intervention, monitoring, evaluation, and acceptability all play a critical role in delivering high-quality and appropriate services to school-aged children and adolescents with ASD.

CASE STUDY

The following case study highlights the benefits of a PST approach to collaborative problem solving and illustrates a behavioral approach to assessment and intervention.

Anusha is a 12-year-old sixth grade learner with a history of behavior problems both at home and at school. Anusha has been identified as having an educational classification of ASD and significant developmental delays. As part of the **problem identification phase**, it was reported that Anusha engages in self-injurious behavior in the form of chin-hitting (striking below her chin with a closed fist), aggression toward others, screaming, tantrums, and refusal to comply with directions. Anusha does not have any verbal language and inconsistently uses sign language and picture cards, instead pointing or grabbing items. The referring issue brought to the PST was that Anusha was engaging in self-injury and screaming behavior during lunch. The special education teacher reported that this occurred every day but did not have any data collected. The PST asked the teacher to record frequency data (or the number of times Anusha engaged in self-injury or screaming) for 3 days during lunch and the school psychologist agreed to assist with data collection on 2 of the 3 days.

During the **problem analysis phase**, the data collected were reviewed and indicated that on each of the 3 days Anusha engaged in self-injury (4, 6, and 3 times) and screaming (8, 7, and 10 times) during lunch. Preceding the problem behavior, the teacher presented Anusha with pictures of food choices for lunch. In response to her behavior, the teacher or paraprofessional commonly prompted Anusha to pick a picture or told her to be quiet. Despite not making a choice, food items were given to her. For example, on Wednesday, Anusha never made a choice and escalated her behavior for 20 min until lunch was over and she was given a preferred item, a cookie to eat on the way out of the lunchroom, which she ate. The PST reviewed the data and during the **data analysis phase**, the hypothesis was made that Anusha engaged in problem behaviors for positive reinforcement in the form of tangible reinforcement, in other words she was using her problem behavior to access food items.

In consultation with the speech-language pathologist during the **plan implementation phase**, it was decided to use the EBP of functional communication training and require Anusha to appropriately communicate for food items to receive them. It had been decided based on baseline data that the **goal** for intervention was 90% consistent use of the switch, one or fewer instances of self-injury, and two or fewer instances of screaming during lunch. Two communication switches were presented, one with a green sticker, and one with a red sticker. During the phase it was decided that the paraprofessional would be trained to present the switches to Anusha along with one food item at a time for Anusha to say "yes" (green switch) or "no" (red switch). One food item behind the two switches was presented to Anusha by the paraprofessional, who used a task analysis checklist of each specific intervention step. If Anusha engaged in screaming or self-injury, the food and switches were removed for 10 s, then represented. Initially, the school psychologist assisted to physically prompt Anusha prior to inappropriate behavior and used a preferred food item, cookies, to reliably teach her to use the switch to access food items.

(continued)

Data were collected during lunch every day for 3 weeks, and by the end of the second week, Anusha was consistently selecting between the two switches 3/5 days (60%) and decreased her self-injury behavior to two or fewer and screaming to four or fewer per lunch period. During the **plan evaluation phase**, data collection was reduced to 3 times per week and within 2 months no additional problem behaviors had been recorded over a 2-week period; formal data collection was stopped and the team agreed that the issue had been resolved, as data were presented and reviewed at the beginning of each PST meeting. Acceptability measures using the TARF-R were completed by the paraprofessional, classroom teacher, and parent and indicated satisfaction with the selection and time needed to implement the intervention. Information on the intervention implementation was also shared with Anusha's family throughout treatment and implementation of the switches was also used at home during dinner with similar success noted over the same period.

APPLICATION ACTIVITIES

1. Why is it important for school-based professionals to understand the role of community-based providers who are involved in service provision for learners with ASD? In what ways might you collaborate with community-based providers in your profession?
2. Identify the four steps in the problem-solving process. Although effective collaboration is not a formal step, why is this important to PST functioning?
3. Why is data collection such an important part of the problem-solving process? Identify three ways in which you could collect objective data consistently in your setting.
4. Evidence-based practices are critical to the problem-solving process but require collection and consideration both of treatment integrity (ensuring the intervention is implemented as intended) and of treatment monitoring (ongoing data collection after the treatment is implemented). What are reasons that they may not be commonplace in school settings? Identify ways in which you would be able to assist with or help to ensure these practices are a part of intervention planning in your setting.
5. How might you collaborate with school professionals you have not had an opportunity to work with? How does this benefit learners with ASD?

ADDITIONAL RESOURCES

Center on Multi-Tiered System of Supports. https://mtss4success.org/
National Clearinghouse on Autism Evidence and Practice. https://ncaep.fpg.unc.edu/
TEACH Teamwork. https://www.apa.org/education/k12/teach-teamwork
UCONN Implementation Science. https://implementationscience.uconn.edu/
Various Organizations/Agencies focused on minoritized families of children with ASD.

1. Autism in Black: https://www.autisminblack.org/
2. Chinese Parents Association for the Disabled: http://www.cpad.org/

3. The Color of Autism Foundation: https://www.thecolorofautism.org/
4. Grupo Salto: https://gruposalto.org/
5. Muhsen: https://muhsen.org/

What Works Clearinghouse. https://ies.ed.gov/ncee/wwc/FWW/Index

NOTE

Partial support for this chapter came from the U.S. Department of Education, Office of Special Education through Personnel Preparation Training Grant H325K190100 and the Institute of Education Sciences, Grant R324A190198 awarded to the University of Wisconsin-Madison.

14

Final Remarks

Katie Wolfe, Laura C. Chezan, and Erik Drasgow

■ ■ ■

Designing and delivering effective supports for learners with ASD can be complex, and we hope that this book has been a useful guide for navigating the process. In this final chapter, we highlight five key themes that recur throughout the book and discuss critical aspects of effective and ethical educational programming and service delivery for learners with ASD. The five themes are (1) focusing on quality of life, (2) connecting assessment and intervention, (3) targeting socially valid and functional behaviors, (4) engaging in ethical practice, and (5) collaborating with the learner, their family, and other stakeholders (see Figure 14.1). Underpinning all of the themes is selecting interventions that are based on rigorous, high-quality research.

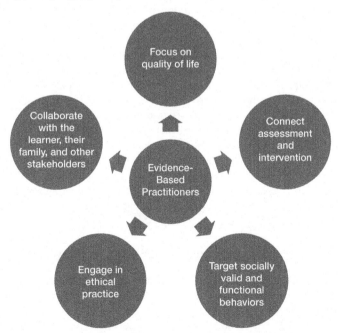

Figure 14.1. Critical aspects of effective supports for learners with autism spectrum disorders

FOCUSING ON QUALITY OF LIFE

When practitioners work with families and the learner to identify goals for intervention, skills and behaviors that will enhance the learner's quality of life should be prioritized. Quality of life refers to an individual's satisfaction with their life (Schalock et al., 2011), and consists of multiple domains including physical and emotional well-being, material well-being, interpersonal relationships, social inclusion, rights and personal development, and self-determination (Schalock & Alonso, 2002). Although one individual, or one culture, may place more or less value on a given domain compared to another individual or culture, the quality-of-life domains are considered to be universal (Schalock & Keith, 2016). Central to the quality-of-life concept is that it is based on the perspective of the individual; that is, only individuals themselves and their families can determine whether they have a poor or good quality of life.

Chapter 1 provided a detailed discussion of quality of life, but we hope that this construct emerged as a common thread throughout all chapters in the book. For example, prioritizing the learner's quality of life means that a practitioner is considering the values and preferences of the learner when selecting goals and interventions within the context of a person-centered approach discussed in Chapter 3. Furthermore, considering the values and preferences of the learner is a critical aspect of the evidence-based intervention selection model discussed in Chapter 4. In Chapter 7, Schwartz and colleagues noted that ethical practitioners seek to improve learner quality of life by targeting meaningful outcomes through the application of evidence-based practices that fit the culture, values, and preferences of the learner and family. In Chapter 10, Rispoli and colleagues discussed the negative impact of problem behavior on learner quality of life and the importance of selecting replacement behaviors that will allow the learner to successfully navigate inclusive environments. The transition to adulthood is a particularly important time to attend to the learner's values and preferences because they take on more independence during this critical juncture (Chapter 11).

In addition to considering the learner's quality of life, effective practitioners also attend to the quality of life of the learner's family. Families of learners with ASD report experiencing more stress than parents of children without disabilities as well as parents of children with other disabilities (Hayes & Watson, 2013). Building the learner's skills by enhancing their social-communication repertoire (Chapter 8) and by reducing challenging behavior (Chapter 10) are likely to minimize family stress and increase their quality of life. However, Meadan and Pearson describe in Chapter 12 additional strategies for supporting family well-being such as sharing resources, helping families navigate service systems, and prioritizing the family's goals for the learner with ASD.

CONNECTING ASSESSMENT AND INTERVENTION

Assessment is an essential step in identifying meaningful and appropriate target behaviors to teach. Considering that ASD is a spectrum disorder, and the characteristics of ASD may manifest in unique ways in different learners, assessment is particularly critical for this population. As described in Chapter 3, assessment is the process of gathering information about a learner's current skills or behaviors. Skills assessment helps pinpoint a learner's strengths and needs and assists practitioners in identifying potential goals for intervention. When a learner engages in challenging behaviors, functional behavior assessment (FBA; Chapter 10) is used to identify the variables that influence the behavior and to develop a function-based intervention. Thus, regardless of the domain, assessment should always precede and inform intervention.

The central role of assessment in goal identification and program planning necessitates that practitioners be familiar with different assessment tools and thoughtful in selecting the appropriate assessment. Because goals are derived from assessment results, the content of the assessment will directly influence the goals that are addressed in intervention programs. Some assessments, such as ecological inventories, evaluate the learner's performance with respect to skills that will be necessary for independent or supported participation (Baumgart et al., 1982) in current and future environments. Other assessments, such as curriculum-based assessments, evaluate the learner's performance on academic standards (Chapter 9) or developmental norms (Chapter 3). These two types of assessments will produce different types of goals for intervention. For example, an ecological inventory may identify that a young child with ASD in preschool would benefit from learning how to unpack her bag independently upon arriving at school, how to request items during snack time, and how to play with her peers. A curriculum-based assessment for this same learner, however, may identify goals such as rote counting, labeling objects, and identifying colors based on her performance relative to developmental standards. A comprehensive approach to assessment that includes multiple types of assessments and multiple sources of information is likely to yield the most well-rounded and impactful programming.

In addition to assessments directly related to the learner's skills and behavior, gathering information about the learner's and their family's preferences, goals, and priorities is an integral part of the assessment process and a key step in the evidence-based intervention selection model. When sharing assessment results with the learner and their family, it is important to first recognize the learner's strengths and then work with the learner and their family to set priorities from the areas of need identified in the assessment (Crais & Roberts, 2004). Questions such as "What is most important to you right now?" or "What would you like [your child] to learn in the next few months?" may help the learner and their family identify goals for intervention (Crais & Roberts, 2004). Stimulus preference assessments and person-centered planning are additional assessments discussed in Chapter 3 that practitioners can use to directly involve the learner with ASD in the process of goal identification and intervention planning.

Ongoing data-based decision making is another area where assessment and intervention are linked. Collecting, graphing, and analyzing learner performance data is a form of assessment, and this assessment should be directly connected to the decisions that practitioners make about whether to continue, modify, or terminate a particular intervention. Chapter 6 describes guidelines for measuring, graphing, and using data to make instructional decisions. Data-based decision making is also a key step in the evidence-based intervention selection model (step 6: reevaluation). We recommend that evidence-based practitioners incorporate data-based decision making into their regular schedule to ensure that there is time for this important activity.

TARGETING SOCIALLY VALID AND FUNCTIONAL BEHAVIORS

One of the main goals of effective educational programming is to equip learners with the behaviors needed to function successfully in the natural environment. Therefore, it is critical that practitioners identify and provide instruction on behaviors that are both socially valid and functional. Socially valid behaviors are behaviors that align with learners' interests, preferences, and values, are relevant for their functioning in the natural environment, and improve quality of life (Falcomata, 2015). Functional behaviors are those behaviors that allow learners to function independently and successfully in the natural environment and have the potential to enhance their active participation in the community, self-determination, and satisfaction with life.

The importance of targeting socially valid and functional behaviors has been emphasized throughout the chapters of this book. In Chapter 8, Sigafoos and colleagues highlight the need to enhance the social competence of learners with ASD, which is critical for becoming an active member of one's community and society and one of the most important domains of learning and development. Fleury and colleagues discuss in Chapter 9 the importance of targeting reading, writing, and mathematics skills that are meaningful and generalizable across settings and allow learners to effectively navigate the natural environment. The importance of targeting functional and socially valid behavior is also reflected in Chapter 10, which highlights the need to promote appropriate behaviors while decreasing problem behavior within the context of function-based interventions. Socially valid and functional behaviors are also critical to ensuring a successful transition into adulthood and allowing learners with ASD to pursue their adulthood or long-term goals and aspirations as described by Plotner and colleagues in Chapter 11.

ENGAGING IN ETHICAL PRACTICE

Ethical practice, regardless of specific discipline, involves the key concepts of confidentiality, competency, and accountability (Chapter 7). Applying the evidence-based intervention selection model (Chapter 4) will support practitioners in engaging in ethical practice, specifically related to competency and accountability. Wilczynski and colleagues describe the importance of practitioners considering the best available scientific evidence; learner values, preferences, and culture; contextual factors; and their own professional competencies when identifying potential interventions. An ethical practitioner, therefore, selects interventions that are within their competence to implement (or train others to implement). If they must select an intervention that is outside of their competence, they should secure appropriate training, supervision, and consultation prior to implementing the intervention. In Chapter 5, Mason and colleagues present several evidence-based training models that can be used to acquire the skills needed to implement an intervention with fidelity. Another critical aspect of being a competent practitioner is remaining current with scientific knowledge. As researchers continue to study interventions and the variables that influence their effectiveness, our knowledge about evidence-based practices will evolve and, thus, it is important to stay in touch with the most current research.

By using the evidence-based intervention selection model, practitioners can ensure that they are accountable for the consequences of their decisions. Being explicit about the steps involved in identifying an intervention can increase transparency for everyone on the team and can provide a forum for discussion and collaboration. Steps 5 and 6 of the model emphasize the importance of ongoing data collection and evaluation both to maintain accountability and to ensure that learners continue to make progress toward their goals and objectives. A practitioner who is accountable for their decisions has objective documentation of learner performance and makes changes when the data suggest that the learner is not progressing as desired.

COLLABORATING WITH OTHERS

Across domains and settings, it is imperative that practitioners working with learners with ASD collaborate with the learner, their family and caregivers, and other professionals to develop an intervention plan that maximizes the learner's potential and promotes their quality of life. Although Chapters 5, 12, and 13 speak most directly to the skills necessary for effective collaboration, each chapter in the book touches on the importance of collaboration when working with learners with ASD. Acknowledging and respecting the perspectives of stakeholders is a key element of being an ethical practitioner (Chapter 7), and incorporating learner values and preferences, and the values, preferences, and cultural norms of caregivers and other professionals, is a key element of the evidence-based intervention selection model (Chapter 4). Thus, establishing meaningful partnerships is a cornerstone of being an ethical and effective practitioner.

Learners with ASD often receive multiple supports and services from a variety of professionals, which heightens the importance of practitioners having the "soft skills" needed to effectively partner with other professionals. Chapter 12 details several of these skills, such as active listening and clear communication, that are often overlooked in preparation programs but critical to establishing partnerships with families and professionals. While collaboration is essential, it is not always easy. Professionals from various disciplines may have different philosophical perspectives about how to approach a challenge, and this difference may produce some friction as the team tries to work together to develop a solution. However, Asmus and colleagues note in Chapter 13 that multidisciplinary teams using a problem-solving team approach have multiple benefits, including a more well-rounded approach to assessment and intervention, enhanced generalization, and an increased impact on the learner's overall quality of life.

SUMMARY

In summary, our main purpose in this book was to provide our audience with useful resources to design and implement evidence-based educational programs that are likely to promote independence, community participation, and life satisfaction across the lifespan for learners with ASD. It is imperative that practitioners select interventions that are supported by high-quality and rigorous research. However, practitioners cannot just select an EBP "off the shelf" and implement it with a learner; they must consider what skill or behavior they are targeting and why. Throughout the book, we emphasized the most important aspects of evidence-based educational programming, including focusing on quality of life, connecting assessment and intervention, targeting socially valid and functional behaviors, engaging in ethical practice, and collaborating with the learner, their family, and other professionals. Critical to effective and evidence-based educational programs are also professional training, implementation of interventions with fidelity, and goals that promote learners' positive outcomes across curricular domains, including academic and quality-of-life domains, such as interpersonal relationships, self-advocacy, self-determination, personal development, and participation in inclusive environments.

References

■ ■ ■

Abadir, C. M., DeBar, R. M., Vladescu, J. C., Reeve, S., & Kupferman, D. M. (2021). Effects of video modeling on abduction-prevention skills by individuals with autism spectrum disorder. *Journal of Applied Behavior Analysis, 54*(3), 1139–1156. https://doi.org/10.1002/jaba.822

Ahearn, W. H., Clark, K. M., MacDonald, R. P. F., & Chung, B. I. (2007). Assessing and treating vocal stereotypy in children with autism. *Journal of Applied Behavior Analysis, 40*(2), 263–275. https://doi.org/10.1901/jaba.2007.30-06

Akemoglu, Y., Muharib, R., & Meadan, H. (2020). A systematic and quality review of parent-implemented language and communication interventions conducted via telepractice. *Journal of Behavioral Education, 29*(2), 282–316. https://doi.org/10.1007/s10864-019-09356-3

Akamoglu, Y., Meadan, H., Pearson, J. N., & Cummings, K. (2018). Getting connected: Speech and language pathologists' perceptions of building rapport via telepractice. *Journal of Developmental and Physical Disabilities, 30*(4), 569–585. https://doi.org/10.1007/s10882-018-9603-3

Akers, J. S., Davis, T. N., Gerow, S., & Avery, S. (2020). Decreasing motor stereotypy in individuals with autism spectrum disorder: A systematic review. *Research in Autism Spectrum Disorders, 77* (September 2019), 101611. https://doi.org/10.1016/j.rasd.2020.101611

Akshoomoff, N. (2006). Use of the Mullen Scales of Early Learning for the assessment of young children with Autism Spectrum Disorders. *Child Neuropsychology, 12*(4–5), 269–277. https://doi.org/10.1080/09297040500473714

Akshoomoff, N., Stahmer, A. C., Corsello, C., & Mahrer, N. E. (2010). What happens next? Follow-up from the children's toddler school program. *Journal of Positive Behavior Interventions, 12*(4), 245–253. https://doi.org/10.1177%2F1098300709343724

Alber, S. R., & Heward, W. L. (2001). Teaching students to recruit positive attention: A review and recommendations. *Journal of Behavioral Education, 10*(4), 177–204. https://doi.org/10.1023/A:1012258231074

Albers, C. A., Elliott, S. N., & Kettler, R. J. (2005). Evaluating intervention outcomes. In R. Brown-Chidsey (Ed.), *Assessment for intervention: A problem-solving approach* (pp. 329–351). Guilford Press.

Albers, C. A., & Kratochwill, T. R. (2006). Teacher and principal consultations: Best practices. In C. Franklin, M. B. Harris, & P. Allen-Meares (Eds.), *The school services sourcebook: A guide for school-based professionals* (pp. 971–976). Oxford University Press.

Alexander, L., & Moore, M. (2020). Deontological ethics. In E. N. Zalta (Ed.), *The Stanford encyclopedia of philosophy.* https://plato.stanford.edu/entries/ethics-deontological/

Algozzine, B., Horner, R., Todd, A., Newton, S., Algozzine, K., & Cusumano, D. (2016). Measuring the process and outcomes of team problem solving. *Journal of Psychoeducational Assessment, 34*(3), 211–229. https://doi.org/10.1177/0734282915592535

Allen, S. J., & Graden, J. L. (2002). Best practices in collaborative problem solving for intervention design. In A. Thomas & J. Grimes (Eds.), *Best practices in school psychology* (4th ed., pp. 565–582). National Association of School Psychologists.

Alsayedhassan, B. T., Banda, D. R., & Griffin-Shirley, N. (2020). Training parents of children with autism to implement the picture exchange communication intervention. *Clinical Archives of Communication Disorders, 5*(1), 31–41. https://doi.org/10.21849/cacd.2019.00171

Alzyoudi, M., Sartawi, A., & Almuhiri, O. (2015). The impact of video modelling on improving social skills in children with autism. *British Journal of Special Education, 42*, 53–68. https://doi.org/10.1111/1467-8578.12057

American Academy of Pediatrics. (2006). Identifying infants and young children with developmental disorders in the medical home: An algorithm for developmental surveillance and screening. *Pediatrics, 118*(1), 405–420. https://doi.org/10.1542/peds.2006-1231

American Association on Intellectual and Developmental Disabilities. (n.d.). *Definition of intellectual disability.* https://www.aaidd.org/intellectual-disability/definition

American Occupational Therapy Association. (2020). *What is the role of the school-based occupational therapy practitioner?* https://www.aota.org/~/media/Corporate/Files/Practice/Children/School-Administrator-Brochure.pdf

American Psychiatric Association. (1980). *Diagnostic and statistical manual of mental disorders* (3rd ed.). American Psychiatric Association.

American Psychiatric Association. (1994). *Diagnostic and statistical manual of mental disorders* (4th ed.). American Psychiatric Association.

American Psychiatric Association. (2013). *Diagnostic and statistical manual of mental disorders* (5th ed.). https://doi.org/10.1176/appi.books.9780890425596

American Psychiatric Association. (2018, August). *What is mental illness?* https://www.psychiatry.org/patients-families/what-is-mental-illness

American Psychological Association. (2005). Policy statement on evidence-based practice in psychology. http://www.apa.org/practice/resources/evidence/evidence-based-statement.pdf

American Psychological Association. (2017). *Ethical principles of psychologists and code of conduct* (2002, amended effective June 1, 2010, and January 1, 2017). http://www.apa.org/ethics/code/index.html

American Speech-Language-Hearing Association. (2005). *Evidence-based practice in communication disorders* (Position Statement). www.asha.org/policy

American Speech-Language-Hearing Association. (2010). *Scope of practice in speech-language pathology.* https://www.asha.org/policy/sp2016-00343/

Anderson, C. M., Rodriguez, B. J., & Campbell, A. (2015). Functional behavior assessment in schools: Current status and future directions. *Journal of Behavioral Education, 24*(3), 338–371. https://doi.org/10.1007/s10864-015-9226-z

Andrews, P., & Sayers, J. (2015). Identifying opportunities for grade one children to acquire foundational number sense: Developing a framework for cross cultural classroom analyses. *Early Childhood Education Journal, 43*(4), 257–267. https://doi.org/10.1007/s10643-014-0653-6

Arciuli, J., & Bailey, B. (2019). Efficacy of ABRACADABRA literacy instruction in a school setting for children with autism spectrum disorders. *Research in Developmental Disabilities, 85*, 104–115. https://doi.org/10.1016/j.ridd.2018.11.003

Arciuli, J., & Bailey, B. (2021). The promise of comprehensive early reading instruction for children with autism and recommendations for future directions. *Language, Speech &*

Hearing Services in Schools, 52(1), 225–238. https://doi.org/10.1044/2020_LSHSS-20-00019

Arias, V. B., Gómez, L. E., Morán, M. L., Alcedo, M. A., Monsalve, A., & Fontanil, Y. (2018). Does quality of life differ for children with autism spectrum disorder and intellectual disability compared to peers without autism? *Journal of Autism and Developmental Disorders, 48*(1), 123–136. https://doi.org/10.1007/s1080 3-017-3289-8

Artiles, A. J. (2003). Special education's changing identity: Paradoxes and dilemmas in views of culture and space. *Harvard Educational Review, 73*(2), 164–202. https://doi.org/10.17763/haer.73.2.j78t573x377j7106

Asperger, H. (1944). Die autistischen psychopathen im kindesalter. Springer.

Asselt-Goverts, A. E., Embregts, P. J. C. M., Hendricks, A. H. C., Wegman, K. M., & Teunisse, J. P. (2015). Do social networks differ? Comparison of the social networks of people with intellectual disabilities, people with autism spectrum disorders and other people living in the community. *Journal of Autism Developmental Disorders, 45*, 1191–1203. https://doi.org./10.1007/s10803-014-2279-3

Assouline, S. G., Foley Nicpon, M., & Dockery, L. (2012). Predicting the academic achievement of gifted students with autism spectrum disorder. *Journal of Autism Developmental Disorders, 42*, 1781–1789. https://doi.org/10.1007/s10803-011-1403-x

Attwood, T. (2003). Understanding and managing circumscribed interests. In M. Prior (Ed.), *Learning and behavior problems in Asperger syndrome* (pp. 126–147). Guilford Press.

Ayres, M., Parr, J. R., Rodgers, J., Mason, D., Avery, L., & Flynn, D. (2018). A systematic review of quality of life of adults on the autism spectrum. *Autism, 22*(7), 774–783. https://doi.org/10.1177/1362361317714988

Azad, G., & Mandell, D. S. (2016). Concerns of parents and teachers of children with autism in elementary school. *Autism, 20*(4), 435–441. https://doi.org/10.1177/136 2361315588199

Bacon, A. C., Dufek, S., Schreibman, L., Stahmer, A. C., Pierce, K., & Courchesne, E. (2014). Measuring outcome in an early intervention program for toddlers with autism spectrum disorder: Use of a curriculum-based assessment. *Autism Research and Treatment, 964704*, 1–9. https://doi.org/10.1155/2014/964704

Bae, Y. S., Chiang, H. M., & Hickson, L. (2015). Mathematical word problem solving ability of children with autism spectrum disorder and their typically developing peers. *Journal of Autism and Developmental Disorders, 45*, 2200–2208. https://doi.org/10.1007/s10803-015-2387-8

Baer, D. M., Wolf, M. M., & Risley, T. R. (1968). Some current dimensions of applied behavior analysis. *Journal of Applied Behavior Analysis, 1*(1), 91–97. https://doi.org/10.1901/jaba.1968.1-91

Bagatell, N. (2010). From cure to community: transforming notions of autism. *Journal of the Society for Psychological Anthropology, 38*(1), 33–55. https://doi.org/10.1111/j.1548-1352.2009.01080.x

Bagwell, C. L., Newcomb, A. F., & Bukowski, W. M. (1998). Preadolescent friendship and peer rejection as predictors of adult adjustment. *Child Development, 69*(1), 140–153. https://doi.org/10.1111/j.1467-8624.1998.tb06139.x

Baker, D. A., & Palmer, R. J. (2006). Examining the effects of perceptions of community and recreation participation on quality of life. *Social Indicators Research, 75*, 395–418. https://doi.org/10.1007/s11205-004-5298-1

Bal, V. H., Farmer, C., & Thurm, A. (2017). Describing function in ASD: Using the DSM-5 and other methods to improve precision. *Journal of Autism and Developmental Disorders, 47*(9), 2938–2941. https://doi.org/10.1007/s10803-017-3204-3

Baldwin, S., Costley, D., & Warren, A. (2014). Employment activities and experiences of adults with high-functioning autism and Asperger's disorder. *Journal of Autism and Developmental Disorders, 44*, 2440–2449. https://doi.org/10.1007/s/10803-014-2112-z

Barger, B., Rice, C., & Roach, A. (2021). Developmental screening and monitoring are associated with increased preschool special education receipt. *Journal of Child and Family Studies, 30*, 1342–1352. https://doi-org.pallas2.tcl.sc.edu/10.1007/s10826 -021-01940-4

Barger, B., Rice, C., Wolf, R., & Roach, A. (2018). Better together: Developmental screening and monitoring best identify children who need early intervention. *Disability and Health Journal, 11*(3), 420–426. https://doi.org/10.1016/j.dhjo.2018.01.002

Barnard-Brak, L. (2019). Educational versus clinical diagnoses of autism spectrum disorder: Updated and expanded findings. *School Psychology Review, 48*(2), 185–189. https://doi.org/10.17105/SPR-2018-0009.V48-2

Barnett, J., & Cleary, S. (2015). Review of evidence-based mathematics interventions for students with autism spectrum disorders. *Education and Training in Autism and Developmental Disabilities, 50*(2), 172–185. http://www.jstor.org/stable/24827533

Barnett, J. H., Trillo, R., & More, C. M. (2018). Visual supports to promote science discourse for middle and high school students with autism spectrum disorders. *Intervention School and Clinic, 53*(5), 292–299. https://doi.org/10.1177/1053451217736865

Baron-Cohen, S., & Wheelwright, S. (2003). The Friendship Questionnaire: An investigation of adults with Asperger syndrome or high-functioning autism and normal sex differences. *Journal of Autism and Developmental Disorders, 33*, 509–517. https://doi.org/10.1023/A:1025879411971

Baroody, A. J., Lai, M. L., & Mix, K. S. (2006). The development of young children's early number and operation sense and its implications for early childhood education. In B. Spodek & O. N. Saracho (Eds.), *Handbook of research on the education of young children* (pp. 187–221). Erlbaum.

Bassey, M. O. (2017). Culturally responsive teaching. *Education in Science, 6*(4), 1–6. https://doi.org/10.3390/educsci6040035

Bates, P. E., Cuvo, T., Miner, C. A., & Korabek, C. A. (2001). Simulated and community based instruction involving persons with mild and moderate mental retardation. *Research in Developmental Disabilities, 22*, 95–115. https://doi.org/10.1016/S0891 -4222(01)00060-9

Batty, G. D., Kivimäki, M., & Deary, I. J. (2010). Intelligence, education, and mortality. *British Medical Journal, 340*, c563. https://doi.org/10.1136/bmj.c563

Bauman, M. L. (2010). Medical comorbidities in autism: Challenges to diagnosis and treatment. *Neurotherapeutics, 7*(3), 320–327. https://doi.org/10.1016/j.nurt.2010.06.001

Baumgart, D., Brown, L., Pumpian, I., Nisbet, J., Ford, A., Sweet, M., Messina, R., & Schroeder, J. (1982). Principle of partial participation and individualized adaptations in educational programs for severely handicapped students. *Research and Practice for Persons with Severe Disabilities, 7*(2), 17–27. https://doi.org/10.1177/154079698200700211

Bauminger, N., & Schulman, C. (2003). The development and maintenance of friendship in high-functioning children with autism: Maternal perceptions. *Autism, 7*(1), 81–97. https://doi.org/10.1177/1362361303007001007

Bauminger, N., Solomon, N., Aviezer, A., Heung, K., Gazit, L., Brown, J., & Rogers, S. J. (2008). Children with autism and their friends: A multidimensional study of friendship in higher-functioning autism spectrum disorder. *Journal of Abnormal Child Psychology, 36*, 135–150. https://doi.org./10.1007/s10802-007-9156-x

Bayley, N. (2005). *Bayley Scales of Infant Development III*. Psychological Corporation.

Beaulieu, L., Addington, J., & Almeida, D. (2019). Behavior analysts' training and practices regarding cultural diversity: The case for culturally competent care. *Behavior Analysis in Practice, 12*(3), 557–575. https://doi.org/10.1007/s40617-018-00313-6

Beavers, G. A., Iwata, B. A., & Lerman, D. C. (2013). Thirty years of research on the functional analysis of problem behavior. *Journal of Applied Behavior Analysis, 46*(1), 1–21. https://doi.org/10.1002/jaba.30

Behavior Analyst Certification Board. (2017). *BCBA task list* (5th ed.). https://www.bacb.com/wp-content/uploads/2020/08/BCBA-task-list-5th-ed-210202.pdf

Behavior Analyst Certification Board. (2020). *Ethics code for behavior analysts*. https://www.bacb.com/ethics-information/ethics-codes/

Bekhet, A. K., Johnson, N. L., & Zauszniewski, J. A. (2012). Resilience in family members of persons with autism spectrum disorder: A review of the literature. *Issues in Mental Health Nursing, 33*(10), 650–656. https://doi.org/10.3109/01612840.2012.671441

Bellini, S., & Akullian, J. (2007). A meta-analysis of video-modeling and video self-modeling interventions for children and adolescents with autism spectrum disorders. *Exceptional Children, 73*(3), 264–287. https://doi.org/10.1177/001440290707300301

Benazzi, L., Horner, R. H., & Good, R. H. (2006). Effects of behavior support team composition on the technical adequacy and contextual fit of behavior support plans. *Journal of Special Education, 40*(3), 160–170. https://doi.org/10.1177/00224669060400030401

Benishek, L. E., Gregory, M., Hodges, K., Newell, M., Hughes, A. M., Marlow, S., Rosenfield, S., Salas, E., & Lacerenza, C. (2016). Bringing the science of team training to school-based teams. *Theory Into Practice, 55*(2), 112–119. https://doi.org/10.1080/00405841.2016.1148987

Berch, D. B., & Mazzocco, M. M. (2007). *Why is math so hard for some children?* Brookes.

Bergan, J. R. (1977). *Behavioral consultation*. Charles Merrill.

Bergan, J., & Kratochwill, T. R. (1990). *Behavioral consultation and therapy*. Plenum Press.

Bethune, K. S., & Wood, C. L. (2013). Effects of wh-question graphic organizers on reading comprehension skills of students with autism spectrum disorders. *Education & Training in Autism & Developmental Disabilities, 48*(2), 236–244. https://www.jstor.org/stable/23880642

Bettelheim, B. (1967). *The Empty fortress*. Simon & Schuster.

Bice-Urbach, B. J., & Kratochwill, T. R. (2016). Teleconsultation: The use of technology to improve evidence-based practices in rural communities. *Journal of School Psychology, 56*, 27–43. https://dx.doi.org/10.1016/j.jsp.2016.02.001

Biggs, E. E., & Carter, E. W. (2016). Quality of life for transition-age youth with autism or intellectual disability. *Journal of Autism and Developmental Disorders, 46*, 190–204. https://doi.org/10.1007/s10803-015-2563-x

Billstedt, E., Gillberg, I. C., & Gillberg, C. (2005). Autism after adolescence: Population-based 13- to 22-year follow-up study of 120 individuals with autism diagnosed in childhood. *Journal of Autism and Developmental Disorders, 35*(3), 351–360. https://doi.org/10.1007/s10803-005-3302-5

Bishop-Fitzpatrick, L., Hong, J., Smith, L. E., Makuch, R. A., Greenber, J. S., & Mailick, M. R. (2016). Characterizing objective quality of life and normative outcomes in adults with autism spectrum disorder: An exploratory latent class analysis. *Journal of Autism and Developmental Disorders, 46*(8), 2707–2719. https://doi.org/10.1007/s10803-016-2816-3

Bitterman, A., Daley, T., Misra, S., Carlson, E., & Markowitz, J. (2008). A national sample of preschoolers with autism spectrum disorders: Special education services and parent satisfaction. *Journal of Autism and Developmental Disorders, 38*(8), 1509–1517. https://doi.org/10.1007/s10803-007-0531-9

Blacher, J., Howell, E., Lauderdale-Littin, S., DiGennaro Reed, F. D., & Laugeson, E. A. (2014). Autism spectrum disorder and the student teacher relationship: A comparison study with peers with intellectual disability and typical development. *Research in Autism Spectrum Disorders, 8*(3), 324–333. https://doi.org/10.1016/j.rasd.2013.12.008

Blair, C., & Razza, R. P. (2007). Relating effortful control, executive function, and false belief understanding to emerging math and literacy ability in kindergarten. *Child Development, 78*(2), 647–663. https://doi.org/10.1111/j.1467-8624.2007.01019.x

Blanchett, W. J., Klingner, J. K., & Harry, B. (2009). The intersection of race, culture, language, and disability implications for urban education. *Urban Education, 44*(4), 389–409. https://doi.org/10.1177/0042085909338686

Blankenship, A. M., Houston, P. D., & Cole, R. W. (2010). *Data-enhanced leadership*. Corwin Press.

Blaska, J. (1993). The power of language: speak and write using "person first." In M. Nagler (Ed.), *Perspectives on Disability*. Health Markets Research.

Bledsoe, R., Smith, B., & Simpson, R. L. (2003). Use of a social story intervention to improve mealtime skills of an adolescent with Asperger syndrome. *Autism, 7*(3), 289–295. https://doi.org/10.1177%2F1362361303007003005

Blue-Banning, M., Summers, J. A., Frankland, H. C., Nelson, L. L., & Beegle, G. (2004). Dimensions of family and professional partnerships: Constructive guidelines for collaboration. *Exceptional Children, 70*(2), 167–184. https://doi.org/10.1177/001440290407000203

Boisvert, M., & Hall, N. (2014). The use of telehealth in early autism training for parents: A scoping review. *Smart Homecare Technology and Telehealth, 2*, 19–27. https://doi.org/10.2147/SHTT.S45353

Bollman, K. A., Silberglitt, B., & Gibbons, K. A. (2007). The St. Croix River Education District model: Incorporating systems-level organization and a multi-tiered problem-solving process for intervention delivery. In S. R. Jimerson, M. K. Burns, & A. M. VanDerHeyden (Eds.), *Handbook of response to intervention: The science and practice of assessment and intervention* (pp. 319–330). Springer.

Bölte, S., Girdler, S., & Marschik, P. B. (2019). The contribution of environmental exposure to the etiology of autism spectrum disorder. *Cellular and Molecular Life Sciences, 76*(7), 1275–1297. https://doi.org/10.1007/s00018-018-2988-4

Bondy, A., & Frost, L. (2001). The picture exchange communication system. *Behavior Modification, 25*(5), 725–744. https://doi.org/10.1177/0145445501255004

Botha, M., Hanlon, J., & Williams, G. L. (2021). Does language matter? Identity-first versus person-first language use in autism research: A response to Vivanti. *Journal of Autism and Developmental Disorders*. Advance online publication. https://doi.org/10.1007/s10803-020-04858-w

Boudett, K. P., City, E. A., & Murnane, R. J. (2006a). The "data wise" improvement process. *Harvard Education Letter, 22*(1), 1–3.

Boudett, K. P., City, E. A., & Murnane, R. J. (2006b). *Data wise: A step-by-step guide to using assessment results to improve teaching and learning*. Harvard Education Press.

Boudett, K. P., & Steele, J. L. (2007). *Data wise in action: Stories of schools using data to improve teaching and learning*. Harvard Education Press.

Bourque, K. S., & Goldstein, H. (2020). Expanding communication modalities and functions for preschoolers with autism spectrum disorder: Secondary analysis of a peer partner speech-generating device intervention. *Journal of Speech, Language, and Hearing Research, 63*(1), 190–205. https://doi.org/10.1044/2019_JSLHR-19-00202

Bradshaw, C. P., Mitchell, M. M., & Leaf, P. J. (2010). Examining the effects of schoolwide positive behavioral interventions and supports on student outcomes: Results from a randomized controlled effectiveness trial in elementary schools. *Journal of Positive Behavior Interventions, 12*(3), 133–148. https://doi.org/10.1177/1098300709334798

Bransford, J. D., & Stein, B. S. (1993). *The IDEAL problem solver: A guide for improving thinking, learning, and creativity* (2nd ed.). W. H. Freeman.

Bridges, D. R., Davidson, R. A., Odegard, P. S., Maki, I. V., & Tomkowiak, J. (2011). Inter-professional collaboration: Three best practice models of interprofessional education. *Medical Education Online, 16*(1), 1–10. https://doi.org/10.3402/meo.v16i0.6035

Brock, M. E., & Carter, E. W. (2013). A systematic review of paraprofessional delivered educational practices to improve outcomes for students with intellectual and developmental disabilities. *Research & Practice for Persons with Severe Disabilities, 38*(4), 211–221. https//doi.org/10.1177/154079691303800401

Brodhead, M. T., Cox, D. J., & Quigley, S. P. (2018). *Practical ethics for effective treatment of autism spectrum disorder.* Academic Press.

Bronfenbrenner, U. (1979). *The ecology of human development: Experiments in nature and design.* Harvard University Press.

Bronfenbrenner, U. (1986). Ecology of the family as a context for human development: Research perspectives. *Developmental Psychology, 22*(6), 723–742. https://doi.org/10.1037/0012-1649.22.6.723

Browder, D., Karvonen, M., Davis, S., Fallin, K., & Courtade-Little, G. (2005). The impact of teacher training on state alternate assessment scores. *Exceptional Children, 71,* 267–282. https://doi.org/10.1177/001440290507100304

Browder, D. M., Root, J. R., Wood, L., & Allison, C. (2015). Conducting and using student assessment. In F. Brown, J. Mcdonnell, & M. Snell (Eds.), *Instruction of students with severe disabilities* (8th ed.) Pearson.

Browder, D. M., Root, J. R., Wood, L., & Allison, C. (2017). Effects of a story-mapping procedure using the iPad on the comprehension of narrative texts by students with autism spectrum disorders. *Focus on Autism and Developmental Disabilities, 32*(4), 243–255. https://doi.org/10.1177/1088357615611387

Browder, D. M., Spooner, F., & Jimenez, B. (2011). Standards-based individualized education plans and progress monitoring. In D. M. Browder & F. Spooner (Eds.), *Teaching students with moderate and severe disabilities* (pp. 42–91). Guilford Press.

Browder, D. M., Wood, L., Thompson, J., & Ribuffo, C. (2014). Evidence-based practices for students with severe disabilities (Document No. IC-3). University of Florida, Collaboration for Effective Educator, Development, Accountability, and Reform Center. https://ceedar.education.ufl.edu/tools/innovation-configurations/

Brown, F., Lehr, D., & Snell, M. E. (2011). Ecological inventories. In M. E. Snell and F. Brown (Eds.), *Instruction of students with severe disabilities* (pp. 93–102). Pearson.

Brown, F., McDonnell, J., & Snell, M. E. (Eds.). (2019). *Instruction of students with severe disabilities.* Pearson.

Brown, F. E., McDonnell, J., & Snell, M. E. (Eds.). (2020). *Instruction of students with severe disabilities* (9th ed.). Pearson.

Brown, H. M., Oram-Cardy, J., & Johnson, A. A. (2013). Meta-analysis of the reading comprehension skills of individuals on the autism spectrum. *Journal of Autism Developmental and Disorders, 43,* 932–955. https://doi.org/10.1007/s10803-012-1638-1

Brown, L., McLean, M. B., Nietupski, S. H., Pumpian, I., Certo, N., & Gruenewald, L. (1979). A strategy for developing chronologically age appropriate and functional curricular content for adolescents and young adults with significant disabilities. *Journal of Special Education, 13*(1), 81–90. https://doi.org/10.1177%2F002246697901300113

Brown, L., Nisbet, J., Ford, A., Sweet, M., Shiraga, B., York, J., & Loomis, R. (1983). The critical need for nonschool instruction in educational programs for severely handicapped students. *Research and Practice for Persons with Severe Disabilities, 8*(3), 71–77. https://doi.org/10.1177%2F154079698300800309

Brown, R. I., & Brown, I. (2005). The application of quality of life. *Journal of Intellectual Disability Research, 49*(10), 718–727. https://doi.org/10.1111/j.1365-2788.2005.00740.x

Bruder, M. B. (2010). Early childhood intervention: A promise to children and families for their future. *Exceptional Children, 76*(3), 339–355. https://doi.org/10.1177/001440291007600306

Bruhn, A. L., Wehby, J. H., & Hasselbring, T. S. (2020). Data-based decision making for social behavior: Setting a research agenda. *Journal of Positive Behavior Interventions, 22*(2), 116–126. https://doi.org/10.1177/1098300719876098

Burgess, A. F., & Gutstein, S. E. (2007). Quality of life for people with autism: Raising the standard for evaluating successful outcomes. *Child and Adolescent Mental Health, 12*(2), 80–85. https://doi.org/10.1111/j.1475-3588.2006.00432.x

Burgess, K. B., Wojslawowicz, J. C., Rubin, K. H., Rose-Krasnor, L., & Booth-LaForce, C. (2006). Social information processing and coping strategies of shy/withdrawn and aggressive children: Does friendship matter? *Child Development, 77*(2), 371–383. https://doi.org/10.1111/j.1467-8624.2006.00876.x

Burke, M. M. (2013). Improving parental involvement: Training special education advocates. *Journal of Disability Policy Studies, 23*, 225–234. https://doi.org/10.1177/1044207311424910

Burke, M. M., & Goldman, S. E. (2018). Special education advocacy among culturally and linguistically diverse families. *Journal of Research in Special Educational Needs, 18*, 3–14. https://doi.org/10.1111/1471-3802.12413

Burke, M. M., & Hodapp, R. M. (2014). Relating stress of mothers of children with developmental disabilities to family-school partnerships. *Intellectual and Developmental Disabilities, 52*, 13–23. https://doi.org/10.1352/1934-9556-52.1.13

Burns, M. K., & Symington, T. (2002). A meta-analysis of pre-referral intervention teams: Student and systemic outcomes. *Journal of School Psychology, 40*(5), 437–447. https://doi.org/10.1016/S0022-4405(02)00106-1

Burns, M. K., VanDerHeyden, A. M., & Boice, C. H. (2008). Best practices in delivery intensive academic interventions. In A. Thomas & J. Grimes (Eds.), *Best practices in school psychology* (5th ed., pp. 1151–1162). National Association of School Psychologists.

Burns, M. K., Vanderwood, M., & Ruby, S. (2005). Evaluating the readiness of prereferral intervention teams for use in a problem-solving model: Review of three levels of research. *School Psychology Quarterly, 20*(1), 89–105. https://doi.org/10.1521/scpq.20.1.89.64192

Burrell, T. L., & Borrego, J., Jr. (2012). Parents' involvement in ASD treatment: What is their role? *Cognitive and Behavioral Practice, 19*(3), 423–432. https://doi.org/10.1016/j.cbpra.2011.04.003

Bury, S. M., Jellett, R., Spoor, J. R., & Hedley, D. (2020). "It defines who I am" or "It's something I have": What language do [autistic] Australian adults [on the Autism Spectrum] prefer? *Journal of Autism and Developmental Disorders*. Advance online publication. https://doi.org/10.1007/s10803-020-04425-3

Cain, K., & Barnes, M. A. (2017). Reading comprehension. In K. Cain, D. L. Compton, & R. K. Parrila (Eds.), *Theories of reading development* (pp. 257–280). John Benjamins Publishing.

Cain, M. K., Kaboski, J. R., & Gilger, J. W. (2019). Profiles and academic trajectories of cognitively gifted children with autism spectrum disorder. *Autism, 23*(7), 1663–1674. https://doi.org/10.1177/1362361318804019

Calzada, E. J., Huang, K. Y., Hernandez, M., Soriano, E., Acra, C. F., Dawson-McClure, S., Kamboukos, D., & Brotman, L. (2015). Family and teacher characteristics as predictors of parent involvement in education during early childhood among Afro-Caribbean and Latino immigrant families. *Urban Education, 50*(7), 870–896. https://doi.org/10.1177/0042085914534862

Campbell, M. L., & Kozloff, M. (2007). Comprehensive training programs for families of children with autism. In J. M. Briesmeister & C. E. Schaefer (Eds.), *Handbook of parent training: Helping parents prevent and solve problem behaviors* (3rd ed., pp. 67–106). Wiley.

Capizzi, A. M., & Alexandra Da Fonte, M. (2012). Supporting paraeducators through a collaborative classroom support plan. *Focus on Exceptional Children, 44*(6), 1–16. https://doi.org/10.17161/fec.v44i6.6685

Capps, L., Kehres, J., & Sigman, M. (1998). Conversational abilities among children with autism and children with developmental delays. *Autism, 2*(4), 325–344. https://doi.org/10.1177/1362361398024002

Carnett, A., Neely, L., Hong, E. R., & Escobar, J. (2019). Choosing a response topography for individuals with autism during functional communication training: A critically appraised topic. *Evidence Based Communication Assessment and Intervention, 13*(1–2), 85–105. https://doi.org/10.1080/17489539.2019.1602298

Carnett, A., Raulston, T., Lang, R., Tostanoski, A., Lee, A., Sigafoos, J. & Machalicek, W. (2014). Effects of a perseverative interest-based token economy on challenging and on-task behavior in a child with autism. *Journal of Behavioral Education, 23*, 368–377. https://doi.org/10.1007/s10864-014-9195-7

Carnett, A., Waddington, H., Hansen, S., Bravo, A., Sigafoos, J., & Lang, R. (2017). Teaching mands to children with autism spectrum disorder using behavior chain interruption strategies: A systematic review. *Advances in Neurodevelopmental Disorders, 1*(4), 203–220. https://doi.org/10.1007/s41252-017-0038-0

Carr, E. G., & Durand, V. M. (1985). Reducing behavior problems through functional communication training. *Journal of Applied Behavior Analysis, 18*(2), 111–126. https://doi.org/10.1901/jaba.1985.18-111

Carr, J. E., Nicolson, A. C., & Higbee, T. S. (2000). Evaluation of a brief multiple-stimulus preference assessment in a naturalistic context. *Journal of Applied Behavior Analysis, 33*(3), 353–357. https://doi.org/10.1901/jaba.2000.33-353

Carroll, J. S., & Johnson, E. (1990). *Decision research: A field guide.* Sage.

Carter, E. W., Common, E. A., Sreckovic, M. A., Huber, H. B., Bottema-Beutel, K., Gustafson, J. R., Dykstra, J., & Hume, K. (2014). Promoting social competence and peer relationships for adolescents with autism spectrum disorders. *Remedial and Special Education, 35*(2), 91–101. https://doi.doi/10.1177/0741932513514618

Carter, E. W., O'Rourke, L., Sisco, L. G., & Pelsue, D. (2009). Knowledge, responsibilities, and training needs of paraprofessionals in elementary and secondary schools. *Remedial and Special Education, 30*(6), 344–359. https://doi.org/10.1177/0741932508324399

Carter, E. W., Owens, L., Trainor, A. A., Sun, Y., & Swedeen, B. (2009). Self-determination skills and opportunities of adolescents with severe intellectual and developmental disabilities. *American Journal on Intellectual and Developmental Disabilities, 114*, 179–192. https://doi.org/doi:10.1352/1944-7558-114.3.179

Cascio, M. A., Weiss, J. A., & Racine, E. (2021). Making autism research inclusive by attending to intersectionality: A review of the research ethics literature. *Review Journal of Autism and Developmental Disorders, 8*(1), 22–36. https://doi.org/10.1007/s40489-020-00204-z

Cassella, M. D., Sidener, T. M., Sidener, D. W., & Progar, P. R. (2011). Response interruption and redirection for vocal stereotypy in children with autism: A systematic replication. *Journal of Applied Behavior Analysis, 44*(1), 169–173. https://doi.org/10.1901/jaba.2011.44-169

Catts, H. W. (2018). The simple view of reading: Advancements and false impressions. *Remedial and Special Education, 39*(5), 317–323. https://doi.org/10.1177/0741932518767563

Catts, H. W., Compton, D., Tomblin, J. B., & Bridges, M. S. (2012). Prevalence and nature of late-emerging poor readers. *Journal of Educational Psychology, 104*(1), 166–181. https://doi.org/10.1037/A0025323

Catts, H. W., Hogan, T. P., & Adlof, S. M. (2005). Developmental changes in reading and reading disabilities. In H. W. Catts & A. G. Kamhi (Eds.), *The connections between language and reading disabilities* (pp. 25–40). Erlbaum.

Catts, H. W., & Kamhi, A. G. (2017). Prologue: Reading comprehension is not a single ability. *Language, Speech, and Hearing Services in Schools, 48*(2), 73–76. https://doi.org/10.1044/2017_LSHSS-16-0033

Cederlund, M., Hagberg, B., Billstedt, E., Gilberg, I. C., & Gilberg, C. (2008). Asperger syndrome and autism: A comparative longitudinal follow-up study more than five years after the original diagnosis. *Journal of Autism and Developmental Disorders, 38*, 72–85. https://doi.org/10.1007/s10803-007-0364-6

Cengher, M., Budd, A., Farrell, N., & Fienup, D. M. (2018). A review of prompt-fading procedures: Implications for effective and efficient skill acquisition. *Journal of Developmental and Physical Disabilities, 30*(2), 155–173. https://doi.org/10.1007/s10882-017-9575-8

Centers for Disease Control and Prevention Autism and Developmental Disabilities Monitoring Network (2018). *Community Report on Autism, Spotlight On: Delay Between First Concern to Accessing Services.* https://www.cdc.gov/ncbddd/autism/addm-community-report/documents/addm-community-report-2018-h.pdf

Centers for Disease Control and Prevention (2020, October 4). *Identifying autism among children: An easy-read summary.* https://www.cdc.gov/ncbddd/autism/addm-community-report/an-easy-read-summary.html

Cermak, S. A., Curtin, C., & Bandini, L. G. (2010). Food selectivity and sensory sensitivity in children with autism spectrum disorders. *Journal of the American Dietetic Association, 110*(2), 238–246. https://doi.org/10.1016/j.jada.2009.10.032

Cervantes, P. E., & Matson, J. L. (2015). Comorbid symptomology in adults with autism spectrum disorder and intellectual disability. *Journal of Autism and Developmental Disorders, 45*(12), 3961–3970. https://doi.org/10.1007/s10803-015-2553-z

Chaidez, V., Hansen, R. L., & Hertz-Picciotto, I. (2014). Gastrointestinal problems in children with autism, developmental delays or typical development. *Journal of Autism and Developmental Disorders, 44*(5), 1117–1127. https://doi.org/10.1007/s10803-013-1973-x

Chalfant, J. C., & Pysh, M. V. (1989). Teacher assistance teams: Five descriptive studies on 96 teams. *Remedial and Special Education, 10*(6), 49–59. https://doi.org/10.1177/074193258901000608

Charman, T., Jones, C., Pickles, A., Simonoff, E., Baird, G., & Happe, F. (2011). Defining the cognitive phenotype of autism. *Brain Research, 1380*, 1021. https://doi.org/10.1016/j.brainres.2010.10.075

Cheack-Zamora, N. C., Maurer-Batjer, A., Malow, B. A., & Coleman, A. (2020). Self-determination in young adults with autism spectrum disorder. *Autism, 24*(3), 605–616. https://doi.org/10.1177/1362361319877329

Cheek, A. E., Rock, M. L., & Jimenez, B. A. (2019). Online module plus eCoaching: The effects on special education teachers' comprehension instruction for students with significant intellectual disability. *Education and Training in Autism and Developmental Disabilities, 54*(4), 343–357.

Chenoweth, K. (2010). Leaving nothing to chance. *Educational Leadership, 68*(3), 16–21.

Chesnut, S. R., Wei, T., Barnard-Brak, L., & Richman, D. M. (2017). A meta-analysis of the social communication questionnaire: Screening for autism spectrum disorder. *Autism, 21*(8), 920–928. https://www.doi.org/10.1177/1362361316660065

Cheung, Y., Lai, C. Y., Cihon, J. H., Leaf, J. B., & Montjoy, T. (2020). Establishing requesting with children diagnosed with autism using embedded instruction in the context of academic activities. *Journal of Behavioral Education*. Advance online publication. https://doi.org/10.1007/s10864-020-09397-z

Chezan, L. C., Drasgow, E., & Grybos, M. E. (2020). Conversation skills and self-initiated interactions in young adults with autism and intellectual disability. *Research in Autism Spectrum Disorders, 75*, 1–12. https://doi.org/10.1016/j.rasd.2020.101554

Chezan, L. C., Liu, J., Cholewicki, J. M., Drasgow, E., Ding, R., & Warman, A. (2022). A psychometric evaluation of the Quality of Life for Children with Autism Spectrum Disorder scale. *Journal of Autism and Developmental Disorders 52*, 1536–1552.

Chezan, L. C., Wolfe, K., & Drasgow, E. (2018). A meta-analysis of functional communication training effects on problem behavior and alternative communicative responses. *Focus on Autism and Other Developmental Disabilities, 33*(4), 195–205. https://doi.org/10.1177/1088357617741294

Chiang, H., Cheung, Y. K., Li, H., & Tsai, L. Y. (2013). Factors associated with participation in employment for high school leavers with autism. *Journal of Autism and Developmental Disorders, 43*, 1832–1842. https://doi.org/10.1007/s10803-012-1732-2

Chiang, H. M., & Lin, Y. H. (2007). Reading comprehension instruction for students with autism spectrum disorders: A review of the literature. *Focus on Autism and Other Developmental Disabilities, 22*(4), 259–267. https://doi.org/10.1177/10883576070220040801

Chiang, H., & Wineman, I. (2014). Factors associated with quality of life in individuals with autism spectrum disorders: A review of literature. *Research in Autism Spectrum Disorders, 8*(8), 974–986. https://doi.org/10.1016/j.rasd.2014.05.003

Chistol, L. T., Bandini, L. G., Must, A., Phillips, S., Cermak, S. A., & Curtin, C. (2018). Sensory sensitivity and food selectivity in children with autism spectrum disorder. *Journal of Autism and Developmental Disorders, 48*(2), 583–591. https://doi.org/10.1007/s10803-017-3340-9

Chiu, Y. D. (2018). The simple view of reading across development: Prediction of grade 3 reading comprehension rom prekindergarten skills. *Remedial and Special Education, 39*(5), 289–303. https://doi.org/10.1177/0741932518762055

Chlebowski, C., Green, J. A., Barton, M. L., & Fein, D. (2010). Using the Childhood Autism Rating Scale to diagnose autism spectrum disorders. *Journal of Autism and Developmental Disorders, 40*(7), 787–799. https://doi.org/10.1007/s10803-009-0926-x

Cholewicki, J., Drasgow, E., & Chezan, L. C. (2019). Parental perception of quality of life for children with autism spectrum disorder. *Journal of Developmental and Physical Disabilities, 31*, 575–592. https://doi.org/10.1007/s10882-019-09660-w

Chou, Y. C., Wehmeyer, M. L., Shogren, K. A., Palmer, S. B., & Lee, J. (2017). Autism and self-determination: Factor analysis of two measures of self-determination. *Focus on Autism and Other Developmental Disabilities, 32*(3), 163–175. https://doi.org/10.1177/1088357615611391

Christenson, D. L., Braun, K. V. N., Baio, J., Bilder, D., Charles, J., Constantino, J. N., Daniels, J., Durkin, M. S., Fitzgerald, R. T., Kurzius-Spencer, M., Lee, L., Pettygrove, S., Robinson, C., Schulz, E., Wells, C., Wingate, M. S., Zahorodny, W., & Yeargin-Allsopp, M. (2016). Prevalence and characteristics of autism spectrum disorder among children aged 8 years. *Morbidity and Mortality Weekly Report: Surveillance Summaries, 65*(3), 1–23. https://doi.org/10.15585/mmwr.ss6503a1

Chung, M. Y., & Meadan, H. (2021). Caregiver involvement in early intervention services: Service providers' perspectives. *Inclusion, 9*(1), 31–45. https://doi.org/10.1352/2326-6988-9.1.31

Cihak, D. F., Moore, E. J., Wright, R. E., McMahon, D. D., Gibbons, M. M., & Smith, C. (2016). Evaluating augmented reality to complete a chain task for elementary students with autism. *Journal of Special Education Technology, 31*(2), 99–108. https://doi.org/10.1177/0162643416651724

Cihon, J. H., Ferguson, J. L., Milne, C. M., Leaf, J. B., McEachin, J., & Leaf, R. (2019). A preliminary evaluation of a token system with a flexible earning requirement. *Behavior Analysis in Practice, 12*, 548–556. https://doi.org/10.1007/s40617-018-00316-3

Cipani, E. (1990). "Excuse me: I'll have . . .": Teaching appropriate attention-getting behavior to young children with severe handicaps. *Mental Retardation, 28*(1), 29–33.

Cirelli, L. K., & Trehub, S. E. (2020). Familiar songs reduce infant distress. *Developmental Psychology, 56*(5), 861–868. https://doi.org/10.1037/dev0000917

Claes, C., Van Hove, G., van Loon, J., Vandevelde, S., & Schalock, R. L. (2010). Quality of life measurement in the field of intellectual disabilities: Eight principles for assessing quality of life-related personal outcomes. *Social Indicators Research, 98*, 61–72. https://doi.org/10.1007/s11205-009-9517-7

Clark, C. A. C., Pritchard, V. E., & Woodward, L. J. (2010). Preschool executive functioning abilities predict early mathematics achievement. *Developmental Psychology, 46*(5), 1176–1191. https://doi.org/10.1037/a0019672

Clements, D. H. (1999). Subitizing: What is it? Why teach it? *Teaching Children Mathematics, 5*(7), 400–405.

Clements, D., & Sarama, J. (2015). Discussion from a mathematics education perspective. *Mathematical Thinking & Learning, 17*(2/3), 244.

Cloutier, H., Malloy, J., Hagner, D., & Cotton, P. (2006). Choice and control over resources: New Hampshire's individual career account demonstration projects. *Journal of Rehabilitation, 72*(2), 4–11.

Coburn, C. E., & Turner, E. O. (2012). The practice of data use: An introduction. *American Journal of Education, 118*(2), 99–111. https://doi.org/10.1086/663272

Cohen, S. (1998). *Targeting autism: What we know, don't know, and can do to help young children with autism and related disorders.* University of California Press.

Čolić, M., Araiba, S., Lovelace, T. S., & Dababnah, S. (2021, January 28). Black caregivers' perspectives on racism in ASD services: Towards culturally responsive ABA practice. https://doi.org/10.31234/osf.io/rp9am

Collier, M., Griffin, M. M., & Wei, Y. (2017). Learning from students about transition needs: Identifying gaps in knowledge and experience. *Journal of Vocational Rehabilitation, 46*(1), 1–10. https://doi.org/10.3233/JVR-160837

Collins, B. C. (2012). *Systematic instruction for students with moderate and severe disabilities.* Brookes.

Conroy, M. A., Asmus, J. M., Boyd, B. A., Ladwig, C. N., & Sellers, J. A. (2007). Antecedent classroom factors and disruptive behaviors of children with autism spectrum disorders. *Journal of Early Intervention, 30*(1), 19–35. https://doi.org/10.1177/105381510703000103

Conroy, M. A., Sutherland, K. S., Algina, J. J., Wilson, R. E., Martinez, J. R., & Whalon, K. J. (2015). Measuring teacher implementation of the BEST in CLASS intervention program and corollary child outcomes. *Journal of Emotional and Behavioral Disorders, 23*(3), 144–155. https://doi.org/10.1177/1063426614532949

Cook, B. G., & Cook, S. C. (2013). Unraveling evidence-based practices in special education. *Journal of Special Education, 47*(2), 71–82. https://doi.org/10.1177/0022466911420877

Cook, C. R., Mayer, G. R., Wright, D. B., Kraemer, B., Wallace, M. D., Dart, E., Collins, T., & Restori, A. (2012). Exploring the link among behavior intervention plans, treatment integrity, and student outcomes under natural educational conditions. *Journal of Special Education, 46*(1), 3–16. https://doi.org/10.1177/0022466910369941

Cooper, J. O., Heron, T. E., & Heward, W. L. (2020). *Applied Behavior Analysis* (3rd ed.). Pearson Education.

Cooper, L. J., Wacker, D. P., Sasso, G. M., Reimers, T. M., & Donn, L. K. (1990). Using parents as therapists to evaluate appropriate behavior of their children: Application to a tertiary diagnostic clinic. *Journal of Applied Behavior Analysis, 23*(3), 285–296. https://doi.org/10.1901/jaba.1990.23-285

Copeland, S. R., & McDonnell, J. (2020). Teaching academic skills. In M. S. Snell & F. Brown (Eds.), *Instruction of students with severe disabilities* (9th ed., pp. 452–490). Pearson.

Cordray, D. S., & Pion, G. M. (2006). Treatment strength and integrity: Models and methods. In R. R. Bootzin & P. E. McKnight (Eds.), *Strengthening research methodology: Psychological measurement and evaluation* (pp. 103–124). American Psychological Association.

Costello, E. J., Mustillo, S., Keeler, G., & Angold, A. (2004). Prevalence of psychiatric disorders in childhood and adolescence. In B. L. Levin, J. Petrila, & K. D. Hennessy (Eds.), *Mental health services: A public health perspective* (pp. 111–128). Oxford University Press.

Council for Exceptional Children. (2010). *Special education professional ethical principles.* https://exceptionalchildren.org/standards/ethical-principles-and-practice-standards

Council for Exceptional Children. (2014). Council for Exceptional Children: Standards for Evidence-Based Practices in Special Education. *Teaching Exceptional Children, 80*(4), 504–511. https://doi.org/10.1177/0040059914531389

Council for Exceptional Children. (2015). *What every special educator must know: Professional ethics and standards.* CEC.

Council for Exceptional Children. (2020, August 14). *K–12 initial standards and components.* https://exceptionalchildren.org/sites/default/files/2021-03/K12%20Initial%20Standards%20and%20Components.pdf

Courchesne, E. (2004). Brain development in autism: Early overgrowth followed by premature arrest of growth. *Mental Retardation and Developmental Disabilities Research Reviews, 10*(2), 106–111. https://doi.org/10.1002/mrdd.20020

Courchesne, E., Carper, R., & Akshoomoff, N. (2003). Evidence of brain overgrowth in the first year of life in autism. *Journal of the American Medical Association, 290*(3), 337–344. https://doi.org/10.1001/jama.290.3.337

Courtade, G., & Browder, D. (2016). *Aligning IEPs to state standards for students with moderate-to-severe disabilities.* Attainment.

Covey, S. R. (1991). *The seven habits of highly effective people.* Covey Leadership Center.

Cowan, R., & Powell, D. (2014). The contributions of domain-general and numerical factors to third-grade arithmetic skills and mathematical learning disability. *Journal of Educational Psychology, 106*(1), 214–229. https://doi.org/10.1037/a0034097

Cox, S. C., Root, J. R., & McConomy, A. M. (2020). Using data to design and evaluate math instruction. In E. C. Bouck, J. R. Root, & B. A. Jimenez (Eds), *Mathematics education for students with autism, intellectual disability, and other developmental disabilities* (pp. 30–75). Division on Autism and Developmental Disabilities.

Coy, J. N., & Kostewicz, D. E. (2020). Noncontingent reinforcement: Enriching the classroom environment to reduce problem behaviors. *Exceptional Children, 50*(5), 301–309. https://doi.org/10.1177/0040059918765460

Crais, E. R., & Roberts, J. E. (2004). Assessing communication skills. In M. McLean, M. Wolery, & D. B. Bailey Jr. (Eds.), *Assessing infants and preschoolers with special needs* (3rd ed., pp. 345–411). Pearson.

Crane, K., & Mooney, M. (2005). Essential tools: Community resource mapping. University of Minnesota, National Center on Secondary Education and Transition. http://project10.info/files/CommunityResourceMapping.Preview.pdf

Crenshaw, K. (1989). Demarginalizing the intersection of race and sex: A black feminist critique of antidiscrimination doctrine. *University of Chicago Legal Forum, 1989* (1), 139–168. https://chicagounbound.uchicago.edu/cgi/viewcontent.cgi?article=1052 &context=uclf

Crimmins, D. B., Durand, V. M., Theuer-Kaufman, K., & Everett, J. (2001). Autism program quality indicators: A self-review and quality improvement guide for schools and programs servicing students with autism spectrum disorders. Office of Vocational and Special Education Services for Individuals with Disabilities, New York State Education Department. https://files.eric.ed.gov/fulltext/ED458767.pdf

Croen, L. A., Zerbo, O., Qian, Y., Massolo, M. L., Rich, S., Sidney, S., & Kripke, C. (2015). The health status of adults on the autism spectrum. *Autism, 19*(7), 814–823. https:// doi.org/ 10.1177/1362361315577517

Cronin, K. (2014). The relationship among oral language, decoding skills, and reading comprehension in children with autism. *Exceptionality, 22*(3), 141–157. https://doi .org/10.1080/09362835.2013.865531

Cummins, D. D., Kintsch, W., Reusser, K., & Weimer, R. (1988). The role of understanding in solving word problems. *Cognitive Psychology, 20*(4), 405–438. https://doi .org/10.1016/0010-0285(88)90011-4

Cummings, R. A. (1997). Assessing quality of life. In R. I. Brown (Ed.), *Assessing quality of life for people with disabilities: Models, research, and practice* (pp. 116–150). Stanley Thornes.

Curtiss, S. L., Lee, G. K., Chun, J., Lee, H., Kuo, H. J., & Ami-Narh, D. (2020). Autistic young adults', parents', and practitioners' expectations of the transition to adulthood. *Career Development and Transition for Exceptional Individuals, 44*(3), 174–185. https://doi.org/10.1177/2165143420967662

Curtiss, S., Pearson, N. J., Akamoglu, Y., Fisher, K. W., Snodgrass, M. R., Meyer, L. E., Meadan, H., & Halle, J. W. (2016). Bringing instructional strategies home: Reaching families online. *TEACHING Exceptional Children, 48*(3), 159–167. https://doi .org/10.1177/0040059915605816

Cushing, L. S., Carter, E. W., Clark, N., Wallis, T., & Kennedy, C. H. (2009). Evaluating inclusive educational practices for students with severe disabilities using the Program Quality Measurement Tool. *Journal of Special Education, 42*(4), 195–208. https://doi .org/10.1177%2F0022466907313352

Dale, B. A., Finch, W. H., Shellabarger, K. A., & Davis, A. (2021). Wechsler Intelligence Scale for Children, Fifth Edition profiles of children with autism spectrum disorders using a classification and regression tree analysis. *Journal of Psychoeducational Assessment, 39*(7), 1–17. https://doi.org/10.1177/07342829211025924

Dales, L., Hammer, S. J., & Smith, N. J. (2001). Time trends in autism and in MMR immunization coverage in California. *Journal of the American Medical Association, 285*(9), 1183–1185. https://doi.org/10.1001/jama.285.9.1183

Dardas, L. A., & Ahmad, M. M. (2014). Validation of the World Health Organization's quality of life questionnaire with parents of children with autistic disorder. *Journal of Autism and Developmental Disorders, 44*, 2257–2263. https://doi.org/10.1007 /s10803-014-2110-1

Davenport, C. A., Alber-Morgan, S. R., & Konrad, M. (2019). Effects of behavioral skills training on teacher implementation of a reading racetrack intervention. *Education and Treatment of Children, 42*(3), 385–408. https://dx.doi.org/10.1353%2Fetc.2019.0018

Davidson, J., & Henderson, V. L. (2010). "Coming out" on the spectrum: Autism, identity, and disclosure. *Social & Cultural Geography, 11*(2), 155–170. https://doi .org/10.1080/14649360903525240

Davignon, M. N., Qian, Y., Massolo, M., & Croen, L. A. (2018). Psychiatric and medical conditions in transition-aged individuals with ASD. *Pediatrics, 141*(Supplement 4), S335–S345. https://doi.org/10.1542/peds.2016-4300K

de Vries, M., & Geurts, H. (2015). Influence of autism traits and executive functioning on quality of life in children with autism spectrum disorder. *Journal of Autism and Developmental Disorders, 45*, 2734–2743. https://doi.org/10.1007/s10803-015-2438-1

Dean, M., Harwood, R., & Kasari, C. (2017). The art of camouflage: Gender differences in the social behaviors of girls and boys with autism spectrum disorder. *Autism, 21*(6), 678–689. https://doi.org/10.1177/1362361316671845

Deavenport-Saman, A., Lu, Y., Smith, K., & Yin, L. (2015). Do children with autism overutilize the emergency department? Examining visit urgency and subsequent hospital admissions. *Maternal and Child Health Journal, 20*(2), 306–314. https://doi.org/10.1007/s10995-015-1830-y

DeGrace, B. W. (2004). The everyday occupation of families with children with autism. *American Journal of Occupational Therapy, 58*(5), 543–550. https://doi.org/10.5014/ajot.58.5.543

Delano, M. E. (2007). Video modeling interventions for individuals with autism. *Remedial and Special Education, 28*(1), 33–42. https://doi.org/10.1177/07419325070280010401

DeLeon, I. G., Iwata, B. A., & Roscoe, E. M. (1997). Displacement of leisure reinforcers by food during preference assessments. *Journal of Applied Behavior Analysis, 30*(3), 475–484. https://doi.org/10.1901/jaba.1997.30-475

Demchak, M., & Sutter, C. (2019). Teachers' perception of use and actual use of a data-based decision-making process. *Education and Training in Autism and Developmental Disabilities, 54*(2), 175–185.

Denny, P. J., & Test, D. W. (1995). Using the One-More-Than technique to teach money counting to individuals with moderate mental retardation: A systematic replication. *Education and Treatment of Children, 18*(4), 422–432. https://www.jstor.org/stable/42899427

Deno, S. L. (1985). Curriculum-based measurement: The emerging alternative. *Exceptional Children, 52*, 219–232. https://doi.org/10.1177%2F001440298505200303

Deno, S. L. (1987). Curriculum-based measurement. *Teaching Exceptional Children, 20*(1), 40–42. https://doi.org/10.1177%2F004005998702000109

Deno, S. L. (2003). Developments in curriculum-based measurement. *Journal of Special Education, 37*(3), 184–192. https://doi.org/10.1177%2F00224669030370030801

DeQuinzio, J. A., Townsend, D. B., & Poulson, C. L. (2008). The effects of forward chaining and contingent social interaction on the acquisition of complex sharing responses by children with autism. *Research in Autism Spectrum Disorders, 2*(2), 264–275. https://doi.org/10.1016/j.rasd.2007.06.006

Didehbani, N., Allen, T., Kandalaft, M., Krawczyk, D., & Chapman, S. (2016). Virtual reality social cognition training for children with high functioning autism. *Computers in Human Behavior, 62*, 703–711. https://doi.org/10.1016/j.chb.2016.04.033

Dietz, S. M., & Malone, L. W. (1985). Stimulus control terminology. *Behavior Analyst, 8*(2), 259–264. https://doi.org/10.1007/BF03393157

DiGennaro Reed, F. D., & Codding, R. S. (2014). Advancements in procedural fidelity assessment and intervention: Introduction to the special issue. *Journal of Behavioral Education, 23*(1), 1–18. https://doi.org/10.1007/s10864-013-9191-3

Division for Early Childhood. (2014). *DEC recommended practices in early intervention/early childhood special education 2014*. http://www.dec-sped.org/recommendedpractices

Dixon, M. R., Belisle, J., Stanley, C., Rowsey, K., Daar, J. H., & Szekely, S. (2015). Toward a behavior analysis of complex language for children with autism: Evaluating the relationship between PEAK and the VB-MAPP. *Journal of Developmental and Physical Disabilities, 27,* 223–233. https://doi.org/10.1007/s10882-014-9410-4

Djulbegovic, B., & Guyatt, G. H. (2017). Progress in evidence-based medicine: A quarter century on. *The Lancet, 390*(10092), 415–423. https://doi.org/10.1016/S0140-6736(16)31592-6

Donnellan, A. M. (1984). The criterion of the least dangerous assumption. *Behavioral Disorders, 9*(2), 141–150. https://doi.org/10.1177/019874298400900201

Donnelly, J. (2013). *Universal Human Rights in Theory and Practice* (3rd ed.). Cornell University Press.

Doren, B., Gau, J. M., & Lindstrom, L. E. (2012). The relationship between parent expectations and postschool outcomes of adolescents with disabilities. *Exceptional Children, 79*(1), 7–23. https://doi.org/10.1177/001440291207900101

Dotto-Fojut, K. M., Reeve, K. F., Townsend, D. B., & Progar, P. R. (2011). Teaching adolescents with autism to describe a problem and request assistance during simulated vocational tasks. *Research in Autism Spectrum Disorders, 5*(2), 826–833. https://doi.org/10.1016/j.rasd.2010.09.012

Douglas, S. N., McNaughton, D., & Light, J. (2013). Online training for paraeducators to support the communication of young children. *Journal of Early Intervention, 35*(3), 223–242. https://doi.org/10.1177/1053815114526782

Dowd-Eagle, S., & Eagle, J. (2014). Team-based school consultation. In P. L. Harrison & A. Thomas (Eds.), *Best practices in school psychology: Data-based and collaborative decision making* (pp. 450–472). National Association of School Psychologists.

Downs, J., Jacoby, P., Leonard, H., Epstein, A., Murphy, N., Davis, E., Reddihough, D., Whitehouse, A., & Williams, K. (2019). Psychometric properties of the Quality of Life Inventory-Disability (QI-Disability) measure. *Quality of Life Research, 28,* 783–794. https://doi.org/10.1007/s11136-018-2057-3

Drame, E. R., Adams, T., Nolden, V. R., & Nardi, J. M. (2020). *The resistance, persistence and resilience of Black families raising children with autism.* Peter Lang Publishing Group.

Drasgow, E., Lowrey, A., Turan, T., Halle, J. W., & Meadan, H. (2008). Social competence interventions for young children with severe disabilities. In W. H. Brown, S. L. Odom, & S. R. McConnel (Eds.), *Competence of young children: Risk, disability, intervention* (pp. 273–299). Paul H. Brookes.

Drasgow, E., Sigafoos, J., Halle, J. W., & Martin, C. A. (2009). Teaching mands to individuals with autism spectrum disorders. In A. Fitzer & P. Sturmey (Eds.), *Language and autism: Applied behavior analysis, evidence, and practice* (pp. 135–168). Pro-Ed.

Driver, J. (2014). The history of utilitarianism. In E. N. Zalta (Ed.), *The Stanford Encyclopedia of Philosophy.* https://plato.stanford.edu/entries/utilitarianism-history/

Dunlap, G., Strain, P., Lee, J. K., Joseph, J., & Leech, N. (2018). A randomized controlled evaluation of Prevent-Teach-Reinforce for young children. *Topics in Early Childhood Special Education, 37*(4), 195–205. https://doi.org/10.1177/0271121417724874

Dunn, L., & Dunn, L. (2007). *Peabody Picture Vocabulary Test* (4th ed.). American Guidance Services.

Dunst, C. J. (2002). Family-centered practices: Birth through high school. *Journal of Special Education, 30*(3), 141–149. https://doi.org/10.1177/00224669020360030401

Dunst, C. J., & Espe-Sherwindt, M. (2016). Family-centered practices in early childhood Intervention. In B. Reichow, B. A. Boyd, E. E. Barton, & S. L. Odom (Eds.), *Handbook of early childhood special education* (pp. 37–55). Springer International.

Dunst, C. J., Trivette, C. M., & Hamby, D. W. (2007). Meta-analysis of family-centered helpgiving practices research. *Mental retardation and developmental disabilities research reviews, 13*(4), 370–378.

Dunst, C. J., Trivette, C. M., & Hamby, D. W. (2012). Meta-analysis of studies incorporating the interests of young children with autism spectrum disorders into early inter-

vention practices. *Autism Research & Treatment*, 1–10. https://doi.org.ezproxy.lib
.purdue.edu/10.1155/2012/462531

Durand, V. M., & Crimmins, D. B. (1988). Identifying the variables maintaining self-
injurious behavior. *Journal of Autism and Developmental Disorders*, 18(1), 99–117.
https://doi.org/10.1007/BF02211821

Durand, V. M., & Moskowitz, L. (2015). Functional communication training. *Topics in Early Childhood Special Education*, 35(2), 116–126. https://doi.org/10.1177
/0271121415569509

Durand, M., & Rost, N. (2005). Does it matter who participates in our studies? A caution when interpreting the research on positive behavioral support. *Journal of Positive Behavior Interventions*, 7(3), 186–188. https://doi.org/10.1177/10983007050
070030801

Dworzynski, K., Ronald, A., Bolton, P., & Happé, F. (2012). How different are girls and
boys above and below the diagnostic threshold for autism spectrum disorders? *Journal of the American Academy of Child & Adolescent Psychiatry*, 51(8), 788–797.
https://doi.org/10.1016/j.jaac.2012.05.018

Dymond, S. K., Gilson, C. L., & Myran, S. P. (2007). Services for children with autism
spectrum disorders: What needs to change? *Journal of Disability Policy Studies*, 18(3),
133–147. https://doi.org/10.1177/10442073070180030201

Dynia, J. M., Brock, M. E., Justice, L. M., & Kaderavek, J. N. (2017). Predictors of decoding for children with autism spectrum disorder in comparison to their peers. *Research
in Autism Spectrum Disorders*, 37, 41–48. https://doi.org/10.1016/j.rasd.2017.02.003

Dynia, J. M., Lawton, K., Logan, J. A. R., & Justice, L. M. (2014). Comparing emer-
gent-literacy skills and home-literacy environment of children with autism and their
peers. *Topics in Early Childhood Special Education*, 34(3), 142–153. https://doi
.org/10.1177/0271121414536784

Education for All Handicapped Children Act of 1975, 20 U.S.C. 1411 § 1400 *et seq.* (1975).
https://www.govinfo.gov/content/pkg/STATUTE-89/pdf/STATUTE-89-Pg773.pdf

Eisenhart, M., Borko, H., Underhill, R., Brown, C., Jones, D., & Agard, P. (1993). Conceptual knowledge falls through the cracks: Complexities of learning to teach mathematics for understanding. *Journal for Research in Mathematics Education*, 24, 8–40.
https://doi.org/10.5951/jresematheduc.24.1.0008

El Zein, F., Gevarter, C., Bryant, B., Son, S. H., Bryant, D., Kim, M., & Solis, M. (2016).
A comparison between iPad-assisted and teacher-directed reading instruction for stu-
dents with autism spectrum disorder (ASD). *Journal of Developmental & Physical
Disabilities*, 28(2), 195–215. https://doi.org/10.1007/s10882-015-9458-9

Elliott, C. D. (1990). *Introductory and technical handbook for the Differential Ability
Scales*. Psychological Corporation.

Elliott, S. N., & Von Brock, T. M. (1991). The Behavior Intervention Rating Scale: Development and validation of a pretreatment acceptability and effectiveness measure. *Journal
of School Psychology*, 29(1), 43–51. https://doi.org/10.1016/0022-4405(91)90014-I

Ellsworth, A. M. (2020). *Walking the talk: The credibility factor in teacher preparation*.
Montana State University.

Emmons, C. L., & Zager, D. (2018). Increasing collaboration self-efficacy to improve educational programming for students with autism. *Focus on Autism and Other Developmental Disabilities*, 33(2), 120–128. https://doi.org/10.1177/1088357616686312

Ennis, R. P., Flemming, S. C., Michael, E., & Lee, E. O. (2020). Using a tiered approach to
support early childhood educators' use of behavioral strategies. *Education & Treatment of Children*, 43(3), 265–277. https://doi.org/10.1007/s43494-020-00027-x

Epstein, J. L. (2001). *School, family, and community partnerships: Preparing educators and
improving schools*. Westview Press.

Epstein, J. L., & Salinas, K. C. (2004). Partnering with families and communities. *School as Learning Communities, 61*(8), 12–18.

Epstein, J. L., Sanders, M. G., Simon, B. S., Salinas, K. C., Jansorn, N. R., & Van Voorhis, F. L. (2002). *School, family, and community partnerships: Your handbook for action* (2nd ed.). Corwin.

Espinoza, O. (2007). Solving the equity–equality conceptual dilemma: A new model for analysis of the educational process. *Educational Research, 49*(4), 343–363. https://doi.org/10.1080/00131880701717198

Estes, A., Rivera, V., Bryan, M., Cali, P., & Dawson G. (2011). Discrepancies between academic achievement and intellectual ability in higher-functioning school-aged children with autism spectrum disorder. *Journal of Autism Development Disorder, 41,* 1044–1052. https://doi.org/10.1007/s10803-010-1127-3

Etscheidt, S. (2006). Least restrictive and natural environments for young children with disabilities: A legal analysis of issues. *Topics in Early Childhood Special Education, 26*(3), 167–178. https://doi.org/10.1177/02711214060260030401

Evans, B. (2013). How autism became autism: The radical transformation of a central concept of child development in Britain. *History of the Human Sciences, 26*(3), 3–31. https://doi.org/10.1177/0952695113484320

Every Student Succeeds Act of 2015, 129 U.S.C. 1802 *et seq.* (2015). https://www.congress.gov/114/plaws/publ95/PLAW-114publ95.pdf

Every Student Succeeds Act, 20 U.S.C. § 6301 (2015). https://www.congress.gov/114/plaws/publ95/PLAW-114publ95.pdf

Fagan, T. K., & Wise, P. S. (2007). *School Psychology: Past, present, and future* (3rd ed.). National Association of School Psychologists.

Fairburn, C. G., & Cooper, Z. (2011). Therapist competence, therapy quality, and therapist training. *Behaviour Research and Therapy, 49*(6–7), 373–378. https://doi.org/10.1016/j.brat.2011.03.005

Falbo, T., Lein, L., & Amador, N. A. (2001). Parental involvement during the transition to high school. *Journal of Adolescent Research, 16*(5), 511–529.

Falcomata, T. (2015). Defining features of applied behavior analysis. In H. R. Roane, J. E. Ringdahl, & T. S. Falcomata (Eds.), *Clinical and organizational applications of applied behavior analysis* (pp. 1–16). Elsevier.

Falcomata, T. S., Roane, H. S., Feeney, B. J., & Stephenson, K. M. (2010). Assessment and treatment of elopement maintained by access to stereotypy. *Journal of Applied Behavior Analysis, 43*(3), 513–517. https://doi.org/10.1901/jaba.2010.43-513

Falcomata, T., Shpall, C., Ferguson, R., Wingate, H., Swinnea, S., & Ringdahl, J. (2017). A comparison of high and low-proficiency mands during functional communication training across multiple functions of problem behavior. *Journal of Developmental & Physical Disabilities, 29*(6), 983–1002. https://doi-org.ezproxy.lib.purdue.edu/10.1007/s10882-017-9571-z

Family Educational Rights and Privacy Act of 1974, 20 U.S.C. § 1232g (1974).

Family Educational Rights and Privacy Act (FERPA). 34 C.F.R. § 99 (2001). http://www2.ed.gov/policy/gen/guid/fpco/ferpa/index.html

Farver, J. M., & Lee-Shin, Y. (2000). Acculturation and Korean-American children's social and play behavior. *Social Development, 9*(3), 316–336. https://doi.org/10.1111/1467-9507.00128

Fein, D., & Dunn, M. A. (2007). *Autism in your classroom: A general educator's guide to students with autism spectrum disorders.* Woodbine House.

Feldman, D. B., & Crandall, C. S. (2006). Dimensions of mental illness stigma: What about mental illness causes social rejection? *Journal of Social and Clinical Psychology, 26*(2), 137–154. https://doi.org/10.1521/jscp.2007.26.2.137

Feldman, E., & Kratochwill, T. (2003). Problem solving consultation in schools: Past, present, and future directions. *Behavior Analyst Today, 4*(3), 318–330. http://dx.doi.org/10.1037/h0100022

Ferguson, C. A. (1976). The structure and use of politeness formulas. *Language in Society, 5*(2), 137–151. https://www.jstor.org/stable/4166867

Ferlazzo, L. (2011). Involvement or engagement? *School, Families, Communities, 68*(8), 10–14.

Ferster, C. B. (1961). Positive reinforcement and behavioral deficits of Autistic children. *Child Development, 32*, 437–456. https://doi.org/10.1007/978-3-662-39876-0_23

Ferster, C. B., & Demyer, M. K. (1961). The development of performances in autistic children in an automatically controlled environment. *Journal of Chronic Diseases, 13*(4), 312–345. https://doi.org/10.1016/0021-9681(61)90059-5

Fiedler, C. R., & Van Haren, B. (2009). A comparison of special education administrators' and teachers' knowledge and application of ethics and professional standards. *Journal of Special Education, 43*(3), 160–173. https://doi.org/10.1177/0022466908319395

Finnegan, E. & Mazin A. L. (2016). Strategies for increasing reading comprehension skills in students with autism spectrum disorder: A review of the literature. *Education and Treatment of Children, 39*(2), 187–220. https://doi.org/10.1353/etc.2016.0007

Fish, W. W. (2008). The IEP meeting: Perceptions of parents of students who receive special education services. *Preventing School Failure, 53*(1), 8–14. *https://doi.org/10.3200/PSFL.53.1.8-14*

Fisher, W. W., Piazza, C. C., Bowman, L. G., & Amari, A. (1996). Integrating caregiver report with a systematic choice assessment to enhance reinforcer identification. *American Journal on Mental Retardation, 101*(1), 15–25.

Fisher, W., Piazza, C. C., Bowman, L. G., Hagopian, L. P., Owen, J. C., & Slevin, I. (1992). A comparison of two approaches for identifying reinforcers for persons with severe and profound disabilities. *Journal of Applied Behavior Analysis, 25*(2), 491–498. https://doi.org/10.1901/jaba.1992.25-491

Fiske, K. E., Isenhouwer, R. W., Bamond, M. J., & Lauderdale-Littin, S. (2020). An analysis of the value of token reinforcement using a multiple-schedule assessment. *Journal of Applied Behavior Analysis, 53*, 563–571. https://doi.org/10.1002/jaba.613

Fixsen, D. L., Naoom, S. F., Blase, K. A., Friedman, R. M., Wallace, F., Burns, B., Carter, W., Paulson, R., Schoenwald, S., Barwick, M., Chambers, D., Petrila, J., Rivard, J., & Shern, D. (2005). *Implementation research: A synthesis of the literature.* National Implementation Research Network. https://nirn.fpg.unc.edu/resources/implementation-research-synthesis-literature

Flannery, K. A., & Wisner-Carlson, R. (2020). Autism and education. *Psychiatric Clinics of North America, 43*(4), 647–671. https://doi.org/10.1016/j.psc.2020.08.004

Flannery, K. B., Fenning, P., Kato, M. M., & McIntosh, K. (2014). Effects of school-wide positive behavioral interventions and supports and fidelity of implementation on problem behavior in high schools. *School Psychology Quarterly, 29*(2), 111–124. https://doi.org/10.1037/spq0000039

Fleming, A. R., Fairweather, J. S., & Leahy, M. J. (2013). Quality of life as a potential rehabilitation service outcome: The relationship between employment, quality of life, and other life areas. *Rehabilitation Counseling Bulletin, 57*(1), 9–22. https://doi.org/10.1177%2F0034355213485992

Fleury, V. P., Hedges, S., Hume, K., Browder, D. M., Thompson, J. L., Fallin, K., El Zein, F., Reutebuch, C. K., & Vaughn, S. (2014). Addressing the academic needs of adolescents with autism spectrum disorder in secondary education. *Remedial and Special Education, 35*(2), 68–79. http://doi.org/0741932513518823

Fleury, V. P., & Lease, E. M. (2018). Early indication of reading difficulty? A descriptive analysis of emergent literacy skills in children with autism spectrum disorder.

Topics in Early Childhood Special Education, 38(2), 82–93. https://doi.org/10.1177/0271121417751626

Flugum, K. R., & Reschly, D. J. (1994). Prereferral interventions: Quality indices and outcomes. *Journal of School Psychology, 32*(1), 1–14. https://doi.org/10.1016/0022-4405(94)90025-6

Flynn, R. M., Lissy, R., Alicea, S., Tazartes, L., & McKay, M. M. (2016). Professional development for teachers plus coaching related to school-wide suspensions for a large urban school system. *Children and Youth Services Review, 62,* 29–39.

Fombonne, E. (2012). Autism in adult life. *Canadian Journal of Psychiatry, 57*(5), 273–274. https://doi.org/10.1177/070674371205700501

Foorman, B. R., Arndt, E. J., & Crawford, E. C. (2011). Important constructs in literacy learning across disciplines. *Topics in Language Disorders, 31*(1) 73–83. https://doi.org/10.1097/TLD.0b013e31820a0b86

Forest, M., & Lusthaus, E. (1987). The kaleidoscope: Challenge to the cascade. In M. Forest (Ed.), *More education/integration* (pp. 1–16). G. Allen Roeher Institute.

Forman, S. G., & Burke, C. R. (2008). Best practices in selecting and implementing evidence-based school interventions. In A. Thomas & J. Grimes (Eds.), *Best practices in school psychology V* (pp. 799–811). National Association of School Psychologists.

Fowler, S. A., Coleman, M. R. B., & Bogdan, W. K. (2019). The state of the special education profession report. *Teaching Exceptional Children, 52*(1), 8–27. https://doi.org/10.1177/0040059919875703

Fox News. (2019, June 19). *America's least-favorite vegetable determined in new survey.* Fox News. https://www.foxnews.com/food-drink/amercas-least-favorite-vegetable-determined-survey

Fredrickson, B. (2004). The broaden-and-build theory of positive emotions. *Philosophical transactions of the Royal Society of London, Series B, Biological Sciences, 359*(1449), 1367–1378.

Frieder, J. E., Peterson, S. M., Woodward, J., Crane, J., & Garner, M. (2009). Teleconsultation in school settings: Linking classroom teachers and behavior analysts through web-based technology. *Behavior Analysis in Practice, 2*(2), 32–39. https://doi.org/10.1007/bf03391746

Friedman, N. D. B., Warfield, M. E., & Parish, S. L. (2013). Transition to adulthood for individuals with autism spectrum disorder: Current issues and future perspectives. *Neuropsychiatry, 3*(2), 181–192.

Fritz, J. N., Jackson, L. M., Stiefler, N. A., Wimberly, B. S., & Richardson, A. R. (2017). Noncontingent reinforcement without extinction plus differential reinforcement of alternative behavior during treatment of problem behavior. *Journal of Applied Behavior Analysis, 50*(3), 590–599. https://doi.org/10.1002/jaba.395

Frolek Clark, G., & Chandler, B. (2014). *Best practices for occupational therapy in schools.* AOTA Press.

Frye, R. E. (2018). Social skills deficits in autism spectrum disorder: Potential biological origins and progress in developing therapeutic agents. *CNS Drugs, 32*(8), 713–734. http://www.doi.org/10.1007/s40263-018-0556-y

Fuchs, D., Fuchs, L. S., Bahr, M. W., Fernstrom, P., & Stecker, P. M. (1990). Prereferral intervention: A prescriptive approach. *Exceptional Children, 56,* 493–513. https://doi.org/10.1177/001440299005600602

Fuchs, L. S., Deno, S. L., & Mirkin, P. K. (1984). The effects of frequent curriculum-based measurement and evaluation on pedagogy, student achievement, and student awareness of learning. *American Educational Research Journal, 21*(2), 449–460. https://doi.org/10.3102/00028312021002449.

Fuchs, L. S., Fuchs, D., Craddock, C., Hollenbeck, K. N., Hamlett, C. L., & Schatschneider, C. (2008). Effects of small-group tutoring with and without validated classroom instruction on at-risk students' math problem solving: Are two tiers of prevention better than one? *Journal of Educational Psychology, 100*(3), 491–509. https://doi .org/10.1037/0022-0663.100.3.491

Fuchs, L. S., Fuchs, D., & Malone, A. S. (2018). The taxonomy of intervention intensity. *Teaching Exceptional Children, 50*(4), 194–202. https://doi.org/10.1177/004 0059918758166

Fuchs, L., S., Fuchs, D., Seethaler, P. M., & Craddock, C. (2020). Improving language comprehension to enhance word problem solving. *Reading & Writing Quarterly, 36*(2), 142–156. https://doi.org/10.1080/10573569.2019.1666760

Fuchs, L. S., Gilbert, J. K., Powell, S. R., Cirino, P. T., Fuchs, D., Hamlett, C. L., Seethaler, P. M., & Tolar, T. D. (2016). The role of cognitive processes, foundational math skill, and calculation accuracy and fluency in word-problem solving versus pre-algebraic knowledge. *Developmental Psychology, 52*(12), 2085–2098. https://doi.org/10.1037 /dev0000227

Fuchs, D., Mock, D., Morgan, P. L., & Young, C. L. (2003). Responsiveness-to-intervention: Definitions, evidence, and implications for the learning disabilities construct. *Learning Disabilities Research and Practice, 18*(6), 157–171. https:// doi.org/10.1177/001440299005600602

Fuchs, L. S., Seethaler, P. M., Sterba, S. K., Craddock, C., Fuchs, D., Compton, D. L., & Changas, P. (2019). Word-problem intervention with and without embedded language comprehension instruction: Causal evidence on language comprehension's contribution to word-problem solving. [unpublished manuscript].

Fung, J., Wong, M. S., & Park, H. (2018). Cultural background and religious beliefs. In M. R. Sanders & A. Morawska (Eds.), *Handbook of parenting and child development across the lifespan*. Springer. https://doi.org/10.1007/978-3-319-94598-9

Gabig, C. S. (2010). Variability in language and reading in high-functioning autism. In M. R. Mohannadi (Ed.), *A Comprehensive Book on Autism* (pp. 63–84). InTechOpen.

Gadaire, D. M., Senn, L., Albert, K. M., Robinson, T. P., Passage, M., Shaham, Y., & Topcuoglu, B. (2021). Differential effects of token production and exchange on responding of children with developmental disabilities. *Learning and Motivation, 73*, 101694. https://doi.org/10.1016/j.lmot.2020.101694

Gagnon, L., Mottron, L., Bherer, L., & Joanette, Y. (2004). Quantification of judgement in high functioning autism: Superior or different. *Journal of Autism and Developmental Disorders, 34*(6), 679–689. https://doi.org/10.1007/s10803-004-5288-9

Gallant, E. E., Reeve, S. A., Brothers, K. J., & Reeve, K. F. (2016). Auditory script location does not affect acquisition and maintenance of vocal initiations by children with autism. *Behavioral Observations, 32*(2), 103–120. https://doi.org/10.1002/bin.1467

Gantman, A., Kapp, S. K., Orenski, K., & Laugeson, E. A. (2012). Social skills training for young adults with high-functioning autism spectrum disorders: A randomized controlled pilot study. *Journal of Autism and Developmental Disorders, 42*(6), 1094–1103. https://doi.org/10.1007/s10803-011-1350-6

Ganz, J. B., Heath, A. K., Lund, E. M., Camargo, S. P. H., Rispoli, J. J., Boles, M., & Plaisance, L. (2012). Effects of peer-mediated implantation of visual scripts in middle school. *Behavior Modification, 36*(3), 378–398. https://doi.org/10.1177%2F0145445512442214

Garbacz, S. A., McIntyre, L. L., & Santiago, R. T. (2016). Family involvement and parent-teacher relationships for students with autism spectrum disorders. *School Psychology Quarterly, 31*(4), 478–490. https://doi.org/10.1037/spq0000157

Gardenier, N. C., MacDonald, R., & Green, G. (2004). Comparison of direct observational methods for measuring stereotypic behavior in children with autism spectrum disorders. *Research in Developmental Disabilities, 25*(2), 99–118. https://doi .org/10.1016/j.ridd.2003.05.004

Gardner, L., Erkfritz-Gay, K., Campbell, J. M., Bradley, T., & Murphy, L. (2016). Purposes of assessment. In J. L. Matson (Ed.), *Handbook of assessment and diagnosis of autism spectrum disorder* (pp. 27–43, Chapter xii). Springer International.

Garland, D., & Dieker, L. (2019). Effects of providing individualized clinical coaching with bug-in-ear technology to novice educators of students with emotional and behavioral disorders in inclusive secondary science classrooms. *Journal of Inquiry and Action in Education, 10*(2), 23–40.

Geary, D. C., & Hoard, M. K. (2005). Learning disabilities in arithmetic and mathematics. In J. I. D. Campbell (Ed.), *Handbook of mathematical cognition* (pp. 253–268). Psychology Press.

Gengoux, G. W. (2015). Priming for social activities: Effects on interactions between children with autism and typically developing peers. *Journal of Positive Behavior Interventions, 17*(3), 181–192. https://doi.org/10.1177/1098300714561862

Gerber, J. S., & Offit, P. A. (2009). Vaccines and autism: A tale of shifting hypotheses. *Clinical Infectious Diseases, 48*(4), 456–461. https://doi.org/10.1086/596476

Gerow, S., Rispoli, M., Ninci, J., Gregori, E. V., & Hagan-Burke, S. (2018). Teaching parents to implement functional communication training for young children with developmental delay. *Topics in Early Childhood Special Education, 38*, 68–81. https://doi.org/10.1177/0271121417740637

Gersten, R., & Chard, D. (1999). Number sense: Rethinking arithmetic instruction for students with mathematical disabilities. *Journal of Special Education, 33*(1), 18–28. https://doi.org/10.1177/002246699903300102

Geurts, H. M., & Jansen M. D. (2012). A retrospective chart study: The pathway to a diagnosis for adults referred for ASD assessment. *Autism, 16*, 299–305. https://doi.org/10.1177/1362361311421775

Gevarter, C., Bryant, D. P., Bryant, B., Watkins, L., Zamora, C., & Sammarco, N. (2016). Mathematics interventions for individuals with autism spectrum disorder: A systematic review. *Journal of Autism and Developmental Disorders, 3*, 224–238. https://doi.org/10.1007/s40489-016-0078-9

Giangreco, M. F., Edelman, S. W., Macfarland, S., & Luiselli, T. E. (1997). Attitudes about educational and related service provision for students with deaf-blindness and multiple disabilities. *Exceptional Children, 63*(3), 329–342.

Gil, V., Bennett, K. D., & Barbetta, P. M. (2019). Teaching young adults with intellectual disability grocery shopping skills in a community setting using least-to-most prompting. *Behavior Analysis in Practice, 12*, 649–653. https://dx.doi.org/10.1007%2Fs40617-019-00340-x

Gilbert, J. H., Yan, J., & Hoffman, S. J. (2010). A WHO report: Framework for action on interprofessional education and collaborative practice. *Journal of Allied Health, 39*, 196–197.

Gilbert, T. F. (1978). *Human competence: Engineering worthy performance.* McGraw-Hill.

Gilliam, J. E. (1995). *Gilliam Autism Rating Scale* (2nd ed.—GARS-2). Pro-Ed. https://doi.org/10.1007/978-1-4419-1698-3_879

Gischlar, K. L., Hojnoski, R. L., & Missall, K. N. (2009). Improving child outcomes with data-based decision making: Interpreting and using data. *Young Exceptional Children, 13*(1), 2–18. https://doi.org/10.1177/1096250609346249

Goin-Kochel, R. P., Myers, B. J., & Mackintosh, V. H. (2007). Parental reports on the use of treatments and therapies for children with autism spectrum disorders. *Research in Autism Spectrum Disorders, 1*(3), 195–209. https://doi.org/10.1016/j.rasd.2006.08.006

Goldman, S. E., Richdale, A. L., Clemons, T., & Malow, B. A. (2012). Parental sleep concerns in autism spectrum disorders: variations from childhood to adolescence. *Jour-*

nal of Autism and Developmental Disorders, 42(4), 531–538. https://doi.org/10.1007/s10803-011-1270-5

Gomez, L. E., Moran, M. L., Alcedo, M. A., Arias, V. B., & Verdugo, M. A. (2020). Addressing quality of life of children with autism spectrum disorder and intellectual disability. *Intellectual and Developmental Disabilities, 59*(5), 393–408. https://doi.org/10.1352/1934-9556-58.5.393

Gomez, L. E., & Verdugo, M. A. (2016). Outcomes evaluation. In R. L. Schalock & Kenneth D. Keith (Eds.), *Cross-cultural quality of life: Enhancing the lives of people with intellectual disabilities* (2nd ed., pp. 71–93). American Association on Intellectual and Developmental Disabilities.

Goodman, A., Joshi, H., Nasim, B., & Tyler, C. (2015). *Social and emotional skills in childhood and their long-term effects on adult life.* Early Intervention Foundation. http://www.eif.org.uk/wp-content/uploads/2015/03/EIF-Strand-1-Report-FINAL1.pdf

Gough, P. B., & Tunmer, W. E. (1986). Decoding, reading, and reading disability. *Remedial and Special Education, 7*(1), 6–10. https://doi.org/10.1177/074193258600700104

Gould, E., Dixon, D. R., Najdowski, A. C., Smith, M., N., & Tarbox, J. (2011). A review of assessments for determining the content of intensive behavioral intervention programs for autism spectrum disorder. *Research in Autism Spectrum Disorders, 5*(3), 990–1002. https://doi.org/10.1016/j.rasd.2011.01.012

Gould, K. M., Collier-Meek, M., DeFouw, E. R., Silva, M., & Kleinert, W. (2019). A systematic review of treatment integrity assessment from 2004 to 2014: Examining behavioral interventions for students with autism spectrum disorder. *Contemporary School Psychology, 23*(3), 220–230. https://doi.org/10.1007/s40688-019-00233-4

Graden, J. L., Casey, A., & Christenson, S. L. (1985). Implementing a prereferral intervention system: Part 1. The model. *Exceptional Children, 51,* 377–384. https://doi.org/10.1177/001440298505100502

Granpeesheh, D., Tarbox, J., Dixon, D. R., Peters, C. A., Thompson, K., & Kenzer, A. (2010). Evaluation of an eLearning tool for training behavioral therapists in academic knowledge of applied behavior analysis. *Research in Autism Spectrum Disorders, 4*(1), 11–17. https://doi.org/10.1016/j.rasd.2009.07.004

Gray, C. A., & Garand, J. D. (1993). Social stories: Improving responses of students with autism with accurate social information. *Focus on Autistic Behavior, 8*(1), 1–10. https://doi.org/10.1177/108835769300800101

Green, L., Chance, P., & Stockholm, M. (2019). Implementation and perceptions of classroom-based service delivery: A survey of public school clinicians. *Language, Speech, and Hearing Services in Schools, 50*(4), 656–672. https://doi.org/10.1044/2019_LSHSS-18-0101

Green, V. A., O'Reilly, M., Itchon, J., & Sigafoos, J. (2005). Persistence of early emerging aberrant behavior in children with developmental disabilities. *Research in Developmental Disabilities, 26*(1), 47–55. https://doi.org/10.1016/j.ridd.2004.07.003

Greene, C. (2014). Transition of culturally and linguistically diverse youth with disabilities: Challenges and opportunities. *Journal of Vocational Rehabilitation, 40*(3), 239–245. https://doi.or/10.3233/JVR-140689

Greenspan, S. (1981). Defining childhood social competence: A proposed working model. *Advances in Special Education, 3,* 1–39.

Gregori, E., Rispoli, M. J., Lory, C., Kim, S. Y., & David, M. (2021). Effects of teachers as coaches for paraprofessionals implementing functional communication training. *Journal of Positive Behavior Interventions.* Advance online publication. https://doi.org/10.1177%2F1098300720983538

Gregori, E., Rispoli, M., Neely, L., Lory, C., Kim, S. Y., & David, M. (2020). Training direct service personnel in functional communication training with adults with disabilities.

Journal of Developmental and Physical Disabilities, 33, 1–24. http://dx.doi.org.proxy
.cc.uic.edu/10.1007/s10882-020-09766-6

Gresham, F. M. (1989). Assessment of treatment integrity in school consultation and prereferral intervention. *School Psychology Review, 18*(1), 37–50. https://doi.org/10.1080
/02796015.1989.12085399

Griffin, M. M., Summer, A. H., McMillan, E. D., Day, T. L., & Hodapp, R. M. (2012).
Attitudes toward including students with intellectual disabilities at college. *Journal of
Policy and Practice in Intellectual Disabilities, 9*(4), 234–239. https://doi.org/10.1111
/jppi.12008

Griffin, M. M., Taylor, J. L., & Urbano, R. C. (2013). Involvement in transition planning
meetings among high school students with autism spectrum disorders. *Journal of Special Education, 47*(4), 256–264. https://doi.org/10.1177/0022466913475668

Grigal, M., & Neubert, D. A. (2004). Parents' in-school values and post-school expectations for transition-aged youth with disabilities. *Career Development for Exceptional
Individuals, 27*, 65–85. https://doi.org/10.1177/088572880402700105

Grigg, N. C., Snell, M. E., & Loyd, B. (1989). Visual analysis of student evaluation data: A
qualitative analysis of teacher decision making. *Journal of the Association for Persons
with Severe Handicaps 14*(1), 23–32. https://doi.org/10.1177/154079698901400104

Grimm, R. P., Solari, E. J., McIntyre, N. S., Zajic, M., & Mundy, P. C. (2018). Comparing
growth in linguistic comprehension and reading comprehension in school-aged children with autism versus typically developing children. *Autism Research, 11*, 624–635.
https://doi.org/10.1002/aur.1914

Groskreutz, N. C., Groskreutz, M. P., Bloom, S. E., & Slocum, T. A. (2014). Generalization
of negatively reinforced mands in children with autism. *Journal of Applied Behavior
Analysis, 47*(3), 560–579. https://doi.org/10.1002/jaba.151

Groth-Marnat, G. (2000). Visions of clinical assessment: Then, now, and a brief history
of the future. *Journal of Clinical Psychology, 56*(3), 349–365. https://doi.org/10.1002
/(SICI)1097-4679(200003)56:3%3C349::AID-JCLP11%3E3.0.CO;2-T

Grygas Coogle, C., Ottley, J. R., Rahn, N. L., & Storie, S. (2018). Bug-in-ear eCoaching:
Impacts on novice early childhood special education teachers. *Journal of Early Intervention, 40*(1), 87–103. https://doi.org/10.1177/1053815117748692

Grygas Coogle, C., Rahn, N. L., & Ottley, J. R. (2015). Pre-service teacher use of communication strategies upon receiving immediate feedback. *Early Childhood Research
Quarterly, 32*, 105–115. https://doi.org/10.1016/j.ecresq.2015.03.003

Guajardo, N. R., & Cartwright, K. B. (2016). The contribution of theory of mind, counter-
factual reasoning, and executive function to pre-readers' language comprehension and
later reading awareness and comprehension in elementary school. *Journal of Experimental Child Psychology, 144*, 27–45. https://doi.org/10.1016/j.jecp.2015.11.004

Gur, A. (2018). Challenging behavior, functioning difficulties, and quality of life of adults
with intellectual disabilities. *International Journal of Developmental Disabilities,
64*(1), 45–52. https://doi.org/10.1080/20473869.2016.1221233

Gurney, J. G., McPheeters, M. L., & Davis, M. M. (2006). Parental report of health conditions and health care use among children with and without autism. *Archives of
Pediatric and Adolescent Medicine, 160*(8), 825–830. https://doi.org/10.1001/arch
pedi.160.8.825

Gutkin, T. B., & Curtis, M. J. (1999). School-based consultation: Theory, techniques, and
research. In T. B. Gutkin & C. R. Reynolds (Eds.), *The handbook of school psychology*
(2nd ed., pp. 577–611). Wiley.

Guyatt, G., Cairns, J., & Churchill, D. (1992). Evidence-based medicine: A new approach
to teaching the practice of medicine. *Journal of the American Medical Association,
268*(17), 2420–2425. https://doi.org/10.1001/jama.1992.03490170092032

Ha, S., Sohn, I. J., Kim, N., Sim, H. J., & Cheon, K. A. (2015). Characteristics of brains in autism spectrum disorder: Structure, function and connectivity across the lifespan. *Experimental Neurobiology, 24*(4), 273. https://doi.org/10.5607/en.2015.24.4.273

Habayeb, S., Dababnah, S., John, A., & Rich, B. (2020). Cultural experiences of Arab American caregivers raising children with autism spectrum disorder. *Journal of Autism and Developmental Disorders, 50*(1), 51–62. https://doi.org/10.1007/s10803-019-04218-3

Hagan-Burke, S., Gilmour, M. W., Gerow, S., & Crowder, W. C. (2015). Identifying academic demands that occasion problem behaviors for students with behavioral disorders: Illustrations at the elementary school level. *Behavior Modification, 39*(1), 215–241. https://doi-org.ezproxy.lib.purdue.edu/10.1177/0145445514566505

Hagner, D., May, J., Kurtz, A., & Cloutier, H. (2014). Person-centered planning for transition-aged youth with autism spectrum disorder. *Journal of Rehabilitation, 80*(1), 4–10.

Hagner, D., McGahie, K., & Cloutier, H. (2001). A model career assistance process for individuals with severe disabilities. *Journal of Employment Counseling, 38*(4), 197–206. https://doi.org/10.1002/j.2161-1920.2001.tb00501.x

Hagopian, L. P., Rooker, G. W., & Zarcone, J. R. (2015). Delineating subtypes of self-injurious behavior maintained by automatic reinforcement. *Journal of Applied Behavior Analysis, 48*(3), 523–543. https://doi.org/10.1002/jaba.236

Halbur, M. E., Kodak, T., Wood, R., & Corrigan, E. (2020). An evaluation of parent preference for prompting procedures. *Journal of Applied Behavior Analysis, 53*(2), 707–726. https://doi.org/10.1002/jaba.616

Hammond, H., Ingalls, L., & Trussell, R. P. (2008). Family members' involvement in the initial individual education program (IEP) meeting and the IEP process: Perceptions and reactions. *International Journal about Parents in Education, 2*, 35–48.

Han, H. S., & Kemple, K. M. (2006). Components of social competence and strategies of support: Considering what to teach and how. *Early Childhood Education Journal, 34*(3), 241–246. https://www.doi.org/10.1007/s10643-006-0139-2

Hanley, G. P. (2012). Functional assessment of problem behavior: Dispelling myths, overcoming implementation obstacles, and developing new lore. *Behavior Analysis in Practice, 5*, 54–72. https://doi.org/10.1007/BF03391818

Hansen, S. G., Raulston, T. J., Machalicek, W., Frantz, R., Drew, C., Erturk, B., & Squires, J. (2019). Peer-mediated joint attention intervention in the preschool classroom. *Journal of Special Education, 53*(2), 96–107. https://doi.org/10.10127274/06062921468689 0178486074464

Happe, F., & Frith, U. (2006). The weak coherence account: Detail-focused cognitive style in autism spectrum disorders. *Journal of Autism and Developmental Disorders, 36*, 5–25. https://doi.org/10.1007/s10803-005-0039-0

Hardy, J. K., & McLeod, R. H. (2020). Using positive reinforcement with young children. *Beyond Behavior, 29*(2), 95–107. https://doi.org/10.1177/1074295620915724

Haring, N. G., & Eaton, M. D. (1978). Systematic instructional procedures: An instructional hierarchy. In N. G. Haring, T. C. Lovitt, M. D. Eaton, & C. L. Hansen (Eds.), *The fourth R: Research in the classroom* (pp. 23–40). Merrill.

Harn, B., Parisi, D., & Stoolmiller, M. (2013). Balancing fidelity with flexibility and fit: What do we really know about fidelity of implementation in schools? *Exceptional Children, 79*(2), 181–193. https://doi.org/10.1177/001440291307900204

Harris, B., Barton, E. E., & McClain, M. B. (2020). Inclusion of racially and ethnically diverse populations in ASD intervention research. *Research in Autism Spectrum Disorders, 73*. https://doi.org/10.1016/j.rasd.2020.101551

Harry, B. (1992). *Cultural diversity, families, and the special education system: Communication and empowerment.* Teachers College Press.

Harry, B. (2008). Collaboration with culturally and linguistically diverse families: Ideal versus reality. *Exceptional Children, 74*(3), 372–388. https://doi.org/10.1177%2F 001440290807400306

Hayes, S. A., & Watson, S. L. (2013). The impact of parenting stress: A meta-analysis of studies comparing the experience of parenting stress in parents of children with and without autism spectrum disorder. *Journal of Autism and Developmental Disorders, 43*(3), 629–642. https://doi.org/10.1007/s10803-012-1604-y

Hazlett, H. C., Gu, H., Munsell, B. C., Kim, S. H., Styner, M., Wolff, J. J., Elison, J.T., Swanson, M. R., Zhu, H., Botteron, K. N., Collins, D. L., Constantino, J. N., Dager, S. R., Estes, A. M., Evans, A. C., Fonov, V. S., Gerig, G., Kostopoulos, P., McKinstry, R. C., & Piven, J. (2017). Early brain development in infants at high risk for autism spectrum disorder. *Nature, 542*(7641), 348–351. https://doi.org/10.1038/nature21369

Health Insurance Portability and Accountability Act. 45 C.F.R. §160 & 164 (2002). https://www.hhs.gov/sites/default/files/privacysummary.pdf

Health Insurance Portability and Accountability Act (HIPAA). (2004). U.S. Dept. of Labor, Employee Benefits Security Administration.

Held, M. F., Thoma, C. A., & Thomas, K. (2004). The John Jones Show: How one teacher facilitates the self-determined planning for a young man with autism. *Focus on Autism and Other Developmental Disabilities, 19*(3), 177–188. https://doi.org/10.1177/108 83576040190030501

Hemmeter, M. L., Snyder, P. A., Fox, L., & Algina, J. (2016). Evaluating the implementation of the Pyramid Model for promoting social-emotional competence in early childhood classrooms. *Topics in Early Childhood Special Education, 36*(3), 133–146. https://doi .org/10.1177/0271121416653386

Henderson, A. T., & Mapp, K. L. (2002). A new wave of evidence: The impact of school, family, and community connections on student achievement. *Annual Synthesis, 2002.*

Henderson, L., Clarke, P. & Snowling, M. (2014). Reading comprehension impairments in autism spectrum disorders. *L'Année Psychologique, 4*(4), 779–797. https://doi .org/10.4074/S0003503314004084

Henning, B., & Intepe, S. (2021). Using number talks to increase the early childhood number sense of students with ASD [manuscript submitted for publication].

Henninger, N. A., & Taylor, J. L. (2012). Outcomes in adults with autism spectrum disorders: A historical perspective. *Autism, 17*(1), 103–116. https://doi.org/10.1177 /1362361312441266

Hewitt, A. S., Stancliff, R. J., Hall-Lande, J., Nord, D., Pettingell, S. L., Hamre, K., & Hallas-Muchow, L. (2017). Characteristics of adults with autism spectrum disorder who use residential services and supports through developmental disability services in the United States. *Research in Autism Spectrum Disorders, 34*, 1–9. https://doi .org/10.1016/j.rasd.2016.11.007

Hill, E. L. (2004). Executive dysfunction in autism. *Trends in Cognitive Sciences, 8*(1), 26–32. https://doi.org/10.1016/j.tics.2003.11.003

Himle, M. B., Miltenberger, R. G., Gatheridge, B. J., & Flessner, C. A. (2004). An evaluation of two procedures for training skills to prevent gun play in children. *Pediatrics, 113*(1), 70–77. https://doi.org/10.1542/peds.113.1.70

Hiremath, C. S., Sagar, K. J. V., Yamini, B. K., Girimaji, A. S., Kumar, R., Sravanti, S. L., Padmanabha, H., Raju, K. N. V., Kishore, M. T., Jacob, P., Saini, J., Bharath, R. D., Seshadri, S. P., & Kumar, M. (2021). Emerging behavioral and neuroimaging biomarkers for early and accurate characterization of autism spectrum disorders: A systematic review. *Translational Psychiatry, 11*(1), 1–12. https://doi.org/10.1038/ s41398-020-01178-6

Ho, T. Q., Gadke, D. L., Henington, C., Evans-McCleon, T. N., & Justice, C. A. (2019). The effects of animated video modeling on joint attention and social engagement in children with autism spectrum disorder. *Research in Autism Spectrum Disorders, 58,* 83–95. https://doi.org/10.1016/j.rasd.2018.09.004

Hobson, R. P., & Lee, A. (1998). Hello and goodbye: A study of social engagement in autism. *Journal of Autism and Developmental Disorders, 28*(2), 117–127. https://doi .org.10.1023/A:1026088531558

Hogan, A., Knez, N., & Kahng, S. (2015). Evaluating the use of behavioral skills training to improve school staffs' implementation of behavior intervention plans. *Journal of Behavioral Education, 24*(2), 242–254. https://doi.org/10.1007/s10864-014-9213-9

Hojnoski, R. L., Caskie, G. I. L., & Young, R. M. (2018). Early numeracy trajectories: Baseline performance levels and growth rates in young children by disability status. *Topics in Early Childhood Special Education, 37,* 206–218. https://doi .org/10.1177/0271121417735901

Holburn, S., Jacobson, J., Schwartz, A., Flory, M. J., & Vietze, P. (2004). The Willowbrook Futures Project: A longitudinal analysis of person-centered planning. *American Journal on Intellectual and Developmental Disabilities, 109*(1), 63–76. https://doi.org/10 .1352/0895-8017(2004)109<63:TWFPAL>2.0.CO;2

Hong, E. R., Ganz, J. B., Mason, R., Morin, K., Davis, J. L., Ninci, J., Neely, L. C., Boles, M. B., & Gilliland, W. D. (2016). The effects of video modeling in teaching functional living skills to persons with ASD: A meta-analysis of single-case studies. *Research in Developmental Disabilities, 57,* 158–169. https://doi.org/10.1016/j.ridd.2016.07.001

Hood, S. A., Luczynski, K. C., & Mitteer, D. R. (2017). Toward meaningful outcomes in teaching conversation and greeting skills to individuals with autism spectrum disorder. *Journal of Applied Behavior Analysis, 50*(3), 459–486. https://doi.org/10.1002 /jaba.388

Hoover, W. A., & Gough, P. B. (1990). The simple view of reading. *Reading and Writing, 2,* 127–160. https://doi.org/10.1007/BF00401799

Horner, R. H., Albin, R. W., Sprague, J. R., & Todd, A. W. (1999). Positive behavior support. In M. E. Snell & F. Brown (Eds.), *Instruction of students with severe disabilities* (5th ed., pp. 207–243). Merrill-Prentice-Hall.

Horner, R. H., Albin, R. A., Todd, A. W., Newton, S. J., & Sprague, J. R. (2010). Designing and implementing individualized positive behavior support. In M. E. Snell & F. Brown (Eds.), *Instruction of students with severe disabilities* (pp. 225–257). Pearson Education.

Horner, R. H., & Kratochwill, T. R. (2012). Synthesizing single-case research to identify evidence-based practices: Some brief reflections. *Journal of Behavioral Education, 21*(3), 266–272. https://doi.org/10.1007/s10864-012-9152-2

Horner, R. H., Newton, J. S., Todd, A. W., Algozzine, B., Algozzine, K., Cusumano, D., & Preston, A. (2017). A randomized waitlist controlled analysis of team-initiated problem solving professional development and use. *Behavioral Disorders, 50*(4), 444–456. https://doi.org/10.1177/0198742917745638

Horton, R. (2004). A statement by the editors of *The Lancet. The Lancet, 363*(9411), 820–821. https://doi.org/10.1016/S0140-6736(04)15699-7

Howlin, P., & Moss, P. (2012). Adults with autism spectrum disorders. *Canadian Journal of Psychiatry, 57*(5), 275–283. https://doi.org/10.1177/070674371205700501

Howlin, P., Moss, P., Savage, S., & Rutter, M. (2013). Social outcomes in mid-to-late adulthood among individuals diagnosed with autism and average nonverbal IQ as children. *Journal of the American Academy of Child & Adolescent Psychiatry, 52*(6), 572–581. https://doi.org/10.1016/j.jaac.2013.02.017

Huemer, S. V., & Mann, V. (2010). A comprehensive profile of decoding and comprehension in autism spectrum disorders. *Journal of Autism & Developmental Disorders, 40*(4), 485–493. https://doi.org/10.1007/s10803-009-0892-3

Huerta, M., & Lord, C. (2012). Diagnostic evaluation of autism spectrum disorders. *Pediatric Clinics of North America, 59*(1), 103–111. https://doi.org/10.1016/j.pcl.2011.10.018

Hume, K., Steinbrenner, J. R., Odom, S. L., Morin, K. L., Nowell, S. W., Tomaszewski, B., Szendrey, S., McIntyre, N. S., Özkan, S. Y., & Savage, M. N. (2021). Evidence-based practices for children, youth, and young adults with autism: Third generation review. *Journal of Autism and Developmental Disorders*. Advance online publication. https://doi.org/10.1007/s10803-020-04844-2

Hunsley, J. (2007). Addressing key challenges in evidence-based practice in psychology. *Professional Psychology: Research and Practice, 38*(2), 113–121. https://doi.org/10.1037/0735-7028.38.2.113

Hyman, S. L., Levy, S. E., & Myers, S. M. (2020). Identification, evaluation, and management of children with autism spectrum disorder. *Pediatrics, 145*(1), e20193447. https://doi.org/10.1542/peds.2019-3447

Individuals with Disabilities Education Improvement Act of 2004, 20 U.S.C. § 1400 *et seq.* (2004). https://sites.ed.gov/idea/statute-chapter-33

Ingersoll, B., & Berger, N. I. (2015). Parent engagement with a telehealth-based parent-mediated intervention program for children with autism spectrum disorders: Predictors of program use and parent outcomes. *Journal of Medical Internet Research, 17*(10), e227. doi:10.2196/jmir.4913

Ingersoll, B., Wainer, A. L., Berger, N. I., Pickard, K. E., & Bonter, N. (2016). Comparison of a self-directed and therapist-assisted telehealth parent-mediated intervention for children with ASD: A pilot RCT. *Journal of Autism and Developmental Disorders, 46*(7), 2275–2284.

International Research Consortium on Evidence-Based Practices (2013). *Organization effectiveness and efficiency scale.* https://sid-inico.usal.es/oees-english/

Iossifov, I., O'Roak, B. J., Sanders, S. J., Ronemus, M., Krumm, N., Levy, D., Stessman, H. A., Witherspoon, K. T., Vives, L., Patterson, K. E., Smith, J. D., Paeper, B., Nickerson, D. A., Dea, J., Dong, S., Gonzales, L. E., Mandell, J., D., Mane, S. M., Murtha, M. T., Sullivan, K. A., Walker, M. F. ... & Wigler, M. (2014). The contribution of de novo coding mutations to autism spectrum disorder. *Nature, 515*(7526), 216–221. https://doi.org/10.1038/nature13908

Iovannone, R., Dunlap, G., Huber, H., & Kincaid, D. (2003). Effective educational practices for students with autism spectrum disorders. *Focus on Autism and Other Developmental Disabilities, 18*, 150–165. https://doi.org/10.1177%2F10883576030180030301

Iwata, B. A., DeLeon, I. G., & Roscoe, E. M. (2013). Reliability and validity of the Functional Analysis Screening Tool. *Journal of Applied Behavior Analysis, 46*(1), 271–284. https://doi.org/10.1002/jaba.31

Iwata, B. A., Dorsey, F. M., Slifer, K. J., Bauman, K. E., & Richman, G., S. (1982). Toward a functional analysis of self-injury. *Analysis and Intervention in Developmental Disabilities, 2*(1), 3–20. https://doi.org/10.1016/0270-4684(82)90003-9

Iwata, B. A., Dorsey, F. M., Slifer, K. J., Bauman, K. E., & Richman, G. S. (1994). Toward a functional analysis of self-injury. *Journal of Applied Behavior Analysis, 27*(2), 197–209. https://doi.org/10.1901/jaba.1994.27-197

Iwata, B. A., & Dozier, C. L. (2008). Clinical application of functional analysis methodology. *Behavior Analysis in Practice, 1*(1), 3–9. https://doi.org/10.1007/BF03391714

Iwata, B. A, Duncan, B. A., Zarcone, J. R., Lerman, D. C., & Shore, B. A. (1994). A sequential, test-control methodology for conducting functional analyses of self-injurious behavior. *Behavior Modification, 18*(3), 289–306. https://doi.org/10.1177%2F014544 55940183003

Iwata, B. A., Pace, G. M., Dorsey, M. F., Zarcone, J. R., Vollmer, T. R., Smith, R. G., Rodgers, T. A., Lerman, D. C., Shore, B. A., Mazaleski, J. L., Goh, H-L., Cowdery, G. E., Kalsher, M. J., McCosh, K. C., & Willis, K. D. (1994). The functions of self-injurious behavior: An experimental-epidemiological analysis. *Journal of Applied Behavior Analysis, 27*(2), 215–240. https://doi.org/10.1901/jaba.1994.27-215

Jacobs, D. W., & Richdale, A. L. (2013). Predicting literacy in children with a high-functioning autism spectrum disorder. *Research in Developmental Disabilities, 34*(8), 2379–2390. https://doi.org/10.1016/j.ridd.2013.04.007

James, R., Sigafoos, J., Green, V. A., Lancioni, G. E., O'Reilly, M. F., Lang, R., Davis, T., Carnett, A., Achmadi, A., Gevarter, C., & Marschik, P. B. (2015). Music therapy for individuals with autism spectrum disorder: A systematic review. *Review Journal of Autism and Developmental Disorders, 2*(1), 39–54. https://www.doi.org/10.1007/s40489-014-0035-4

Jayanthi, M., & Friend, M. (1992). Interpersonal problem solving: A selective literature review to guide practice. *Journal of Educational and Psychological Consultation, 3*(1), 39–53. https://doi.org/10.1207/s1532768xjepc0301_3

Jenaro, C., Verdugo, M. A., Caballo, C., Balboni, G., Lachapelle Y., Otbrebski, W., & Schalock, R. L. (2005). Cross-cultural study of person-centered quality of life domains and indicators: A replication. *Journal of Intellectual Disability Research, 49*(10), 734–739. https://doi.org/10.1111/j.1365-2788.2005.00742.x

Jenkins, S. R., & DiGennaro Reed, F. D. (2017). A parametric analysis of rehearsal opportunities on procedural integrity: ERRATUM. *Journal of Organizational Behavior Management, 37*(1), 119. http://dx.doi.org.proxy.cc.uic.edu/10.1080/01608061.2017.1270181

Jeynes, W. (2003). A meta-analysis: The effects of parental involvement on minority children's academic achievement. *Education & Urban Society, 35,* 202–218. https://doi.org/10.1177%2F0013124502239392

Jeynes, W. H. (2017). A meta-analysis: The relationship between parental involvement and Latino student outcomes. *Education and Urban Society, 49*(1), 4–28. https://doi.org/10.1177/0013124516630596

Jimenez, B. A., & Kemmery, M. (2013). Building the early numeracy skills of students with moderate intellectual disability. *Education and Training in Autism and Developmental Disabilities, 48*(4), 479–490. https://www.jstor.org/stable/24232505

John-Steiner, V., & Mahn, H. (1996). Sociocultural approaches to learning and development: A Vygotskian framework. *Educational Psychologist, 31*(3–4), 191–206. https://doi.org/10.1207/s15326985ep3103&4_4

Johnson, C. P., & Meyers, S. M. (2007). Identification and evaluation of children with autism spectrum disorders. *Pediatrics, 120*(5), 1183–1215. https://doi.or/10.1542/peds.2007-2361

Johnson, D. R., Thurlow, M. L., Wu, Y., LaVelle, J. M., & Davenport, E. C. (2020). IEP/Transition planning participation among students with the most significant disabilities: Findings from NLTS 2012. *Career Development and Transition for Exceptional Individuals, 43*(4), 226–239. https://doi.org/10.1177/2165143420952050

Johnson, S. B., Johnson, C. M., & Vladescu, J. C. (2008). A comprehensive model for assessing the unique characteristics of children with autism. *Journal of Psychoeducational Assessment, 26*(4), 325–338. https://doi.org/10.1177%2F0734282908316952

Johnson, S. L., Elam, K., Rogers, A. A., & Hilley, C. (2018). A meta-analysis of parenting practices and child psychosocial outcomes in trauma-informed parenting interventions after violence exposure. *Prevention Science, 19*(7), 927–938. https://doi.org/10.1007/s11121-018-0943-0

Johnson-Martin, N. M., Attermeier, S. M., & Hacker, B. J. (2004). *The Carolina curriculum for infants and toddlers with special needs (CCITSN)* (3rd ed.). Brookes Publishing.

Jones, C. R., Happé, F., Golden, H., Marsden, A. J., Tregay, J., Simonoff, E., Pickles, A., Baird, G., & Charman, T. (2009). Reading and arithmetic in adolescents with autism spectrum disorders: Peaks and dips in attainment. *Neuropsychology, 23*(6), 718–728. https://doi.org/10.1037/a0016360

Jordan, N. C., & Levine, S. C. (2009). Socioeconomic variation, number competence, and mathematics learning difficulties in young children. *Developmental Disabilities Research Reviews, 15*(1), 60–68. https://doi.org/10.1002/ddrr.46

Jorgensen, J. D., Scheier, I. H., & Fautsko, T. F. (1981). *Solving problems in meetings.* Nelson-Hall.

Junge, C., Valkenburg, P. M., Dekovic, M., & Branje, S. (2020, September 18). The building blocks of social competence: Contributions of the Consortium of Individual Development. *Developmental Cognitive Neuroscience, 45.* Epub. https://doi.org/10.1016/j.den.2020.100861

Kagohara, D., Achmadi, D., van der Meer, L., Lancioni, G. E., O'Reilly, M. F., Lang, R., Marschik, P. B., Sutherland, D., Ramdoss, S., Green, V. A., & Sigafoos, J. (2013). Teaching two students with Asperger syndrome to greet adults using Social Stories™ and video modeling. *Journal of Developmental and Physical Disabilities, 25*(2), 241–251. https://doi.org/10.1007/s10882-012-9300-6

Kahn, K. S., & Justice, L. M. (2020). Continuities between early language development and reading comprehension. In P. D. Pearson, R. Barr, M. L. Kamil, P. Mosenthal, E. B. Moje, P. Afflerbach, P. Enciso, & N. K. Lesaux (Eds.), *Handbook of reading research* (Vol. V). Longman.

Kaiser, A. P., & Roberts, M. Y. (2013). Parents as communication partners: An evidence-based strategy for improving parent support for language and communication in everyday settings. *Perspectives on Language Learning and Education, 20*(3), 96–111. https://doi.org/10.1044/lle20.3.96

Kalyanpur, M., & Harry, B. (2012). *Cultural reciprocity in special education: Building family-professional relationships.* Paul H. Brookes.

Kamhi, A. G., & Catts, H. W. (2012). *Language And Reading Disabilities* (3rd ed.). Pearson.

Kamp-Becker, I., Schröder, J., Muehlan, H., Remschidt, H., Becker, K., & Bachmann, C. J. (2011). Health-related quality of life in children and adolescents with autism spectrum disorder. *Zietschrift fur Kinder Judenpsychiatrei und Psychotherapie, 39*(2), 13–31. https://doi.org/10.1024/1422-4917/a000098.

Kanner, L. (1943). Autistic disturbances of affective contact. *Nervous child, 2*(3), 217–250.

Kapp, S. K., Gillespie-Lynch, K., Sherman, L. E., & Hutman, T. (2012). Deficit, difference, or both? Autism and neurodiversity. *Developmental Psychology, 49*(1), 59–71. https://doi.org/10.1037/a0028353

Karren, B. C. (2017). Test review: Gilliam, J. E. (2014). Gilliam Autism Rating Scale-Third Edition (GARS-3). Pro-Ed. *Journal of Psychoeducational Assessment, 35*(3), 342–346. https://doi.org/10.1177/0734282916635465

Kazdin, A. E. (1980). Acceptability of alternative treatments for deviant child behavior. *Journal of Applied Behavior Analysis, 13*(2), 259–273. https://doi.org/10.1901/jaba.1980.13-259

Keen, D., Meadan, H., Brady, N. C., & Halle, J. W. (Eds.). (2016). *Prelinguistic and minimally verbal communicators on the autism spectrum.* Springer.

Keen, D., Webster, A., & Ridley, G. (2016). How well are children with autism spectrum disorder doing academically at school? An overview of the literature. *Autism, 20*(3), 276–294. https://doi.org/10.1177/1362361315580962

Keith, K. D., Heal, L. W., & Schalock, R. L. (1996). Cross-cultural measurement of critical quality of life concepts. *Journal of Intellectual and Developmental Disability, 21*(4), 273–293. https://doi.org/10.1080/13668259600033201

Keith, K. D., & Schalock, R. L. (2016). People speaking for themselves. In R. L. Schalock & K. D. Keith (Eds.), *Cross-cultural quality of life: Enhancing the lives of people with intellectual disabilities* (pp. 35–49). American Association on Intellectual and Developmental Disabilities.

Kelley, M. E., Lerman, D. C., Fisher, W. W., Roane, H. S., & Zangrillo, A. N. (2011). Reinforcement delay fading during differential reinforcement of communication: The effects of signals on response maintenance. *Journal of the Experimental Analysis of Behavior, 96*(1), 107–122. https://doi.org/10.1901/jeab.2011.96-107

Kelly, A., & Tincani, M. (2013). Collaborative training and practice among applied behavior analysts who support individuals with autism spectrum disorder. *Education and Training in Autism and Developmental Disabilities, 48*(1), 120–131. https://www.jstor.org/stable/23879891

Kelly, E. M., Greeny, K., Rosenberg, N., & Schwartz, I. (2020). When rules are not enough: Developing principles to guide ethical conduct. *Behavior Analysis in Practice, 14*, 491–498. https://doi.org/10.1007/s40617-020-00515-x

Kendeou, P. (2020). The assessment of reading for understanding. In P. D. Pearson, A. S. Palincsar, G. Biancarosa, & A. I. Berman (Eds.), *Reaping the rewards of the reading for understanding initiative* (pp. 67–142). National Academy of Education.

Kenny, L., Hattersley, C., Molins, B., Buckley, C., Povey, C., & Pellicano, E. (2016). Which terms should be used to describe autism? Perspectives from the UK autism community. *Autism, 20*(4), 442–462. https://doi.org/10.1177/1362361315588200

Kern, P., Wolery, M., & Aldridge, D. (2007). Use of songs to promote independence in morning greeting routines for young children with autism. *Journal of Autism and Developmental Disorders, 37*(7), 1264–1271. https://doi.org/10.1007/s10803-006-0272-1

Kerr, M. E., & Bowen, M. (1988). *Family evaluation: An approach based on Bowen theory.* Norton.

Kidder, R. M. (2005). *Moral courage.* HarperCollins.

Kidder, R. M. (2009). *How good people make tough choices: Resolving the dilemmas of ethical living* (rev. ed.). HarperCollins.

Kim, I., Dababnah, S., & Lee, J. (2020). The influence of race and ethnicity on the relationship between family resilience and parenting stress in caregivers of children with autism. *Journal of Autism and Developmental Disorders, 50*(2), 650–658. https://doi.org/10.1007/s10803-019-04269-6

Kim, S. Y. (2019). The experiences of adults with autism spectrum disorder: Self-determination and quality of life. *Research in Autism Spectrum Disorders, 60*, 1–15. https://doi.org/10.1016/j.rasd.2018.12.002

Kim, Y. G. (2017). Why the simple view of reading is not simplistic: Unpacking component skills of reading using a direct and indirect effect model of reading (DIER). *Scientific Studies of Reading, 21*(4), 310–333. https://doi.org/10.1080/10888438.2017.1291643

King, S. A., Lemons, C. J., & Davidson, K. A. (2016). Math interventions for students with autism spectrum disorder: A best-evidence synthesis. *Exceptional Children, 82*(4), 443–462. https://doi.org/10.1177/0014402915625066

Kintsch, W., & Greeno, J. G. (1985). Understanding and solving word arithmetic problems. *Psychological Review, 92*(1), 109–129. https://doi.org/10.1037//0033-295X.92.1.109

Kirby, A. V., Baranek, G. T., & Fox, L. (2016). Longitudinal predictors of outcomes for adults with autism spectrum disorder: Systematic review. *OTJR: Occupation, Participation and Health, 36*(2), 55–64. https://doi.org/10.1177%2F1539449216650182

Kirby, M. (2017). Implicit assumptions in special education policy: Promoting full inclusion for students with learning disabilities. *Child & Youth Care Forum, 46*(2), 175–191.

Kirkpatrick, M., Akers, J., & Rivera, G. (2019). Use of behavioral skills training with teachers: A systematic review. *Journal of Behavioral Education, 28*(3), 344–361. https://doi.org/10.1007/s10864-019-09322-z

Kleinert, W. L., Silva, M. R., Codding, R. S., Feinberg, A. B., & St. James, P. S. (2017). Enhancing classroom management using the classroom check-up consultation model with in-vivo coaching and goal setting components. *School Psychology Forum: Research in Practice, 11*(1), 5–19.

Klin, A., Saulnier, C., Tsatsanis, K., & Volkmar, F. R. (2005). Clinical evaluation in autism spectrum disorders: Psychological assessment within a transdisciplinary framework. In F. R. Volkmar, R. Paul, A. Klin, & D. Cohen (Eds.), *Handbook of autism and pervasive developmental disorders* (3rd ed., pp. 772–798). Wiley.

Knight, E., Blacher, J., & Eisenhower, A. (2019). Predicting reading comprehension in young children with autism spectrum disorder. *School Psychological Quarterly, 34*(2), 168–177. http://dx.doi.org/10.1037/spq0000277

Knight, V., Sartini, E., & Spriggs, A. D. (2014). Evaluating visual activity schedules as evidence-based practice for individuals with autism spectrum disorders. *Journal of Autism and Developmental Disorders, 45*(1), 157–178. https://doi.org/10.1007/s10803-014-2201-z

Knoster, T., & Kincaid, D. (2005). Long-term supports and ongoing evaluation. In L. M. Bambara & L. Kern (Eds.), *Individualized supports for students with problem behaviors: Designing positive behavior plans* (pp. 303–333). Guilford Press.

Kobak, K. A., Craske, M. G., Rose, R. D., & Wolitsky-Taylor, K. (2013). Web-based therapist training on cognitive behavior therapy for anxiety disorders: A pilot study. *Psychotherapy, 50*(2), 235–247. https://doi.org/10.1037/a003050568

Kober, R. (2011). *Enhancing the quality of life of people with intellectual disabilities: From theory to practice.* Springer.

Kober, R., & Eggleton, I. R. C. (2005). The effect of different types of employment on quality of life. *Journal of Intellectual Disability Research, 49*(10), 756–760. https://doi.org/10.1111/j.1365-2788.2005.00746.x

Koegel, L. K., Bryan, K. M., Su, P. L., Vaidya, M., & Camarata, S. (2020). Definitions of nonverbal and minimally verbal in research for autism: A systematic review of the literature. *Journal of Autism and Developmental Disorders, 50*(2), 2957–2972. https://doi.org/10.1007/s10803-020-04402-w

Koegel, L. K., Koegel, R. L., Harrower, J. K., & Carter, C. M. (1999). Pivotal response interventions I: Overview of approach. *Research and Practice for Persons with Severe Disabilities, 24*(3), 174–185. https://doi.org/10.2511%2Frpsd.24.3.174

Koegel, L., Matos-Freden, R., Lang, R., & Koegel, R. (2012). Interventions for children with autism spectrum disorders in inclusive school settings. *Cognitive and Behavioral Practice, 19*(3), 401–412. https://doi.org/10.1016/j.cbpra.2010.11.003

Koegel, R. L., Fredeen, R., Kim, S., Danial, J., Rubinstein, D., & Koegel, L. (2012). Using perseverative interests to improve interactions between adolescents with autism and their typical peers in school settings. *Journal of Positive Behavior Intervention, 14*, 133–141. https://doi.org./10.1177/1098300712437043

Koegel, R. L., & Koegel, L. K. (1988). Generalized responsivity and pivotal behaviors. In R. H. Horner, G. Dunlap, & R. L. Koegel (Eds.), *Generalization and maintenance: Lifestyle changes in applied settings* (pp. 41–66). Paul H. Brookes.

Kohane, I. S., McMurry, A., Weber, G., MacFadden, D., Rappaport, L., Kunkel, L., Bickel, J., Wattanasin, N., Spence, S., Murphy, S., & Churchill, S. (2012). The co-morbidity burden of children and young adults with autism spectrum disorders. *PloS One, 7*(4), e33224. https://doi.org/10.1371/journal.pone.0033224

Kohler, F. W. (1999). Examining the services received by young children with autism and their families: A survey of parent responses. *Focus on Autism and Other Developmental Disabilities, 14*(3), 150–158. https://doi.org/10.1177/108835769901400304

Kohler, P. D., & Field, S. (2003). Transition-focused education: Foundation for the future. *Journal of Special Education, 37*(3), 174–183. https://doi.org/10.1177/00224669030370030701

Kohler, P. D., Gothberg, J. E., Fowler, C., & Coyle, J. (2016). *Taxonomy for transition programming 2.0: A model for planning, organizing, and evaluating transition education, services, and programs.* Western Michigan University. www.transitionta.org.

Kourassanis, J., Jones, E. A., & Fienup, D. M. (2015). Peer-video modeling: Teaching chained social game behaviors to children with ASD. *Journal of Developmental and Physical Disabilities, 27*(1), 25–36. http://dx.doi.org/10.1007/s10882-014-9399-8

Kratochwill, T. R. (2006). Evidence-based interventions and practices in school psychology: The scientific basis of the profession. In R. Subotnik & H. Walberg (Eds.), *The scientific basis of educational productivity* (pp. 229–267). American Psychological Association.

Kratochwill, T. R. (2008). Best practices in school-based problem-solving consultation: Applications in prevention and intervention systems. In A. Thomas & J. Grimes (Eds.), *Best practices in school psychology V* (pp. 1673–1687). National Association of School Psychologists.

Kratochwill, T. R., Albers, C. A., & Shernoff, E. (2004). School-based interventions. *Child and Adolescent Psychiatric Clinics of North America, 13*(4), 885–903. https://doi.org/10.1016/j.chc.2004.05.003

Kratochwill, T. R., Altschaefl, M. A., & Bice-Urbach, B. (2014). Best practices in school-based problem solving consultation: Applications in prevention and intervention systems. In A. Thomas & P. Harrison (Eds.), *Best practices in school psychology VI* (pp. 461–482). National Association of School Psychologists.

Kratochwill, T. R., Elliott, S. N., & Callan-Stoiber, K. (2002). Best practices in school-based problem-solving consultation. In A. Thomas & J. Grimes (Eds.), *Best practices in school psychology IV* (pp. 583–604). National Association of School Psychologists.

Kratochwill, T. R., Elliott, S. N., & Rotto, P. C. (1995). Best practices in school-based behavioral consultation. In A. Thomas & J. Grimes (Eds.), *Best Practices in School Psychology III* (pp. 519–538). National Association of School Psychologists.

Kratochwill, T. R., & Stoiber, K. C. (2002). Evidence-based interventions within school psychology: Conceptual foundations of the procedural and coding manual of Division 16 and the Society for the Study of School Psychology Task Force. *School Psychology Quarterly, 17,* 341–389. https://doi.org/10.1521/scpq.17.4.341.20872

Kratz, H., Locke, J., Piotrowski, Z., Ouellette, R., Xie, M., Stahmer, A., & Mandell, D. (2014). All together now: Measuring staff cohesion in special education classrooms. *Journal of Psychoeducational Assessment, 33*(4), 329–338. https://doi.org/10.1177/0734282914554853

Krieger, B., Kinebanian, A., Prodinger, B., & Heigl, A. (2012). Becoming a member of the work force: perceptions of adults with Asperger syndrome. *Work, 43*(2), 141–157. https://doi.org/10.3233/WOR-2012-1392

Kubina, R. M., & Wolfe, P. S. (2005). Potential applications of behavioral fluency for students with autism. *Exceptionality, 13,* 35–44. https://doi.org/10.1207/s15327035ex1301_5

Kuhlthau, K., Orlich, F., Hall, T. A., Sikora, D., Kovacs, E. A., Delahaye, J., & Clemons, T. E. (2010). Health-related quality of life in children with autism spectrum disorders: Results from the autism treatment network. *Journal of Autism and Developmental Disabilities, 40,* 721–729. https://doi.org/10.1007/s/10803-009-0921-2

Kunnavatana, S. S., Bloom, S. E., Samaha, A. L., & Dayton, E. (2013). Training teachers to conduct trial-based functional analyses. *Behavior Modification, 37*(6), 707–722. http://dx.doi.org.proxy.cc.uic.edu/10.1177/0145445513490950

Kuo, C. C., Tseng, Y. C., Chang, C. F., Chen, C. S., Li, Y. J., & Wang, H. T. (2019). Using video-modeling package on improving workplace social skills of young adults with talent traits and autism: A case study. *Universal Journal of Educational Research, 7*(12), 2806–2816. https://doi.org/10.13189/ujer.2019.071231

Kuravackel, G. M., Ruble, L. A., Reese, R. J., Ables, A. P., Rodgers, A. D., & Toland, M. D. (2018). Compass for hope: Evaluating the effectiveness of a parent training and support program for children with ASD. *Journal of Autism and Developmental Disorders, 48*(2), 404–416. https://doi.org/10.1007/s10803-017-3333-8

Kusché, C. A., Mackey, A. L., & Kusché, J. B. R. (2020). Emotional and social competence (ESC) for adults: Keys for health, happiness, and success. In D. W. Nangle, C. A. Erdley, & R. A. Schwartz-Mette (Eds.), *Social skills across the lifespan: Theory, assessment and intervention* (pp. 277–293). Academic Press. https://doi.org/10.1016/B978-0-12-817752-5.00014-7

LaBrot, Z. C., Dufrene, B. A., Whipple, H., McCargo, M., & Pasqua, J. L. (2020). Targeted and intensive consultation for increasing head start and elementary teachers' behavior-specific praise. *Journal of Behavioral Education, 29*(4), 717–740. http://dx.doi.org.proxy.cc.uic.edu/10.1007/s10864-019-09342-9

Lachapelle, Y., Wehmeyer, M. L., Haelewyck, C., Courbois, Y., Keith, K. D., Schalock, R., Verdugo, M. A., & Walsh, P. N. (2005). The relationships between quality of life and self-determination: An international study. *Journal of Intellectual Disability Research, 49*(10), 740–744. https://doi.org/10.1111/j.1365-2788.2005.00743.x

Lai, M. C., Kassee, C., Besney, R., Bonato, S., Hull, L., Mandy, W., Szatmari, P., & Ameis, S. H. (2019). Prevalence of co-occurring mental health diagnoses in the autism population: A systematic review and meta-analysis. *The Lancet Psychiatry, 6*(10), 819–829. https://doi.org/10.1016/S2215-0366(19)30289-5

Lambert-Lee, K. A., Jones, R., O'Sullivan, J., Hastings, R. P., Douglas-Cobane, E., Thomas, J. E., Hughes, C., & Griffith, G. (2015). Translating evidence-based practice into a comprehensive educational model within an autism-specific special school. *British Journal of Special Education, 42*(1), 69–86. https://doi.org/10.1111/1467-8578.12090

Lang, R., Didden, R., Machalicek, W., Rispoli, M., Sigafoos, J., Lancioni, J., Mulloy, A., Regester, A., Pierce, N., & Kang, S. (2010). Behavioral treatment of chronic skin picking in individuals with developmental disabilities: A systematic review. *Research in Developmental Disabilities, 31*(2), 304–315. https://doi.org/10.1016/j.ridd.2009.10.017

Lang, R., Machalicek, W., Rispoli, M., O'Reilly, M., Sigafoos, J., Lancioni, G., Peters-Scheffer, N., & Didden, R. (2014). Play skills taught via behavioral intervention generalize, maintain, and persist in the absence of socially mediated reinforcement in children with autism. *Research in Autism Spectrum Disorders, 8*(7), 860–872. https://doi.org/10.1016/j.rasd.2014.04.007

Lang, R., Muharib, R., Lessner, P., Davenport, K., Ledbetter-Cho, K., & Rispoli, M. (2020). Increasing play and decreasing stereotypy for children with autism on a playground. *Advances in Neurodevelopmental Disorders, 4,* 146–154. https://doi.org/10.1007/s41252-020-00150-1

Lang, R., & Sturmey, P. (Eds.) (2021). *Adaptive behavior strategies for individuals with intellectual and developmental disabilities.* Springer. https://doi.org/10.1007/978-3-030-66441-1

Language for Learning. (2008). McGraw Hill.

Lanovaz, M. J., & Argumedes, M. (2009). Using the three-component multiple-schedule to examine the effects of treatments on stereotypy. *Journal on Developmental Disabilities, 15*(3), 64–68.

Lanovaz, M. J., Rapp, J. T., & Ferguson, S. (2012). The utility of assessing musical preference before implementation of noncontingent music to reduce vocal stereotypy. *Journal of Applied Behavior Analysis, 45*(4), 845–851. https://doi.org/10.1901/jaba.2012.45-845

Lanovaz, M. J., Rapp, J. T., Maciw, I., Prégent-Pelletier, É., Dorion, C., Ferguson, S., & Saade, S. (2014). Effects of multiple interventions for reducing vocal stereotypy:

Developing a sequential intervention model. *Research in Autism Spectrum Disorders*, 8(5), 529–545. https://doi.org/10.1016/j.rasd.2014.01.009

Laugeson, E. A., & Ellingsen, R. (2014). Social skills training for adolescents and adults with autism spectrum disorder. In F. R. Volkmar, B. Reichow, & J. C. McPartland (Eds.), *Adolescents and adults with autism spectrum disorders* (pp. 61–87). Springer.

Laugeson, E. A., Frankel, F., Gantman, A., Dillon, A. R., & Mogil, C. (2012). Evidence-based social skills training for adolescents with autism spectrum disorder: The UCLA PEERS program. *Journal of Autism and Developmental Disorders, 42*, 1025–1036. https://doi.org./10.1007/s10803-011-1339-1

Leaf, J. B., Ferguson, J. L., Cihon, J. H., Milne, C. M., Leaf, R., & McEachin, J. (2020). A critical review of social narratives. *Journal of Developmental and Physical Disabilities, 32*(2), 241–256. https://doi.org/10.1007/s10882-019-09692-2

Leblanc, M. P., Ricciardi, J. N., & Luiselli, J. K. (2005). Improving discrete trial instruction by paraprofessional staff through an abbreviated performance feedback intervention. *Education and Treatment of Children, 28*(1), 76–82. https://www.jstor.org/stable/42899829

Ledbetter-Cho, K., Lang, R., Watkins, L., O'Reilly, M., & Zamora, C. (2017). Systematic review of collateral effects of focused interventions for children with autism spectrum disorder. *Autism & Developmental Language Impairments, 2*, 1–22. https://doi.org/10.1177/2396941517737536

Lee, S. Y., Lo, Y-Y., & Lo, Y. (2017). Teaching functional play skills to a young child with autism spectrum disorder through video self-modeling. *Journal of Autism and Developmental Disorders, 47*, 2295–2306. https://doi-org.proxy.bsu.edu/10.1007/s10803-017-3147-8

Lee, S., Poston, D., & Poston, A. J. (2007). Lessons learned through implementing a positive behavior support at home: A case study on self-management with a student with autism and his mother. *Education and Training in Developmental Disabilities, 42*(4), 418–427. https://www.jstor.org/stable/23879847

Lehmkuhl, H. D., Storch, E. A., Bodfish, J. W., & Geffken, G. R. (2008). Brief report: Exposure and response prevention for obsessive compulsive disorder in a 12-year-old with autism. *Journal of Autism and Developmental Disorders, 38*, 977–981. https://doi.org/10.1007/s10803-007-0457-2

Leithwood, K. (2010). Characteristics of school districts that are exceptionally effective in closing the achievement gap. *Leadership and Policy in Schools, 9*(3), 245–291. https://doi.org/10.1080/15700761003731500

Lerman, D. C., Iwata, B. A., & Hanley, G. P. (2013). Applied behavior analysis. In G. J. Madden (Ed.), *APA handbook of behavior analysis* (pp. 81–104). American Psychological Association.

Levy, A., & Perry, A. (2011). Outcomes in adolescents and adults with autism: A review of the literature. *Research in Autism Spectrum Disorders, 5*(4), 1271–1282. https://doi.org/10.1016/j.rasd.2011.01.023

Liao, C. Y., Ganz, J. B., Vannest, K. J., Wattanawongwan, S., Pierson, L. M., Yllades, V., & Li, Y. F. (2020). Caregiver involvement in communication skills for individuals with ASD and IDD: A meta-analytic review of single-case research on the English, Chinese, and Japanese literature. *Review Journal of Autism and Developmental Disorders*. Advance online publication. https://doi.org/10.1007/s40489-020-00223-w

Liber, D. B., Frea, W. D., & Symon, J. B. G. (2008). Using time-delay to improve social play skills with peers for children with autism. *Journal of Autism and Developmental Disorders, 38*, 312–323. https://doi.org/10.1007/s10803-007-0395-z

Lieb, R. W., & Bohnert, A. M. (2017). Relations between executive functions, social impairment, and friendship quality on adjustment among high functioning youth with autism spectrum disorder. *Journal of Autism and Developmental Disorders, 47*(9), 2861–2872. https://doi.org/10.1007/s10803-017-3205-2

Lindsay, S., Proulx, M., Scott, H., & Thomson, N. (2014). Exploring teachers' strategies for including children with autism spectrum disorder in mainstream classrooms. *International Journal of Inclusive Education, 18*(2), 101–122. https://doi.org/10.1080/1360 3116.2012.758320

Lindstrom, L., Doren, B., & Miesch, J. (2011). Waging a living: Career development long-term employment outcomes for young adults with disabilities. *Exceptional Children, 77*(4), 423–434. https://doi.org/10.1177/001440291107700403

Lipkin, P. H., Baer, B., Macias, M. M., Hyman, S. L., Levy, S. E., Coury, D., Wolfe, A., & Sisk, B. (2017, May 6–9). *Trends in standardized developmental screening: Results from national surveys of pediatricians, 2002–2016.* Paper Presented at the Pediatric Academic Societies Annual Meeting, San Francisco, CA.

Lipkin, P. H., Macias, M. M., & Council on Children with Disabilities, Section on Developmental and Behavioral Pediatrics. (2020). Promoting optimal development: Identifying infants and young children with developmental disorders through developmental surveillance and screening. *Pediatrics 145*(1), e20193449. https://doi.org/10.1542 /peds.2019-3449

Lipscomb, S., Haimson, J., Liu, A. Y., Burghardt, J., Johnson, D. R., & Thurlow, M. L. (2017). Preparing for life after high school: The characteristics and experiences of youth in special education. Findings from the National Longitudinal Transition Study 2012. Volume 1: Comparisons with other youth: Full report (NCEE 2017-4016). U.S. Department of Education, Institute of Education Sciences, National Center for Education Evaluation and Regional Assistance. https://ies.ed.gov/ncee/projects/evaluation /disabilities_nlts2012.asp.

Litras, S., Moore, D. W., & Anderson, A. (2010, June 9). Using video self-modelled Social Stories to teach social skills to a young child with autism. *Autism Research and Treatment.* Epub. https://doi.org/10.1155/2010/834979

Little, S. G., Swangler, J., & Akin-Little, A. (2017). Defining social skills. In J. L. Matson (Ed.), *Handbook of social behavior and skills in children* (pp. 9–17). Springer. https:// doi.org/10.1007/978-3-319-64592-6_2

Liu, Q., Hsieh, W. Y., & Chen, G. (2020). A systematic review and meta-analysis of parent-mediated intervention for children and adolescents with autism spectrum disorder in mainland China, Hong Kong, and Taiwan. *Autism, 24*(8), 1960–1979. https://doi .org/10.1177/1362361320943380

Locke, J., Ishijima, E. H., & Kasari, C. (2010). Loneliness, friendship quality and the social networks of adolescents with high-functioning autism in an inclusive school setting. *Journal of Research in Special Education Needs, 10,* 74–81. https://doi.org/10.1111 /j.1471-3802.2010.01148.x

Lombardi, M., & Croce, L. (2016). Aligning supports planning within a quality-of-life outcomes framework. In R. L. Schalock & K. D. Keith (Eds.), *Cross-cultural quality of life: Enhancing the lives of people with intellectual disabilities* (pp. 81–93). American Association on Intellectual and Developmental Disabilities.

Lorah, E. R., Crouser, J., Gilroy, S. P., Tincani, M., & Hantula, D. (2014). Within stimulus prompting to teach symbol discrimination using an iPad® speech generating device. *Journal of Developmental and Physical Disabilities, 26,* 335–346. https://doi .org/10.1007/s10882-014-9369-1

Lorah, E. R., Gilroy, S. P., & Hineline, P. N. (2014). Acquisition of peer manding and listener responding in young children with autism. *Research in Autism Spectrum Disorders, 8*(2), 61–67. http://dx.doi.org/10.1016/j.rasd.2013.10.009

Lorah, E. R., Karnes, A., Miller, J., & Welsch-Beardsley, J. (2019). Establishing peer manding in young children with autism using a speech-generating device. *Journal of Developmental and Physical Disabilities, 31*, 791–801. https://doi.org/10.1007/s10882-019-09679-z

Lord, C., Rutter, M., DiLavore, P., Risi, S., Gotham, K., & Bishop, S. L. (2012). *Autism diagnostic observation schedule* (2nd ed.). Western Psychological Services.

Lord, C., Rutter, M., & Le Couteur, A. (1994). Autism Diagnostic Interview-Revised: A revised version of a diagnostic interview for caregivers of individuals with possible pervasive developmental disorders. *Journal of Autism and Developmental Disorders, 24*, 659–685. https://doi.org/10.1007/BF02172145

Loukusa, S., Mäkinen, L., Kuusikko-Gauffin, S., Ebeling, H., & Leinonen, E. (2018). Assessing social-pragmatic inferencing skills in children with autism spectrum disorder. *Journal of Communication Disorders, 73*(1), 91–105. https://doi.org/10.1016/j.jcomdis.2018.01.006

Lovaas, O. I., Schreibman, L., Koegel, R. L., & Rehm, R. (1971). Selective responding by autistic children to multiple sensory input. *Journal of Abnormal Psychology, 77*(3), 211–222. https://psycnet.apa.org/doi/10.1037/h0031015

Love, J. J., Miguel, C. F., Fernand, J. K., & LaBrie, J. K. (2012). The effects of matched stimulation and response interruption and redirection on vocal stereotypy. *Journal of Applied Behavior Analysis, 45*(3), 549–564. https://doi.org/10.1901/jaba.2012.45-549

Love, J. R., Carr, J. E., & LeBlanc, L. A. (2009). Functional assessment of problem behavior in children with autism spectrum disorders: A summary of 32 outpatient cases. *Journal of Autism and Developmental Disorders, 39*(2), 363–372. https://doi.org/10.1007/s10803-008-0633-z

Lucas, R., & Norbury, C. (2014). Levels of text comprehension in children with autism spectrum disorders (ASD): The influence of language phenotype. *Journal of Autism & Developmental Disorders, 44*(11), 2756–2768. https://doi.org/10.1007/s10803-014-2133-7

Lucas, R., & Norbury, C. (2015). Making inferences from text: It's vocabulary that matters. *Journal of Speech, Language & Hearing Research, 58*(4), 1224–1232. https://doi.org/10.1044/2015_JSLHR-L-14-0330

Lukmanji, S., Manji, S. A., Kadhim, S., Sauro, K. M., Wirrell, E. C., Kwon, C. S., & Jetté, N. (2019). The co-occurrence of epilepsy and autism: A systematic review. *Epilepsy & Behavior, 98*, 238–248. https://doi.org/10.1016/j.yebeh.2019.07.037

Lydon, S., Healy, O., & Dwyer, M. (2013). An examination of heart rate during challenging behavior in autism spectrum disorder. *Journal of Developmental and Physical Disabilities, 25*(1), 149–170. https://doi.org/10.1007/s10882-012-9324-y

Lyons, V., & Fitzgerald, M. (2007). Asperger (1906–1980) and Kanner (1894–1981), the two pioneers of autism. *Journal of Autism and Developmental Disorders, 37*(10), 2022–2023. https://doi.org/10.1007/s10803-007-0383-3

MacDuff, G. S., Krantz, P. J., & McClannahan, L. E. (2001). Prompts and prompt-fading strategies for people with autism. In C. Maurice, G. Green, & R. M. Foxx (Eds.), *Making a difference: Behavioral intervention for autism* (p. 37–50). Pro-Ed.

Machalicek, W., O'Reilly, M. F., Beretvas, N., Sigafoos, J., & Lancioni, G. E. (2007). A review of interventions to reduce challenging behavior in school settings for students with autism spectrum disorders. *Research in Autism Spectrum Disorders, 1*(3), 229–246. https://doi.org/10.1016/j.rasd.2006.10.005

Machalicek, W., Shogren, K., Lang, R., Rispoli, M., O'Reilly, M. F., Franco, J. H., & Sigafoos, J. (2009). Increasing play and decreasing the challenging behavior of children with autism during recess with activity schedules and task correspondence training. *Research in Autism Spectrum Disorders, 3*(2), 547–555. https://doi.org/10.1016/j.rasd.2008.11.003.

Madden, G. J., Dube, W. V., Hackenberg, T. D., Hanley, G. P., & Lattal, K. A. (Eds.). (2013). *APA handbooks in psychology®. APA handbook of behavior analysis* (Vol. 1). *Methods and principles.* American Psychological Association. https://doi.org/10.1037/13937-000

Maenner, M. J., Shaw, K. A., & Baio, J. (2020). Prevalence of autism spectrum disorder among children aged 8 years—autism and developmental disabilities monitoring network, 11 sites, United States, 2016. *MMWR Surveillance Summaries, 69*(4), 1. https://doi.org/10.15585/mmwr.ss6904a1

Magaña, S., Lopez, K., Aguinaga, A., & Morton, H. (2013). Access to diagnosis and treatment services among Latino children with autism spectrum disorders. *Intellectual and developmental disabilities, 51*(3), 141–153. https://doi.org/10.1352/1934-9556-51.3.141

Magaña, S., Machalicek, W., Lopez, K., & Iland, E. (2018). Padres en Accion: A parent education program for Latino parents of children with ASD. In J. Lutzker & K. Guastaferro (Eds.), *A guide to programs for parenting children with autism spectrum disorder, intellectual disabilities or developmental disabilities: Evidence-based guidance for professionals.* Jessica Kingsley Publishers.

Maggin, D. M., Chafouleas, S. M., Goddard, K. M., & Johnson, A. H. (2011). A systematic evaluation of token economies as a classroom management tool for students with challenging behavior. *Journal of School Psychology, 49*(5), 529–554. https://doi.org/10.1016/j.jsp.2011.05.001

Magiati, I., Moss, J., Yates, R., Charman, T., & Howlin, P. (2011). Is the Autism Treatment Evaluation Checklist a useful tool for monitoring progress in children with autism spectrum disorders? *Journal of Intellectual Disability Research, 55*(3), 302–312. https://doi.org/10.1111/j.1365-2788.2010.01359.x

Magiati, I., Tay, X. W., & Howlin, P. (2014). Cognitive, language, social and behavioural outcomes in adults with autism spectrum disorders: A systematic review of longitudinal follow-up studies in adulthood. *Clinical Psychology Review, 34*(1), 78–86. https://doi.org/10.1016/j.cpr.2013.11.002

Mahoney, B., Johnson, A., McCarthy, M., & White, C. (2018). Systematic review: Comparative efficacy of the Picture Exchange Communication System (PECS) to other augmentative communication systems in increasing social communication skills in children with autism spectrum disorder. *Communication Sciences and Disorders: Systematic Review Publications, 4.* https://scholarworks.uvm.edu/csdms/4

Mandell, D. S., Stahmer, A. C., Shin, S., Xie, M., Reisinger, E., & Marcus, S. C. (2013). The role of treatment fidelity on outcomes during a randomized field trial of an autism intervention. *Autism: The International Journal of Research and Practice, 17*(3), 281–295. https://doi.org/10.1177/1362361312473666

Mandell, D. S., Wiggins, L. D., Arnstein Carpenter, L., Daniels, J., DiGuiseppi, C., Durkin, M. S., Giarelli, E., Morrier, M., J., Nicholas, J. S., Pinto-Martin, J. A., Shattuck, P. T., Thomas, K. C., Yeargin-Allsopp, M., & Kirby, R. S. (2009). Racial/ethnic disparities in the identification of children with autism spectrum disorders. *American Journal of Public Health, 99*(3), 493–498. https://doi.org/10.2105/AJPH.2007.131243

Manz, P. H., Fantuzzo, J. W., & Power, T. J. (2004). Multidimensional assessment of family involvement among urban elementary students. *Journal of School Psychology, 42*, 461–475. https://doi.org/10.1016/j.jsp.2004.08.002

Mapp, K. L., & Kuttner, P. J. (2013). Partners in education: A dual capacity-building framework for family-school partnerships. SEDL, US Department of Education.

Marsh, J. A., McCombs, J. S., & Martorell, F. (2010). How instructional coaches support data-driven decision making: Policy implementation and effects in Florida middle schools. *Educational Policy, 24*(6), 872–907. https://doi.org/10.1177/0895904809341467

Martens, B. K., Witt, J. C., Elliott, S. N., & Darveaux, D. (1985). Teacher judgments concerning the acceptability of school-based interventions. *Professional Psychology: Research and Practice, 16*(2), 191–198. https://doi.org/10.1037/0735-7028.16.2.191

Martinez, C. K., Betz, A. M., Liddon, C. J., & Werle, R. L. (2016). A progression to transfer RIRD to the natural environment. *Behavioral Interventions, 31*, 144–162. https://doi.org/10.1002/bin

Martorell, A., Gutierrez-Recacha, P., Pereda, A., & Ayuso-Mateos, J. L. (2008). Identification of personal factors that determine work outcome for adults with intellectual disability. *Journal of Intellectual Disability Research, 52*, 1091–1101. https://doi.org/10.1111/j.1365-2788.2008.01098.x

Mas, J. M., Dunst, C. J., Balcells-Balcells, A., Garcia-Ventura, S., Gine, C., & Canadas, M. (2019). Family-centered practices and the parental well-being of young children with disabilities and developmental delay. *Research in Developmental Disabilities, 94*, 1–13, https://doi.org/10.1016/j.ridd.2019.103495

Mason, R. A., Ganz, J. B., Parker, R. I., Burke, M. D., & Camargo, S. P. (2012). Moderating factors of video-modeling with other as model: A meta-analysis of single-case studies. *Research in Developmental Disabilities, 33*(4), 1076–1086. https://doi.org/10.1016/j.ridd.2012.01.016

Mason, R. A., Gunersel, A. B., Irvin, D. W., Wills, H. P., Gregori, E., An, Z. G., & Ingram, P. B. (2021). From the frontlines: Perceptions of paraprofessionals' roles and responsibilities. *Teacher Education and Special Education, 44*(2) 97–116. https://doi.org/10.1177/0888406419896627

Mason, R. A., Schnitz, A. G., Wills, H. P., Rosenbloom, R., Kamps, D. M., & Bast, D. (2017). Impact of a teacher-as-coach model: Improving paraprofessionals fidelity of implementation of discrete trial training for students with moderate-to-severe developmental disabilities. *Journal of Autism and Developmental Disorders, 47*(6), 1696–1707. https://doi.org/10.1007/s10803-017-3086-4

Mather, M., Jacobsen, L. A., Jarosz, B., Kilduff, L., Lee, A., Pollard, K. M., Scommegna, P., & Vanorman, A. (2019). American's changing population. Population Reference Bureau (PRB), *Population Bulletin, 74*(1). https://www.prb.org/wp-content/uploads/2019/06/PRB-PopBulletin-2020-Census.pdf

Matson, J. L. (2007). Determining treatment outcome in early intervention programs for autism spectrum disorders: A critical analysis of measurement issues in learning-based interventions. *Research in Developmental Disabilities, 28*, 207–218. https://doi.org/10.1016/j.ridd.2005.07.006

Matson, J. L., & LoVullo, S. V. (2008). A review of behavioral treatments for self-injurious behaviors of persons with autism spectrum disorders. *Behavior Modification, 32*(1), 61–76. https://doi.org/10.1177/0145445507304581

Matson, J. L., Tureck, K., & Rieske, R. (2012). The Questions About Behavioral Function (QABF): Current status as a method of functional assessment. *Research in Developmental Disabilities, 33*(2), 630–634. https://doi.org/10.1016/j.ridd.2011.11.006

Matson, J. L., Wilkins, J., & Macken, J. (2008). The relationship of challenging behaviors to severity and symptoms of autism spectrum disorders. *Journal of Mental Health Research in Intellectual Disabilities, 2*(1), 29–44. https://doi.org/10.1080/19315860802611415

Mattison, M. (2000). Ethical decision making: The person in the process. *Social Work, 45*(3), 201–212. https://doi.org/10.1093/sw/45.3.201

May, T., Rinehart, N., Wilding, J., & Cornish, K. (2013). The role of attention in the academic attainment of children with autism spectrum disorder. *Journal of Autism and Developmental Disorders, 43*, 2147–2158. https://doi.org/10.1007/s10803-013-1766-2

Mayes, S. D., & Calhoun, S. L. (2003). Ability profiles in children with autism: Influence of age and IQ. *Autism, 7*(1), 65–80. https://doi.org/10.1177/1362361303007001006

Mayes, S. D., Gorman, A. A., Hillwig-Garcia, J., & Syed, E. (2013). Suicide ideation and attempts in children with autism. *Research in Autism Spectrum Disorders, 7*(1), 109–119. https://doi.org/10.1016/j.rasd.2012.07.009

Mazurek, M., & Kanne, S. (2010). Friendship and internalizing symptoms among children and adolescents with ASD. *Journal of Autism and Developmental Disorders, 40*(12), 1512–1520. https://doi.org/10.1007/s10803-010-1014-y

Mazzone, L., Postorino, V., Siracusano, M., Riccioni, A., & Curatolo, P. (2018). The relationship between sleep problems, neurobiological alterations, core symptoms of autism spectrum disorder, and psychiatric comorbidities. *Journal of Clinical Medicine, 7*(5), 102. https://doi.org/10.3390/jcm7050102

Mazzotti, V. L., Rowe, D., Kwiatek, S., Voggt, A., Chang, W., Fowler, C. H., Poppen, M., Sinclair, J., & Test, D. W. (2021). Secondary transition predictors of post-school success: An update for the field. *Career Development and Transition for Exceptional Individuals, 44*(1), 47–64. https://doi.org/10.1177/2165143420959793

Mazzotti, V. L., Rowe, D. A., Sinclair, J., Poppen, M., Woods, W. E., & Shearer, M. (2016). Predictors of post-school success: A systematic review of NLTS2 secondary analyses. *Career Development and Transition for Exceptional Individuals, 39*(4), 196–215. https://doi.org/10.1177/2165143415588047

McAuliffe, D., & Chenoweth, L. (2008). Leave no stone unturned: The inclusive model of ethical decision making. *Ethics and social welfare, 2*(1), 38–49. https://doi.org/10.1080/17496530801948739

McCahill, J., Healy, O., Lydon, S., & Ramey, D. (2014). Training educational staff in functional behavioral assessment: A systematic review. *Journal of Developmental and Physical Disabilities, 26*(4), 479–505. https://doi.org/10.1007/s10882-014-9378-0

McCay, L. O., & Keyes, D. W. (2001). Developing social competence in the inclusive primary classroom. *Childhood Education, 78*(2), 70–78. https://doi.org/10.1080/00094056.2002.10522707

McComas, J. J., Goddard, C., & Hoch, H. (2002). The effects of preferred activities during academic work breaks on task engagement and negatively reinforced destructive behavior. *Education and Treatment of Children, 25*(1), 103–112. https://www.jstor.org/stable/42900518

McConachie, H., & Diggle, T. (2007). Parent implemented early intervention for young children with autism spectrum disorder: A systematic review. *Journal of evaluation in clinical practice, 13*(1), 120–129. https://doi.org/10.1111/j.1365-2753.2006.00674.x

McConachie, H., & Robinson, G. (2006). What services do young children with autism spectrum disorder receive? *Child Care, Health and Development, 32*(5), 553–557. https://doi.org/10.1111/j.1365-2214.2006.00672.x

McCulloch, E. B., & Noonan, M. J. (2013). Impact of online training videos on the implementation of mand training by three elementary school paraprofessionals. *Education and Training in Autism and Developmental Disabilities, 48*(1), 132–141. https://www.jstor.org/stable/23879892

McDaniel, S. & Bloomfield, B. (2020). School-wide positive behavior support telecoaching in a rural district. *Journal of Educational Technology Systems, 48*(3), 335–355. https://doi.org/ 10.1177/0047239519886283

McDuffie, A., Machalicek, W., Oakes, A., Haebig, E., Weismer, S. E., & Abbeduto, L. (2013). Distance video-teleconferencing in early intervention: Pilot study of a naturalistic parent-implemented language intervention. *Topics in Early Childhood Special Education, 33*(3), 1–14. https://doi.org/10.1177/0271121413476348

McGreevy, P., Fry, T., & Cornwall, C. (2014). *Essential for Living.* Patrick McGreevy.

McGuire, J., & McDonnell, J. (2008). Relationships between recreation and levels of self-determination for adolescents and young adults with disabilities. *Career Development for Exceptional Individuals, 31*(3), 154–163. https://doi.org/10.1177/0885728808315333

McIntosh, A., Reys, B. J., & Reys, R. E. (1992). A proposed framework for examining basic number sense. *For the Learning of Mathematics, 12*(3), 2–44. https://www.jstor.org/stable/40248053

McIntyre, N. S., Grimm, R. P., Solari, E. J., Zajic, M. C., & Mundy, P. C. (2020). Growth in narrative retelling and inference abilities and relations with reading comprehension in children and adolescents with autism spectrum disorder. *Autism & Developmental Language Impairments, 5*, 1–16. https://doi.org/10.1177/2396941520968028

McIntyre, N. S., Oswald, T. M., Solari, E. J., Zajic, M. C., Lerro, L. E., Hughes, C., Devine, R. T., & Mundy, P. C. (2018). Social cognition and reading comprehension in children and adolescents with autism spectrum disorders or typical development. *Research in Autism Spectrum Disorders, 54*, 9–20. https://doi.org/10.1016/j.rasd.2018.06.004

McIntyre, N. S., Solari, E. J., & Gonzales, J. E. (2017). The scope and nature of reading comprehension impairments in school-aged children with higher-functioning autism spectrum disorder. *Journal of Autism and Developmental Disorders, 47*, 2838–2860. https://doi.org/10.1007/s10803-017-3209-y

McIntyre, N. S., Solari, E. J., Grimm, R. P., Lerro, L. E., Gonzales, J. E., & Mundy, P. C. (2017). A comprehensive examination of reading heterogeneity in students with high functioning autism: Distinct reading profiles and their relation to autism symptom severity. *Journal of Autism and Developmental Disorders, 47*, 1086–1101. https://doi.org/10.1007/s10803-017-3029-0

McKinney, T., & Vasquez, E., III. (2014). There's a bug in your ear! Using technology to increase the accuracy of DTT implementation. *Education and Training in Autism and Developmental Disabilities, 49*(4), 594–600. https://www.jstor.org/stable/24582354

McLaughlin, T., Aspden, K., & Clarke, L. (2017). How do teachers support children's social-emotional competence? *Early Childhood Folio, 21*(2), 21–27. https://doi.org/10.18296/ecf.0041

McLaughlin, T. W., Denney, M. K., Snyder, P. A., & Welsh, J. L. (2011). Behavior support interventions implemented by families of young children: Examination of contextual fit. *Journal of Positive Behavior Interventions, 14*(2), 87–97. https://doi.org/10.1177/1098300711411305

McLeskey, J., Barringer, M-D., Billingsley, B., Brownell, M., Jackson, D., Kennedy, M., Lewis, T., Maheady, L., Rodriguez, J., Scheeler, M. C., Winn, J., & Ziegler, D. (2017, January). *High-leverage practices in special education.* Council for Exceptional Children & CEEDAR Center.

McNamara, K., Rasheed, H., & Delamatre, J. (2008). A statewide study of school-based intervention teams: Characteristics, member perceptions, and outcomes. *Journal of Educational and Psychological Consultation, 18*(1), 5–30. https://doi.org/10.1080/10474410701864107

Meadan, H., & Daczewitz, M. E. (2015). Internet-based intervention training for parents of young children with disabilities: A promising service-delivery model. *Early Child Development and Care, 185*(1), 155–169. https://doi.org/10.1080/03004430.2014.908866

Meadan, H., Halle, J. W., & Ebata, T. A. (2010). Families of children who have autism spectrum disorder: Stress and support. *Exceptional Children, 77*(1), 7–36. https://doi.org/10.1177/001440291007700101

Meadan, H., Snodgrass, M. R., Meyer, L. E., Fisher, K. W., Chung, M. Y., & Halle, J. W. (2016). Internet-based parent-implemented intervention for young children with autism: A pilot study. *Journal of Early Intervention, 38*(1), 3–23. https://doi.org/10.1177/1053815116630327

Mehling, M. H., & Tassé, M. J. (2016). Severity of autism spectrum disorders: Current conceptualization, and transition to DSM-5. *Journal of Autism and Developmental Disorders, 46*(6), 2000–2016. https://doi.org/10.1007/s10803-016-2731-7

Meleshkevich, O., Axe, J. B., & Espinosa, F. D. (2020). Effects of time delay and requiring echoics on answering questions about visual stimuli. *Journal of Applied Behavior Analysis, 54*(2), 725–743. https://doi.org/10.1002/jaba.790

Mells Yavuz, H., Selcuk, B., & Korkmaz, B. (2019). Social competence in children with autism. *International Journal of Developmental Disabilities*, 65(1), 10–19. https://doi.org/10.1080/20473869.2017.1346224

Meltzer, L. (2018). *Executive function in education: From theory to practice* (2nd ed.). Guilford Press.

Menchetti, B., & Garcia, L. (2003). Personal and employment outcomes for person-centered planning. *Education and Training in Developmental Disabilities*, 38(2), 145–156. https://www.jstor.org/stable/23879592

Mercier, C., Mottron, L., & Belleville, S. (2000). A psychosocial study on restricted interests in high functioning persons with pervasive developmental disorders. *Autism*, 4(4), 406–425. https://doi.org/10.1177/1362361300004004006

Metz, A., Halle, T., Bartley, L., & Blasberg, A. (2013). The key components of successful implementation. In T. Halle, A. Metz, & I. Martinez-Beck (Eds.), *Applying implementation science in early childhood programs and systems* (pp. 21–42). Brookes.

Meyers, B., Valentino, C. T., Meyers, J., Boretti, M., & Brent, D. (1996). Implementing prereferral intervention teams as an approach to school-based consultation in an urban school system. *Journal of Educational and Psychological Consultation*, 7(2), 119–149. https://doi.org/10.1207/s1532768xjepc0702_2

Michael, J. L. (2004). *Concepts and Principles of Behavior Analysis* (rev. ed.). Association for Behavior Analysis International.

Miller, K. L., Re Cruz, A., & Ala'i-Rosales, S. (2019). Inherent tensions and possibilities: Behavior analysis and cultural responsiveness. *Behavior and Social Issues*, 28, 16–36. https://doi.org/10.1007/s42822-019-00010-1

Miltenberger, R. G. (2011). Chaining. In T. Matray, P. Hovanessian, & S. DeNola (Eds.), *Behavior modification: Principles and procedures* (5th ed., p. 207). Wadsworth.

Minshew, N. J., Meyer, J., Goldstein, G. (2002). Abstract reasoning in autism: a dissociation between concept formation and concept identification. *Neuropsychology*, 16(3), 327–334. https://psycnet.apa.org/doi/10.1037/0894-4105.16.3.327

Moes, D. R., & Frea, W. D. (2000). Using family context to inform intervention planning for the treatment of a child with autism. *Journal of Positive Behavior Interventions*, 2, 40–46. https://doi.org/10.1177/109830070000200106

Montague, M. (1997). Student perception, mathematical problem solving, and learning disabilities. *Remedial and Special Education*, 18(1), 46–53. https://doi.org/10.1177/074193259701800108

Montgomery, J. M., Duncan, C. R., & Francis, G. C. (2007). Test Review: Siegel, B. (2004). Pervasive Developmental Disorder Screening Test-II (PDDST-II). Harcourt. *Journal of Psychoeducational Assessment*, 25(3), 299–306. https://doi.org/10.1177/0734282906298469

Moore, J. W., & Quintero, L. M. (2018). Comparing forward and backward chaining in teaching Olympic weightlifting. *Journal of Applied Behavior Analysis*, 52(1), 50–59. https://doi.org/10.1002/jaba.517

Moran, M. L., Gomez, L. F., Alcedo, M. A., & Pedrosa, I. (2019). Gender differences in social inclusion of youth with autism and intellectual disabilities. *Journal of Autism and Developmental Disorders*, 49, 2980–2989. https://doi.org/10.1007/s10803-019-04030-z

Mount, B. (1992). *Person-centered planning: A sourcebook of values, ideas, and methods to encourage person-centered development*. Graphic Futures.

Mount, B. (2000). *Person-Centered Planning: Finding directions for change using personal futures planning*. Capacity Works.

Mount, B., & Zwernik, K. (1988). *It's never too early, it's never too late: A booklet about personal future planning for persons with developmental disabilities, their families and friends, case managers, service providers, and advocates* (Publication No. 42-88-109). Governor's Council on Developmental Disabilities.

Mowbray, C. T., Holter, M. C., Teague, G. B., & Bybee, D. (2003). Fidelity criteria: Development, measurement, and validation. *American Journal of Evaluation, 24*(3), 315–340. https://doi.org/10.1177/109821400302400303

Mueller, M. M., Palkovic, C. M., & Maynard, C. S. (2007). Errorless learning: Review and practical application for teaching children with pervasive developmental disorders. *Psychology in the Schools, 44*(7), 691–700. https://doi.org/10.1002/pits.20258

Mueller, T. G., & Carranza, F. (2011). An examination of special education due process hearings. *Journal of Disability Policy Studies, 22*(3), 131–139. https://doi.org/10.1177%2F1044207311392762

Murch, S. H., Anthony, A., Casson, D. H., Malik, M., Berelowitz, M., Dhillon, A. P., Thomson, A., Valentine, A., Davies, S. E., & Walker-Smith, J. A. (2004). Retraction of an interpretation. *The Lancet, 363*(9411), 750. https://doi.org/10.1016/S0140-6736(04)15715-2

Murnane, R., Sharkey, N. S., & Boudett, K. P. (2005). Using student-assessment results to improve instruction: Lessons from a workshop. *Journal of Education for Students Placed at Risk, 10*(3), 269–280. https://doi.org/10.1207/s15327671espr1003_3

Murphy, G. H., Beadle-Brown, J., Wing, L., Gould, J., Shah, A., & Holmes, N. (2005). Chronicity of challenging behaviours in people with severe intellectual disabilities and/or autism: A total population sample. *Journal of Autism and Developmental Disorders, 35*(4), 405–418. https://doi.org/10.1007/s10803-005-5030-2

Najdowski, A. C., Gould, E. R., Lanagan, T. M., & Bishop, M. R. (2014). Designing curriculum programs for children with autism. In J. Tarbox, D. R. Dixon, P. Sturmey, & J. L. Matson (Eds.), *Handbook of early intervention for autism spectrum disorders: Research, policy, and practice* (pp. 227–259). Springer.

Nation, K. (2019). Children's reading difficulties, language, and reflections on the simple view of reading. *Australian Journal of Learning Difficulties, 24*(1), 47–73. https://doi.org/10.1080/19404158.2019.1609272

Nation, K., & Castles, A. (2017). Putting the learning into orthographic learning. In K. Cain, D. L. Compton, & R. K. Parrila (Eds.), *Theories of reading development* (pp. 147–168). John Benjamins Publishing. https://doi.org./10.1075/swll.15.09nat

Nation, K., Clarke, P., Wright, B., & Williams, C. (2006). Patterns of reading ability in children with autism spectrum disorder. *Journal of Autism and Developmental Disorders, 36*, 911–919. https://doi.org/10.1007/s10803-006-0130-1

National Association of School Psychologists. (2020a). *Model for comprehensive and integrated school psychological services.* https://www.nasponline.org/standards-and-certification/nasp-practice-model/nasp-practice-model-implementation-guide/section-i-nasp-practice-model-overview/nasp-practice-model-overview

National Association of School Psychologists. (2020b). *Principles for professional ethics.* https://doi.org/10.1080/02796015.2010.12087782

National Association of School Psychologists. (2020c). *Who are school psychologists?* https://www.nasponline.org/about-school-psychology/who-are-school-psychologists

National Association of Social Workers. (2017). *Code of ethics of the national association of social workers.* https://www.socialworkers.org/About/Ethics/Code-of-Ethics/Code-of-Ethics-English

National Association of State Directors of Special Education. (2005). *Response to intervention: Policy considerations and implementation.* NASDSE.

National Center and State Collaborative *2015 Operational Assessment Technical Manual* (2016). http://www.ncscpartners.org/Media/Default/PDFs/Resources/NCSC15_NCSC_TechnicalManualNarrative.pdf

National Center for Education Statistics. (2020). https://nces.ed.gov

National Center for Quality Teaching and Learning. (2014). *Practice-based coaching.* http://eclkc.ohs.acf.hhs.gov/hslc/tta-system/teaching/development/coaching.html

National Center on Educational Outcomes. (2016). https://nceo.info/Resources

National Council of Teachers of Mathematics. (2000). *Principles and standards for school mathematics*. NCTM.

National Early Literacy Panel. (2008). *Developing early literacy.* https://lincs.ed.gov/publications/pdf/NELPReport09.pdf

National Education Association. (2020, September 14). *Code of Ethics for Educators.* https://www.nea.org/resource-library/code-ethics-educators

National Reading Panel. (2000). Teaching children to read: an evidence-based research assessment of the scientific research literature on reading and its implications in reading instruction: Reports of the subgroups. https://www.nichd.nih.gov/sites/default/files/publications/pubs/nrp/Documents/report.pdf

National Research Council. 2001. *Educating children with autism*. National Academies Press. https://doi.org/10.17226/10017

Neuhaus, E., Bernier, R. A., Tham, S. W., & Webb, S. J. (2018). Gastrointestinal and psychiatric symptoms among children and adolescents with autism spectrum disorder. *Frontiers in Psychiatry, 9,* 515. https://doi.org/10.3389/fpsyt.2018.00515

Nevill, R. E., Lecavalier, L., & Stratis, E. A. (2018). Meta-analysis of parent-mediated interventions for young children with autism spectrum disorder. *Autism, 22*(2), 84–98. https://doi.org/10.1177/1362361316677838

Newman, L. (2005). Family involvement in the educational development of youth with disabilities: A special topic report of findings from the National Longitudinal Transition Study-2 (NLTS2). Office of Special Education Programs, U.S. Department of Education. https://files.eric.ed.gov/fulltext/ED489979.pdf

Newman, L., Wagner, M., Cameto, R., & Knokey, A. M. (2009). The post-high school outcomes of youth with disabilities up to 4 years after high school: A report from the National Longitudinal Transition Study-2 (NLTS2). NCSER 2009-3017. National Center for Special Education Research. https://eric.ed.gov/?id=ED505448

Newman, L., Wagner, M., Knokey, A. M., Marder, C., Nagle, K., Shaver, D., Wei, X., Cameto, R., Contreras, E., Ferguson, K., Greene, S., & Schwarting, M. (2011). *The post-high school outcomes of young adults with disabilities up to 8 years after high school*. A report from the National Longitudinal Transition Study-2. SRI International. www.nlts2.org/reports/

Newman, T. M., Macomber, D., Naples, A. J., Babitz T., Volkmar, F. & Grigorenko, E. L. (2007). Hyperlexia in children with autism spectrum disorders. *Journal of Autism and Developmental Disorders, 37,* 760–774 (2007). https://doi.org/10.1007/s10803-006-0206-y

Newton, J. S., Horner, R. H., Algozzine, B., Todd, A. W., & Algozzine, K. (2012). A randomized wait-list controlled analysis of the implementation integrity of team-initiated problem solving processes. *Journal of School Psychology, 50*(4), 421–441. https://doi.org/10.1016/j.jsp.2012.04.002

Nguyen, T., Watts, T. W., Duncan, G. J., Clements, D. H., Sarama, J. S., Wolfe, C., & Spitler, M. E. (2016). Which preschool mathematics competencies are most predictive of fifth grade achievement? *Early Childhood Research Quarterly, 36,* 550–560. https://doi.org/10.1016/j.ecresq.2016.02.003

Nicolaidis, C. (2012). What can physicians learn from the neurodiversity movement? *Virtual Mentor: American Medical Association Journal of Ethics, 14,* 503–510. https://doi.org/10.1001/virtualmentor.2012.14.6.oped1-1206

Ninci, J., Gerow, S., Rispoli, M., & Boles, M. (2017). Systematic review of vocational preferences on behavioral outcomes of individuals with disabilities. *Journal of Developmental and Physical Disabilities, 29,* 875–894. https://doi.org/10.1007/s10882-017-9560-2

Nirje, B. (1969). The normalization principle and its human management implications. In R. Kugel & W. Wolfensberger (Eds.), *Changing patterns in residential services for the mentally retarded* (pp. 179–195). President's Commission on Mental Retardation.

Nirje, B. (1994). The normalization principle and its human management implications. *The International Social Role Valorization Journal, 1*(2), 19–23.

No Child Left Behind Act of 2001, Pub. L. No. 107-110, 115 Stat. 1425. (2002).

Noble, T., & McGrath, H. (2014). Well-being and resilience in school settings. In G. A. Fava & C. Ruini (Eds.), *Increasing psychological well-being in clinical and educational settings: Interventions and cultural contexts* (pp. 135–152). Springer.

Norbury, C., & Nation, K. (2011). Understanding variability in reading comprehension in adolescents with autism spectrum disorders: Interactions with language status and decoding skill. *Scientific Studies of Reading, 15*(3), 191–210, https://dor.org/10.1080/10888431003623553

Norbury, C. F., & Sparks, A. (2013). Difference or disorder? Cultural issues in understanding neurodevelopmental disorders. *Developmental Psychology, 49*(1), 45–58. http://dx.doi.org/10.1037/a0027446

Northup, J. (2000). Further evaluation of the accuracy of reinforcer surveys: A systematic replication. *Journal of Applied Behavior Analysis, 33*(3), 335–338. https://doi.org/10.1901/jaba.2000.33-335

Nota, L., Ferrari, L., Soresi, S., & Wehmeyer, M. (2007). Self-determination, social abilities, and the quality of life of people with intellectual disability. *Journal of Intellectual Disability Research, 51*, 850–865. https://doi.org/10.1111/j.1365-2788.2006.00939.x

Oakhill, J., Cain, K., & Elbro, C. (2015). *Understanding and teaching reading comprehension: A handbook*. Routledge.

O'Brien, J., Mount, B., & O'Brien, C. L. (1990). *The personal profile*. Responsive Systems Associates.

O'Brien, J., O'Brien, C. L., & Mount, B. (1997). Person-centered planning has arrived . . . or has it? *Mental Retardation, 35*(6), 480–488. https://doi.org/10.1352/0047-6765(1997)035<0480:PPHAOH>2.0.CO;2

Odom, S. L., Cox, A. W., Brock, M. E., & the National Professional Development Center on ASD. (2013). Implementation science, professional development, and autism spectrum disorders. *Exceptional Children, 79*(3), 233–251. https://doi.org/10.1177/001440291307900207

Odom, S. L., Hall, L. J., Morin, K. L., Kraemer, B. R., Hume, K. A., McIntyre, N. S., Nowell, S. W., Steinbrenner, J. R., Tomaszewski, B., Sam, A. M., & DaWalt, L. (2021). Educational interventions for children and youth with autism: A 40-year perspective. *Journal of Autism and Developmental Disorders, 51*, 4354–4369. https://doi.org/10.1007/s10803-021-04990-1

Office of Special Education Programs. (2020). *OSEP expectations for engaging families in discretionary grants*. https://osepideasthatwork.org/sites/default/files/OSEP%20Expectations%20for%20Family%20Engagement%20in%20Discretionary%20Grants%28May2020%29-508%20%281%29.pdf

Ogletree, B. T., Rose, A., & Hambrecht, G. (2019). Evidence-based methods for teaching school aged children and youth with autism spectrum disorder and complex communication needs. In J. B. Ganz & R. L. Simpson (Eds.), *Interventions for individuals with autism spectrum disorders and complex communication needs* (pp. 193–223). Paul H. Brookes.

Olmstead, C. (2013). Using technology to increase parent involvement in schools. *TechTrends, 57*, 28–37. https://doi.org/10.1007/s11528-013-0699-0

O'Neill, R. E., Albin, R. W., Storey, K., Horner, R. H., & Sprague, J. R. (2015). *Functional assessment and program development for problem behavior: A practical handbook.* (3rd ed.). Brooks/Cole Publishing.

O'Neill, S. J., McDowell, C., & Leslie, J. C. (2018). A comparison of prompt delays with trial-and-error instruction in conditional discrimination training. *Behavior Analysis in Practice, 11*(4), 370–380. https://doi.org/10.1007/s40617-018-0261-9

O'Reilly, M. F., Renzaglia, A., & Lee, S. (1994). An analysis of acquisition, generalization and maintenance of systematic instruction competencies by preservice teachers using behavioral supervision techniques. *Education and Training in Mental Retardation and Developmental Disabilities, 29*(1), 22–33. https://www.jstor.org/stable/23879183

Orland, M. (2015). Research and policy perspectives on data-based decision making in education. *Teachers College Record, 117*(4), 1–10. https://www.tcrecord.org/Home.asp

Orpinas, P. (2010). Social competence. In I. B. Weiner & W. E. Craighead (Eds.), *The Corsini encyclopedia of psychology* (n.p.). John Wiley & Sons. https://doi-org.helicon.vuw.ac.nz/10.1002/9780470479216.corpsy0887

Orpinas, P., & Horne, A. M. (2006). *Bully prevention: Creating a positive school climate and developing social competence.* American Psychological Association. https://doi.org/10.1037/11330-000

Orsmond, G. I., Krauss, M. W., & Sletzer, M. M. (2004). Peer relationships and social and recreational activities among adolescents and adults with autism. *Journal of Autism and Developmental Disorders, 34,* 245–256. https://doi.org/10.1023/B:JADD.0000029547.96610.df

Osburn, J. (2006). An overview of social role valorization theory. *SRV Journal, 1*(1), 4–13.

Oswald, T. M., Beck, J. S., Iosif, A. M., McCauley, J. B., Gilhooly, L. J., Matter, J. C., & Solomon, M. (2016). Clinical and cognitive characteristics associated with mathematics problem solving in adolescents with autism spectrum disorder. *Autism Research, 9*(4), 480–490. https://doi.org/10.1002/aur.1524

Ottley, J. R., Coogle, C. G. & Rahn, N. L., (2015). The social validity of bug-in-ear coaching: Findings from two studies implemented in inclusive early childhood environments. *Journal of Early Childhood Teacher Education, 36*(4), 342–361. https://doi.org/10.1080/10901027.2015.1100146

Owens, T. L., Lo, Y.-Y., & Collins, B. C. (2020). Using tiered coaching and bug-in-ear technology to promote teacher implementation fidelity. *Journal of Special Education, 54*(2), 67–79. https://doi.org/10.1177/0022466919852706

Ozonoff, S., Goodlin-Jones, B. L., & Solomon, M. (2005). Evidence-based assessment of autism spectrum disorders in children and adolescents. *Journal of Clinical Child & Adolescent Psychology, 34*(3), 523–540. https://doi.org/10.1207/s15374424jccp3403_8

Pace, G. M., Ivancic, M. T., Edwards, G. L., Iwata, B. L., & Page, T. A. (1985). Assessment of stimulus preference and reinforcer value with profoundly retarded individuals. *Journal of Applied Behavior Analysis, 18*(3), 249–255. https://doi.org/10.1901/jaba.1985.18-249

Paden, A. R., Kodak, T., Fisher, W. W., Gawley-Bullington, E. M., & Bouxsein, K. J. (2012). Teaching children with autism to engage in peer-directed mands using a picture exchange communication system. *Journal of Applied Behavior Analysis, 45*(2), 425–429. https://doi.org/10.1901/jaba.2012.45-425

Page, M. J., Moher, D., Bossuyt, P. M., Boutron, I., Hoffmann, T. C., Mulrow, C. D., Shamseer, L., Tetzlaff, J. M., Akl, E. A., Brennan, S. E., Chou, R., Glanville, J., Grimshaw, J. M., Hróbjartsson, A., Lalu, M. M., Li, T., Loder, E. W., Mayo-Wilson, E., McDonald, S. . . . & McKenzie, J. E. (2021). PRISMA 2020 explanation and elaboration: Updated guidance and exemplars for reporting systematic reviews. *British Medical Journal, 372*(160), 1–36. https://doi.org/10.1136/bmj.n160

Paode, P. (2020). *Housing for adults with autism and/or intellectual and developmental disabilities: Shortcomings of federal programs.* Daniel Jordan Fiddle Foundation Adult Autism Public Policy Agenda.

Paparella, T., Goods, K. S., Freeman, S., & Kasari, C. (2011). The emergence of nonverbal joint attention and requesting skills in young children with autism. *Journal of Communication Disorders, 44*(6), 569–583. https://doi.org/10.1016/j.comdis.2011.08.002

Paramore, N. W., & Higbee, T. S. (2005). An evaluation of a brief multiple-stimulus preference assessment with adolescents with emotional-behavioral disorders in an educational setting. *Journal of Applied Behavior Analysis, 38*(3), 399–403. https://doi.org/10.1901/jaba.2005.76-04

Parker, D., & Kamps, D., (2011). Effects of task analysis and self-monitoring for children with autism in multiple social settings. *Focus on Autism and Other Developmental Disabilities, 26*(3), 131–142. https://doi.org/10.1177/1088357610376945

Parrish, S. (2014). *Number talks: Helping children build mental math and computation strategies, grades K–5, updated with common core connections.* Math Solutions.

Partington, J. W. (2010). *The Assessment of Basic Language and Learning Skills-Revised (ABLLS-R): An assessment, curriculum guide, and skills tracking for children with autism and other developmental disabilities.* Behavior Analysts Inc.

Pearpoint, J., O'Brien, J., & Forest, M. (1996). *Planning alternative tomorrows with hope: A workbook for planning possible and positive futures.* Inclusive Press.

Pearson, J. N., Akamoglu, Y., Chung, M., & Meadan, H. (2019). Building family-professional partnerships with culturally, linguistically, and economically diverse families of young children. *Multicultural Perspectives, 21*(4), 208–216. https://doi.org/10.1080/15210960.2019.1686381

Pearson, J. N., & Meadan, H. (2018). African American mothers' perceptions of diagnosis and services for children with autism. *Education and Training in Autism and Developmental Disabilities, 53*, 17–32. https://www.jstor.org/stable/26420424

Pearson, J. N. & Meadan, H. (2021). FACES: An advocacy intervention for African American parents of children with autism. *Intellectual and Developmental Disabilities, 59*(2), 155–171. https://doi.org/10.1352/1934-9556-59.2.155

Pearson, P. D., & Cervetti, G. N. (2017). The roots of reading comprehension instruction. In S. E. Israel (Ed.), *Handbook of research on reading comprehension* (2nd ed., pp. 12–56). Guilford Press.

Pennington, R. C., & Carpenter, M. (2019). Teaching written expression to students with autism spectrum disorder and complex communication needs. *Topics in Language Disorders, 39*(2), 191–207. https://doi.org/0000000000000181

Pennington, R., Flick, A., & Smith-Wehr, K. (2018). The use of response prompting and frames for teaching sentence writing to students with moderate intellectual disability. *Focus on Autism and Other Developmental Disabilities, 33*(3), 142–159. https://doi.org/10.1177/1088357616673568

Perry, J., Allen, D. G., Pimm, C., Meek, A., Lowe, K., Groves, S., & Felce, D. (2013). Adults with intellectual disabilities and challenging behaviour: The costs and outcomes of in- and out-of-area placements. *Journal of Intellectual Disability Research, 57*(2), 139–152. https://doi.org/10.1111/j.1365-2788.2012.01558.x

Petcu, S., Chezan, L. C., & Van Horn, M. L. (2015). Employment support services for students with intellectual and developmental disabilities attending postsecondary education programs. *Journal of Postsecondary Education and Disability, 28*(3), 359–374.

Petrina, N., Carter, M., & Stephenson, J. (2015). Parental perception of the importance of friendship and other outcome priorities in children with autism spectrum disorder. *European Journal of Special Needs Education, 30*(1), 61–74. https://doi.org/10.1080/08856257.2014.943566

Pfeiffer, B., Piller, A., Giazzo-Fialko, T., & Chainani, A. (2017). Meaningful outcomes for enhancing quality of life for individuals with autism spectrum disorder. *Journal of Intellectual and Developmental Disability, 47*(1), 90–100. https://doi.org/10.3109/13668250.2016.1197893

Pinkelman, S. E., & Horner, R. H. (2017). Improving implementation of function-based interventions: Self-monitoring, data collection and data review. *Journal of Positive Behavior Intervention, 19*(4), 228–238. https://doi.org/10.1177/1098300716683634

Pituch, K. A., Green, V. A., Didden, R., Lang, R., O'Reilly, M. F., Lancioni, G. E., & Sigafoos, J. (2011). Parent reported treatment priorities for children with autism spectrum disorders. *Research in Autism Spectrum Disorders, 5*(1), 135–143. https://doi.org/10.1016/j.rasd.2010.03.003

Plavnick, J. B. (2013). A practical strategy for teaching a child with autism to attend to and imitate a portable video model. *Research and Practice for Persons with Severe Disabilities, 37*(4), 263–270. http://doi.org/10.2511/027494813805327250

Plotner, A. J., Mazzotti, V., Rose, C., & Teasley, K. (2020). Perceptions of interagency collaboration: Relationships between secondary transition roles, communication, and collaboration. *Remedial and Special Education, 41*(1), 28–39. https://doi.org/10.1177/0741932518778029

Potter, J. N., Hanley, G. P., Augustine, M., Clay, C. J., & Phelps, M. C. (2013). Treating stereotypy in adolescents diagnosed with autism by refining the tactic of "using stereotypy as reinforcement." *Journal of Applied Behavior Analysis, 46*(2), 407–423. https://doi.org/10.1002/jaba.52

Povenmire-Kirk, T. C., Test, D. W., Flowers, C. P., Diegelmann, K. M., Bunch-Crump, K., Kemp-Inman, A., & Goodnight, C. I. (2018). CIRCLES: Building an interagency network for transition planning. *Journal of Vocational Rehabilitation, 49*(1), 45–57. https://doi.org/10.3233/JVR-180953

Radley, K. C., Dart, E. H., Brennan, K. J., Helbig, K. A., Lehman, E. L., Silberman, M., & Mendanhall, K. (2020). Social skills training for individuals with autism spectrum disorder: a systematic review. *Advances in Neurodevelopmental Disorders, 4*(3), 215–226. https://doi.org/10.1007/s41252-020-00170-x

Ramirez, H., Cengher, M., & Fienup, D. (2014). The effects of simultaneous prompting on the acquisition of calculating elapsed time in children with autism. *Journal of Developmental & Physical Disabilities, 26*(6), 763–774. https://doi.org/10.1007/s1088201493940

RAND (2002). *Reading for understanding: Toward an R&D program in reading comprehension.* RAND.

Randolph, K. M., & Duffy, M. L. (2019). Using iCoaching to support teachers' implementation of evidence-based practices. *Journal of Special Education Apprenticeship, 8*(2), 1–7. https://files.eric.ed.gov/fulltext/EJ1231820.pdf

Randolph, K. M., Duffy, M. Lou, Brady, M. P., Wilson, C. L., & Scheeler, M. C. (2020). The impact of iCoaching on teacher-delivered opportunities to respond. *Journal of Special Education Technology, 35*(1), 15–25. https://doi.org/10.1177/0162643419836414

Range, B. G., Scherz, S., Holt, C. R., & Young, S. (2011). Supervision and evaluation: The Wyoming perspective. *Educational Assessment, Evaluation, and Accountability, 23*, 243–265. https://doi.org/10.1007/s11092-011-9123-5

Rapp, J. T. (2004). Effects of prior access and environmental enrichment on stereotypy. *Behavioral Interventions, 19*(4), 287–295. https://doi.org/10.1002/bin.166

Rapp, J. T., Swanson, G., Sheridan, S. M., Enloe, K. A., Maltese, D., Sennott, L. A., Shrader, L., Carroll, R. A., Richling, S. M., Long, E. S., & Lanovaz, M. J. (2013). Immediate and subsequent effects of matched and unmatched stimuli on targeted vocal stereotypy and untargeted motor stereotypy. *Behavior Modification, 37*(4), 543–567. https://doi.org/10.1177/0145445512461650

Rapp, J. T., & Vollmer, T. R. (2005). Stereotypy II: A review of neurobiological interpretations and suggestions for an integration with behavioral methods. *Research in Developmental Disabilities, 26*(6), 548–564. https://doi.org/10.1016/j.ridd.2004.11.006

Rayner, K., Foorman, B. R., Perfetti, C. A., Pesetsky, D., & Seidenberg, M. S. (2001). How psychological science informs the teaching of reading. *Psychological Science in the Public Interest, 2*(2), 31–74. https://doi.org/10.1111/1529-1006.00004

Regan, K., & Weiss, M. P. (2020). Bug-in-ear coaching for teacher candidates: What, why, and how to get started. *Intervention in School and Clinic, 55*(3), 178–184. https://doi.org/10.1177/1053451219842218

Reichle, J., Ganz, J., Drager, K., & Parker-McGowen, Q. (2016). Augmentative and alternative communication applications for persons with ASD and complex communication needs. In D. Keen, H. Meadan, N. C. Brady, & J. W. Halle (Eds.), *Prelinguistic and minimally verbal communicators in the autism spectrum* (pp. 179–213). Springer.

Reichle, J., & Wacker, D. P. (2017). *Functional communication training for problem behavior.* Guilford Press.

Reichow, B., & Sabornie, E. J. (2009). Brief report: Increasing verbal greeting initiations for a student with autism via a Social Story™ intervention. *Journal of Autism and Developmental Disorders, 39*(12), 1740–1743. http://www.doi.org/10.1007/s10803-009-0814-4

Reid, B., & Batten, A. (2006). *B is for Bullied.* National Autistic Society.

Reimers, T. M., Wacker, D. P., Cooper, L. J., & DeRaad, A. O. (1992). Acceptability of behavioral treatments for children: Analog and naturalistic evaluations by parents. *School Psychology Review, 21*(4), 628–643.

Reinke, W. M., Stormont, M., Webster-Stratton, C., Newcomer, L. L., & Herman, K. C. (2012). The incredible years teacher classroom management program: Using coaching to support generalization to real-world classroom settings. *Psychology in the Schools, 49*(5), 416–428. https://doi.org/10.1002/pits.21608

Renzaglia, A., Karvonen, M., Drasgow, E., & Stoxen, C. (2003). Promoting a lifetime of inclusion. *Focus on Autism and Other Developmental Disabilities, 18*(3), 140–149. https://doi.org/10.1177/10883576030180030201

Reschly, D. J., & Bergstrom, M. K. (2009). Response to intervention. In T. B. Gutkin & C. R. Reynolds (Eds.), *The handbook of school psychology* (4th ed., pp. 434–460). Wiley.

Reynhout, G., & Carter, M. (2006). Social Stories for children with disabilities. *Journal of Autism and Developmental Disorders, 36*(4), 445–469. https://doi.org/10.1007/s10803-006-0086-1

Richards, C., Oliver, C., Nelson, L., & Moss, J. (2012). Self-injurious behaviour in individuals with autism spectrum disorder and intellectual disability. *Journal of Intellectual Disability Research, 56,* 476–489. https://doi.org/10.1111/j.1365-2788.2012.01537.x

Richards, J. (2012). Examining the exclusion of employees with Asperger syndrome from the workplace. *Personnel Review, 41*(5), 630–646. https://doi.org/10.1108/00483481211249148

Ricketts, J., Davies, R., Masterson, J., Stuart, M., & Duff, F. J. (2016). Evidence for semantic involvement in regular and exception word reading in emergent readers of English. *Journal of Experimental Child Psychology, 150,* 330–345. https://doi.org/10.1016/j.jecp.2016.05.013

Ricketts, J., Jones, C. R. G., Happe, F., & Charman, T. (2013). Reading comprehension in autism spectrum disorders: The role of oral language and social functioning. *Journal of Autism and Developmental Disorders, 43,* 807–816. https://doi.org/10.1007/s10803-012-1619-4

Rimland, B. (1964). *Infantile autism.* Appleton-Century-Crofts.

Rios, D., Schenk, Y. A., Eldrige, R. R., & Peterson, S. M. (2020). The effects of remote behavioral skills training on conducting functional analyses. *Journal of Behavioral Education, 29,* 449–468. https://doi.org/10.1007/s10864-020-09385-3

Risley, T. R. (2005). Montrose M. Wolf (1935–2004). *Journal of Applied Behavior Analysis, 38*(2), 279–287. https://doi.org/10.1901/jaba.2005.165-04

Rispoli, M., Camargo, S., Machalicek, W., Lang, R., & Sigafoos, J. (2014). Functional communication training in the treatment of problem behavior maintained by access to rituals. *Journal of Applied Behavior Analysis, 47*(3), 580–593. https://doi.org/10.1002 /jaba.130

Rispoli, M., Ganz, J., Neely, L., & Goodwyn, F. (2013). The effect of noncontingent positive versus negative reinforcement on multiply controlled behavior during discrete trial training. *Journal of Developmental & Physical Disabilities, 25*(1), 135–148. https://doi-org.ezproxy.lib.purdue.edu/10.1007/s10882-012-9315-z

Rispoli, M., Lang, R., Neely, L., Camargo, S., Hutchins, N., Davenport, K., & Goodwyn, F. (2013). A comparison of within- and across-activity choices for reducing challenging behavior in children with autism spectrum disorders. *Journal of Behavioral Education, 22*(1), 66–83. https://doi.org/10.1007/s10864-012-9164-y

Rispoli, M., & Machalicek, W. (2020). Advances in telehealth and behavioral assessment and intervention in education: Introduction to the special issue. *Journal of Behavioral Education, 29*, 189–194. https://doi.org/10.1007/s10864-020-09383-5

Rispoli, M., Neely, L., Healy, O., & Gregori, E. (2016). Training public school special educators to implement two functional analysis models. *Journal of Behavioral Education, 25*(3), 249–274. http://dx.doi.org.proxy.cc.uic.edu/10.1007/s10864-016-9247-2

Rispoli, M., Neely, L., Lang, R., & Ganz, J. B. (2011). Training paraprofessionals to implement interventions for people autism spectrum disorders: A systematic review. *Developmental Neurorehabilitation, 14*(6), 378–388. https://doi.org/10.3109/17518423 .2011.620577

Rispoli, M., Zaini, S., Mason, R., Brodhead, M., Burke, M. D., & Gregori, E. (2017). A systematic review of teacher self-monitoring on implementation of behavioral practices. *Teaching and Teacher Education, 63*, 58–72. https://doi.org/10.1016/j.tate .2016.12.007

Rittle-Johnson, B. (2017). Developing mathematics knowledge. *Child Developmental Perspectives, 11*(3), 184–190. https://doi.org/10.1111/cdep.12229

Rittle-Johnson, B., & Schneider, M. (2015). Developing conceptual knowledge of mathematics. In R. C. Kadosh & A. Dowker (Eds.), *The Oxford handbook of numerical cognition* (pp. 1118–1134). https://doi.org/10.1093/oxfordhb/9780199642342.013.014

Roberts, M. L., Marshall, J., Nelson, J. R., & Albers, C. A. (2001). Curriculum-based assessment procedures embedded within the functional behavioral assessments: Identifying escape-motivated behaviors in a general education classroom. *School Psychology Review, 30*(2), 264–277. https://doi.org/10.1080/02796015.2001.12086115

Robins, D. L., Fein, D., Barton, M. L., & Green, J. A. (2001). The Modified-Checklist for Autism in Toddlers (M-CHAT): An initial investigation in the early detection of autism and pervasive developmental disorders. *Journal of Autism Developmental Disorders, 31*(2), 131–144. https://doi-org.pallas2.tcl.sc.edu/10.1023/A:1010738829569

Robins, D. L., Fein, D., & Barton, M. L. (2009). *The Modified-Checklist for Autism in Toddlers, Revised, with Follow-Up*. Self-Published. https://mchatscreen.com

Robinson, S. E. (2011). Teaching paraprofessionals of students with autism to implement pivotal response treatment in inclusive school settings using a brief video feedback training package. *Focus on Autism and Other Developmental Disabilities, 26*(2), 105–118. https://doi.org/10.1177/1088357611407063

Rodriguez, N. M., & Thompson, R. H. (2015). Behavioral variability and autism spectrum disorder. *Journal of Applied Behavior Analysis, 48*(1), 167–187. https://doi .org/10.1002/jaba.164

Romanczyk, R. G., Wiseman, K., & Morton, H. (2017). Curriculum-based assessment of social development: Goal selection and sequencing. In J. B. Leaf (Ed.), *Handbook of social skills and autism spectrum disorder* (pp. 113–135). Springer.

Ronald, A., & Hoekstra, R. A. (2011). Autism spectrum disorders and autistic traits: A decade of new twin studies. *American Journal of Medical Genetics Part B: Neuropsychiatric Genetics, 156*(3), 255–274. https://doi.org/10.1002/ajmg.b.31159

Root, J. R., Henning, B., & Boccumini, E. (2018). Teaching students with autism and intellectual disability to solve algebraic word problems. *Education and Training in Autism and Developmental Disabilities, 53*(3), 325–338. https://www.jstor.org/stable/26563472

Root, J. R., Henning, B., & Jimenez, B. (2019). Building the early number sense of kindergarteners with autism: A replication study. *Remedial and Special Education, 41*(6), 378–388. https://doi.org/10.1177/0741932519873121

Root, J. R., Wood, L., & Browder, D. M. (2020). Assessment and planning. In M. S. Snell & F. Brown (Eds.), *Instruction of students with severe disabilities* (9th ed., pp. 60–97). Pearson.

Rosales, R., Stone, K., & Rehfeldt, R. A. (2009). The effects of behavioral skills training on implementation of the picture exchange communication system. *Journal of Applied Behavior Analysis, 42*(3), 541–549. https://doi.org/10.1901/jaba.2009.42-541

Rosenberg, N. E., Artman-Meeker, K., Kelly, E., & Yang, X. (2020). The effects of a bug-in-ear coaching package on implementation of incidental teaching by paraprofessionals in a K–12 school. *Journal of Behavioral Education, 29*(2), 409–432. https://doi.org.ezproxy.lib.purdue.edu/10.1007/s10864-020-09379-1

Rosenberg, N. E., & Schwartz, I. S. (2019). Guidance or compliance: What makes an ethical behavior analyst? *Behavior Analysis in Practice, 12*(2), 473–482. https://doi.org/10.1007/s40617-018-00287-5

Rosenfield, S. (1992). Developing school-based consultation teams. *School Psychology Quarterly, 7*(1), 22–46. https://doi.org/10.1037/h0088248

Rosenfield, S. A., & Gravois, T. A. (1996). *Instructional consultation teams: Collaborating for change.* Guilford Press.

Rosenfield, S., Newell, M., Zwolski, S., & Benishek, L. E. (2018). Evaluating problem-solving teams in K–12 schools: Do they work? *American Psychologist, 73*(4), 407–419. https://doi.org/10.1037/amp0000254

Rotholz, D., Kinsman, A. M., Lacy, K. K., & Charles, J. (2017). Improving early identification and intervention for children at risk for autism spectrum disorder. *Pediatrics, 139*(2), 2–7. https://doi-org.proxy.lib.odu.edu/10.1542/peds.2016-1061

Roux, A. M., Garfield, T., & Shattuck, P. T. (2019). Employment policy and autism: Analysis of state Workforce Innovation and Opportunity Act (WIOA) implementation plans. *Journal of Vocational Rehabilitation, 51*(3), 285–298. https://doi.org/10.3233/JVR-191046

Roux, A. M., Shattuck, P. T., Cooper, B. P., Anderson, K. A., Wagner, M., & Narendorf, S. C. (2013). Postsecondary employment experiences among young adults with autism spectrum disorder. *Journal of the American Academy of Child & Adolescent Psychiatry, 52*(9), 931–939. https://doi.org/10.1016/j.jaac.2013.05.019

Roux, A. M., Shattuck, P. T., Rast, J. E., Rava, J. A., & Anderson, K. A. (2015). *National Autism Indicators Report: Transition into Young Adulthood.* Life Course Outcomes Research Programme, A. J. Drexel Autism Institute, Drexel University.

Rowe, D. A., Mazzotti, V. L., Fowler, C. H., Test, D. W., Mitchell, V. J., Clark, K. A., Holzberg, D., Owens, T. L., Rusher, D., Seaman-Tullis, R. L., Gushanas, C. M., Castle, H., Chang, W., Voggt, A., Kwiatek, S., & Dean, J. C. (2021). Updating the secondary transition research base: Evidence- and research-based practices in functional skills. *Career Development and Transition for Exceptional Individuals, 44*(1), 28–46. https://doi.org/10.1177/2165143420958674

Ruble, L. A., & Dalrymple, N. J. (2002). Compass: A parent-teacher collaborative model for students with autism. *Focus on Autism and Other Developmental Disabilities, 17*(2), 76–83. https://doi.org/10.1177/10883576020170020201

Ruble, L. A., & McGrew, J. H. (2007). Community services outcomes for families and children with autism spectrum disorders. *Research in Autism Spectrum Disorders, 1*(4), 360–372. https://doi.org/10.1016/j.rasd.2007.01.002

Ruble, L. A., McGrew, J. H., Wong, W. H., & Missall, K. N. (2018). Special education teachers' perceptions and intentions toward data collection. *Journal of Early Intervention, 40*(2), 177–191. https://doi.org/10.1177/1053815118771391

Rush, D. D., & Shelden, M. L. (2008). Common misperceptions about coaching in early intervention. *CASEinPoint, 4*(1), 1–4. https://fipp.ncdhhs.gov/wp-content/uploads/caseinpoint_vol4_no1.pdf

Rutter, M., Le Couteur, A., & Lord, C. (2003). *ADI-R: Autism Diagnostic Interview Revised*. Western Psychological Services.

Rylaarsdam, L., & Guemez-Gamboa, A. (2019). Genetic causes and modifiers of autism spectrum disorder. *Frontiers in Cellular Neuroscience, 13*, 385. https://doi.org/10.3389/fncel.2019.00385

Sacco, R., Gabriele, S., & Persico, A. M. (2015). Head circumference and brain size in autism spectrum disorder: A systematic review and meta-analysis. *Psychiatry Research: Neuroimaging, 234*(2), 239–251. https://doi.org/10.1016/j.pscychresns.2015.08.016

Salley, B., Brady, N. C., Hoffman, L., & Fleming, K. (2020). Preverbal communication complexity in infants. *Infancy, 25*(1), 4–21. https://doi.org/10.1111/infa.12318

Sam, A., & AFIRM Team. (2015). *Prompting*. National Professional Development Center on Autism Spectrum Disorder, FPG Child Development Center, University of North Carolina. http://afirm.fpg.unc.edu/prompting

Sam, A., Steinbrenner, J., Morgan, W., Chin, J., & AFIRM for Paras Team. (2019). *Visual Cues*. FPG Child Development Institute, University of North Carolina. https://afirm.fpg.unc.edu/visual-cues-introduction-practice

Sandall, S. R., Schwartz, I. L., & Lacroix, B. (2004). Interventionists' perspectives about data collection in integrated early childhood classrooms. *Journal of Early Intervention, 26*(3), 161–174. https://doi.org/10.1177/105381510402600301

Sandin, S., Lichtenstein, P., Kuja-Halkola, R., Hultman, C., Larsson, H., & Reichenberg, A. (2017). The heritability of autism spectrum disorder. *Journal of the American Medical Association, 318*(12), 1182–1184. https://doi.org/10.1001/jama.2017.12141

Sandin, S., Schendel, D., Magnusson, P., Hultman, C., Surén, P., Susser, E., Grønborg, T., Gissler, M., Gunnes, N., Gross, R., Henning, M., Bresnahan, M., Sourander, A., Hornig, M., Carter, K., Francis, R., Parner, E., Leonard, H., Rosanoff, M., Stoltenberg, C., . . . Reichenberg, A. (2016). Autism risk associated with parental age and with increasing difference in age between the parents. *Molecular Psychiatry, 21*(5), 693–700. https://doi.org/10.1038/mp.2015.70

Sandoval-Norton, A. H., & Shkedy, G. (2019). How much compliance is too much compliance: Is long-term ABA therapy abuse? *Cogent Psychology, 6* (1), 1–8.

Sanetti, L. M. H., & Collier-Meek, M. C. (2019). *Supporting successful interventions in schools: Tools to plan, evaluate, and sustain effective implementation*. Guilford Press.

Sanetti, L. M., & Kratochwill, T. R. (2014). *Treatment integrity: A foundation for evidence-based practice in applied psychology*. American Psychological Association.

Sarama, J., & Clements, D. H. (2009). *Early childhood mathematics education research: Learning trajectories for young children*. Routledge.

Saunders, A. F. (2020). Contextualizing mathematics standards. In E. C. Bouck, J. R. Root, & B. A. Jimenez (Eds.), *Mathematics education for students with autism, intellectual disability, and other developmental disabilities* (pp. 7–29). Division on Autism and Developmental Disabilities.

Saunders, A. F., Root, J. R., & Jimenez, B. A. (2019). Recommendations for inclusive educational practices in mathematics for students with extensive support needs. *Inclusion, 7*(2), 75–91. https://doi.org/10.1352/2326-6988-7.2.75

Saylor, S., Sidener, T. M., Reeve, S. A., Fetherston, A., & Progar, P. R. (2012). Effects of three types of noncontingent auditory stimulation on vocal stereotypy in children with autism. *Journal of Applied Behavior Analysis, 45*(1), 185–190. https://doi.org/10.1901/jaba.2012.45-185

Scattone, D. (2007). Social skills interventions for children with autism. *Psychology in the Schools, 44*(7), 717–726. https://doi.org/10.1002/pits.20260

Schaak, G., Sloane, A., Arienti, F., & Zovistoski, A. (2017). Priced out: The housing crisis for people with disabilities. Technical Assistance Collaborative. https://www.tacinc.org/wp-content/uploads/2020/04/priced-out-in-2016.pdf

Schaefer, J. M., & Ottley, J. R. (2018). Evaluating immediate feedback via bug-in-ear as an evidence-based practice for professional development. *Journal of Special Education Technology, 33*(4), 247–258. https://doi.org/10.1177/0162643418766870

Schall, C. (2009). Educational and transition planning. In P. Wehman (Ed.), *Autism and the transition to adulthood: Success beyond the classroom* (pp. 39–94). Paul H. Brookes.

Schall, C., & Wehman, P. (2009). Understanding the transition from school to adulthood for students with autism. In P. Wehman (Ed.), *Autism and the transition to adulthood: Success beyond the classroom* (pp. 1–14). Paul H. Brookes.

Schalock, R. L. (2000). Three decades of quality of life. *Focus on Autism and Other Developmental Disabilities, 15*(2), 116–127. https://doi.org/10.1177/108835760001500207

Schalock, R. L. (2004). The concept of quality of life: What we know and do not know. *Journal of Intellectual Disability Research, 48*(3), 203–216. https://doi.org/10.1111/j.1365-2788.2003.00558.x

Schalock, R. L., & Alonso, M. A. V. (2002). *Handbook on quality of life for human service practitioners.* American Association on Mental Retardation.

Schalock, R. L., & Keith, K. D. (2016). *Cross-cultural quality of life: Enhancing the lives of people with intellectual disability* (2nd edition). American Association on Intellectual and Developmental Disabilities.

Schalock, R. L., Keith, K. D., Verdugo, M. A., & Gomez, L. E. (2011). Quality of life model development and use in the field of intellectual disability. In R. Kober (Ed.), *Enhancing the quality of life of people with intellectual disabilities: From theory to practice.* Springer.

Schalock, R. L., & Verdugo, M. A. (2002). *Quality of life for human service practitioners.* American Association on Mental Retardation.

Schalock, R. L., & Verdugo, M. A. (2013). The transformation of disability organization. *Journal of Intellectual and Developmental Disabilities, 51*(4), 273–286. https://doi.org/10.1352/1934-9556-51.4.273

Schalock, R. L., Verdugo, M. A., Jenaro, C., Wang, M., Wehmeyer, M., Xu, J., & Lachapelle, Y. (2005). A cross-cultural study of quality of life indicators. *American Journal on Mental Retardation, 110*(4), 298–311. https://doi.org/10.1352/0895-8017(2005)110[298:CSOQOL]2.0.CO;2

Scheeler, M. C., & Lee, D. L. (2002). Using technology to deliver immediate corrective feedback to preservice teachers. *Journal of Behavioral Education, 11*(4), 231–241. https://doi.org/10.1023/A:1021158805714

Scheeler, M. C., McAfee, J. K., Ruhl, K. L., & Lee, D. L. (2006). Effects of corrective feedback delivered via wireless technology on preservice teacher performance and student behavior. *Teacher Education and Special Education, 29*(1), 12–25. https://doi.org/10.1177/088840640602900103

Scheeler, M. C., McKinnon, K., & Stout, J. (2012). Effects of immediate feedback delivered via webcam and bug-in-ear technology on preservice teacher performance. *Teacher*

Education and Special Education, 35(1), 77–90. https://doi.org/10.1177/0888
406411401919

Scheeler, M. C., Morano, S., & Lee, D. L. (2018). Effects of immediate feedback using bug-in-ear with paraeducators working with students with autism. *Teacher Education and Special Education, 41*(1), 24–38. https://doi.org/10.1177/0888406416666645

Schieve, L. A., Gonzalez, V., Boulet, S. L., Visser, S. N., Rice, C. E., Van Naarden Braun, K., & Boyle, C. A. (2012). Concurrent medical conditions and health care use and needs among children with learning and behavioral developmental disabilities, National Health Interview Survey, 2006–2010. *Research in Developmental Disabilities, 33*(2), 467–476. https://doi.org/10.1016/j.ridd.2011.10.008

Schmidt, J. D., Drasgow, E., Halle, J. W., Martin, C. A., & Bliss, S. A. (2014). Discrete-trial functional analysis and functional communication training with three individuals with autism and severe problem behavior. *Journal of Positive Behavior Interventions, 16*(1), 44–55. https://doi.org/10.1177/1098300712470519

Schnell, L. K., Vladescu, J. C., Kisamore, A. N., DeBar, R. M., Kahng, S., & Marano, K. (2020). Assessment to identify learner-specific prompt and prompt-fading procedures for children with autism spectrum disorder. *Journal of Applied Behavior Analysis, 53*, 1111–1129. https://doi.org/10.1002/jaba.623

Schoenfeld, A. H., & Herrmann, D. J. (1982). Problem perception and knowledge structure in expert and novice mathematical problem solvers. *Journal of Experimental Psychology: Learning, Memory, and Cognition, 8*(5), 484. https://doi.org/10.1037/0278-7393.8.5.484

School Social Work Association of America. (2020). *Role of school social worker*. https://www.sswaa.org/school-social-work

Schopler, E., Reichler, R., & Rochen Renner, B. (1988). *The childhood autism rating scale*. Western Psychological Services.

Schrandt, J. A., Townsend, D. B., & Poulson, C. L. (2009). Teaching empathy skills to children with autism. *Journal of Applied Behavior Analysis, 42*(1), 17–32. https://doi.org/10.1901/jaba.2009.42-17

Schrank, F. A., McGrew, K. S., & Woodcock, R. W. (2001). *Woodcock-Johnson III Technical Abstract*. Riverside Publishing.

Scott, J., Clark, C., & Brady, M. (2000). *Students with autism: Characteristics and instruction programming*. Thompson Wadsworth.

Scott, L. A., & Alexander, Q. (2019). Strategies for recruiting and retaining black male special education teachers. *Remedial and Special Education, 40*(4), 236–247. https://doi.org/10.1177/0741932517732636

Scott, M., Milbourn, B., Falkmer, M., Black, M., Bolte, S., Halladay, A., Lerner, M., Taylor, J. L., & Girdler, S. (2019). Factors impacting employment for people with autism spectrum disorder: A scoping review. *Autism, 23*(4), 869–901. https://doi.org/10.1177%2F1362361318787789

Sedgewick, F., Hill, V., Yates, R., Pickering, L., & Pellicano, E. (2016). Gender differences in the social motivation and friendship experiences of autistic and non-autistic adolescents. *Journal of Autism and Developmental Disorders, 46*(4), 1297–1306. https://doi.org/10.1007/s10803-015-2669-1

Segrin, C., & Taylor, M. (2007). Positive interpersonal relationships mediate the association between social skills and psychological well-being. *Personality and Individual Differences, 43*(4), 637–646. https://doi.org/10.1016/j.paid.2007.01.017

Seltzer, M. M., Wyngaarden Krauss, M., Shattuck, P. T., Orsmond, G., Swe, A., & Lord, C. (2003). The symptoms of autism spectrum disorders in adolescence and adulthood. *Journal of Autism and Developmental Disorders, 33*, 565–581. https://doi.org/10.1023/B:JADD.0000005995.02453.0b

Semrud-Clikeman, M. (2007). *Social competence in children*. Springer. https://www.doi
.org/10.1007/978-0-387-71366-3

Sevlever, M., Mg, J., & Ferguson, B. (2015). Improving conversational skills of children
with autism spectrum disorders: A pilot study of the Teaching Interaction Procedure (TIP). *International Journal of School and Cognitive Psychology*, S1. https://doi
.org/10.4172/2469-9837.S1-006

Sharma, P., Heywood, A., & Rajkumar, D. (2010). Brief report: IBI training: Social and
play skills upon entry as predictors of outcome in children with autism spectrum disorder. *Journal of Developmental Disabilities*, 16(3), 76–77.

Shattuck, P. T., Narendorf, S. C., Cooper, B., Sterzing, P. R., Wagner, M., & Taylor, L. (2012).
Postsecondary education and employment among youth with an autism spectrum disorder. *Paediatrics*, 129(6), 1042–1049. https://doi.org/10.1542/peds.2011-2864

Shattuck, P. T., Roux, A. M., Hudson, L. E., Taylor, J. L., Maenner, M. J., & Trani, J. (2012).
Services for adults with an autism spectrum disorder. *Canadian Journal of Psychiatry*,
57(5), 284–291. https://doi.org/10.1177%2F070674371205700503

Shattuck, P. T., Wagner, M., Narendorf, S. C., Sterzing, P. R., & Hensley, M. (2011). Post-
high school service use among young adults with an autism spectrum disorder. *Archives
of Pediatrics & Adolescent Medicine*, 165(2), 141–146. https://doi.org/10.1001/arch
pediatrics.2010.279

Shaw, S. R. (Ed.). (2011). Expanding the role of school psychologists for children with
autism spectrum disorders. *School Psychology Forum: Research in Practice*, 5(4).

Sheldon, S. B., & Epstein, J. L. (2005). Involvement counts: Family and community partnerships and mathematics achievement. *Journal of Educational Research*, 98, 196–
206. https://doi.org/10.3200/JOER.98.4.196-207

Sheridan, S. M., Holmes, S. R., Coutts, M. J., Smith, T. E., Kunz, G. M., & Witte, A. L. (2013).
CBC in rural schools: Preliminary results of a randomized trial (CYFS Working Paper
2013-1). Nebraska Center for Research on Children, Youth, Families and Schools.

Sheridan, S. M., & Kratochwill, T. R. (2008). *Conjoint behavioral consultation: Promoting
family-school connections and interventions*. Springer Science & Business Media.

Sheridan, S. M., Kratochwill, T. R., & Bergan, J. R. (1996). *Conjoint behavioral consultation: A procedural guide*. Plenum.

Sheridan, S. M., Smith, T. E., Kim, E. M., Beretvas, S. N., & Park, S. (2019). A meta-analysis
of family-school interventions and children's social-emotional functioning: Modera-
tors and components of efficacy. *Review of Educational Research*, 89(2), 296–332.
https://doi.org/10.3102/0034654318825437

Sheridan, S. M., & Wheeler, L. A. (2017). Building strong family–school partnerships:
Transitioning from basic findings to possible practices. *Family Relations*, 66(4), 670–
683. https://doi.org/10.1111/fare.12271

Shinn, M. (2014). Curriculum-based measurement. In A. Thomas & J. Grimes (Eds.), *Best
practices in school psychology IV* (pp. 243–262). National Association of School
Psychologists.

Shogren, K. A., Wehmeyer M. L., & Palmer S. B. (2017). Causal Agency Theory. In
M. Wehmeyer, K. Shogren, T. Little, & S. Lopez (Eds.), *Development of self-determination through the life-course*. Springer. https://doi.org/10.1007/978-94-024-1042-6_5

Shogren, K. A., Wehmeyer, M. L., Palmer, S. B., Rifenbark, G. G., & Little, T. D.
(2015). Relationships between self-determination and postschool outcomes for
youth with disabilities. *Journal of Special Education*, 48(4), 256–267. https://doi
.org/10.1177%2F0022466913489733

Shore, S. (n.d.). *Leading Perspectives on Disability: A Q&A with Dr. Stephen Shore* [Inter-
view transcript]. https://www.limeconnect.com/opportunities_news/detail/leading-per
spectives-on-disability-a-qa-with-dr-stephen-shore

Shorey, S., Ng, E. D., Haugan, G., & Law, E. (2019). The parenting experiences and needs of Asian primary caregivers of children with autism: A meta-synthesis. *Autism, 24*(3), 591–604. https://doi.org/10.1177/1362361319886513

Shurr, J. C., Jimenez, B. A., & Bouck, E. C. (Eds.). (2019). Book 1: *Research-Based Practices and Education Science. Educating students with Intellectual Disability and Autism Spectrum Disorder.* Council for Exceptional Children.

Sigafoos, J. (2000). Communication development and aberrant behavior in children with developmental disabilities. *Education & Training in Mental Retardation & Developmental Disabilities, 35*(2), 168–176. https://www.jstor.org/stable/23879941

Sigafoos, J. (2021). Teaching communication skills to people with intellectual and developmental disabilities. In R. Lang & P. Sturmey (Eds.), *Adaptive behavior strategies for individuals with intellectual and developmental disabilities* (pp. 73–102). Springer. https://doi.org/10.1007/978-3-030-66441-1_4

Sigafoos, J., Drasgow, E., Reichle, J., O'Reilly, M. F., Green, V. A., & Tait, K. (2004). Tutorial: Teaching communicative requesting to children with severe disabilities. *American Journal of Speech-Language Pathology, 13*(1), 31–42. https://doi.org/10.1044/1058 -0360(2004/005)

Sigafoos, J., & Kerr, M. (1994). Provision of leisure activities for the reduction of challenging behavior. *Behavioral Interventions, 9,* 43–53. https://doi.org/10.1002/bin .2360090105

Sigafoos, J., & Meikle, B. (1996). Functional communication training for the treatment of multiply determined challenging behavior in two boys with autism. *Behavior Modification, 20*(1), 60–84. https://doi.org/10.1177/01454455960201003

Sigafoos, J., & Saggers, E. (1995). A discrete-trial approach to the functional analysis of aggressive behaviour in two boys with autism. *Australia & New Zealand Journal of Developmental Disabilities, 20*(4), 287–297. https://doi.org/10.1080/07263869500035621

Sigafoos, J., Schlosser, R. W., Green, V. A., O'Reilly, M. F., & Lancioni, G. E. (2008). Communication and social skills assessment. In J. L. Matson (Ed.), *Clinical assessment and intervention for autism spectrum disorders* (pp. 165–192). Elsevier. http://www.doi .org/10.1016/B978-012373606-2.50008-5

Sigafoos, J., & York, J. (1991). Using ecological inventories to promote functional communication. In J. Reichle, J. York, & J. Sigafoos (Eds.), *Implementing augmentative and alternative communication: Strategies for learners with severe disabilities.* Paul H. Brookes.

Silbaugh, B. C., & Falcomata, T. S. (2019). Effects of a lag schedule with progressive time delay on sign mand variability in a boy with autism. *Behavior Analysis in Practice, 12*(1), 124–132. https://doi.org/10.1007/s40617-018-00273-x

Singer, J. (1999). Why can't you be normal for once in your life? From a "problem with no name" to the emergence of a new category of difference. In M. Corker & S. French (Eds.), *Disability Discourse* (pp. 57–59). Open University Press.

Sivaraman, M., & Rapp, J. T. (2020). Further analysis of the immediate and subsequent effect of RIRD on vocal stereotypy. *Behavior Modification, 44*(5), 646–669. https:// doi.org/10.1177/0145445519838826

Skinner, B. F. (1969). Contingencies of reinforcement: A theoretical analysis. Appleton-Century-Crofts.

Slocum, S. K., Grauerholz-Fisher, E., Peters, K. P., & Vollmer, T. R. (2018). A multicomponent approach to thinning reinforcer delivery during noncontingent reinforcement schedules. *Journal of Applied Behavior Analysis, 51*(1), 61–69. https://doi .org/10.1002/jaba.427

Slocum, T. A., Detrich, R., Wilczynski, S. M., Spencer, T. D., Lewis, T., & Wolfe, K. (2014). The evidence-based practice of applied behavior analysis. *Behavior Analyst, 37*(1), 41–56. https://doi.org/10.1007/s40614-014-0005-2

Smeltzer, S. S., Graff, R. B., Ahearn, W. H., & Libby, M. E. (2009). Effect of choice of task sequence on responding. *Research in Autism Spectrum Disorders, 3*(3), 734–742. https://doi.org/10.1016/j.rasd.2009.02.002

Smith, C. J., Lang, C. M., Kryzak, L., Reichenberg, A., Hollander, E., & Silverman, J. M. (2009). Familial associations of intense preoccupations, an empirical factor of the restricted, repetitive behaviors and interests domain of autism. *Journal of Child Psychology and Psychiatry, 50*(8), 982–990. https://doi.org/10.1111/j.1469 -7610.2009.02060.x

Smith, G. J., McDougall, D., & Edelen-Smith, P. (2006). Behavioral cusps: A person-centered concept for establishing pivotal individual, family, and community behaviors and repertoires. *Focus on Autism and Other Developmental Disabilities, 21*(4), 223–229. https://doi.org/10.1177/10883576060210040301

Smith, R. G., Iwata, B. A., & Shore, B. A. (1995). Effects of subject-versus experimenter-selected reinforcers on the behavior of individuals with profound developmental disabilities. *Journal of Applied Behavior Analysis, 28*, 61–71. https://doi.org/10.1901 /jaba.1995.28-61

Smith, T. (2013). What is evidence-based behavior analysis? *Behavior Analyst, 36*(1), 7–33. https://doi.org/10.1007/BF03392290

Smull, L. (2005). *Essential lifestyle planning for everyone.* The Learning Company.

Sng, C. Y., Carter, M., Stephenson, J. (2018). A systematic review of comparative pragmatic differences in conversational skills of individuals with autism. *Autism and Developmental Language Impairments, 3*(1), 1–24. http://doi.org/10.1177/2396941518803806

Snell, M. E., & Brown, F. (2011). *Instruction of students with severe disabilities* (7th ed.). Pearson.

Snell, M. E., & Janney, R. E. (2000). *Practices for inclusive schools: Social relationships and peer support.* Paul H. Brookes.

Snodgrass, M. R., Chung, M. Y., Biller, M. F., Appel, K. E., Meadan, H., & Halle, J. W. (2017). Telepractice in speech-language therapy: The use of online technologies for parent training and coaching. *Communication Disorders Quarterly, 38*(4), 242–254. https://doi.org/10.1177/15257 40116 68042 4

Snow, C. E. (2018). Simple and not-so-simple views of reading. *Remedial and Special Education, 39*(5), 313–316. https://doi.org/10.1177/0741932518770288

Snyder, P. A., Hemmeter, M. L., & Fox, L. (2015). Supporting implementation of evidence-based practices through practice-based coaching. *Topics in Early Childhood Special Education, 35*(3), 133–143. https://doi.org/10.1177/0271121415594925

Snyder, P., & Wolfe, B. (2008). The big three process components of effective professional development: Needs assessment, evaluation, and follow-up. In P. Winton, J. McCollum, & C. Catlett (Eds.), *Practical approaches to early childhood professional development: Evidence, strategies, and resources* (pp. 13–51). Zero to Three.

Soenksen, D., & Alper, S. (2006). Teaching a young child to appropriately gain attention of peers using a Social Story intervention. *Focus on Autism and Other Developmental Disabilities, 21*(1), 36–44. https://www.doi.org/10.1177/10883576060210010501

Solari, E. J., Grimm, R., McIntyre, N. S., Lerro, L. S., Zajic, M., & Mundy, P. C. (2017). The relation between text reading fluency and reading comprehension for students with autism spectrum disorders. *Research in Autism Spectrum Disorders, 41–42*, 8–19. https://doi.org/10.1016/j.rasd.2017.07.002

Solari, E. J., Grimm, R. P., McIntyre, N. S., Zajic, M., & Mundy, P. C. (2019). Longitudinal stability of reading profiles in individuals with higher functioning autism. *Autism, 23*(8), 1911–1926. https://doi.org/10.1177/1362361318812423

Solomon, B., Klein, S., & Politylo, B. (2012). The effect of performance feedback on teachers' treatment integrity: A meta-analysis of the single-case literature. *School Psychology Review, 41*(2), 160–175. https://doi.org/10.1080/02796015.2012.12087518

Sosnowy, C., Silverman, C., & Shattuck, P. (2018). Parents' and young adults' perspectives on transition outcomes for young adults with autism. *Autism, 22*(1), 29–39. https://doi.org/10.1177%2F1362361317699585

South, M., Ozonoff, S., & McMahon, W. M. (2005). Repetitive behavior profiles in Asperger syndrome and high-functioning autism. *Journal of Autism and Developmental Disorders, 35*(2), 145–158. https://doi.org/10.1007/s10803-004-1992-8

Sparapani, N., Connor, C. M., McLean, L., Wood, T., Toste, J., & Day, S. (2018). Direct and reciprocal effects among social skills, vocabulary, and reading comprehension in first grade. *Contemporary Educational Psychology, 53*, 159–167. https://doi.org/10.1016/j.cedpsych.2018.03.003

Spence, S. H. (2003). Social skills training with children and young people: Theory, evidence, and practice. *Child and Adolescent Mental Health, 8*, 84–96. https://doi.org/10.1111/1475-3588.00051

Spencer, T. D., Detrich, R., & Slocum, T. A. (2012). Evidence-Based Practice: A framework for making effective decisions. *Education and Treatment of Children, 35*(2), 127–151. https://doi.org/10.1353/etc.2012.0013

Sreckovic, M. A., Brunsting, N. C., & Able, H. (2014). Victimization of students with autism spectrum disorder: A review of prevalence and risk factors. *Research in autism spectrum disorders, 8*(9), 1155–1172. https://doi.org/10.1016/j.rasd.2014.06.004

Sreckovic, M. A., Hume, K., & Able, H. (2017). Examining the efficacy of peer network interventions on the social interactions of high school students with autism spectrum disorder. *Journal of Autism and Developmental Disorders, 47*, 2556–2574. https://doi.org/10.1007/s10803-017-3171-8

Stahmer, A. C., & Carter, C. (2005). An empirical examination of toddler development in inclusive childcare. *Early Child Development and Care, 175*(4), 321–333. https://doi.org/10.1080/0300443042000266231

Stahmer, A. C., Ingersoll, B., & Carter, C. (2013). Behavioral approaches to promoting play. *Autism, 7*(4), 401–413. https://doi.org/10.1177/1362361303007004006

Star, J. R. (2005). Reconceptualizing procedural knowledge. *Journal for Research in Mathematics Education, 36*(5), 404–411. https://doi.org/10.2307/30034943

Stecker, P. M., & Fuchs, L. S. (2000). Effecting superior achievement using curriculum-based measurement: The importance of individual progress monitoring. *Learning Disabilities Research & Practice, 15*(3), 128–134. https://doi.org/10.1207/SLDRP1503_2

Stecker, P. M., Lembke, E. S., & Foegen, A. (2008). Using progress-monitoring data to improve instructional decision making. *Preventing School Failure: Alternative Education for Children and Youth, 52*(2), 48–58. https://doi.org/10.3200/PSFL.52.2.48-58

Steele, J. L., & Boudett, K. P. (2008a). The collaborative advantage. *Educational Leadership, 66*(4), 54–59.

Steele, J. L., & Boudett, K. P. (2008b). Leadership lessons from schools becoming "data wise." *Harvard Education Letter, 24*(1), 1–2.

Steinbrenner, J. R., Hume, K., Odom, S. L., Morin, K. L., Nowell, S. W., Tomaszewski, B., Szendrey, S., McIntyre, N. S., Yücesoy-Özkan, S., & Savage, M. N. (2020). *Evidence-based practices for children, youth, and young adults with autism.* University of North Carolina at Chapel Hill, Frank Porter Graham Child Development Institute, National Clearinghouse on Autism Evidence and Practice Review Team.

Stichter, J. P., Herzog, M. J., Owens, S. A., & Malugen, E. (2016). Manualization, feasibility, and effectiveness of the school-based social competence intervention for adolescents (SCI-A). *Psychology in the Schools, 53*(6), 583–600. https://doi.org/10.1002/pits.21928

Stodden, R. A., & Mruzek, D. W. (2010). An introduction to postsecondary education and employment of persons with autism and developmental disabilities. *Focus on Autism and Other Developmental Disabilities, 25*(3), 131–133. https://doi.org/10.1177/1088357610371637

Stokes, T., & Baer, D. M. (1977). An implicit technology of generalization. *Journal of Applied Behavior Analysis, 10*(2), 349–367. https://doi.org/10.1901/jaba.1977.10-349

Stone, W. L., Ousley, O. Y., Yoder, P. J., Hogan, K. L., & Hepburn, L. (1997). Nonverbal communication in two- and three-year-old children with autism. *Journal of Autism and Developmental Disorders, 27*(6), 20. https://://doi.org/10.1023/a:1025854816091

Sturmey, P., & Didden, R. (Eds.). (2014). *Evidence-based practice and intellectual disability*. Wiley Blackwell.

Sugai, G., & Horner, R. R. (2006). A promising approach to expanding and sustaining school-wide positive behavior support. *School Psychology Review, 35*(2), 245–259. https://doi.org/10.1080/02796015.2006.12087989

Sugai, G., Lewis-Palmer, T., Todd, A., & Horner, E. H. (2001). *School-wide evaluation tool*. University of Oregon.

Sugai, G., & Simonsen, B. (2020). Reinforcement foundations of a function-based behavioral approach for students with challenging behavior. *Beyond Behavior, 29*(2), 78–85. https://doi.org/10.1177/1074295620902444

Suhrheinrich, J., & Chan, J. (2017). Exploring the effect of immediate video feedback on coaching. *Journal of Special Education Technology, 32*(1), 47–53. https://doi.org/10.1177/0162643416681163

Sullivan, L., Mundy, P., & Mastergeorge, A. M. (2015). Joint attention in preschool children: Is it a meaningful measure. *International Journal School Cognitive Psychology, 2*(1), 120. https://doi.org/10.4172/2469-9837.1000120

Summers, J. A., Marquis, J., Mannan, H., Turnbull, A. P., Fleming, K., Poston, D. G., Wang, M., & Kupzyk, K. (2007). Relationship of perceived adequacy of services, family-professional partnerships, and family quality of life in early childhood service programmes. *International Journal of Disability, Development, & Education, 54*, 319–338. https://doi.org/10.1080/10349120701488848

Sundberg, M. L. (2014). *Verbal behavior milestones assessment and placement program (VB-MAPP)* (2nd ed.). AVB Press.

Swain, R., Lane, J. D., & Gast, D. L. (2015). Comparison of constant time delay and simultaneous prompting procedures: Teaching functional sight words to students with intellectual disabilities and autism spectrum disorder. *Journal of Behavioral Education, 24*, 210–229. https://doi.org/10.1007/s10864-014-9209-5

Sylvester, L., Ogletree, B. T., & Lunnen, K. (2017). Cotreatment as a vehicle for interprofessional collaborative practice: Physical therapists and speech-language pathologists collaborating in the care of children with severe disabilities. *American Journal of Speech-Language Pathology, 26*(2), 206–216. https://doi.org/10.1044/2017_AJSLP-15-0179

Szidon, K., & Franzone, E. (2009). *Task Analysis*. National Professional Developmental Center on Autism Spectrum Disorders, Waisman Center, University of Wisconsin.

Tadevosyan-Leyfer, O., Dowd, M., Mankoski, R., Winklosky, B., Putnam, S., McGrath, L., Tager-Flusberg, H., & Folstein, S. (2003). A principal components analysis of the Autism Diagnostic Interview—Revised. *Journal of the American Academy of Child and Adolescent Psychiatry, 42*(7), 864–872. https://doi.org/10.1097/01.CHI.0000046870.56865.90

Tager-Flusberg, H., & Kasari, C. (2013). Minimally verbal school-aged children with autism spectrum disorder: The neglected end of the spectrum. *Autism Research, 6*(6), 468–478. https://doi.org/10.1002/aur.1329

Tamm, L., Duncan, A., Vaughn, A., McDade, R., Estell, N., Birnschein, A., & Crosby, L. (2020). Academic needs in middle school: Perspectives of parents and youth with autism. *Journal of Autism & Developmental Disorders, 50*(9), 3126–3139. https://doi .org/10.1007/s10803-019-03995-1

Tarbox, R. S. F., Ghezzi, P. M., & Wilson, G. (2006). The effects of token reinforcement on attending in a young child with autism. *Behavioral Interventions, 21*(3), 155–164. https://doi.org/10.1002/bin.213

Targett, P. S., & Smith, M. D. (2009). Living in the community. In P. Wehman (Ed.), *Autism and the transition to adulthood: Success beyond the classroom* (pp. 163–188). Paul H. Brookes.

Tarnowski, K. J., & Simonian, S. J. (1992). Assessing treatment acceptance: The abbreviated acceptability rating profile. *Journal of Behavior Therapy & Experimental Psychiatry, 23*(2), 101–106. https://doi.org/10.1016/0005-7916(92)90007-6

Tarver, J., Palmer, M., Webb, S., Scott, S., Slonims, V., Simonoff, E., & Charman, T. (2019). Child and parent outcomes following parent interventions for child emotional and behavioral problems in autism spectrum disorders: A systematic review and meta-analysis. *Autism, 23*(7), 1630–1644.

Tassé, M. J., Luckasson, R., & Schalock, R. L. (2016). The relation between intellectual functioning and adaptive behavior in the diagnosis of intellectual disability. *Intellectual and Developmental Disabilities, 54*(6), 381–390. https://doi.org/10.1352/1934 -9556-54.6.381

Tavernor, L., Barron, E., Rodgers, J., & McConachie, H. (2013). Finding out what matters: Validity of quality of life measurement in young people with ASD. *Child: Care, Health, and Development, 39*(4), 592–601. https://doi.org/10.1111/j.1365 -2214.2012.01377.x

Taylor, J. L., & Seltzer, M. M. (2011). Employment and post-secondary educational activities for young adults with autism spectrum disorders during the transition to adulthood. *Journal of Autism and Developmental Disorders, 41,* 566–574. https://doi .org/10.1007/s10803-010-1070-3

Test, D. W., Fowler, C. H., Richter, S., White, J. A., Mazzotti, V. L., Walker, A. R., Kohler, P., & Kortering, L. (2009). Evidence-based practices in secondary transition. *Career Development for Exceptional Individuals, 32*(2), 115–128. https://doi .org/10.1177/0885728809336859

Test, D. W., Mazzotti, V. L., Mustian, A. L., Fowler, C. H., Kortering, L. J., & Kohler, P. H. (2009). Evidence-based secondary transition predictors for improving post-school outcomes for students with disabilities. *Career Development for Exceptional Individuals, 32*(3), 160–181. https://doi.org/10.1177/0885728809346960

Test, D. W., Spooner, F., Keul, P. K., & Grossi, T. (1990). Teaching adolescents with severe disabilities to use the public telephone. *Behavior Modification, 14*(2), 157–171. https:// doi.org/10.1177/01454455900142003

Tharp, R. G., & Wetzel, R. J. (1969). *Behavior modification in the natural environment.* Academic Press.

Thomas, K. C., Morrissey, J. P., & McLaurin, C. (2007). Use of autism-related services by families and children. *Journal of Autism and Developmental Disorders, 37*(5), 818–829. https://doi.org/10.1007/s10803-006-0208-9

Thornton, A., McKissick, B. R., Spooner, F., Lo, Y.-Y., & Anderson, A. L. (2015). Effects of collaborative preteaching on science performance of high school students with specific learning disabilities. *Education and Treatment of Children, 38*(3), 277–304. https:// doi.org/10.1353/etc.2015.0027

Thurm, A., Farmer, C., Salzman, E., Lord, C., & Bishop, S. (2019). State of the field: Differentiating intellectual disability from autism spectrum disorder. *Frontiers in Psychiatry, 10,* 526. https://doi.org/10.3389/fpsyt.2019.00526

Tilly, W. D. (2008). The evolution of school psychology to a science-based practice: Problem solving and the three-tiered model. In J. Grimes & A. Thomas (Eds.), *Best practices in school psychology V* (pp. 17–36). National Association of School Psychologists.

Tirado, M., & Saldaña, D. (2016). Readers with autism can produce inferences, but they cannot answer inferential questions. *Journal of Autism & Developmental Disorders, 46*(3), 1025–1037. https://doi.org/10.1007/s10803-015-2648-6

Titeca, D., Roeyers, H., Josephy, H., Ceulemans, A., & Desoete, A. (2014). Preschool predictors of mathematics in first grade children with autism spectrum disorder. *Research in Developmental Disabilities, 35*, 2714–2727. https://doi.org/10.1016/j.ridd.2014.07.012

Titeca, D., Roeyers, H., Loeys, T., Ceulemans, A., & Desoete, A. (2015). Mathematical abilities in elementary school children with autism spectrum disorder. *Infant and Child Development, 24*(6), 606–623. https://doi.org/10.1002/icd.1909

Tobin, M. C., Drager, K. D. R., & Richardson, L. F. (2014). A systematic review of social participation for adults with autism spectrum disorders: Support, social functioning, and quality of life. *Research in Autism Spectrum Disorders, 8*(3), 214–229. https://doi.org/10.1016/j.rasd.2013.12.002

Todd, A. W., Algozzine, B., Horner, R. H., Preston, A. I., Cusumano, D., & Algozzine, K. (2017). A descriptive study of school-based problem-solving. *Journal of Emotional and Behavioral Disorders, 27*(1), 14–24. https://doi.org/10.1177/1063426617733717

Topor, D. R., Keane, S. P., Shelton, T. L., & Calkins, S. D. (2010). Parent involvement and student academic performance: A multiple mediational analysis. *Journal of Prevention & Intervention in the Community, 38*(3), 183–197. https://doi.org/10.1080/10852352.2010.486297

Toth, K., Munson, J., Meltzoff, A. N., & Dawson, G. (2006). Early predictors of communication development in young children with autism spectrum disorder: Joint attention, imitation, and toy play. *Journal of Autism and Developmental Disorders, 36*(8), 993–1005. https://doi.org/10.1007/s10803-006-0137-7

Touchette, P. E. (1971). Transfer of stimulus control: measuring the moment of transfer. *Journal of Experimental Analysis of Behavior, 15*(3), 347–354. https://doi.org/10.1901/jeab.1971.15-347

Trainor, A. A. (2010). Diverse approaches to parent advocacy during special education home-school interactions: Identification and use of cultural and social capital. *Remedial and Special Education, 31*(1), 34–47. https://doi.org/10.1177/0741932508324401

Trainor, A. A., & Bal, A. (2014). Development and preliminary analysis of a rubric for culturally responsive research. *Journal of Special Education, 47*(4), 203–216. https://doi.org/10.1177%2F0022466912436397

Trainor, A. A., Carter, E. W., Karpur, A., Martin, J. E., Mazzotti, V. L., Morningstar, M. E., Newman, L., & Rojewski, J. W. (2020). A framework for research in transition: Identifying important areas and intersections for future study. *Career Development and Transition for Exceptional Individuals, 43*(1), 5–17. https://doi.org/10.1177/2165143419864551

Tripp, T. R., & Rich, P. J. (2012). The influence of video analysis on the process of teacher change. *Teaching and Teacher Education, 28*, 728–739. https://doi.org/10.1016/j.tate.2012.01.011

Trivette, C. M., Dunst, C. J., & Hamby, D. W. (2010). Influences of family-systems intervention practices on parent-child interactions and child development. *Topics in Early Childhood Special Education, 30*(1), 3–19. https://doi.org/10.1177/0271121410364250

Tsatsanis, K. (2005). Neuropsychological characteristics of autism and related conditions. In R. R. Volkmar, R. Paul, A. Klin, & D. Cohen (Eds.), *Handbook of autism and developmental disorders*. Wiley.

Turnbull, A. A., Turnbull, H. R., Erwin, E. J., Soodak, L. C., & Shogren, K. A. (2011). *Families, professionals, and exceptionality: Positive outcomes through partnerships and trust.* Pearson.

Turner, M. (1999). Annotation: Repetitive behaviour in autism: A review of psychological research. *Journal of Child Psychology and Psychiatry, 40*(6), 839–849. https://doi.org/10.1111/1469-7610.00502

Turner-Brown, L. M., Lam, L. S. L., Holtzclaw, T. N., Dichter, G. S., & Bodfish, J. W. (2011). Phenomenology and measurement of circumscribed interests in autism spectrum disorders. *Autism: The International Journal of Research and Practice, 15*(4), 437–456. https://doi.org/10.1177/1362361310386507

Tyrer, P., Nagar, J., Evans, R., Oliver, P., Bassett, P., Liedtka, N., & Tarabi, A. (2016). The Problem Behaviour Checklist: short scale to assess challenging behaviours. *British Journal of Psychiatry Open, 2*(1), 45–49. https://doi.org/10.1192/bjpo.bp.115.002360

U.S. Bureau of Labor Statistics. (2017). *Occupational outlook handbook: Teacher assistants.* U.S. Department of Labor. https://www.bls.gov/ooh/education-training-and library/teacher-assistants.htm

U.S. Census Bureau. (2020). *America's families and living arrangements.* https://www.census.gov/newsroom/press-releases/2020/estimates-families-living-arrangements.html

U.S. Department of Education. (2020). *42nd Annual Report to Congress on the implementation of the Individuals with Disabilities Education Act.* https://sites.ed.gov/idea/2020-annual-report-congress-idea/#Key-Findings-3-21

U.S. Department of Education (ED) and U.S. Department of Health and Human Services (HHS). (2016). *Policy statement on family engagement form the early years to the early grades.* U. S. Department of Health and Human Services and U.S. Department of Education. https://www2.ed.gov/about/inits/ed/earlylearning/files/policy-statement-on-family-engagement.pdf

U.S. Department of Health and Human Services, National Institutes of Health, National Institute on Deafness and Other Communication Disorders. (2014). *Communication problems in children with autism spectrum disorder.* https://www.nidcd.nih.gov/sites/default/files/Documents/health/voice/NIDCD-Communication-Problems-in-Children-with-Autism-FS_0.pdf

Vandercook, T., York, J., & Forest, M. (1989). The McGill Action Planning System (MAPS): A strategy for building the vision. *Journal of the Association for Persons with Severe Handicaps, 14*(3), 205–215. https://doi.org/10.1177/154079698901400306

Van Dooren, W. V., Bock, D. D., & Verschaffel, L. (2010). From addition to multiplication . . . and back: The development of students' additive and multiplicative reasoning skills. *Cognition and Instruction, 28*(3), 360–381. https://doi.org/10.1080/07370008.2010.488306

van Heijst, B. F. C., & Geurts, H. M. (2015). Quality of life in autism across the life span: A meta-analysis. *Autism, 19*(2), 158–167. https://doi.org/10.1177/1362361313517053

Van Loon, J., & Van Wijk, P. (2016). Organizational transformation. In R. L. Schalock & K. D. Keith (Eds.), *Cross-cultural quality of life: Enhancing the lives of people with intellectual disabilities* (2nd ed., pp. 109–118). American Association on Intellectual and Developmental Disabilities.

Vannest, K. J., Davis, J. L., & Parker, R. I. (2013). *Single case research in schools: Practical guidelines for school-based professionals.* Routledge/Taylor & Francis Group.

Van Steensel, F. J., Bogels, S. M., & Perrin, S. (2011). Anxiety disorders in children and adolescents with autistic spectrum disorders: A meta-analysis. *Clinical Child and Family Psychology Review, 14*(3), 302–317. https://doi.org/10.1007/s10567-011-0097-0

Van Vondel, S., Steenbeek, H., Van Dijk, M., & Van Geert, P. (2018). The effects of video feedback coaching for teachers on scientific knowledge of primary students. *Research in Science Education (Australasian Science Education Research Association)*, 48(2), 301–324. https://doi.org/10.1007/s11165-016-9569-z

Vargason, T., Frye, R. E., McGuinness, D. L., & Hahn, J. (2019). Clustering of co-occurring conditions in autism spectrum disorder during early childhood: A retrospective analysis of medical claims data. *Autism Research*, 12(8), 1275–1285. https://doi.org/10.1002/aur.2128

Vaughan, C. (2011). Test Review: E. Schopler, M. E. Van Bourgondien, G. J. Wellman, & S. R. *Love Childhood Autism Rating Scale* (2nd ed.). Western Psychological Services.

Vespa, J., Armstrong, D. M., & Medina, L. (2018). *Demographic turning points for the United States: Population projections for 2020 to 2060*. U.S. Census Bureau. https://www.census.gov/content/dam/Census/library/publications/2020/demo/p25-1144.pdf

Vine Foggo, R. S., & Webster, A. A. (2017). Understanding the social experiences of adolescent females on the autism spectrum. *Research in Autism Spectrum Disorders*, 35, 74–85. https://doi.org/10.1016/j.rasd.2016.11.006

Vivanti, G. (2020). Ask the editor: What is the most appropriate way to talk about individuals with a diagnosis of autism? *Journal of Autism and Developmental Disabilities*, 50(2), 691–693. https://doi.org/10.1007/s10803-019-04280-x

Volkmar, F. R., Cohen, D. J., & Paul, R. (1986). An evaluation of DSM-III criteria for infantile autism. *Journal of the American Academy of Child Psychiatry*, 25(2), 190–197. https://doi.org/10.1016/s0002-7138(09)60226-0

Volkmar, F. R., Langford Booth, L., McPartland, J. C., & Wiesner, L. A. (2014). Clinical evaluation in multidisciplinary settings. In F. Volkmar, S. Rogers, R. Paul, & K. Pelphrey (Eds.), *Handbook of autism and pervasive developmental disorders* (4th ed.). Wiley & Sons.

Vollmer, T. R., Marcus, B. A., & LeBlanc, L. (1994). Treatment of self-injury and hand mouthing following inconclusive functional analyses. *Journal of Applied Behavior Analysis*, 27(2), 331–344. https://doi.org/10.1901/jaba.1994.27-331

Vollmer, T. R., Peters, K. P., & Slocum, S. K. (2015). Treatment of severe behavior disorders. In H. S. Roane, J. E. Ringdahl, & T. S. Falcomata (Eds.), *Clinical and Organizational Applications of Applied Behavior Analysis* (pp. 47–67). Elsevier.

Vygotsky, L. S. (1978). *Mind in society: The development of higher psychological processes*. Harvard University Press.

Wagner, A., Lecavalier, L., Eugene Arnold, L., Aman, M. G., Scahill, L., Stigler, K. A., Johnson, C. R., McDougle, C. J., & Vitiello, B. (2007). Developmental disabilities modification of the Children's Global Assessment scale. *Biological Psychiatry*, 61(4), 504–511. https://doi.org/10.1016/j.biopsych.2007.01.001

Wagner, M., Newman, L., Cameto, R., Levine, P., & Garza, N. (2005). *An overview of findings from wave 2 of the National Longitudinal Transition Study-2 (NLTS-2)*. SRI International. https://www.nlts2.org/reports/2006_08/nlts2_report_2006_08_complete.pdf

Wakefield, A. J., Murch, S. H., Anthony, A., Linnell, J., Casson, D. M., Malik, M., Berelowitz, M., Dhillon, A. P., Thomson, M. A., Harvey, P., Valentine, A., Davies, S. E., & Walker-Smith, J. A. (1998). RETRACTED: Ileal-lymphoid-nodular hyperplasia, non-specific colitis, and pervasive developmental disorder in children. *The Lancet*, 351(9103), 637–641. https://doi.org/10.1016/S0140-6736(97)11096-0

Walsh, E., Holloway, J., & Lydon, H. (2017). An evaluation of a social skills intervention for adults with autism spectrum disorder and intellectual disabilities preparing for employment in Ireland: A pilot study. *Journal of Autism and Developmental Disorders*, 48, 1727–1741. https://doi.org/10.1007/s10803-017-3441-5

Wanberg, C. R. (2012). The individual experience of unemployment. *Annual Review of Psychology*, 63, 369–396. https://doi.org/10.1146/annurev-psych-120710-100500

Wang, D., Mason, R. A., Lory, C., Kim, S. Y., & David, M. (2020). Vocal stereotypy and autism spectrum disorder: A systematic review of interventions. *Research in Autism Spectrum Disorders, 78*(19), 101647. https://doi.org/10.1016/j.rasd.2020.101647

Wang, M., Mannan, H., Poston, D., Turnbull, A. P., & Summers, J. A. (2004). Parents' perceptions of advocacy activities and their impact on family quality of life. *Research and Practice for Persons with Severe Disabilities, 29*, 144–155. https://doi.org/10.1007/s10803-014-2351-z

Ward-Horner, J., & Sturmey, P. (2012). Component analysis of behavior skills training in functional analysis. *Behavioral Interventions, 27*(2), 75–92. http://dx.doi.org.proxy.cc.uic.edu/10.1002/bin.1339

Watanabe, M., & Sturmey, P. (2003). The effect of choice-making opportunities during activity schedules on task engagement of adults with autism. *Journal of Autism and Developmental Disorders, 33*(5), 535–538. https://doi.org/10.1023/A:1025835729718

Watkins, L., Ledbetter-Cho, K., O'Reilly, M., Barnard-Brak, L., & Garcia-Grau, P. (2019). Interventions for students with autism in inclusive settings: A best-evidence synthesis and meta-analysis. *Psychological Bulletin, 145*(5), 490–507. https://doi.org/10.1037/bul0000190

Watson, S. M. R., & Keith, K. D. (2002). Comparing the quality of life of school-age children with and without disabilities. *Intellectual and Developmental Disabilities, 40*(4), 304–312. https://doi.org/10.1352/0047-6765(2002)040<0304:CTQOLO>2.0.CO;2

Wechsler, D. (2003). *Wechsler Intelligence Scale for Children (WISC-IV)*. Psychological Corporation.

Wehman, P. (2013). Transition from school to work: Where are we and where do we need to go? *Career Development and Transition for Exceptional Individuals, 36*(1), 58–66. https://doi.org/10.1177/2165143413482137

Wehman, P., Schall, C., Carr, S., Targett, P., West, M., & Cifu, G. (2014). Transition from school to adulthood for youth with autism spectrum disorder: What we know and what we need to know. *Journal of Disability Policy Studies, 25*(1), 30–40. https://doi.org/10.1177/1044207313518071

Wehman, P., Schall, C., McDonough, J., Molinelli, A., Riehle, E., Ham, W., & This, W. R. (2013). Project SEARCH for youth with autism spectrum disorders: Increasing competitive employment on transition from high school. *Journal of Positive Behavior Interventions, 15*(3), 144–155. https://doi.org/10.1177%2F1098300712459760

Wehmeyer, M. L. (2005). Self-determination and individuals with severe disabilities: Re-examining meanings and misinterpretations. *Research and Practice for Persons with Severe Disabilities, 30*, 113–120. https://doi.org/10.2511/rpsd.30.3.113

Wehmeyer, M. L., & Shogren, K. (2008). Self-determination and learners with autism spectrum disorders. In R. Simpson & B. Myles (Eds.), *Educating children and youth with autism: Strategies for effective practice* (pp. 433–476, 2nd ed.). Pro-Ed Publishers.

Wehmeyer, M. L., Shogren, K. A., & Kurth, J. (2020). The state of inclusion with students with intellectual and developmental disabilities in the United States. *Journal of Policy and Practice in Intellectual Disabilities, 18*(1), 36–43. https://doi.org/10.1111/jppi.12332

Wehmeyer, M. L., Shogren, K. A., Zager, D., Smith, T. E. C., & Simpson, R. (2010). Research-based principles and practice for educating students with autism: Self-determination and social interactions. *Education and Training in Autism and Developmental Disabilities, 45*(4), 475–486. https://www.jstor.org/stable/23879754

Wei, X., Christiano, E. R., Yu, W. J., Wagner, M., & Spiker, D. (2014). Reading and math achievement profiles and longitudinal growth trajectories of children with an autism spectrum disorder. *Autism, 19*(2), 1–11. https://doi.org/10.1177/1362361313516549

Wei, X., Wagner, M., Christiano, E. R. A., Shattuck, P., & Yu, J. W. (2014). Special education services received by students with autism spectrum disorders from preschool through high school. *Journal of Special Education, 48*(3), 167–179. https://doi.org/10.1177/0022466913483576

Wentzel, K. R., Donlan, A., & Morrison, D. (2012). Peer relationships and social motivational processes. In A. M. Ryan & G. W. Ladd (Eds.), *Peer relationships and adjustment at school* (pp. 79–108). Information Age Publishing.

Werner, R. (2018). Music, movement and memory: Pedagogical songs as mnemonic aids. *TESOL Journal, 9*(4), 1–11. https://doi.org/10.1002/tesj.387

West, E. A. (2008). Effects of verbal cues versus pictorial cues on the transfer of stimulus control for children with autism. *Focus on Autism and Other Developmental Disabilities, 23*(4), 229–241. https://doi.org/10.1177/1088357608324715

West, E. A., Travers, J. C., Kemper, T. D., Liberty, L. M., Cote, D. L., McCollow, M. M., & Stansberry Brusnahan, L. L. (2016). Racial and ethnic diversity of participants in research supporting evidence-based practices for learners with autism spectrum disorder. *Journal of Special Education, 50*(3), 151–163. https://doi.org/10.1177/0022466916632495

Westerveld, M., Paynter, J., Trembath, D., Webster, A., Hodge, A., & Roberts, J. (2017). The emergent literacy skills of preschool children with autism spectrum disorder. *Journal of Autism & Developmental Disorders, 47*(2), 424–438. https://doi.org/10.1007/s10803-016-2964-5

Westling, D. L., & Fox, L. (2009). *Teaching students with severe disabilities* (4th ed.). Merrill Prentice Hall.

Weston, R., Hodges, A., & Davis, T. N. (2018). Differential reinforcement of other behaviors to treat challenging behaviors among children with autism: A systematic and quality review. *Behavior Modification, 42*(4), 584–609. https://doi.org/10.1177/0145445517743487

Whalon, K. (2018). Enhancing the reading development of learners with autism spectrum disorder. *Seminars in Speech and Language, 39*(2), 144–157. https://doi.org/10.1055/s-0038-1628366

Whalon, K. J., Al Otaiba, S., & Delano, M. E. (2009). Evidence-based reading instruction for individuals with autism spectrum disorders. *Focus on Autism and Other Developmental Disabilities, 24*(1), 3–16. https://doi.org/10.1177/1088357608328515

Whitacre, I., Henning, B., & Atabas, S. (2017). *Disentangling the research literature on "number sense": Three constructs, one name.* Proceedings of the 39th annual meeting of the North America Chapter of the International Group for the Psychology of Mathematics Education.

White, S., Frith, U., Milne, E., Rosen, S., Swettenham, J., & Ramus, F. (2006). A double dissociation between sensorimotor impairments and reading disability: A comparison of autistic and dyslexic children, *Cognitive Neuropsychology, 23*, 748–761. https://doi.org/10.1080/02643290500438607

White, S., Keonig, K., & Scahill, L. (2007). Social skills development in children with autism spectrum disorders: A review of the intervention research. *Journal of Autism and Developmental Disorders, 37*(10), 1858–1868. https://doi.org/10.1007/w10803-006-0320-x

White, S. W., Koenig, K., & Scahill, L. (2010). Group social skills instruction for adolescents with high-functioning autism spectrum disorders. *Focus on Autism and Other Developmental Disabilities, 25*(4), 209–219. https://doi.org/10.1177/1088357610380595

White, S. W., Scahill, L., Klin, A., Koenig, K., & Volkmar, F. R. (2007). Educational placements and service use patterns of individuals with autism spectrum disorders. *Journal of Autism and Developmental Disorders, 37*(8), 1403–1412. https://doi.org/10.1007/s10803-006-0281-0

Whitehouse, A. J. O., Barry, J. G., & Bishop, D. V. M. (2007). The broader language phenotype of autism: A comparison with specific language impairment. *Journal of*

Child Psychology and Psychiatry, 48(8), 822–830. https://doi.org/10.1111/j.1469-7610.2007.01765.x

Whitehouse, C. M., Vollmer, T. R., & Colbert, B. (2014). Evaluating the use of computerized stimulus preference assessments in foster care. *Journal of Applied Behavior Analysis, 47*(3), 470–484. https://doi.org/10.1002/jaba.148

White-Koning, M., Grandjean, H., Colver, A., & Arnaud, C. (2008). Parent and professional reports of the quality of life of children with cerebral palsy and associated intellectual impairment. *Developmental Medicine and Child Neurology, 50*(8), 618–624. https://doi.org/10.1111/j.1469-8749.2008.03026.x

Whitley, D. M., Kelley, S. J., & Campos, P. E. (2011). Perceptions of family empowerment in African American custodial grandmothers raising grandchildren: Thoughts for research and practice. *Families in Society: Journal of Contemporary Social Services, 92*, 383–389. https://doi.org/10.1606/1044-3894.4148

Whittenburg, H. N., Sims, K. A., Wehman, P., & Walther-Thomas, C. (2018). Strategies for developing work experiences for youth with intellectual and developmental disabilities. *Career Development and Transition for Exceptional Individuals, 42*(4), 259–264. https://doi.org/10.1177/2165143418813900

Wichnick-Gillis, A. M., Vener, S. M., & Poulson, C. L. (2019). Script fading for children with autism: Generalization of social initiation skills from school to home. *Journal of Applied Behavior Analysis, 52*(2), 451–466. https://doi.org/10.1002/jaba.534

Wilczynski, S. M. (2012). Risk and strategic decision-making in developing evidence-based practice guidelines. *Education and Treatment of Children, 35*(2), 291–311. http://doi.org/10.1353/etc.2012.0012

Wilczynski, S. M. (2017). *A practical guide to finding treatments that work for people with autism.* Elsevier Inc.

Wilczynski, S. M., Connolly, S., Dubard, M., Henderson, A., & McIntosh, D. (2015). Assessment, prevention, and intervention for abuse among individuals with disabilities. *Psychology in Schools, 52*(1), https://doi.org/10.1002/pits.21808

Wilczynski, S. M., Fisher, L., Sutro, L., Bass, J., Mudgal, D., Zeiger, V., Christian, L., & Logue, J. (2011). Evidence-based practice and autism spectrum disorders. In M. A. Bray & T. J. Kehle (Eds.), *The Oxford Handbook of School Psychology* (pp. 567–592). Oxford University Press.

Wilczynski, S. M., Henderson, A., Harris, N. R., Kosmala, S. D., & Bostic, J. (2016). Evidence-based practice, culture, and young children with autism spectrum disorder. *Perspectives in Early Childhood Psychology and Education, 1*(2), 141–160.

Wilczynski, S. M., Kazee, A., & Sundberg, S. L. (2021). *The evidence-based treatment selection prompts ethical and culturally sensitive service delivery.* [Manuscript submitted for publication]. Department of Special Education, Ball State University.

Wilczynski, S. M., Trammell, B. A., Caugherty, T. N., Shellabarger, K., McIntosh, C. E., & Kaake, A. (2016). Integrating evidence-based practice into early childhood alternative settings with children with ASD. *Perspectives in Early Childhood Psychology and Education, 1*(2), 73–91.

Wilder, D. A., Atwell, J., & Wine, B. (2006). The effects of varying levels of treatment integrity on child compliance during treatment with a three-step prompting procedure. *Journal of Applied Behavior Analysis, 39*(3), 369–373. https://doi.org/10.1901/jaba.2006.144-05

Wilkinson, L. A. (2017). *A best practice guide to assessment and intervention for autism spectrum disorder in schools* (2nd ed.). Jessica Kingsley Publishers.

Wilson, K. P. (2013). Teaching social-communication skills to preschoolers with autism: Efficacy of video versus in vivo modeling in the classroom. *Journal of Autism and Developmental Disorders, 43*(8), 1819–1831. https://doi.org/10.1007/s10803-012-1731-5

Wing, L. (1981). Asperger's syndrome: a clinical account. *Psychological Medicine, 11*(1), 115–129. https://doi.org/10.1017/S0033291700053332

Wing, L., & Gould, J. (1979). Severe impairments of social interaction and associated abnormalities in children: Epidemiology and classification. *Journal of Autism and Developmental Disorders, 9*(1), 11–29. https://doi.org/10.1007/BF01531288

Witt, J. C., & Elliott, S. N. (1985). Acceptability of classroom intervention strategies. In T. Kratochwill (Ed.), *Advances in school psychology* (Vol. 4, pp. 251–288). Erlbaum.

Wójcik, M., Eikeseth, S., Eldevik, S., & Budzinska, A. (2020). Teaching children with autism to request items using audio scripts, interrupted chain procedure and sufficient exemplar training. *Behavioral Interventions, 36*, 40–57. https://doi.org/10.1002/bin.1761

Wolf, M. M. (1978). Social validity: The case for subjective measurement or how applied behavior analysis is finding its heart. *Journal of Applied Behavior Analysis, 11* (2), 203–214. https://doi.org/10.1901/jaba.1978.11-203

Wolfe, K., Blankenship, A., & Rispoli, M. (2018). Generalization of skills acquired in Language for Learning by young children with autism spectrum disorder. *Journal of Developmental and Physical Disabilities, 30*, 1–16. https://doi.org/10.1007/s10882-017-9572-y

Wolfe, K., McCammon, M. N., LeJeune, L. M., & Holt, A. K. (2021). Training preservice practitioners to make data-based instructional decisions. *Journal of Behavioral Education*, 1–20. https://doi.org/10.1007/s10864-021-09439-0

Wolfe, K., Pound, S., McCammon, M. N., Chezan, L. C., & Drasgow, E. (2019). A systematic review of interventions to promote varied social-communication behavior in individuals with autism spectrum disorder. *Behavior Modification, 43*(6), 790–818. https://doi.org/10.1177/0145445519859803

Wolfensberger, W. (1983). Social Role Valorization: A proposed new term for the principle of Normalization. *Mental Retardation, 21*(6), 234–239.

Wolfensberger, W., & Thomas, S. (2005). *Introductory Social Role Valorization workshop training package*. Training Institute for Human Service Planning, Leadership, and Change Agentry (Syracuse University).

Wong, C., Odom, S. L., Hume, K. A., Cox, A. W., Fettig, A., Kucharczyk, S., Brock, M. E., Plavnick, J. B., Fleury, V. P., & Schultz, T. R. (2015). Evidence-based practices for children, youth, and young adults with autism spectrum disorder: A comprehensive review. *Journal of Autism and Developmental Disorders, 45*, 1951–1966. https://doi.org/10.1007/s10803-014-2351-z

Wood, L., Root., J., & Thompson, J. (2018). Academics. In B. Jimenez, J. Shurr, & E. Bouck (Eds.), *Evidence-based practices and instructional information for students with intellectual disability & autism spectrum disorders* (pp. 5–21). Council for Exceptional Children.

Workforce Innovation and Opportunity Act of 2014, 29 U.S.C. 3101 *et seq.* (2014). https://www.govinfo.gov/content/pkg/PLAW-113publ128/pdf/PLAW-113publ128.pdf

World Health Organization and Division of Mental Health and Prevention of Substance Abuse (1997). *WHOQOL: Measuring quality of life.* World Health Organization.

Wu, S., Wu, F., Ding, Y., Hou, J., Bi, J., & Zhang, Z. (2017). Advanced parental age and autism risk in children: A systematic review and meta-analysis. *Acta Psychiatrica Scandinavica, 135*(1), 29–41. https://doi.org/10.1111/acps.12666

Yates, K., & Le Couteur, A. (2016). Diagnosing autism/autism spectrum disorders. *Paediatrics and Child Health, 26*(12), 513–518. https://doi.org/10.1016/j.paed.2016.08.004

Yeargin-Allsopp, M., Rice, C., Karapurkar, T., Doernberg, N., Boyle, C., & Murphy, C. (2003). Prevalence of autism in a U. S. metropolitan area. *Journal of the American Medical Association, 289*(1), 49–55. https://doi.org/10.1001/jama.289.1.49

Yell, M. (2019). *The law and special education* (5th ed.). Pearson.

Yell, M. L., & Bateman, D. F. (2017). Endrew F. v. Douglas county school district (2017) FAPE and the US supreme court. *Teaching Exceptional Children, 50*(1), 7–15.

Yell, M. L., Drasgow, E., Lowrey, K. A. (2005). No Child Left Behind and students with autism spectrum disorders. *Focus on Autism and Other Developmental Disabilities, 20*(3), 130–139. https://doi.org/10.1177/10883576050200030101

Ysseldyke, J., Burns, M., Dawson, P., Kelley, B., Morrison, D., Ortiz, S., Rosenfield, S., & Telzrow, C. (2006). *School psychology: A blueprint for training and practice III.* National Association of School Psychologists.

Zablotsky, B., Bradshaw, C. P., Anderson, C., & Law, P. A. (2013). The association between bullying and the psychological functioning of children with autism spectrum disorders. *Journal of Developmental and Behavioral Pediatrics, 34*(1), 1–8. https://doi.org/10.1097/DBP.0b013e31827a7c3a

Zablotsky, B., Boswell, K., & Smith, C. (2021). An evaluation of school involvement and satisfaction of parents of children with autism spectrum disorders. *American Journal of Intellectual and Developmental Disabilities, 117*(4), 316–330. https://doi.org/10.1352/1944-7558-117.4.316

Zentall, S. (2007). Math performance of students with ADHD. In D. B. Berch & M. M. Mazzocco (Eds.), *Why is math so hard for some children?* (pp. 219–243). Brookes.

Zhang, Q., Oetzel, J. G., Gao, X., Wilcox, R. G., & Takai, J. (2007). Teacher Immediacy Scales: Testing for validity across cultures. *Communication Education, 56*(2), 228–248. http://dx.doi.org/10.1080/0363452060108909

Zins, J. E., & Erchul, W. P. (2002). Best practices in school consultation. In A. Thomas & J. Grimes (Eds.), *Best practices in school psychology-IV* (pp. 625–639). National Association of School Psychologists.

Zoder-Martell, K. A., Markelz, A. M., Floress, M. T., Skriba, H. A., & Sayyah, L. E. N. (2020). Technology to facilitate telehealth in applied behavior analysis. *Behavior Analysis in Practice, 13,* 596–603. https://doi.org/10.1007/s40617-020-00449-4

Zuckerman, K. E., Lindly, O. J., Reyes, N. M., Chavez, A. E., Macias, K., Smith, K. N., & Reynolds, A. (2017). Disparities in diagnosis and treatment of autism in Latino and non-Latino white families. *Pediatrics, 139*(5). https://doi.org/10.1542/peds.2016-3010

Index

Page numbers followed by *f* refer to figures and *t* to tables.

About the Editors and Contributors

■ ■ ■

EDITORS

Laura C. Chezan is an associate professor of special education in the Darden College of Education and Professional Studies at Old Dominion University. She received her doctorate at the University of South Carolina and is a Board Certified Behavior Analyst–Doctoral. Her research interests focus on social-communication interventions for individuals with autism spectrum disorder, positive behavior support, and postsecondary education for individuals with autism spectrum disorder and other developmental disabilities. She has coauthored book chapters and published peer-reviewed articles in scholarly journals in the field of education and behavior analysis. Dr. Chezan has also presented at local, state, and national conferences on topics related to communication and behavioral interventions for individuals with autism spectrum disorder and other developmental disabilities. She serves as an associate editor for *Preventing School Failure* and as an editorial board member for six peer-reviewed journals in the fields of special education and applied behavior analysis. Dr. Chezan is a recipient of the Sara and Rufus Tonelson Award for Excellence in Teaching, Research, and Service from Old Dominion University and the Star Reviewer Award from the *Journal of Behavioral Education*.

Katie Wolfe is an associate professor of special education in the Department of Educational Studies at the University of South Carolina. She received her doctorate in disability disciplines and applied behavior analysis at Utah State University. She is a Board Certified Behavior Analyst–Doctoral who has worked with children with autism spectrum disorder for more than 15 years. She conducts research on behavioral interventions to promote language and communication in children with autism spectrum disorder, on methods of training practitioners to make data-based instructional decisions, and on the visual analysis of single-case research data. Dr. Wolfe has published chapters and peer-reviewed articles in scholarly journals related to these interests and serves on the editorial board of five peer-reviewed journals in the fields of applied behavior analysis and special education. She regularly presents at national conferences and conducts workshops related to interventions for children with autism spectrum disorder and related disabilities.

Erik Drasgow is professor of special education and chair of the Department of Educational Studies at the University of South Carolina. He has been in the field of special education for more than 30 years. Dr. Drasgow has published in such journals as the *Journal of Applied Behavior Analysis*, *Behavior Modification*, and *Focus on Autism and Other Developmental Disabilities*. His research and personnel preparation efforts have been funded by the U.S. Department of Education. He has conducted workshops and given presentations across the country in his areas of expertise and has provided technical assistance for more than 35 years to families, teachers, related practitioners, and paraprofessionals.

CONTRIBUTORS

Jennifer M. Asmus is a professor of school psychology in the Department of Educational Psychology at the University of Wisconsin–Madison, with 20 years of experience in applied behavior analysis, developmental disabilities, autism, social skills, severe challenging behavior, and family and school-based consultation. She has served as principal investigator (PI) and co-PI of federally directed research grants that investigated the use of applied behavior analysis strategies for school-aged students with autism in inclusive classrooms, as well as collaborative federal training grants focused on developing school-based professional competency in autism and school-based problem solving. Prior to her work in academia, Dr. Asmus spent three years as director of the biobehavioral inpatient service at the University of Iowa, where she carried out evaluation and intervention services for children and adults with developmental disabilities with resistant problem behaviors. She has an extensive publication and presentation record and has served on the editorial board for the *Journal of Applied Behavior Analysis*.

Amanda Austin is a licensed special education teacher, Board Certified Behavior Analyst, and doctoral student in special education at Purdue University. She has experience as a public-school special educator and district-wide behavior specialist in a large urban school district. Her research interests include applying principles of adult learning, implementation science, and organizational behavior management to improve the adoption, implementation, and sustainability of evidence-based behavioral practices for students with disabilities in public school settings.

Amarie Carnett is a senior lecturer in educational psychology at Victoria University of Wellington, New Zealand, and an adjunct professor at the University of Texas–San Antonio in the applied behavior analysis program. She is a doctorate-level Board Certified Behavior Analyst (BCBA-D). Dr. Carnett initially trained in applied behavior analysis (ABA) at Texas State University during her master's program. She completed her doctorate degree in educational psychology, specializing in ABA and communication interventions, at Victoria University of Wellington. Dr. Carnett has written 35 peer-reviewed articles, 21 related to communication interventions, and 14 related to adaptive functioning.

Wen-hsuan Chang is a postdoctoral associate in the Young Adults Empowerment, Leadership, and Learning (YELL) lab at the University of Florida. She received her doctoral degree in special education at the University of North Carolina at Charlotte. Her research aimed to understand parents' perceptions of existing challenges and to develop family-focused evidence-based practices.

Aaron R. Check received his degree in child psychology with a minor in youth studies from the University of Minnesota in 2006. After graduating, he worked in a clinical setting in Minneapolis, implementing applied behavior analysis with children with autism. In 2008, he moved to Columbia, South Carolina, where he continued to work in clinical and home settings while completing a master's degree and earning a BCBA in 2011. In 2013, he opened his own practice in the Charleston, South Carolina, area, contracting with school districts and providing in-home services for children and adults with a variety of disabilities. He is currently pursuing a PhD in special education from the University of South Carolina with a focus on applying the principles of behavior analysis within the process of transition.

Hannah Crosley is a doctoral student in special education at Purdue University. She has five years of experience implementing applied behavior analysis procedures with individuals with high support needs between the ages of 3 and 16. Her research focus is on the use of implementation science to increase the adoption of evidence-based practices, specifically peer-mediated interventions, at the secondary and postsecondary level.

Taylor P. Dorlack is a graduate of the School Psychology Program at the University of Wisconsin–Madison. She recently completed her doctoral internship in behavioral psychology at the Kennedy Krieger Institute/Johns Hopkins School of Medicine in Baltimore, Maryland, and will soon begin her postdoctoral fellowship in clinical psychology with the Autism Assessment, Research, Treatment, and Services Center at Rush University Medical Center in Chicago, Illinois. She is actively pursuing credentialing both as a Licensed Psychologist and as a Board Certified Behavior Analyst. Her clinical, research, and teaching interests include the promotion of early identification, diagnosis, and behavioral intervention for children with autism spectrum disorders and neurodevelopmental disabilities.

Veronica P. Fleury is an associate professor of special education at Florida State University. She engages in applied research focused on optimizing learning opportunities for individuals with autism spectrum disorder (ASD). Dr. Fleury has served as PI or co-PI on grants from the Organization for Autism Research, Autism Science Foundation, U.S. Department of Education's Office of Special Education Programs (OSEP) and Institution of Education Sciences (IES), including an IES early career and mentoring award. Dr. Fleury earned her doctorate in special education from the University of Washington and completed an IES postdoctoral research fellowship focused on autism interventions with the Frank Porter Graham Child Development Institute at the University of North Carolina at Chapel Hill. She is a former special education preschool teacher and a Board Certified Behavior Analyst (BCBA) who has worked with special education teachers, children with ASD, and their families for more than 20 years.

Kaitlin Greeny is a teaching associate in the applied behavior analysis program at the University of Washington. She teaches and coordinates clinical supervision in the on-campus and online programs. She received her PhD in special education from the University of Washington and is a Board Certified Behavior Analyst (BCBA). She has experience in early childhood special education, as a clinical BCBA, and as a supervisor in the University of Washington ABA program. Dr. Greeny's research interests include effective supervision and ethics in special education and ABA. She recently completed her dissertation, which looked at recommended supervision practices in ABA.

Emily Gregori is an assistant professor of special education at the University of Illinois at Chicago and a Board Certified Behavior Analyst. She has more than 10 years of professional experience in special education and behavior analysis with students with disabilities across the lifespan. Her research examines the assessment and treatment of problem behavior in individuals with disabilities and methods for caregivers to implement evidence-based behavioral interventions.

Elizabeth M. Kelly is an instructor in special education and a research scientist in the Haring Center for Inclusive Education at the University of Washington. She earned a PhD in special education with an emphasis in applied behavior analysis (ABA) at the University of Washington. Dr. Kelly's research interests include collaborative coaching with parents and professionals, family-practitioner partnerships, and ethical practices in special education and ABA. Dr. Kelly is currently working on a project to support the implementation of a unique coaching model in early childhood settings.

Stephen M. Kwiatek, at the time of this work, was a graduate research assistant at the National Technical Assistance Center on Transition and a doctoral candidate at University of North Carolina at Charlotte. He is currently a postdoctoral research associate with the Illinois Center for Transition and Work at the University of Illinois at Urbana-Champaign. His research interests include general education involvement in college and career readiness efforts, secondary transition evidence-based practices and predictors, and interagency collaboration.

Giulio E. Lancioni, PhD, is a professor in the Department of Basic Medical Sciences, Neuroscience and Sense Organs of the University "Aldo Moro" of Bari in Italy. His research interests include, among others, the development and assessment of assistive technologies for (a) people with intellectual and developmental disabilities; (b) people with consciousness disorders, lack of speech, and pervasive motor impairments; and (c) people with neurodegenerative diseases such as Alzheimer's disease and amyotrophic lateral sclerosis. The assistive technologies are mainly used for promoting positive interaction with the environment and supporting alternative communication strategies and social and occupational skills among the aforementioned groups of people.

Catharine Lory is a postdoctoral research associate in educational psychology at Baylor University and a Board Certified Behavior Analyst. Her work has a primary focus on designing effective assessments and interventions to address the behavioral needs of children with autism and developmental disabilities. She also provides specialized training to support educators, service providers, and caregivers to engage in evidence-based practices with children with autism in natural environments.

Abby Magnusen is a behavior specialist in a large suburban school district. She is a Board Certified Behavior Analyst and licensed special education administrator and teacher who has worked in public PK–12 school settings. Early in her career she worked as a behavior analyst providing in-home applied behavior analysis services to young autistic children. She is currently working on her doctoral dissertation at Ball State University.

Rose A. Mason is an associate professor of special education at Purdue University and a Board Certified Behavior Analyst–Doctoral Level. She has 20 years of experience consulting with and training service providers including special education teachers and parents. Her research interests include identification of mechanisms to increase access to evidence-based practices for individuals with autism including practice-based coaching, training via telehealth, and utilizing technology to deliver interventions for adolescents and adults with autism.

Valerie L. Mazzotti is a professor of special education at the University of North Carolina at Charlotte. Her research interests include self-determination, secondary transition evidence-based practices and predictors of post-school success, and interagency collaboration for students with disabilities.

Meka N. McCammon is an assistant professor of instruction and practicum coordinator at the University of South Florida. She has 15 years of experience providing ABA therapy to children and young adults with autism spectrum disorder (ASD) in homes and clinic settings. Her research interests include developing and evaluating interventions to promote communication skills in children with ASD, evaluating the effectiveness and efficiency of training methods for caregivers and educators in the implementation of evidence-based practices, and single-case methodology.

Lindsay M. McCary is a senior scientist at the University of Wisconsin–Madison. She holds affiliate faculty appointments in educational psychology and pediatrics at University of Wisconsin–Madison. Dr. McCary received her doctorate in school psychology from the University of South Carolina. As a licensed psychologist, she serves as director of psychological services at an outpatient autism clinic. Dr. McCary's professional interests have focused on high-quality clinical training of school psychologists, speech-language pathologists, occupational therapists, and social workers to work with children and youth with autism spectrum disorder and related developmental disabilities within interprofessional settings.

Hedda Meadan is a professor and the head of the Department of Special Education at the University of Illinois at Urbana-Champaign. She is a Goldstick Family Scholar and a Board Certified Behavior Analyst. Her research focuses on social-communication skills and challenging behavior of children with autism and other developmental disabilities and intervention methods to enhance these spheres of functioning. Dr. Meadan and her team use a cascading intervention model in which they train and coach, via telepractice, natural change agents (e.g., family members, service providers, behavior analysts) to use evidence-based strategies to promote social-communication skills of children with autism in the natural environment. She has published widely on topics related to interventions for children with autism and their families and on the use of technology to enhance these interventions.

Abigail Mojica is the assistant director of academics and family engagement for the CarolinaLIFE program, an inclusive postsecondary education program for students with intellectual and developmental disabilities at the University of South Carolina. She obtained her MAT in special education from the University of South Carolina and taught special education at the middle-school level for two years. Currently, she is pursuing her PhD in special education; her research interests focus on self-determination and transfer of rights issues and options for youth with disabilities.

Mark F. O'Reilly received his PhD in Special Education from the University of Illinois at Urbana-Champaign. He has taught at the University College Dublin and the University of Texas at Austin. He is currently professor and chair in the Department of Special Education at the University of Texas at Austin. He is editor-in-chief of the *Journal of Developmental and Physical Disabilities*. He is interested in the assessment and support of individuals with developmental disabilities and their families.

Jamie N. Pearson, a former behavioral interventionist and autism program consultant, is an assistant professor of special education in the Department of Teacher Education and Learning Sciences at North Carolina State University. Dr. Pearson earned her PhD in special education from the University of Illinois at Urbana-Champaign, where she developed FACES (Fostering Advocacy, Communication, Empowerment, and Support), a parent advocacy program designed to support Black families of children with autism. Dr. Pearson's research focuses on (a) disparities in autism identification, service access, and service utilization; (b) the impact of parent-advocacy and empowerment training on child and family outcomes; and (c) strategies to promote positive parent-professional partnerships between educators and historically marginalized communities. Dr. Pearson's FACES program is funded by a 2021 Early Career Development and Mentoring Grant from the Institute of Education Sciences (R324B210003). She is also a co-PI on a project designed to promote STEM career development in high school students with autism, funded by the National Science Foundation. Her work has been published in several peer-reviewed journals in the fields of special education and racial and ethnic disparities, and she has written several invited and refereed book chapters on autism, families, and racial and ethnic disparities in special education.

Anthony J. Plotner is professor in the Department of Educational Studies at the University of South Carolina. He received his PhD in special education from the

University of Illinois. As a scholar, his work has focused on improving postschool outcomes for youth and young adults with disabilities. He was recently awarded a Distinguished Mary Switzer Fellowship from the National Institute on Disability, Independent Living, and Rehabilitation Research. Dr. Plotner has published more than 50 peer-reviewed publications and book chapters in the field of rehabilitation counseling and special education.

Mandy Rispoli is a professor of special education at Purdue University and a Board Certified Behavior Analyst–Doctoral level. She is the co-editor-in-chief of the *Journal of Positive Behavior Interventions.* Operating from a behavior analytic framework, Dr. Rispoli's scholarship is built upon sustained university-community partnerships to improve teachers' meaningful involvement in functional behavior assessment and intervention and to promote positive outcomes for young children with autism and developmental disabilities. Dr. Rispoli's research explores (a) improving the efficiency, effectiveness, and feasibility of functional behavior assessments and function-based interventions in educational settings, and (b) innovations in professional development for teachers of young children with autism and challenging behavior. Dr. Rispoli has published more than 120 peer-reviewed research articles and book chapters concerning behavioral interventions for children with autism and developmental disabilities.

Jenny R. Root is an associate professor of special education at Florida State University. Her research focuses on how to teach meaningful academic skills to students with autism and intellectual disability, particularly in the area of mathematics. She is a former special education teacher and Board Certified Behavior Analyst (BCBA). Dr. Root earned her doctorate in special education from the University of North Carolina at Charlotte with a focus on severe disabilities and applied behavior analysis. She has more than a decade of experience conducting research and training teachers of students with disabilities. Dr. Root has published more than 45 articles and book chapters related to instruction and assessment of individuals with autism and intellectual disability. Her research has been funded by the Organization for Autism Research, Autism Science Foundation, American Education Research Association, U.S. Department of Education Office of Special Education Programs, and Institution of Education Sciences (IES), including through an IES early career and mentoring award.

Ilene S. Schwartz is a professor of special education at the University of Washington and the director of the Haring Center for Inclusive Education at University of Washington. She earned her PhD in child and developmental psychology from the University of Kansas and is a Board Certified Behavior Analyst-Doctoral (BCBA-D). Dr. Schwartz has an active research and professional training agenda with primary interests in autism, inclusive education, and the sustainability of educational interventions. She serves on a number of editorial review boards including the *Topics in Early Childhood Special Education* and the *Journal of Early Intervention.* Dr. Schwartz is the director of Project DATA, a model preschool program for children with autism that has been in operation since 1997 and was started as a model demonstration project with OSEP funding. She is currently working on projects to improve the quality of instruction students with disabilities receive in charter schools and strategies that can be used to improve access to services for young children with ASD in under-resourced areas.

Benjamin Seifert is a Board Certified Behavior Analyst and has served in various capacities in the field of applied behavior analysis for almost 20 years. He is currently the director of community outreach for Central Texas Autism Center and is part of the consulting team of Dr. Patrick McGreevy and Associates. He has also been an adjunct professor instructing ABA courses at Ball State University. He specializes in working with adolescents and adults with autism and other developmental delays. His current research focus is using behavior skills training to instruct interventionists to fade prompts efficiently and effectively. He plans to continue this line of research to teach employments skills to individuals who require very substantial supports.

Eric N. Shannon is a doctoral student in special education at Purdue University. For the past decade, he has implemented evidence-based practices to improve social and communication skills and reduce problem behavior in children with ASD. Eric's primary research interests are the use of naturalistic communication interventions to treat young children with ASD, and to train caregivers and other stakeholders to implement evidence-based practices within the home and school settings.

Jeff Sigafoos received his PhD in educational psychology from the University of Minnesota in 1990. Since then, he has held academic appointments at the University of Queensland, University of Sydney, and the University of Texas at Austin. He is currently a professor of educational psychology at Victoria University of Wellington in New Zealand. He is also currently co-editor-in-chief for the journal *Evidence-Based Communication Assessment and Intervention.* His teaching and research interests are focused on educational provision and communication intervention for students and adults with developmental and physical disabilities.

Jennifer Elaine Smith is a clinical assistant professor of special education at Purdue University. She has 15 years of experience teaching at the elementary level. Dr. Smith's research interests include preparation of pre-service and in-service educators to increase positive outcomes for students with disabilities and developing creativity for students with disabilities to prepare for positive postsecondary outcomes.

Emily Stover is currently a doctoral student in special education at Florida State University. Prior to her doctoral studies, Emily was an educator at the elementary school level. Most recently, she was a special education resource teacher for students with specific learning disabilities for two years. Prior to that she was a classroom teacher for students with extensive intellectual and developmental disabilities for seven years. Emily earned her bachelor's degree and master's degree in special education from the University of Florida. Her teaching certifications include elementary K–6 and exceptional student education K–12 and also holds endorsement in autism spectrum disorders. Emily is supported through the Project RAISE (Research-based Academic Interventions for Students with Extensive Support Needs) grant. Her research interests are focused on increasing culturally responsive practices in special education and building literacy in students with ASD and other extensive support needs.

Shawnna Sundberg received a BA in psychology from Purdue University in 2008, and an MA in special education with certifications in ABA and autism from Ball State University in 2015. Shawnna is a Board Certified Behavior Analyst (BCBA) with more than 13 years of experience working in the mental health and ABA/VB field. Shawnna is currently a PhD student in special education at Ball State University, where she will be completing her dissertation on prompting methods to reduce ableism used to support autistic students. She focuses both her clinical and research efforts on dismantling ableism and ABA reform as well as training other behavior analysts and parents on issues of social justice–diversity, equity, and inclusion in the field of ABA. She has a special interest in sexuality education for autistics. Previously in her career, Shawnna was a parent training coordinator focusing supporting families in home. In addition, Shawnna was the 2018–2019 Hoosier Association for Behavior Analysis secretary, assisting with licensure for BCBAs in the state of Indiana. She has published two chapters on using interventions with autistic children and three peer-reviewed chapters accepted for publication that focus on sexuality education, self-management, and college alternatives for transition-aged autistic students.

Charissa Voorhis is a doctoral student in the special education department at Purdue University. She is a Board Certified Behavior Analyst and a licensed special education teacher. Charissa taught in special education for four years while completing her MSEd in special education. Her research interests involve working with in-service and pre-service teachers on addressing challenging behavior in the classroom setting.

Charles (Charlie) Walters is a PhD student in special education. He currently coordinates the college access and preparation program for CarolinaLIFE and serves as a member of the National Technical Assistance Center on Transition's Project-Related Outcomes Team. Charlie is active in training and consultation related to the support of alternatives to guardianship through his work with the South Carolina Supported Decision-Making Project.

Kelly Whalon is an associate professor in special education. She earned her PhD in special education in 2005 with an emphasis in autism spectrum disorder (ASD). She has served children with ASD for more than 20 years in the role of teacher or researcher. Dr. Whalon has prepared future teachers and researchers at the undergraduate, graduate, and doctoral level in a variety of program areas (e.g., general and special education, school psychology, school counseling). Her research interests include interventions to enhance the language, literacy, and social communication skills of children with ASD. Dr. Whalon has published many refereed articles and chapters and presented at numerous conferences on topics related to literacy development and social competence of children with ASD.

Susan M. Wilczynski is the Plassman Family Distinguished Professor of Special Education and Applied Behavior Analysis. She regularly works to expand her scope of competence on the topics of sexuality for autistics and how this topic interacts with ableism. She also works on actively dismantling ableism on the practice of behavior analysis. Susan is the coordinator for the ABAI's Practice Board and is a currently an associate editor for *Behavior Analysis in Practice*. Earlier in her career, she served as the executive director of the National Autism Center, where she chaired the first National Standards Project. In addition, she developed the first center-based treatment program at the University of Nebraska Medical Center. She is a licensed psychologist, and a BCBA-D. Susan has edited and/or written multiple books including her upcoming book, *Postsecondary Transition for College- or Career-Bound Autistic Students* and published scholarly works in *Behavior Analysis in Practice*, *Journal of Applied Behavior Analysis*, *Behavior Modification*, *Focus on Autism and Other Developmental Disabilities*, and *Psychology in the Schools*. She a licensed psychologist, and a Board Certified Behavior Analyst.

Alice Williams is a doctoral student in special education at Florida State University. She earned her MS in communication sciences and disorders in 2006 from Florida State University. She is a former speech-language pathologist and classroom teacher of students with extensive support needs who worked with children with autism spectrum disorders and their families for more than 15 years. Her research interests include interventions to increase literacy skills and enhance language abilities in students with extensive support needs who have complex communication needs.

Made in the USA
Coppell, TX
30 April 2023

16260648R00260